BY THE SAME AUTHOR

The Gentle Zionists

'Baffy':
The Diaries of Blanche Dugdale

Vansittart: Study of a Diplomat

Lewis Namier and Zionism

Chaim Weizmann: A Biography

Churchill: An Unruly Life

The Cliveden Set:
Portrait of an Exclusive Fraternity

HAROLD NICOLSON

HAROLD NICOLSON

Norman Rose

JONATHAN CAPE
LONDON

Published by Jonathan Cape 2005

2 4 6 8 10 9 7 5 3 1

Copyright © Norman Rose 2005

Norman Rose has asserted his right under the Copyright, Designs
and Patents Act 1988 to be identified as the author of this work

First published in Great Britain in 2005 by
Jonathan Cape
Random House, 20 Vauxhall Bridge Road,
London SW1V 2SA

Random House Australia (Pty) Limited
20 Alfred Street, Milsons Point, Sydney,
New South Wales 2061, Australia

Random House New Zealand Limited
18 Poland Road, Glenfield,
Auckland 10, New Zealand

Random House South Africa (Pty) Limited
Endulini, 5A Jubilee Road, Parktown 2193, South Africa

The Random House Group Limited Reg. No. 954009
www.randomhouse.co.uk

A CIP catalogue record for this book
is available from the British Library

ISBN 0-224-06218-2

Papers used by The Random House Group Limited are natural,
recyclable products made from wood grown in sustainable forests;
the manufacturing processes conform to the environmental
regulations of the country of origin

Typeset in Ehrhardt by Palimpsest Book Production Limited,
Polmont, Stirlingshire
Printed and bound in Great Britain by
William Clowes Ltd, Beccles, Suffolk

Map of Europe post-1918 drawn by Reginald Piggott
Map of Sissinghurst House and Garden copyright © Stuart and Christine Page

For My Mother

CONTENTS

EUROPE
POST-1918

Boundaries created by
the Versailles Peace
Settlement

.... Pre-settlement boundaries

[1918/20] Date of independence

EDEN

Baltic Sea

hagen

ESTONIA [1918/20]

[1918/20]

LATVIA

Danzig Free City 1919

LITHUANIA [1918/20]

EAST PRUSSIA

-lin

Posen

R. Vistula

Warsaw

USSR

Y

POLAND [1916/18]

N

to Poland 1918/19

Prague

TESCHEN

to Poland 1921

to Czech. 1919/20

CECH
oravia

OSLOVAKIA Ruthenia

[1918/20]

Slovakia

R. Dniester

BESSARABIA to Romania 1918/20

Vienna

IA

Budapest

HUNGARY [1918/19]

to Yugoslavia 1919

to Romania 1919/20

ROMANIA

Black Sea

Belgrade

YUGOSLAVIA [1918]

MONTENEGRO to Yugoslavia 1921

Bucharest

R. Danube

SERBIA

Sofia

BULGARIA

ZONE OF THE STRAITS
(armed occupation)

riatic Sea

ALBANIA

Occ. by Greece 1920/22

to Greece 1919

Y

GREECE

Aegean Sea

TURKEY

Athens

n Sea

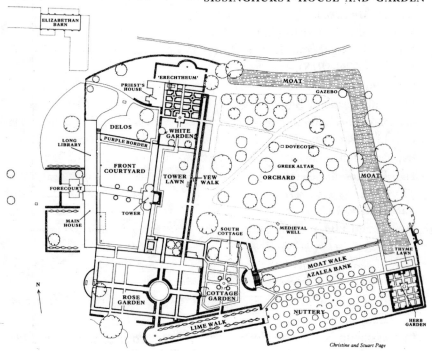

SISSINGHURST HOUSE AND GARDEN

ELIZABETHAN BARN

PRIEST'S HOUSE

'ERECHTHEUM'

MOAT

GAZEBO

DELOS

LONG LIBRARY

PURPLE BORDER

WHITE GARDEN

DOVECOTE

GREEK ALTAR

FRONT COURTYARD

TOWER LAWN

YEW WALK

ORCHARD

MOAT

FORECOURT

MAIN HOUSE

TOWER

SOUTH COTTAGE

MEDIEVAL WELL

THYME LAWN

N

MOAT WALK

AZALEA BANK

ROSE GARDEN

COTTAGE GARDEN

NUTTERY

HERB GARDEN

LIME WALK

Christine and Stuart Page

ILLUSTRATIONS

1. Harold Nicolson and Vita Sackville-West at a flower show in Sevenoaks, 1914 (*National Portrait Gallery, London*).
2. Harold at the Paris Peace Conference, 1919 (*reproduced by kind permission of the Estates of Harold Nicolson and Vita Sackville-West*).
3. Vita Sackville-West in 1918, painting by William Strang (*Glasgow City Council Museums*).
4. Violet Trefusis in 1919 (*Camera Press*).
5. Vita with Nigel and Ben at Long Barn, 1924 (© *Hulton-Deutsch Collection/CORBIS*).
6. Sissinghurst Castle from the air in 1932 (*Simmons Aerofilms Ltd.*).
7. Vita and Harold at Smoke Tree Ranch, California, 1933 (*reproduced by kind permission of the Estates of Harold Nicolson and Vita Sackville-West*).
8. Harold as the New Party candidate for the Combined Universities at the general election of 1931 (*Hulton-Deutsch Collection/CORBIS*).
9. Harold after his election as MP for West Leicester, November 1935 (*reproduced by kind permission of the Estates of Harold Nicolson and Vita Sackville-West*).
10. Harold and Vita at Sissinghurst, 1938 (*reproduced by kind permission of the Estates of Harold Nicolson and Vita Sackville-West*).
11. Harold setting up his lathe ready for an evening's work helping in the war production (*Hulton Archive/Getty Images*).
12. Harold at his typewriter at Sissinghurst (*reproduced by kind permission of the Estates of Harold Nicolson and Vita Sackville-West*).
13. Canvassing in North Croydon, 1948 (*reproduced by kind permission of the Estates of Harold Nicolson and Vita Sackville-West*).
14. Bertrand Russell, Harold Nicolson and Lord Samuel at the BBC before the discussion 'Why defend liberty?' on 24 January 1951 (*BBC*).
15. Vita and Harold in 1959 (*Philip Turner*).
16. Harold with Nigel and grandson Adam in 1962 (*Edwin Smith*).

Every effort has been made to trace and contact copyright holders. The publishers will be pleased to correct any mistakes or omissions in future editions.

ACKNOWLEDGEMENTS

Realising a project of this nature depends upon the good will, encouragement and co-operation of many individuals. I remain deeply in debt to the late Mr Nigel Nicolson for his hospitality and for allowing me to examine family papers in his possession at Sissinghurst Castle; and also for granting me access to archival material for which he holds the copyright. I remain grateful also to my numerous friends and colleagues for having (deliberately) taxed their patience, often picking their brains in what perhaps appeared to them as little more than casual conversations. Particular thanks are due to: the late Sir Isaiah Berlin; the late Lord Bullock; Professor David Cannadine; Sir Edward Cazalet; Professor Ellis Joffe; Professor Wm. Roger Louis; Martin Lubowski; Professor Susan Pedersen; Diana Reich; Professor Adam Roberts; Dr Inbal Rose; Mrs Janice Rossen; Dr Steve Uran; and Professor Donald Watt.

I am especially grateful to the Director and Staff of the Institute for Advanced Studies at Princeton for inviting me to spend a year with them. The Institute received me most warmly and ensured that my stay there was both congenial and fruitful. It was in these exceptionally agreeable and stimulating surroundings that I completed the research for this book. Thanks are also due to Professor Wm. Roger Louis for inviting me to appear at his British Studies Seminar at the University of Austin, Texas, where I first laid out in public the main themes of this book.

Crown copyright material at the National Archives (formerly the Public Record Office) at Kew, London, is reproduced by kind permission of the Controller of Her Majesty's Stationery Office. I would also like to thank the authors and publishers – listed in the bibliography – for quotations I have used from works of which they hold the copyright; and to register in advance my apologies for those cases that I have inadvertently overlooked.

I remain greatly in debt to the staffs of the numerous archives, libraries and institutions that generously extended their facilities to me: to the Library at Balliol College, Oxford; to the Berg Collection at the New York Public Library; the Bodleian Library, Oxford; the British Council Library, Jerusalem; the British Library and its Manuscripts Room, London, and its Newspaper Collection at Colindale; the British Library of Political and Economic Science at the London School of Economics; Churchill Archives Centre at Churchill College, Cambridge; the Firestone Library, Princeton University, and its Special Reading Room; the Harry Ransom Research Center at the University of Texas, Austin; the House of Lords Record Office; the Institute of Historical Research, Senate House, London; the Library for Humanities and Social Sciences and the National Library at the Hebrew University, Jerusalem; the Library at King's College, Cambridge, and its Archive Centre; the Lilly Library at the University of Indiana, Bloomington; and Temple University Library, Philadelphia, and its Special Collections Department.

I also owe more than I can express to Dr Inbal Rose and Andrew Lownie for reading the manuscript and subjecting it to the most apposite comments. I am most grateful for their help. A special word of thanks is due to my long-standing friend, Ellis Joffe, for cheerfully sustaining my all too often flagging spirits, for his persistence in reminding me that writing a biography was really a very simple matter. 'You see,' Eli would say, 'he was born; he lived; he died. Nothing to it!'

Andrew Lownie has been the most patient, optimistic and supportive of literary agents, cheerfully sustaining this project from the outset: I owe him much. Many thanks are due to the staff at Jonathan Cape (Random House), in particular to my editor Will Sulkin, for his expertise and tact, and no less, his sense of humour; also to Jörg Hensgen, whose keen eye and proficiency saved me from many mistakes; and to Ros Porter, for her tact in combating my computer illiteracy. Altogether a lively and highly efficient team: their skill and professionalism guided this venture to a fruitful outcome. Extra thanks are due to Beth Humphries, the copy-editor, and Vicki Robinson, the indexer, for their behind-the-scenes expertise that contributed much to the final version of this venture.

As always my greatest debt belongs to my family: to my wife, Tslilla, and my daughter and son-in-law, Inbal and Amit, for their patience and understanding. Authorship is a solitary business. Without their mutual support and encouragement this book would not have been written.

Norman Rose,
Ba'aka, Jerusalem,
March 2004

HAROLD NICOLSON

ONE

'Silver Spoons'

How extraordinary, it was said of the Hon. Harold George Nicolson – Knight Commander of the Royal Victorian Order, Commander of Legion of Honour, Companion of St Michael and St George, Fellow of the Royal Society of Literature, Governor of the BBC, Honorary Fellow of Balliol College, Oxford, President of the Classical Association, and member of the Boards of the National Trust, the London Library and the National Portrait Gallery – 'to be born with your mouth full of silver spoons'.[1]

Harold would not have disagreed, although he might not have put it so bluntly. His earliest memories were of the sumptuous legations or embassies, presided over by his father or his most illustrious relative, the Marquess of Dufferin and Ava, and of the great country houses of County Down, Ireland, patrimony of his mother's kinsfolk.

He recalled:

At breakfast, each of the three footmen wore powdered suits. My eyes wandered upwards from their buckled shoes, their silk stockings, their velvet breeches, to the frontage of their upper vesture. Enraptured – my gaze fixed itself upon their heads. The hair of each of them had that morning been drenched in oil; upon the agglutinated foundation thus achieved some early-rising hairdresser had puffed, sprinkled or thrown a preparation of powdered chalk. He had then, with a wide-pronged comb, striated this starched amalgam; parting it ruthlessly on the right side of the head; clawing it backwards above the ears.

Perplexed, the young Harold was at a loss to explain this exotic vision. 'Mummy,' he asked, 'why has this man got white hair?'[2] Bewilderment soon gave way to a distinct penchant for such settings, as these scenes, with slight variations according to place and period, pursued him with pleasing regularity throughout his life.

The British Legation at Tehran, recorded an entranced Gertrude Bell, was housed in a 'rambling pale stone house, with long hallways, where liveried servants would bow as one passed'. Chancing upon 'capacious dining rooms, drawing rooms, and billiard rooms, countless sitting rooms and bedrooms for family and guests', she recalled that 'everywhere one could smell the scent of roses and hear the sound of nightingales'. As for the grounds, they were akin to 'the Garden of Eden'. Dotted among the lawns and the trees and the running streams were located the bungalow-like residences of the diplomatic staff.

The Legation was surrounded by the vastness of the desert: 'miles and miles of it with nothing, *nothing* growing; ringed in with bleak bare mountains snow crowned and furrowed with the deep courses of currents . . . it is a very wonderful thing to see'. But it was only a short half-hour drive to Gulhek, where the diplomatists would escape from the torrid summer heat of Tehran. 'Life at Gulhek was almost a dream of delight.' A little work until about midday, a plunge into the very cold waters of the bathing pool, a glass of sherry, luncheon, an obligatory siesta in the burning heat of the summer afternoon, tea, tennis, and finally an admirable dinner. 'What could be a more delightful programme.'[3] It was in these relaxed, civilised surroundings that Harold George Nicolson was born on 21 November 1886, third son to Arthur Nicolson, Secretary to the British Legation, and Mary Catherine Rowan.*

Arthur Nicolson, after a frustrating spell as a naval recruit, had turned to diplomacy. His lineage was ancient. Family lore held that the clan was founded by Norwegian raiders, the Nicols'sens, who, in the twelfth century, established their ascendancy over the Hebrides, in particular over Lewis and Skye. Dominating in particular the promentory of Totternish on Skye, a certain Andrew Nicolson constructed there the mighty stronghold of Scorrybreck. Nothing now remains of Scorrybreck, though the name Nicolson still survives throughout the region. A distant cousin, so it was claimed, fell at Flodden Field in 1513, fighting valiantly for the losing side.[4] In 1570, a branch of the family, now Anglicised as the Nicolsons, moved from Skye to Edinburgh where they established themselves as lawyers, acquiring substantial properties at Carnock and Tillicoultrie, patiently climbing the social ladder. In 1629, John Nicolson, by now a figure of local substance, was rewarded with a baronetcy. Suspected of Jacobite tendencies, several of Nicolson's immediate forebears sought refuge among the Scottish regiments serving in the Low Countries, living Dutch lives and

*Catherine bore Arthur three more children, Frederick Archibald (b. 1883), Erskine (Eric) Arthur (b. 1884), and Gwendolen (b. 1896).

dying at Breda and Ypres. Though not entirely impoverished, the Nicolsons founded no great fortunes; nor did they rise above the level of provincial dignitaries. However, the baronetcy passed from generation to generation, until, in 1899, Arthur Nicolson succeeded as the eleventh baronet.

Mary Catherine Rowan Hamilton (or Hamilton Rowan), Harold's mother, could boast of far grander aristocratic connections. Irish-based, her kin embraced the Sheridan, the Blackwood and the Hamilton families. Centred in County Down, the expansive estates of Killyleagh, Shanganagh and Clandeboye splendidly upheld their rank and status. By far the most celebrated of Harold's closest relatives was Uncle Duff, otherwise known as Frederick Temple-Hamilton Blackwood, first Marquess of Dufferin and Ava, one-time Governor-General of Canada, Viceroy of India, Ambassador at St Petersberg, Constantinople, Rome and Paris, and Warden of the Cinque Ports, who had married Mary Catherine's sister, Hariot ('Lal'). In time, Harold developed the deepest of attachments to his family's Irish ancestral homes, relishing the privileges they offered. It was a cocooned existence – and it found nostalgic expression in his subsequent writings. Here, Harold confessed, he felt secure, anchored in a time-honoured past.[5]

Arthur Nicolson remained three years in Tehran, and then moved on to Hungary (as Consul-General), Constantinople (Secretary of Embassy), Bulgaria (Agent and Consul-General), Morocco (Envoy Extraordinary and Minister Plenipotentiary), Madrid and St Petersburg (Ambassador), before returning to the Foreign Office in 1910 as Permanent Under-Secretary. Until he reached school age, Harold followed his parents from place to place. Children of the aristocracy customarily regarded their parents from afar. Finding that their mothers and fathers were too preoccupied with their own affairs – whether high-level statecraft or top-drawer socialising – they routinely attached themselves to surrogate figures, invariably enigmatic governesses or eccentric servants – or perhaps both.

Harold was no exception. He would later acknowledge that 'we were always strangers to our parents'.[6] In any case, Arthur Nicolson was a remote figure. An unhappy childhood and the rigours and limitations of his early education 'had rendered him, even for an Englishman, unduly diffident and reserved'. After concluding his training on the HMS *Britannia*, he refused to follow his father's example and pursue a naval career. Did he find the false camaraderie, the schoolboyish brutality too much for him? No reason is given. At Rugby his fate was no better. Arthur's final report read: 'Your boy has been an absolute failure . . . We can only hope that he will be less of a failure in after life.' There was no improvement at Brasenose College, where his tutors found him 'indolent, undisciplined and untidy'. Arthur left Oxford without taking his degree.[7]

At home, things were not much better. Arthur encountered ill humour, if not outright animosity at the hands of his parents. His father, Admiral Sir Frederick William Erskine Nicolson, appeared to epitomise the cliché, 'a crusty old sea dog'. Having apparently committed a colossal, though unspecified, 'error of judgment' during the Crimean War, he was virtually axed from the Navy three years later and received no further command. No less controversial was the Admiral's conduct of his personal affairs, at least in the eyes of those who determined the social mores of the age. It was whispered that the circumstances of his second marriage to Augusta Sarah were not such as to 'commend themselves to Osborne'. Harold would later describe her as 'a tart'. Nor could his third marriage have inspired greater respect, for it was no secret that Arthur's second stepmother, Anne, was addicted to the bottle. She disliked Arthur and the Admiral followed suit, only too ready to believe that his youngest son was 'a wastrel' and regarding him with 'disapproval and almost dislike'. The young Harold recalled the air of 'gloom', of overall neglect, that enveloped his grandfather's house at 15, William Street, Knightsbridge. When not interfering 'with the liberty and feelings of his children', the Admiral dined daily at the Travellers' Club – on partridges and champagne – read a French novel a day, and attended meetings of the Thames Conservancy Board, of which he became chairman.

Eventually, Arthur found refuge from the adversities at home in the relative calm of the Foreign Office. A late starter, it was only after leaving Oxford that he began to apply himself to his studies. Fluent in French and German, he passed out first in the Foreign Office examinations, gaining 772 marks out of a maximum of 930. He entered the Foreign Office in 1870, spent thirty-five years abroad, returned in 1910 as head of the Office, and retired six years later. Effective as a diplomat, Arthur Nicolson subsequently admitted to his youngest son that he 'was not a good head of an office. I am too easy-going. I do so hate rows' – words that Harold would echo time and again when contemplating the vicissitudes of his own public career. Although they were never intimate, Harold always exhibited the greatest respect and affection for his father. Later he came to write a filial biography of Sir Arthur Nicolson, resuscitating in glowing terms the Old Diplomacy as personified by his father, the Old-Style Diplomat who was 'neither imaginative nor intellectual: he was merely intelligent, honest, sensible, high-minded and fair'.[8]

On the other hand, Harold doted on his mother, Catherine ('Katie'). She hovered constantly in the background, often on call to help combat the everyday cares of his young life. During his earliest years he was cared for by his nurse 'Anna, my dear Anna, who was German and had a sewing-machine and used to eat raw bacon on a green plate'.[9] Later, and inevitably, his so-called champion in these matters was his governess. Who was she? In his writings, Harold invariably referred to her as Miss Plimsoll, a habit, for the sake of convenience, retained in the ensuing narrative.* So, the ubiquitous Edith Plimsoll was forever to be found at Harold's elbow, gently, if not always tactfully, monitoring his every move. 'Not so much noise, dears, please, *please*,' Miss Plimsoll would irritatingly entreat her charges; or else she would resort to her 'boatswain's voice', calling her little ones to 'Breakfast' or La-unch'. When at tea she would enquire, 'Sugar dear?' 'Yes please Miss Plimsoll; two.' 'No, not two dear, but you can have one of those dear little cakes.' You must not screw up your eyes, Harold was told, 'it's an affected habit'. Whereupon Harold would open them wide in what seemed to be 'a meaningless stare'.

Miss Plimsoll was not 'an excellent governess', Harold sadly acknowledged – even though she had taught him the multiplication tables. 'Sums first,' she would intone, 'and then we must do history. The Kings, you know . . . of England.' What particularly incensed him were her persistent pleas that he embrace visible 'forms of sturdiness' in his day-to-day behaviour. Her constant reproaches produced in him 'a feeling of constant inadequacy', and left Harold ill suited to face his schooldays 'with an ardent smile'. 'The fibres of my own virility, such as they were,' he reflected later, 'were by this process twisted into unnatural shapes.'[10] Were these remarks a belated attempt to fathom the causes of his own sexual preferences as they evolved later in his life?

Was he a nervous child? he asked his mother. Quite the contrary, she replied, 'you were always doing such dangerous things', and she reminded him of the time when he skipped recklessly along the battlements at Walmer Castle. Harold was forward in other ways. Prompted by his Aunt 'Lal', he was placed on a chair, recited a now long-forgotten poem to an audience of girls, and was rewarded with a Kodak camera – sufficient reward apparently to shield his embarrassment. Every evening he said his prayers in English

---

*Nicolson implied (*Helen's Tower*, 105) that Miss Edith Plimsoll was a real person, comparing her unfavourably with his two other governesses, a Miss Corrin and a Miss Woods. Yet James Lees-Milne notes (*Harold Nicolson. A Biography*, Chatto and Windus, 1980, i, 311) that Nicolson had told an American acquaintance that Miss Plimsoll never existed at all, and that neither Miss Corrin nor Miss Woods remotely resembled Miss Plimsoll. Instead, Nicolson went on, the prototype for Edith Plimsoll was 'an unnamed typist' he had once worked with at the Foreign Office. But why pick on an 'unnamed typist' at the Foreign Office? Perhaps Nicolson was being his usual tactful self, unwilling to load on to Misses Corrin's and Woods's (slender?) shoulders Miss Plimsoll's harmless idiosyncrasies. In the above narrative I have chosen to follow Nicolson's example, naming Miss Plimsoll as his governess, assuming, I hope logically, that she is indeed a composite of all his governesses.

and German (a language no doubt picked up from his 'dear Anna'). And, or so Catherine claimed, he was always saying 'very clever and original things'. One aspect of Harold's behaviour disturbed his parents. He was frightened of the dark: night-times became an ordeal. Only a passing phase, said the family doctor. But it wasn't. Consumed by 'night-fears', he lay awake 'shaking in the dark', menaced by imaginary 'bears and lions, burglars and ghosts'. Harold later admitted: 'I did not get over it.'[11]

A 'motif of fear' ran through Harold's childhood memories, as 'successive terrors' tortured his imagination. His humour could not have improved when he encountered Sir Richard Burton who thrust his dark, bearded face into Harold's, barking, 'Hello, little Tehran!' Harold yelled. He screamed and screamed until Lady Burton, large and benign in a dove-coloured silk frock, appeared to rescue him. The memory of the notorious adventurer's 'questing panther eyes' remained with him for ever 'as a thrill of terror and delight'. Somewhat less frightening, but no less intimidating, was his encounter with Prince Ferdinand of Bulgaria. 'A sinister man', clad in a 'green Bulgarian uniform, with the stars of many orders strewn across his breast,' his gloved hands rested menacingly 'upon the hilt of a cavalry sword'. The occasion for this apparition watching over Harold was the birthday of the future King Boris III, Ferdinand's son. Sugared buns and walnuts dipped in toffee, however, more than compensated for Ferdinand's scary presence.[12]

Harold's most vivid childhood memories centred on his father's postings abroad. In his young mind, he graded them according to the magnificence of their dining rooms. Starting with the cramped accommodation in Andrassy Street, Budapest – which robbed it 'of stately ease' – they included the grander establishments at Constantinople – 'where the napkins ran in rows like bishops' mitres . . . and the soft Bosphorus sunset slid across the white dinner table in slatted shafts of orange and blue' – and Tangier – where the table, weighed down with exotic flowers, formed 'a covert among which nestled little silver bowls for sweets . . . and sugared almonds of all colours, and crystallized cherries'. In Madrid, the embassy was located in a beautiful but inconvenient cardinal's palace in the Calle Torrijos. A gloomy place, it lacked bathrooms, and the electric light was apt to flicker on and off. But its dining room, walls hung in scarlet damask and adorned with huge royal portraits, looked out over a cobbled courtyard, from which wafted up the 'smell of stables mingling, not unpleasantly, with the scent of food'. By the time Harold frequented the palatial splendour of the St Petersburg embassy he was a junior clerk in the Foreign Office.[13]

But nothing could match the glamour of Uncle Duff's Paris embassy on the fashionable rue du Faubourg St Honoré, as Harold, aged six, remembered it in May 1892. Aunt 'Lal', as always 'detached, slim and stately', met the Nicolsons at the Gare de l'Est. Attended by two footmen in fawn-coloured greatcoats, they drove in a brougham to the embassy in circuitous fashion, crossing by the Pont au Change and returning by the Concorde so that Harold could see the lights of the bridges spiralling downwards into the shadowy waters of the Seine. On arrival at the embassy, Miss Plimsoll remarked, 'it is like a *palace*, dear, isn't it?' Edith Plimsoll was nearer to the mark than she knew, for at one time it had been the residence of Pauline Borghese, the flirtatious and scandal-ridden younger sister of the great Napoleon. This made little impression on Harold. When shown Pauline's bed, he thought it 'nothing more than a heap of stuff'. But the black and white marble pavement of the great hall, the ornate, sweeping staircase, the magnificent ballroom, the two separate dining rooms, one for small, intimate dinners, the other a spacious room that could hold up to fifty diners, were quite another thing. And always, hovering discreetly in the background, a continuous procession of finely dressed servants. These colourful impressions stuck in Harold's memory.

It was at the Paris embassy that Harold first encountered the figure of Benjamin Constant (later a subject for one of his biographies). '*Beautiful*,' gasped Miss Plimsoll, captivated by Constant's portrait of Uncle Duff, 'perfectly beautiful.' Harold also thought it 'grand'. (Afterwards he changed his mind, damning Constant as an 'incompetent' portraitist who had failed to catch Uncle Duff's Irish personality.) One evening, Harold stood by his bedroom window that overlooked the courtyard to the *porte-cochère*, admiring the steady procession of lamp-lit carriages drawing up at the carpeted steps that led to the front entrance. An official dinner and reception was being held. Harold's cousin, Lord Terance (later, second Marquess of Dufferin and Ava), had betrothed himself to an American lady. Miss Plimsoll, who had now joined Harold, was visibly upset, despite the gaiety of the occasion. Distressed and unhappy at the ramifications of this projected union, she clarified her feelings to her young ward. 'You would not understand, dear, and you mustn't say I told you. But your cousin, Lord Terance, has become engaged to an *American*.' '*To an American*,' she repeated tragically, introducing Harold to the complexities of the 'special relationship'.[14]

Harold's Irish relatives cast an authentic spell over him, a constant fascination. Certainly, he never devoted as much time or energy to exploring the past of his Scottish ancestors, whom he once described as 'a landless tribe'. Uncle Duff was the close relative he most revered. For one thing, Dufferin's achievements and social status set him apart. But no less, aspects of his political philosophy held a certain appeal for the more mature Harold. Shortly after coming of age, Dufferin had declared himself a Whig, an act of faith that brought him an English peerage in addition to his Irish title. As an improving landlord, Harold wrote of him that 'he pitied' the Irish peasant 'but did not really love' him. He reflected further that 'He wanted to better the plight of the masses, but they should know their place',[15] sentiments that would later trip easily from Harold's lips.

Yet despite his illustrious career, the closing chapter of Dufferin's life was anything but gratifying. He had innocently accepted the chairmanship of a suspect firm, the London and Globe, that speculated in mining stock. The company folded. Dufferin, his reputation damaged, had not only ruined others – albeit inadvertently – but had also sustained heavy losses himself, severely depleting the family fortune. So, was Uncle Dufferin a great man? Harold asked. Reluctantly, Harold was forced to concede that he was not. Kind, charming, greatly gifted, a man of integrity and moral courage, certainly. But he possessed none of the required vision and imagination, the swollen ego, the autocratic instinct, the iron will that marked out the truly great. Was he capable, even when pressed, of trampling on the opposition to carry his policies through to a successful conclusion? Harold would only say that Dufferin was 'a very great diplomatist'. There is much in Harold's interpretation of Dufferin's personality and career résumé that, with minor adjustments, might well be applied to his own. Harold's relationship with his Aunt 'Lal' was more complex, at least from her point of view. Tea-time gossip had it that she 'disliked' Harold as a small boy, finding him overly spoilt and self-indulgent. Time did not improve matters. Later, when Aunt 'Lal' learned about Harold's scandalous, *demi-monde* way of life in Berlin in the late 1920s, she 'took against him in a big way'.[16]

Still, Harold identified Ireland with the happiness of his 'dawn–golden days'. As a child he would spend his holidays being shuttled back and forth between the estates held by the Blackwood–Hamilton families: Clandeboye or Killyleagh Castle, County Down – a distance of only twelve miles separating them; or Shanganagh Castle, near Bray, County Wicklow. All conjured up different associations. Clandeboye – Uncle Duff's country seat – was a commodious Georgian building plastered in greyish chalk, a style typical of Anglo–Irish mansions of that period. Dufferin remedied whatever structural defects he thought marred his inheritance. Harbouring pretensions as an amateur architect, he redesigned the house. A new, more imposing entrance, with stone cannon balls guarding it, was added. Additional rooms for family, guests and receptions were tacked on; an agreeable library – 'one of the pleasantest rooms on earth' – was constructed; and a vast series of domestic offices appended, sheltering under glass roofing and skylights, his consuming passion. But the net effect of this assault, at least in Harold's eyes, was 'one of structural confusion'. The grounds, however, suffered none of these imperfections. Consisting of a sequence of lakes, islands, gulfs, channels, hidden reefs and peninsulas, they culminated in Helen's Tower, a monument raised in the memory of Dufferin's mother, perched on the summit of a rounded hill dominating the sea.

Harold would often visit Shanganagh Castle, a late Georgian pile that belonged to his maternal grandmother, a strong-willed lady who championed women's rights and higher education long before they became fashionable. Revisiting the castle many years later, 'Old fears, memories of my childhood', surfaced. Its overgrown garden, littered with Roman statues, its turrets and winding staircases revived 'old terrors'; his old nursery rekindled 'that sense of night-fears'. Yet how strange, for his mother assured him that he was a constantly cheerful child, bubbling over with laughter. 'The gayest of my children,' she assured Harold.[17]

Catherine Rowan herself was born at Killyleagh, which is situated on the western shore of Strangford Lough. Again, years later, Harold returned to the castle, now abandoned, 'in search of the past'. Once again, as he roamed its deserted garden he could recall only the memory of his 'nervous childhood days'. Yet Killyleagh also roused memories of more turbulent days, of rebellion, of betrayal and deception, of sectarian fanaticism as Ulster Volunteers challenged Irish Nationalists, for Killyleagh had been the home of his most notorious ancestor. 'Tell me,' he asked his mother one day, 'who was Hamilton Rowan?' 'He was my great-grandfather,' she replied. 'He was a rebel. We do not talk about him much. I think we are rather ashamed of him in a way.' But Archibald Hamilton Rowan caught Harold's imagination. Here indeed was a romantic moving tale of a dedicated nonconformist. Rusticated from Cambridge, Hamilton Rowan schemed with Theobald Wolfe Tone and Sir Edward Fitzgerald to found the Society of the United Irishmen. Betrayed by a government spy, imprisoned and condemned to be hanged, he succeeded in escaping to Paris where he consorted with Robespierre before finally finding refuge in the newly created United States. After ten years in exile he successfully petitioned the King for mercy and returned to Killyleagh. A rebel to the last, he lobbied for Catholic Emancipation, ending his days in Dublin in 1834, aged eighty-three. Harold came to write a charitable biography of this 'black sheep' of the family. In it he (half admiringly) characterised his great-great-grandfather as subject to 'Laziness, penury, domestic worries, vivacity, fluency, courage and a most impatient mind',[18] an odd collection of characteristics, typical, or so Harold thought, of the revolutionary mind. While appealing on paper, the life of an authentic revolutionary, of a resolute nonconformist, held few attractions for Harold in practice.

Harold came to regard these baronial castles as his 'anchors in a drifting life'. Here, he owned up, 'I ceased to be a pot-plant forever bedded out in alien soil.'[19] But even this comforting thought soon faded. It came as something as a shock for him to learn that his own family were little more than immigrants – admittedly, of three hundred years' standing – outsiders living among foreigners. All around were the dreaded 'Catholics', dangerous, difficult people who had casually surrendered their liberties to 'Fenians and Priests'. Among the servants at Clandeboye were fierce Orangemen who warned Harold that Catholics were 'evil men', 'alien, intractable, sly'. These impressions could only have been reinforced by Miss Plimsoll's paranoia, for she would manipulate every incident, however trivial, to uncover the odious Fenians; or even by the often tendentious conversations he overheard when lunching at the Private Secretary's Lodge in Phoenix Park.[20] Something of this rubbed off, for in later life Harold frowned upon 'candlesticks' holding high positions of state, deprecating in particular John Kennedy's election as President of the United States.[21]

It was at Clandeboye – Dufferin's family seat – that Harold decided that 'the Protestant ascendancy was established'. His own attitude to the Irish question was very much in the manner of a tepid Foreign Office employee grappling with an intractable international crisis: he proposed 'benevolent neutrality'. 'I rejoice,' he wrote, 'that I am not concerned with any Irish controversy.' For all that, when pressed, he was drawn back to the hero of his family memoir. 'Is it atavism which dulls my sympathy for the Calvinism of Ulster and sends my heart winging backwards to Hamilton Rowan of Killyleagh?' Perhaps the day will come, he speculated, when their animosities will be shelved and the 'whole thirty-two counties will be peopled by United Irishmen'.[22]

In 1895, at the age of nine, Harold was sent to the Grange, a preparatory school near Folkestone, where he remained for four years. By his own admission he was haunted by 'child terrors', powerless to escape his 'nervous childhood days'. But he also bore another heavy handicap. Three years earlier, at a toyshop on the rue de Rivoli, he had humiliatingly failed to spin a top. From this fiasco, he derived 'the sad theory' that he was 'bad at games'. Such inhibition was not the best preparation for an English upper-class, public school education.

Harold retained few joyful memories of the Grange. He wrote later that 'We were cold and underfed: we were incessantly being bothered to live up to our moral tone', the highest of any school in England, they were assured. None of this bothered Mr Hussey, the headmaster, who violated in the most savage manner the high moral tone he preached. A brutal martinet, he would 'kick us if we made the slightest noise'. Hussey 'spanked me for missing a music lesson,' he wrote to his mother, 'and said he would cain me next time. On Monday at 12½ he cained me, and then next at 2, and he cained me and found out it wasn't my fault he said that next time I ought to be cained he would let me off . . . Your *loving, loving, loving* son Harold.'

Given such a terrifying example, bullying was rife in the school. In one case, of a boy called 'Jack', Harold intervened to prevent the ragging: but with no success. Nor did Harold establish rapport with any of the other masters. Scolded for being untidy – he and his brother, Eric, were known as 'Rags and Tatters' owing to their chronically grubby appearance – he was mocked for drawing irreverent sketches in class. Small wonder that he dreamed of warmer climes and an abundance of appetising food. 'Neither the games nor the lessons nor the high moral tone,' he glumly concluded, 'were things in which, somehow, the masters expected me to share.'

Harold's discomfort was compounded by the unorthodox political stance he adopted. Not only did he defend Dreyfus from abuse, he also took up the cause of the Boers, defying the jingoistic fervour of the time. In assuming the mantle of a self-appointed martyr, he sustained his image as something of an oddball. Things worsened, became more personal, when in the ensuing Boer War the British army sustained an early defeat at a place called 'Nicholsen's Nek'. Patriotic cries of the loyalists would mock Harold during the morning break. Sometimes 'a few racket balls' would be 'dextrously aimed' at him. On one occasion he was subjected to 'the methods of the Inquisition'. 'You *are* a freak, aren't you?' suggested Alan Herbert (soon to be barrister, author, humorist; and, in time, Independent MP for Oxford). 'None of your cheek,' countered Harold, putting down Herbert who was a few years his junior. Occasionally there was some comic relief, provided by Miss Plimsoll. She turned up one day, on the eve of their departure to join their parents. Standing upon one of the ramparts of Caesar's Camp at Folkestone, her hand raised with middle and index fingers pointing threateningly across the Channel, she cried, 'Now boys, all together, Eastward Ho! Eastward Ho!' And the Nicolson boys obediently chorused, 'Eastward Ho! Eastward Ho!', only to be forced to repeat the drill for good effect. Harold estimated that they journeyed 'Eastward Ho!' thirty-six times during his childhood.

Whatever difficulties Harold encountered socially, he proved to be an able pupil. Once, when confined to the school infirmary with a severe cough, he wrote home: 'Darling Mummy, it is so dull. On Saturday we had half an hour to learn the <u>whole</u> of England and Wales in and then we had to do a map of it out of our heads putting in the counties and the towns. It was so hard. I did the second best.' At a school prize-giving ceremony years later, an old master, a Mr Nettleton, told him that although his written work had been 'disgustingly untidy', he was 'keen' at his lessons and 'really good at Greek'. Harold, he went on, had been 'certain to get a scholarship', but apparently Hussey would not allow it. Hussey, Nettleton acknowledged, was really 'rather a bully'. Reminiscing about the Grange in October 1950 Harold realised that 'the regime of old Hussey seems to have been perpetuated by his successor . . . I can see that you [Jocelyn Brooke] were just as cold and miserable there as I was myself.' He gained the oddest of impressions as he recaptured the past when he had been 'so unhappy . . . Now if, as a little boy, I could have a vision of myself today I should have been less unhappy. What oppressed me then was fear and a sense of failure.' Was parental indifference the cause of this sorry state of affairs? Harold, typically, apportioned the blame in an even-handed manner. 'Clearly it was a better thing to have been loved and sent to The Grange, Folkestone, than never to have been loved at all.'[23]

Wellington College was founded in 1852 in memory of the Great Duke. Formally opened in 1859 by Queen Victoria, it was intended to care for the 'education and bringing up, maintaining and clothing of the children of deceased officers, who may have borne commissions either in Our Royal Army or the Army of East India Company, and no others . . .' By the time Harold arrived in January 1900 the college was clearly in breach of these by now outmoded regulations. It was said that Wellington College was the creation of its first headmaster, the Reverend Edward White Benson (later Archbishop of Canterbury). Recognised as a 'stern disciplinarian', he was obsessed with the 'vice' of homosexuality, bent on ensuring that his charges remained pure. Wire entanglements were placed along the top of the dormitory cubicles to prevent any illicit toing and froing. At bedtime, doors would be locked from the outside while the matron and steward would patrol the middle of the dormitory. Every conceivable measure was taken to deter forbidden contact. By the time Harold's headmaster, the Reverend Bertram Pollock (later Bishop of Norwich) appeared, these draconian regulations had eased somewhat, though the spirit of Benson's regime lived on.[24]

Wellington sought social eminence. Under Benson it had enjoyed the patronage of Prince Albert, a practice perpetuated by Queen Victoria after his death in 1861. Under Pollock, the striving for social distinction soared as he conscripted two princes, three dukes, three earls, three bishops, six baronets, and a former prime minister to serve as its governors. Several days after the relief of Mafeking (17–18 May 1900) Queen Victoria visited Wellington College. By now Harold had tempered his radical views on the Boer War, perhaps reflecting that discretion should now give way to valour. At any rate, he 'shouted and hallooed with the rest', saluting the Queen in the appropriate manner. As the Queen, hunched in her seat, drove off in her barouche, Harold ran alongside it, clinging to the mudguard of the royal carriage until it left the school grounds and disappeared from sight. He recalled glimpsing 'one large pendulent, and surprisingly pink cheek; . . . the glint of gold spectacles above; and . . . a band beneath the bonnet of beautifully brushed hair – the colour of dried straw'. [25]

Harold was not unhappy at Wellington, but he was 'terribly and increasingly bored'. The grinding, repetitive timetable imposed from above wore him down: 'One ceased so completely to be an individual, to have any but a corporate identity.' Deprived of privacy and granted no leisure time, 'One was just a name, or rather a number, on the list.' Harold tried hard at games, or 'exercise' as it was called at Wellington, but only managed to 'flounder about'. To actually kick a ball was quite a gamble, as it would inevitably 'wriggle off sideways somewhere'. His inability to master the art of kicking a ball straight hindered his advancement through the school hierarchy. Eventually, in his last year, he was promoted to the rank of dormitory prefect, an unforeseen status owing nothing to his athletic prowess and everything to his scholastic achievements. Even so, until he came into direct contact with Bertram Pollock he claimed to have learned 'nothing serious' at Wellington. [26]

There were those who thought Pollock had inaugurated Wellington's 'Golden Age'; others thought that he had founded 'a military Lycée'. Harold phrased it differently, recalling an 'oppressive sense of regimentation', an environment so restrictive that in the four years he spent at Wellington his training in human relationships was limited to the ten boys who happened more or less to be his contemporaries. Pollock was plainly an authoritarian figure. Supremely confident of his own powers, he held those of his staff in contempt. 'If all the staff resigned today,' he notified one of them, 'I could easily supply all their places tomorrow.' Until Harold entered the Upper Sixth, the master appeared to him as 'a remote and rather alarming mystery . . . a mixture of fearful curiosity and religious awe'. From afar, Harold would spot his tall, slim, theocratic figure, silken gown billowing, striding rapidly through the cloisters, trailing 'a faint but pleasant smell of hairwash' behind him.

Pollock was undoubtedly a teacher of singular talent, at least in Harold's eyes: elegant, charming, erudite, exuding a self-conscious superiority, possessed of a sardonic turn of humour, sympathetic and subtle in his method.

His lessons held Harold spellbound to the point where he felt they formed 'part of my central consciousness'. He imbued in Harold a love of the classics.

> His method of teaching Latin was wholly personal . . . he would present one with a little printed card containing what in his mind were the five or six most beautiful lines in the Latin language. Of these the one he himself most preferred was the startling line of Persius: 'Virtutem videant intabescantque relicta [Let them look upon virtue and pine because they have lost her].' Often and often he would murmur that line, sighing to himself, sighing with the words 'and all the dreary round of sin' . . . How carefully would he read to us, how gently would he almost intone, the Sirmio elegy of Catullus, swinging suddenly, from the sad Latin words to the lovely song of Tennyson 'Row us out from Desenzano to your Sirmione, row.'

Pollock, no doubt to add spice to his coaching, would vary the settings of his tutorials, some more opulent than others. At times his pupils would 'sprawl on pine needles in his garden'; at others, they would 'lounge beside the fire on his floor'. Served coffee and cakes, and waited upon by two footmen bearing Georgian silver and Wedgwood cups, the Master would read from Lucretius, or a page of Shelley, or even from an article by Max Beerbohm. The effect was exhilarating. Overcome, Harold was swept up by 'a sense of Olympian ease and privilege'. 'If I have since understood in any way the meaning and the purposes of culture,' he wrote later, 'my understanding is due entirely and absolutely to Dr Pollock. And I render thanks.'[27]

By the autumn of 1903 Harold was preparing to leave Wellington for Balliol College, Oxford. An enthusiastic classics scholar, he successfully passed his finals in Latin – inspired by Pollock – and Greek – stimulated by a Mr Perkins, 'most exact of hellenists, most meticulous of scholiasts'. He was not sorry to quit Wellington, comparing it to being released from prison.* He wrote home.

---

*By chance, Wellington College, located near Crowthorne, Berkshire, happened to be within striking distance of Broadmoor, an institution for the criminally insane. At Broadmoor they tested the escape sirens every Monday morning; 'the banshee wails,' it was said, 'were spine-chilling' – so much so that the locals reported that the birds remained silent, frightened for many minutes. See Simon Winchester, *The Surgeon of Crowthorne* (Penguin Books, 1999), 106.

I cannot say I am in the least sorry, in work I have succeeded here above my expectations, yet I should not say I was top of the tree. It is so funny to think that it is nearly over and how happy and unhappy I have been . . . I shall be sorry to say goodbye to Pollock, Kemp [his house-master, Mr Kempthorne] & to Mr Perkins. They have all done their best for me & I don't think I shall ever forget it. I am beginning to see that brain counts for little but that character counts [for] every-thing, & it is not a pleasant thought as my character is weak and easily influenced.[28]

In October he went up to Balliol for his oral examination. Asked to trans-late a Horatian ode, he succumbed to a fit of nerves. Tongue-tied, he strug-gled with his assignment. His examiners, three superior Balliol dons, gave no quarter as they raised their upper lips 'in a sarcastic sneer'. But despite their intimidating, not to say arrogant, posturing, Harold must have done something right, for he passed the test. How 'nice to think I am a commoner of Balliol,' he informed his mother.[29] Harold's schooldays had come to an end. From the comfort and experience of middle age Harold asked himself whether he would willingly live his life again. Yes, he answered emphati-cally. Without doubt. 'But only on condition that I started at eighteen . . . Anything before that is dull and disagreeable to me.' Although he confessed to having a happy childhood, the 'whole period passed under a cloud of boredom. I was bored, bored, bored . . .'[30]

In nostalgic mood, Harold recalled his schooldays, employing some fine-sounding phrases. What he remembered most was the 'smell of varnished wood and Sunlight soap, the smell of linseed oil in the pavilion, the white light of acetylene gas upon a Latin grammar'. Yet he also called to mind being beaten twenty-four times at his prep and public schools. Did these repeated floggings leave any scars upon his soul, did they break his spirit? Not at all, or so he claimed much later. They were 'not humiliating; anger, resentment, or mortification were not aroused; and subsequent relations between the beaten and beatee remained amicable, respectful and often comradely . . . one bore these consequences with friendliness and such courage as one could muster. That was all.' Harold put this aptitude to absorb corporal punishment in a dignified and chummy way down to 'the English character', a variation of the legendary 'stiff upper lip'. Naturally, it applied neither to Germans nor Japanese, he hastened to add.[31]

Harold defined his social skills in a negative sense. 'I was not, I think, unpopular,' he said. At any rate, he made few firm friends at Wellington. A certain 'Dainty' (McEuan ?) , with whom he used to exchange notes through a slit in the woodwork of the partition dividing their adjoining cubicles, is casually mentioned. Probably his only real friend was Reggie Cooper, 'the most stimulating of companions'.* They became inseparable, despite their periodic rows, and remained on the friendliest terms for life. Yet Harold by nature was a gregarious creature. But at Wellington, excluded from the camaraderie of the 'hearties', he fell back – *faute de mieux* – upon his own company, or else favoured the society of those of similar disposition. This left him much time for reading. He read extensively and widely, from the historical adventure stories of G. A. Henty and Henry Seton Merriman to Anthony Hope's swashbuckling tales of Ruritania, traditional schoolboy fare. He was already developing a fondness for poetry. He knew well *Idylls of the King*, Lord Tennyson's connected poems cultivating the Arthurian legends. Familiar with Swinburne's works, he was also, like so many, charmed by Alfred Housman's *A Shropshire Lad*. On the other hand, he failed to work up any enthusiasm for Dickens or Walter Scott. And he positively disliked Edmund Spenser. When reading 'the cloying pages' of *The Faerie Queene*, and detesting 'allegory in any form', he became 'bored and bewildered by the whole story': 'this meandering and inconclusive poem . . . [is] not a poem that should appeal to any healthy child'. Turning to history, and as they were 'handy to hold', he ploughed through the intimidating volumes of William Edward Lecky's *History of England in the Eighteenth Century*, and was astonished to learn of the 'greed' of his Irish ancestors. In a lighter vein, Harold was positively discouraged from enjoying the escapades of Arthur Conan Doyle's best-selling hero, Sherlock Holmes, a ban which he no doubt evaded, for he later became quite a fan of detective fiction, relaxing with Agatha Christie, Ellery Queen and Georges Simenon – whom he held in the highest regard.[32]

Harold always spoke of Dr Pollock in glowing terms, praising his shining example, for he had shown Harold the true 'meaning and purposes of culture'. Yet on reflection Harold became acutely conscious of the one-dimensional nature of Pollock's reading of 'culture'. True, his passion for classical studies sprang from Pollock's scholarship and teaching skills. But the closed, cosseted world that was Wellington, that Pollock represented in the broadest sense, had little relevance to the real world outside. Harold knew it. Nearly thirty years on, he remarked: 'I have no affection for the school whatsoever and no pride in it. I feel a grievance against it for having retarded my development.' 'My grievance against the school,' he went on, 'was that the rigid system did not fit one enough for social life, and that when I went up to

*Reginald A. Cooper: served in Diplomatic Service; with Harold at Constantinople, 1913; served in First World War; promoted to Colonel and awarded DSO.

Balliol I thought that I was mentally and socially a whole year younger than my contemporaries.' No doubt he exaggerated – slightly? – when he put on record that 'I entered Wellington as a puzzled baby and left it as a puzzled child.' [33]

'Puzzled' he may have been, but by now Harold had acquired certain patterns of behaviour that would remain with him for ever. The 'rigid system', the grinding, repetitive timetable he complained about so bitterly came to serve him well. He adopted Wellington's rigorous work routine as a way of life. Self-discipline, an essential factor in any successful writer's make-up, underpinned his literary career. What else can explain his phenomenal industry as an adult?

Harold was often accused of being an inveterate snob, a dedicated élitist. Wellington provided him with a philosophy to justify his élitism.

I am conscious . . . of a marked distaste for those who have not bene-fited by a public school education. This distaste is based on no super-ficial prejudice; it is founded on experience. People who have not endured the restrictive shaping of an English public school are apt in after life to be egocentric, formless and inconsiderate. These are irri-tating faults. They are inclined, also, to show off. This objectionable form of vanity is in turn destructive of the more creative form of intelligence.[34]

In the future, his sense of class superiority considerably sharpened. He would display a barely concealed contempt towards those unfortunates who had not received a public school education. 'I hate them,' he once remarked of the lower classes. 'I do not want them to become like me.'[35]

It has been noted that 'intense passions and romantic friendships' consumed practically all public-school boys.[36] Harold was no exception. It is as certain as anything can be that he experienced his first homo-sexual adventures at Wellington. The evidence, though circumstantial, is entirely convincing. In their desire to stamp out any trace of 'illicit inter-course', the authorities at Wellington would divert the attention of the boys from the temptations of 'Satan' by devising a precise occupation 'for every hour and every minute, whether in the form of compulsory games or in that of compulsory lessons'. At least, that was the intention. But it was counter-productive. For 'Satan' lay in wait, ambushing the innocent, and, as Harold confessed, 'the vices which this system was supposed to repress flourished incessantly and universally, losing in their furtive squalor any educative value which they might otherwise have possessed'.[37] For many public-school boys this was a passing phase. Not for Harold.

An engaged homosexual throughout his life, his sexual preferences never changed.

But the most profound legacy Harold took away from Wellington was a deep sense of personal inadequacy. Time and again he would cry, 'What oppressed me then was fear and a sense of failure.' 'I am so fearfully sensitive,' he told his mother, 'that I mind awfully what people say to me . . . Altogether I am a fool, and I'll never get on in the world.' This perceived character flaw haunted him for the remainder of his life. Forty years on, he still admitted to 'a profound disbelief in myself'.[38] It was not that he lacked courage, or ability, or ambition. But these qualities, if not anchored to an assertive self-confidence (or colossal ego), were insufficient to bring them to fruition. Unfortunate side-effects followed. Adopting affectations, flaunting his cleverness, parading his wit, cultivating a mocking sense of humour, he all too often left the impression on his contemporaries that he was a 'lightweight', not to be taken too seriously.

Six months were to elapse before Harold went up to Balliol. As usual, holidays were spent on the family estates in Ireland or at his parents' embassies abroad. Often seasick on these 'Eastward Ho' journeys, he would be revived by swallowing 'cheap Medoc and little bits of cake'. Tangier was his preferred choice. It was primitive by Western standards, lacking electric light and paved streets, and one moved from place to place by sedan chair or on horse, picking one's way through mud and garbage and open sewers. Yet Harold chose to recall its romantic side, 'disturbing and aromatic, with wide nights beside the campfire, the smell of gum-cistus, the rootling of wild boar in the swamp behind the hill, the boom of a warmed Atlantic on a distant beach'. For him, Tangier, locked in a far distant past, conjured up memories not of the decadent East but of the ancient civilisations of Rome and Athens that had captivated him as a schoolboy.[39]

Harold also spent much time on the Continent, brushing up his foreign languages. For some months he lodged with the British Chaplain at Weimar, the Reverend F. E. Freese. He read Goethe, saw his plays, but never succumbed to the Goethe cult. Nor was he impressed by what he considered the excessive – even ridiculous – degree of regimentation tolerated by the Germans. All the pavements have 'footway' painted on them at intervals, he pointed out, clearly to save a few unruly Germans from fatal road accidents. He was introduced to foreign artists and intellectuals. He attended the opera on at least twenty-five occasions. Later, he claimed to dislike music: in some circles it was put out that he was tone deaf. Perhaps this misfortune struck him in middle age. 'I enjoyed it most frightfully,' he wrote, after applauding Wagner's *Tristan und Isolde*. 'It is a wonderful piece of music – I wish one could always have such a safety valve.'[40]

That summer Harold accompanied the Freeses on a walking holiday in Switzerland. He roughed it, after a fashion. Based at a pension on Lac Champex, near St Bernard's Pass, their daily treks led to wooden cabins in which they camped on the mountainside. Arriving late at their destination, Harold would bathe, 'with Pears soap', in an icy pool by moonlight in the early hours of the morning. The party almost came to grief when climbing the Grand Combin. Roped together, they somehow lost their footing and 'glissaded' down the frozen slopes. Still, mastering the mountain was an achievement he long savoured.[41]

Tired, but content, Harold returned to Weimar towards the end of August 1904. After bidding farewell to the Freeses, he left for England, stayed overnight in London, and then continued to Ireland to spend his last holiday of the season at Clandeboye. Oxford lay ahead.

TWO

'Effortless Superiority'

Balliol College. The name, long shrouded in mystique, has acquired a legendary status that somewhat belies the inauspicious circumstances that led to its foundation. Around 1254 John Balliol of Barnard Castle, a scion of a prominent Scottish family, insulted the Bishop of Durham when drunk. As a penance, Balliol agreed to support several scholars at Oxford, an act of conscience-stricken altruism that led ultimately to the establishment of the college a decade later. Situated on Broad Street, Balliol is a mixture achitecturally, sporting a Gothic revival façade that conceals older as well as newer buildings, revealing themselves as one quadrangle leads off into another.

It was in the early to mid-nineteenth century that Balliol began to consolidate its mythical reputation. Its cast of alumni was star-studded: Herbert Henry Asquith, Lord Curzon, Lord Milner, Lord Baden-Powell, Hilaire Belloc, Graham Greene, Harold Macmillan, Aldous Huxley, Edward Heath, and so on and so on. Here were prime minsters, proconsuls, scholars, lawyers, senior civil servants and distinguished men of letters in abundance, a vintage social and intellectual freemasonry, a brilliant host of movers and shakers. Sir Herbert Samuel, yet another Balliol graduate, noted gratefuly that 'Life is one Balliol man after another.' When Harrovians sang, 'The Balliol come to us now and then,' they acknowledged that 'a Balliol scholarship was prized higher by headmasters than that of any other college'.[1] Balliol radiated a flawless aura.

People spoke freely about the 'Balliol mind'. What was it? Whether admired or rejected, it has been regarded as 'an immutable phenomenon: public spirited, but somewhat aloof; cultivated but not necessarily cultured; earnest, but never strenuous in its exertions; and methodical, but often tinged with an unfeeling sterility'. Its devotees deemed it a combination of 'brain-power and wordly influence'. 'Eclectic, humanist, and a little worldly,' thought others. Not everyone was enamoured of the 'Balliol mind'. Alfred

George Gardiner, the celebrated journalist, noted provocatively that 'The Balliol mind distrusts "great thoughts" even if it thinks them. It believes they come from weak minds and soft hearts – from zealous persons with good emotions but defective intellects. Balliol . . . is really atrophy of the heart. It is exhaustion of the emotions.' Although it had produced the finest mental machines of its generation, 'they are sometimes cold and cheerless . . . We admire them, we respect them: we do not love them, for we feel that they would be insulted by the offer of so irrational a thing as love.'

The person held mainly responsible for this mind-set was Benjamin Jowett, Regius Professor of Greek at Oxford and Master of Balliol from 1870 to 1893.

First come I my name is J-W-TT.
There's no knowledge but I know it.
I am Master of this College.
What I don't know isn't knowledge.

Asquith offered a different perspective, alleging that Jowett's conversation had 'more bouquet than body'.[2] Jowett was not a path-breaking scholar. His translation of Plato's *Republic*, for many years a standard school text, was his most lasting contribution to scholarship. But he was one of the formative figures in the history of English education in late Victorian Britain. It was widely presumed that he held advanced views. A student of Hegelian philosophy, he was suspected of heresy owing to the liberality of his religious views. Fearful of the University being possessed by the 'gentry', he advocated reforms to lessen the expenses of an Oxford career, founding more scholarships and exhibitions for the less fortunate. He instituted reading parties known as 'Jowett's Jumbles' in the long vacation. He orchestrated the right mix of undergraduates for these happenings. In particular, he fostered a sense of loyalty to the college. By promoting the tutorial system he strengthened the bond between the Fellows and their pupils. A tutor's first duty, Jowett decreed, was 'to look after his men'. He set an example: it was rumoured that he saw every undergraduate at Balliol at least once a week.

At times ingenuous, at others ruthless, Jowett – nicknamed 'the Jowler' – reflected the earnest spirit of the age. 'A cherubic, shrill-voiced, fresh-faced little man', he was apparently incapable of small talk, though he was perfectly capable of putting down gauche undergraduates or disagreeable academics with a caustic remark. 'I hope you in Oxford don't think we hate you?' asked Professor Blackie, an innocent from Glasgow University. 'We don't think of you at all,' Jowett promptly countered. Autocratic by nature, his mode of governing the college took root. When Alexander ('Sandy')

Lindsay, a future Master of the College, found himself in a minority of one, he terminated the meeting by proclaiming, 'I see we are deadlocked.' Dedicated to producing a ruling élite, Jowett aspired 'to inoculate England' with Balliol alumni.[3]

Harold arrived at Balliol at the beginning of Michaelmas term, October 1904. His rooms, located on the ground floor on staircase X, were situated at the far end of the Garden Quad. Everything seemed perfect: furniture neatly arranged, pictures already hung, fire blazing in the grate. Yet his first impressions of Balliol were far from favourable. He heard too many 'strange accents', saw too many 'blacks and Rhodes Scholars', exotic creatures to be shunned. Even worse, impudent and assertive female students disturbed his peace of mind. Of course, they were not bona fide, certified members of the University, but through unofficial associations or societies without college status they had gradually infiltrated *Universitas Oxoniensis*. Harold found their presence intolerable, particularly as they were given to appalling slang, 'leckers' for lectures, or 'Jaggers' for Jesus. Nor was he overly impressed with the incumbent Master, Edward Caid. Although Caid was a philosopher of some distinction, Harold dismissed him as 'very dull and stupid', something akin to a 'Scottish Minister'.[4] The arrogance of youth? Perhaps. But his remarks betrayed the ingrained prejudice, a conviction that never left him, that mankind was divided into two categories: a racial, social and intellectual aristocracy, to which, naturally, he belonged; and the rest, philistines in taste, who, by definition, were excluded from his gilded circles. Harold clung to this belief. It was his birthright: he never abandoned it.

Harold soon settled down. He made friends: Hughe Knatchbull-Hugessen and the Hon. Arthur ('Tata') Bertie, both of whom would later join him at the Foreign Office. He gave himself to pleasure. He went riding in Wytham Park, skating at Blenheim Palace, and swam in the Cherwell. Occasionally, 'Tata' Bertie would take Harold to dine at Wytham Abbey, 'a grim gray building in a lovely park', the country seat of his father, Lord Abingdon, a mile or so outside Oxford. One Saturday evening he met there, to his delight, 'a young man with reddish hair who stooped and slouched . . . [and] who talked a great deal'. Winston Churchill, he recalled admiringly, 'only thirty-four and already a member of the Cabinet'.[5] Inevitably, he indulged in undergraduate high jinks. It was reported that while riding in a hired coach he squirted his fellow passengers with soda water and threw bananas at passing bicyclists. He even gambled, though his skill at roulette brought him no profit.[6] Elected to the Brackenbury Club, one of the more fashionable Balliol societies, he began to mingle with the so-called smart set. Harold even took up rowing. He formed part of 'the Morrison Fours'. Later memories would flood back of 'chill afternoons', of training 'with knees blue with cold', of the 'soap-sud congestion of the changing room, when my dislike of nudity merged with my dislike of stuffy cold'. To add to this torture, 'a man on the bank would jump off his bicycle and say things to me through a megaphone which were sharp and rude'. 'Brutish and short', this disagreeable – not to say uncharacteristic – ordeal was swiftly terminated.[7] Of course, it could be argued that these contrived activities showed Harold as playing to the gallery, merely gimmicks intended to win over his peers, a consequence of his inherent lack of self-confidence. But despite such desperate bids for approval, did Harold really fit in? At least one contemporary of his, Sir Charles Travis Clay (later Librarian of the House of Lords), thought not. Harold, he recalled, had made little impression at Balliol and was generally regarded as a negative character. Clay added, charitably, that Harold was believed to be a late developer.[8]

One leading light at Balliol saw in Harold qualities that had perhaps eluded others. About a month after Harold entered college, Francis Fortescue ('Sligger', or 'the sleek one') Urquhart invited him to lunch. So began a relationship that lasted until 'Sligger's' death. Over time Urquhart assumed legendary status in the annals of the college. The first Catholic to be elected to a fellowship since the Reformation, he entertained his pupils in his rooms that overlooked the back gate facing the Protestant Martyrs Memorial in St. Giles, a curious outlook for such a devout Catholic. A widely read history tutor, 'Sligger' made little original contribution to scholarship. He did not regard writing esoteric articles as his calling. His purpose was to educate, in the most general sense of the word, his young men. He cast his net wide. Not only his own history students were favoured, but any Balliol under-graduate whom he felt worthy of his patronage. So Harold fell under his spell. 'Sligger' was not an intellectual. Lengthy, intricate discourses failed to excite him, and he would cut them short by an abrupt transition to another subject. But he was a cultivated and tolerant man who had an undoubted talent for social catalysis. Probably Balliol's most renowned tutor, 'he emanated a stream of gentle sympathy that brought others out'. 'Although he was the hub of Balliol life for many years', 'Sligger's' presumed homo-sexuality hindered his election to the mastership in 1924, though it was also widely felt that he lacked the dynamism necessary to fill the top job.[9]

'Sligger' and Harold hit it off from the start. Harold would visit his rooms whenever he felt the need for advice or encouragement. They would take meals together regularly. 'Sligger' favoured Harold with an invitation to one of his exclusive reading parties at his Chalet des Mélèzes in the Haute Savoie, where conditions were spartan and the work timetable rigorous. Over time they began a correspondence that continued until 'Sligger's' death in 1934. In the future, whenever Harold was called to Oxford he would make his mandatory pilgrimage to 'Sligger's' rooms. What was the secret of this relationship? (Contrary to much gossip, there is no evidence that there was a sexual bond, though their shared sexual preferences, presumed or otherwise, may have drawn Harold closer to 'Sligger'.) Years later Harold noted that 'Sligger'

> imposed nothing while suggesting everything. He suggested to young men that they would grow out of their affectations and attain their own realities. He taught them that their failings and even their vices were unimportant and that they must surely possess inside themselves an inner core of energy and righteousness. He inspired confidence in the young. [10]

In other words, he cut away at Harold's lack of self-confidence, boosting his belief in himself, in his own abilities. For Harold, this was of inestimable moment.

During his three years at Balliol, apart from the stimulation gained from 'Sligger's' tête-à-têtes, Harold had displayed a rather casual approach to his studies, favouring instead the social merry-go-round. The result showed in his finals: a disappointing third in Greats. Neither the examination room nor the playing field had brought him great distinction. True, he had made some friends, but the immediate result of his Oxford sojourn apparently left him distinctly soured. As he recalled, 'I never learned to cope with Balliol until after I had left it.' Its 'effect upon my development was salutary and overpowering. But it didn't work at the time.'[11] As the years passed, and with growing experience, no doubt spiced by a liberal dose of nostalgia, all this would change – radically!

Oxford left an indelible mark on Harold. It confirmed his sense of 'effortless superiority', of 'the fastidiousness with which they differentiate between knowledge and learning', of his belonging to an exclusive fraternity, of his sense of élitism, all of which remained permanent features of his character throughout his life. He never tired of remarking that he was always carried away by the mention of Oxford, 'even on a pot of marmalade'. And at the centre of his Oxford fixation stood Balliol. The Balliol anthem inspired him. 'Balliol made me, Balliol fed me,/Whatever I had she gave me again:/And the best of Balliol loved and led me./God be with you, Balliol men' – words that Harold would recite with absolute conviction. The honorary fellowship at Balliol awarded him in 1953 was, he triumphantly claimed, the 'one honour I most desire'.[12] When his youngest son, Nigel, was about to go up to Balliol, he offered him the following advice:

> The main thing to remember is that Balliol is half a school and half not a school. In other words you cannot treat it as a Summer Fields

boy would treat Eton when he first goes there. Balliol does not care over much for the extent of a man's knowledge: it cares dreadfully for the state of his mind. Remember that what they want to find out is whether you are intelligent, not whether you are *learned*. They judge intelligence by the extent to which you avoid saying something stupid, rather than by the extent to which you manage to say something right.[13]

It was taken for granted that Harold would seek a diplomatic career. Other options – the law, Church, army – were not considered, or at least there is no evidence of it. Vacations were spent visiting his parents in Madrid or St Petersburg, where Sir Arthur was serving as ambassador, or else travelling the Continent, boarding with French or German or Italian families, honing his linguistic skills. This pattern repeated itself for another two years after Harold came down from Oxford, as he prepared himself for the entry examinations to the Diplomatic Service.

His continental excursions were not without interest. At an embassy luncheon in Madrid he chanced upon Ronald Firbank. The same age as Harold, Firbank was already a published author. Dandy, aesthete, exotic, homosexual, given to tiresome affectations, Firbank flaunted a camp lifestyle – reflected in his literary works – that offended Harold's sense of propriety. Forever wearing a velours hat, tilted angularly, 'it would be impossible,' Harold sensed, 'to be as decadent' as his luncheon guest looked. But as he came to know Firbank better, Harold began to appreciate his erudition, in particular his illuminating grasp of the finer points of literature and the arts. Harold readily admitted that Firbank 'represented my first contact with the literary mind'. Later, Firbank became the subject – disguised as Lambert Orme – of a cutting pen-portrait in Harold's engaging stab at autobiography, *Some People*.

In August 1906 Harold visited his parents at the embassy in St Petersburg. The embassy, 'an immense though low-storied house, washed in blood red', stood at the corner of the Troitzky bridge. Outside ran the 'twisted waters' of the Neva. Graced with elegant reception rooms, a spacious white ballroom and a capacious oval dining room, it boasted a majestic staircase, with pile-carpeted landings, decorated by Empire statues. In short, Sir Arthur entertained in grand style, marred only, Harold recalled, 'when the windows were open' and 'the peculiar stench of Russia – that strange smell of leather and fish-oil – would puff into the silken drawing-room as if the scent of blood'.

During Harold's stay, an attempt was made on the life of the Russian Prime Minister, Count Peter Stolypin. Sir Arthur held Stolypin in the highest regard. He asked Harold to make his way to Stolypin's residence on Apothecary's Island to find out what exactly had happened.

I went round there immediately . . . the whole front of the house was blown in; and in the roadway were two landaus tilted sideways with their horses lying in a pool of blood. They were carrying stretchers out from the garden and loading them into ambulances. I felt very sick and hurried away.

Twenty-five people had been killed and thirty wounded. Stolypin had escaped, bruised but unhurt, even though his children, his daughter of fifteen and an infant son, were badly injured. Naturally, Sir Arthur was delighted to learn of Stolypin's narrow escape. He held an extravagant belief in Stolypin's ability to stem Russia's revolutionary groundswell. He even put forward the highly improbable notion that had Stolypin survived – eventually, he was assassinated, in the presence of the Tsar, while attending an opera in a Kiev theatre in September 1911 – Russian history might have taken a different course, that is, the Russian revolution would have been avoided. Harold was never party to this fantasy. Recalling the botched assassination attempt, Harold remarked: 'My disbelief in the reality of St Petersburg society was not diminished by this episode.' Still, this barbaric incident must have been an eye-opening introduction for him to the savage, intractable nature of Russian politics.

There was another, less violent, upshot of his periodic visits to St Petersburg. Late in life Harold claimed to have 'always hated the Tories', a prejudice he had first become aware of at the ripe age of ten. How had this come about? he was asked. The people who had attended his father's sumptuous, not to say ostentatious, diplomatic receptions, he replied, 'believed above all in pomp and grandeur'. Apparently, not so the young Harold. 'And then there was the diplomatic body,' he went on, 'that strange cosmopolitan family, the leading members of which have been bored with each other for thirty years.' The tedious, arrogant, pretentious nature of these occasions repelled him. At St Petersburg, these perceptions were reinforced. Harold observed 'the behaviour at the Russian Court', and thought 'it was horrible'. 'To me, St Petersburg society as I saw it, was florid and inane.' And so, by a crude act of transference, he transmitted his 'hatred of their cruelty, indifference and selfishness to their opposite numbers at home – the Tories'. This sounds like special pleading, a provocative afterthought. One point can be made with absolute certainty: Harold was not immune to pomp and grandeur. He may well have been disgusted by the corruption at the Russian Court, but this did not prevent him, when in pursuit of a political career, of putting himself forward as a Tory candidate for Sevenoaks. He was not adopted!

Another matter disturbed Harold. 'Never could one get away from that sense of oppression and secrecy which is the bane of Holy Russia. We knew that our hall-porter was in the pay of the secret police.' Nerves were on edge. This led to a comic scene involving the ambassador, Harold, and the attaché to the embassy, Nevile Henderson. Henderson and Harold had been to the theatre to see a production of Sherlock Holmes. They returned to the embassy and retired. At about three in the morning, Harold heard suspicious noises coming from the Chancery. He alerted both his father and Henderson. The latter, accompanied by Harold, went to investigate, slipping a revolver in the pocket of his dressing gown, 'where fortunately he forgot all about it'. Meanwhile, an impatient Sir Arthur Nicolson decided to take matters into his own hands and advanced alone towards the Chancery. Glimpsing a faint shadow blocking his path, Henderson threw himself at it. Sir Arthur went flying. Henderson pounced. 'There was a shout, a crash, a gurgle. "Animal", yelled Nevile Henderson, "You devil, I've got you".' Harold rushed in, turned on the switch, only to observe his father struggling violently in the hands of Henderson, who had grabbed him by the throat. Sir Arthur faintly cried out, 'Look out, it's only me.' Henderson, embarrassed no end, disengaged. To Harold's considerable discomfort, it took two or three days in bed before his father was able to resume normal duties. The true culprit of this fracas, it was discovered later, was a large brown cat that had been trapped in the Chancery.

From these early pre-1914 visits Harold retained impressions of Russia that he clung to for the remainder of his life. Unlike his father, who 'loved the Russians and their fickle ways', Harold regarded those who lived on the eastern marches of the Continent as barely European. The Slav character, earthy, emotional, gloomy, confused him. 'Our special values' eluded it, nor was it 'a true inheritor of the European tradition'. 'Asia,' Harold eventually ruled, 'began on the east bank of the Niemen.' Fundamentally, nothing had changed, nor would it. 'You have that same incompetence in little things, you have that same delight in extremes, the same hatred for the middle course; you have above all that same Asianism and that extraordinary mysticism . . .'[14]

When not visiting his parents, Harold travelled the Continent, spending two to three months at a time with foreign families, learning their languages. On these tours he saw in turn Blois, Frankfurt am Main, Hanover, Wiesbaden, Torre Pellice and Siena. From Frankfurt he reported to 'Sligger', 'I am working here at this language and feel more grateful for the Norman Conquest than ever – & more sick of Goethe, & Bismarck, & Maximilian Harden, & Oscar Wilde & other German national heroes, than I have ever been before.'[15] Harold gravitated towards Paris, where one memorable evening he saw Sarah Bernhardt in *Phèdre*. He met up with Reggie Cooper at Versailles and bicycled into Paris every morning, where they left their machines at the Gare St Lazare.[16] But the main attraction for Harold was quartered at 174, rue de la Pompe, the residence of the redoubtable Jeanne de Hénault, the Mecca of many ambitious would-be candidates for the Diplomatic or Foreign Service. Jeanne first received Harold in January 1907. Apparently, he met her approval, for he returned on a number of occasions thereafter to perfect his French. Jeanne was already something of a legend. Ensconced in her fifth-floor apartment overlooking the Bois de Boulogne, surrounded by her cats and her aged mother – whom she disliked – she imposed upon her young men an enigmatic discipline understood fully only by herself. Of medium height and indeterminate age, shrouded perpetually in cigarette smoke, she would instruct her charges in a rich baritone voice, correcting their lessons with a khaki-coloured fountain pen dripping green ink. As Harold remembered her, 'the skin of the face was uniform in texture, smooth and yet unhealthy like a large, soft, yellow apple: slightly soiled and bruised'.

Supremely confident in her ability to translate the subtleties of the French language, Jeannne 'believed sincerely that God had granted to her the mission to coach young Englishmen for the Diplomatic Service'. She had a mesmeric hold over her pupils. Her crowded apartment could accommodate only three at a time. Harold – who had brought his dog, Rajah, with him for congenial company – remembered sharing its amenities with Lord Eustace Percy and Harold Handaside Duncan (who would later reappear as the luckless J. D. Marstock in *Some People*), two other young hopefuls for diplomacy. They would rise at five and drop exhausted into their beds at midnight. Meals were frugal affairs, served by Jeanne's long-suffering maid, Eugénie. Afternoons might be spent relaxing in the Bois or the Avenue des Acacias, memorising French vocabulary. Jeanne did not much care for Duncan. In fact, she regarded him with some contempt, sensing that he had less intellectual distinction than her usual run of quick-witted, well-bred students. Not so Eustace Percy, deeply religious, idealistic, high-minded, somewhat lacking in humour, but clearly destined for great things. So impressed was Jeanne – an ultra-royalist – with Percy's potential, that, in a flight of fancy, she toyed with the idea that one day he would become King of France. '*Voilà,*' Jeanne would solemnly say, '*mon candidat.*' Modestly, and with no rancour, Harold concluded that he would never figure so prominently in Jeanne's reveries. Compared to the blaze of Percy's comet, his own star looked 'a trifle dimmed'.[17]

It was still customary for all candidates to secure the Foreign Secretary's nomination before entering the competitive examination for the Diplomatic Service. In June 1909 Harold passed this test, shyly convincing a board of veteran diplomatists, chaired by the commanding figure of Sir Charles

Hardinge, the Permanent Under-Secretary, of his merits as an attaché. The next few weeks were spent either polishing up his language skills, or at a crammer's at 129 Adelaide Road, Hampstead, swotting up political economy, geography and history. In August he sat for the examination. This was no simple matter. True, it was heavily loaded in favour of those endowed with linguistic ability, and on this score Harold need have no fear – even though he later professed that 'the gift of tongues' eluded him.[18] But apart from papers in French and German, he had to muster sufficient marks in arithmetic, handwriting, orthography, English composition, précis, general intelligence, geography, the history of Europe, and an extra language paper – Harold chose Italian. He passed with distinction, second in his year, squeezed between Jeanne de Hénault's future 'King of France', Eustace Percy, who came in first, and 'Tata' Bertie, Harold's friend from Balliol. That year only Percy and Harold passed into the Foreign Office. Harold's acceptance into the Civil Service was now a matter of form. He gave as his referees 'Sligger' Urquhart and the Revd Dr Bertram Pollock. When asked whether he suffered from 'nervousness or overwork', Harold disarmingly replied: 'Slightly run down after the August exam.' He stood at 5 foot 10½ inches, with a chest measurement of 36 inches, weighing in at 10 stone 8 pounds. Of slim build (though his expanding figure would cause him much concern later on), conventionally attractive in appearance, his hair was brushed sharply back over a high brow above keenly inquisitive eyes and he had a smudge of a moustache. He admitted to wearing reading glasses. These qualities satisfied the Civil Service Commission.[19] His success was a great confidence-booster for Harold, as well as cause for much rejoicing in his family.

It has been suggested that there was a qualitative difference in the standard required for the Foreign Office and Diplomatic Service candidates: the former attracting the intellectual high-flyers; the latter, the weaker candidates. Diplomacy was recognised as an élitist service. One candidate, who appeared before the selection board dressed simply in an ordinary suit, was horrified to find all his rivals attired in grand fashion, 'in tail coats!'[20] By 1914, career diplomatists numbered no more than 150, forming a closed, gilded circle, staffed in the main by the sons of peers, landowners and aspiring gentry, and drawn primarily from the prestige public schools and Oxbridge colleges.

One compelling reason for this state of affairs was money, for attachés received no salary for the first two years of their service, and it was assumed that they commanded a private income of around £400 per annum to maintain themselves, a not inconsiderable sum in those days.[21] By the time Harold entered the service some flexibility had crept in about the required amount. Although the Nicolsons did not consider themselves a wealthy family, financing Harold's career does not appear to have been a problem; or if it was there was no mention of it. Still, Harold constantly complained of being in straitened circumstances. The situation did not materially improve over the years. Ten years later, now married with two sons to support, and holding the rank of third secretary, Harold grumbled that his net salary amounted to a paltry £86 a year.[22]

On 19 October 1909 Harold received a note from the Civil Service Commission instructing him to take up his duties at the Foreign Office. To facilitate his smooth entry into the service he went out and bought 'a subdued tie & had [his] boots cleaned'.[23] Before taking up his first posting abroad, he was required to undergo a brief period of training. Harold was twenty-three years old.

It has been noted that 'All the clichés about the Foreign Office staff were true', that it was truly the stronghold of the aristocracy where everything was done to preserve its class character and clannish structure.[24] This image stemmed in large measure from its methods of recruitment. Only the wealthy, the highly placed, the correctly educated dared to put themselves forward for nomination. Those without the required social graces hesitated to apply for fear that, if accepted, they would find themselves out of their element.

Of the two services the Diplomatic was the more socially exclusive. The glamour and romance ascribed to service abroad in an atmosphere still dominated by courtiers and an aristocratic society made this inevitable. Interchange between the two services was rare. Foreign Office officials were reluctant to take up posts abroad, mainly because of the heavy extra expenses involved. This was particularly true at the lower end of the scale. Only at the highest level was there some tradition of transfer. This sharp distinction between the diplomats and the officials came under increasing criticism, and there was a steady movement towards the idea of amalgamation. It met with entrenched opposition, almost entirely fuelled by the veterans of the Foreign Office who tended to regard the diplomatists as dilettantes and social butterflies. Quite naturally a degree of competition, if not latent hostility, developed between the two services, which continued until 1919 when formal amalgamation took place.

Nevertheless, some improvements were made in the years immediately preceding the First World War. Lord Hardinge, after becoming Permanent Under-Secretary in 1906, and possibly influenced by his own career, encouraged more interchange between the two services at the lower level. When they did take place, exchanges were almost always set in motion on the personal initiative of the clerk or diplomat concerned. Even then questions of rank and allowance intruded, and the number of exchanges permitted in any single year was severely restricted. Deciding which service to enter was, therefore, a matter of considerable importance. Once having made a decision it was extremely difficult, and often impossible, to reverse it.

By the time Harold entered the service the days of the old-style Foreign Office were numbered. Gradually, changes were set in motion. No longer would even the Permanent Under-Secretary be considered little more than a 'super-clerk'. A Registry system was introduced, registering and filing dispatches in an orderly manner, relieving the first division clerks of much tedious drudgery. Labour-saving office devices were viewed by the old-timers with some suspicion. One junior was caught fingering a typewriter, only to be warned off by a senior clerk explaining, 'Don't you know we're in a hurry.'[25] But by 1914 a separate department of eleven typists was at work. At about the same time telephones were put into regular use, each department having at least one at its disposal. Most importantly, the so-called Hardinge reforms of 1906 allowed juniors more initiative in their work. Now they could not only read dispatches and collate extra material, but also, on occasion, recommend a possible course of action. As their minutes gradually filtered upwards, drawing the attention of the upper echelons of the Office, they began to contribute to the foreign policy decision-making process.[26]

Harold was far too junior to benefit immediately from these reforms. For his initiation into Office routine, he was sent to the China department. 'They were all very shy & I was too,' he told his family about his introduction to his colleagues. When set to work indexing files, he acknowledged, ironically, 'the value of a liberal education'.[27] His duties were not particularly onerous. Reporting at 10.30 in the morning, he found the pace of work leisurely, though at times unbearably dreary. One mid-nineteenth-century Foreign Office wit had scratched on a window pane the following ditty: *Je suis / Affreux métier / Joyeux ou triste / Toujours copier!*[28] Since then, things had changed marginally for the better. But Harold and his contemporaries were still chiefly preoccupied with minor chores: filing, indexing, copying. He grumbled about his unhappy situation almost from the first day he entered the service. After only three months he concluded: 'The F.O. is so silly . . . They are idiots. I hope if [?] gets here (which is unlikely) he will do more to fuse the two services – & the sort of mutual suspicion and secretiveness is idiotic.' Two weeks later, practically in despair, he commented: 'I do such silly work: e.g. this morning I wrote drafts about a typewriter to be sent to Tokyo.' There is so much 'red tape', he protested. Twenty years later little seemed to have changed for him. He charged 'that whereas the Foreign Office is run today on the system of 1930, the Diplomatic Service is still to a large extent conducted on the system of 1842. And the energetic Civil Servant, when relegated to Diplomacy, is thus apt to resign.'[29] (Harold, restless at the irrational constraints imposed upon him from the outset, resigned the same year that he wrote these comments.)

When Harold joined the Diplomatic Service a Liberal government had been in office for three years. In foreign policy there was a striking degree of continuity with the previous Conservative administration. The so-called New Course in British policy was by now firmly rooted. In January 1902 an alliance with Japan had been concluded. Designed to thwart Russian encroachment in the Far East and the possibility of a Russo-Japanese deal in the area at Britain's expense, it was a visible indication of the unease prevalent in ruling circles that Britain was only able to safeguard her imperial commitments by coming to a bargain with her potential rivals. The Anglo-French entente of April 1904 followed a similar pattern, as did the entente with Russia in August 1907. On the face of it these were mere colonial arrangements;* and in the eyes of many British statesmen and officials had little if any relevance to the European balance of power. But this was a misleading assumption. Often the spirit of an agreement assumes a greater significance than its clauses. Fuelled by international crises, it generates a momentum of its own, pushing its partners into ever closer co-operation and mutual commitment. Certainly this was true of the Anglo-French entente.

Harold had no quarrel with these shifts in British policy. Indeed, it is clear that, given the choice, he would have defined the imprecise arrangements in a much more meaningful manner. His starting-point was the breakdown of the Anglo-German talks at the turn of the century. Had they succeeded, 'a treaty of alliance, certainly a definite *Entente*' would have been concluded that would have rendered the entente system 'a diplomatic impossibility' – hinting that the First World War could therefore have been avoided. It was only the machinations of that 'demented hyena', Friedrich von Holstein, the highly intelligent but machiavellian Assistant Under-Secretary at the German Foreign Ministry, that blocked such a beneficial settlement. With Germany now playing the role of a rogue state, Harold thought it 'an historical disaster' that the Anglo-French entente was not transformed into 'an overt offensive and defensive alliance', a combination that would have deterred Germany from embarking upon its fatal policy of

---

*The Anglo-French entente ('Entente Cordiale') was signed on 8 April 1904. By it the two countries settled oustanding disputes in West Africa, Siam, Madagascar, the New Hebrides, and fishing rights off Newfoundland. Above all, it balanced a free hand for Britain in Egypt against a free hand for France in Morocco, provided that no fortifications were erected to threaten Gibraltar and that Spanish historic claims were respected.

On 31 August 1907 the Anglo-Russian entente was concluded. This settlement defined spheres of influence in Persia and the attitude of both countries towards Afghanistan and Tibet.

brinkmanship. Harold remained a lifelong enthusiast for the French connection. Nor would he have argued with his father, who at the same time was pressing for a Russian alliance, by definition to rein in Germany.[30]

'The Balance of Power', thought Harold, was the best method, short of world government, 'of avoiding a major war'. He was restating what had long been regarded as a prerequisite of British policy. In 1820 Lord Castlereagh spoke of 'Pieces on the board' that play 'the game of Publick Safety', arguing that when 'the Territorial Balance of Europe is disturbed, [Britain] can interfere with effect'. Almost ninety years later Eyre Cowe, head of the Western Department at the Foreign Office, wrote of preserving the balance of power as 'an historical truism to identify England's secular policy'. Castlereagh was concerned at a resurgence of French power; Crowe was troubled by the prospect of the establishment of 'a German primacy in the world of international politics at the cost and to the detriment of other nations'.[31] As far as British policy was concerned, the principle remained the same.

Crowe's memorandum of January 1907 is now generally acknowledged to be a classic statement of the foundations of Britain's foreign policy. It identified Germany in unequivocal terms as a threat to the existing world order, challenging Britain's global ascendancy; it also gave a fresh impetus to the mounting anti-German mood in the Foreign Office. Harold was probably aware of Crowe's paper, but would have been far too junior to have dared voice an opinion about it in public. However, in time he came to embrace Crowe's views. For Harold, Crowe was 'the perfect type of British Civil Servant – industrious, loyal, expert, accurate, beloved, obedient, and courageous', a vision enhanced for Harold by Crowe's bold practice of indicating to his political masters that at times 'they were not only ill-informed but also weak and silly'. Extolling Crowe's 'nobility of nature', Harold regarded this austere figure with something akin to hero worship.[32]

Harold's relationship with another prominent figure at the Foreign Office, Sir William Tyrrell, was more problematical. Tyrrell served as principal private secretary to the Foreign Secretary, Sir Edward Grey. His style was very different to that of Crowe. He had acquired, or so it was asserted, 'seemingly oblique approaches to problems and personalities'. One high official put it plainly: 'Where Crowe would fearlessly confront a situation, Tyrrell would take avoiding action and let the thing blow itself out.' Malicious tongues put this down to Tyrrell's origins. Born in India, he was thought to be tainted with 'oriental blood'. Clemenceau dubbed him 'le petit Japonais au bord de la Tamise'. Permanently on duty at the Foreign Secretary's side, his influence was considerable. Grey valued Tyrrell highly. He agreed with those who thought him endowed with 'a keen and brilliant wit and the surest eye for its personal equations'.[33] Preoccupied with domestic matters, Grey was only too willing to delegate many of his routine duties to Tyrrell's capable hands. Of special importance to Grey were Tyrrell's multifarious contacts with the press and politicians. In a sense, Tyrrell acted as a necessary buffer between Grey and his political critics.

All this chipped away at the authority of Sir Arthur Nicolson, who had returned, grudgingly, to the Foreign Office in 1910 to act as its Permanent Under-Secretary. Many thought that Tyrrell's immense influence exceeded that of the Permanent Under-Secretary, in theory the Foreign Secretary's chief adviser. One experienced observer concluded, guardedly, that Nicolson's 'personal influence over his Chief is not as great as it should be'. Inevitably, a measure of gentlemanly rivalry crept in between Nicolson – upheld by Crowe – and Tyrrell. All this was compounded by Nicolson's self-perceived failings. 'I am afraid that I am not a good head of an office,' he confessed candidly to his son, and continued (in words that Harold would later paraphrase about himself), 'I am too easy-going . . . I do so hate rows.'[34] This was tantamount to admitting defeat almost before the first shot had been fired. But differences of policy, not so much in substance as in emphasis, separated these officials. Nicolson – together with Crowe – was convinced of the German menace, and aimed to turn the entente system into something more binding. They claimed that the existing arrangements with France and Russia possessed all the disadvantages, and none of the benefits, of an alliance. Tyrrell was more circumspect. Acutely aware of the parliamentary and party constraints that bore down upon his master, he steered Grey away from taking too clear-cut a stand on the German threat. These differences of attitude were to lead to painful scenes between Nicolson and Grey in the days immediately preceding the outbreak of the First World War. Harold, though aware of the conflicting currents of opinion, would have taken no part in these high-level exchanges. Even so, he was mindful enough to warn his father to 'be very careful not to put anything silly in his private letters to Sir Charles [Hardinge] – as they go all round the Cabinet, and, what is more important, they are seen by juniors in the office'.[35]

Something of the barely concealed rivalry between his father and Tyrrell seemed to have rubbed off on Harold. His remarks about Tyrrell's abilities were less than laudatory, certainly when compared with the effusive compliments he showered upon Crowe. Tyrrell, Harold reflected, 'excelled in examining the outer radius of international problems', he believed in 'personal relations', in 'atmosphere', while his conversations were 'intangible but suggestive'.[35] Perhaps not surprisingly, late in his own diplomatic career Harold fell foul of Tyrrell's reign as Permanent Under-Secretary at the Foreign Office.

Life in the Foreign Office dragged on. There was one brief moment of excitement. Two delegates from the Haitian Republic had arrived in London for King Edward VII's funeral. Less than overjoyed, Harold was dispatched to ferry them around London. He met them at Victoria station. 'Take the beastly niggers to F.O. and then round by Tower to see London.' The following day he went along to the Cecil Hotel: 'Pick niggers up . . . and take them down to Windsor for the funeral.' Harold's wards seriously embarrassed him. Not only had they brought a too gaudily decorated wreath, which Harold had to change for a more dignified one, but their unseemly behaviour on entering the precincts of St George's Chapel – ostentatiously waving highly coloured bandanna handkerchiefs – ruffled him even more. It was a very hot day, which no doubt contributed to already frayed nerves. Making their way back to the Haitian Legation, Harold's two companions, who for some reason did not see eye to eye, came to blows over who should claim the right-hand window seat in the carriage. It was Harold's first diplomatic assignment. Not, he must have thought, a very auspicious start to a glittering career.[37]

Bored with the tedium of his Foreign Office chores, other, more lively, aspects of life beckoned. A personable, well-connected young man, equipped with social graces and literary airs, he sought a place in Edwardian society. He joined a club, St James's – 'where the grandest diplomats go'. Less physically imposing than other fashionable London clubs, its rooms were smaller, its servants more unobtrusive, its décor – a green motif dominating – more restful, or so its proud members claimed. He played the country house circuit. Later, he boasted of having exposed 'the jade and lobster of the Edwardian epoch'.[38] But at the time, he seemed to enjoy the fun and games well enough. He weekended at Stoke Church – 'tennis and all sorts of silly games . . . Jolly party'; Kirtlington Park; Stratfield Saye – 'quite dreadful'; The Vine; Dormy House – 'We do nothing but play golf. I am frightfully keen about it'; and Knole House. He holidayed at the family estates in Ireland. He frequented bridge parties, went skating at Olympia, and tried his luck at dancing, but came away bored: 'I don't much like Bohemia,' he remarked dismissively.

Harold was not excessively overworked. Sport – golf, tennis and riding – occupied much of his time. He saw the world-renowned ballerina, Anna Pavlova, dance and attended the opera: *La Bohème* was 'simply thrilling' and *Tristan and Isolde* 'wonderful'. Beethoven and Brahms concerts were also included on his itinerary.* Naturally, he read voraciously: Paul Verlaine, Byron, Yeats, Walt Whitman, Plato, Theocritus – and Edgar Allan Poe. He frequented the theatre. *The Merry Wives of Windsor*, starring Ellen Terry,

---

*It has been contended that Harold was tone deaf. If so, this was an affliction that struck him much later in life.

he judged 'rather bad'. One play touched upon a sensitive subject that pursued Harold all his life. It concerned 'a Catholic who has a loathing for Jews', he reported home. The Catholic challenges a Jew to a duel only to discover that the Jew is his father. 'I must say I sympathise with the Catholic & not a bit with the Jew father . . . I don't think Jews will be able satisfactorily to write about their own race because they do not see the funny side of it. I think when I grow up I shall try to write a pro-semitic piece.'[39] He never did.

Eminently clubbable, Harold dined and gossiped with long-standing friends from his Wellington–Oxford days as well as with newer acquaintances from the Foreign Office, mainly Reggie Cooper, Gerry Wellesley, 'Tata' Bertie, Gerry Villiers, Gerald Tyrwhitt (Berners), Alan ('Tommy') Lascelles, and Archie Clark Kerr.[40] His socialising also extended to affairs with other young men about town, one known only as 'Uppie', and another named 'Greg': 'Dine and sleep at cottage with Greg – jolly,' he noted.[41]

In April 1909 Lloyd George introduced his so-called 'People's Budget'. It was, he declared, 'a war budget'. It called for increased direct taxation, a supertax on the rich, and, most damning of all, land duties, a levy that struck particularly at those landowners made rich from the growth of urban centres. Widely interpreted by the governing classes as a devastating blow at their way of life, it created a political sensation.[42] For over two hundred and fifty years the Upper Chamber had not dared to reject a finance bill. Now, defying tradition and good sense, it voted down the budget. In their folly, the Lords had recklessly precipitated a political-constitutional crisis that dragged on until August 1911 and that was to cost them dear. Eventually, after two stormy election campaigns, the Lloyd George budget was passed, as was a Parliament Bill that effectively clipped the powers of the House of Lords. Harold's perspective on these events reflected the interests of the social milieu he cultivated. 'I fear the "People" means nothing to me except ugliness,' he observed. 'I suppose I ought to have been an Elizabethan.'[43] It was his first recorded political comment. It could just as easily have been his last, for it set the tone for his subsequent class-ridden convictions that never fundamentally changed for the rest of his life.

In June 1910 Harold learned, 'to his sorrow', that he had been transferred to the Eastern (Europe) Department. So far, he was moderately pleased with his accomplishments as a Foreign Office clerk. Setting his own, characteristic, order of priorities, he remarked: 'I do not think I have gained a reputation for efficiency . . . [but] I do think I have been popular.' Despite his popularity, he was anxious to be posted abroad. London, he had discovered, was 'far too expensive'. He was earmarked for Spain, a prospect he dreaded for he placed Madrid on a par with Blackpool.[44] Blackpool notwithstanding, he arrived in Madrid in February 1911. His ambassador, Sir Maurice de Bunsen, a diplomat of some distinction, on excellent terms with the Spanish royal family, greeted Harold warmly. Harold's duties were not demanding or time-consuming, allowing him ample time to enjoy the glittering ceremonies of the Spanish court and whatever other delights Spanish society offered. That September these distractions were brought to an abrupt end. Harold was compelled to leave Spain in compromising circumstances: he fell ill. As he confessed much later to a close friend: 'I had (I really blush to state) gonorrhoea. It all came from Spain and the effect of Andalusia and a desire to establish my sex . . .'[45] Harold returned to London for a cure. He accepted his affliction in a philosophical manner, as did his father, who also served as his professional chief. To 'Sligger' Urquhart he speculated, 'perhaps the lesson has been valuable'. By the end of 1911, now fully recovered, he was promoted to third secretary and had passed an examination in international law. Harold was all set to be transferred to the embassy at Constantinople.

These months saw a sharp turn in his life. In the past he had flirted innocently with casual female acquaintances at dances or dinner parties, unwilling or unable to form any lasting relationship. For a brief period he was unofficially – and half-heartedly – engaged to Lady Eileen Wellesley, Gerald's sister. Now, suddenly, the prospect of marriage acquired a new urgency. 'I wish I could get married,' he cried. 'I hate this vague sort of luggage life. Besides I do so want a wife'; though he was careful to reassure his family, 'But you needn't fuss, because I won't.'[46] This had little to do with his homosexuality. Perhaps Harold thought that he was still going through a prolonged adolescent stage of sexual experimentation and should now settle down. At any rate, convention required that he lead a married life and raise a family as prescribed by the established norms of his class. On 29 June 1910, at a dinner at Apsley House, the London home of the Wellingtons, Harold first met Victoria ('Vita') Sackville-West. Just over three years later, on Wednesday, 1 October 1913, they were married in the chapel at Knole House, Kent, the Sackville-Wests' family seat.[47] Their marriage survived until Vita's death in June 1962.

THREE

Vita

The Hon. Victoria (Vita) Mary Sackville-West was born on 9 March 1892 at Knole House, near Sevenoaks, Kent.[1] Vita's aristocratic lineage was far grander than Harold's. Her forebears can be traced back to the Doomsday survey, while Knole House, the family country seat, was awarded to Thomas Sackville (created Baron Buckhurst, 1567; Earl of Dorset, 1604), Lord High Treasurer of England, by his cousin, Elizabeth I. Knole was a princely estate. Built by Archbishop Thomas Bourchier in the 1460s, it was appropriated by Henry VIII as a handsome gift to be granted – if deemed expedient – to anyone who chanced to command royal favour. Enlarged and improved upon over the years, Knole impressed as an imposing complex of largely fifteenth-century stone buildings set off by its spacious parks and woodlands. Covering more than six acres, it contained – or so it was claimed – 365 rooms, fifty-two staircases, and seven courtyards. Fifty servants maintained this magnificent pile, which reminded Vita of 'a medieval village with its square turrets and its grey walls, its hundred chimneys sending blue threads up into the air'.

Vita was obsessed by Knole, by its traditions and the family obligations it entailed. She wrote extensively about it, bringing to life its Great Hall, where occasionally she would encounter a stag sheltering from the cold or heat, and where, every Christmas, her mother dispensed gifts to the estate children. She recalled its three state bedrooms – unslept in 'for two hundred years'; its library – 'lined with unread bound volumes'; its ballroom and galleries – 'preserving their ancient furnishings, their gildings and velvets'; its chapel – 'hung with Gothic tapestries'; and Poets' Parlour, where Pope, Dryden, Congreve and Rochester were rumoured to have dined and gossiped. In 1813 Lady Elizabeth Sackville, upon whom the holdings had devolved, married John West, fifth Earl de La Warr, and fused the names as Sackville-West. Her eldest son, Mortimer Sackville-West, newly created Lord Sackville, inherited on Elizabeth's death. And it was upon his death, in 1888, that the Knole estates, now sadly diminished in extent and value as the family fortunes fluctuated, were inherited by his younger brother, Lionel, Vita's grandfather.

Vita's paternal ancestors were impeccably high-born. Her maternal lineage was more controversial, with outlandish, exotic overtones. Legend had it – and it was one that Vita chose to believe until late in life – that her grandmother, Josefa ('Pepita') Durán, was the illegitimate love child of a gypsy and a Spanish duke, reputedly of Osuna. 'My maternal ancestry is hard to beat for sheer picturesqueness,' Vita would brag. The truth was more prosaic. Pepita's mother, Catalina Ortega, an ex-acrobat, had been married to a barber from Málaga, Pedro Durán. On his early death, Catalina supported her family by repairing and selling old clothes. Pepita herself struggled hard before rising to international fame as a dancer, known throughout Europe as the 'Star of Andalusia'. Aged twenty, she married one Juan de la Oliva, another Spanish dancer. But the marriage soon broke down, and Pepita was free to take on as many lovers as she chose – and, it was said, 'she chose many'. In time, she formed a liaison with Lionel Sackville-West, giving birth to five of his children. Their first daughter was christened Victoria Josefa Dolores Catalina. According to her birth certificate she was *une fille de père inconnu*, but she adopted her father's surname, Sackville-West.

Supported by Lionel, Pepita moved her *ménage* to Arcachon, a coastal resort near Bordeaux. Upon her death in 1871, Lionel enrolled Victoria – and her sisters, Flora and Amalia – at the Convent of St Joseph in Paris, where she remained for seven years, and then to another religious institution in London. Aged nineteen, she was rescued from this cloistered existence by her father. In need of a hostess, Lionel, a run-of-the-mill English diplomat, brought her to Washington, where he had recently been appointed Minister at the British Legation. For the young Victoria this abrupt change in lifestyle must have been exhilarating: a sudden launch from the sheltered surroundings of a spiritual, God-fearing retreat into the grand world of embassy receptions and diplomatic soirées. She adjusted easily. She proved to be a more than efficient society hostess, and would brook no argument or disobedience to her wishes. She made a huge impression on Washington's social and political élite. Society columnists wrote of her 'beauty, charm, modesty, grace, clothes and taste'. She claimed that she had rejected twenty-five suitors, including the President of the United States, Chester Alan Arthur, a widower, and two young English diplomats destined to rise to the highest ranks, Charles Hardinge and Cecil Spring-Rice. Later, she boasted that her years in Washington were 'the first and greatest triumph of her life'.

This pleasant existence was brought to an abrupt end by the so-called Murchison Letter affair. Charles Murchison, a former British citizen now a resident of California, had sought Lionel's advice regarding the forthcoming presidential elections. Lionel favoured President Grover Cleveland, running for a second term, over the Republican contender, Benjamin Harrison. Injudiciously, he replied to Murchison in this vein. His letter was leaked to the press. Patriotic political commentators had a field day, damning 'The British Lion's Paw Thrust into American Politics'. The State Department, up in arms, demanded Lionel's dismissal. And so it turned out. Forced to return to England, Lionel's diplomatic gaffe cost him his career. Nor, apparently, was his advice widely heeded, for Cleveland lost the election.[2]

Lionel, now the master of Knole – his elder brother Mortimer had died a month after the Murchison affair broke – returned to England towards the end of 1888, accompanied by Victoria, destined to fulfil her role as its chatelaine. Having rejected many suitors, Victoria eventually chose her first cousin, another Lionel, five years her junior. They were married at Knole in June 1890. The union was not viewed with overt enthusiasm by the Sackvilles. For one thing, it was considered unsuitable that first cousins should marry. For another, Victoria was a Catholic, and although she refused to heed her Church's decree that any children of the marriage must be brought up in the Catholic faith – an act of independence for which she was excommunicated by Cardinal Manning – a degree of apprehension remained. There was also Victoria's alleged 'bad Spanish blood'. How this mysterious ingredient would affect the family's fortunes remained an open question for some of the Sackvilles.

On one score at least there was no need to worry. Victoria, self-opinionated, strong-willed, overbearing, discharged her duties punctiliously. She dominated the household, playing both 'master and mistress', benefiting from (old) Lionel's indifference to the day-to-day running of the estate. Even when her husband inherited Knole in 1908 nothing changed, for it was acknowledged that (young) Lionel 'lacked bite and grasp'. Victoria went her own way, her behaviour becoming ever more authoritarian, not to say capricious and unbalanced. She also took lovers – as did young Lionel. Her most devoted admirer was Sir John Murray Scott, fifteen years older than herself, known affectionately to the family as 'Seery'. Scott had been the secretary and adopted son of Sir Richard and Lady Wallace and upon their death he inherited a substantial share of their considerable fortune. Now a phenomenally affluent bachelor, he held the lease on Hertford House, London, with its priceless collection of furniture and paintings known as the Wallace Collection. Apart from owning extensive holdings in Ireland and Suffolk, 'Seery' retained an opulent *pied-à-terre* at 2, rue Lafitte, Paris, packed with art treasures, together with 'a country cottage', in fact a pavilion, situated in sixty acres in the Bois de Boulogne, that had once belonged to Marie Antoinette. Standing well over six feet, weighing 25 stone and with a five-foot waist, 'Seery's' gargantuan proportions matched his fortune.

'Seery' and Victoria quarrelled constantly. 'Go away you little Spanish beggar,' he would scold her time and again. These storms blew over as quickly as they erupted. Of an easy disposition, 'Seery' repeatedly reconciled himself to Victoria's tantrums. He was devoted to her – though whether their relationship was ever physically consummated remains a matter of speculation – and treated Vita 'like a daughter'. Generous, perhaps to a fault, 'Seery' showered Victoria with gifts. He also rescued Knole House from ruin. The estate's annual income amounted to £13,000 a year, a paltry sum and one insufficient to meet Victoria's improvements and the family's running expenses. 'Seery' balanced the books. During his lifetime, it was estimated that he contributed over £84,000 to save the estate from insolvency. Moreover, he vowed to make Victoria financially independent. In his will he bequeathed her £150,000 in cash, 'in gratitude for all your affection and kindness to me'. As an added bonus, he left her the apartment at rue Lafitte, including its contents, a treasure trove valued at £350,000. To Vita he left only a diamond necklace; but his expectation was that Victoria would pass on to Vita the bulk of this fortune when she died.

On 'Seery's' death in 1912 his family contested his will, portraying Victoria as a scheming hussy who had manipulated 'Seery's' feelings for her own mercenary advantage. It was a charge that drew headlines. Here were two well-known society families, who had retained *the* luminaries of the English Bar, Sir Edward Carson – appearing for Victoria – and F. E. Smith – representing the plaintiffs – feuding over a massive inheritance. Sex and money: heady ingredients indeed, that resulted in one of the most sensational court cases of the period. Vita was called to the witness box. She acquitted herself admirably, endorsing her mother's protestations that she was innocent of any misdeeds. After conferring for only twelve minutes, the jury found in favour of the Sackvilles.* Victoria's financial future was secured. So also, in the long run, was Vita and Harold's, though their expensive tastes led to constant complaints of being out of pocket.

Vita was brought up at Knole. It was her first passion. She longed to possess it, and believed it to be hers, but as Knole was entailed to the male-line descendants of the Sackvilles she never would. Instead, her first cousin, Edward

---

* This was the second time that the Sackville inheritance had been challenged. In 1908, Henry, Victoria's brother, claimed that their father, Lionel (second Lord Sackville), had secretly married Pepita. If he could prove his claim, and hence his legitimacy, he, and not Vita's father (Lionel, third Lord Sackville), would inherit Knole. In February 1910 – four months before Vita and Harold met – the court case adjudicated decisively against Henry, upholding the young Lionel's inheritance.

Sackville-West, would inherit the estate. 'I used to hate Eddy when he was a baby and I wasn't much more, because he would have Knole,' Vita once admitted, adding disingenuously, 'But now I don't want it.' Of course, this was far from the truth; a half-hearted attempt to face reality. Vita's obsession with Knole never wavered. 'If only I had been Dada's son, instead of his daughter!' she once lamented.[3] It has even been suggested that her fixation on Knole defined her sexual preferences. Was it not possible that by 'some peculiar permutation of nature, might she not become a male if she put her mind to it? . . . is it too far-fetched to surmise that [her infatuation with Knole] also determined in adolescence her sexual instincts and urges?'[4] And all to become master-mistress of Knole! But these are indeed deep waters, never to be fathomed.

As an only child, Vita led a solitary existence. Left alone for long periods with her increasingly eccentric grandfather, her relationship with her parents lacked real intimacy. Victoria was the dominant figure. But from the outset there existed an inbuilt tension between Vita and her mother, a tension that at times spilled over into outright antagonism as Victoria's behaviour grew more erratic. (In close family circles Lady Victoria Sackville-West was known, ironically, as B.M. – Bonne Mama.) Eager to make Knole a social focal point, Victoria's weekend house parties, which Vita was required to attend, had the reverse effect on her daughter. Here were gathered scores of people, Vita later inferred, who, 'By virtue of their position are accustomed to the intimate society of princes, politicians, financiers, wits, beauties, and other makers of history, yet are apparently content with desultory chatter and make-believe occupation throughout the long hours of an idle day.' The beau monde never held any attraction for Vita.

Nor were Vita's efforts at making friends with local children of her own age any more successful. Flaunting her social position, she would display a cruel streak, taking a special delight in treating them with contempt, humiliating them, 'stuffing their nostrils with putty' or 'beating a little boy with stinging-nettles'. The result was predictable: 'none of the local children would come to tea with me except those who had acted as my allies and lieutenants'.[5] Vita's sense of alienation from the outside world never left her; indeed in later life she would glorify her estrangement from society.

There were compensations, however. Knole filled her life. To wander through its rooms and galleries, to explore its grounds, was an endless adventure, a journey of discovery. At every turn she was overwhelmed by its history and her family traditions. Other great family houses, Blenheim and Chatsworth, she dismissed as 'an incongruity', foreign to the spirit of England, in contrast to Knole which was 'of England'; as for the Sackvilles, she extolled them as being 'portraits representing the whole of English history'.[6] But was she herself a 'portrait from English history'? Her Spanish background intruded. Later, she would refer to herself, with a touch of pride, as 'not being wholly English'.[7]

Inspired by Edmond Rostand's *Cyrano de Bergerac*, she began writing – the loneliest of occupations – at about the age of twelve: 'I never stopped writing after that.' Ballads, plays, historical novels were rapidly put to paper on a hit-or-miss basis. She often wrote in French. One play of hers, *Chatterton*, as she recollected, was 'of quite unequalled gloom'. Alone, she acted it out for herself in the attic at Knole, 'moved to tears every time' by her own performance.

Vita's formal education befitted her class and station. Governesses at home and then on to an exclusive day school in Mayfair run by a Miss Woolf. She excelled at her lessons. 'I beat everybody there, sooner or later,' she triumphed. Although Vita confessed to being 'the worst person in the world at making friends', it was at Miss Woolf's school that she first met Rosamund Grosvenor and Violet Keppel (later Trefusis) with whom she was to form the closest of relationships and who would figure prominently in her life. How did the few friends she had regard Vita? Curious to know, Vita asked one to write a character sketch of her.

I think you are '*very very passionate* – came back the reply –

> and *loyal and generous*! but that you can hate as much as you can love! You are emotional in a great many things especially where you are concerned – you are very easily hurt by unkindness. You are *very* ambitious and always want to be first . . . You are very frightened at being laughed at . . . You like compliments. You are *very* jealous but try and hide your feelings as much as possible. You have a great longing for sympathy, and at times can be very sympathetic yourself.[8]

Passionate, loyal, generous, ambitious, emotional, intensely jealous, highly competitive, able to love and hate in equal proportions, easily wounded but easily appeased, and craving sympathy. Certainly a mixed bag of character traits. But it might be pertinent to add self-absorption to the point of acute selfishness, leading at times to a total disregard for the feelings of others that brought to the surface an element of ruthlessness, a streak of merci-lessness. Vita admitted it. 'I feel passionately, and am vindictive and uncon-trollable when my emotions are aroused.' Harold would subsequently agonise over her 'dual personality', one 'tender, wise and with such a sense of responsibility. And the other rather cruel and extravagant.' The latter 'has always alarmed me', he conceded, acknowledging that he despaired at ever 'coping with the more violent side in yourself'.[9]

Vita 'came out' in June 1910, 'a distasteful and unsuccessful process', she recollected, 'but the death of the King [Edward VII] saved me many festivities. Thus can the tragedies of great Kings be turned to the uses of little people.' Later that month she was introduced to Harold at a small dinner party at Apsley House. He had arrived late. When asked to play host to the company, he replied, 'What fun', a spontaneous reaction that appealed to Vita. 'I liked his irrepressible brown curls, his laughing eyes, his charming smile, and his boyishness.' Three days later, on 2 July, yielding to Vita's invitation, Harold paid his first visit to Knole. The company was mixed: Herbert Asquith, the Prime Minister, presiding, accompanied by Ellen Terry, the celebrated actress, among others. It poured with rain. Lady Sackville took him on a tour of the house and grounds. Persuaded to stay on, he enjoyed 'a pleasant dinner', deciding, finally, that he had spent 'a jolly day'. From then on Harold and Vita met regularly, either at lunch or dinner parties or at Knole, where Harold became a regular fixture, driving through the Kent countryside to his tête-à-têtes with Vita in his 'little green Archie', his Morris Oxford car.[10]

Vita was not entirely lacking in sexual experience. At the age of eleven she had been introduced to some of the facts of life, the outcome of adolescent fumbling at the hands of Jackie, a local farmer's son. 'He didn't rape me,' Vita wrote later. 'He masturbated instead.' More was to follow. Later a crony of 'Seery's' '[tried] to rape me when I was sixteen, and frequently after that, when I was fortunately better able to deal with the situation.'[11] Vita coped as best she could. 'Men didn't attract me,' she acknowledged, 'I didn't think of them in what is called "that way",' adding that women did arouse her in 'that way'. At the same time that Vita first met Harold, and was encouraging him to visit Knole, she began an intimate affair with her school friend, Rosamund Grosvenor, while simultaneously cultivating a romantic relationship with Violet Keppel, who responded willingly: 'I love you Vita because I've seen your soul.'[12]

It was not that Vita did not have, or encourage, suitors. There was 'poor little Pucci', the Marchese Orazio Pucci, scion of a distinguished Florentine family, who chased Vita all over Italy, confronted her in Monte Carlo, and even turned up at Knole. Closer to home there appeared Lord Lascelles, heir to the earldom of Harewood, and Lord Granby, heir to the Duke of Rutland, 'a curious and rather morose person',[13] both of whom competed, unsuccessfully, for her favours. And then there was Harold. Struck by his *joie de vivre*, his charm, his keen wit and cleverness, Vita welcomed Harold as a favoured visitor at Knole; and other assignations were arranged. A pattern that was to become all too familiar began to emerge. With Harold abroad, in Madrid and Constantinople, and with both of them conducting homosexual affairs at the time, their affair, if subdued and low-key by conventional standards, flourished.

In January 1912, after eighteen months of chaste courtship – 'He had never kissed me' – Harold proposed to Vita at a ball at Hatfield House.

He had never made love to me – not by a single word – and I only knew he liked me because he always tried to be with me, and wrote to me whenever he had to go away . . . He was very shy, and pulled the buttons one by one off his gloves . . . He didn't kiss me, but we sat rather bewildered over supper afterwards, and talked excitedly though vaguely about the flat we would have in Rome . . .

Vita accepted, if somewhat hesitantly.

When informed of Harold's proposal, Lord Sackville felt let down, disappointed that Vita had not made 'a great match with a great title'. Lady Sackville agreed, but was, uncharacteristically, more discreet in her remarks. Still, she laid down strict guidelines for the happy couple's future behaviour. For one thing, the 'Seery' inheritance case was pending. With the future so uncertain, she resolved that there could be no official engagement for at least a year. 'Where is the money to come from?' she asked. Family gossip spoke of Harold as 'a penniless Third Secretary'. Lady Sackville took matters into her own hands. Vita, she firmly ruled, must be 'absolutely free' of any obligation, and moreover their correspondence must be pure, free of any words of endearment. Harold despaired of ever getting married 'till this beastly case is over'.[14] Deeply in love and left with no alternative, he agreed. Harold and Vita had to wait patiently until October 1913 before they stood before the altar. But there would be other pitfalls on the way to Knole Chapel.

In the meantime, Vita's affair with Rosamund deepened. Vita saw this as something quite natural.

'It never struck me as wrong that I should be more or less engaged to Harold, and at the same time very much in love with Rosamund.' She saw Harold 'far more as a playfellow' than in any other light. 'Our relationship was so fresh, so intellectual, so unphysical, that I never thought of him in that aspect at all.' She concluded that it was all rather Harold's 'fault', for she maintained he was far too 'over-respectful': clearly, Vita added, Harold was not 'the lover-type of man'.

Some years earlier Vita had written a 120,000–word unpublished novel, *Behind the Mask* (1910), in which she revealed her unorthodox attitude towards marriage. It tells of a young heroine thrown into the 'matrimonial fishpond' by an ambitious, assertive mother. Surrendering to pressure, she marries a devoted Frenchman whom she does not love, rejecting the man she does love, 'a playmate, clever and gay, with whom she feels an effortless affinity'. Although married, she does not abandon her 'playmate'. Quite the contrary, ultimately she scoops up both her 'devoted husband' *and* her 'playmate'. Controlling events, she manoeuvres husband and playmate to play out their allotted, distinct roles in her life.[15] Here was the harsh reality that lay behind the mask. Unwittingly, Vita had written the scenario of her own life; but she would add an original twist. In her fiction, the 'young heroine' determined both the spirit and the substance of her marriage. So it would be in real life. But Vita ensured that her 'devoted husband' and her 'playmate' would fuse in the figure of Harold, while true passion would lie elsewhere, outside marriage. This turned out to be more than congenial for Harold, for he too sought a 'playmate' and a 'devoted' wife. Like Vita, Harold solicited true passion elsewhere, though of a more restrained nature.

The guidelines of their future relationship were set out well before the marriage ceremony actually took place. Vita, thinking of Harold's prolonged absences on service, had already decided that 'It is rather good for us to have a chance of thoroughly missing each other.' Despairing of the social merry-go-round that she was forced to ride, Vita elevated herself, and Harold, to a different level. After a particularly frivolous fancy dress ball, she concluded: 'This is very primitive and unsubtle for literary people like us.' These were clearly Vita's judgements, not necessarily shared by Harold, for he was saddened by the long separations and enjoyed playing the social circuit, though he rose naturally to the bait of 'literary people like us'. And what of Harold's diplomatic career? Vita carelessly promised, appeasing Harold, that she would 'always be ready to go to dinner parties if you want me to'. But it was an empty pledge. As in most things, Vita thoughtlessly wrote her own rules of the game. Did she sense Harold's easygoing, tolerant nature, already secure in the knowledge that she could mould him to her will? Or did Harold sense Vita's dominant personality, already apprehensive that under pressure he would cave in? Harold speculated about acting out the role of the proverbial husband of Victorian-Edwardian times: authoritative, decisive, bossy. But no sooner had he contemplated it than he abandoned it. 'About big things I am to have the upper hand,' he bragged, but then he buckled under: 'Remember that whatever you do . . . I shall know that you were right'. These terms of reference of their marriage held firm until the end. It survived, not only because the rules of the game, so to speak, had been decided from the outset, but also because they discovered, and then fostered, other interests: literature, gardens, family. As Harold acutely observed at the time, it was going to be an 'amazing marriage'.[16] And so it was.

Whenever Harold was home on leave he was usually to be found at Knole. Time drifted by. Weekend parties, tennis, long walks or motoring around the Kent countryside occupied their time. On a rainy weekend at the end of September 1912 Harold finally faced up to Vita. 'He kissed me! He kissed me! I love him. *Io l'amo tanto,*' Vita cried after it had happened in the Venetian Ambassador's Bedroom at Knole. 'But I so much want to see R[osamund] again,' she wistfully added. One weekend Harold met Rosamund there. Although he was unaware of the true nature of Vita's relationship with her, Rosamund saw in him a serious rival. At the same time Violet Keppel was fiercely protesting her love for Vita. Having already seen into Vita's 'soul', she promised, 'I will show you madness Vita, madness, do you hear?' At Knole, they walked together around the park. 'She was crazy,' Vita remembered. 'She embraced me as she never has before, talking to me like a lover. Rosamund doesn't know that I was with Violet tonight.' To Harold, Vita referred innocently to Violet as 'her erratic friend' who 'will amuse you more than anybody'. 'How you will hate her, or perhaps you will be completely bowled over, so on the whole I think you had better not meet.'[17] They did meet, however, in September 1912. But Harold would never be amused by Violet who, to his utter misery, fulfilled her promise to bring 'madness' into Vita's life and by so doing almost wrecked his own.

Torn between Rosamund and Violet at home, and with Harold waiting patiently abroad, Vita wavered. 'Sometimes,' she wrote to him in Constantinople, 'I feel it would be simpler to give it all up.' Alarmed, he telegraphed: '*Dernière lettre incompréhensible et inquiétante. Dois-je la prendre au sérieux? Réponds télégraphiquement oui ou non. Très anxieux.*' Vita replied the same day, 18 May 1913, setting Harold's doubts at rest. '*Non. T'en demande pardon. N'en crois un mot.*' 'Mea culpa! Mea maxima culpa!' Vita confessed, 'I come to you in sack-cloth and ashes, and humble myself to the dust at your feet, a bad naughty Mar* who hardly dares hope to be forgiven.'[18] Harold was only too willing to forgive and forget. Some weeks later the 'Seery' case was settled in Lady Sackville's favour, with Harold, Vita, Rosamund and Violet present to witness her triumph. 'Summing up of judge excellent,' Harold applauded. 'Jubilant dinner at Rubens.'† Now that the family finances were secure, and with Vita persuaded that Harold would serve as her 'refuge', her 'lifebelt'[19] – in other words, 'a playmate, clever and gay' – the wedding could go ahead. Lady Sackville gave her consent, and the ceremony took place at Knole Chapel on 1 October 1913, the Bishop of

*'Mar' was the Sackville vernacular for 'small', referring in general to a child. Lady Sackville invariably called Vita 'Mar', and Harold adopted the habit. Vita retaliated by dubbing Harold as 'Hadji' (pilgrim), Sir Arthur's pet name for his son.
†The Rubenses were Walter Rubens – a golf partner of Harold's, but still 'a bit of a bounder and low bred' –and his wife Olive, the mistress of Vita's father, Lionel, third Lord Sackville. See **ND**, 7 July 1913.

Rochester presiding. Walter Rubens played the organ, accompanying his wife Olive, who sang an aria from Gounod's *Redemption*. Lady Sackville herself was absent, allegedly ill in bed; but Rosamund, as bridesmaid, escorted Vita to the altar, together with Gwen, Harold's sister, while Freddy, Harold's elder brother, clad in the uniform of the 15th Hussars, served as best man.

Throughout the ups and downs of this offbeat courtship, Harold was earning his living as 'a penniless Third Secretary' in Madrid and Constantinople. From Madrid he sent Vita a wooden effigy of Saint Barbara, worm-eaten and 21 inches high. Barbara would accompany them everywhere on their travels during their married life: it now rests at Sissinghurst. It was a highly symbolic gift. According to legend, Saint Barbara – a Christian martyr – was the extremely beautiful daughter of a wealthy heathen. Because of her singular beauty, and fearful that she be demanded in marriage, he shut her up in a tower to shield her from the corrupt distractions of the outside world. In religious works, Saint Barbara is typically seen standing by a high tower. Vita sensed an immediate affinity with Barbara. She told Lady Sackville that she would like 'to live alone in a tower with her books'.[20] To Harold she admitted that she was 'an unsociable and unnatural mar'.[21] At Sissinghurst, Vita lived out Barbara's story as she isolated herself in her Elizabethan tower, brooking no irksome interruptions, declaring it forbidden territory for all except the most privileged.

After spending six months in Madrid, from February to September 1911, Harold returned to London to undergo a cure for gonorrhoea. Medical treatment apart, he returned also to resume his social hob-nobbing, while putting in the obligatory hours at the Foreign Office as a matter of course. At leisurely dinner and lunch parties he would unwind in the company of friends – Archie Clark Kerr, Reggie Cooper, 'Tata' Bertie, among others – enjoying the comforts of London's clubland. He played some golf and tennis, and even attended an occasional concert: 'Boy violinist [probably Samuel Kutcher]. Quite wonderful.' Christmas and the New Year found Harold at Knole, courting Vita. Then he crossed over to County Down where he spent a fortnight at Clandeboye, resting, walking, playing golf, despite the bad weather. After another brief visit to Knole, Harold left London on 24 January to take up his new posting as third secretary at the embassy in Constantinople. He travelled overland via Munich, Vienna and Sofia, arriving safely at his destination on the 27th.[22]

Harold served almost two years in Constantinople, years that coincided with a most turbulent period in the history of the Ottoman Empire: internal unrest and revolution at home, wars and defeat abroad. Four years before his arrival, an abortive movement for reform led by the so-called 'Young Turks' (or Committee of Union and Progress) forced the despotic Sultan,

Abdul Hamid II, to summon a parliament and restore the liberal constitution of 1876.* A year later he was sent into exile, found guilty of backing a counter-revolution, proof, apparently, of the Young Turks' good intentions. Initially, British policy viewed the Young Turks' aspirations for reform with great sympathy. Sir Edward Grey, the Foreign Secretary, hailed their 'revolution', 'keen that the new order should have every chance'; Sir Gerard Lowther, the British ambassador at the Porte, fantasised that the Young Turks would inaugurate a constitutional monarchy on the British model.

These high hopes soon turned sour. The British quickly discovered that the Young Turks were very much like the 'Old Turks', their regime characterised by an aggressive pan-Ottomanism (that eventually shaded off into pan-Turkism and pan-Turanianism) and an inability, or unwillingness, to establish effective constitutional rule. These policies, or lack of them, clashed with fundamental British interests. With a slight stretch of the imagination, the Young Turks' 'isms' could reach as far as Egypt, or the Persian Gulf, or even India. But no less, they also touched upon the future of the Ottomans' Christian subjects at a time when the Balkan peoples, backed by Russia, Britain's entente partner, were flaunting an assertive nationalism. Faced with the necessity of safeguarding vital imperial interests and preserving the entente system, Britain's Eastern policy was unravelling. It was Italy, bent on territorial aggrandisement, that escalated events to crisis point.

In October 1911, relying on previous Great Power agreements, and banking on Turkish weakness, Italy landed a force at Tripoli – then a province of the Ottoman Empire – and annexed it the following month. The Italians continued on their path to imperial glory. In April 1912 they bombarded the Dardanelles, forcing the Turks to close the Straights, an act that caused much damage to the Russians. Soon after they occupied Rhodes and other Dodecanese islands. These matters were brought to a close by the treaty of Ouchy (later, of Lausanne) in October. By it, Italy acquired Tripoli, but agreed, eventually, to evacuate the islands. The same month, October 1912, saw the Balkan League – Bulgaria, Serbia, Greece and Montenegro – a creature of Russian diplomacy, attack Turkey: its aim was to partition Macedonia, another province of the decaying Ottoman Empire. The League gained startling victories. The Bulgars, within days, had advanced to the Chatalja lines, the last line of defence before Constantinople, though they failed to break through. At the same time the Serbs swept through northern Albania, reaching the Adriatic, outdoing more modest gains by the Greeks and the

---

*The constitution of 1876 declared the indivisibility of the Ottoman Empire; liberty of the individual; freedom of conscience, the press and education; equality of taxation; irremovability of judges; and parliamentary government based on general representation.

Montenegrans. All this alarmed the powers. With Grey playing a major role, a treaty was signed at London on 30 May 1913 bringing the war to an end, Turkey ceding all its territories west of a line from Enos to Midia. A month later the second Balkan war broke out, the victors squabbling over the spoils, a situation that saw Bulgaria humbled and that allowed the Turks to intervene and to recover some lost territory.

The net effect of these wars was to reduce Turkey in Europe to an area around Adrianople and Constantinople; to strengthen the Balkan League countries, in particular Serbia; and to leave Bulgaria bitterly resentful at having been forced to cede some of its gains from the first war.

In January 1913 British policy took a further blow. Enver Bey, a leading pan-Turanian, heading a pro-German faction, led a *coup d'état* against his government that had been humiliated in war by Italy and the Balkan states. Turkey slipped further out of the British orbit and into Germany's grasp. Neither Lowther nor his successor, Sir Louis Mallet, whose 'extravagant flatteries' directed at Enver and his intimates fell on deaf ears, could stop the drift. By 5 November 1914, the three entente powers, Britain, France and Russia, were at war with Turkey, now an ally of Germany.[23]

These dramatic events found little expression in Harold's diaries or letters. 'How tiresome,' he recorded laconically, when Greece joined in the war against Turkey. 'How dull!' he thought, when he heard that peace negotiations had been decided upon. There was one spark of excitement, however. As the Bulgars advanced on Adrianople, Harold, disguised as a doctor, bearing a red crescent and wearing a fez, made his way to the front as an observer. Understandably, he was racked by nerves. But he managed to rescue twenty-two wounded Turkish soldiers, bringing them to safety in a motor launch while under fire. When he told them that Adrianople had been captured, they murmured, 'as God wills'. Proud of his exploit, he boasted to Vita: 'But it was capable of me to get out . . . So who says I am not capable.'[24]

Harold attempted to interest Vita in the complicated diplomacy of the Balkan conflict. 'You see the whole question is like this,' he began, and went on to detail the powers' response to the fighting. 'Does this interest you?' he asked. 'Do you know what it means? It may mean anything – war, revolution or peace.' But Vita was not really interested. 'I hate you for making me tell you,' she retorted, 'but I suppose I must. Sometimes I think you are really quite happy there with your Gerry [Wellesley] and your wars, and I am not by any means all-important.' Apart from a profound indifference to the art of diplomacy, Vita had other things on her mind: the court case and its repercussions; her tangled relationships with Rosamund and Violet; and pleasure trips to Italy and Spain – 'this is the life for me: gypsies, dancing, disreputable artists, bull fights'. A contrite Harold regaled Vita with generous portions of Turkish Delight, laced with 'monkey nuts', for which Vita was forever grateful.[25]

Harold's sporadic comments on politics and diplomacy were more than matched by his crowded social calendar: balls, parties, picnics, concerts, dances, golf, squash, tennis, swimming. He took up sailing, a pastime not without its dangers: 'sail in a gale out to Marmora and am nearly drowned'. He kept a horse called Bottle, and doted on his dog, Mikki. Close friends – Gerry Wellesley, Reggie Cooper, Gerald Tyrwhitt – were also seconded to the embassy, familiar company that helped to pass the hours. Another old acquaintance appeared, Ronald Firbank. When they had first met in Madrid he had offended Harold with his overtly camp mannerisms. But fascinated by Firbank's erudition, Harold made arrangements to see him again, planning to take him sailing on the Bosphorus, perhaps as far as the Black Sea. Everything was settled, including a picnic lunch. It was an ideal spring day for sailing, but Firbank failed to show up. He sent Harold a note: 'let us keep today as something marvellous that did not occur'. Furious, Harold dashed round to his hotel, the Pera Palace, but Firbank had already left to inspect churches and other tourist attractions. Harold scribbled 'silly ass' on his card and left it for the 'ridiculous' Firbank. He went sailing, 'alone and indignant'. When he returned home he found his sitting room full of Madonna lilies. His servant greeted him with a grin. '*C'est un Monsieur qui vous a apporté tous ça.*' '*Quel Monsieur?*' '*Un Monsieur qui porte le chapeau de travers*' – Firbank's trademark.[26]

In July 1912, another camp figure turned up, more impressive than the 'ridiculous' Firbank. Pierre de Lacretelle, 'slender, dark, vivacious and highly intelligent', was the cause of Harold's infatuation. Harold thought him 'one of the most brilliant people I have ever known'. A master of the subtleties of modern French literature, he would help Harold with his books and articles on French poets and authors. Well born, Pierre inherited great wealth, but opium and obsessive gambling ruined him. This was far in the future. That summer they enjoyed each other's company. They spent a happy week together, sailing and sunbathing, 'dallying in a low-ceilinged room in Therapia . . . all the while reciting and talking about French poetry . . . a golden week'. By September Harold was back at Knole. After wooing Vita, he hurried over to Paris to Pierre, where they spent a weekend together at the Astoria Hotel, and where Pierre introduced him to Jean Cocteau.*

* * *

*Pierre de Lacretelle was the main prototype for the composite figure, the Marquess de Chaumont, in *Some People*, although Pierre himself also makes an appearance in the essay. See also Lees-Milne, *Harold Nicolson*, i, 54–56.

After their wedding, Harold and Vita left for Constantinople, arriving at the beginning of November. They stopped off at Florence where Harold tried his hand at watercolour painting, not, apparently, with much success. Dutiful tourists, they visited the Uffizi and the Duomo; and, in an act of 'dreadful *manque de délicatesse*' – Vita's expression – they stayed in the 'little cottage' that she had shared with Rosamund only eighteen months earlier. From Brindisi – accompanied by Vita's maid, Emily, and Harold's valet, William ('Wuffy') Booth – they set sail for Egypt. They did all the expected things: visited the Pyramids; travelled up the Nile to Luxor where they wandered through the intimidating colonnades of the great temple at Karnak. In Cairo, Ronald Storrs, the scholarly Oriental Secretary at the embassy, escorted them to mosques and bazaars and showed off his own Egyptian *objets d'arts*. They dined with Lord Kitchener, the all-powerful British Agent in Egypt, but his ill-bred behaviour and philistinism held no appeal for the Nicolsons. When discussing Egyptian art, the Field Marshal growled: 'I can't think much of a people who drew cats the same way for four thousand years.'[27]

Harold was keen to reach Constantinople. 'Bored – and impatient,' he recorded, as they sailed through the Marmora. Immediately upon arrival they began to look for a home. They chose 'the most attractive house you have ever seen', wrote Vita to a friend; a wooden Turkish structure at Cospoli, overlooking the Golden Horn and St Sophia. It was a large house, with a little garden and a pergola of grapes and fruit trees. 'I find it lovely,' Vita said. It needed seven servants to maintain it. It was here that Vita, aided by Harold, first experimented with gardening, creating a terraced garden on the grounds that sloped down to the sea. Together they went sailing, searched the bazaars for bric-à-brac, pieces of white jade and Persian pottery, gaining 'an alarming reputation for originality and "art treasures" '.[28]

Harold was occupied at the embassy, dealing with the repercussions of the Balkan wars and the consequences of increased German penetration at the Porte that came to a head over the Liman von Sanders affair in November–December 1913. General von Sanders had arrived at the Porte as head of a German military mission with the task of reorganising the Turkish army after the débâcles of the Balkan wars. He was given command of the First Army Corps at Constantinople and other far-reaching powers. The Russians protested violently at what they considered to be a hostile incursion into their sphere of influence. France, their ally, lent them vigorous support; Britain too backed its entente partners, though in a more restrained manner. But this combined pressure proved sufficient. Von Sanders was forced to stand down from his original appointment. Instead, he assumed the post of Inspector-General of the Turkish army, in which capacity he did much to improve the fighting ability of the Turkish army, a fact that worked against the entente powers when war broke out.

For the first, and only, time in her life Vita played the traditional role expected of a diplomatist's wife. She dutifully attended teas, dinners, dances and receptions. She performed well. 'Vita splendid,' Harold remarked. Congenial visitors relieved the tedium: Rosamund arrived, as did the Rubenses, escorted by Olive's paramour, Lionel, Vita's father. Uncle Bertie (Sackville-West), then Inspector of the Ottoman Public Debt, was also close at hand. So too were Harold's bosom friends, Reggie Cooper, Gerry Wellesley and Mark Sykes, as well as Pierre, who provided amusing, stimulating company when called upon. But Vita's adherence to the rules of the game was only surface deep, something that Harold knew well but was helpless to change.

'Vita bored,' Harold confided to his diary. There were times when Harold returned home after a day at the embassy and a brooding Vita would simply ignore him. Harold made the best of a potentially embarrassing situation. 'I long to see my darling – and be soundly snubbed when I come in . . . do you remember? You used to go on writing with your pretty little head over your table refusing to turn round.'[29] The implications of these ostentatious gestures of disapproval could not have been lost on Harold, who was always sensitive to negative body language. Vita was not bored by the sightseeing, the acquisition of oriental treasures, the gardening, or by Harold's intimate circle of companions. She was not bored with Harold. But she was bored by the role her marriage to Harold had forced upon her. Vita would not make the same mistake again.

Just before Christmas Vita became pregnant and they arranged to return to England for the birth, due in early August. They left Constantinople in mid-June 1914, storing all their furnishings, fully expecting to return.* Harold had spent two and a half years in Constantinople. If his superiors became disillusioned at the Young Turks' capacity for reform, Harold came to hold the Turks in absolute contempt. 'I can't understand the pro-Turk attitude – I see nothing in this servile and inglorious decay,' he told his family. Even after due consideration, his position did not mellow: 'For the Turk I had, and have, no sympathy whatsoever. Long residence at Constantinople had convinced me that behind his mask of indolence, the Turk conceals impulses of the most brutal savagery.'[30] This was the harshest of verdicts; but, Harold would argue, it was based firmly on solid evidence. After all, what could be more compelling than his first-hand experience of Turkish misrule? His attitude scarcely altered, even when faced with entirely

*Harold did return to Constantinople, but as a character in a novel he wrote, *Sweet Waters* (1921), about diplomatic life in pre-1914 Constantinople (see Chapter 6, p. 113).

different circumstances in the immediate post-war era, and when he was in a position to influence the course of events. Eyre Crowe once told him, not without good cause, that he was 'a sentimental Philhellene'[31] – the other side of the coin. This anti-Turk bias, common to many British decision-makers, was to have disastrous consequences for British policy.

On their return to England the Nicolsons made straight for Knole, where they stayed for a few weeks. However, they soon moved into rented accommodation at 182, Ebury Street, Pimlico, the pressures of living in such close proximity to Lady Sackville having proved too much for the young couple's nerves. While at Knole, news reached them at the end of June that the Archduke Franz Ferdinand, heir to the crown of the Austro-Hungarian Empire, and his wife Sophia, had been assassinated at Sarejevo. As the 'July crisis' escalated, Harold was recalled to the Foreign Office. He was placed, finally, in the newly fashioned War Department (an amalgamation of the Western and Eastern Departments), supervised initially by his mentor, Sir Eyre Crowe – 'He was so human. He was so super-human'[32] – where he remained well into the post-war years, having been transferred officially on 1 October from the Diplomatic Service to the Foreign Office.

The Office had undergone little change since he had left it. Sir Arthur still served as its Permanent Under-Secretary, though he found himself increasingly isolated. His relations with Grey, the Foreign Secretary, were strained over Ulster; and he had even clashed with Crowe, whom he greatly respected and whose views he fully accepted. But his principal bugbear was William Tyrrell who, as Grey's private secretary, stood permanently on guard at his chief's shoulder. Tyrrell openly expressed his distrust and dislike of Sir Arthur. He charged him with 'grave disloyalty' towards Grey, claiming that Nicolson had criticised Grey's policy to foreign diplomatists. There was something in his charge. Two years earlier Nicolson had written to Paul Cambon, the French ambassador, proposing an Anglo-French alliance, only 'This radical-socialist cabinet' would not agree to it. He spoke contemptuously of the 'financiers, pacifists, faddists and others' who strove for closer relations with Germany, concluding: 'the cabinet will not last, it is done for, and, with the Conservatives, you will get something precise'. This was strong stuff for such a mild-mannered man, a highly placed civil servant whose political leanings should remain hidden from the public. It was probably indiscretions of this kind that reached Tyrrell's ears.

Nicolson's barbed remarks to Cambon were probably directed against Tyrrell – still considered by some as the strongman at the Foreign Office – among others. It was the Prince Karl Max Lichnowsky, German ambassador in London, who bore witness that Tyrrell, 'This highly intelligent official [who] had been at school in Germany . . . became a convinced advocate of an understanding. He influenced Sir Edward Grey, with whom he was very intimate, in this direction.'[33] Something of Tyrrell's hostility towards Sir Arthur spilled over into Tyrrell's relations with Harold. It was eventually to prove a key factor in determining Harold's career at the Foreign Office.

With country and Cabinet preoccupied with the troubles in Ulster, the gravity of the European crisis did not register immediately. But the uncompromising Austrian ultimatum to Serbia on 23 July compelled the government to turn its attention to the Balkan imbroglio. Grey declared it 'unexpectedly severe; harsher in tone and more humiliating in its terms than any communication of which we had recollection addressed by one independent Government to another'.[34] The alliance system was set in motion: Germany backing Austria, Russia (sustained by its ally, France) defending Serbia. Military timetables heightened the tension, in particular the German (Schlieffen) plan which necessitated a first strike. Nine days after the Austrian ultimatum, German troops crossed over into Luxembourg and Belgium. Britain, having no contractual obligations to come to the aid of either side, and checked at home by so-called 'peace camps' in Parliament and the Cabinet, held back until the last moment. But by 4 August Britain too was at war in defence of its traditional interests, to maintain the European balance of power, to secure the independence of the Low Countries, but also to preserve Western democratic principles. Sir Eyre Crowe put it plainly: 'Our interests are tied up with France and Russia in this struggle, which is not for the possession of Servia, but one between Germany aiming at a political dictatorship in Europe, and the powers who desire to retain individual freedom.'[35] A committed Francophile all his life, Harold would not have taken issue with Crowe's sentiments.

As a very junior official Harold played no significant role in these great events. But, paradoxically, he did step into the pages of history simply because he happened to be 'the youngest member of the staff'. During the last hours of peace, muddled signals had been exchanged between Germany and Britain. On hearing that German troops had crossed over into Belgium, Grey had issued a moderately worded ultimatum to Berlin – intended to come into force on 4 August at 12 p.m. London time – warning that unless Germany backed down Britain would be obliged to take 'all steps' necessary to uphold the neutrality of Belgium. While waiting for the German reply – which never arrived – someone recalled that German time was an hour in advance of Greenwich mean time. For reasons that remain obscure – protocol, perhaps – it was decided that the ultimatum should expire according to the time in Berlin. Other complications intruded. A news agency reported that Germany had already declared war on Britain. A note to Lichnowsky – which reflected the changed situation – was rapidly redrafted and sent off. When it became clear that the agency reports were entirely unfounded, and that no German reply to Grey's ultimatum would be forthcoming, meaning that a state of war would exist by midnight, it became imperative to retrieve the by now out-of-date communiqué to Lichnowsky and substitute the correct declaration of war. This was Harold's humble task, or as he put it, his 'invidious mission'.

It was just after 11 p.m. when Harold arrived at the embassy. Met by a footman, he was told that the ambassador was asleep and in no circumstances could be disturbed. Harold insisted. The butler was summoned. Harold clarified to him the gravity of the situation. Finally convinced, he escorted Harold to Lichnowsky's bedroom. They found the ambassador in his pyjamas reclining on his bed. Harold stated his mission: 'there had been a slight error in the document previously delivered and that he had come to substitute for it another, and more correct, version'. 'You will find it there,' Lichnowsky replied in despair, barely moving, and waved Harold over to the writing table by the window where the papers lay, apparently unexamined. Harold made the exchange. Just as the ambassador was acknowledging receipt of the proper declaration of war, 'the sound of shouting came up from the Mall, [accompanied by] the strains of the Marseillaise'. Excited crowds were streaming back from Buckingham Palace, celebrating in their own fashion the warlike mood. Lichnowsky turned away from Harold, signalling that the interview had come to an end. But he was a diplomatist schooled in the old ways. 'Give my best regards to your father,' he entreated Harold. 'I shall not in all probability see him before my departure.'[36]

Writing in 1929, Harold examined the responsibility of the powers for the outbreak of the First World War. The war of 1914–18, he expounded, was caused 'by a false conception of international values'. 'Unselfishness, humanity and intelligence' were out of favour, not part of the international dialogue. Instead, 'national egoism' was paramount. Shunning co-operation, the powers viewed each other as deadly rivals. 'The European community of nations was not an organised community, and for them the ultimate appeal was not to law but force.' Was Harold thinking of Thomas Hobbes? 'The condition of man . . . is a condition of war of everyone against everyone.'

On one point Harold had no doubt. He concurred with his father, and with Crowe, that 'there was good cause' to fear 'the German menace'. But was Germany responsible? Harold wavered, presenting an even-handed proposition. He distinguished between the 'origins (1900–1914)' and the 'causes (1500–1900)' of the war. 'As regard the origins I consider Germany at fault. Though even then, less at fault than Austria or Russia. As regards the causes I consider that the main onus falls on England.' Harold elaborated.

By 1900, having absorbed the Dutch republics in South Africa, the British Empire was satiated . . . This placed her in a defensive position . . . Our own predatory period – and it was disgraceful enough – dated from 1500 to 1900. During that period we were far more violent and untruthful than were the Germans during those fourteen years which preceded the war . . . Before we blame Germany, we must first blame our own Elizabethans. The spirit was exactly the same: the Germans, however, owing to a higher state of culture and rectitude, behaved less blatantly; and were less successful . . . The Germans, during the period which I cover, were fired by exactly the same motives and energies which illumine what we still regard as one of the most noble passages in our early history. [37]

Harold's reasoning reflected a popular view at the time; but it was stretching historical interpretation almost to breaking point.

Harold's reference to Austria and Russia being more 'at fault' than Germany can be traced to stories told him by Richard von Kühlmann, who had served as Counsellor at the German embassy in London from 1908 to 1914. Serious doubts have been raised as to Kühlmann's 'veracity or memory'. Lewis Namier called him 'a frustrated intriguer', inaccurate 'in matters big and small', moved only by 'an innate disregard for truth'. Harold too thought of Kühlmann as being 'not too scrupulous' and as lacking 'strength of character', even though he was a 'remarkable' and 'intelligent' man.[38] Still, Harold seemingly accepted his gossipy tales at face value.

They met in Berlin in the late 1920s. Kühlmann told the following story. It all began, he said, with Count Alois Lex von Aerenthal's, the Austrian Foreign Minister, long-standing agenda to annex Bosnia and Herzegovina. But Aerenthal knew that his game plan, if realised, was certain to have far-reaching international repercussions. To ensure success, he would have first to square matters with Austria's ally, Germany. So he decided to play a little trick. He invited Baron Wilhelm von Schoen, the German Foreign Minister, to dinner, feigned drunkenness and began spouting all kinds of nonsense. As they were leaving the room, Aerenthal, supposedly intoxicated, said jocularly: 'I shall have to annex Bosnia and Herzegovina.' Von Schoen, dismissing Aerenthal's threat as foolish after-dinner chatter, refused to take it seriously and never reported it. However, when Aerenthal actually annexed the provinces in October 1908, precipitating a crisis with Russia, he was able to say, 'But I told von Schoen – I warned him.' In any case, a month earlier, at a conference at Buchlau, Aerenthal believed that he had taken action to avert a European crisis. He had come to an arrangement with Alexander Izvolski, the Russian Foreign Minister, that, in exchange for Russia sanctioning the annexation, Austria would not oppose the opening of the Straits to Russian warships, under certain conditions. As such a wide-ranging deal would require the consent of the powers, Izvolski set off on a tour of the European capitals to test diplomatic opinion. It was while he was negotiating in Paris that he heard that Aerenthal had reneged on their deal and had seized Bosnia and Herzegovina before securing the powers' consent. Izvolski was left empty-handed – and furious!

The Bosnian crisis brought Europe to the brink of war. The powers lined up. Austria backed by Germany; Serbia – which had long looked upon the provinces as its legacy to the future – sustained by Russia. But it was Germany's combativeness that won the day for Aerenthal. Prince von Bülow, the German Chancellor, told him: 'I shall regard whatever decision you come to as the appropriate one.' Faced with an Austro-German united front, Russia yielded, aware that both France – its ally – and Britain – its entente partner – resented strongly Izvolski's furtive diplomacy. Ultimately, the powers, including Turkey, deferred to the annexation as a *fait accompli*. The Bosnia-Herzegovina affair has widely been considered as a dress rehearsal for the 'July crisis': the same actors manoeuvring for position over yet another Balkan squabble, though on this occasion the drift to war proved impossible to arrest.

According to Külhmann's account to Harold, Isvolski, deceived at Buchlau and humiliated over Bosnia and Herzegovina, was bent on revenge. He was prepared to offer Germany 'anything on this earth – a treaty of alliance – if Germany would abandon Austria to his mercy'. During the July 1914 crisis, Izvolski had told Kühlmann: 'Look here – I don't want war with you – but I must have my revenge on Austria.'[39] But by then Izvolski was Russian ambassador at Paris, out of favour at St Petersburg, his influence minimal. It remains unclear whether Harold swallowed whole Kühlmann's colourful account of these events. He recorded these reminiscences without comment. But it is crystal clear that he held Austrian policy mainly responsible for the outbreak of war, with Russia trailing a close second.

With the outbreak of war Harold returned to the Foreign Office, where he was to remain until he took up another diplomatic posting in 1925, impressing his professional competence upon his masters, slowly climbing the ladder of preferment.

FOUR

War Games

The war passed slowly for Harold. Like so many of his contemporaries, his first inclination was to volunteer for active service. Many of his close friends had set him an example. Reggie Cooper and Gerry Wellesley, diplomatists like Harold, went off to fight on the western front, as did his brother Freddy, a professional soldier. Harold stayed on at the Foreign Office. Not that he lacked physical courage – after all, he had rescued twenty-two wounded Turkish soldiers under fire during the Balkan wars – and although of nervous disposition, he was always on the lookout for signs that would attest to his bravery. But he remained in Whitehall for the convincing reason that his masters considered his services too valuable to lose. Others were placed in the same position, the gifted Robert Vansittart for example.

Harold was assigned to the newly created War Department. Set up to deal with political, military and naval matters, it was under the general supervision of Eyre Crowe, an arrangement much to Harold's liking. Nothing could dislodge Crowe from the high pedestal upon which Harold, and others, had placed him. He felt strongly when his revered chief was subjected to scurrilous attacks in the press on account of his German origins. After a few months Crowe moved over to take charge of economic affairs, his position taken over by Sir Arthur Nicolson, Harold's father. Harold's immediate superior was George Clerk, who had been appointed head of the War Department. Harold knew him well, for they had served together in Constantinople. Something of a dandy, sporting a monocle and spats, always immaculately dressed in an old-fashioned way, he and Harold got on famously. 'George Clerk is such an angel to work with: so appreciative and encouraging and stimulating. He never snubs one for being uppish . . .'[1]

Owing to the exigencies of war Britain's foreign policy, having also to consider its allies' interests, ceased to have a separate identity. But there were other constraints on the work of the Foreign Office. As the war progressed its authority was scaled down, its negotiating duties often being commandeered by the Cabinet and/or the Prime Minister's Office. Reflecting on these matters, Harold warned against confusing the framing of 'foreign policy' by the Cabinet, contingent upon 'the approval of the elected representatives of the people', with 'negotiation', the implementation of that policy, which 'should generally be left to professionals of experience and discretion'. The latter, he affirmed confidently, 'is diplomacy'.[2] He was of course aware that during the war both of his riders were disregarded, or at least side-stepped. But Harold profited from this mingling of functions. A knowledgeable, industrious and skilful draftsman of position papers, he now found himself helping to frame foreign policy, albeit at a junior level, but not implement it. Considering his rank, his input was impressive.

Much of allied wartime diplomacy centred on the future of the Austro-Hungarian and Ottoman Empires: how to control the emergence of new national entities in central Europe; how to reconcile conflicting national claims among the Balkan countries; how to avoid or approve the break-up of Turkey itself; and how to resolve the clash of rival allied demands with local nationalist movements in the Arab East. The treaties of Constantinople (4 March–10 April 1915) – that promised Russian ascendancy at Constantinople and the Dardanelles, provided that Britain and France 'achieve their aims in the Near East and elsewhere' – and London (26 April 1915) – a bribe to Italy to enter the war that went far beyond *Italia Irredenta* (Trentino, South Tyrol, Istria, Trieste) to include the Dodecanese Islands and the Turkish province of Adalia – passed across his desk. Was it possible to square these concessions with the concept of self-determination, then much in vogue? In particular, the payoff to Italy stuck in the throat of the Foreign Office. It was accepted, reluctantly, as a 'war necessity'. But Sir Edward Grey, pleading illness, retired to the country, disgusted at Italy's grasping behaviour, while Sir Arthur Nicolson bluntly told the Marchese Imperiali, the Italian ambassador to London, that Britain had 'purchased' Italy's support, not the most diplomatic of remarks.[3]

As the war progressed so too did Harold's self-confidence, as did his masters' belief in him. His initials began to appear with increasing regularity on Foreign Office papers as he ventured opinions on topics that had hitherto passed him by. The future of the Balkans absorbed him. How would its post-war map look? One complication was the drive and ambition of Bulgaria, an ally of Germany, 'the only strong power in the Balkans'. Any solution that would leave Bulgaria 'unsatisfied but still dominant' would damage British interests: it would entail 'the indefinite maintenance of our "protectorate" of Greece and Serbia'; and it would perpetuate Bulgarian and Turkish dependence on the Central Powers, thereby rendering the area 'infinitely more inflammable than before the war'. To appease Bulgaria Harold offered her a share in a future international regime for Macdeonia: 'Otherwise Bulgaria would conquer the territory at a future date, adding to the instability of the region.' Lord Robert Cecil, then Assistant Secretary of State for Foreign Affairs, felt 'disposed to agree with Mr. Nicolson'. Eleutherios Venizelos, the charismatic Greek leader who had brought Greece into the war on the allied side, and an interested party, decidedly did not. For him, Bulgaria was a rapacious, imperialistic force. To allow it into Macedonia would 'entail the cession of Salonika and the spoliation of Greece'. His own position, Venizelos clarified, would not survive such an arrangement. Harold thought Venizelos's attitude 'extremely disheartening', much as he would have liked to have placated him. Tongue in cheek, he fell back on two solutions: either 'Bulgarian hegemony in the Peninsula'; or, 'the internationalisation of (an autonomous) Macedonia'.

Harold's mind was fixed. Even after Bulgaria had surrendered to the allied powers he was lamenting that 'emotional feeling' might prevent territory being 'ceded to Bulgaria' and so intensify friction in the Balkans. Still, he was honest enough to admit that 'However desirable, from an academic point of view, the conciliation of Bulgarian rights in Macedonia may be, it is questionable whether public opinion in France or this country would tolerate the cession to Bulgaria of territory at present Serbian or Greek.' Let us wait for the American President, he advised. 'Mr. Wilson alone,' he optimistically presumed, 'can cut the Gordian knot.'[4]

Mollifying Bulgaria was only part of a broader scheme Harold envisaged to calm the Balkans. He thought in terms of a generation ahead. 'The ultimate policy of HMG,' he suggested, 'is the creation of a Balkan Federation such as will constitute an effective barrier to German Eastern expansion.' In the meantime, determined to give voice to the fashionable principle of national self-determination and conscious of the need to limit French ambitions in the area, he offered the following formula:

The Allied Powers for their part undertake in the event of Serbia and Romania attaining unity with their co-nationals at present incorporated in the Austro-Hungarian Empire, to use their good offices as between Bulgaria, Serbia and Romania for such rectifications of the frontiers established under the Treaty of Bucharest [of 7 May 1918, whereby Romania ceded the Dobrudja area to Bulgaria] as may be in conformity with the doctrine of nationality, the wishes of the population concerned, and the vital national interests of Serbia and Romania.[5]

There was also the problem of central Europe and the disintegrating Austro-Hungarian Empire. The Czechs, riding high on a wave of national fervour, were claiming German-speaking Bohemia, for strategic and economic reasons, and Slovakia, on ethnographic grounds. Leo Amery, Political Secretary to the War Cabinet, would have none of this. He submitted a paper challenging these demands. Convinced that the emerging national states in the area would not be viable entities and would inevitably contribute to the instability of the region, 'the Balkanisation of Central Europe', he fell back upon one of his pet schemes: reorganising the world system into a few closely knit blocs. He proposed a large 'non-national superstate', 'a federated Austria-Hungary in federation with Germany'. Robert Cecil expressed 'considerable sympathy' with Amery's views. Unless 'we can induce the small states' to move along these lines, he warned, 'the last state of Europe may well be worse than the first'. He called upon 'the skilled technical assistance' of the Political Intelligence Department of the Foreign Office to examine Amery's scheme.

Lewis Namier responded. A member of the PID, and an acknowledged, if opinionated, expert on the national question in central and eastern Europe, he subjected Amery's ideas to microscopic scrutiny. Harold assisted him. Together they unpicked Amery's grand design. The disruption of the Habsburg Empire, they argued, will not add to the number of states in Europe, 'but merely render their frontiers more reasonable'. Nothing could be done to arrest the drive for Yugoslav or Romanian unity into sovereign states. Yugoslavia will replace Serbia, Transylvania will form part of a Greater Romania: neither will constitute 'a new problem for the future'. As for the union Amery proposed, it would be self-defeating. The Germans would not play Amery's game. Inevitably, they would dominate the Federation, in which case 'so far from restoring a balance against Germany, an Austrian federation under German leadership would merely increase the difficulties caused by the collapse of Russia'. It would turn south-east Europe into a German sphere of influence. Namier and Harold held firmly to the view that the Old Empire was doomed. To reverse – by what means? – what was taking place on the ground would be to allow Germany to absorb the whole of German Bohemia and to abet the Magyars in maintaining their oppressive domination of the Slovaks. These options, the pair agreed, 'would be quixotic'.

There remained only Hungary and Bohemia, where the situation was so confused that it would be 'wiser for us to form no settled policy, or even opinion, as regards the future status of these countries'. They turned to the uncertain outlook for Czecho-Slovakia, recognising immediately that the incorporation of Germans into it 'will be a weakness'. But 'if in some particular districts, as seems to be really the case, the paramount strategic and economic interests of the Czechs, though contrary to the national principle, are such as cannot be disregarded', then the doctrine of self-determination would have to be applied in a more flexible manner. German Bohemia in the west and the Slav areas in the south and east, they judged, were essential to maintain a secure and prosperous Czech state. 'I agree,' minuted Hardinge. So did Cecil. Discarding Amery, he adopted Harold and Namier's line as 'very sound'.[6]

The new Czecho-Slovakia that emerged after the war contained German-speaking Bohemia – the Sudetenland – and Slovakia, much as Harold (and Namier) had wanted. But its problems – 'self-determination will inevitably lead to much confusion and rivalry', they had cautioned – would not go away: they remained, even sharpened. And were to re-emerge with devastating effect during the Munich crisis of 1938. The 'options' first envisaged by Namier and Harold would no longer be 'quixotic' but would lead to war.

The break-up of the Ottoman Empire, coinciding as it did with the collapse of Russia, raised questions of an entirely different nature. Here, tangible British interests were at stake. They had been set out in various internal departmental assessments and wartime agreements, particularly the de Bunsen report and the Sykes-Picot accord.* Having lost the Arab East, it was widely feared that the dying Ottoman Empire would seek compensation elsewhere, that Turkey would strive to unite under its leadership the Turkish-speaking peoples of Russian central Asia, North-West Persia, and Afghanistan. India would be threatened 'in the gravest way', warned Arnold Toynbee, Namier's colleague in the Political Intelligence Department. It was a nightmare scenario for old-style imperialists. In August 1918 Harold pronounced against a separate peace with Turkey, believing that it would only encourage 'Pan-Turanism'. What would be the implications for Persia? he asked. On one point he was absolutely clear. Extending the concession of the Anglo-Persian Oil Company must 'form one of the main points in

---

*The de Bunsen Report (June 1915) anchored British interests in the Near East on the Suez Canal and its hinterland and the Persian Gulf, and the need for easy access between these areas, aims that necessitated a measure of British influence in Palestine. It was considered crucial to keep the French as far away as possible from these salient imperial areas. (Report and its minutes are in NA, CAB.27/1).

By the Sykes–Picot Agreement (May 1916), the French were to rule directly or indirectly the area north of a line running from Acre to a point on the Tigrus some 70 miles south of Mosul, while the British were to have the same rights in the area south of that line extending as far as Aqaba and along the Saudi Arabian border. Palestine, defined in the agreement as the area bordered by the Jordan river in the east, the sea in the west, and from Acre in the north to a line from El Arish to Be'ersheva in the south, would be governed by an international regime. (See Sykes–Picot memorandum, 5 Jan. 1916, NA, FO.371/2767/2522; Also H. W. V. Temperley, ed., *A History of the Peace Conference of Paris* (Royal Institute of International Affairs, 1924), 16–17.

our future policy in Persia'. To do this it would be necessary to appease 'Persian national sentiment', perhaps, he indicated, by suspending the Anglo-Russian agreement of 1907 that had divided Persia into spheres of influence.[7] As it happened, the Anglo-Russian entente died a natural death as the Bolsheviks repudiated all deals concocted in the pre-revolutionary era as 'imperialist'. However, replacing it, while simultaneously soothing Persian nationalism, proved far more complex.

Harold's suggestions were picked up by the government a year later. An Anglo-Persian agreement was signed in August 1919 that, had it been ratified, would have assured British ascendancy in the country. But the Majlis (Persian Parliament), fired by an extreme national sentiment that Harold wished to humour, would have none of it. Oil continued to flow from the wells of the Anglo-Persian Oil Company, but Anglo-Persian relations entered a period of mounting tension. This was not to be Harold's final say in the affairs of Persia. Stationed at Tehran in the mid-twenties, he made another bid to reform Anglo-Persian relations, reiterating his advocacy of a more liberal approach to Persian nationalism. But this time his comments backfired. His seniors took umbrage at his audacity, and his diplomatic career wobbled off course to continue under a cloud.

Combating 'pan-Turanism' in Persia was an offshoot – a vital one, no doubt – of 'the Turkish puzzle', of the by now defunct Ottoman Empire, and how to solve it. Here again, Harold put forward clear-cut answers. He urged, first, that the Straits be opened to 'our Fleets . . . under supreme British Command'. 'Our essential aims . . . as modified or extended by present conditions', he unhesitatingly proposed, should encompass 'a full revision of the Sykes–Picot agreement and the Italian agreement regarding spheres of influence in Asia Minor'.[8] Aggressive Italian demands had no place on Harold's agenda for a more equitable world order. Nor did the Sykes–Picot agreement (of May 1916), an old-fashioned imperialist plot – or so Harold thought – fit into his conception of how international affairs should now be conducted; moreover, it brought France perilously close to the Suez Canal. British interests in the area, Harold believed, could be preserved by more plain-speaking arrangements.

When the old Emperor, Franz Josef, died in November 1916, his successor, his great-nephew, Karl, put out feelers for a separate peace between the crumbling Austro-Hungarian Empire and the Allies. Harold, apparently a lone voice in the Office, was in favour. 'I suggested peace with Austria against everybody's views,' he told Vita. One complication was that the British suspected the Germans of pushing the Austrians forward as front-runners. 'Simply explore any proposals Germany might have to make,' instructed

Balfour, completely misreading the situation. The first stage of the negotiations dragged on until late August 1917, but eventually broke down owing to the Italians insisting that the precise terms of the treaty of London be upheld, including its demand for Trieste, a claim the Austrians were unwilling to concede. Later, as the Austro-Hungarian Empire continued to fall apart, Harold proposed that the United States should handle the negotiations. There were definite advantages to be gained from involving the Americans. First, the United States, as an associate power of the Allies, was not committed to any contractual arrangements with Italy. America could also tempt Vienna with financial aid. Lastly – and of immense importance for Harold – there was Wilson's 'immense prestige' which 'rests on a base at once more solid and more spiritual than that of the older belligerents'. Now voicing the Foreign Office view, Harold favoured extensive concessions to Austria; 'dazzling' Austria to wean her away from Germany's grasp. He spoke, for example, of 'the Austrian solution' in Poland, of the recovery of non-Polish Silesia, and the succession to 'the moral heritage of Slav hegemony'. None of these 'dazzling' inducements came to fruition. In September 1919, at the château of St Germain near Paris, a treaty of extreme severity was imposed upon Austria, reducing it to a rump state, dependent for its survival on massive allied aid.[9]

Across the Atlantic, in November 1916, President Woodrow Wilson had been re-elected for a second term of office. It was a close race – 277 electoral votes to 254 – a narrow victory generally ascribed to the backing of pacifist and non-interventionist groups. Wilson too was committed to a peace initiative, 'a peace without victory', as he dispassionately put it. Lloyd George was not. He told an American journalist in his celebrated 'Knock-Out Blow' interview that Britain would be 'justifiably suspicious of any suggestion that President Wilson should choose this moment to "butt in" with a proposal to stop the war before we could achieve victory'. In December Wilson 'butted in'. Proposing an exchange of views on peace terms, he contended that all the belligerents had the same war aims. He did not elaborate, except in the most high-flown – and, let it be said, meaningless – language. For the British, this was to confuse the aggressor with its victims. The German reply was couched very much in Wilson's style: all generalities, no specifics. Harold, reviewing this material, saw immediately the 'German character of Mr Wilson's demarche', a conclusion shared by his political masters.[10] The allied reply took a diametrically opposite line: all specifics, no generalities. It called for the restoration of all territories occupied by the Central Powers, with just reparations. Nothing came of Wilson's initiative. Four months after these barren exchanges the United States entered the war against Germany as an associate power of the Allies.

As one peace proposal faded away, another took its place, this one sponsored by the Vatican. Taking a high moral tone, Pope Benedict XV's proposals
were far-reaching in principle, touching in a noncommittal way upon topics
such as disarmament, arbitration, freedom of the seas, renunciation of indem-
nities, and the evacuation and restoration of occupied territories. Far too
much was left to be clarified in detail. In the Pope's note, only the full restoration of Belgium was mentioned without question. But what of the recovery
of Alsace and Lorraine by France? And what of the Italian obsession with
Italia Irredenta? Was Benedict XV simply proposing a return to the status
quo of 1914? Harold took it upon himself, 'for convenience of reference', to
assess this muddled affair. The Pope's cloudy ideas regarding the 'freedom
of the seas', an issue of supreme importance to Britain, aroused immediate
suspicion. Nor were any of Britain's allies impressed with the papal initiative, hoping that it would die a natural death. The Americans employed altogether tougher language, seeing it as 'a blind adventure' leading only 'to a
return to the status quo ante'. Like those around him, Harold succumbed
to the view that the Pope's initiative was inspired by Germany, as seemed
abundantly clear from its contents. 'My inquiries,' he concluded authoritatively, 'indicate beyond a doubt that the Papal move was indirectly, if not
directly, inspired from enemy sources.' Harold's superiors, Cecil and Crowe,
took note of his initiative and prescience. Lord Hardinge – who had replaced
Sir Arthur Nicolson as Permanent Under-Secretary – 'told [Lancelot]
Oliphant who told me that he was much impressed with my work'.[11] The
government decided not to decide. No British reply was sent to the Pope
and the 'peace offensives' of 1917 petered out as casually as they had started.

Towards the autumn of 1917 Harold became involved in one of the most
controversial foreign policy decisions any British government has ever made:
the issuance of the Balfour Declaration. He was seconded to work with Sir
Mark Sykes, one of two political secretaries to the Cabinet, the other being
Leopold Amery, appointments made in the wake of Lloyd George's reconstruction of the government machine. Together, they were told, they would
function 'as a kind of informal "brains trust" '. Sykes has been portrayed
as the classic illustration of that truly authentic figure of British public life,
the amateur. Heir to an estate at Sledmere, Yorkshire, he had travelled extensively in the Near East in his youth. He was not conversant with its languages
– Arabic, Turkish, Hebrew or Persian; he had no formal training in oriental
studies, nor as a professional diplomat. None of this tarnished his reputation. A prolific author and skilful cartoonist, and moving in the right circles,
he came to be recognised as an expert on the area. By the natural order of
things he dealt with Near Eastern affairs. Harold was greatly taken by

Sykes's effervescent charm, even while deploring his lack of Civil Service discipline.[12]

Sykes acted as the main channel of communication between the government and the Zionist movement. He had been negotiating with Chaim Weizmann and Nahum Sokolov - the two leading Zionists in Britain – since the beginning of the year, as they worked together to draft a pro-Zionist pledge. Sykes saw no contradiction between this and his staunchly pro-Arab outlook. Indeed, he told himself, one would complement the other: indebted to Britain, both views would serve British imperial interests. Later developments proved these presumptions wildly optimistic, but at the time most British policy-makers were party to them. Harold was no exception. His pro-Zionism did not stem from a deep knowledge of recent Jewish history. Nor was he on intimate terms with any Jews. Indeed, Jews hardly figured, if at all, in his social calendar. 'Although I loathe anti-semitism,' he once said, 'I do dislike Jews.' This was a subtle difference, as one thing could so easily lead to another. For all that, a trace of anti-Semitism also fuelled his Zionism – as it did with so many other Gentile Zionists. Zionism, they claimed, would repair perceived defects in the Jewish character. It would restore to the Jews their dignity, that corporate national confidence and self-respect they so clearly lacked: it would, so to speak, stiffen the backbone of the Jewish people. Once given a National Home, they would no longer misuse their considerable gifts for mischievous ends. It 'would be a nice place,' Harold reflected, 'in which to collect all the Jews of the world, as Butlin's collects the noisy holidaymakers.'[13]

There were other aspects of Gentile Zionism, more historical and spiritual, that would have appealed to a classicist like Harold. It was best expressed by Balfour:

Their [the Jews'] position and their history, their connection with world religion and with world politics is absolutely unique. There is no parallel to it . . . in any other branch of world history' . . . [They have been] deported, then scattered, then driven out of [Palestine] altogether into every part of the world, and yet maintaining continuity of religion and racial tradition of which we have no parallel elsewhere . . . Consider how they have been subject to tyranny and persecution, consider whether . . . our whole religious organisation of Europe has not from time to time proved itself guilty of great crimes against this race . . . [and] do not forget what part they have played in the intellectual, the artistic, the philosophic and scientific development of the world.

'Christendom is not oblivious of their faith,' he went on to tell the House of Lords, 'is not unmindful of the service they have rendered to the great religions of the world.' Nor would it have escaped Harold's notice that of the three great races of the ancient world, the Greeks, the Romans and the Jews, only the Jews had yet to gain national self-determination.[14] Harold remained a pro-Zionist all his life, in contact, on and off, with Weizmann, whom he greatly admired.[15]

Having supported Sykes and Amery in this 'adventure' – to use Balfour's expression – Harold was at pains to point out that the Balfour Declaration was not an 'impulsive and ill-considered' statement; nor could its authors be accused of 'ignorance or cynicism'. It took months to negotiate, went through five drafts, and was debated at three sessions of the War Cabinet before it was finally approved on 31 October 1917. Writing in 1947, after 'almost thirty years of bitter experience', he admitted that it would now be drafted in 'far different terms'. Unduly 'optimistic' it may have been. But he vehemently defended Balfour against accusations 'of cynicism, of opportunism, of imperialism'. He remained silent about Lloyd George's role in this affair, which had been crucial.*

Harold's growing confidence and expertise, particularly in drafting letters, telegrams and memoranda in clear and precise prose, commanded respect and marked him out as a figure of promise. The Foreign Office, understandably, was much impressed with his work. Yet despite his impressive record, there were signs that Harold himself was becoming increasingly restless, frustrated, at being tied down to an anonymous Whitehall desk while more dramatic scenarios were being played out elsewhere. Was he simply bored, or lonely? 'Oh! solitude, Oh *pauvreté*,' he confided to Vita, and went on to describe in painful detail his daily routine, a blow-by-blow account of how he would wait upon Balfour's every need, of how he would make his way alone on foot across a rainy London, ending up at his club, St James's, to eat a tasteless dinner only to be reminded, '*Mais! comme on mange mal en temps de guerre*', and for him to wearily note yet again, 'Oh! solitude, Oh *pauvreté*': it was a dreary existence relieved only by drawing 'piccies for my mar'.[16]

*The Balfour Declaration is contained in a letter to Lord Rothschild from Balfour, sent on 2 November 1917. Its key paragraph reads: 'His Majesty's Government view with favour the establishment in Palestine of a national home for the Jewish people, and will use their best endeavours to facilitate the achievement of this object, it being clearly understood that nothing shall be done which may prejudice the civil and religious rights of existing non-Jewish communities in Palestine, or the rights and political status enjoyed by Jews in any other country.'
See Harold's essay, 'The Balfour Declaration', in *Comments, 1944–1948*.

Friends suggested that he transfer to the Rome embassy; he even toyed with the idea of enlisting for active service. But there was to be no escape from his daily chores at the Foreign Office. George Clerk wouldn't hear of it: 'the whole war department would collapse if he went, and besides if I let him go (which I never will) Hardinge would never hear of it'. On reading one of Harold's memoranda Hardinge himself complimented Nicolson's flair: 'You know, really it represents a very able view of the [overall war] situation. I can't think how you managed to concentrate so many ideas in so small a space.'[17] Nor did Balfour forget to chip in, introducing him as 'young Nicolson, my staunchest adviser'. The door was slammed shut by Lord Denman's committee, appointed to adjudicate on exempting civil servants from military service. The report read:

[Mr Nicolson] has dealt with certain subjects from the outbreak of the war, and has an intimate knowledge of many difficult and intricate European problems. His technical experience and facility for writing memoranda render him quite invaluable when information on the Balkans and other problems is called for by the War Cabinet at short notice. Mr. Balfour, whose opinion was solicited, stated that he did not know how Mr Nicolson could be replaced: that, indeed, he had no hesitation in saying that it would be almost impossible to do so.

'So that's that,' he confided to Vita, 'and I think I am safe for this war. I can't say that I am really glad about it, or that I feel they had the facts put honestly before them. It was true in 1917. I doubt whether it is true now.'[18]

So Harold spent the remainder of the war as a top-class bureaucrat, a recognised authority on 'the Balkans and other problems', writing papers for the War Cabinet, tutoring his political chiefs as they prepared for the forthcoming peace conference to be held in Paris. He wrote a memorandum on Holland, about which 'I know nothing and am wretched about it, and overwhelmed'. There were other problems concerning the Lowlands – Belgian claims on Dutch Flanders to acquire territories 'on the left bank of the Scheldt between Antwerp and the sea'. Crowe wouldn't hear of it. Neither would Curzon, though he phrased it more delicately: the subject would be brought up at the peace conference, 'to the harmony of whose proceedings it does not appear likely to contribute'. And Harold would not have disagreed.[19]

Once again he was concerned with regulating the borders of a new Balkans, usually to Bulgaria's, Romania's, and Greece's advantage, while scrupulously abiding by the latest canon of world politics, national self-determination –

if at all possible.[20] Of particular note was his latest blueprint for the Balkans, ideas put together with his scholarly colleague and friend, Allen Leeper – the 'prototype of the new diplomatist' and a firm believer in 'compact national states' – and helped along by the expertise of Lewis Namier and Professor Seton-Watson. They proposed to create two new states, Czechoslovakia and Yugoslavia, with territorial bonuses for Greece, Romania and Bulgaria.[21] The post-war settlement of the Balkans that was conjured up from the ruins of the Austro-Hungarian Empire was mapped out roughly in accordance with these ideas. True, 'compact national states' were left half done, and deep-rooted religious prejudices were papered over. But sensitive to the constraints of Balkan in-fighting, diplomatic and warlike, and relying on the spirit of co-operation and goodwill so prevalent at the time, or on wise (or dictatorial) leadership, the system was to last until it broke down irreparably in the 1990s, surviving 'the short twentieth century'. At any rate, the Romanian and Yugoslav governments, delighted at the services Harold had rendered them, wished to bestow upon him orders of decoration, only for the recommendations to be 'bowled out in accordance with the standing rule against acceptance of foreign decorations by members of the Foreign Office and Diplomatic Service'.[22]

'I should like Mr. Nicolson in the first instance to try his hand at this. It will give full scope to the imagination,' instructed Hardinge. 'Yes,' agreed Nicolson, 'apparently we are thought to be endowed with prophetic gifts.' Hardinge was responding to a Lloyd George initiative. He had asked General Sir Henry Wilson, Chief of the Imperial General Staff, to report on the possibility of a 'favourable decision to the war by military means in 1919, or at some later date'. Wilson, in turn, requested that the Foreign Office assess 'the prospects of any change in the grouping of the opposing Powers, either by 1919 or later, and as to any military or naval action which . . . is likely to bring about such a change'. This was Harold's task. It resulted in a closely worded ten-page memorandum, the 'Consideration of Future Political and Diplomatic Developments', dated 10 March 1918, that was eventually circulated to the War Cabinet.[23] His main conclusions fell into two interrelated categories: the relative staying power of the protagonists; and the relative cohesion of the two rival camps. Distinct advantages were accorded to Germany regarding the first of these factors. 'The tonnage situation' troubled Harold: '[it could] force upon us either capitulation or a serious diminution of energy'. And adding to this Germany's ambitions and conquests in the east – where the treaty of Brest-Litovsk had been signed on 3 March 1918 with vast gains for Germany – Germany would be inclined to 'an indefinite prolongation of the war', an option backed by 'the great

mass of opinion in Germany'. The weak link was Austria. Its peace over-
tures only shelved, Austria 'will, in the first place, press for a general peace,
or at least a military decision during the present year'. Harold summed up:

> our whole energies and resources should be concentrating on upholding
> our own *morale* or preventing the enemy from this year obtaining a
> military decision, and on conducting with all energy and with every
> confidence a concentrated political offensive against Austria, which
> consitutes at once the most vital and the weakest link in the chain of
> the central Alliance.

Harold's assessment was greeted with paeans. 'The memorandum reflects
the greatest credit on Mr. Nicolson,' said Lancelot Oliphant, a close friend
and confidant of Harold's. 'I entirely agree,' added Cecil. Not to be outdone,
Hardinge thought it 'an excellent and carefully thought-out memorandum,
and the conclusions at which Mr. Nicolson has arrived seem absolutely sound'.
Eleven days after Harold's assessment was completed, the Germans launched
their great, but ultimately self-defeating, offensive in the west. All forecasts
were pitched out of kilter. Apart from prolonging the war, as Harold had
anticipated, the Germans had gambled everything on a last desperate throw,
causing a 'serious diminution of [allied] energy' on the western front. Wisely,
Harold had prepared for himself an escape hatch, presciently warning his
masters that it is a truism that in war 'military events alone dictate the course
of political development'. The massive German attack petered out, leaving
the way open for an allied counter-offensive that finally led to the disinte-
gration of the Habsburg Empire and the capitulation of Germany. But
Harold's memorandum, together with his chiefs' fulsome tributes to his
shining ability, remained on record for future reference.

In October 1918, Harold made a brief trip to Rome for talks with the
ambassador, Sir Rennell Rodd, taking time off to see the city with his old
chums Gerry Wellesley and Lord Berners, both serving at the embassy. The
following month he met and lunched with the beguiling Venizelos, one of
Harold's favourites. Like many others, Harold fell under Venizelos's spell,
and was perhaps also a victim to his ambitions. Back in London, on 11
November he recorded 'A strange, hectic, flag-waving day in which I have
endeavoured to work on unaffected by the cheers and jubilation outside.' It
was Armistice Day. Harold was busy working on the complications of the
Strumnitza enclave (a remote area subject to rival claims by Serbia, Bulgaria
and Greece), when he was drawn to a window overlooking 10, Downing
Street. There he saw 'a plump and smiling' Lloyd George, 'hatless, white-
haired and flushed', waving to a tiny knot of people who had gathered there.

'At eleven o'clock this morning the war will be over,' he told them. Cheering wildly, and then standing silent, 'they bared their heads and sang "God Save the King"'. After this impromptu ceremony, Lloyd George pushed himself 'backwards through a sea of hands, faces and flags into his little garden gate'. Bantering with his secretaries, the Prime Minister disappeared into the quietude of the house. 'It was a moving scene.'[24] With some help from the Americans, Lloyd George had brought off his 'Knock-Out Blow'. The Great War was at an end.

By any reckoning Harold had served the Foreign Office with great distinction. Crowe, Hardinge, Balfour, Cecil – even Lloyd George – were alert to his gifts. On 8 November 1918 he was told that he would be going to Paris, a member of the British Delegation to the peace conference.[25] There could be no greater compliment. Aged thirty-two, still only a third secretary, a brilliant diplomatic career beckoned. Three weeks later Harold left for Paris.

FIVE

Personal Distractions

If Harold's professional life ran smoothly, along well-worn tracks, his personal, private affairs were more problematical, hitting highs but also striking lows. Two days after the outbreak of war Vita gave birth to their first son. Lady Sackville insisted on taking charge of the christening. His first name must be Lionel, in the family tradition, and not Benedict as Harold and Vita wished. No argument would move Bonne Mama, who threatened to withhold Vita's inheritance and ruin Harold's career unless she got her way. When Harold tried to reason with her she insulted him in front of the servants. After she abused his parents, Harold's self-control cracked, but he quickly apologised. Finally, he and Vita capitulated. Their first-born was named Lionel Benedict, known to all as Ben. 'This can't go on, my dear one,' Harold wrote to Vita. 'We must make . . . a treaty of defence' against 'B.M.'s destructive personality [that] might in the end intrude between us – between *us* my darling who love each other so passionately'. This did not work out quite as Harold planned. No 'treaty of defence' could fully withstand Lady Sackville's 'destructive personality'. The rows continued, some more acrimonious than others, until B.M. died in 1936.[1]

In June 1915 Harold and Vita acquired Long Barn, a half-ruined cottage, 'all untidy and tinkly' in Harold's words. An antique, dilapidated structure, where, local legend had it, William Caxton was born, it was situated midway down a hill at the edge of Sevenoaks-Weald, a village two miles from Knole. They renovated it after their own fashion, adding a large extension at right angles to the cottage, the wings setting off a modest courtyard. By the time they had completed their improvements, seven main bedrooms, four bathrooms, and a fifty-foot-long drawing-room would serve their every purpose. It was not a simple procedure to revamp such a timeworn property – and it showed: parts of the roofs appeared lopsided, some of the internal beams were askew, Vita's bedroom floor sloped, and pieces of furniture had to be propped up by blocks of wood. Harold and Vita enjoyed the privacy of separate studies and bedrooms. And after Nigel, their second surviving son, was born,[2] he and Ben were lodged in a separate cottage higher up the hill. 'This physical separation of the family was symptomatic of our relationship,' Nigel later wrote. 'Each person must have a room of his own, but there must be, and was, a common room where we could periodically unite.'[3]

Harold planned much of the rebuilding of Long Barn. As has been noted, Harold was 'the strategist', who also designed the layout of the gardens, allowing Vita, 'the tactician', to hone her talents as a gardener. Clearing away piles of rubble and patches of rank weeds, they dug and planted in a joint undertaking that resulted in a series of lawns and walled terraces falling away to the surrounding shrubbery. There was even space to put in a tennis court. Here, it was said, they 'flexed their muscles' for their exquisite creation at Sissinghurst.[4]

Although they continually complained of lack of funds, this fine establishment, or 'our little mud pie' or 'cottage', as Harold was wont to call it, was maintained by three domestic servants and two gardeners. Part of the funds came from an unexpected source: Lady Sackville. For a brief period relations returned to a more even keel. B.M. bought them a Rolls-Royce, paid the salary of one of their gardeners, and purchased for £700 Brook Farm, a property adjacent to Long Barn that considerably added to Harold and Vita's estate. She also lent them sufficient funds to buy the house in Ebury Street, which until then they had been renting. Notoriously unpredictable, Lady Sackville came to their rescue at a convenient time, at least for a few months. Harold's attachment to Long Barn was absolute. He shared his feelings with Vita:

[Long Barn] which we both love so childishly and which for both of us is the place where we have been so happy, darling. I don't think we could ever leave the cottage: there is not one crook in the wall, or one stain in the carpet, which does not mean something to you and me which it could never mean to strangers . . . And with it all a sense of permanence . . . And I shall think of the Rodin and the blue [Egyptian porcelain] crocodile and the figure of St. Barbara – and the London *Mercury* [magazine] upon the stool . . . [5]

Regardless of wartime conditions, which might have called for a modicum of self-restraint, Harold and Vita turned weekend parties at Long Barn into agreeable social occasions; and these gay get-togethers continued well into the 1920s. At a typical weekend old friends, Gerry Wellesley and Reggie Cooper, when free from military duty, would appear, as would other friends, Oswald ('Ozzie') Dickinson, Edwin Lutyens, Hugh Walpole, Maurice Baring and, now and then, Violet Keppel. In the 1920s their social horizons widened to include the intellectual aristos of Bloomsbury, Virginia and Leonard Woolf, Duncan Grant and Clive Bell. Harold's special friend, Raymond Mortimer, was always welcome. Roy Campbell, the poet, and his wife Mary, were often in attendance, as were diplomats like Gladwyn Jebb and favoured politicians such as Venizelos. At one Long Barn party, Harold, 'curled up on Vita's sofa', regarded 'Desmond [MacCarthy], Clive [Bell], Ethel Sands, Cynthia Noble engaged to Gladwyn [Jebb], and Gladwyn engaged to Cynthia Noble, and Francesco Mendelsohn who played the cello to an indifferent and ignorant audience'.[6]

Harold was also much sought after as a dinner guest. He graced the tables of London's leading hostesses, the Ladies Greville, Colefax, Cunard, Astor, and 'Circe', the Marchioness of Londonderry – although with the latter two ladies he was often at odds politically. Harold, never a dull companion, gained something of a reputation as a raconteur. James Lees-Milne, who came to know him well, thought that he was bound to enliven a flagging conversation. 'In a misleadingly hesitant manner' he would begin with 'an amusing anecdote . . . and would develop his story with a mounting enthusiasm that held his audience spellbound. As a talker he had few rivals . . . the natural overflow of a well-stocked mind, the unavoidable outlet of his high spirits.' His natural high spirits begat an incurable optimism. After returning from an especially dull party, he conceded ironically: 'I enjoyed it. I always enjoy everything. That is dreadful. I must pull myself together and be bored for once.'[7]

Towards the end of October 1917 the Nicolsons were invited to a weekend party at Knebworth House, Hertfordshire, the country estate of Lord Lytton, parliamentary secretary to the Admiralty. Other guests included Sir John Lavery, the painter; Edward Marsh, civil servant and Churchill's private secretary, scholar and patron of the arts; the diplomatists, Sir Horace Rumbold and Sir Louis Mallet, and Osbert Sitwell, the writer. A week later Harold suspected that he had caught a venereal infection from one of the male guests (or servants) at Knebworth. In torment, he wrote to Vita: 'But I can't laugh over it all. I am so flight [frightened] about it. It will be such an awful business if the [doctor's] report is not satisfactory. I simply *dread* it. Darling you hated me today, how much will you hate me if it really does come? I haven't the courage to face it all.'[8] Distressed that he might have passed it on to her, Harold, understandably, was terrified at the possible consequences of his casual sexual encounter, both for himself and for Vita. His consultant had advised them not to have sex for the coming six months. It is impossible to know precisely what Vita was thinking. But apart from Harold having endangered her health, his confession surely confirmed what she already must have suspected about Harold's sexual predilections. Did this incident prove to be 'a turning point' in their relationship, as has been suggested? Did it give Vita an excuse to give full rein to her own sexual preferences – and perhaps also to 'punish' Harold for putting her in danger? As if to justify her future behaviour she began to gossip about Harold's lack of finesse as a lover. Lady Sackville heard from her daughter that Harold is 'too quick and too sleepy' as a lover, that he is 'physically cold'. The gossip, and its source, reached Harold's ears. Angry and humiliated, he would snap at Vita in public and scold her in private, behaviour quite out of character for someone of Harold's placid temperament. Oswald ('Ozzie') Dickinson joined in the tongue-wagging. A lifelong bachelor and a close friend of Harold's, but also a favourite of Lady Sackville's, he elaborated further to B.M. about 'the most intimate things' concerning Harold and Vita's married life.[9]

By chance, Harold found comfort in Marie Stopes's *Married Love* (1918): 'It is wonderful: it goes into every detail. There is a whole chapter which explains why Hadji goes to sleep and Mar doesn't. I find I am the *rule* and not the exception.' Appalled at his own ignorance, he accepted that Vita 'must have suffered terribly – and that only a splendid character like yours could have kept from hating me.' Harold attempted to placate Vita. His doctor had assured him that by 20 April there would be no risk: 'Darling do you mind awfully having a diseased husband?' Like his doctor, he was 'frightfully opty' about it not happening again. But was it too late?

In April 1918, the six-month waiting period barely over, Vita's extraordinary, scandalous adventure with Violet Keppel began. Violet, tempestuous and passionate, had always been in the background. She had acted as Ben's godmother and was a regular, if sporadic, visitor at Long Barn. She and Vita met socially, at teas or lunches, and went to matinées and saw exhibitions together. 'Darling,' she wrote to Vita at the end of October 1917, 'I simply can't get on without a periodical glimpse of your radiant domesticity . . . We are absolutely essential to one another, at least in *my* eyes!' Long ago Violet had seen into Vita's 'soul' and, protesting her love for her, had vowed to show Vita 'madness'.[10]

On 13 April Violet came to stay for a fortnight at Long Barn. Five days later Vita recollected 'that wild irresponsible day . . . Violet had struck the secret of my duality'. They stayed up all night, talking, kissing, petting. The upshot was that they decided to go away together. They turned to Harold for help – and Harold obliged. He wrote to his friend Hugh Walpole: 'Do you happen to know of a suitable inn or hotel in your *farouche* [wild, fierce] county of Cornwall where my wife and Violet Keppel can go for the [inside ?] of a week? They have a sudden desire to see the sea, but do not wish to go where they will find Jews or other people.'[11] Walpole complied. He put his cottage at Polperro at their disposal. In this manner their love affair, which would last almost three years, began. They were to run away together for a second time to Cornwall, but also to France and Italy, sometimes absconding for months at a time. Their definitive game plan, to elope and live together in a house in Sicily, never quite materialised.[12]

Whenever Vita ran into a snag, she turned to Harold. And Harold, following a pattern, would usually respond positively. If Vita and Violet needed passes to travel through war-torn France, Harold provided them. At Monte Carlo, a desperate Vita appealed for funds: Harold sent her £130. Their correspondence is replete with protestations of enduring love. But every so often he would snap. 'What frightens me so, is that I feel now I don't *want* to see you.' But he would soon repent, accepting part of the responsibility for what was happening. 'Of course I blame myself chiefly,' he said on one occasion, adding on another, '[I] hope you will be very happy with your new companion.' He would reassure her: 'I want you to feel that I shall always take your point-of-view and that I realize . . . it is *not* your fault.' Harold's diplomatic training sought a compromise. He proposed – ironically? – that Vita acquire 'a little cottage in Cornwall or elsewhere', but on condition.

Then the Padlock [Sackville vernacular for an unbreakable promise] is that Hadji never goes there and can't (by the rules of the Padlock) even be asked – or even know when she is there or who she has got with her. It will make a real escape from the YOKE [of marriage]. And when I am rich, I shall have one too, just the same and on the same condition.

Darling, take the idea seriously and think over it.[13]

If Vita wasn't at fault, who then was the guilty party? Vita laid some of the blame at Harold's door, murmuring that he should have been more audacious, more resolute, acted more vigorously to keep her in check, to curb the 'Wanderlust' that was taking her away from him. 'I was never fit to marry someone so sane, so good, so sweet, so limpid, as yourself,' she told Harold. 'I try to *make* you fight for yourself, but you never will; you just say "Darling Mar!" and leave me to invent my own conviction out of your silence.' Later, after much thought, she went on to say that Harold could at any moment have reclaimed her, 'but for some extraordinary reason you wouldn't. I used to beg you to; I *wanted* to be rescued, and you wouldn't hold out a hand.' Much, much later, Harold Macmillan saw in Harold something of a 'martyr' with a 'slightly masochistic' temperament.[14]

For Harold, there could only be one culpable party. To charge Vita was unthinkable – though Vita would every so often confess to her own weaknesses. Harold targeted his preferred *bête noire*, 'that swine Violet who seems to addle your brain'. 'I wish Violet were dead,' he declared. 'She is like some fierce orchid, glimmering and stinking in the recesses of life and throwing cadaverous sweetness on the morning breeze. Darling, she is evil and I am not evil.' He spoke of Violet's 'evil eye'. 'Don't let her see my babies,' he pleaded.[15] Harold's bitter antipathy towards Violet was perfectly understandable, even if it was slightly out of focus.

On 26 March 1919 *The Times* announced the engagement of Violet Keppel to Major Denys Trefusis, MC, of the Royal Horse Guards, lending yet another extraordinary twist to this extraordinary story. When Denys had first proposed, Violet rejected him outright, assuring Vita, '*Je t'aime, je t'aime*'. But Mrs Keppel, the late Edward VII's mistress, herself the soul of discretion, insisted that her daughter honour established society values. In other circumstances, Denys and Vita might have been good friends. She found him 'a very splendid person', 'intelligent', and absorbed in 'un-sordid things'. But she reacted furiously to the news of Violet's impending marriage. 'Mrs Denys Trefusis, that name is a stab to me every time I hear it.' As the fateful day approached – 16 June 1919 – she became 'ABSOLUTELY TERRI- FIED'. She longed to discard moribund Victorian values and move into the modern age where women would have the same freedom as men.

O Hadji, if you knew how it would amuse me to scandalise the whole of London! It's so secure, so fatuous, so conventional, so hypocritical, so whited-sepulchre, so cynical, so humbugging, so mean, so ungenerous, so self-defensive, so well-policed, so beautifully legislated, so well-dressed, so up-to-date, so hierarchical, so virtually vicious, so viciously virtuous. I'd like to tweak away the chair just as it's going to sit down.

Immediately after their wedding in London Violet and Denys left for Paris. Vita was waiting – fuming with envy. She took Violet to the small hotel where she was staying and 'treated her savagely'. 'I made love to her, I had her, I didn't care, I only wanted to hurt Denys.' In the words of her biographer, 'She behaved like a madwoman. She had lost all control.'[16] This was to take sexual possessiveness to an extreme degree.

Vita had 'tweaked away the chair' from under London society long before this occurred, not that it brought her much comfort. All London and Paris 'hummed' with gossip at her and Violet's escapades. At Long Barn in April 1918 Vita, on sudden impulse, had put on breeches and gaiters and found a freedom she hadn't imagined existed. Pursued by Violet, 'I ran, I shouted, I jumped, I climbed, I vaulted over gates, I felt like a schoolboy let out on holiday.' The cross-dressing continued. Now metamorphosed as Mitya (Vita) and Lushka (Violet), or as Julian and Eve, they would parade the streets of London or Paris or Monte Carlo, smoking and dancing in public.[17] Harold was appalled at this brazen, exhibitionist behaviour. 'I have heard an awful story that you and Violet danced together in public at some charity show. Of course, I don't believe it, because, my darling, you *can't* dance & never could. But did you do *anything* which could have given the grounds for such a story?' The gossip persisted. 'I can't forgive you if you have really done something as vulgar and dangerous as that,' he wrote, adding, typically, 'I am still cross about it, but I will forgive you anything.' Lady Sackville was not as forgiving. Although she saw Violet as 'a sexual pervert, pernicious, amoral, a snake in the grass' who had 'demoralized' Vita, she abhorred her daughter's behaviour. 'I don't want them [Ben and Nigel] to blush when their mother's name is mentioned.'[18]

Lady Sackville also adamantly opposed the publication of *Challenge*, a novel Vita began in May 1918. Dedicated to Violet, it constitutes 'the best evidence of Vita's feelings' for her, and reads as a thinly disguised fictional version of their relationship. The main characters were all too easily recognisable. Julian (Vita), a rich young Englishman living in a small republic on the Greek coast, incites the offshore islanders of Aphros (Harold) to revolt and so becomes their illegal president. Eve (Violet), his cousin, joins him there and they become 'happy lovers'. But Julian's commitment to Aphros leads an insanely jealous Eve, who wants Julian absolutely, to betray him, throwing all convention to the wind. At one point Eve pleads, ' "Come with me, gypsy!"/ . . . "Away from Aphros"? he said, losing his head/ "All over the world"/ He was suddenly swept away by the full force of her wild, irresponsible seduction/ "Anywhere you choose, Eve".' Even to have countenanced publication of this transparent work would have invited a dreadful scandal. So thought Lady Sackville, and Mrs Keppel, no less determined a character, joined her. Joint pressure brought to bear by these two formidable mothers ensured that it would be shelved. Collins returned the rights for £150. (Although published in the United States in 1923, it was not until 1974 that Collins renewed its contract to bring out *Challenge*.) Harold's response was more ambivalent. He found little of merit in the manuscript. He nicknamed it 'Smuts', and implored Vita to 'Keep Eve the little prig she is.'[19] But he refused to take as forceful a stand as Lady Sackville and Mrs Keppel. Perhaps he hoped that the very act of writing would purge Vita's body of the dybbuk that had infected it. It was not to be.

In the early New Year of 1920, only weeks after Vita had completed the final draft of *Challenge*, she told Harold that she intended to elope with Violet, for ever. Her decision, she implied, was final: it brooked no argument. Like Julian, she 'was suddenly swept away by the full force of [Eve's] wild, irresponsible seduction'. Already depressed by the racy gossip surrounding Vita – at times he toyed with the idea of divorce, even of exile – Harold broke down and wept. If this was his way of fighting back, it had no effect. He was also physically run-down. Lame, hobbling about with the aid of two canes, he had arrived home from Paris on sick leave, anticipating an operation for an abscess in his knee. After an interlude of a fortnight spent at Knole, where he 'made no allusion' to the ongoing crisis, Harold left for Paris and the peace conference while Vita left for Lincoln with Violet, where it was 'bitterly cold but we were happy'.[20] On 9 February the two lovers travelled to Dover. They were to proceed separately to Calais and meet up again at Amiens, and would then, perhaps, go on to Sicily.

At this point, for the disinterested observer, the affair takes on some of the characteristics of a French farce. To Vita's surprise she met Denys at Dover. Without recriminations, they sailed together for Calais, crossing the Channel in gale force winds and heavy rain, joking about 'sea-sick remedies'. (Unknown to them, Harold was crossing in the opposite direction, searching for Vita.) At Calais they were astonished to find Violet, looking ill and under-nourished. All three took adjoining rooms at the same hotel. The following day they departed for Amiens, Denys 'crying the whole way', saying he would leave them at Amiens and go off to London by himself, 'never to see Violet again'. His resolve was short-lived. Back in London it was arranged by the indomitable Mrs Keppel that he should fly in a two-seater private plane to Amiens, rescue Violet from Vita's clutches and, for the time being, keep her out of England to avoid a great scandal. Lady Sackville, sizing up its dramatic potential, heard of the scheme and persuaded Denys to take Harold with him. 'Quite like a sensational novel,' she recorded in her diary.[21]

Landing at Amiens they went straight to the Hôtel du Rhin where Vita and Violet were staying. Husbands confronted wives. Harold asked Vita to pack; Denys remained silent. Vita made no move, while Violet abused Denys, telling him how much she 'loathed' him. It was a stalemate until Harold said to Vita: 'Are you sure Violet is as faithful to you as she makes you believe? Because Denys has told your mother a different story.' Denys refused to confirm or deny the story, an admission of guilt in Vita's eyes. But Violet, when confronted by Vita, confessed to having 'belonged' to him. 'Blind with passion and pain' at Violet's betrayal, Vita determined to leave her at once, 'to get away at all costs'. Acting like one possessed – her behaviour has been described as 'temporarily, clinically insane' – she packed and left with Harold for Paris. While they were dining at their hotel restaurant, Violet and Denys walked in. After another cross-examination, Denys denied that he had had sexual relations with Violet – 'perjuring himself', he later told Harold, to quell Vita's hysteria. It was not good enough for Vita. Violet had deceived her, 'even to a certain extent', and just when Vita was ready 'to give up everything in the world for her'. Vita, her passions still running high, told Violet that she could not 'bear to see her for at least two months'.[22]

After the denouement at the Hôtel du Rhin, the affair faded away. But the two lovers continued to meet. And when they did 'it was like two flames leaping together'. They 'spent four absolutely unclouded days' together at Violet's house in the country. They travelled further afield, to Avignon and San Remo, Venice and Hyères, the last flickerings of a blazing fire. Vita agonised, unable 'to reconcile my house, my garden, my fields, and Harold . . . that pleaded only by their own merits of purity, simplicity, and faith', with Violet, 'fighting wildly for me . . . riding roughshod over those gentle defenceless things'.[23] There would be no reconciliation, however. Instead, she favoured Harold over Violet, claiming that Violet had destroyed all trust between them, making it inconceivable that they should ever live together. But this was only partially true. Having boxed herself into a corner, Vita was searching for an escape route. Despite having adopted the revolutionary *nom de plume* of Mishka, Vita lacked the true revolutionary instinct, or the character, to live openly with another woman, defying all social etiquette, fulfilling the unquestioned nature of her sexual preferences. Unlike the famous 'Ladies of Llangollen' (Lady Eleanor Butler and Miss Sarah Ponsonby), when put to the test Vita opted for her 'playfellow' Harold, for her family, for Knole and Long Barn, for all the trappings of a conventional life, for the veneer of respectability that would allow her to continue writing and gardening – and to carry on with her transient infidelities – with the least possible disruption.

In one way, Harold's reaction to the affair was crystal clear. Violet was the 'poisonous orchid', the odious villain of the piece. It could hardly have been otherwise, for it would have been unbearable for him to have placed the burden of blame on Vita's shoulders. He was always very considerate of his 'little Mar', ready to forgive her 'muddles', as he was wont to call her liaisons. For Harold, the threat of Violet always hung in the air. A year after Amiens, he sensed something 'hopeless about Vita', who was holidaying at Hyères with Violet. A few days later Harold recorded: 'Received a letter from Denys saying that he has decided to divorce Violet. Damn!'[24]

Throughout the affair Harold had acted passively, waiting upon events rather than initiating them, painfully patient, understanding, chivalrous.

Even to reach Amiens he had, so to speak, to be pushed into the cockpit of the aeroplane. His outward display of sang-froid was by no means contrived, but did it reveal all that he was undergoing?

'I fear I am going downhill without you,' he wrote to Vita, 'and I get so awfully depressed that I drink too much, and I spend my time with rather low people, but I am ashamed to go into society, so I live in the demi-monde and I don't like it much.' Vita had shunted him aside sexually. 'You say you want to *tromper* me with myself. But that's *impossible*, darling, there can't be anything of *that* now – just now I mean.'[25] In what could be interpreted as a kind of game of sexual tit-for-tat, Harold sought distractions elsewhere, with those more attuned to his own sensual pleasures. In December 1918 he began a casual affair with Victor Cunard, a nephew by marriage to Lady Cunard. Victor was twenty years old, brash in manner, exuding self-confidence, and was openly gay. They weekended together at Victor's family home in Leicester and at Vita's estate at Knole. In Paris, just over a year later, Edward Molyneux, a well-known fashion designer, appeared. 'I have got such a funny new friend . . . with a charming flat at the Rond Point . . . My dressmaker is only 27 – and it is rather sporting to launch out into so elaborate an adventure at that age. Mar would like my new friend, I think – very attractive.' At the same time, while grappling with the complexities of the postwar treaties and writing a biography of the homosexual poet, Paul Verlaine, he encountered Jean de Gaigneron, a *risqué* Parisian socialite, promiscuous in habit, who introduced Harold to Marcel Proust and Jean Cocteau. 'Jean is a nice friend for Hadji as he knows all the clevers.' Would Vita 'arrange with B.M. for Jean to sleep at Hill Street with me (!!)', he asked innocently.[26]

Harold's affairs posed no threat to Vita, or their marriage; nor were they intended to. Never as passionate or committed as Vita, he entered into his fleeting dalliances in rapid succession, sometimes, as seems apparent, even pursuing them simultaneously. At heart, Vita must have understood what moved Harold, and should have been kindly disposed to his sexual urges. But outwardly she showed little forbearance, as she spoke ironically, scornfully, cruelly of his 'non-masculine' men friends: 'Victor [Cunard] is a nice, easy, pleasant, ineffectual little thing. What contempt one has, *au fond*, for the Victors, Eddie Marshes and Ozzies [Dickinson] of this world.'[27]

In general, Violet has had a bad press. It has been noted that she was 'a true neurotic' and 'a manipulator' who played on Vita's fantasies. It is true that Violet's behaviour was histrionic to an extreme degree, that she displayed her emotions on her sleeve. But, to a greater or lesser extent, much the same could be said of Vita. Time and again she spun out of control. Older and more experienced than Violet, she in fact controlled the affair. She admitted it: 'My old domination over her had never been diminished.'[28] It was Vita who led Violet along, who raised her hopes that theirs would be a permanent relationship. It was Vita's decision to break off the relationship when she came to the conclusion that it was in her interest to do so. As for Violet, she was left with no option but to accept Vita's ruling – and damn the consequences!

This was to become a familiar pattern. Vita could pursue her affairs with or without Violet, as she did, one passion supplanting another as it suited her purpose. A long string of lovers replaced Violet: Dorothy ('Dottie') Wellesley, Pat Dansey, Mary Campbell, Hilda Matheson, Margaret Voigt, Evelyn Irons, Olive Rinder, Gwen St Aubyn, Avilde Lees-Milne, and most famously, Virginia Woolf. In her son's words, 'her only problem was to free herself of one love affair in order to begin the next'. She discarded lovers with an arrogant ease. Vita's behaviour, it has been noted, was 'reckless and cruel'. She penned the following lines: 'Those cheap and easy loves! But what were they,/ Those rank intruders into darkest lairs?/ We take a heart and leave our own intact.' Pat Dansey called Vita 'a romantic young man who treats his women badly'.[29] In this way she benefited from all worlds: security on one hand, affairs galore on the other.

The Trefusis affair was the defining crisis of Harold and Vita's marriage, a turning point. They never shared a bedroom again. After such an emotional and physical roller-coaster, it must be asked, how did their marriage survive at all? Was it because of Harold's widely admired patience, his acclaimed tolerance, his adept diplomatic handling of the situation? Or was it simply because Vita decided that it should endure? Not that she loved Violet less than Harold, but because she remained shackled to the established traditions of her class, to the rights and duties involved, to the presumed respectability that placed family and home and children above all else. Harold was the perfect partner for the role mapped out for him, and as their marriage moved forward, so too did their mutual affection, their love for each other. In some ways their love affair struck deeper roots. But their lovemaking was practised by remote control, enriched by frequent absences and letter-writing (10,529 at the Lilly Library alone). 'You are my only anchor,' Vita repeatedly told him; and there can be no doubt that it worked both ways. Was their love enhanced by the freedom they allowed each other? They were always absolutely frank about their entanglements, her 'muddles', his 'fun', insisting that in the long run their dalliances would not be allowed to disrupt the smooth progress of their union. 'Our two lives,' Vita boasted, 'outside and inside, are rich lives – not little meagre repetitions of meagre cerebral habits.'[30]

Little of this came out when the BBC invited them to broadcast to a mass audience their views on a successful marriage.[31] Harold led the discussion,

Vita followed. They agreed on the basics. A thriving marriage, 'the greatest of human benefits', should be based on 'love guided by intelligence' and 'a common sense of values', bolstered by 'give and take' and 'mutual esteem'. Marriage, they concurred, should be compared to an organic growth, to 'a plant' and not to 'a piece of furniture'. 'It grows, it changes; it develops. You must tend its growth.' All marriages are initially on trial, similar to 'pot plants under eight years'. To guide the partners safely through the tricky first stage they need to display 'modesty, good humour and, above all, occupation'. These were not especially profound or provocative observations, however elegantly put. Vita livened up the discourse when she took issue with some of the ramifications of the 'plant' analogy. Quite, agreed Vita, except that men regard themselves as 'the plant' and women as 'the soil', a self-defeating point of view since it taught men to be 'dominant and inconsiderate' and women to be 'sly'. When Harold argued that a man's work was a necessity while a woman's career was a luxury, Vita again protested. What of independent callings, she remonstrated? And no, she countered emphatically, 'the joys of motherhood' were no compensation. Harold cut dangerously close to the bone when he began to talk of 'temperamental differences between the sexes' being so acute as to be only 'superficially affected by forms of sexual aberrations', and tacked on for good measure that in any case 'sex lasts a short time, from three weeks only to three years'. Here was a subtext that went undetected by most listeners. No doubt it was these comments that caused some eyebrows to be raised. But for the predominantly middle-class audience that heard the broadcast, it was deemed a considerable success.

The Trefusis affair confirmed Vita's dominance in her relationship with Harold. She not only held the purse-strings, but also the emotional strings. The impression remains strong that Harold was at times overawed by Vita's commanding personality. 'A crushed life is what I lead,' he once complained to Vita, 'similar to that of the hen you ran over the other day.' He considered whether Vita would have been happier had she married 'a more determined and less sensitive man':

> On the one hand you would have hated any sense of control or management, and other men might not have understood your desire for independence. I have always respected that, and you have often mistaken it for aloofness on my part. What bothers me is whether I have given way too much to your eccentricities . . . What has always worried me is your dual personality. The one tender, wise and with such a sense of responsibility. And the other rather cruel and extravagant. The former has been what I have always clung to as the essential you, but the latter

has always alarmed me . . . I do not think you have quite realised how deeply unhappy your eccentric side has often rendered me. When I am unhappy I shut up like an oyster.

All of which leads one to speculate whether Vita married Harold, not only for all the customary reasons, but also because she sensed that he lacked those qualities that he now so candidly admitted to.[32]

For Harold ending Vita and Violet's affair was crucial, not only to preserve his marriage, albeit on a fresh basis, but also to preserve his career. All London 'hummed' with the affair, but all London meant in effect the exclusive circles in which Vita and Harold moved. Had the scandal become public knowledge in the fullest sense, it would have opened a Pandora's box and would surely have destroyed Harold's diplomatic career. Those were still the days when homosexuality was a criminal offence: even now, Oscar Wilde's tragic fate cast its long shadow.

One other aspect of his marriage disturbed Harold's peace of mind. He was vexed by the superior social standing of the Sackvilles when compared with his own family roots, even though the Nicolsons could boast of a baronetcy dating from the mid-seventeenth century. But how could this compare to a family tree that began with Herbrand de Sackville, reputedly a companion of William the Conqueror, and included a royal connection to Elizabeth I? Harold railed at the Sackville 'toffs' and their 'Norman blood'. He owned up: 'I have always hated the name Nicolson as being a common, plebeian name.' 'Amused' to find in himself 'a fat grub of snobbishness', he thirsted after a peerage. And if it would come about – it didn't – he would change his name to the more aristocratic-sounding Cranfield.* Lady Sackville in turn saw Harold's parents 'as very ugly and very small and unsmart looking': Lady Nicolson in particular appeared 'deadly dull and *génée*; most unattractive; but *une brave femme*. I said nothing to her.'[33]

Although never stated openly, the Nicolsons could easily have been pigeon-holed as 'bedint'.† Did something of this seep through to Harold's immediate

---

*Despite his railing at 'Sackville toffs', Harold had chanced (?) upon an old Sackville title, inherited from 'a Jacobean grocer whom the Nicolsons of that time had despised as a howling vulgarian'. See Hugh Trevor-Roper, 'Lord Cranfield As He Wasn't', *Spectator*, 6 Sept. 1968.

† A corruption from the German *bedienen*, to serve or wait upon. Originally used by the Sackvilles to refer to servants, it was corrupted further by Sackville–Nicolson double-speak to put down anyone they considered as vulgar or common or as lacking in social distinction: by definition, it included the lower and middle classes – but often those of their own class who did not measure up to their inflexible, self-determined social standards.

family? Neither Vita nor Nigel nor Ben cared much for Harold's mother – whom Harold cherished. At times, Vita found Lady Carnock's perceived possessiveness unbearable. She boiled over. 'She is a damned selfish grasping old woman, that's what she is . . . I hate her, I hate her, I hate her . . . I wish she were dead.' Nor did Vita appreciate the delights of Clandeboye – the most tangible symbol of Harold's aristocratic pedigree, and where he had spent many happy days – when she first visited it in August 1952, putting it down as 'lugubrious', 'an ugly County Down house'. Harold's brother, Freddy (the second Lord Carnock), was another casualty. A chronic alcoholic, Vita hotly opposed to him moving into 10, Neville Place – where Harold and the boys were living at the time – so that they could take care of him. When Nigel told Harold that he felt more Sackville than Nicolson, Harold noted ruefully: 'It is quite true that neither of our boys regards any of my family as belonging in the same way they regard Eddy, Lionel, etc. as belonging. So there I am next to Sackville Street [he was then living at C.1. Albany, Piccadilly] and imposed upon, crushed, humiliated by that melancholic breed.'[34] Harold, not without feelings of resentment, had succumbed to the aristocratic Sackville myth.

The Trefusis affair moved into overdrive at precisely the time Harold was coming to the notice of leading government ministers and his superiors at the Foreign Office. Now a delegate to the peace conference, his opportunity had arrived to prove to his masters that he was indeed 'a coming man'. Understandably, the Trefusis 'muddle' left him frustrated, confused, bitter and depressed. It put Harold under an intolerable strain: 'Oh Darling, Why did you get me into this hateful muddle? I do hate it so – & I am dead with work and worry.' But Vita would not relent. 'All the sun has gone from Paris – which has become a cold, grey meaningless city where there is a Conference going on somewhere, a conference which meant so much to me yesterday, and today is something detached, unreal and inanimate.' After 'a frightful row' at work, he confided to his diary:

So even my personal position in the Office is gone wrong now. No home. No affection. No money. No happiness. Oh, *Viti, Viti* – what have you to answer for . . . What a bloody thing it is to have so thin a skin . . . and I am a harmless, happy creature by nature. If only I did [not ?] care for her it would help. But I love her so. Even the thought of exile is painful. [35]

These cries, with their potentially devastating effect on Harold's diplomatic career, did not influence Vita to any marked degree. Towards the end of their life together Harold candidly admitted to a close friend that '[Vita] is not an easy person to manage.'[36]

SIX

Back to Diplomacy

At 11 a.m. on 3 January 1919 Harold left Charing Cross station for Paris. He arrived at the Gare du Nord twelve hours later and drove without delay to the the Hôtel Majestic on the Avenue Kléber – 'a vast caravanserai . . . constructed almost entirely of onyx for the benefit of Brazilian ladies who, before the war, could come to Paris to buy their clothes' – that was to house the British delegation. The onyx remained, but the Brazilian ladies had long since departed. Instead, Alwyn Parker, a Middle East specialist now responsible for the well-being of the British delegates, had instituted a security-conscious, morally uplifting, home-cooking environment consistent with sound British standards. Staffed by British domestics, and reinforced by nameless security agents, it was intended to ensure that there would be 'no Metternich nonsense about the Conference of Paris'. The catering standards were, apparently, tasteless in the extreme. 'It has been a sad joke,' Eyre Crowe, renowned throughout the service for his austere lifestyle, wryly noted. 'The coffee,' Harold added mockingly, 'was British to the core.'[1] The logic of this arrangement escaped Harold as the delegation worked at the adjoining Hôtel Astoria, where all its papers and maps were kept, and which was staffed by French nationals. Those who could, fled from Parker's spartan regime to seek the relative comfort and privacy of a *pied-à-terre*. Harold made his move at the beginning of February, not only to escape from Parker's watchdogs, but also because he was expecting Vita to join him in Paris. (She failed to turn up, preferring to remain in Monte Carlo with Violet, though she did budget him four days in mid-March.)

A century earlier, Simon Bolivar, the 'Liberator' of Latin America, had impressed upon one of his aides the niceties of diplomatic technique:

I will give you a good maxim for diplomatic matters: calm, calm, calm; delay, delay, delay; compliments; vague words; consultations; examinations; twisting of arguments and requests; references to a new Congress;

digressions on the nature of the issues and documents . . . and at all times be slow, be very laconic so as not to give anything away to your opponent . . . Above all, be always firm where good principles and universal justice is concerned . . . Let us conduct ourselves properly and let time work miracles.[2]

Whether or not Harold was aware of Bolivar's dictum, it provided him, in the main, with sound guidelines for his own diplomatic method, even though at times it left him frustrated at the lack of foresight of others.

Overworked – 'Boxes full. Work! Work! Work! Work!' – and underpaid (he drew a salary of £86 net per annum at the conference), Harold served as a technical adviser on the committees that were busy drawing up new maps for central Europe and the Balkans. Sketching in fresh boundaries for Czechoslovakia, Romania, Yugoslavia, Hungary and Greece – and by implication, for Turkey – consumed his working hours. Although he found the work 'passionately interesting', it was not all smooth going. At times he was conscious-stricken at the burdens imposed upon him. 'How fallible one feels here! A map – a pencil – tracing paper. Yet my courage fails at the thought of people whom our errant lines enclose or exclude, the happiness of several thousands of people.' Perceived national characteristics also intruded: 'Nobody who has not had experience of Committee work in actual practice can conceive of the difficulty of inducing a Frenchman, an Italian, an American and an Englishman to agree on anything.'[3]

These committees were not concerned with constructing the framework of the newborn League of Nations, President Wilson's obsessive brainchild. Still, they stood at the heart of the conference's deliberations, dealing with the fate of national minorities, reconciling the all too often conflicting, and exaggerated, claims of both the great and the small powers – it was approvingly noted that Clemenceau, 'always audible', was 'equally rude' to both. And as at the plenary sessions of the conference the powers had neither the time nor the knowledge to challenge the recommendations of the 'experts', they became, in effect, the arbiters of these disputes, 'the final court of appeal'. It was a responsibility that Harold could have done without.[4]

Interminable committee meetings, drafting endless position papers, irregular hours, hurried meals, late nights, and competing with closed-minded politicians, all put Harold under an intolerable strain, a state of mind not eased by Vita's escapades. Exhausted, he had reached the point when he found himself 'reading sentences twice over', an ominous sign. He sought advice from Balfour. He found the Foreign Secretary, languid in his habits, usually draped over a chair, 'always affable and benign', at his apartment in the rue Nitot. 'You're feeling stale?' Balfour asked. 'Sir,' Harold replied, 'I feel I want a thorough change.' Perhaps a few days at Dieppe, or Fontainebleau, or even a quick dash down to Nice. Out of the question, murmured Balfour, what you require is 'a holiday, not a distraction': they are two quite different things, Balfour clarified. 'You will,' he continued,

> return at once to the Majestic – arrived there, you will go to bed. For luncheon you will drink a bottle of Nuits St George and eat all that you can possibly swallow. You will then sleep until four. You will then read some books which I shall lend you [a selection of his favourite thrillers]. For dinner you will have champagne and foie gras – a light dinner. You repeat this treatment until Sunday at three – when you drive alone to Versailles and back. In the evening of Sunday you dine – again alone, that is essential – at Larue and go to a play. By Monday you will be cured.

And so it turned out. By Monday, Harold cheerfully noted, 'I felt again a young and vigorous man.' Refreshed, he returned to attend to his duties – which included faithfully serving Balfour's needs.[5]

Harold worked in close tandem with Allen Leeper. Australian by birth, Anglo-Catholic by choice, Leeper – a Balliol man, he had gained a first in Greats – was an ideal partner for Harold. Academically inclined, of unfailing energy and flagging health, he possessed a working knowledge of many languages, including French, German, Italian, Spanish, Dutch, Flemish, Russian, Greek, Latin, Hebrew, Serbo-Croat and Ladino. True to the *Zeitgeist*, he favoured compact nation states – to unite the Poles, the Yugoslavs, the Romanians, the Arabs, the Greeks – a process that would pave the way for the demise of the old, discredited system ruled by the Great Powers and lead to a new era regulated by the League of Nations and Wilsonism. For Harold, at the time, these ideas were 'as always, admirable'. Later, writing in 1935, he thought they might appear utopian, but added: 'to many of us it still remains the most valid of all our visions'.[6]

There were other colleagues whom he admired and with whom he was only too pleased to co-operate. Naturally, Crowe topped the list. 'It is a joy to be working under someone so acute and precise. My mind is, with him, always at ease.' Crowe reciprocated. 'Nicolson works with me a great deal and I have got to like him particularly, both personally and on account of his excellent work.' (After a 'two minute' introduction, Vita also made a favourable impression on the strait-laced Crowe, 'contrary to what I had anticipated'.) Robert Vansittart and Eric Forbes-Adam, two rising stars of the Foreign Office, also ranked high in Harold's esteem. Not so Hardinge, who strutted about in such a pompous way 'that he almost fell over backwards'. Irredeemably stuffy in outlook, Hardinge sent for poor Harold, and 'solemnly cursed' him 'for coming to a dance in day clothes'. It came as no surprise when Harold coolly refused Hardinge's tempting offer that he should serve as 'HIS PRIVATE SECRETARY', even though it would have been recognised as a step up the promotion ladder. 'I remained unmoved however – and while my head swam – I refused it. You can never say again that I am ambitious!' Harold reported to Vita.[7]

But more than anything Harold wished to work in tandem with the Americans. The New World had arrived to reshape the Old. The Americans had prepared for the conference with their characteristic industry. An 'Inquiry', under the supervision of Colonel Edward Mandell House – Wilson's confidential adviser – had prepared for every eventuality likely to arise at the Paris gathering, sixty reports for the Far East alone. In scenes of high drama, President Woodrow Wilson, his reputation at a peak, had been received as a saviour by ecstatic crowds in the capitals of Europe. He promised a new era in the conduct of international relations. The Old Adam of pre-war diplomacy would be cast out; in its place he pledged to erect a trail-blazing international system based on national rights, co-operation and trust. These ideas struck a deep chord with the younger generation in the Foreign Office, Harold included. Arriving in Paris, they would not have been embarrassed to identify themselves as 'Wilsonians'.

Even before the conference formally began the British sought out the Americans. Wary of openly forming an Anglo-Saxon bloc, Harold and Leeper met their American counterparts in what had once been a *cabinet particulier* at Maxim's. As Harold mischievously put it, he aimed at 'secret covenants secretly arrived at'. They might have been conducting an academic seminar as the British experts faced Professor Clive Day of Yale, 'pale, slim, arid, decent'; Professor Charles Seymour, also of Yale, 'young dark, might be a major in the Sappers'; Dr Lybyer, 'silent, somewhat remote'; and Captain Rhys Carpenter, a philologist and archaeologist, 'a cultured mind', and moreover a Balliol man. They conducted a particularly wide ranging discussion – and more were to follow – covering the future of the Balkans, the fate of the secret Italian treaties of London (April 1915) and St Jean de Maurienne (April 1917),* and the prospects for Asiatic Turkey.[8] Harold was encouraged by the degree of expertise the Americans brought to these subjects. Impressed

---

*By the London treaty, signed by Britain, France, Russia and Italy, Italy was promised confirmation of its conquests, Libya and the Dodecanese islands, which it had seized in 1911–12, together with extensive territories in the Tyrol and along the Dalmatian coast, if it would enter the war: Italy entered the war at the end of May 1915.

The treaty of St Jean de Maurienne, concocted by Britain, France and Italy, conceded to Italy considerable gains at the expense of a partitioned Ottoman Empire.

by their 'very beautiful' relief map of the Adriatic, he concluded that 'they evidently know their subject backwards'. 'Intelligent, not too distrustful, alert', the American scholars proved to be an ideal sounding board for the British diplomatists. Over some matters – Czechoslovakia and Romania – they held 'identical views'; over others – exaggerated Greek claims, for example – there were differences of emphasis. But 'the net result of these discussions is a most satisfactory unanimity in regard to general policy'.

For all Harold's cheerful interpretation of these talks, there were several sticking points that Crowe and Hardinge were quick to pick up. The Americans were too favourably disposed towards Bulgaria, but 'it is neither right, nor can we afford, to quarrel with Greece and Roumania, and Serbia in order to be tender to the Bulgarians', minuted Crowe. Hardinge concurred. Questionable Greek claims were also scrutinised, forcing Harold to sadly admit: they were 'perhaps naturally, less in sympathy with M. Venizelos, than I was myself . . . and to whom we had incurred deep moral obligations'. Somewhat suprisingly there was a meeting of minds over Greek demands to seize Smyrna – a most controversial proposition. The Americans 'are very keen on a Greek zone at Smyrna', Harold noted; and they were even prepared to hand over the Dodecanese islands to Greece. This was all the more unexpected as the Americans emphasised that they were not bound by any wartime agreements regarding the future of the Ottoman Empire as the United States had never declared war on Turkey – a potentially threatening opening gambit. Fortunately, like the British, they favoured the expulsion of the Turks from Europe and supported an international zone at the Straits, though how it was to be administered was left open. But the main stumbling block was the Allies' wartime commitments to Italy. The Americans 'made it abundantly clear that President Wilson would never accept any final solution which might be based on the Italian treaties'. This threw out of kilter the whole substance of the proposed settlements regarding the Adriatic and central Europe and Turkey.

One intriguing idea, in keeping with the spirit of the time, was floated for consideration. The Americans hinted that Britain might well show other nations an example, with the Italians well in mind, and surrender Cyprus. Harold, rightly, made no comment at the time. But something must have struck home. Two days later he broached the matter with Crowe. The answer was a resounding No! 'I am distressed about Cyprus,' Harold sadly noted. 'The British Empire Delegation have decided to retain it on strategical and other grounds. They are wrong entirely: its retention compromises our whole moral position in regard to the Italians.'

* * *

The conference opened officially on 18 January 1919 at the Quai d'Orsay. Raymond Poincaré, the French President, greeted the delegates, but Clemenceau soon took command in typical high-handed fashion. '*Y a-t-il d'objections? Non? . . . Adopté.* Like a machine gun.' At first Harold found his work 'passionately interesting'. He was absorbed with the minutiae of the territorial commission's deliberations, niggling questions that at a distance seem esoteric to an extreme but which at the time took on a grave importance: deciding, for example, on the Enos–Midia line to cut off Turkey-in-Europe from Greece and Bulgaria; or plotting with Arnold Toynbee about Constantinople and the Straits.

> We agree, therefore, to propose to cut the Gordian knot. Let the Turks have Anatolia as their own. Give the Greeks European Turkey only. And let the Straights be kept open by a 'Commission Fluviale' with powers analogous to those of the Danube Commission. Such a solution would at least have the merit of finality. All other solutions would entail trouble in the future. We put this down on paper; we will sign it with our names; we send it in. It will not be considered.[9]

Other matters seized Harold's attention. He explained to Balfour why the Italians should not be awarded Fiume, a judgement that was upheld by Wilson and Lloyd George. Considered also a Czech expert, and impressed with Beneš, the Czech Foreign Minister – 'altogether an intelligent, young, plausible, little man with broad views', who based his case not so much on securing national rights as on sustaining the stability of central Europe – Harold agreed: '*Parfaitement, Excellence,*' and confidently told the Supreme Council that 'Bohemia and Moravia, historical frontier justified, in spite of the fact that many Germans would be included. Teschen, Silesia, Oderburg justified . . . Hungarian Ruthenes justified and desirable.' Having indulged Beneš, he waited for Venizelos to appear. 'Such a darling,' Harold enthused. 'His charm lights up the room.' But Venizelos's charm did not blind Harold to the exaggerated nature of some of his demands. Although on the whole supportive of Greek claims, Harold was also mindful of the fact that Venizelos's 'line in Asia Minor [was] excessive'. When the Greeks were granted the 'Smyrna–Aivali zone and a mandate over most of the Vilayet of Aidin', Harold protested to his diary: 'It is immoral and impracticable. But I obey my orders. The Greeks are getting *too* much.' He wrote to Vita: 'There is a thunderstorm brewing here against Lloyd George. It is all about this Asia Minor business. I feel it difficult for me to guide my tiny row-boat in and out of these crashing Dreadnoughts.'[10] In this instance, Harold was certainly right. Still, Venizelos gained 'a personal triumph' when, on 6 May, he was given the green light to land a division at Smyrna, a move that set off a prolonged international crisis. But neither would the Czech settlement, as promoted by Harold, stand the test of time.

As the conference moved forward, Harold became increasingly depressed. Naturally, Vita's intemperate behaviour preyed heavily upon his mind. But so did the self-centred, ill-informed, arrogant behaviour of the world's leaders who had gathered in Paris. Ion Bratianu, the Romanian Prime Minister, was 'a bearded woman, a forceful humbug, a Bucharest intellectual, a most unpleasing man' who aspired to the 'status of a Great Power'; the Baron Sidney Sonnino, the Italian Foreign Minister, emerged as 'the evil genius of the piece', obstructing everything, whose 'obstinacy and malevolence' were 'quite unrealisable', while Signor Vittorio Orlando, the Italian Prime Minister, was never 'able to rise to the level of his own intelligence'. When the Italians decided to leave Paris in protest at their allies' refusal to meet them half-way, Harold waved them off with a hearty 'good riddance' (they returned two weeks later). Even the ever-fascinating Venizelos continually overplayed his hand, much to Harold's distress.[11]

Reluctantly, he concluded that the conference generally was 'proceeding in a rather irresponsible and intermittent way'. And for this sorry state of affairs the Big Three were held accountable, notably Wilson. Hampered by 'his spiritual arrogance' and the 'hard but narrow texture of his mind', he appeared 'conceited, obstinate, nonconformist . . . obsessed', in fact no better than 'a presbyterian dominie [schoolmaster, pedagogue]'. Nor was Harold alone in thinking so. These characteristics were soon picked up by the Parisian press. Bitter at these public assaults on his character, Wilson, prickly to a fault, contemplated moving the conference to Geneva where he hoped to benefit from the tolerance of the more sober-minded Swiss.[12] (Nothing came of his plan, though Harold, for different reasons, favoured it.) Nor did Lloyd George escape Harold's sharp tongue. Lloyd George – dressed in a 'bedint grey suit' – 'hasn't the faintest idea of what he is talking about,' complained Harold. He tried to ginger up Balfour to protest at Lloyd George's 'madcap schemes', but Balfour proved 'infinitely tiresome' and fobbed him off with a typical aside: 'Yes, that's all very well, but what you say is pure aethestics!' Before long, Harold came to appreciate Lloyd George's uphill struggle at the conference against those who were more extreme. 'Quick as a kingfisher,' Harold thought, as he saw Lloyd George fending off excessive Italian or French demands, not always with complete success. He fights 'like a Welsh terrier', Harold reported to his father, as Lloyd George strove to modify the 'punitive' terms of the German treaty.[13]

Wilson, Harold believed, was also responsible for what he, and others, thought a totally impractical timetable. Instead of giving first priority to the main purpose of the conference – settling the peace treaty with Germany – Wilson kept his colleagues busy playing word games when drafting the Covenant of the League of Nations, his pet pastime, and by fiddling with the maps of central and eastern Europe and Asia Minor. In this way, the German treaty was effectively put on hold until the end of March, nine weeks after the conference had opened. Invited to attend meetings of the Big Three in his capacity as an expert, Harold witnessed their capricious handling of affairs. 'Darling, it is appalling, those three ignorant and irresponsible men cutting Asia Minor to bits as if they were dividing a cake, and with no one there except Hadji . . . Isn't it terrible – the happiness of millions being decided in that way.' When Harold politely protested, he was condescendingly put down: '*Mais, voyez-vous, jeune homme . . . Il faut aboutir.*' There were opportunities to advise and influence. 'The door opens and Hankey tells me to come in. A heavily furnished study with my huge map on the carpet. Bending over it (bubble, bubble, toil and trouble) are Clemenceau, Ll.G. and P.W.' Lloyd George explains their plan. Harold makes some 'minor suggestions'. 'P.W says, "And what about the [Dodecanese] Islands?" "They are," I answer firmly, "Greek Islands, Mr. President." "Then they should go to Greece?" H.N. "Rath*er*!" P.W. "Rat*HAR*!"'[14]

Already dispirited at the way the conference was, or to be more accurate, was not, proceeding, Harold's gloomy state of mind was compounded by news of the death of his friend, Mark Sykes, aged only thirty-nine, a victim of the influenza epidemic then devastating Europe. 'I shall miss him . . . boisterous, witty, untidy, fat, kindly, excitable . . . I feel glum and saddened.'[15] A month after Sykes's death in mid-February, matters had only deteriorated; and so had Harold's mood. He wrote to his father:

> The Council of Ten are atrophied by the mass of material which pours in upon them . . . We are losing the peace rapidly and all the hard work is being wasted. The Ten haven't really finished off anything, except the League of Nations, and what does that mean to starving people at Kishineff, Hermannstadt and Prague? It is despairing.

'What we want is a dictator for Europe and we haven't got one. And never will have!' he added.[16]

Life in Paris wasn't all work. There was his 'funny friend' with the 'charming flat at the Rond Point', Edward Molyneux. Or equally, his 'nice friend', Jean de Gaigneron, who 'knows all the clevers'. Through Jean he renewed his acquaintence with Jean Cocteau and met André Gide. At a 'swell dinner' at the Ritz he saw a 'white, unshaven, grubby, slip-faced' person clad in a fur coat and white kid gloves, the much-lauded Marcel Proust, no less. He interrogated Harold in a style true to the author of *À la Recherche du temps perdu*: '*Mais non, mais non, vous allez trop vite. Recommencez. Vous prenez la voiture de la Délégation. Vous descendez au Quai d'Orsay. Vous montez l'escalier. Vous entrez dans la Salle. Et alors? Précisez, mon cher, précisez.*' 'Why this? Why that?' he persisted. Amused, Harold told him 'everything'. At another dinner at the Ritz he discussed 'inversion' with Proust who, apart from his normal shabby appearance, looked 'very Hebrew'. 'He says it is a matter of habit. I say, "surely not." He says, "No – that was silly of me – what I meant was that it's a matter of delicacy." He is not very intelligent on the subject.'[17]

There was another festive interlude when all the Balliol men – reportedly forming 60 per cent of the British delegation – met for a celebratory dinner at the Majestic. 'We feel proud,' Harold modestly noted. He was also immensely cheered when he heard Lionel Curtis make 'a really admirable speech' to promote the formation of an 'Anglo-American Institute of Foreign Affairs' to enlighten public opinion by research and discussion. Crowe opposed the idea: Cecil spoke up strongly in favour. Harold hoped the scheme would 'materialize and prosper'. It did; but not quite in the manner Curtis or Harold anticipated, for while the American aspect languished, the British side prospered. In July 1920, at a glittering affair held at Lord and Lady Astor's mansion in St James's Square, the British (later Royal) Institute of International Affairs (more commonly known as 'Chatham House') was launched. Chatham House would be the scene for many of Harold's more informative lectures on foreign affairs.[18]

On April Fool's Day, Harold, in the company of Leeper, left Paris on a special mission headed by General Jan Smuts, the South African member of the War Cabinet. They were bound for Budapest where, on 21 March, a communist revolution led by Bela Kun had taken place; their assignment was to investigate its ramifications. For the world's leaders gathered in Paris, the spectre of Bolshevism was truly haunting Europe: it threatened widespread starvation, social chaos, economic ruin, anarchy, a violent, shocking end to the old order. Harold wrote to Vita: 'They [the Germans] have always got the trump card, *i.e.* Bolshevism – and they will go Bolshevist the moment they feel it is hopeless to get good terms.'[19] (This was one of the main themes of Lloyd George's cogently argued but largely ignored Fontainebleau memorandum.) Small wonder that Bela Kun's strike for communism triggered many anxious moments for the Supreme Council.

Smuts's specially prepared train stopped over in Vienna to warn Bela Kun of their imminent arrival and to ensure their safe passage. Harold was sent to the Hungarian Bolshevik headquarters to make the initial contact. He found it crowded with 'men, women and children scrambling for passports. Nearly all are Jews, struggling to get to Buda Pesth and the hope of loot.' After much telephoning, the commissar in charge, a Chicago-educated Galician Jew, secured the necessary assurances; and as Bela Kun spoke only Magyar, he was brought along to translate. The next morning Harold woke up to find their train resting in a siding at the Ostbahnhof, Budapest, encircled by Red Guards with 'fixed bayonets and scarlet brassards'. Smuts insisted on conducting the negotiations from the wagon-lit, as to have done otherwise would have implied recognition of the new regime. 'The Jew Bolshevik' Bela Kun was called for. Harold met him and saw 'A little man of about 30: puffy white face and loose wet lips: shaven head: impression of red hair: shifty suspicious eyes: he has the face of a sulky uncertain criminal.' Harold regarded the Hungarian Foreign Minister accompanying Bela Kun with equally hostile eyes: 'a little oily Jew – fur-coat rather moth-eaten – stringy green tie – dirty collar'. It rained continuously. There was also an energy crisis, with supplies of gas and electricity at a premium. As they spoke, 'rain still patters on the roof and glistens in the light of our candles, golden drops upon the pane'. The negotiations centred on whether or not the Bolsheviks would accept the Allies' armistice proposals, lines that would commit them to considerable territorial losses, particularly to the Romanians. They hesitated all day. In the interval Harold decided to explore Budapest, a city he had last visited in 1912. 'The whole place is wretched – sad – unkempt.' He took tea at the Hungaria, Budapest's leading hotel. Although it had been 'communised', it flew 'a huge Union Jack and Tricolour', a gesture of good intent. Red Guards with bayonets patrolled the hall, but in the foyer what remained of Budapest society 'huddled sadly together with anxious eyes and in complete, ghastly silence', sipping their lemonade 'while the band played'. 'I shudder and feel cold,' Harold remarked. 'We leave as soon as possible. Silent eyes search out at us as we go.'

Later that evening Bela Kun returned to the train's dining-car, accompanied by his senior ministers, and handed Smuts his answer. Smuts read it twice, and then handed it to Harold who studied it and shook his head. Smuts responded: 'No gentlemen, this is a a Note which I cannot accept. There must be no reservations.' Although prepared to offer minor concessions, Smuts's terms of reference were uncompromising. Bela Kun had first to agree to the occupation by allied forces of a neutral zone separating the Bolshevik forces from the Romanian army; if he complied, the Allies would be prepared to raise their blockade strangling his regime. Bela Kun desperately needed allied recognition of his government, but he inserted a clause to Smuts's draft agreement that the Romanian forces should withdraw to a line east of the neutral zone, in effect to evacuate Transylvania. Smuts would not countenance such a deal. He made a final appeal to reason. But the Bolsheviks, 'silent and sullen', proved obdurate. 'They looked like convicts standing [before] the Director of the Prison.' His patience exhausted, Smuts, always behaving with 'exquisite courtesy', brought these pointless exchanges to an end, having already concluded that 'Bela Kun is just an incident and not worth taking seriously'.* 'Well, gentlemen,' he said, 'I must bid you goodbye.' Bela Kun and his aides failed to understand Smuts's meaning. And so, with 'whistles already blowing . . . our special glided out into the night', leaving Bela Kun and company 'bewildered'. Stranded on the platform, they looked up at the departing train 'in blank astonishment'. Three days later Harold relaxed in the comfort of his room at the Majestic, took a 'much-needed bath' and partook of Parisian restaurants, a welcome relief from the wartime austerity rations of 'bully beef and beans' that Smuts had imposed upon the mission.[20]

The Bela Kun interlude was Harold's first intimate acquaintance with Smuts. He was smitten by the South African's exemplary character, so 'simple and intricate'. 'What a man!' he pointed out. 'A spendid, wide-horizoned man – for whom I have the deepest admiration.'[21] There were cracks, however, in this glowing assessment. Widely esteemed by the general public, respected by most politicians, Smuts could always be relied upon to drop the right words in the right ears at the right time. But he was not above pursuing narrow, partisan interests when it suited his purpose, as Harold would soon find out.

During Harold's absence from Paris the prospects for a settlement based on Wilson's new world order had receded. The French, having suffered two German invasions within living memory, now put forward extreme ideas that would extend French sovereignty or influence into the Rhineland. Lloyd George and Wilson hotly opposed these demands, seeing in them the seeds of another war. Eventually, a compromise was worked out that called for an allied occupation of the Rhineland with staged withdrawals, backed by an Anglo-American guarantee of French frontiers. But Harold, and many

---

*The impression that Bela Kun was just 'an incident' proved to be only too true. On 10 April, a day after Harold's account to Vita, a provisional government was set up in Budapest that reflected the old ruling Hungarian cliques: Count Julius Karolyi, Count Stephen Bethlen, and Admiral Horthy de Nagybanya, Nicholas. On 1 August, Bela Kun fled the capital in the face of invading Romanian armies. Some months later, in February 1920, after the Romanians had retreated, taking everything moveable with them, Horthy was appointed Regent and head of state. Bela Kun ended his days in Russia. He died in 1936: the exact circumstances of his death remain unclear, but he is believed to have been a victim of one of Stalin's innumerable purges.

others, harboured a 'ghastly suspicion' that the United States would not honour the signature of its delegates: 'it became the ghost at all our feasts'. From mid-May to mid-June the German treaty hung on a razor's edge. Word reached Paris that the German government was prepared to sign it but that public opinion would not allow it without allied concessions. Harold was at one with the German public. 'The more I read [the treaty], the sicker it makes me . . . If I were the Germans I shouldn't sign for a moment . . . The great crime is the reparations clauses, which were drawn up solely to please the House of Commons.'[22] Harold was referring to article 231, the notorious 'war guilt' clause, that compelled Germany and her allies to accept full responsibility for 'causing all the loss and damage to which the Allied and Associated Governments and their nationals have been subjected as a consequence of the war imposed upon them by the aggression of Germany and her allies'. At Paris, there was no agreement on the total sum of reparations to be paid by Germany. But there was much talk about what items should be included in the reparations bill. Smuts – Harold's 'spendid, wide-horizoned man' – now showed that his character, though 'simple', was also exceptionally 'intricate'. Concerned that the bulk of the reparations would go to France, he concocted a creative formula to include separation allowances for soldiers' families, as well as pensions for widows and orphans. His prescription effectively doubled the potential bill and would not have been to Harold's liking. (It was eventually fixed in April 1921 by a special allied commission at £6,600 million plus interest.) For promoting this atmosphere of winner take all, Harold indicted 'the iniquity of Northcliffe jingoism'.[23]

Could anyone salvage something from this mess? Surprisingly, Harold hit upon the figure of Lloyd George. Surprising, because hitherto Harold had been sharply critical of Lloyd George's policies, particularly in Asia Minor (that were finally to lead to his political downfall): the image of three witches – 'bubble, bubble, toil and trouble' – brewing an unholy blend sticks. As the Prime Minister strove to scale down the reparations bill – 'immoral and senseless' – revise the territorial settlement in Silesia to Germany's advantage, and grant Germany membership of the League of Nations, Harold's admiration grew, particularly as he fought alone. The French, naturally, were furious at him for what they considered to be a betrayal of their interests. But it was Wilson's passivity that infuriated Harold. 'Cannot understand [him],' Harold recorded. 'Here is a chance of improving the thing and he won't take it.' The draft treaty stood. Harold, voicing the general view of the up-and-coming generation of British diplomatists, wrote to his father: 'There is not a single person among the younger people here who is not unhappy and disappointed at the terms. The only people who approve are the old fire-eaters.'[14]

After much hesitation, and under the threat of renewed force, the German government accepted the treaty. 'What a relief,' sighed Harold, conscious that another round of warfare was a far worse alternative. The treaty was signed on 28 June 1919 in the Galerie des Glaces at the palace of Versailles. Harold witnessed the occasion and recorded it in careful detail. 'It will amuse Ben and Nigel [aged five and two respectively],' he considerately remarked.[25]

Dressed in tails and a black slouch hat, and excited by the historic occasion he was about to witness, Harold drove up the avenue leading to the château, which was lined with 'cavalry in steel-blue helmets', the 'pennants of their lances fluttering red and white in the sun'. *Gardes républicains* were stationed everywhere, flashing their sabres, saluting the guests. The salons leading into the Galerie were magnificently furnished with Aubusson tapestries and carpets and 'the gems of the Louvre'. The Galerie itself was crowded, with seats for over a thousand. Clemenceau, 'small and yellow. A crunched homunculus,' orchestrated the proceedings. '*Faites entrer les Allemands,*' he called out. And Dr Hermann Müller and Dr Johannes Bell, heads held high, eyes studying the ceiling, one looking like 'the second fiddle' in a string ensemble, the other resembling 'a privat-dozent', were led to the table to sign the treaty. No one spoke or moved. Having committed Germany to the treaty of Versailles, they were escorted from the hall 'like prisoners from the dock'. Over the 'breathless silence', Clemenceau rasped: '*Messieurs, la séance est levée.*' Outside, salvoes were fired, while a squadron of aeroplanes flew overhead. Fountains played in the gardens, the crowds cheering and yelling '*Vive Clemenceau*', adding, as Harold drove away, '*Vive l'Angleterre.*' After the ceremony Clemenceau with tears in his eyes, was overheard to say: '*Oui, c'est une belle journée.*' But not for Harold. '*Vae victis*' – woe to the defeated – he would reply. Exhausted at the end of this extraordinary day, Harold lamented that 'It has all been horrible . . . To bed, sick of life.'

Harold's views on the 'mistakes' and 'misfortunes' of the treaties scarcely changed over the years.[26] He would argue that Britain's freedom of action had been severely restricted by its wartime treaties with Italy, with France, with Romania, and with the Arabs, in the short run beneficial, in the long run positively harmful. He would further argue that democratic diplomacy, being captive to narrow, partisan domestic pressures, was 'irresponsible', and that the fundamental error of Versailles was the 'spirit not the letter' of the treaty. He blamed the peacemakers. They had not combined to elaborate a 'formal procedure', nor had they settled upon an 'established programme', the upshot being that their deliberations were 'uncertain, intermittent and confused'. As a consequence, they vacillated between the Americans, who contended that under the auspices of the League of Nations all international disputes would be settled by 'sweet reasonableness', and the French, who, obsessed with their own security, suffered from no such illusion. Harold took his reasoning a step further (into uncharted waters, it must be said). In a flight of optimism, he claimed that if only the British had wholeheartedly supported either the American or the French perception of peace, a golden age of worldwide tranquillity and harmony might have been inaugurated for a century.

Inevitably, with the passing of time there were some inconsistencies. Writing in 1939, after war had broken out, Harold made a curious confession. At Paris, the French had asked for the Rhine frontier, a demand he had then rejected as a manifestation of French intransigence: 'I now think they were right. I did not think so at the time.' On the same pages, when considering the reasons for Hitler's rise to power, he marginalised the effect of the Versailles treaty: 'It would be more accurate to say that [Hitler] owed his success to Raymond Poincaré,' the hardline French President who would happily have settled for a French advance up to the Rhine, and who later, in 1923, occupied for a few tense months the Ruhr basin. Harold laboured under the mistaken impression that by 1922 Germany had reconciled itself to the terms of the Versailles treaty.[27]

Nevertheless, on the main issues Harold showed a remarkable consistency in his views. War-torn Paris, its streets crying out for revenge, was clearly the wrong venue for a peace conference. Geneva would have been a more judicious choice. Given these circumstances, with passions running high and distorting public opinion, he would have preferred to see a preliminary treaty followed by a final one, after a suitable cooling-off period. With the Congress of Vienna in mind, he argued that it was a grave mistake to have treated Germany as a pariah state: the stability of Europe would have been better served had she been invited to participate in the conference, particularly as Bolshevism threatened to despoil a crushed and humiliated Germany. He damned the reparations claims as 'manifestly absurd' and was appalled (as was his father) by the infamous 'war guilt clause'. As a result, 'The peace which emerged was unjust enough to cause resentment, but not forcible enough to render such resentment impotent.'[28]

Personalities also intruded. Harold had come into close contact with the world's leaders. He had seen them at work, 'ignorant and irresponsible men' cutting up the world as though it were a cake. These manipulative politicians, all plying their own nationalistic agendas, had left him with a poor impression of their qualifications to negotiate intricate agreements; such work, he always contended, was best left to the professionals. Viewing the politicians with extreme disdain, he accused them of employing 'jesuitical phraseology' to justify the unjustifiable. For the Bulgarians he harboured nothing but 'feelings of contempt'. Bratianu, the Romanian, was distinguished only by his 'follies . . . vanities and . . . obstinate blindness'. As for the Turks, they were simply 'a race of Anatolian marauders'. He despised the Italians, who always behaved like 'sulky children' with their 'incessant ill-temper, untruthfulness, and cheating'. Although sympathetic to France's security problems, he was repelled by Poincaré's style, which he saw as far too dogmatic and militant – though he had a sneaking admiration for Clemenceau. For the Germans he admitted to a feeling compounded of 'fear, admiration, sympathy and distrust'. But Harold knew where to place the blame for the failure, as he saw it, of the Paris conference. His most telling criticism was levelled at Woodrow Wilson, who had betrayed his own much-lauded Fourteen Points, and hence betrayed those – like Harold – who had believed implicitly in them. Wilson, guided by his 'sacro egoiso' and 'fanatical mysticism', and trapped by the 'rigidity and spiritual arrogance' of his 'one track mind', should have remained locked up in the White House.[29] 'We came to Paris confident that the new order was about to be established; we left it convinced that the new order had merely fouled the old. We arrived as fervent apprentices in the school of Woodrow Wilson: we left as renegades.'[30] If Harold had to choose a hero at Paris, he would surely have chosen Lloyd George, fighting valiantly for a moderate peace, with Venizelos and Smuts running a close second and third.

Two weeks after witnessing the humiliating scenes in the Galerie des Glaces, he watched the allied victory procession make its way through the Arc de Triomphe. Perched high on the roof of the Hôtel Astoria, he was overcome by a wave of patriotic fervour as he applauded the British Grenadiers and behind them 'hundreds and hundreds of British regimental flags – stiff, imperial, heavy with gold lettering, "Busaco", "Inkerman", "Waterloo" – while the crowd roared with enthusiasm'. Cries of 'Good Old Blighty' were heard. Harold wept at the spectacle of 'the most glorious, the most democratic and the most final' of Britain's victories.[31] For Harold, these months in Paris, despite his private agony and professional frustration, ended on an emotional high.

On 8 May, while drawing up the new frontiers of Austria, Harold was suddenly asked by Sir Eric Drummond, a senior Foreign Office mandarin and designate Secretary-General of the League of Nations, whether he would like to join his staff. 'I should love to,' Harold replied without hesitation, 'I am delighted beyond words.' An idea of sending him to Athens was precipitately dropped. Harold was supremely confident that the League was 'a body which is certain to become of vital importance': at long last he had found 'a job, a cause, a chief' worth serving. He would also receive an increase in salary, £1,200 tax free plus a subsistence allowance, a factor of some importance as he was forever complaining that he was living on an overdraft. His enthusiasm knew no bounds. He thought of the League as 'a great experiment', to be protected at all costs. At times it would necessitate him becoming 'anti-English . . . and when necessary pro-Italian', a tough admission for Harold to make as he so admired 'the sturdy, unenlightened, un-intellectual muzzy British way of looking at things', and so despised the Italian wheeling and dealing at the conference. He preached the virtues of the League to Vita – even though it has been established that Vita had no idea what the League of Nations was. Would Mar please think about the League? he begged, and 'tonic Hadji when he becomes too national and anti-dago'. 'Think only of the League point of view,' he pleaded, 'where Right is the ultimate sanction, and where compromise is a crime.' Longing to get away from Paris, 'where improvisations flit above the mists of ignorance like dragon-flies above a marsh', he went off to Geneva to look for a house, suspecting all the while that 'the Geneva temperament will be rather Hampstead Garden Suburb'.[32]

Harold's chief, Hardinge, asked him why he was so determined to work for the League. Harold murmured, 'interest', 'hope', 'the new future'. Hardinge argued, hoping to tempt Harold away from the time-wasting talking-shop of Geneva by offering him a more senior post at the Foreign Office. Harold stood his ground, a posture that could not have endeared him to his chief. Nothing came of Harold's doggedness, or of his high hopes. Seconded for service under the League only from October 1919 until May 1920, he commuted between Paris and London, mainly concerned with organising the League's international secretariat. He then returned to routine duties at the Foreign Office.

Until the end of 1919 Harold was based mainly in Paris, not only working for the League but also putting the final touches to the treaties with Austria, Hungary, Romania, Bulgaria and Turkey. Crowe was now in charge of the British delegation, Lloyd George and Balfour having left Paris to immerse themselves in Westminster politics. Harold benefited from this arrangement. Much committee work was delegated to him, in particular on those bodies dealing with the Czech and Greek questions. He scored a minor success regarding the vexed question of Teschen, a border area, rich in coal resources and the centre of a major railway network, that lay between Poland and Czechoslovakia. 'How many members ever heard of Teschen?' Lloyd George asked the House of Commons, disarmingly admitting that until recently he had not. Ethnically Polish (by a ratio of two to one), Teschen was considered essential to Czechoslovakia's economic well-being. In early 1919 fighting had broken out between the rival parties, a ceasefire being imposed by the Allies with some difficulty. Teschen presented the peacemakers with an intriguing problem: whether to honour the sacrosanct principle of national self-determination; or whether to secure the prosperity of a model, demo-cratic state emerging in central Europe. Sound out Dr Edvard Beneš, Crowe instructed Harold. Shrewdly, Beneš told him that the fate of Teschen depended upon 'the attitude adopted by the British Delegation'. In his report to Crowe, Harold balked at taking a definite stand. Instead, clearly and lucidly, he set out the options: either appeasing Polish nationalism, or more precisely, chauvinism; or allowing Czechoslovakia an economic breathing space. 'It is for you and Mr. Balfour to instruct as to which of these two solutions [we ?] should support.'

To Vita he was more outspoken, if not entirely accurate. He boasted of his 'deeply Machiavellian' triumph, having suggested to Beneš that Poland should keep the coal mines but allow the Czechs free access to them. Nothing of this appears in the official reports, but with a touch of imagination it can be seen as the basis for a workable compromise for the Teschen imbroglio. By the final settlement, reached only after strong French pressure, the region was effectively partitioned: the Czechs acquired the coal mines, and hence, most of the industrial basin, approximately 1,300 square kilometres; the city of Teschen was divided, the old quarters awarded to Poland, the remainder to Czechoslovakia, including the invaluable railway station; while the essential energy sources, gas and electricity, were divided between them. Imposed by the Allies, it was a kind of Solomon's choice, a trade-off that infuriated both parties, and that broke down in 1938.[33]

Then there were the preposterous Italians, once again parading their insa-tiable territorial ambitions. Having acquired Trieste under the treaty of London, Italy now wished to consolidate its control over the northern Adriatic – and if possible the entire Dalmatian coast down to, and including, Albania. Istria and the port of Fiume, 'the jewel of the Adriatic', which became a symbol of Italian nationalism, were placed at the centre of Italian demands. In August 1919 Harold attended an allied meeting in Paris convened to sort out these problems. Italy put forward a series of transparent formulas designed to mask its true aims. Fiume and its hinterland, M. Scialoga, the Italian delegate, suggested, should be recognised as a 'free state', but the island of Cherso, which dominated and effectively blocked the Gulf of Fiume, should be annexed to Italy, as should the high ground surrounding the port. The railway system, extending from Fiume inland, should also be under Italian control. Abandoning all claims to Dalmatia, Scialoga insisted that the Dalmatian coast be neutralised, and called for Italian sovereignty over certain key areas, the zone of Zara, for example. Lastly, Scialoga put in a claim for a mandate over Albania. In this under-the-counter manner Italy hoped to achieve mastery of the Adriatic. These stratagems fell on deaf ears, except for those of the French who were prepared for a deal 'on any terms'. The American delegate, Major Johnson,

however, would have none of it. Harold backed the Americans in firmly repu-
diating Italian claims to Fiume and Istria. This was the key issue: who would
control the northern Adriatic? Elsewhere, Harold was more accommodating:
Cherso, on ethnic grounds; perhaps the Zara enclave; even possibly an Italian
mandate for Albania. Crowe agreed immediately. Balfour, on the other hand,
and typically, thought that 'we must have an oral discussion' first. Eventually,
it was agreed to set up Fiume as 'a free city' – an arrangement ultimately
accepted by Yugoslavia and Italy .

A month after these talks, in September 1919, Gabriele d'Annunzio, at
the head of a legion of ultra-nationalist volunteers, seized Fiume, defying
the Allies and throwing their talks into disarray. D'Annunzio was the renowed
author of 'highly coloured *fin-de-siècle* verse and prose', endowed with a
genius for self-advertisement. Harold rather admired him as a poet but
considered him a political dimwit, now barnstorming out of 'of sheer swank'.
D'Annunzio's posturing proved him right. At the end of 1920, d'Annunzio
declared war on Italy, an act of sheer lunacy. Left with no option, an embarrassed Italian government expelled him and his cohorts by force in January
1921. D'Annunzio, in the name of a resurgent Italy, had held the contested
region for fifteen months. The endgame worked very much to Italy's advantage. In March 1922 a Fascist coup overthrew the Fiume government and
Italian troops occupied the town, a less theatrical but more durable riposte
to d'Annunzio's stunt. And exactly three years after d'Annunzio's undoing,
Mussolini completed the takeover, negotiating a treaty with Yugoslavia that
gave him Fiume. Italy had attained command of the northern Adriatic.[34]

The Greek question fared even worse. It began on a high note, with virtual
agreement between the British and American delegations on how to resolve
the Greek puzzle. It turned on meeting most of Venizelos's territorial goals,
which included Smyrna and its hinterland (roughly corresponding with the
Ottoman *vilayet* of Aydin), some form of international regime over
Constantinople, and the whole of western and eastern Thrace up to the
vicinity of the Turkish capital, claims that, if realised, would in effect have
given the Greeks control over the Straits. Matters were considerably complicated by Venizelos's beguiling personality.

> Veniselos Veniselos!
> Do not fail us! Thou'lt not fail us!
> Righteousness is on thy face;
> Strength thou hast to rule our race;
> Great in war and great in peace,
> Thou, our second Perikles

So wrote, without a trace of irony, a leading Anglo-philhellene.* Not many could withstand Venizelos's charm. Harold too fell before it. But he soon recognised, as did the Americans, that Venizelos's extravagant empire-building heralded disaster. Together with the American diplomat and lawyer, Frank Polk, Harold was instructed to inform Venizelos that there would have to be a compromise regarding the future of Thrace. 'It was very painful. I simply loathed it,' he told Vita. 'It was *bloody*.' Not surprisingly, he offered to a tearful Venizelos far more than the Americans were prepared to give: the southern portion of eastern Thrace and almost all of western Thrace. 'A *bloody* solution' for Greece, he called it, but one that he managed to persuade Balfour and André Tardieu – a prominent member of the French delegation and an intimate associate of Clemenceau – to agree to.[35] Even his '*bloody* solution' did not stand the test of time. The Smyrna landings – besmirched by Greek atrocities against the local Turkish population – sparked off a Turkish nationalist revival under Mustafa Kemal's (Atatürk's) leadership that, eventually, expelled the Greeks from Turkish Anatolia, thereby dismantling almost all of Harold's generous compromise to Venizelos.

Other affairs held his interest – the Austrian and Bulgarian treaties, or delineating Albania's frontiers in the face of Yugoslavia's demands. He clashed with Lloyd George over Italian policy, Harold arguing for a tougher line in view of Italy's recent mischievous behaviour. Lloyd George reacted angrily: 'The Foreign Office always blocks me in whatever I wish to do.' But the most pressing issue that engaged Harold was to how meet the British commitment to Greece, an undertaking that was slowly but relentlessly unravelling. On 10 August 1920, a year after Harold had confronted a tearful Venizelos, the treaty of Sèvres was signed. It gave Venizelos almost all he wanted: the Smyrna region was to be administered by Greece for another five years, after which there would be a plebiscite; and while the Dodecanese islands and Rhodes went to Italy, virtually all of Thrace and the remaining Turkish islands in the Aegean were assigned to Greece. Venizelos's supporters celebrated the creation by their idol of a Greece of 'the two Continents and of the five seas'.[36]

His triumph proved to be short-lived. Two months after Sèvres, by one of those accidents of history, King Alexander, amenable to Venizelos, was bitten in the leg by his pet monkey while walking in the gardens of Tatoi: blood poisoning set in and he died soon after. He was replaced by his father Constantine, who had quarrelled violently with Venizelos and who, in 1917,

---

*The writer of this verse, 'Song of the Hellenes to Veniselos the Cretan', was Professor Ronald Burrows, Principal of King's College, London (1913–20), a distinguished scholar of modern Greece. Quoted by Richard Clogg, *Arnold Toynbee and the Koraes Chair. Politics and the Academy* (Frank Cass, London, 1986), 1.

owing to his pro-German policies, had been forced off the throne and out of the country (without formally abdicating) by the entente powers. The political climate in Greece changed dramatically. New elections were held: Venizelos fell from power. But nothing, apparently, could dim Harold's admiration for Venizelos. 'He *is* my hero,' Harold told Vita, 'dear old man in his skull cap and his charming Christ-like smile . . . I'd chuck everything for what V. represents. You see, he is the *winged reason*.'[37] His seniors were more sceptical. Fully aware of Harold's attachment to Venizelos, the Foreign Office asked him to assess this potentially damaging shift in Greek affairs.

The most that Harold could say was that British policy had to choose between various alternatives. But what alternatives? To support Constantine, for the Allies – and Harold – a 'corrupt and inefficient' ruler, a 'tool of the Hohenzollerns', the perpetrator of 'brutal murders and gross betrayal'? Or to withdraw all support from Constantine? And then what? Perhaps to compromise by allowing the Crown Prince, George, to return as King. Or perhaps to intervene and ensure that Venizelos was restored to power. And what of Sèvres? Should the Allies stick by it? Or should they acknowledge that circumstances had changed and seek to revise it? And if so, would not the Bulgarian and German treaties be subject to the same treatment? There was a Micawber-like quality to these computations. But would something useful turn up? Matters were further complicated by the manipulative policies of Britain's allies, France and Italy, both out to exploit the situation to their own advantage, thereby damaging British interests, a fact confirmed for Harold when considering the outcome of a series of inter-allied discussions held in Paris and London in the winter months of 1921.[38]

Harold's own position seemed clear enough. Speaking to Philip Kerr, Lloyd George's influential private secretary, he harped on the need to either 'buy France off with concessions, or break with her'. A day later, on 7 January 1921, he planned 'to force the PM and Lord Curzon [who had replaced Balfour as Foreign Secretary in October 1919] into realizing that we cannot maintain the Treaty of Sèvres without an effort and that this effort will be costly. If it is considered *too* costly then we should say so at once and not [deceive ?] the Greeks with false hopes.' Senior officials, Crowe and Tyrrell, took the view that 'we have been beaten by [Mustafa] Kemal', implying that a revision of Sèvres was inevitable. Curzon joined in the chorus: '[he] makes a long speech to me about the Near East. He thinks we shall have to modify Sèvres.' But was Harold entirely convinced, despite his diary jottings? His official papers register a more muted tone, mainly one suspects because of his attachment to Venizelos whom he considered 'morally and physically a more permanent phenomenon than King Constantine. That he will return one day is not to be questioned.' But 'to what will he return?'

Harold couldn't resist asking. He then went on, in a position paper of 18 January, to argue cogently against revision:

Greece constitutes a very positive asset in British imperial policy and so long as we have an Empire, our policy is bound to be imperial. We now propose to surrender this asset in deference to France . . . The revision of the Treaty of Sèvres will face us with a discontented and possibly an actively recalcitrant Greece. I feel that it is imprudent to hope that we shall be compensated for this by having a contented and pacific Turkey. A compromise on the question will not either please Greece, placate Turkey or be loyally subscribed to by the French.

Crowe was won over, at least temporarily; or perhaps Harold put an extra gloss on his chief's praise. 'For him, he is complimentary & I would rather have a look of interest from him than endless [tributes ?] from others.' Harold's spirits rose when he met Venizelos in an overheated room at the Hôtel Majestic in Paris. Propped up in bed, 'the old man . . . who seemed in excellent health gave me the impression of regarding the present crisis as little more than an irritating interruption in his work for Greece. He was not in the least resentful or dispirited . . .' Venizelos's uncalled for optimism gelled with Harold's own instincts.[39]

From Harold's standpoint the Greek–Turkish situation deteriorated throughout 1921–22. King Constantine was reinstated; Mustafa Kemal consolidated his standing, militarily and diplomatically; Anglo-French relations worsened. Even Crowe threw up his hands in despair. 'I hate the Balkans,' he confessed, after yet another attempt to reach an agreed allied policy had collapsed.[40] Nor did Curzon live up to Harold's immediate expectations as a competent foreign minister: 'he has gone quite off his head and changes his mind every day'. He clashed with Viscount Field Marshal Edmund Allenby, High Commissioner for Egypt, going back on his word by suppressing a dispatch by Allenby that proposed concessions for Egypt. When Allenby confronted him with the truth, Curzon began to cry. 'He [Curzon] is a coward and has shown A. that he is a shit . . . now he is picking grievances with us . . . Not a very estimable man.'[41] Was Curzon capable of nursing the Near East crisis through to a satisfactory outcome? Harold could not be certain.

In March 1922 the Greeks declared their willingness to accept a British proposal for a compromise peace based on the evacuation of their forces from Smyrna, to be balanced by a League protectorate over the Greeks of Asia Minor. But Mustafa Kemal, by now brimming with self-confidence, would countenance nothing less than the evacuation of every Greek soldier from Asia Minor and cutting off Greek access to the Black Sea. So desperate was the situation that even Harold gave up on Sèvres, though not on Venizelos.[42] It was clear to Harold that events on the ground had overtaken Sèvres – and any compromise formula, however much he hankered after one. Mustafa Kemal, knowing that the military tide had turned in his favour, launched a massive offensive on 26 August. His armies occupied Smyrna a few days later, slaughtering some 30,000 Greek and Armenian Christians. Harold grieved: 'Poor darlings,' he mourned.[43] Left with no option, Constantine abdicated, a move that brought Venizelos back to a position of influence. But British policy was in ruins. Deserted by France and Italy – both countries had made their peace with Kemal – Britain was virtually isolated. But Lloyd George, harnessing Churchill's and Lord Birkenhead's combativeness, was in a bellicose mood. Even the Dominions – apart from Newfoundland and New Zealand – refused to back him when a small British force, hopelessly outnumbered and ill-equipped, confronted the victorious Turkish troops at Chanak, an obscure outpost in the neutral zone, situated on the Asian coast of the Dardanelles. 'Le coup de Janak,' wrote Harold on 18 September, when he heard of the Cabinet's decision to hold the Straits, with or without the French, a ruling he was authorised to pass on to Venizelos via an intermediary.[44]

Curzon crossed over to Paris to meet Poincaré, hoping to repair Anglo-French relations, anticipating, perhaps, resurrection of a joint allied policy. Instead, Harold heard that 'a terrific row' had broken out. An enraged Poincaré had discovered that Curzon – in accordance with a cabinet decision – had gone behind his back to enquire whether Romania – linked to France through the Little Entente – would be prepared to send troops to Chanak to aid the British contingent. He lashed into Curzon in no uncertain manner: 'precise but cutting phrases' spilling over. A broken Curzon fled the conference chamber, collapsed on to 'a scarlet settee', and wept. 'Charley,' he mumbled to Lord Hardinge, then British ambassador in Paris, 'I can't bear that horrid little man. I can't bear him. I can't bear him.'[45] The situation at Chanak remained tense.

Harold was not a passive bystander to these events. Encouraged by the Foreign Office, he kept in touch with Venizelos, and found him 'calm' but 'rather bitter'. Pending the outcome of the crisis, he was asked to write a memorandum on the perennial question of the future status of the Straits. 'In its essence,' he wrote, 'the problem is Anglo-Russian not Anglo-Turkish. And freedom of the Straights means essentially the right of passage of warships *through* the Straights to the Black Sea.' Curzon thought this an 'able' judgement. Another paper that he helped to prepare argued in favour of constructing a Balkan bloc to balance Turkish influence, concluding that

'it would be more prudent, while doing everything to encourage an agreement on the political aspect between ourselves and the Balkan States, to
approach the military problem as one which, if we cannot secure the co-
operation of France and Italy, we shall be in the end obliged to face [Kemal]
on our own resources'.[46]

Did Lloyd George take note? Perversely, knowing full well that France
and Italy were lost, he refused to back down. Early on in the crisis he had
said: '[I] could take no part or lot in any policy which would have the result
of placing the Christian population of Smyrna and Thrace back under the
Turkish heel. Such a policy undertaken by the Allies would be regarded by
the world and history as infamous and cowardly.'[47] It was, therefore, well in
keeping with Lloyd George's views that instructions were sent to General
Harington, the British commander at Chanak, to deliver an ultimatum to
the Turks ordering them to withdraw. Wisely, Harington – encouraged by
Sir Horace Rumbold, High Commissioner at Constantinople – procrastinated, his common sense winning Harold's approval. 'Our war party is
discredited,' he applauded, praising Curzon for aborting an attempt by the
said 'war party' to censure the wayward General.

Having thwarted the 'the hawks', Curzon made another, more successful,
attempt to appease Poincaré. A rejuvenated, if shaky, Anglo–French front
confronted Kemal at Mudanya. By 11 October a bargain had been agreed
upon: the neutral zone at the Straits would be respected until the conclusion of a final peace, but eastern Thrace and Adrianople would be returned
to Turkey. However these events are juggled, the outcome was a triumph
for Kemal. He had split the Allies, defied them, and prevailed. Lloyd George
paid the heaviest price of all. Towards the end of October his coalition disin-
tegrated: he resigned, never to hold office again. With Sèvres shattered, a
fresh treaty had to be negotiated. On 13 October Harold was informed that
he would accompany Curzon to Lausanne, where Sèvres would be revised.

There were moments of relaxation from the pressures of work. In the New
Year's Honours List of January 1920 Harold was created a Companion of
St Michael and St George (CMG) for services rendered during the Paris
conference; at the same time he was promoted in rank to first secretary.
There were long weekends at Long Barn where Harold would amuse his
two boys, hone his talents as a gardener, and entertain friends. Visitors might
include Augustus John, resembling 'a burly and debouched Christ'; John
Drinkwater, playwright and poet, 'rather overcome with his own good looks';
the writer, Algernon Blackwood, 'shy, attractive with rolling blue eyes'; Clive
Bell, a pillar of Bloomsbury; or Gerry and Dorothy ('Dottie') Wellesley,
particular friends, whose failing marriage would cause the Nicolsons much

anguish. More intimate companions, Victor Cunard and Raymond Mortimer, would arrive, as would favoured colleagues from the Office. In London, Harold enjoyed the social merry-go-round, luncheons, dinner parties, and the pleasures of its exclusive clubland, his favourite clubs now being the Marlborough and Buck's. At the Savoy Hotel he saw Smuts, who castigated President Wilson for his 'egoism and vanity' but spoke highly of Lord Robert Cecil, regretting only that 'he was too much Savonarola and too little John Bull'. Brief holidays were spent sailing on Southampton Water and round the south-west coast on Lord Sackville's yacht, *Sumerun*, or off Yarmouth and Lowestoft.

In October 1921 he took three weeks' leave. Setting out for Rome, he passed through Paris, where he dined at the Tour d'Argent, a symbolic last supper, for two days later his doctor told him he 'mustn't touch wine or meat for five days'. 'A cruel blow,' Harold complained. In Rome he met up with Gerald Berners – noting appreciatively his chauffeur, 'William the Adonis', perched on the box of Berners's Rolls-Royce – Gerry Wellesley, and 'a nice Prince', Prince Philip of Hesse (later to be an emissary of Hitler). Sightseeing was high on the agenda, though Harold was not by inclination an enthusiastic tourist. Gerry Wellesley took the initiative. They toured familiar sights: the Trevi Fountain, Palazzo Barberini, the Forum and the Colosseum, the Pantheon, and Keats's house, located just below the Spanish Steps. They motored out to Frascati and Castel Gondolfo, the war poet Siegfried Sassoon joining them. At Castel Gondolfo they indulged in some high jinks, launching paper boats down a cascade as Siegfried Sassoon flung his cap into the foaming waters. Harold enjoyed Sassoon's company. At dinner, they gossiped about Robbie Ross and Alfred Douglas, two of Oscar Wilde's conquests. Sassoon had dared to dedicate a poem to Ross, provoking an enraged Douglas to abuse Sassoon as 'a degenerate Jew'. 'It was so unfair,' Sassoon protested, 'as he knew me personally and must have seen that I have no very marked semitic characteristics, and am not effeminate in appearance.'

At midnight on 6 October Harold was awakened by a rattle at the door. Vita stood there, 'My darling Viti.' Only weeks earlier, still recovering from the fallout of the Trefusis affair, his emotions had tugged him in a different direction: 'Oh, Viti, Viti,' he sighed, 'what have you to answer for.' Theirs was still very much a stop-start relationship, softened by mutual vows of eternal love, genuinely felt. Accompanied by the Wellesleys, the Nicolsons made their way back to London, stopping off at Trieste, Venice and Vienna. In Munich Harold indulged himself and bought twelve pairs of silk socks, 'straight off . . . just like that'. By 24 October they had reached London.[48]

* * *

During the peace conference, Harold was often to be found in the company of Michael Sadleir. Sadleir was a member of the British Delegation (later, he too was seconded to work at the Secretariat of the League of Nations), a Balliol man, an author, and a publisher at Constable & Co. One day in January 1920, as they descended the staircase of the Hôtel Majestic, he suggested that Harold write a life of the French poet, Paul Verlaine, an idea that Harold had long been contemplating. Vita was enthusiastic. 'You *must* write the Life of Verlaine. You would do it so excellently well.' She urged Harold to seek literary as well as diplomatic distinction.[49] The book appeared in March 1921. Others were to follow in rapid succession: *Sweet Waters* (November 1921), *Tennyson* (March 1923), *Byron: The Last Journey* (February 1924) and *Swinburne* (June 1926).

Anxious to achieve literary prominence, Harold canvassed acquaintances to review his first book, *Paul Verlaine*. He lobbied Sir Edmund Gosse in the lavatory at the Marlborough Club, but the great man refused to commit himself. 'What does this mean?' he nervously asked Sadleir. (Gosse later repented and wrote a favourable review in the *Sunday Times*.) The *Times Literary Supplement* accused Harold of 'vulgarity' and 'inaccuracies' in his portrayal of Verlaine. But on the whole a cheerful Harold thought that the reviews ranged from 'good' to 'excellent'. The book also sold quite well, 500 copies by mid-April. At lunch at Lady Cunard's, he saw *Verlaine* on top of a pile of books that included Lytton Strachey's *Victoria* and Peter Wright's *Supreme War Council*. So, 'it's Strachey the Ace, Peter Wright the Knave, and I the Queen. I think that is very satisfactory.'[50]

But Strachey, who had written *Landmarks in French Literature*, a work that Harold held in high regard, disliked *Verlaine*: he found it too general in its portrayal of its main characters. Edmund Wilson, in a famous but critical survey of Harold's literary *oeuvre*, put it more bluntly, pointing out that Harold had discreetly skated over the more notorious aspects of his subject's life: Verlaine's violent homosexual affair with Arthur Rimbaud, his imprisonment, his descent into 'drink and debauchery', shamelessly enjoying the company of ageing prostitutes. He had no doubt that Harold possessed 'a genuine literary gift', but 'it was childish [of him] to be shocked by Verlaine . . . and to dismiss him with with a sharp tone of reprimand'. In fact, Harold had violated his own first rule of 'pure biography', which was to reveal 'the wider veracity of complete and accurate portraiture', while considerations such as 'loyalty', 'reverence', 'discretion', were to be derisively brushed aside as hagiography. Of course, Harold added, 'all malice or all unnecessary infliction of pain must be avoided'. Nor should the biographer stain 'the morals of the age'. But if unable to abide by these principles, 'he should not sully his conscience by the suggestion of untruth but rather abandon his project, and wait until the passage of time shall render his disclosures less scandalous or painful'.[51] By his own standards Harold had sullied his conscience; or to be more gracious, he told the truth, but not the whole truth. But hardly surprisingly, given his own lifestyle, Harold was always guided by the innate fastidiousness, an instinctive discreetness, that habitually distinguished his behaviour. Still, Harold had much cause for self-satisfaction. Contemporary reviewers treated *Verlaine* favourably; society readers thought of him as a serious author. Even that superior person Curzon considered him 'a clever boy'.[52]

No sooner had Harold finished one book than he began another, 'a splendidly psychoanalytical, obscene novel', as he put it to Michael Sadleir. After receiving the manuscript, Sadleir told him to 'tone down its modernity'. Harold agreed.[53] If they were referring to *Sweet Waters*, the finished product, it was far from being 'splendidly psychoanalytical', or 'obscene'. It was, however, a novel, based loosely on Harold's period of service at the British embassy in pre-war Constantinople. Harold weaved himself into the plot as Angus Field, a junior clerk, young, dandyish in taste, lacking in self-confidence, but something of a know-all, 'a little sodomitic cad',[54] who pursues a lackadaisical, passionless affair with Eirene (a faint echo of Vita). Angus, having committed a monumental gaffe – he had not shown the 'required (diplomatic) reticence' when speaking with local government officials – was packed off home, to Tunbridge Wells, Kent. He took his leave of Eirene. '"Leaving?" she echoed in amazement . . . "Oh, but how mean of you!" she cried . . . "How mean! You should have warned me. You have not given me time." He leaned towards her. "Time, Eirene? Time for what?" . . . The wind from Asia came softly upon the waters, laden with the scent of cistus and of thyme. The scent of spring. There was no longer any silence between them.'[55] Over-intense in style, the dialogue stilted, *Sweet Waters* would fail to strike a chord for the contemporary reader of fiction. But for the historian there are some evocative descriptive scenes of pre-war Constantinople, of expatriate life there, of the ins and outs of diplomatic manoeuvrings in the Turkish capital.

By January 1922 *Sweet Waters* had sold a respectable 3,000 copies and had brought in about £150 for Harold, though Michael Sadleir was quick to point out that both *Paul Verlaine* and *Sweet Waters* had been published at a loss.[56] As he handed in the manuscript of *Tennyson*, Harold made another move to advance his literary career. He found a literary agent, Alexander Strathan Watt, so that 'the material side' should be thrashed out between Watt and Constable & Co., while 'the spiritual side' would be discussed between himself and Sadleir. He wrote *Tennyson* at a prodigious speed. Begun in April 1922, it was finished in August. One of Sadleir's readers gave it an enthusiastic notice: 'first-rate', an 'admirable work', 'should rank as *the* book on Tennyson', though he also laboured the point that Harold had missed the 'essential fact' that Tennyson was 'a mystic'.[57] Vita was ecstatic: 'a brilliant piece of work with none of the shallowness of mere brilliance'. Although one review was 'wishy-washy', the others were mainly complimentary, Gosse, to Harold's satisfaction, joining in the chorus of praise, as did 'Sligger' Urquhart. In Gordon Square, however, the snooty Bloomsberries thought differently. The Nicolsons had dined there on 15 March 1923, the day that *Tennyson* was published. 'Light eggs show dark patches,' Virginia Woolf recorded in her diary. 'I mean we judged them both incurably stupid. He is bluff, but oh so obvious; she, Duncan [Grant] thought, took the cue from him, & had nothing free to say. There was Lytton, supple and subtle as an old leather glove, to emphasise their stiffness.' When she came to read *Tennyson* some months later she threw it 'onto the floor in disgust', dismissing it as a soiled imitation of Lytton Strachey's works. Strachey's reaction was no less severe: 'I'm sorry to say I can't face Lord Tennyson . . . Harold N's book is so disgusting and stupid.'[58]

Between the 'Ace', Strachey, and the 'Queen', Harold, there existed an almost unbridgeable status gap. Strachey, flamboyant and serpentine, was already a literary celebrity; Harold, circumspect and above board, aspired to become one. Strachey could afford to be condescending, at times churlish, towards Harold. Harold's feelings remained ambivalent: he admired Strachey as a writer, but disliked him as a person. 'Lytton Strachey has the meanest intelligence going,' he told Raymond Mortimer. To Vita he promised: 'I shall *not* become a flabby old sod like Lytton. I won't. I won't. I won't.' Passing years had not mellowed his opinion. 'Lytton,' he told Strachey's biographer, 'resembled a bearded and bitchy old woman, rude rather than witty in society, injecting with his unnaturally treble voice jets of stinging poison into otherwise convivial gatherings.' And Vita concurred: 'the drooping Lytton must have done its [Bloomsbury's] cause a great deal of harm. I hated Lytton.' Yet both recognised Harold's debt to Strachey. Vita, like Virginia Woolf and many others, had also noticed that *Tennyson* was influenced by Strachey's impressionistic approach: an exercise in dismantling a Victorian legend, though Harold, typically, was careful not to strip the popularly acclaimed Poet Laureate completely bare. When Harold received 'warm messages of approval' from Strachey via Vita, he assumed (rightly or wrongly) that Strachey had 'forgiven me for aping him'.[59]

Harold invariably felt himself at a disadvantage when confronting the self-centred, opinionated highbrows of Bloomsbury. They have 'such sly minds', he reminded Raymond Mortimer. Bloomsbury offered nothing but pitfalls. At times, it was 'a gift from heaven'. With an air of resignation, Harold conceded that it 'refines or checks what, in my writing, I recognize and deplore as a flabby vulgarity. It is a distinction I lack.' Was he aware of Lytton's and Virginia's feelings of 'disgust' at his *Tennyson*? It hardly seems likely. Nor could he have been mindful of Virginia Woolf's verdict on his *Byron*: she dismissed it as 'tawdry and melodramatic'. There was another reason why Harold valued the opinion of the Bloomsbury set. He felt that 'their only real prejudice is that against shams'.[60] But did they regard him as 'a sham'? Unconventional themselves – it was said that the Bloomsberries 'loved in threes and lived in Squares' – they must have been aware of Harold's unconventional private life. Yet this stuffy, uptight man from the Foreign Office represented for them all the values that they delighted in mocking: King and Country and Empire, excessive respect for a class-ridden society. Small wonder that Virginia Woolf continually pressed Vita to press Harold to quit the stifling, enervative atmosphere of the Foreign Office.

Five books published in the space of five years indicates a phenomenal work ethic, particularly as Harold was also engaged full time at the Foreign Office. He possessed an amazing facility for writing. '10,000 words in one day! – 40,000 in one week!'[61] he recorded when writing *Byron*, numbers well outside the scope of most writers, professional or otherwise. He maintained this self-discipline until the end of his life. Harold received some help from Eddie Marsh before delivering the finished manuscripts to Sadleir. Marsh, 'accurate and fussy' according to Harold, proof-read and, where necessary, amended his drafts. (Marsh had considerable experience of this kind of thing for he performed the same function for many of Winston Churchill's books.) Marsh found some of Harold's work slovenly, a failing that Harold acknowledged since he wrote at such 'a rattling pace'. The finished products owed much to Marsh's rigorous editing, as Harold readily admitted.[62] It has been noted that Harold was fascinated by 'the more scandalous type of poets' – Verlaine, Swinburne and Byron:[63] he later wrote biographies of Benjamin Constant, the Franco-Swiss novelist, and Sainte-Beuve (Charles Augustin), the French literary critic. Perhaps there is a psychological explanation for this. Or perhaps these were subjects that simply appealed to his gradually expanding reading public. Or then again, perhaps this was merely smart publishing strategy. Whatever the explanation, probably a combination of all three, Harold was pleased with the end result. *Verlaine* had given him a positive start; *Tennyson*, 'a settled reputation'; *Byron*, 'a good position'; while *Swinburne*, Harold had no doubt, was 'A GOOD BOOK'.[64] All this boosted his self-confidence as an author with a future. In March 1924, he started reviewing books for the *Nation*.[65] By design, Harold had created for himself a new and promising career.

SEVEN

'But you see Britannia has ruled here'

Harold arrived at Victoria station shortly after one o'clock in the afternoon of 17 November 1922. The party assembled: Sir William Tyrrell, Allen Leeper, typists and secretaries and servants. Red dispatch boxes had been safely stored in the carriages. Only the leading actor, Curzon, was missing. 'Is the Marquis often as late as this?' asked one reporter. 'Lord Curzon is never late,' replied Harold. And then, 'majestically', His Excellency appeared, with literally seconds to spare, walking at a dignified pace 'as if he were carrying himself on a howdah' towards his Pullman car, shrugging off impatient journalists with their impertinent questions, while turning to give a winning smile to energetic photographers. At precisely two o'clock the Golden Arrow glided out of the station bound for Paris: its final destination, Lausanne.[1]

After stopping at the Ritz Hotel, Paris, the delegation, accompanied by the French, moved on to the Hôtel Beau Rivage Ouchy-Lausanne, where the hall was crowded with journalists of international repute. They were to be momentarily disappointed, for Mussolini, triumphant from his recent so-called 'March on Rome', dragged Curzon and Poincaré back to Vevey for a late night conference, to be continued the following morning in Curzon's suite of rooms at the Beau Rivage. The official conference opened at 4 p.m. that afternoon in the casino of the Hôtel du Château. Attending were delegations from Britain, France, Italy, Greece, Romania, the Soviet Union and Turkey, as well as 'the glum delegates' of the Serbs, Croats and the Slovenes, and American observers. Curzon, as the highest-ranking public figure present, presided. His aim: to revise the abortive Sèvres agreement of August 1920, forced upon the defeated Ottoman Empire but effectively dismantled by the military triumphs and diplomatic skills of Mustafa Kemal (Atatürk).

Harold had been far from idle. Seeing to Curzon's needs, preparing position papers, arranging conference procedures, active on various subcommittees, placating other delegates, kept him fully occupied. On one occasion – daring to draft a full treaty instead of a preliminary one – he even acted independently of Curzon's instructions. Curzon gasped at this impertinence: 'You have done this,' he snapped angrily, 'knowing that it was in direct contradiction to my own decision.' Harold defended himself: 'it seemed the only sensible thing to do'. On reflection, Curzon grudgingly admitted, 'Well, I suppose you were right.' When free from routine conference business and the occasional contretemps with his chief, Harold, a mark of his industry, kept himself fully occupied by correcting the proofs of *Tennyson* and sketching out the first draft of his *Byron*.[2]

For the British, three main issues were at stake: that most contentious of questions, the freedom of the Straits; the future status of Mosul in northern Mesopotamia, an area rich in oil reserves; and the need to break the Turkish–Soviet connection. As with all international gatherings of this kind it came down to reconciling disparate, at times conflicting, national interests. Compromise was inevitable. Curzon, no doubt with Lloyd George's conference diplomacy in mind, had little faith in such dramatic stagings as they tended to boost public anticipation and hence subordinate tangible achievements to illusory results. Harold noted with distaste how the other delegations played to the gallery. The Turks became 'very tiresome', their eyes fixed on western Thrace. Curzon disillusioned them: it was out of the question, he said: 'on this point the allies are unanimous'. The Italians, angling after economic consortiums and participation in mandates, put Curzon in 'a frightful state'. He curbed their inflated ambitions, but not before he succumbed 'to a fit of violent trembling' which much alarmed his aides. At home, he was pilloried – most unfairly – in the press for abandoning the Greeks. His Lordship had no doubt who was behind these calumnies: those 'dirty dogs' Lord Birkenhead and Lloyd George.[3]

Harold's bias in favour of Greece and Venizelos was an accepted fact in Foreign Office folklore. But when news came through, on 28 November, of 'the Athens atrocities', even Harold's patience broke. A group of Venezelist officers had seized power, led by Colonel (later General) Nikolaos Plastiras: six so-called traitors – those thought responsible for the Smyrna débâcle – were summarily executed by firing squad, including Dimitrios Gounaris, the former Prime Minister. Harold exploded: 'This is the third time the Greeks have let us down: first politically, by getting rid of Venizelos: the second militarily, by being beaten by the Turks: and now morally by this business.' Still ambitious for office, and as one of Britain's most faithful partners, Venizelos had been invited to Lausanne. 'You seem to be able to manage the Cretan,' Curzon once told Harold. Profiting from Curzon's confidence in him, Harold met Venizelos on a number of occasions.[4] He clarified to 'the Cretan' that Britain would not countenance a renewal of the war with Turkey, despite Greek 'sacrifices' and 'humiliations', though he could not resist adding: 'We may be right in urging M. Venizelos in no circumstances to make war, but he is also right in urging us to help him to make peace.' Harold reckoned that for some odd reason Curzon 'hated' Venizelos. 'How unpleasant that man is,' he told Harold. Taken aback, Harold replied that he was still 'very fond of him'. But to himself he reluctantly admitted that Venizelos was 'not quite the man he was'.[5]

Curzon soon had things well under control. At the Foreign Office it was noticed with gratification that he had imposed his authority upon the conference. 'I watch with daily delight the masterly way in which you lead and dominate the Conference,' wrote Eyre Crowe. 'What a contrast with the old Peace Conference and Genoa!' he added, an obvious dig at Lloyd George, to Curzon's distinct advantage.[6] The Straits question was resolved much as Curzon had wanted. Harold had drafted a lengthy memorandum on this problematic issue. His first priority was to free the Straits to navigation by warships. This was little more than wishful thinking, given the predictable Turkish and Russian objections, cemented by the current close relations between those two countries. Curzon grasped this immediately. 'In present circumstances,' he claimed, 'we cannot obtain unrestricted "freedom of the Straights" for warships.' Inevitably, Harold fell back on some kind of international control or inspection that would at least guarantee commercial freedom of the waterways, in fact a rehash of the abortive settlement at Sèvres. Curzon's scheme, accepted by the conference except for a few minor details, proposed a sensible compromise. Warships were to be allowed freedom of navigation in times of peace subject to limitation of number, which should not exceed that of the maximum naval forces of any one Black Sea power; they would also be restricted as to their length of stay. Commercial shipping would be granted absolute freedom of navigation in times of peace; in times of war, ships of the belligerent powers would be excluded.[7] Although the Straits Convention dragged on, by mid-December Curzon had accomplished much: he had cracked the Turkish–Russian alliance; reached shaky accords with the French and Italians, thereby maintaining allied solidarity; attained significant gains at the Straits; and had forcefully demonstrated that Britain was still a major force in international affairs.

Within days the international climate had changed. On 31 December Curzon met Bonar Law, Prime Minister since 23 October, in Paris. Noting his chief's gloomy disposition on his return, Harold remarked: 'it is obvious that Mr Bonar Law was not encouraging.' '[His] feet,' Curzon answered, were 'positively glacial'. Conscious of an impending Anglo-French crisis over reparations, Bonar Law wished to bring the Lausanne conference to a rapid end, regardless of the consequences. He longed 'to clear out of Mosul, the Straights, Constantinople', Curzon complained to his wife. He was 'willing to give up everything and anything rather than have a row': he was prepared 'for me to back down everywhere'.[8] The day after receiving Curzon's disheartening report, Harold, with other members of the delegation, took a day off. From Montreux, they went 'in a funny funicular to a place called Gstaadt'. At the hotel, after dinner, there was a fancy dress ball that 'rather bored' him. The following morning he made up for it. He went skiing, with more enthusiasm than skill: 'I have never fallen about so much or so often.' Although 'wet, frightened, bruised and hungry', he insisted to Vita that it was all 'great fun'.[9]

On 11 January – Curzon's birthday – the row Bonar Law feared erupted. French and Belgian troops occupied the Ruhr, citing Germany's default on a timber assignment as their excuse. Anglo-French relations fell into a deep crisis, not the most conducive of backgrounds against which to tie up the loose ends of the Lausanne meeting. For all that, Curzon struggled on. But Harold was pessimistic about his chances of success. 'A bad day . . . the conference breaking down,' he asserted gloomily. Too gloomily perhaps, for the following day, eight days after meeting Bonar Law, Curzon presented a preliminary treaty, prepared in part by Harold. 'There,' he claimed triumphantly, 'I said I could do it in two hours. I have done it in one hour and three-quarters. I am content.' Things were not quite so simple. Keen to exploit the rift in Anglo-Turkish relations to France's advantage, Curzon's bane, Poincaré, threatened to go it alone, but quickly backed down, sensing that if he did not co-operate fully he would be excluded from the final treaty, so damaging French interests. Mosul was a sticking point – for the French and the Turks – but that too was settled, if not amicably, then in a busi-nesslike fashion, at least from the British point of view. After protracted negotiations, the Mosul region was retained for Iraq – a British mandate – its oil reserves to be parcelled out between Britain and France.

Nor were the Turks quite as accommodating as at first anticipated. When they suggested 'that they must be allowed to dig up our graves at Gallipoli and put them in one cemetery', Harold flared up. 'I simply saw red . . . Really, they are quite, quite mad – and if they want war they will get it . . . I told them that the British Empire would never NEVER evacuate Gallipoli until our graves were safeguarded.' Despite Atatürk's victories, the Turks had lost much. At the last moment they balked at putting their signatures to the treaty. Curzon, looking pointedly at his watch, told the chief Turkish delegate, General Ismet Pasha, 'You have only half an hour in which to save your country.' Fending off appeals and threats, Ismet Pasha remained obdu-rate. The half-hour passed without issue. '*Nous partons*,' Harold told the stationmaster, and 'slowly the great train slides into the night'. By 7 February Harold was back in London.[10]

This was not the end of the Turkish settlement. Other conferences followed, at London and again at Lausanne. Meanwhile, Ismet Pasha had pushed through the Turkish National Assembly a motion approving of Curzon's draft subject to certain modifications, particularly regarding the capitulation and economic clauses. These were examined and an agreement reached. The Lausanne treaty was finally signed on 24 July 1923, and ratified by the Turkish Assembly the following August.* Curzon's own work at the first conference remained largely untouched, a tribute to his perseverance and sure touch.

One incident occurred at Lausanne that, it could be argued, would affect Harold's diplomatic career. He and his father had never been favourites of William Tyrrell, at one time Grey's powerful private secretary and now Curzon's principal adviser at Lausanne. His biographer suggests that Tyrrell was 'nervous and sensitive' by temperament.[11] Both of his sons had been killed in the war, a terrible loss that resulted in some kind of breakdown. At Lausanne Harold was 'furious' with Tyrrell for having 'ratted' on an agreed arrangement to deal with the repercussions of 'the Athens atrocities'.† Justifying himself later, Tyrrell claimed that he had been busy dressing and had not fully taken in Harold's 'wildcat scheme'. Was he drunk at the time?

Tyrrell's drinking problem was well known in most Foreign Office circles. At Lausanne, Harold had found Tyrrell 'dead-drunk'. He informed Crowe, 'who brought Tyrrell home on ground that his wife was ill'. Curzon, Harold

---

*The final terms of the Lausanne treaty read as follows: Turkey surrendered all claims to the non-Turkish territories lost as a result of the war, but recovered eastern Thrace to the Moritsa river, Adrianople, and Smyrna; under the supervision of a League of Nations Commission the Straits were to be demilitarised with a zone on either bank: they were to be open to ships of all nations in time of peace and in time of war if Turkey remained neutral – but if Turkey was at war, enemy ships, but not neutrals, might be excluded (a clause was added stipulating that no naval force larger than the strongest Black Sea fleet might be sent in peacetime into the Black Sea by a non-Black Sea state); Greece retained possession of all the Aegean islands except Imbrosa and Tenedos, which were handed over to Turkey; Turkey recognised the annexations of Cyprus by Britain and the Dodecanese islands by Italy; the capitulations agreements were abolished, Turkey in turn promising to implement judicial reforms; Turkey also agreed to treaties protecting minorities' rights; and no reparations were demanded of Turkey.

A separate Turkish–Greek agreement provided for the exchange of populations: one million Greeks to be transferred from Turkey, 350,000 Turks to be exiled from Greece.

†The arrangement turned on sending an intermediary, Gerald Talbot, naval attaché at the Athens embassy, then in Lausanne, back to Athens with instructions to restrain the Greek officers and to attempt to rescue Prince Andrew.

added, eventually 'found out more about Tyrrell's ways', in particular over 'the Athens atrocities' affair when he had 'let all the blame fall on Harold!' It is inconceivable that Curzon was unaware of Tyrrell's drinking habits (whether he actually saw Tyrrell 'dead-drunk' in public is another matter). At the height of the Lausanne conference Curzon wrote to his wife: 'I begin to see that Tyrrell, for all his quickness and superficial intelligence is a really small man. He has no knowledge of reading or width of view. He has a sort of nimbleness of wits and likes negotiation and palavering and intellectual jig-saw work. But he could not grapple with big situations or make a good Ambassador.' To many it appeared as though Tyrrell's career had burned out. But he soon recovered and went on to become Permanent Under-Secretary (1925–28) and lastly Ambassador at Paris (1928–34). When Tyrrell retired, Harold settled long-standing accounts both for his father and himself. Here was 'a little man . . . whose intrigues and drunkenness did much to darken and discredit the FO system. To my mind he was the greatest *cabotin* [bungler or double-crosser] I have known . . . For serious or prolonged thinking he was of no value whatever . . . he was a drunken little half-caste, not brave or honest, and completely unaware of the real traditions of our service.' At Lausanne, Harold had shielded Tyrrell. Had Curzon found out that Tyrrell was 'a dipsomaniac . . . he would have sacked him. So I enabled W.T. to become head of the Office and Ambassador in Paris. And he never forgave me.'[12]

There was another tippler at Lausanne, Chippendale, Curzon's wayward valet, the inspiration for a wonderful (partially fictitious) comic incident. In a bout of alcoholic stupor the inebriated Chippendale boldly strutted the ballroom at the Beau Rivage, ambitiously flirting with the fashionably clad ladies. He was sacked and sent home for his impudence; and, throwing what little discretion he had left to the wind, hid all of Curzon's trousers in revenge. Harold witnessed these surreal scenes and brilliantly recorded them in *Some People*, the delightful Arkentall hiccuping his way to perdition as Curzon's disgraceful valet.[13]

'Haughty, self-opinionated and conservative', never 'grateful' or even 'averagely considerate to his subordinates', Curzon was admired but not loved by his officials. Unwittingly he would irritate his aides. On more than one occasion Harold referred to Curzon as 'a shit', quick to add 'but a decent one' with a sense of humour, able to laugh at himself. With his quaint accent, that 'eccentric amalgam of Derbyshire and Eton', and his patrician values – 'how positively ghastly', he cried, when gazing across Lake Geneva to the lights of Evian from his hotel rooms – he was an easy figure to poke fun at. Of far more consequence, Harold did not rate Curzon very highly as a Foreign Secretary. 'Not the most creative of our Foreign Secretaries,' he concluded. But more than anything, Harold thought that Curzon lacked a sense of proportion.[14]

Yet even Harold conceded that Curzon had brought off a great coup at Lausanne. From Berlin, the British ambassador, Lord D'Abernon, listed Curzon's achievements: he had healed Anglo-Turkish relations; outmanoeuvred the French; and unhinged the Soviet-Turkish relationship. Harold agreed, adding: 'He had restored British prestige in the East.' On the eve of their departure from Lausanne, Harold wrote: 'When I thought he was wrong, he was right, and when I thought he was right, he was much righter than I thought. I give him 100 marks out of 100 and I am so proud of him. So *awfully* proud. He is a great man and one day England will know it.'[15] Others were less certain. The *Daily Mail* wrote of Curzon's 'failure'; the *Daily Express* campaigned for the abandonment of Iraq, 'bag and baggage'. What is certain is that by the time the Lausanne treaty was ratified British primacy had been established in the Middle East from Egypt to the Persian Gulf, for good or ill. 'But you see,' Harold told Vita, 'Britannia *has* ruled here.'[16] In Harold's eyes, Lausanne did much to redeem Curzon's reputation. A triumph for British policy, it was also a personal triumph for Curzon. It was the high point of his political career: his fading reputation faded no longer. Of no less importance for Harold, Lausanne was a triumph for the Foreign Office, of late eclipsed by Lloyd George's individual-style diplomacy. And so, by implication, a victory for those officials who had guided Curzon to his present august station.

Once in London, Harold made his way to his house in Ebury Street to rejoin his family. When he had asked Vita to accompany him to Lausanne, she had prevaricated, and eventually decided to stay in London. She did turn up at the Beau Rivage on 12 January and left nine days later. They socialised, dined out, visited tourist attractions such as Chillon Castle. But the visit was not a success. The pain of Vita's departure left Harold 'in a dark mood of gloom'.[17] The enduring problem of Vita's flings came between them. Although her affair with Violet had died down, Vita's behaviour remained a cause of concern for Harold. Would the same madness ever repeat itself? It did not; but the thought that it might nagged at Harold's psyche. At Lausanne, he wondered about Dorothy (Dottie) Wellesley, Gerry's wife, another unpredictable character. Was Vita having an affair with her, with its attendant poisonous gossip? In fact she was, but it petered out, as would all of Vita's affairs in the future. Never again would she provoke Harold with the same apparent passionate commitment that she had invested in Violet.

On 14 December 1922, Vita met Virginia Woolf for the first time at a dinner party given by Clive Bell, Virginia's brother-in-law. 'Did she look very mad?' Harold asked pointedly. Before she had time to answer, Vita wrote: 'I simply adore Virginia Woolf . . . At first you think she is quite plain, then a sort of spiritual beauty imposes itself . . . I've rarely taken a fancy to anyone, and I think she likes me. Darling I have quite lost my heart.' Virginia was no less frank, but from a different perspective. 'Muzzy headed' from her encounter with 'the lovely gifted aristocratic Sackville-West', she found Vita, on reflection, 'not much to my severer taste – florid, moustached, parakeet coloured, with all the supple ease of the aristocracy, but not the wit of the artist . . . a grenadier; hard; handsome, manly; inclined to double chin.' It was Vita, the 'high aristocrat . . . virginal, savage, patrician', that fascinated Virginia Woolf, not her reputation as a writer. Some months earlier she had heard by word of mouth that 'Mrs Nicolson thinks me the best woman writer – and I have almost got used to Mrs Nicolson having heard of me.' At the time, Vita – now largely forgotten – by far outsold Virginia Woolf – now a cult figure. Virginia remained adamantly unimpressed. In private, she scorned Vita's writing skills; Vita churned out her books – fifteen pages a day – wielding a 'pen of brass', as she once famously noted. (Leonard, her husband and Vita's publisher, was not quite as scathing, but was not exactly complimentary either: 'Inside Vita was an honest, simple, sentimental, romantic, naive, and competent writer.')[18]

Vita was intrigued by, perhaps envied, Virginia's writing style, at once more allusive, imaginative and subtle than her own. Did Virginia persuade her to put down her 'pen of brass'? 'You asked me to write a story for you,' Vita wrote to Virginia, and immediately took up the challenge. The result was *Seducers in Ecuador*, published by the Hogarth Press, which was owned and run by Leonard and Virginia Woolf. Virginia liked this novel that had its hero caught up in a series of fantasies, his own and other people's. There were those, family and friends, who thought that she had succumbed too easily to the Bloomsbury mode. Vita herself had no doubts: 'You ask which of my novels I prefer,' she wrote to her American publisher, 'I dislike them all, – *Seducers in Ecuador* is the only one I might save from the rubbish-heap.' Harold, apparently, was less sure, observing grudgingly that 'they [Bloomsbury] imagine that they have "discovered" you'.[19] Generally flattering about Vita's literary works, he remained conspicuously silent about *Seducers*. On two occasions he listed the books for which he thought Vita would be best remembered. *Seducers* did not appear on either list, perhaps a reflection of his ambiguity towards the Bloomsbury crowd.[20]

Virginia and Vita's relationship deepened on other levels. Soon after they first met, they dined alone. Overjoyed, Vita wrote gushingly to Harold of her 'darling Mrs Woolf . . . I love Mrs Woolf with a sick passion . . . Oh dear, how much I love that woman.' Virginia reacted cautiously: 'She is a pronounced Sapphist, & may, thinks Ethel Sands [the American painter], have an eye on me, old though I am.'²¹ (Aged forty-three, she was ten years older than Vita.) In December 1925 they began a love affair that lasted about three years, just when Vita's 'improbable' affair with Geoffrey Scott was finally tapering off.*

Given Virginia's history of mental instability leaving her open to suicidal tendencies, Harold was naturally uneasy about how Vita's latest intimacy would develop. Would it be a repetition of the Trefusis affair, but with an even more disastrous denouement? 'Don't be nervous!' Vita assured him, 'I love her, but couldn't fall "in love" with her.' 'But she does love me,' Vita confessed some months later, 'and I did sleep with her at Rodmell. That does not constitute a muddle though.' Harold, by now far away in Tehran, was not convinced. 'Oh my dear, I do hope that Virginia is not going to be a muddle. It is like smoking over a petrol tank.' Did Vita realise the danger? She rationalised her conduct. Vita thought of it as a 'spiritual', an 'intellectual' affair. That Virginia loved her, flattered and pleased her. But, she assured Harold, and

> this is all strictly padlock private – I am scared to death of arousing physical feelings in her, because of the madness . . . that is a fire with which I have no wish to play . . . Also she has never lived with anyone but Leonard, which was a terrible failure, and was abandoned quite soon . . . [besides] I have got too many dogs not to let them lie where

*Scott, it has been noted, conducted an 'improbable but passionate' affair with Vita from 1923 to 1925. 'Improbable', because at New College, Oxford he had acquired a reputation as a homosexual, and although he later married, he was not, as his daughter remarked, 'by temperament, a husband'. So his love affair with Vita was highly 'improbable' on both sides. Vita had first met him in 1911 in Florence. For two years Scott had acted as Bernard Berenson's secretary: a professional architect, he later remodelled the library and gardens at I Tatti. Described as 'a very tall, black-haired sallow man, rather saturnine in appearance', with 'a strong streak of melancholy', he met Vita again in 1923 at the Villa Medici, Fiesole, where he was living with his wife, Lady Sybil (Cutting), daughter of the fifth Earl of Dorset. His brief affair with Vita led to the breakdown of his marriage and to a divorce in 1927.

Scott was also an author of distinction. His influential *Architecture of Humanism* (1914), a plea for classicism, was extremely well received; as was his *Portrait of Zelide* (1925), an ironical biography of the eighteenth-century bluestocking, Madame de Charriore, with whom Boswell fell in love. He was asked to edit a collection of Boswell's papers, and *The Private Papers of Boswell at Malahide Castle* (1928–34) appeared in eighteen volumes, the majority of them after his untimely death from pneumonia in New York in 1929 (see *DNB*).

they *are* asleep . . . and I don't want to get landed in an affair which might get beyond my control before I knew where I was . . . I *have* gone to bed with her (twice), but that's all.

Harold was relieved that Vita saw 'the danger and will be wise'. But he couldn't resist stressing that 'it's not merely playing with fire; it's playing with gelignite'. Still, he added, 'Don't let's worry about these things. I know that your love for me is central, as is my love for you, and it's quite unaffected by what happens at the outer edge.'[22]

It has been suggested that 'it is a travesty of their [Vita and Virginia's] relationship to call it an affair'.[23] Why so? Possibly because, as the same authority surmised, they had only 'slept together perhaps a dozen times'. Does this really make it less of an affair? On the assumption that an 'affair' involves emotional commitment as well as physical pleasure, it would be a travesty not to call their relationship an affair. Certainly, by the late 1920s Vita had found other lovers, Mary Campbell and Hilda Matheson to name but two. There are indications that Virginia took this very much to heart. 'And aint it wretched you care for me no longer,' she wrote to Vita. 'I always said you were a promiscuous brute – Is it a Mary again; or a Jenny? Eh? . . . Am I to be wearing my heart out for a woman who goes with any girl from an Inn!' She wrote, despondently, of Vita's 'queer traits', her passions 'for the earnest middle-class intellectual, however drab & dreary'. 'Do you love me?' she asked sadly.[24] Were these her true feelings, heartfelt emotions disguised as deliberately casual throwaways? The possibility cannot be dismissed out of hand. One thing is certain: Harold was more at ease with Vita's 'earnest middle-class intellectual', than with unpredictable bluestockings like Virginia or Violet.

Once their affair had died down, Harold reconciled himself to other aspects of their relationship that suited his purpose. He told Lady Sackville, who had complained of Virginia's injurious influence on Vita, 'I know that there is a side of Vita which Virginia understands better than I could. Vita has little interest in my political life and I do not expect to find in her companionship in political matters. Similarly in literary matters Virginia means a great deal to her. This is right and inevitable. Virginia's influence on her has been nothing but admirable.'[25]

'All in all it has been a good year,' recorded Harold, looking back on 1923. 'I have been well in health and spirits: my piles and constipation better: very happy with my darling Vita . . . : not really distressed by the approach of middle age and the consequent extension of my figure and thinning of my hair.' Although delighted with his boys' progress, he could find nothing complimentary to say about Ben, but Nigel had 'come on tremendously . . . and is a gay and jolly person – obviously quick, clever, and courageous'. He had no doubt that his own literary and diplomatic career had blossomed. *Tennyson* had given him 'a settled reputation', while his accomplishments at Lausanne had boosted his standing at the Office.

Despite Harold's rosy summing up of 1923, things had not gone quite as smoothly as he judged, privately or publicly. His old friends, Gerry and Dorothy Wellesley, presented a problem. Their marriage had long been a shambles: they had separated – and 'their rows have occupied much of our time'.[26] In August the Corfu incident broke out. An Italian general and four members of his staff had been killed while delineating the Greek–Albanian frontier. Mussolini saw this as a national insult and reacted violently: he demanded reparations from Greece and dispatched his forces to bombard and occupy Corfu. The Greeks appealed to the League for justice. Curzon at first favoured this approach, but later backed down owing to French indifference and Mussolini's obduracy. So the matter was referred to the Council of Ambassadors, a concession that prompted Mussolini to evacuate his forces from Corfu. The Council, as he no doubt anticipated, adjudicated in favour of most of the Italian demands, including the payment of a considerable indemnity. Harold was horrified. He held that a great opportunity to stamp the authority of the League upon the new world order had been lost. Instead, it had been defied and its authority eroded. He clashed with Tyrrell once again – 'because he is for an arrangement at any price, and had no intellectual principle or moral stability' – and the faint-hearted Curzon, 'because his inordinate vanity was affected by the Harmsworth press attacks'. Harold recorded: 'We had a chance of calling the new world into being in order to redress the balance of the old . . . [but] the result was that we killed the League and fortified Poincaré. Terribly distressed by this lack of strength and guidance.'[27] It was too early to talk of killing off the League: that would come later. The League was scarred but not (yet) mortally wounded. But Harold's reaction was all too typical of his generation as it witnessed with dismay the systematic demise of Wilsonism.

The New Year brought in a new resolution – 'I decide to resolve to be less irresponsible, not to have claret for luncheon, and to suffer fools more gladly' – and a new government. 'A Labour triumph,' Harold crowed, greeting its electoral victory in December 1923, not sorry to learn of the 'Unionist fiasco'. It was not the greatest of triumphs, however. Ramsay MacDonald headed a minority government, kept in office by the benevolent neutrality of the Liberals. In the new Commons, the Conservatives held 258 seats, the Liberals 159, and Labour, 191.

Ramsay MacDonald also took charge of the Foreign Office. It was rumoured that Harold was the preferred choice as MacDonald's private secretary, a mark of his current standing in the Office. Coyly, he protested to his diary that he didn't want the job, but when he learned that Walford Selby had been appointed he confessed to being 'disappointed and mortified'. Apparently, Tyrrell (and Crowe) wanted someone 'safe and sound . . . they regarded me as not wholly safe nor temperamentally sound'. Curzon arranged a farewell reunion for 'the more aged members of the Foreign Office'. Harold was invited. He turned up at 1, Carlton House Terrace to attend a subdued dinner party. Curzon talked without ceasing, but not to Crowe, who felt slighted, and who in turn chatted with Robert Vansittart about the modern French novel. The food was inferior in quality. All balked at making a speech complimenting Curzon. 'A sorry ceremonial', concluded Harold, as they filed past Curzon murmuring their good-nights.[28]

Harold went to the Central Department, replacing Selby. 'The Labour people are very bad at reading papers,' he complained, 'they don't seem to stick in their minds . . . continually landing themselves in messes from which we have to extricate them.' According to Harold, MacDonald had wanted to delegate most of his foreign affairs work to Arthur Ponsonby, his Under-Secretary at the Foreign Office. Crowe had bluntly told him: 'You would have to see ambassadors, read papers, and make minutes of your meetings . . . Ramsay said he wouldn't. Crowe said he would have to. Then he went away.'[29] Crowe was a stickler for protocol, but had Harold, allowing his patrician instincts to get the better of him, garbled Crowe's orders to his untested, inexperienced master? Punctilious almost to a fault, MacDonald, in fact, was reluctant to delegate responsibility: it was reported that, even when in office, he checked train schedules for one of his secretaries.[30] Perhaps MacDonald was not quite as conscientious as Curzon – who was? – but he certainly knew his own mind and clearly read the material sent to him. MacDonald called for a reappraisal of Anglo–French relations in the aftermath of the Ruhr crisis. Old memoranda were dug out; new papers were prepared. Harold saw two outstanding problems: security, to be settled under the auspices of the League; and reparations, which required American assistance before a complete solution could be attained. The real problem, Harold argued, was that Britain had lost the high moral ground. 'M. Poincaré . . . has continually endeavoured to obscure the essential issues by drawing us on to the debatable ground of treaty interpretation . . . we have been edged away not only from the spirit and letter of the Treaty of Versailles, but from our own principles.' Let us evade Poincaré's 'enmeshing' tactics, Harold advised, and cling 'firmly to the main principles which inspire our attitude'. To prove his point, he drafted a letter incorporating these ideas for MacDonald to send to Poincaré. Crowe approved, as did MacDonald: 'This is an admirable minute.' The letter was published in the press on 3 March.[31]

During 1924 views were traded between the War Office and the Foreign Office about the future of the Rhineland, a topic that reflected upon Anglo-French-German relations. The essential problem was how to ensure France's permanent security. No one had a convincing answer. Harold dismissed the permanent occupation of the Rhineland as impractical; an Anglo-French alliance equally so, as it entailed 'a continental commitment on our part which we cannot agree to undertake'. The War Office's 'bold assumption' that an Anglo-French war was as impossible as an Anglo-German war was inevitable was shot down without hesitation by senior officials at the Foreign Office, including Harold. He confidently dismissed 'The assumption that Germany and Germany alone is the future enemy' as 'too theoretical'. One idea that was floated in the Central Department suggested the creation of a European balance based on France and Germany neutralising each other, thereby reducing British involvement on the Continent to a minimum, an argument in favour of isolationism. A policy of wait and see was preferred. Miles Lampson, Harold's immediate chief, mildly recommended that they 'wait upon events'. Crowe agreed. So did Harold. Prior to a League meeting in Geneva, when it was intended to propose a protocol (which was subsequently drafted, though never ratified) encompassing security, arbitration and disarmament questions, Harold aired his own ideas. He feared rushing into something which, though harmless and incidental in itself, would commit Britain to backing French policy.

> Whatever the French may say, they wish, under the guise of the League, to forge iron chains which will encircle Germany and keep her captive: whatever we may say, we wish, while aiming at general pacification and disarmament, to avoid in any way committing ourselves to military intervention in Europe. We suspect the French of wishing to use the League as a cloak for militarism: they suspect us of wishing to use vague formulae such as disarmament and arbitration as an excuse for a policy of selfish isolation.

For Harold, at present, there was only one possible policy, that 'of absolute reserve'.[32]

There were other matters. Italian duplicity, for example, an ongoing headache for Harold since the Paris conference. Was it possible to deal with Mussolini, 'the greatest rascal in the worrrld', in MacDonald's words? The future of Jubaland, a rich cotton-growing area in southern Somalia, was under consideration. Harold had drafted a reasonable compromise: Italy would take Jubaland; in return, Greek minority rights on the Dodecanese islands would be guaranteed. At first, MacDonald prevaricated. Eventually, Harold's note was sent off, but not before contradictory, and false, statements were made in the Commons about the entire question. Harold flared up, seeing in this episode a prime example of the government's incompetence and inefficiency. In the end, the Jubaland question was settled roughly in accordance with Harold's note. But could the Italians ever be trusted? His attention then turned to the Balkans, the intention again being to thwart bloated Italian ambitions. They had never disguised their aim to swallow Albania, or partition it (with Yugoslavia), leading the way to Italian primacy in the region. More concerned with safeguarding Greek (and hence British) interests as a way of blocking the Italians, Harold was not averse to promoting Britain as a rival to Italian interests in Albania.[33] In May 1924, the University of Athens conferred upon Harold an honorary degree in recognition of his services to Greece. Heartened by the award, he went and ordered three new suits: tweed, brown and flannel, together with a blue shirt.[34]

At the same time, the Americans were co-operating in unravelling the reparations problem, brought to a head by the Ruhr crisis. (General) Charles G. Dawes, an American banker, presented his report to the Allied Reparations Committee in April 1924. It proposed instituting annual payments of reparations on a fixed scale; reorganising the German State Bank to stabilise the mark; and to prop up Germany by foreign loans, 'priming the German pump', as it was called. An inter-allied conference opened in London in July to consider his plan. After much haggling with the French and the Germans, and some caveats put forward by Philip Snowden, MacDonald's Chancellor of the Exchequer – who possessed a 'temperament as rigid as his intellect' – it was accepted by the powers in August. From his position in the Central Department – occasionally he stood in as its head – Harold attended these negotiations and witnessed their successful conclusion. 'A great triumph for MacDonald,' he recorded. The prospect for stability and peace in Europe was more favourable than at any time since the end of hostilities. It has been noted that 'It was the high point of [MacDonald's] Government – perhaps of his career.'[35]

There were distractions of another kind. Harold renewed his acquaintance with Oswald (Tom) Mosley, and watched with approval Mosley's drift from Tory to Labour. Mosley had first met Harold at a country house weekend at the end of the war. Invalided out of the army, he then spent some time working in the Foreign Office and was a part-time colleague of Harold's. For a time they were close politically as well as socially, Lady Cynthia,

Mosley's first wife and Curzon's daughter, providing a link between friendship and office chores. Harold lunched with Curzon, who, to his great relief, did not 'pump him about the Labour Government'. Invited to Hackwood, Curzon's rented mansion near Basingstoke, he found 'The Marquis in delightful form' as they partook of gargantuan meals and listened to 'coon songs' after dinner. He was also an intermittent visitor at the Wharf, the Asquiths' house at Sutton Courteney, Oxfordshire – later in life Harold would proudly pronounce himself an Asquithian Liberal. At Chartwell, he was subject to Churchill's sumptuous hospitality. He thought Churchill's newly acquired estate 'rather nice', but not a red-haired Australian journalist named Brendan Bracken he met there: 'A most self-confident and I should think wrong-headed young man.' At lunch at the house of Sir John (the distinguished portrait painter) and Lady Hazel Lavery, he encountered George Bernard Shaw whose conversation was 'affable but dull' but who looked like 'a freckled bargee'. Hilaire Belloc, on the other hand, he found most 'stimulating'. Belloc pontificated about three types of literary style: poetry, rhetoric and prose. 'The latter,' he asserted, 'consists of conveying a lucid passage to the stupidist man.' Perhaps they had spoken of Harold's style, for his *Byron* had just been published. It was the great poet's centenary, so Harold, in a gesture of extraordinary generosity, suggested to MacDonald that the Elgin Marbles be returned to Greece: but his 'minute was not a success and causes bad blood'.[36]

Bloomsbury was another diversion, though it aroused in Harold mixed emotions. One party at Virginia Woolf's house in Tavistock Square he ruled 'a failure', as all he saw there were Lytton Strachey and Duncan Grant – with whom, it was said, Harold had 'tucked up'[37] – 'mooning about helplessly [?] among epicene young men'. Such affectations were not Harold's style. He had another 'foolish tiff' with Strachey when they met up at George (Dadie) Rylands's, though he discreetly declined to disclose the grounds for their quarrel. Strachey irritated him. On the whole, he found the Bloomsberries an exasperating clutch of highbrows, 'a narrow but stimulating lot'. Over one luncheon party, Clive Bell, Virginia Woolf and Roger Fry vigorously denied being snobbish, 'either socially or intellectually', an accusation often levelled at them, often with ample justification. Harold brushed aside their arguments, though his good sense made little impact on their second nature. If he was not allowed to compete with them, he could at least puncture their superior airs. 'In the summer of 1925 I went to a party in Bloomsbury,' he remembered. 'I went with much diffidence, alarmed at entering the Areopagus of British culture. They treated me with distant but not unfriendly courtesy.' Courting the Nicolsons, Virginia Woolf somewhat distanced herself from 'Gloomsbury', Vita's sharp phrase. Harold greatly admired Virginia's writing skills. When *Mrs Dalloway* appeared, he was 'very excited by it', and this set a pattern for the abundant praise he lavished upon her books.[38]

There were other matters. Harold's father suffered a heart attack, a cause for much immediate concern, though he made an early recovery. Another row erupted between Vita and Lady Sackville: 'Vita doesn't want to take any more money from her.' It soon blew over. Bonne Mama, rewarding Vita for seemingly shunning Geoffrey Scott, made over the house at Ebury Street to Vita and Harold, cancelling the loan she had made them. At the same time, she agreed to pay them £500 a year for its upkeep and £200 a year towards Ben's education. 'They are *delighted*, bless them.' Harold was gladdened at Vita's neglect of Scott. 'I dislike Geoffrey because: a) he talks better than I do; b) he worries you; c) he has a yellow face & sits up late & is flabby; d) because he is more emotional than I am, and because you [Vita] are impressed by emotion.'[39]

Ben's place at Summer Field's preparatory school, Oxford, was now secure. 'He is very sweet. He cries when we go,' Harold recorded after one visit: Nigel spent his time being shunted between Ebury Street, Long Barn and Knole. One Easter break, Harold and Vita took Ben on an extended visit to northern Italy. They toured Lake Como, Verona, Venice and Murano, the glass island. Harold gorged himself, 'all that spaghetti', fell ill, and put on weight. In the spring of 1924, Harold, together with Vita and 'Dottie' Wellesley, motored westwards to the Wye Valley and Tintern Abbey, stopping off at Monmouth and Ludlow, staying with Reggie Cooper, Harold's old school chum, on the way. In July they were off on a walking holiday in the Tyrol. The trip was not a great success. The slopes of the mountain they were scaling proved too steep for Vita to climb, and to add to their discomfort they lost their way and were caught by a storm. After relaxing in Venice for a few days, shopping and sightseeing, they returned to London.[40]

One morning, while walking across Horse Guards Parade, Harold was accosted 'by a Tommy in uniform with an untidy tam-o'-shanter and a weatherbeaten unshaven face'. 'Is Rodd in the Office?' he asked. Harold studied the spectacle before him. 'I see it is little Lawrence of Arabia. What an odd shifty charlatan that man is. A mixture of a brute and a schoolboy, he tells me that his book is so conceived as to mystify the bibliophile – no two copies being quite the same.' Harold disliked Lawrence, 'mainly because he was so frightfully untruthful and treacherous'.[41] They had first met at the Paris peace conference. A member of the British delegation, and considered an expert on the Middle East, he was seen constantly at Sherif Feisal's side, posturing in Arab robes, acting as the adviser to the head of the Arab delegation. Lawrence's mystifying book was his *Seven Pillars of Wisdom*. By

1923, at its third draft, eight copies had been printed by the *Oxford Times* and circulated to Lawrence's close friends, including George Bernard Shaw and his wife, who had corrected the grammar and punctuation. (The revised text was privately printed and published in 128 copies in 1926.) Harold's connections extended to Max Beerbohm, who wished to draw a caricature of him depicting him as 'the angel of pity'. And to William Rothenstein, who much admired Harold's *Verlaine*. He sketched a revealing portrait of Harold in red chalk, showing the approach of middle age. The result greatly pleased Harold.[42]

EIGHT

'Not really interested in foreign politics'

At the end of 1924 Harold reviewed his position in the Office. 'I have got into rather a rut', he felt. 'I must try to get out of it.' If Hardinge was 'an insufferable die-hard', Tyrrell was his chief bugbear, pulling strings behind the scenes, bad-mouthing Curzon, his 'tortuousness and secretiveness' unnerving Harold. Only Crowe, upright, trustworthy, since 1920 Permanent Under-Secretary at the Foreign Office, retained Harold's full confidence, and affection. How 'I adore and respect that man,' he said, applauding Crowe yet again. In October there were rumours of the government falling owing to its inept handling of the Campbell affair. There had long been an impression, unfounded, that MacDonald was unduly subservient to his radical Clydeside supporters. On assuming office he had recognised the Soviet Union, a presumed signal that his Cabinet had surrendered to its backbench Russophiles. When shortly afterwards his government entered negotiations to guarantee a loan to the Soviet Union, that impression was greatly reinforced. In August, a fierce Liberal–Conservative parliamentary onslaught forced the government to abruptly reverse its previous intention. Its prestige already damaged, it decided at about the same time to abandon the prosecution of the journalist, J. R. Campbell, a communist charged with inciting the armed forces to mutiny, a ruling roundly condemned by the opposition as a concession to subversive forces outside the government.

Elections were scheduled for 29 October. MacDonald, clearly panicking under the combined assault of the press and the opposition who claimed that he had caved in to a seditious cabal, turned on the Foreign Office as being 'lazy, incompetent and ignorant'. Harold took this reproof personally. 'His object doubtless is to disprove the suggestion that he did nothing and we did it all. But to go so far . . . is really a mean and shifty thing to do. It destroyed all my faith in him and all my liking.' Then, a few days before the elections, a copy of the so-called Zinoviev letter reached the Foreign Office. The letter, allegedly sent by Grigory Zinoviev, chairman of the

Comintern, urged the British communists to overturn the government through acts of sedition. 'Organize a campaign of disclosure of the foreign policy of MacDonald,' it ordered. And continued: 'Armed warfare must preceded by a struggle against the inclinations to compromise which are imbedded among the majority of British workmen, against the ideas of evolution and peaceful extermination of capitalism. Only then will it be possible to count on complete success of an armed insurrection.'

When the Office heard that the *Daily Mail* was about to publish the letter, it decided 'to forward criticism by publishing [it] ourselves'. It was a catastrophic blunder that served to strengthen the general impression that the Labour government was discreditably subservient to extremist influences. At the election Labour lost forty-one seats, and power. Who was responsible for this blunder? Crowe at first accused MacDonald, but after some humming and hawing he owned up that MacDonald had minuted the instruction approving publication, 'Let me see it again.' Harold was horrified at his beloved chief's error of judgement, to say nothing of his uncharacteristic cover-up.[1]

Stanley Baldwin formed his second government in November 1924. Harold feared that Curzon would return to the Foreign Office and that he would be appointed Curzon's private secretary, an honour he was desperately anxious to avoid.[2] But Curzon was passed over. Instead, Austen Chamberlain took over the Foreign Office. On 22 January he met with senior members of his staff in his room to discuss future policy. 'We all sit around a table with a blue cloth on it and smoke cigarettes.' Opinions varied. Owen O'Malley favoured isolation; Gerry Villiers was 'for supporting France in any circumstances'; Headlam-Morley argued 'for the reconstruction of the "Concert of Europe"'. Harold plumped 'for nothing except fulfilling our debts of honour'. Crowe, summing up, rejected isolationism, but thought there was an urgent need to amend the Covenant of the League, to bring it more into keeping with British interests, and to come to agreement with France to defend the Channel ports. 'Have we got a Dominion or a Downing Street Foreign Policy?' Harold asked his diary, slightly puzzled by the rambling discussion. 'The two things are very different – cannot be confused without trouble.' Chamberlain invited Harold to prepare a paper setting out the options for British policy in Europe. It was submitted on 20 February.[3]

'One half of Europe is dangerously angry; the other half is dangerously afraid,' Harold began, considering Britain's former allies and enemies. He foresaw a German revival of power: 'sooner or later [it] will become a powerful military factor' and will attempt to right 'the two most objectionable provisions of the Peace Settlement, namely the Polish Corridor and the partition of Silesia'. In the West, France feared renewed German aggression. Let down by the unfulfilled pledge of an Anglo-American guarantee, France sought compensation elsewhere: in a Polish alliance, in links to the Little Entente, in the so-called French eastern system, 'a policy of desperation' that made the French all the more recalcitrant, reluctant to evacuate the Rhineland unless given some 'compensating guarantee'. France must be secured against the German menace, Harold contended, otherwise 'she will be driven to expedients which in the end will only provoke the German revenge of which she stands in terror'. The League, whatever its pretensions, was a body incapable of curbing a Great Power's ambitions.

Turning to British interests, Harold ruled out a return to 'Splendid Isolation'. Taking his cue from his mentor, Eyre Crowe, he stressed Britain's worldwide commitments: the need to protect its Empire, its Dominions, the sea lanes linking them, all of which were essential to the defence of Britain itself. Again echoing Crowe, he argued that Britain's security depended largely upon preserving the European balance of power. No 'single power shall be in a position to occupy or to dominate all the Channel and North Sea ports', he laid down. He went a step further. He advised guaranteeing publicly French and Belgian territorial integrity. Such a commitment would 'constitute a very important contribution to European security' – and by implication, to Britain. It would also induce France to pursue a less provocative policy. In this way 'a nucleus of stability' would be created in Europe that, eventually, would include Germany. If Germany becomes a member of the League, Harold speculated, 'we may look forward to agreed treaty revision – particularly regarding 'the Polish Corridor and Silesia'. There was one sticking point. It was imperative to follow a policy that public opinion, both in Britain and Europe, would endorse. But the bottom line was written in bold letters. 'The essential interests of Imperial Defence are thus closely related to a policy of European security. The first hope of stability in Europe lies in a new entente between the British Empire and France.' Only by clarifying British policy beyond peradventure would another catastrophe on the scale of 1914–18 be averted. All this was a radical departure from his previous policy of 'absolute reserve'.

It was the most significant paper that Harold wrote at the Foreign Office. In it, some of the core themes of the forthcoming Locarno treaties can be detected.* Austen Chamberlain was 'very laudatory' and instructed that it

---

*The treaties were signed on 1 December 1925. The linchpin pact, guaranteed by Britain and Italy, confirmed the inviolability of the Franco–German, Belgian–German frontiers, and the demilitarisation of the Rhineland. There were also arbitration conventions between Germany and France, Belgium, Poland and Czechoslavakia; and treaties of mutual guarantee between France and Poland and Czechoslavakia. The treaties inaugurated the so-called 'Locarno era', a period of hope and international co-operation, of fulfilment of the peace treaties eased by the prospect of treaty revision. It proved to be short-lived.

be circulated as a cabinet paper, a compliment for any diplomatist or official. Harold – giving way to false modesty? – thought differently: 'I *know* that the memo. is a bad memo.' In any case, he did not rate Austen Chamberlain very highly. Chamberlain was not only a 'fool' and an 'ass', but far too susceptible to Tyrrell's roguish influence.[4] In some ways Harold missed Curzon, idiosyncrasies and all. Curzon died on 20 March 1925. After attending the funeral at Westminster Abbey, Harold was included among the chosen few to dignify the interment at Kedleston, Derbyshire. Three months later, Jonathan Cape asked him to write a biography of Curzon. Harold refused, claiming he didn't know enough about India. He was however prepared to write a monograph, after Curzon's official biography had been published.[5] It duly appeared as *Curzon. The Last Phase, 1919–1925. A Study in Post-War Diplomacy* (1934), a rather lengthy monograph as it turned out.

Far more significant for Harold, Eyre Crowe died at the end of April. 'Tyrrell reigns in his place,' he sadly recorded. His thoughts moved rapidly forward:

Feeling bored with FO: not really interested in Foreign Politics and rather out of it personally . . . this requires serious thinking over. I know I couldn't do much better at literature than I am doing already: so if I chuck in Office it will only mean doing what I do already a little more but not necessarily a little better. Don't want to abandon my second string merely because it is out of tune.

In August he was still feeling 'depressed' and 'out of it'. Convinced that Tyrrell 'has put Austen against me', his minutes were 'markedly ignored' while those of others were 'marked out for notice and commendation'. Where was all this leading? By mid-September he knew. Walford Selby, Chamberlain's private secretary, asked him whether he would like to go as Counsellor to Peking or Tehran. At first, Harold refused, pleading 'family affairs', meaning Vita and the boys (and also perhaps his most recent partner, Raymond Mortimer). He agonised over his future. 'Don't want to be selfish about it. After all it is my career that benefits and not Vita's. She gains nothing by the project and loses more than I do. On the other hand it [Tehran] really is the turning point and if I miss this I shall be down in the [?] . . . and of all foreign posts it will be the one Vita will dislike least.' He consulted his father and Lancelot Oliphant, Assistant Under-Secretary at the Foreign Office, who, although no substitute for Crowe, repeatedly lent a sympathetic ear to Harold's travails. Both advised him to accept the offer, which he did, to Vita's dismay. After a round of emotional farewells, Harold left for Tehran on 4 November. 'Here finishes my career as a civil servant,' he noted, adding: 'I have been civil but not servile.'[6] Towards Tyrrell? The thought that Tyrrell, manipulative, scheming, hostile, had banished him to Persia could not have been far from his mind.

'Poor little Tray cries.' 'Tray' was Raymond Mortimer, self-proclaimed hedonist and renowned literary and art critic. He and Harold had just spent a weekend together at Long Barn on the eve of Harold's departure for Persia. Although Harold had – and would have – many affairs, his intimacy with Mortimer was the most meaningful of them. He once wrote: 'physical pleasures rarely, very rarely, provide intellectual or moral pleasures which are in any way commensurate'.[7] With Mortimer he found that they did. They had first met at the Foreign Office at the end of the First World War where Mortimer had been seconded to work in the Cypher Department. They renewed their acquaintance in 1923–24, when their affair blossomed. After a few days together in Paris in August 1925, Harold returned to London 'very depressed'. (Mortimer had gone on to St Tropez from where he sent Harold a vivid description of 'Eugene going off into the bushes with two fishermen' – and other equally arousing incidents.) For Harold, their parting was unbearable. 'Is it all worse for you or for me?' he asked. 'Oh Raymond – I do miss you so . . . I long for your return with a hidden dread.' In one tender gesture of fidelity, he placed Mortimer's tie on his blue pyjamas: 'I can't tell you how nice it looked.'[8]

Harold's exile to Persia worsened matters. 'My dear Tray – how happy I should be here if I had a proper companion. I am feeling rather restless in the sex way – but there is nowhere safe to rest my head.' He felt 'starved physically and intellectually. I am really rather fussed about my physical cravings.' Is this due to 'the climate or unwonted abstinence'? he asked Mortimer. Whatever it was, it was 'a great bore. And masturbation is not enough. I can't even write to you without being assailed. It is too silly and school-boyish . . . What they call, I am told, "libido senilis".' Anyway, he promised 'not to lose my head or do anything silly . . . Besides I don't like the Savoy Bath business – even if it were available here, which it only is in a degraded and highly dangerous form.' 'The idea of a gentleman of birth and education sleeping with a guardsman,' he added later, 'is repugnant to me.' There were times, however, when the temptation proved too strong.

Mortimer arrived in Tehran in March for a visit: he departed three months later, 'very silent and wretched'. Harold consoled him: 'Dearest Tray you are so much to me . . . Anyway you know that there is someone in the world to whom you are of supreme importance.' Now middle-aged – he was forty years old – he felt twenty-five, 'And I look so young too.' So how does one deal with the problem of 'ineffective desire', he quizzed

Mortimer? And answered: 'I fear the only answer is "self-control" . . . I fear it is only lust which keeps one's mind buoyant – & if one has to drive that out of one's life one is driving out the impetus of all interest.'[9] 'Dearest Tray,' Harold observed, 'you are the ideal companion. Always there when wanted, never there when not . . . In this I shall always be grateful to you. And for so much else.' Their affair lasted a few years. Even when it died down, 'Tray' remained an intimate friend of the family.

Contemplating these matters when in Persia, Harold wrote to Vita about 'the two dominant things' in his life: '1. You. 2. b.s.' (backstairs: Sackville shorthand for something common or gossipy – but came to mean homosexual attitudes and behaviour).[10] To a close friend, James Lees-Milne, he extolled the advantages of homosexuality, the relationships between men that allowed individual independence. Vita, he emphasised, was 'an exceptional wife'. They kept no secrets from each other. They had pledged to tell one another the moment one of them fell in love, but not to confess to casual affairs because that was rather squalid.

He said that in his whole life he had only been in love three times, and these times were before his marriage, with two subsequent ambassadors, and a 'bedint' young man of no consequence, called Eric Upton, whose only recommendation was extreme beauty.

Oh, I may have once fallen a fourth time, with R[aymond]. I told Vita about this fall and she was wonderful.

To the same confidant, he later clarified that he 'never lied except over sex matters'.[11]

Harold's sexual preferences were an open secret to a closed circle. Vita, of course, was privy to his 'falls', if not to all his casual affairs. But so too were his sons. Bedridden and going blind, Lady Sackville, eccentric to the last, revealed to Ben the nature of his parents' sexual peccadilloes, 'the boys [Harold] had had in Persia and in all the capitals of Europe', and how Vita was prepared to wreck her marriage and desert her children for the favours of Violet, and 'That Mrs Woolf, who described in that book [*Orlando*] how your mother *changed her sex*!' Enraged, Harold compared her to Iago; Vita, to a 'genius gone wrong'. In a midnight talk with Ben – 'the first intimate talk we had ever had', he recalled – Vita told all. 'Everything was true except the part about Virginia endangering their marriage, but none of it mattered a hoot because the love they bore each other was so powerful that it could withstand anything.' Ben and Nigel took these revelations in their stride. One fine Sunday afternoon, James Lees-Milne, together with some of his Oxford friends, motored over to Sissinghurst. Ben and Nigel were swimming in the lake. 'As we approached we heard one say – no doubt he thought *sotto voce* – to the other, breast-stroking beside him, "Who is that little pansy in the yellow pullover?" "Oh!" said the other disdainfully, "presumably one of Daddy's new friends".'[12]

Harold was concerned about Ben's future. Sulky, morose, unkempt, Ben's relations with Vita were always precariously balanced on the brink of a precipice. His attitude never improved. He could not abide her, nor bear to remain in the same room as her: at mealtimes he would remain deliberately silent in her company. Harold feared that he would grow up to be 'a high-brow', not 'a jolly intellectual like you [Raymond] . . . but a grim prig . . . And not very clever at that.'[13] Unaware of the stark contrasts – 'a jolly intellectual' or a 'grim prig' – facing him, Ben, a Balliol scholar, approached his father about his own 'sex worries'. On the eve of Ben's departure for Eton, Harold had told him to put off masturbation 'as long as he possibly could – and then he must only do it on Saturdays'. At Oxford, Ben, clearly anxious, raised doubts about his own sexual orientation. Harold willingly replied, shedding light also on his own attitude to homosexuality, the second most decisive influence on his life. He consoled his eldest son. Do not despair of never being attracted to women: 'After all you have met so few attractive women and besides you might be a late-flowering plant in that respect.'

> But even if you are condemned to prefer your own sex, do not go and get an inferiority complex about it. As Raymond [Mortimer] says, 'it is better than having a bad squint or an incurable stammer'. You may find it inconvenient at Oxford where the whole practice is much looked down upon by the people you would like, and frequently indulged in by people, such as Richard Rumbold, whom you would not like. The line to take is the most natural line. As if you liked oysters done in sherry: not a thing to be particularly ashamed of or particularly proud of. Most homosexuals either slink in shame or become arrogant about it. Both attitudes are equally silly. It is quite possible with a reserve and an amount of gaiety, to enable the thing to become quite bright.

Apparently Ben was having an affair with one 'Jeremy' at Oxford. 'And what a good thing!' Harold cried. 'But do tell him if he mentions it to be discreet . . . Ben can have all the fun he wants if he is quiet about it and does not dress like a *tapette* [French slang for 'a pansy'].'[14]

'Oysters done in sherry'? Judging from his supportive remarks to Ben, Harold was plainly at ease with his own sexuality. He put it down to 'some strange [ab]normality in our thyroid or our pituitary glands' that ensured his membership of "'the Third Sex'", not yet 'officially recognized', but for which 'the movements of the mind – the movements of the heart, if you will – are more vital than the movements of the body'. After being examined by his doctor, Sir Kenneth Goadby, and studying his X-ray, 'it seems that my skull is thicker than that of most people and that this has inhibited the full expansion of the pituitary gland. It may be owing to this excess of calcium in babyhood that I became homosexual.'*

Harold was treading lightly around the subject, for there were more menacing aspects to his homosexuality that must have persistently preyed upon his peace of mind. Sections of society, high and low, loathed homosexuals. George V, commonly assumed to personify Middle England, was overheard saying, 'I thought men like that shot themselves.' But far more to the point, homosexuality was a criminal offence. Were Harold to be prosecuted and found guilty under the Criminal Law Amendment Act, he would face certain imprisonment – and then what? Exile! Ruin! The fate of Oscar Wilde was within living memory. On the day Wilde was arrested, six hundred gentlemen were said to have fled across the Channel from Dover to Calais or Dieppe – the normal traffic was about sixty – including Aubrey Beardsley, James Whistler and Walter Sickert. Harold, however, had to look no farther than William Lygon, seventh earl of Beauchamp, a popular Liberal minister, Knight of the Garter, Lord Warden of the Cinque Ports, and Chancellor of the University of London. Rather than face a trial by the House of Lords for homosexual offences, he had hurriedly left England in 1931. In exile, Vita met up with him in Touggourt, Algeria, where he turned up at a party accompanied 'by a sulky, embarrassed and bored young man called George'. Beauchamp never returned to England and died in New York.[15]

In this sense at least, Harold must have lived on a knife's edge. Although not a sexual marauder like Vita, some of his lovers are known. Apart from his three (unnamed) 'falls' before marriage and all his 'casuals', it is possible to identify Raymond Mortimer, Edward Molyneux, Jean de Gaigneron, Duncan Grant, Bobby Sharpe, Sandy Baird, David Herbert, Richard

*These comments are voiced by John Shorland (Assistant Private Secretary to the Foreign Secretary, and a Fellow of All Souls) to Jane Campbell (Parliamentary Under-Secretary at the Foreign Office) in Nicolson's novel, *Public Faces* (Constable, 1932, pp. 142–43). John is unmistakably Harold, while Jane, underlining 'how much my independence, my single-mindedness, my combative singleness, my being just Jane Campbell, has always meant to me', faithfully echoes Vita's feelings.

For results of his X-ray, see **ND**, 23 Sept. 1941. Recent research – admittedly inconclusive – has shown that 'Dissections of their forebrain hypothalamus found that the glands in both the women and the gay men were less than half the size of those in the straight men . . . [this finding] suggests that sexual orientation has a biological substrate.' See 'Gays and Genes', *New York Review of Books*, 27 Mar. 2003.

Rumbold, James Pope-Hennessy, Ivor Novello and James Lees-Milne. Harold was nothing if not discreet – although he was known to 'cruise' the bars of Berlin in the late 1920s and New York in the early '30s. He was also discreet on Vita's behalf. Vita sought his advice on a series of 'love poems' that she had written, concerned that people would think them 'Lesbian'. Harold advised against publication, claiming, diplomatically, not to care about 'their lesbian implication', but holding rather that the poems were not good enough for publication, a response that took Vita aback.[16] When Harold's cousin by marriage, Eddy Sackville-West published his *risqué* novel, *The Ruin: A Gothic Novel* (1926), Harold called it 'very personal and very decadent'. Eddy was one of those 'arrogant', aggressive homosexuals that Harold so much disliked. Vita once saw him at Knole, 'mincing in black velvet'. 'I don't object to homosexuality,' she remarked, accurately reflecting Harold's frame of mind, 'but I do hate decadence.'[17]

Harold was lampooned four times in books: twice by friends, the third time by a so-called friend, and the fourth by an enemy. But first Virginia Woolf introduced Harold in her fantastical biography, *Orlando* (1928), which traces the history of the youthful, beautiful, aristocratic Orlando (Vita) through four centuries and both male and female manifestations. Harold appears as Marmaduke Bonthrop Shelmerdine Esq., a 'romantic and chivalrous, passionate, melancholy, yet determined' character. The subtext was clear to those in the know. Orlando and Marmaduke became lovers. '"Tell me Mar," Orlando would say . . . "You're a woman, Shel!" she cried, "You're a man Orlando!" he cried.' Harold was so overwhelmed by Virginia Woolf's writing style that he took all this in his stride. 'The whole thing has a beauty which makes one catch one's breath . . . It is far *more* than brilliant. I simply cannot believe that such a book will not survive.'[18]

He was less understanding about what followed. Gerald Tyrwhitt (Lord Berners) portrayed him as 'Mr "Lollipop" Jenkins, 'a well-known author, journalist and member of Parliament . . . an *enfant terrible* who was growing middle-aged and slightly pompous', whose more thoughtful friends 'scented the presence of the invisible worm' and who 'seemed to prefer the company of quite unimportant young men'. Harold immediately recognised his character sketch. 'An unhappy day. I begin by glancing at Berner's new novel *Far From the Madding War*, and am horrified to feel that Mr Lollipop Jenkins must be a portrait of myself.' But Berners was the soul of discretion when compared with Richard Rumbold, one of Harold's lovers. His creation, Mr Henry Armitage, was an outrageous figure. A noted social and literary butterfly, he was also a 'lecherous old beast', a leading player in explicit scenes of homosexual orgies who enjoyed 'rescuing pretty boys'. As for Isabella Armitage (Vita), her scurrilous behaviour as 'one of London's most

renowned Lesbians and seducers of young men' left nothing to the imagination. 'Dark . . . and very fat . . . She speaks like a man in a deep bass
voice . . . She is horribly ugly . . . and gives lurid, detailed accounts of her
affairs. She started at sixteen and has kept going pretty well ever since.'
Harold was appalled. 'Read Richard Rumbold's novel which enrages one so
that I fling it away.' He later wrote 'quite frankly' to Rumbold, a most
disturbed young man, always on the brink of a nervous breakdown, 'that he
was wrong to do me harm in this way'. And then there was Evelyn Waugh,
who, maliciously if privately, claimed that 'Sir Ralph Brompton', a patrician
diplomatist of homosexual tastes who appears in his wartime trilogy, *Sword
of Honour*, was modelled on Harold.[19]

By far and away the most savage and vindictive of these lampoonists was
Roy Campbell, the South African poet. The Campbells were staying at the
gardener's cottage at Long Barn in the late 1920s. Campbell took extreme
umbrage when he learned that Vita was conducting an affair with his wife,
Mary. He threatened to commit suicide; and even proposed a suicide pact
with Mary. But he took his revenge in the manner best suited to his talents.
His poem, *The Georgiad*, starred Harold as 'Androgyna' and Vita as
'Georgiana'.

The Stately Homes of England open their door,
To piping Nancy-boys and crushing bores
How Nicolson who in his weekly crack,
Will slap the meanest scribbler on the back
[They lecture] Upon the radio, about married life,
as if their life were one protracted kiss,
And they the models of connubial bliss
From bed to bed to amorous fury flies,
The beds, late soothed with homosexual snores
To Bloomsberry, to Fabians, to Sissies. [20]

Although cruelly mocked in public in this manner, Harold, wisely, never
sought satisfaction except in his diaries and letters. There would be no risky
lawsuits for him. He moved securely in a close-knit network that protected
its own.

Harold left for Persia on 4 November 1926. Writing letters to Vita and
Mortimer on the way, he passed through Paris, Trieste and Alexandria,
crossed the Sinai desert to Lydda and Jerusalem before embarking on the
hazardous journey overland by motor convoy to Tehran via Baghdad.
Although Tehran lacked the comforts and sophistication of London, the

British Legation there has been described as a veritable 'Garden of Eden', while opinion was unanimous that life at the summer Legation at Gulhek was 'a dream of delight'.²¹ He was assured of a warm reception. Sir Percy Loraine, the British Minister at Tehran, had told him: 'No appointment could be more welcome or more completely suitable.'

As usual, the internal politics of Persia were complex. Curzon had appointed Loraine with the express purpose of salvaging something from a convention that the Persians had reneged upon earlier. In August 1919, British forces had intervened in Persia to put down domestic unrest and a potential Bolshevik incursion. As a result, a convention was signed that provided for the British administration of the Persian army, treasury and railways in return for a phased evacuation of British troops. The following year, in June 1920, extreme nationalist agitation compelled the Shah to suspend the convention, a considerable setback for Curzon, a self-proclaimed authority on the region, who had just taken over at the Foreign Office.

Loraine quickly recognised Reza Khan as the coming strongman of Persia. Reza, a former colonel in the Cossack Brigade, had seized power in 1921 in a British-orchestrated coup. Now War Minister, he negotiated first the speedy evacuation of Russian forces and then those of the British. In October 1925 – a month before Harold's arrival – he deposed the reigning Shah, Ahmed Mirza, and proclaimed himself as Reza Shah Pahlevi, the head of a new dynasty. Loraine, tall, discreet, immaculately dressed, conventional, stuffy in manner, had established a harmonious rapport with Reza Khan. But Loraine's assignment was dogged by long-standing, and conflicting, British obligations to the sheikh of Mohammerah, an independent feudal despot who ruled the oil province of Arabistan and had been worsted by Reza in the contest to control Persia. In bad faith, Reza had seized the sheikh, 'a tiresome old man' in Harold's opinion, and removed him to Tehran, where, as Harold more generously put it, he was held 'as an honoured prisoner' for ransom. (He later died there.) The Legation spent much effort trying to correct this injustice.

Reza Khan's seizure of power had not brought peace and stability to the country, at least not in the short run. The overall situation was 'gloomy', Harold reported: 'mutiny' in Azerbaijan; 'serious uprisings' in the provinces; 'unrest' among the Kurds; banditry on the highways a daily occurrence; rising tension between the Majlis and the Shah; the sheikh still 'in jug'; the Russians up to their usual tricks. 'The old story' persisted: 'oppression, corruption, lack of pay'. To the east, Dost Mohammed, a local warlord, had advanced on a railway in Indian territory. The Government of India reacted angrily, ordering Harold to issue an ultimatum to the Persian government: 'if you don't send troops to restore order, we shall'. Harold thought this 'a rotten idea', and advised the Indian government to act first 'and explain later'. The Foreign Office dilly-dallied, blowing hot – send the ultimatum – and then cold – 'suspend action'. It was all a hopeless muddle. 'Now these are facts & not opinions – & surely they justify a little pessimism.'[22]

Loraine and Reza consulted frequently. All too often, the subject was Russian encroachment from the north, a perennial problem. 'Reza says he plays with the Russians, that he doesn't like them, that he sometimes has to give way to them in minor matters . . . but in all vital matters he can trust the Majlis to refuse to surrender . . . Percy Loraine comes back very pleased.'[23] But Harold couldn't help wondering whether Reza was simply telling Loraine what he wished to hear.

Still, Harold regarded Loraine in great esteem: 'You know what I feel about your amazing kindness to me – & I won't become soppy. But it has been a splendid education working with you.' Whatever the strength of their personal relationship, they differed greatly regarding the probity of the Shah and the Persians. Reza, Harold noted, was a violent man, not above striking his aides, and given to drink and opium.

You [Loraine] feel he is something reliable and solid. I think him infi-nitely untrustworthy and sly. Again, you believe, somewhere, in the Persians. I think them the most contemptible race on earth. You believe in good relations as something positive: I only believe in them as some-thing negative, i.e. they won't get us what we want, but they prevent us being bothered by pin-pricks. The Persians have heaps of pins (Gulchek, Capitulations, Gulf) which they could use if they wanted to be nasty. Good relations prevent them from being nasty: but it doesn't make them nice . . . I feel the whole, in truth, is pretty bloody . . .

Backtracking marginally, Harold continued: 'He [Reza] remains a mystery to me. I still think he is a sly bully and nothing more. But I admit that these qualities may yet save poor Persia. But it is all rather hopeless!'[24]

'You see this sort of life is really what I like best,' he told Vita: 'work, riding, hot weather, reading, writing, bathing. But it seems to have no point without you.'[25] There was much work, but also much leisure time. Apart from reading, writing, bathing and riding, there were innumerable paper chases and tennis matches, as well as playing host to a steady stream of visi-tors, snapping up bargains at bazaars; and quite a few poker games. In August a 'slim Adonis' arrived by the name of Buchan-Hepburn: 'Amazingly beautiful'. Harold's hopes were raised as 'he was intimate with some of Eddy's [Sackville-West's] friends'. These hopes were soon dashed when it became apparent that 'he was not in the least b.s.', as he explained to Vita.

There was also Leigh Ashton, a visitor who turned up in February 1927. They slept in the same room, but 'No,' he reassured Mortimer, 'I didn't sleep with him.' In fact, he found Ashton rather a bore. 'But in principle I like him.'[26] Harold's constant companion was Gladwyn Jebb, third secretary at the Legation. 'His eyelashes do not make up for something rather unyielding in his personality – something a little too heterosexual even for me.' 'Charming and handsome . . . normal and manly, which is also a good thing. We ride together & shoot woodcock in ruined gardens & motor after gazelles.'[27]

In March 1926 Vita arrived, having negotiated successfully the perilous overland journey from Baghdad. Harold greeted her in a snow-covered village on the Persian frontier late at night. 'Wild excitement,' he rejoiced at being reunited at last with Vita, who was wearing 'a little fur cap' and cradling 'a Saluki [Persian greyhound] on her knee'. Mortimer arrived four weeks later. Tehran did not impress Vita: 'except for the bazaars, [it] lacks charm . . . it is a squalid city of bad roads, rubbish-heaps, and pariah dogs'. They attended the Shah's birthday. Harold – who detested dressing up for official ceremonies – in '[full] uniform and gold lace, little sword getting between his legs; Vita derisive, but decked in emeralds; escort in scarlet and white'. There were numerous expeditions to the countryside, where they found the local flora and shrubs of much interest. And one long and exhausting journey to Isfahan and then on to Kum, travelling over high tablelands of perhaps six thousand feet. On 25 April they witnessed the Shah's coronation. There was much bowing and scraping. 'Now what can be more absurd than a coronation?' Vita asked, as she watched the Shah advance imperially towards the Peacock Throne. 'With his own hands he removed the cap from his head, with his own hands he raised and assumed the crown, while two ministers stood by, holding the dishonoured tiaras of the Kajar dynasty. Then from outside came a salvo of guns, making the windows rattle, proclaiming to the crowds in the streets that Reza Khan was King of Kings and Centre of the Universe.'[28] Vita left on 1 May, but would return the following February.

Vita's departure has been described as 'a watershed in their marriage'. The farewell scenes were painful and tear-ridden. Harold was overcome with 'a giddy agony, which made the whole house swing and wobble'. He cried incessantly, tears pouring down his face, 'splashing on the dark floor'. He vowed to Vita: 'Oh my dear, we can't go through this again. It is mad to inflict such suffering on each other.' Vita was equally distressed. 'I feel lightheaded with pain. Never, never, never, again. I cannot bear it, and if Providence forgives me for having tempted it and allows me to be with you again, we will not leave each other any more . . . I simply can't live without you.'[29] A turning-point in their marriage? It would be offensive to challenge such deeply felt emotions. But the logic of their relationship meant that it would be Harold who would have to make the most agonising of decisions. As there was no prospect whatsoever of Vita agreeing to traipse after Harold from one embassy to another, he would have to decide whether to abandon or to continue his diplomatic career – for which he was most eminently suited. Would he be able to withstand the pressure? 'So my dear Tray,' Vita promised, 'you may expect to have us with you again before so very long, and we'll all be happy again, and we'll see what we can do to keep Harold in England, though he's very stubborn about it so far – and more determined than ever to be an Empire-builder'.[30]

In July 1926 Loraine left Tehran for a new appointment, Athens. At his farewell party Harold made his familiar 'Empire builder's speech', one that made Mortimer 'almost sick . . . and aroused Tray's anti-virility complex'.[31] His replacement, Sir Robert Clive, was not expected until November. In the interim period Harold acted as the Legation's *chargé d'affaires*. Awaiting Clive's arrival, he decided 'to review the present state of Anglo-Persian relation'.[32] He examined the time-honoured axioms of British policy that saw Persia as a bastion of imperial strategy, defending India, pushing back the Soviet Union, maintaining primacy in the Gulf, and protecting, if necessary by force, the Anglo-Persian oilfields. Perhaps the moment had arrived to re-examine and reaffirm these truisms, he suggested. It was the lack of clarification of these principles that made British policy 'so empirical and at times so disheartening', so 'tentative . . . illogical and confused'. The idea that there would soon emerge 'a stable and self-dependent' Persia was, Harold thought, 'chimerical'. Persia, he had no doubt, was on the verge of chaos: the army 'mutinous', the tribes 'restless', the people 'impoverished', the Civil Service 'unpaid, corrupt, and incompetent'. Nor was it possible to rely on the Shah. Capricious and untrustworthy, at odds with the Majlis, his policy of centralisation a failure, Reza Khan would soon lose his throne. Only the Soviets benefited from this abysmal situation, Harold claimed, comparing Russia's influence, 'a healthy weed', with that of Britain's, 'a very frail little seedling'. There was, he hastened to point out, a 'negative value of good relations': 'they produce no immediate positive result'. On the surface, this was a direct challenge to strongly held conventional wisdoms, an invitation to the Foreign Office to rethink its Persian policy. But Harold's bottom line was more than conventional in itself. 'I trust that I have made it clear that I do not for one moment advocate any change in the policy at present being pursued.' His aim was merely 'to dispel any misapprehensions regarding its productive value'.

Harold's superiors, Lancelot Oliphant, William Tyrrell and Austen Chamberlain, were not impressed. Oliphant was outraged at Harold's 'unduly alarmist and not altogether logical despatch', and particularly incensed at his lack of tact and his arrogance in criticising his highly regarded chief, Sir Percy Loraine, Oliphant's cousin.[33] (One must assume that Loraine was also privy to Harold's paper and was no less offended.) Austen Chamberlain had already warned Harold that 'he has no policy in Persia beyond that of Percy Loraine'.[34] So it could have come as no surprise that Chamberlain pooh-poohed the idea of submitting Harold's views 'to a meticulous examination', alluding caustically to the 'doubts and obscurities in Mr Nicolson's mind in regard to the purpose and principles' of British policy. Unlike Harold, he believed in the Shah's ability to survive (as he did until 1941, when he was sent into exile by the British and the Russians) and strongly approved of Reza's policy of centralisation. Chamberlain framed British interests in much the same manner as Harold, though in more general terms. And like Harold, he argued for more of the same, but in a more direct, unambiguous way.

> To sum up, good relations, which in Mr Nicolson's opinion do not lead anywhere and are merely negative, are in my opinion the key without which no doors open, but with which most doors open sooner or later. The cultivation of good relations is in fact the first condition for the attainment of the ends which HMG have ever in view, whether positive or negative. Rightly understood and practised it is not a passive but an active and constructive policy, upon which all else depends.

It was not so much the contents of Harold's paper that grated upon Foreign Office ears as the style in which it was presented, its haughty and self-assured phrasing. In the strait-laced atmosphere of the Foreign Office, such audacity was considered unbecoming for a mere *chargé d'affaires*. 'If Mr Nicolson were a fool, I should remove him,' Chamberlin minuted.[35] Harold's reputation for cleverness, or perhaps being too clever by half, had saved him – for the time being!

Not for one moment did Harold regret having provoked his masters. If he had annoyed them, he was equally irritated by their over-the-top reaction. He let off steam to Mortimer:

> It [his paper] merely tried to tell the truth & diminish some of the cant in which we endeavour to hide our impotence & lack of purpose. It was quite calmly and moderately written but it provoked a reply in which I could detect the hand and brain of our beloved Foreign Secretary & from which I could detect that the latter was seriously annoyed. You see they don't like the truth at the FO. They like to be

told that everything is going quite splendidly. For instance I said that our own policy of doing nothing in Persia was doubtless inevitable owing to the difficulty of doing anything: that there was no harm, if we liked, in calling this absence of policy 'the policy of good relations and non-intervention': but then the FO must realise that the Persians didn't understand good relations, and that our policy was therefore entirely negative & unproductive.

Nicolson then paraphrased Chamberlain's response, which lauded 'the important results obtained by Sir P. Loraine's patient and understanding interpretation of the intentions of HMG'.

Doesn't that make you wild, Tray? What would Sir A. Chamberlain reply if I asked him 'What important results'. There *are* none except in Loraine's own despatches. I must say it is rather irritating to see the suggestibility of the herd reflected in the mind of our Foreign Minister. I really think that the assishness of that man is a public danger: look at the way he toadies Mussolini! It makes me ill. I hate him. So there!

As a final thrust, Harold told of the latest Persian 'prize-packet', its repudiation of an agreement with Imperial Airways for landing rights to service the air route to India.[36]

When free of the Foreign Office, and with his own case clearly in mind, he wrote of the conventional British diplomatist as a timid creature, 'frightened of "causing trouble"'. Of the Foreign Office preferring 'diplomatists who say soothing and optimistic things to diplomatists who tell home truths in defiant language'. Of the 'smugness, rather than outspoken realism', that colours so many diplomatic reports, inducing a 'narcotic quality' that clouds the official mind. Bitter at his masters' inability to rise to his own level of analysis, Harold would not lay his resentment to rest.[37]

His paper, replete with 'home truths', was to have far-reaching consequences for Harold's career. Oliphant, usually sympathetic to Harold's problems, was now highly critical; he could not rely on Tyrrell, an acknowledged enemy; nor could he be counted among Chamberlain's favourites. Reviewing 1926, he thought it 'A bloody year. But I don't regret having come to Tehran. It braced me.' But for what? The fallout from his Persian memorandum coincided with Vita's second visit to Persia. One morning after her arrival Harold woke up 'with a conviction that I shall chuck the diplomatic service. I have been fussing and worrying about this problem for months – and then this morning I woke up with a calm certain conviction as if it had come to me from outside.' A few days later he sensed 'the end of my brilliant career in diplomacy'. It would be no less accurate to state that Vita – egged on by Virginia Woolf – had been 'fussing and worrying about this problem', not for months, but for years. Harold went to see Sir John Cadman, chairman of Anglo-Persian Oil, about a job in the company's London office; but nothing came of his first bid for independence. However, the two Vs' pressure would continue unabated. It was simply a matter of time before Harold succumbed.

At the end of March he and Vita made ready to return to England, but not before they made an adventurous trip across the Bakhtiari mountains.[38] They arrived at Victoria station on 5 May.

On 23 June 1927 Harold's original stab at autobiography, *Some People*, was published. In some ways no less innovative than Lytton Strachey's new style of biography, it remains his most attractive and original book.* Drawing on Max Beerbohm and Strachey, lightly written with a touch of humour, it has lasted well and still remains in print. Deftly combining fact and fiction, he recounts the various stages of his life, from childhood to Tehran, by introducing eight fictitious characters, based on real, identifiable people, and one living person, and shows in a most amusing way how their lives interwined with his. The chapter headings of *Some People* read: 'Miss Plimsoll', based, Harold later explained, on an unnamed typist who had once worked for him in the Foreign Office. (Why it should not have drawn on his two actual governesses, Miss Corrin and Miss Wood, remains a mystery. But then perhaps it did.); 'J. D. Marstock', relied on an old Wellingtonian, J. R. Parsons, and a Balliol contemporary, Harold Handaside Duncan; for 'Lambert Orme', see Ronald Firbank, novelist, dandy and homosexual; 'The Marquis de Chaumont', based largely on Pierre de Lacretelle, but also on Jean de Gaigneron, two of Harold's intimate friends; 'Jeanne de Hénault', the legendary figure who taught French from her fifth-floor flat at 174, rue de la Pompe, Paris, to hundreds of Foreign Office hopefuls; 'Titty' was Arthur Hope Vere, a diplomat, who had served with Harold at Constantinople; 'Professor Malone', drew on D. J. Dillon, a philologist, and Henry Wickham Steed, editor of *The Times*; 'Arketall', unmistakably

---

*The origins of *Some People* lay in an essay, 'Jeanne de Hénaut', Harold wrote in 1924. Published by the Hogarth Press, it was distributed privately. So enthusiastic was its reception by its chosen audience that Harold was encouraged to to write other sketches in the same vein. Once the book was finished, however, Harold decided it was 'not good enough for the Woolfs': he marked it down as 'too silly', unsuitable 'for their imprimatur'. Instead, it went to Michael Sadleir's Constable and Company Ltd. Later, he relented: 'If ever I write a good book, I shall give it to them.' He never did. (Harold to Vita, 31 Dec. 1926, LL, and Nigel to Raymond Mortimer, 13 Nov. 1968, RMP.)

Chippendale, Curzon's jinxed valet; and 'Miriam Codd', an unsuspecting American lady whom Harold had encountered on his way to Tehran.

Harold began the book on the journey to Tehran. He claimed not to take it seriously. 'Reads like babbling idiocy', even after he had taken Mortimer's advice to 'get rid of the A. A. Milne element'. He also scrapped a chapter about Vita entitled 'Atalanta in Bloomsbury'; in fact, Harold explained, 'I shall cut you out of all the stories. Too sacred.' Although he insisted it was 'a silly book', he took great pleasure in writing it, '& I think one or two people may be amused by it'.[39]

If he really thought *Some People* trivial – perhaps compared with his earlier works – he must have been equally aware that his mischievous sense of humour, his inclination to poke fun at Foreign Office etiquette, at stuffy officialdom, might harm his career. If so, he was not to be disappointed. Tyrrell assured Harold that *he* had not found *Some People* 'indiscreet' – but could he be trusted? And the implication was that others *had* found it imprudent.[40] 'Ponderous Percy [Loraine]' – he appears in *Some People* as the faintly absurd figure of Lord Bognor in 'Titty' – called it 'a cad's book'. Harold, distressed at being 'in disgrace' with his former chief, readily admitted to his faults: 'I expect you are right about my lack of judgment. Moreover my habit of ridiculing everybody from myself upwards may often land me in appearances of disloyalty.' The coincidence of his Persian dispatch – that 'bids fair to be my swan-song' – and *Some People* – which showed 'that I did not take the F.O. or diplomacy very seriously' – seriously damaged Harold's prospects of professional advancement. 'I loathe the processions and gholams [couriers] and sowars [cavalrymen] and uniform and tail coats and all that – I can't hide my loathing' – not quite the thing to tell Oliphant, otherwise known as 'the Prince of Protocol'.[41] Lack of tact, along with intellectual arrogance, exposing his superiors' phoniness, disdain for diplomatic conventions, were not the characteristics expected of a sound Foreign Office man.

Others were not as fussy. Harold's father, on reflection, thought it '*so* good', but only after he had learned that George V was heard laughing out loud at some of its passages. A brash young Cyril Connolly struck a sour note – in private. Over a meal, he had told Harold that he thought *Some People* 'an important work. IMPORTANT!!' To Gladwyn Jebb, he said that it was one of three twentieth-century novels worth reading, the others being Norman Douglas's *South Wind* and Aldous Huxley's *Antic Hay*. In his diary, however, he deemed it 'a most unpleasant book' that might have been written 'by an undergraduate trying to combine Max Beerbohm and Aldous Huxley with a touch of Beverley Nichols'.[42] Virginia Woolf was far more charitable.

I must scribble a line in haste to say how absolutely delightful I think it – how I laughed out loud to myself again and again. Yet at the same time it is rather serious – I can't make out how you combine the advantages of fact and fiction as you do. I am also jealous – I can't help it – that all these things should have happened to you, not to me . . . You must write another, and for goodness sake, send it to the Wolves.

She cast her net wider, asking questions about 'The New Biography'.

He [Harold] has devised a method of writing about people and about himself as though they were at once real and imaginary. He has succeeded remarkably, if not entirely . . . *Some People* is not fiction because it has the substance, the reality of truth. It is not biography because it has the freedom, the artistry of fiction . . . And the victory is definite enough to leave us asking what territory it has won for the art of biography.[43]

Other distinguished literary figures wrote of it no less enthusiastically. Edmund Wilson, normally a fierce critic of Harold's, wrote that it was 'the one very good book' that he had written. And for a later generation, John Raymond described it as 'his most perfect book'.[44]

Throughout his life Harold claimed to believe that *Some People* was an exercise – albeit a successful one – in trivia, 'the one book of his which old ladies, the proletariat and the Earl of Athlone remembered' – in other words, an assorted mixture of 'bedints' from workers to a minor Royal. It is true that Harold wrote his vignettes in great haste. 'They just live in a drawer of my table and are pulled out when I have an off moment.' But whatever doubts he might have had about publication, it is difficult to accept Harold's later misgivings entirely at face value. *Some People* was an instantaneous success, acclaimed immediately as a minor classic, portraying candidly – perhaps a little too forthrightly for some – the social and intellectual élites of his times. Published simultaneously in Britain and the United States, it was kindly reviewed and sold well, fulfilling Harold's mercenary instinct that 'I must look upon [it] as a means of making money.'[45] The book's success with the general public, and even with Bloomsbury, 'gave him pleasure and surprise.'[46] But equally it earned him a reputation for 'frivolity'. He was a serious man – but would others take him all that seriously? It was a question that hovered above him throughout his public career.

NINE

From Diplomacy to Grub Street

London – Long Barn – the summer of 1927. Harold seemed to be marking time. His position at the Foreign Office was under review, an ominous signal. But these months, free of diplomatic routine in faraway exotic places, also brought a degree of solace to his personal life, his relationship with his sons and with Vita, as he renewed old friendships and extended his social and literary contacts. At the end of June, in the company of Leonard and Virginia Woolf, Quentin Bell and Eddy Sackville-West, the Nicolsons travelled by night train to Bardon Fell, north Yorkshire, from where they would view a total eclipse of the sun, the first for two hundred years. On the journey, 'H. curled up with his head on V's knee.' Apparently, he 'was very kind & attentive' throughout the expedition, though the eclipse itself came as something of an anticlimax. Two weeks later Harold engaged Leonard Woolf in a discussion about imperialism. 'Leonard says it is not whether it is right or wrong, but that it is *practically* impossible. I fear he may be right. But it saddens me as I feel our national genius [expresses itself] that way and that way only.' He remained confident, however, that Britain would be great again 'in intellectual matters'. A few days later he left for Paris where he spent the weekend with Mortimer and took in the Folies Bergères. He met Maurice Couve de Murville, the future French Prime Minister, and signed him on as his sons' French tutor. On his return to London he learned that Nigel had gained a prize for French. Nonplussed, he exclaimed, 'Good God!'[1]

On 20 August Harold's manservant, Moody, brought him a note from the Foreign Office. It said that Austen Chamberlain had decided not to send him back to Tehran, a wholly positive step, but that there was no place for him at the Foreign Office, and that he was to be demoted from Counsellor to first secretary. He was offered a posting in Budapest. Harold thought the proposal 'grotesque' and considered refusing it outright. Vita, no doubt scenting a crisis, was 'very sweet and calm and wise, bless her'. As he had 'no desire to be a Minister or an Ambassador', Harold's first choice would have been to remain in London, working in the Foreign Office, following in his beloved Crowe's footsteps. Now 'Willie Tyrrell' had intervened. He was told that Tyrrell refused to have people in the Office 'who he feels are hostile to him'. 'Will he never forgive me for having seen him in a state of dipsomania at Lausanne?' Harold asked. Humiliated, Harold retired to his study to consider his position. Thumbing abstractedly through Virgil's *Aeneid* he came across the line: 'Greater is the story that opens before me; greater is the task I essay.' But being neither 'superstitious' nor a believer in 'necromancy', Harold remained 'muddled and distressed'. He agonised over his next move, acutely conscious that his Persian memorandum had heralded his 'swan-song'. He refused Budapest on social grounds – as he could neither 'shoot nor dance' – but also for political reasons, as he had been too involved in defining Hungary's frontiers at Paris. He suggested to Walford Selby, Chamberlain's private secretary, that he put the matter 'on hold for six months'.

Two days later he was still agonising. Wandering around the garden, 'calmly and without resentment', he considered his future. 'I have Vita and the boys – and that is more than a compensation for anything material. I have my home and my love of nature. I have my friends. I have my energy and my talent for writing. I shall be free. I can tell the truth. There is no truth now that I cannot tell.' He would write 'a trenchant book' on the conduct and administration of the Foreign Service. Still, he prevaricated. Would you consider Rome? Selby asked him. 'Might consider that,' Harold replied. Nothing came of Rome. (It later came to his knowledge that Sir Ronald Graham, the ambassador at Rome, had vetoed Harold's appointment 'for fear I should laugh at him'. *Some People* cast a long shadow.)[2] He conducted 'long talks about the purpose of life' with Vita and Virginia Woolf, but not, one must assume, 'the purpose of life' at the Foreign Office. Harold still vacillated. On 14 October Selby made a final offer: Berlin. Harold must have realised that it was either Berlin or resignation. Grudgingly, he agreed to be sent abroad, degraded in rank. 'There are few [postings] which I should dislike more – and it is bad luck on my darling. But I won't chuck it if I can. So I accept. Gloomily.' The humiliation clearly rankled. But whatever its shortcomings, diplomacy still appeared to him a noble calling; and more to the point, one best suited to his talents. None of this could bottle up his foul mood. In a fierce temper, he (uncharacteristically) abused his parents 'for encouraging me to go to Berlin'. He left for Berlin on 24 October 1927. Knowing he had disappointed Vita, he wrote: 'Little one, do not be angry with me for being so obstinate and selfish . . . [Diplomacy] is Othello's occupation – and however much it may depress and irritate me, I feel that without it I should become *not* a cup of tea but a large jug of tepid milk.' When Harold finally arrived at the German capital the following day, his mood took a turn for the worse. On entering his apartment at 24, Brücken Allee in north-west Berlin, he found it 'so ghastly that it is almost funny . . . I hate my flat.' He soon improved it by importing a consignment of furniture from home.³

Harold summed up 1927 in a slightly more upbeat manner:

> Not a bad aeon . . . The Hawthornden Prize for Vita [for *The Land*, a long, nostalgic poem of bygone rural life]* and for me the very real success of *Some People* [he had also completed *The Development of English Biography*]. Trouble with the F.O . . . and some disgrace and disgruntling for a bit . . . But all this is nothing as to the joy of my own home life . . . Health good – and morals pretty bad – drink and indulgence a little exaggerated for my age. But not serious. Am definitely getting stout . . . Brain and energy unimpaired.⁴

By the New Year Harold had regained his previous rank of Counsellor. No sooner had Harold arrived in Berlin, than his appetite for the diplomatic life returned. He quickly established easy relations with his ambassador, Sir Ronald Lindsay, a workaday diplomat, but an amiable, good-humoured Wykhamist, a far cry from the strait-laced Loraine. You see, 'I love foreign politics,' he told Vita,

> and I get them here in a really enthralling form. If I chucked them merely for emotional reasons I should feel a worm – unworthy of what is one of the few serious and virile sides to my nature. 'Yes,' you say, 'that's all very well – but what about me?' . . . But somewhere right deep down in you must realise that Hadji's willingness to do hard drudging work merely because it is interesting is a very respectable form of looniness. It should give you, somewhere, deep down a twiddle of respect. Doesn't it? So bear with me my sweet. I won't undergo anything *intolerable* for this idea: but Berlin is not *intolerable* and I can't pretend that it is.

Did Vita give 'a twiddle of respect' for Harold's renewed enthusiasm for diplomacy? Not to judge from the evidence. 'Oh my darling!' Vita remarked, 'I *don't* like perfect diplomatists, no I don't. I like Hadji's soft collars – and

---

*Others have refused to succumb to the bucolic charm of *The Land*. John Carey, Merton Professor of English at Oxford, a former chair of Booker Prize judges and a distinguished literary critic, wrote of it as, 'at best well-meaning minor verse . . . weighed down, like all her writing, by arty pretension'.

his laughing eyes – not that white cardboard round his neck and that severe expression. Oh my darling, where have you gone? and what become?'[5]

The pressure continued. And if Vita softened, there was always Virginia Woolf to stiffen her resolve. 'Have you talked to Harold about giving up silk stockings and gold lace and humbug and nonsense and becoming a sensible man,' she asked. And continued: 'If only Harold would do a man's work there [in England] instead of a flunkey's in Berlin.' At times Harold was compelled to face reality, even if in a roundabout way. 'Look here!' he told Virginia, 'This Vita of mine is not made to be the wife of a diplomatist – not, that is, of a successful diplomatist.'[6] At heart, Harold knew that his time as a 'successful diplomat' was limited.

Germany in 1928 appeared to be on the brink of recovery. Affairs proceeded smoothly, or at least with no undue friction. The Foreign Minister, Gustav Stresemann, was still in office, a key figure in any German government. His prudent strategy of 'fulfilment' of the Versailles treaty, of negotiating treaty revision that by definition worked to Germany's advantage, had reaped rich dividends. The Locarno treaties were still in play; Germany was now a member of the League; the Dawes plan (that scaled down the original reparations agreement; stabilised the German mark after the hyperinflation of recent years; and 'primed' the German economy with short-term loans, mainly from the United States) was in operation, and a further reparations agreement was in the offing. Franco-German relations, if not excessively friendly, were not overtly hostile – and Anglo-German relations followed suit. Harold, smothered by his excruciatingly dull routine at the embassy, yearned for some excitement. 'I hope ardently that some interesting crisis will arise,' he confided to his parents. 'The new German government, however, is so mild and peaceful that I foresee no alarums ahead.'[7]

There were some outstanding issues, substantial in themselves but mostly leftovers from previous agreements. Reparations and the phased evacuation of allied forces from the Rhineland were matters still pending a final settlement. There was also the question of assessing German-Soviet relations, potentially an explosive issue. At times, the Germans could prove awkward. Harold explained to Chamberlain why 'the German Government may have caused you disappointment'. In doubt 'about their own intelligence', they cover up their lack of 'self-confidence' by 'bluster and at times by an over accumulation of facts'. German pride, in tatters after the defeat, is now 'a strained and battered object of extreme sensitiveness', and leads them to construe 'as interference what is a mere request for cooperation . . . Their apparent unreasonableness and ingratitude are to be interpreted in terms of over-sensitive pride.' Harold's message appeared to be that to advance

Anglo-German relations it would be necessary to pander to wounded German pride: 'they will hesitate to do anything for us unless we can offer them in return something more remunerative and more concrete than polite appreciation'. Everything hinged on Stresemann. Without his firm hand, German policy lacked 'definition'. Harold ended his review on a speculative note, for it was common knowledge that Stresemann was ill, perhaps fatally so. Should he disappear from the scene, nothing could be taken for granted.[8]

Recalling his days in Berlin, Harold advised young diplomats to cultivate the society of journalists. 'I am grateful for hours I devoted to talking to journalists in the Adlon Bar. I learned more from them than I did from any other form of social relations . . . It was the journalists who first warned me of the coming of the Nazi movement. Diplomatic field work often misleads.' In November 1929 he reported that the outstanding feature of the recent local elections was the 'emergence of the National-Socialists'. Whether 'red fascists, or left-wing jingoes', they were 'dangerous people', 'akin to the Hitlerites of Bavaria' – an odd, and misleading, comment. He quoted from the 'Twenty-Five Points', their 'vigorous, if utopian' programme, noting its commitment to totally erase the Versailles treaty, to introduce a policy of extreme centralisation; above all, to execute a rabid anti-Semitic programme. Harold saw the danger, even if he couched it in curious turns of phrase. 'The refreshing vigour of the young National-Socialist party,' he began, 'is certain to make an increasing appeal to German youth, who are always impressed by extreme idealism.' Although he considered the internal situation to be outwardly healthy, it showed 'symptoms of septic inflammation'. But was it sufficiently inflamed, sufficiently septic to awaken the bourgeois parties from their 'apparent apathy' and resuscitate the body politic? He left the question unanswered.[9] But as the world economic crisis struck at Germany, German policy took a more extreme path. Harold recorded not only the emergence of the Nazis, but also the initiatives of Alfred Hugenberg, a bigoted German nationalist who controlled a media empire and led the German National Party, and Dr Hjalmar Schacht, the influential President of the Reichbank, that in effect called for the unilateral abrogation of Germany's post-war contractual obligations, and demanded the restoration to Germany of the 'lost provinces' in the East. These instances of direct action, Harold warned the Foreign Office, 'cannot but strengthen the hands of those who are continually contending that democratic institutions are not suited to Germany, and that Government by Parliamentary coalitions means only weakness and confusion of purpose'.

At the beginning of July 1928 Lindsay left Berlin for the Foreign Office, where he assumed the post of Permanent Under-Secretary. His replacement, Sir Horace Rumbold, arrived a month later. In the interim period

Harold acted as *chargé d'affaires* (though he would not exploit the time to write a German equivalent of his by now notorious Persian memorandum). Harold met 'old Rumbie' – as he was wont to call his new chief – at the station. 'He is a nice old bumble bee – and I am quite happy with him. But he is *not* Lindsay – no no.' But Rumbold was 'a bumble bee' with a sting. Appearances deceive. Putting aside his public persona, that of a mild-mannered, suburban bank manager, Rumbold was in reality an astute, hard-headed diplomatist. Few saw with greater clarity the Nazi menace than he, so trenchantly expressed in his well-known 'Mein Kampf' memorandum. Quoting extensively from *Mein Kampf*, he showed that the inner dynamics of Nazism would inevitably lead to war. On leaving Berlin, Rumbold categorised Hitler, Goering and Goebbels as 'notoriously pathological cases' driven by an 'aggressive nationalism'.[10]

In the course of his duties, Harold met with most of the leading figures of the Weimar Republic, including Konrad Adenauer, Lord Mayor of Cologne, 'a rather remarkable figure', who, it was widely tipped, would 'establish some form of fascismo' should parliamentary government break down.[11] He lunched with President Paul von Hindenburg. 'It was rather fun . . . [he] is an old darling: he has a trick of raising his eyebrows and laughing like a schoolboy: he talks very simply, almost boyishly, but is pretty shrewd . . . A splendid old man.' There was one amusing incident. When Harold translated, on behalf of an Indian guest, a remark referring to the bravery of the Gurkhas as 'sind auch die Gurken', Hindenburg again raised his eyebrows, understandably misconstruing 'Gurken' as 'cucumbers'. The Duke and Duchess of York – later King George VI and Queen Elizabeth – arrived. Harold took them to a golf club for lunch. 'She is really a delightful person, incredibly gay and simple. It is simply a tragedy that she should be royalty.' She spoke 'intelligently about *Some People*, whereas he had clearly only read the Arketall story and got it wrong . . . her charm is quite overwhelming. He is just a snipe from the great Windsor marches.' John Maynard Keynes, 'looking very clean and tidy', turned up with good news. An astonished Harold heard that Keynes had been 'studying "transmitted genius" and has found out that I am descended from Boswell. How funny!'[12]

Harold hosted many figures of note who passed through Berlin: the authors, H. G. Wells, Sinclair Lewis, Dorothy Thompson, Pirandello – 'a simple vivid little old man with sly uncertain eyes'; show business personalities, Noël Coward – 'He is a bounder of course – but I don't mind that when combined with real talent and energy', Ivor Novello – 'completely unspoilt by his success and absolutely *thrilling* about his life', and for whom Harold fostered a '*béguin*' – and Ramon Novarro – 'a film king of little charm'. He frequented the opera, enjoying Mozart's *Don Giovanni* and *Die*

Zauberflöte, Kurt Weill's *Die Dreigroschenoper* (The Threepenny Opera), and Gershwin's *Porgy and Bess,* 'about niggers'. He found 'scaringly funny' Charlie Chaplin's film, *The Circus*, and Al Jolson's *The Singing Fool*, 'most entertaining'.[13] He mixed with local literati, such as Thomas Mann and Emil Ludwig. 'I had an odd luncheon party yesterday,' Harold disclosed. The Ludwigs, Sir Horace Rumbold and his daughter, Constantia, and Eddy Sackville-West arrived on time; Ethel Smyth, the composer and suffragette, aged seventy, verbose, animated and practically stone deaf, made a late entry. Noticeably agitated, her tricorne falling over her eyes, she screamed at Ludwig – and his friends – for having destroyed 'the Old German culture' and brought into being 'the Jewish [Weimar] republic'. Ludwig, understandably, 'was hurt' by these smears. But the 'torrent of invective' flowed on, only to be partially stilled after 'three glasses of Rieslinger Auslee'.[14]

Harold, no doubt, was appalled by Smyth's bad manners. But her comments struck a raw nerve, for he nurtured an inbred prejudice against Jews. Like many others, he must have been mindful of the persistent allegations that Jews dominated Germany's economic, financial and cultural life, out of all proportion to their numbers: that they were seated 'too arrogantly' at tables in fashionable restaurants that had once been the exclusive preserve of senior officers and the social élite of Wilhelmine Germany. He would habitually employ the loaded adjective 'oily' to describe Jews he knew. Harold rated Emil Ludwig 'a rather disgusting creature'. After reading his book, *Juli 1914*, he remarked, '[it] amazes me. That man makes me feel anti-semitic.'[15] This was the least attractive feature of Harold's character. And it worsened with advancing years.

Long Barn was readily accessible to Harold from Berlin. Visits, though regulated by his work, were relatively frequent. Once there, Harold fell easily into an Office-free routine: there was his family, his garden, his cronies and London clubland, and re-establishing his place on the social circuit, pastimes that were never far from his thoughts. Early in the New Year he was summoned urgently to England. Vita's father, Lionel, the third Lord, was critically ill, having contracted pericarditus brought on by pneumonia. Harold, much attached to his father-in-law, rushed over to Knole. He managed to raise Lionel's spirits by reading aloud to him 'The Secret of Father Brown' by G. K. Chesterton. But there was nothing to be done. Lord Horder, the King's doctor, had pronounced Lionel's condition terminal. He died on 28 January. His body was interred in Knole chapel, where a huge crowd attended a 'fine service', mercifully 'very short!' When they returned home, Vita broke down. Apart from the trauma of losing her father, Vita was confronted with the fact that she had lost Knole for ever, no less an emotional shock. Owing to the family's inheritance laws, Knole passed to her 'Uncle Charlie' and from him to her cousin, Eddy. But her childhood obsession with Knole remained. She fantasised to Harold: 'I would be quite ready to take it off their hands. I want Knole . . . I've got an idea about it: shall we take it some day?' When *Orlando* was published Harold encouraged her possessiveness. *Orlando*, he wrote, '[is a book] in which you and Knole are identified for ever, a book that will perpetuate that identity into years when both you and I are dead'.[16]

Ten months after Lord Sackville died, Harold's father became 'seriously ill'. He had been unwell for some time. Again, Harold hurried over to England. Lord Carnock, bedridden and desperately weak, bade farewell to his servants and family. To Harold he indicated how pleased he was that 'I stayed in the Service'.[17] On 5 November he fell into a coma and died. The title passed to Harold's elder brother, Freddy.

Harold's relations with his father had been harmonious and congenial rather than intimate. His feelings can perhaps best be gauged from the filial biography he wrote of Lord Carnock. It set out to express 'Affection for my father. Interest in diplomacy. Love of truth. Hatred of war', to show 'that father was very just to Germany really – & much objected to her being humiliated by the Treaty of Versailles. People will thus be left with the final impression of his essential fairness.' Largely uncritical, interspersed with Harold's recollections of events he had witnessed, it flattered the 'Old Diplomacy' of the pre-war era and its most typical representative, Lord Carnock. Harold later came to rate *Lord Carnock* as his best book. He did not think so at the time. 'It really is a bad book,' he told Vita. It revealed himself 'without trimmings or excuses', he confessed to Mortimer, for what he really was, 'a petty chatty chatterboxy thing. I am Mr Gossip.'[18] He handed in the final draft of *Carnock* a month before he left Berlin – and the Foreign Office: a decision his father would certainly have frowned upon.

When Harold referred to Berlin as not being '*intolerable*', he may well have been alluding to Berlin's racy night life that he was beginning to enjoy. As Christopher Isherwood famously said, 'Berlin meant Boys'. Apart from the Ivor Novello interlude, Harold was involved with Sandy Baird, a feckless Old Etonian who powdered his face and who, in Harold's lurid phrase, 'was an absolute little bum boy'. There was also 'Bobby' (Sharpe), a young American artist and aspiring playwright. 'Very conjugal and bliss,' Harold noted after one encounter. Bobby read to him his play. 'It is very young. Go on with him to Todd [?] and then to visit a haunt in North Berlin.'[19] Many visitors passed through 24, Brücken Allee. Cyril Connolly, 'terribly untidy', 'like a young Beethoven with spots'. 'Cyril and Tray are very suspicious of each other, and stalk round each other with their hackles up like two poodles'. Others who benefited from Harold's hospitality included Gladwyn Jebb, Christopher Sykes, Lord Berners, David Herbert, Victor Cazalet, Edward James and Eddy Sackville-West, almost on a regular basis. Vita came four times. She hated Berlin. All that she saw confirmed her worst impressions of diplomatic life. 'Oh, that filthy, filthy place. How I loathe it . . . This is a bloody place, to be sure; and my feelings which if I gave way to them would be all rebellion and despair.'[20] She brought Ben and Nigel with her during the summer vacation of 1928, and later in the year for Christmas. This last visit coincided with the arrival of Leonard and Virginia Woolf, accompanied by Vanessa Bell and Duncan Grant. The visit was a disaster. Duncan was 'approached' by Eddy, with Harold looking on. Leonard refused to attend political meetings that Harold had arranged for him. (Although Harold admired Leonard Woolf, Woolf did not hold Harold in high regard.[21]) Virginia detested Berlin and Harold's diplomatic 'posturing' as much as Vita. Vanessa refused to consider 'the Nicholsons [*sic*]' – as she insisted on calling them – as authentic Bloomsbury types: '[they] seem to me such an unnecessary importation into our society'.[22]

In October 1928, Ramsay MacDonald appeared, accompanied by Oswald and Cynthia Mosley. One evening Harold took the Mosleys and Frau Stresemann on a tour of Berlin night life. 'Cimmie and I had never seen anything like that night in our lives. In several of the many resorts to which we were taken, the sexes had simply exchanged clothes, make-up and the habits of Nature in crudest form. Scenes of decadence and depravity suggested a nation sunk so deep that it could never rise again.'[23]

A familiar pattern emerged. Once official work was over – or perhaps when Harold was at a loss how to entertain his guests – he would introduce them to Berlin's by now notorious night life, with which he was all too familiar. 'We went to the sodomites ball [*Ball der Jugend*, an annual affair],' Vita revealed to Virginia Woolf. 'A lot of them were dressed as women, but I fancy I was the only genuine article in the room. A very odd sight.' Perhaps they would frequent the 'Cosy Corner', a favourite hang-out at Zollenstrasse 7 patronised by homosexuals and rent-boys. Eddy Sackville-West talked of being 'dragged about at night from one homosexual bar to another. The behaviour is perfectly open . . . I was kissed indiscriminately . . . The night passed like a dream.' Christopher Isherwood, who immortalised Berlin's free-and-easy lifestyle of the 1920s, recalled that many homosexuals thought working-class bars – the 'Cosy Corner'? – too 'rough' and 'felt safer in the high-class bars of the West End which only admitted boys who were neatly dressed . . . [here] there were also dens of pseudo-vice catering to hetero-sexual tourists. Here, screaming boys in drag and monocled Eton-cropped girls in dinner-jackets play-acted the high jinks of Sodom and Gommorrah, horrifying the onlookers and reassuring them that Berlin was still the most decadent city in Europe.'[24] Could these be the kinds of haunts that Harold introduced to his guests?

Throughout 1928–29 Harold had been receiving the broadest hints from Vita (and Virginia) that he should leave the Diplomatic Service, abandoning the world of flummery for a calling better suited to his talents. Even Frau Stresemann advised him to leave diplomacy, as he was 'clearly unsuited for it'.[25] But what else could he do? Above all, he needed a secure income. Living beyond his means, he became 'very depressed' about money, a condition made more hazardous by Lady Sackville's bizarre behaviour. 'I funk all bills,' he told Vita.[26] Did he fancy a political career? He daydreamed of behaving 'with conspicuous courage' during a debate in the House of Commons. 'Tom' Mosley advised him to return to the Foreign Office for two years and then enter politics as a Labour member. 'He will speak to Henderson about it,' Harold gratefully noted. He felt at one with the new Labour government, at least conceptually. 'I fully agree with Labour policy in regard to Foreign, Dominion, and Imperial affairs. With my head I also agree to their socialist policy, only my selfish interest makes me frightened they will impoverish me.' If only Mosley would go to the Foreign Office, then 'I might have a chance of getting home'.[27] Although Harold favoured the amalgamation of the Consular and Diplomatic Services, a positive move in itself, he was no less concerned about the dumbing down of the Office, of the dreadful prospect that 'in a few years Embassies will be composed of trade experts and coal experts and mining experts and labour experts and electrical experts, all drawn from places like the Treasury and Board of Trade and that the regular diplomatic staff will degenerate into mere clerks'.[28] Yet for all Harold's doubts, the moment a rumour cropped up about a new diplomatic appointment that would advance his career, the agonising began afresh.[29]

On 22 July Harold wrote to Vita that Bruce Lockhart, 'an attractive scamp', previously a Foreign Office colleague and currently masquerading as 'Londoner', the gossip columnist of Lord Beaverbrook's *Evening Standard*, had brought him the offer of a job from his boss. It would entail writing and editing a page 'like the Londoner's Diary'. Harold set out the pros and cons. 'It means London, liberty, scope, salary, freedom of time and opinion, plus a tremendous score over the Foreign Office.' As he told Lockhart, 'Being Counsellor in Berlin is very like being First Secretary at Stockholm. I am a stepney [spare] wheel of a car that is seldom taken out of the garage.' There was another point, unsaid to Lockhart but preying heavily upon

Harold's and Vita's minds. B.M. was out of control: her violent behaviour and abusive language had brought them to the verge of despair.* 'She has done nothing but attempt to ruin us financially and morally . . . We have decided not to stand this humiliation any longer and plan to take "drastic action",' meaning cutting loose from B.M.'s purse-strings. But the cons were no less telling. Harold had no desire to be associated with Beaverbrook's unsavoury reputation and the *Evening Standard*'s 'dirty politics'. Would such an affiliation stymie his chances of a political career? Would it not erode his reputation 'of being a high-brow of unquestioned integrity'? Also, he was bad at 'lobbying', useless at 'worming things' out of cabinet ministers. Nor, he stressed, would he surrender his freedom of expression or 'abandon his radical views.' In a somewhat muddled fashion, he put his so-called 'radical views' on record:

> I am by politics and conviction a left-liberal or right-labour. On the one hand I am a pacifist and believe strongly in good relations with America at any sacrifice. On the other hand I am an Imperialist in the modern sense of the term, and I am by no means a passionate free-trader. I could not agree to express opinions which conflicted with these principles.

Lockhart brokered the deal with Beaverbrook. Despite Beaverbrook's 'unsavoury reputation', his dictatorial telephone interventions to his editors, his impish, often malicious ways, he allowed remarkable leeway to the journalists and cartoonists he employed. There was some haggling over Harold's salary. Beaverbrook offered £3,000 a year. Harold held out for more, but eventually accepted the offer. By mid-September, after meeting and dining with Beaverbrook, and again insisting that he must retain his 'political independence', the compact was struck.[31] On the whole Vita approved of the offer, as did Virginia and Leonard Woolf, who had also been consulted. Virginia had never disguised her feelings. She wrote to Harold saying, 'She feels almost ashamed of having a friend who is married to man who will (not "may" mark you) be an Ambassador.' Overjoyed at the news, Virginia cross-examined Vita: 'But what I want to know is as much as you think discreet to

---

*Vita suffered many tongue-lashings at the hands of her mother. At a meeting at the family's lawyers, to discuss Lord Sackville's estate, Bonne Mama raged hysterically at her daughter. 'Thief and Liar!' she screamed, threatening to physically assault Vita, demanding that Vita return all the jewels she had given her. Harold recorded that 'BM has renounced the trusteeship' that guaranteed Vita's annuity. This was not so. But Vita, visibly shaken, decided never again to accept gifts, either in kind or of money, from her mother: a courageous decision, but one difficult to uphold in all circumstances. (See ND, 14 Feb. 1928; Vita to Harold, 26 Nov. 1929, LL; and Glendinning, *Vita*, 192–93.)

say about Beaverbrook and Harold's job – what is it? What is the pay? – my word I think you are lucky to have brushed off the bloom of diplomacy and then off to another flower while the sun still shines – What a stallion, what a young blood mare you are, to fling your head, kicking your heels.'[32] The Foreign Office was told. Lindsay, the Permanent Under-Secretary, took the news 'calmly, and very sympathetically', graciously wishing Harold 'all success in your new occupation'. Rumbold, whose opinion Harold valued more than most, expressed his 'deep regret'. You could have had 'a glittering career', he reminded Harold, 'certainly you could have been a young ambassador'.[33]

Of course, Harold needed no reminding of the 'glittering career' that he had let slip from his fingers. For the remainder of his working life he wondered whether or not he had made the right decision. And never more so than in the immediate period before he broke finally with the Foreign Office. In one obvious sense he had been hustled into quitting diplomacy. And for what? It nagged at his conscience. Had fate played him 'a scurvy trick'? He had heard that the Athens Legation was about 'to be filled'. He saw before him the (certain) prospect of 'Five years in Athens and then an Embassy'. 'Poor Hadji,' he sighed, 'not much of a success in life. Everybody will think me quite, quite loony' – and all for 'having become a hack-journalist'. After burying himself in the *Evening Standard* and *Daily Express* for three days he was filled with alarm. He felt unable 'to write the sort of sob-stuff they want . . . I do loathe slush'. 'Now what shall I do in such a *galère?*' he asked Vita. Mortimer was another confidant. So,

I enter the service of Lord Beaverbrook. God give me, in his goodness, moral courage. What I fear is the thin edge of the wedge. Requests that I should just write a paragraph about this or that: requests which it [would] be ungracious to refuse, but the acceptance of which will edge me further & further away from independence & integrity . . . Anyhow I am going to write a play. That will illumine the darkness.

In truth, he pined for the diplomatic life: 'The tug always at my heart of diplomacy in all its forms.' Even the Viceroyalty of India was not excluded from his private ambition.[34]

Two factors finally tipped the scales in favour of hack journalism: the need to escape from B.M.'s financial embrace; and the necessity to put an end to the protracted separations from Vita, a problem that had seemingly been smouldering for ever. 'Once she has repaid the Knole capital, we shall take nothing more from her. Not one penny,' Harold vowed. This proved to be in large measure a paper declaration. Although Harold's financial situation marginally improved – he was set to write twenty-four articles for

Vanity Fair for 'untold sums', in fact, £1,200; and had contracted to deliver five talks on 'People and Things' for the BBC at fifteen guineas a broadcast – his dependence on B.M.'s largesse never entirely faded: hampers of food from Selfridges would arrive, as would consignments of furniture to adorn the Nicolsons' new acquisition, Sissinghurst Castle, purchased with moneys raised by the family's trustees, with B.M's consent.[35] Harold always found himself hard pressed for money – a perennial worry – and felt that he could amplify his capital in the outside world, an optimistic assessment as it turned out. (Of course, being hard pressed for money is a relative matter. While Harold continually complained of living just above the breadline, the Nicolsons were served at Sissinghurst – an estate of some 400 acres – by a cook, handyman-chauffeur, two secretaries, a lady's maid, a valet and three gardeners. They also maintained for a number of years a flat in the Inner Temple, and a yacht, the *Mar*.)[36] Although Harold was now to return to England, in a curious way the Nicolsons still led separate lives: Harold working and socialising hard in London; Vita, increasingly retreating into a reclusive existence at Sissinghurst.

Harold left Berlin to a round of farewell dinners. At the Buccaneers' Club forty guests assembled to hear 'old Rumbie' make a provocative speech which left 'a lump' in Harold's throat. The Foreign Office ought to have been able to retain Harold's services, said the ambassador, in the presence of the press, 'had they possessed more imagination'. Three days later there was another dinner at the embassy. 'I am presented with a cactus. The end of my diplomatic career,' Harold noted – perhaps interpreting the going-away present as symbolic.[37] He left Berlin on 20 December to move into 4, King's Bench Walk, Inner Temple, a flat that became available to him because his brother Freddy, a barrister, had relinquished his right to it. Vita had spent some time preparing these rooms for Harold's arrival. 'I know what she has done,' Harold responded. 'She has put his modern pictures in the bedroom. Well, I expect she's right. Get a large basin for me to be sick into.' Was this tongue-in-cheek? He had previously thought that 'KBW is BEDINT', adding graciously, 'But I think I shall like it.' Conveniently situated for Harold's future work as a journalist, it was, by most standards, a prestigious and attractive address. Turning south from where the Strand merges into Fleet Street, one enters into a maze of courtyards and passageways, open spaces and broad avenues and carefully cultivated gardens: King's Bench Walk remains a pleasing tree-lined avenue leading down to the Embankment and river. There was an added bonus. As an Oxford MA Harold enjoyed certain privileges at Inner Temple: 'rooms without question; parking rights; lunch in Hall; food sent over from kitchen; use library; use chapel'.[38]

On 1 January 1930 Harold joined Beaverbrook's team at 47, Shoe Lane, the offices of the *Evening Standard*. Encounter with his new colleagues confirmed his worst suspicions. 'They didn't seem in the least pleased to see me. So unlike the FO or an Embassy. That's what happens when one works with bedints, they are all so tied up and *manquent d'amabilité* [lacking in politeness/courtesy]. Not hostile exactly, but always on the defensive.' 'End of a bloody aeon,' was how Harold summed up 1929.[39]

TEN

Interregnum

Harold persevered at Shoe Lane for twenty months. As a contributor to the *Evening Standard*'s 'London Diary', he was little more than a sophisticated gossip columnist, covering the social, political and literary scenes. After only two months on the job, he realised that he was 'not much good as a journalist'. All the assets he possessed, a first-class education and a certain facility for writing, were wasted. 'The things I know and care about are of little interest to the British Public.' Quite useless at 'bothering people', the information that he did manage to squeeze out of his friends was 'not generally of a nature to be published'. Even more, his worst fears had transpired. Not only was he working with 'bedints', he was pandering to their insatiable appetite for tittle-tattle. Harold knew it – and hated it. 'I simply loathe working for a newspaper . . . I feel I simply cannot stand it for another two years . . . it covers all my days with a dark cloud of shame.' If he found his work repugnant, some of his colleagues were no less so. George Gilliat, his editor, he spurned as 'a horrid man, a cautious and sly man'. By August 1931, pleased that his last days as a 'London Diarist' had finally arrived, Harold registered his delight at leaving 'that urinal of futility'.[1]

For all that, the 'London Diary' was the prelude to a long and distinguished journalistic career, albeit now on Harold's own terms. He began reviewing for the *Daily Telegraph*, fifteen books a month, which brought in a welcome £1,000, and later – from 1949 to 1963 – for the *Observer*, a trade that he honed to a fine art, though he seldom reviewed novels. In December 1938 he accepted an invitation from Wilson Harris to write for the *Spectator* a weekly op-ed feature. 'Marginal Comment' appeared for the next fourteen years, 670 pieces in all.[2] At the same time, Harold began to broadcast regularly for the BBC, though not without some clashes with its creator, Sir John Reith, by temperament 'neither subtle nor supple'. Harold was scheduled to give a series of talks on 'Literature', but he found no common ground with Reith. 'The man's head is made entirely of bone and it's impossible to talk to him as to an intelligent human being,' Harold tartly remarked. 'Wants me to induce illiterate members of the population to read Milton instead of going on bicycle excursions.' Despite these run-ins, Harold went on to become a regular, and popular, broadcaster. His proficiency as a broadcaster and public speaker lent him a national standing. But he did not survive Reith's authoritarian regime for long. His series of topical talks, 'People and Things', was brought to an abrupt end when Reith refused to allow him to mention the forbidden novel, *Ulysses*. Harold profited greatly from his role as a publicist; but he remained ambivalent about his new means of livelihood. In this way, he once concluded, 'we increase our fame and lower our reputation'.[3]

It is fortunate that Harold's crude description of Shoe Lane never reached the ears of Lord Beaverbrook. Depressed by the fatuous trivia he was forced to write about, and always apprehensive about working for Beaverbrook, his relations with his chief were also coloured by his political choices. Harold had elected to join Oswald Mosley's 'New Party'. They were, of course, friends of long standing. Mosley, previously a Conservative MP, was returned to Parliament as the Labour member for Smethwick in December 1925. During the 1920s he and his wife Lady Cynthia, Curzon's daughter, had acquired something of a 'gilded couple' reputation, decorating the smart set. Handsome, rich, an inspiring orator, and claiming to speak for the 'Lost Generation', Mosley was widely tipped as a possible leader of the Labour Party. In November 1929 he had been appointed to the Cabinet as Chancellor of the Duchy of Lancaster in Ramsay MacDonald's second administration. The following May, at odds with his colleagues over how to deal with mounting unemployment and the economic crisis, he resigned from the government when his 'dynamic' recommendations for economic recovery – which focused on massive state intervention to stabilise prices, regulate tariffs, control banking practices, and to set in motion public works to expand domestic purchasing power – were rejected as impracticable by both the Cabinet and the Party. So in March 1931 he launched his 'New Party' that quickly degenerated into the British Union of Fascists. Overly ambitious and self-seeking, Mosley's political objectives were offset by his arrogance, self-confidence and lack of judgement.

Harold's decision to link his political fortunes with such a suspect character as Mosley was not to Beaverbrook's liking: he was running his own crusade, 'Empire Free Trade'. Beaverbrook thought Harold was making 'a mistake'. Wait, he advised. Aiming to 'obtain control of the Conservative Party', Beaverbrook promised his unhappy gossip columnist 'a safe seat and a fat job'. Harold, glum and obstinate, refused outright. 'Go to Hell with you Harold,' Beaverbrook retorted, 'do what you like and my blessings are with ye.' They parted, Harold agreeing 'not to boost you [Mosley] unduly in the *Evening Standard*. Later, Beaverbrook hinted broadly that Harold might have the editorship of the *Evening Standard* if only he were to abandon Mosley. But once again, Harold refused to rise to the bait.[4]

Harold was bent on pursuing a political career. This had always been his aim. For him, 'Londoner's Diary' was little more than a convenient stopover, particularly as Mosley, while still a member of the Labour Cabinet, had virtually promised him a seat in Parliament in the Labour interest. After his resignation from the Foreign Office, each of the major parties had approached him. But he was already committed to Mosley's New Party – and not only for reasons of personal friendship. Many well-meaning people were attracted by Mosley's (Keynesian) economic programme. Harold had given it public recognition when he praised it in a BBC talk. Vita – who 'loathed Tom. He gives her the creeps' – readily acknowledged that Harold had joined Mosley 'out of conviction'. As did many others, including Allan Young, John Strachey, the Sitwells, Cyril Joad, Peter Howard, the rugger star, and Ted 'Kid' Lewis, the champion boxer. Other famous names flirted with Mosley, Maynard Keynes, Lloyd George and Churchill among them.[5]

It has been suggested, however, that Harold attached himself to Mosley for less commendable reasons. As one of a number of 'exotic intellectuals and literary figures', he apparently felt the attraction of 'the weak . . . to the strong' to be irresistible; or as one observer more picturesquely put it: Harold was 'wetter than the wettest sponge in a full bath'. And further, that as an active homosexual he was drawn 'to the manly and virile youths of the better classes' that he introduced to the New Party.[6] There is no convincing evidence to justify these speculations. Harold had never lacked sexual partners, and was certainly not in need of a volatile political framework to augment his conquests – in any case, a most dangerous path to take! Nor was the political scene wanting in 'strong' leaders. Harold backed Mosley because he was young, dynamic, charismatic. In the political firmament, he shone brightly. But more than anything, Mosley had drummed up a compelling answer to the political malaise that had struck Britain down.

These years saw a widespread feeling that the current political system had failed. Democracy 'is dead', Mosley proclaimed. Harold agreed: 'and so it is for me too.' He was present at a gathering attended by Oliver Stanley, Walter Elliot and Bob Boothby – leading lights of the Conservative Party – and Mosley. 'They talk about the decay of democracy and parliamentarism . . . They discuss whether it would be well to have a Fascist coup.' Who would save England? Harold conjured up a fantasy scenario – a Fascist coup orchestrated by Mosley? – with Ramsay MacDonald and J. H. Thomas interned on the Isle of Wight and 'the roll of drums around Westminster'.[7]

Such was Harold's faith in Mosley's abilities that in his novel, *Public Faces* (1932), he envisaged a future Mosley administration, ready and able to resolve the crisis in Britain's affairs during the 1930s.

Harold greatly admired Mosley, who, he considered, was 'striving to achieve an era of Tory socialism'. He also found Mosley's 'revivalist' barnstorming style breathtaking. There he goes, 'striding up and down the rather frail platform with great panther steps and gesticulating with a pointing, and occasionally a stabbing, index', whipping up 'real enthusiasm [so that] one had the feeling that 90 per cent of the audience were certainly convinced at the moment'.[8] Still, Harold was beset by certain doubts about the New Party's strategy, its final goals, its methods of putting across its case. Harold urged Mosley to adopt 'a new attitude of mind', to cultivate 'an intellectual appeal': in one rare moment of fancy he saw himself (and Cyril Joad) as the 'philosopher-kings' of the New Party.[9]

The formation of a National Government in August 1931 led Harold to reappraise the New Party's strategy. Fearful that it would fall between two stools, Labour soaking up 'oppositionist groups', while the National Government relied on 'patriotic' support, Harold argued that the New Party would prosper only if it marched under 'the National banner'. But this was too tame for Mosley: he was all for activism, for doing something 'dramatic'. Harold advised caution, fearful that the Party would draw on 'eccentrics', 'the disgruntled', and other undesirables; and that 'our candidates will be of the inferiority complex type'. 'The curse of our Party is that we attract all the ninnies and all the bores,' Harold noted gloomily. Was Harold thinking also of the Prince of Wales, who had indicated his support for the New Party, and whom Mosley wished to recruit as a high-profile member? An indignant Harold urged Mosley 'not to be so foolish or unscrupulous'. Troubled at the way the New Party was developing, he went to see Allan Young, its secretary. Young was uneasy lest the Party be 'forced into Hitlerism . . . He does not approve of the idea that we should meet communist force with fascist force . . . [and] is deeply opposed to the Youth Movement, which, to his mind, is either meaningless or else means disciplined force. I wholly agree with him.' Three months later Harold took a different line. After a violent meeting in Glasgow, the Party's leadership convened to consider its reaction. Mosley insisted on raising a 'trained and disciplined force'. 'We discuss their uniforms,' Harold noted, and suggested, characteristically, 'grey flannel trousers and shirts'. This was not the kind of battledress that Mosley had in mind. He launched his Youth Movement (NUPA), also known, and not without cause, as the 'Biff Boys'. Harold would soon complain that the Party had failed to attract 'the better class of manual workers'.[10]

Despite these misgivings, Harold soldiered on. He drafted the Party's manifesto on foreign policy: he proposed a policy of 'complete internationalism abroad and sacred egoism at home'. It was greeted with 'high praise' and was approved with minor modifications.[11] In August Harold left the *Evening Standard* to become editor of the New Party's weekly, *Action*, an enterprise he undertook 'with great zest'. He was promised a yearly salary of £3,000 with £15,000 a year running expenses, largely paper promises as it turned out. The first issue appeared on 8 October. His opening editorial struck a suitably upbeat note. 'The old world is dead,' he assured his readers; 'from its ashes will arise a new world, more scientific, more human and far more enjoyable. Week by week we shall put before you new vistas into the future. Week by week you will see the sunlight glimmering at the end of the dark forest.' He retained a bevy of distinguished contributors: Christopher Isherwood, Osbert Sitwell, Francis Birrell, Peter Quennell, Christopher Hobhouse, and inevitably Vita on gardening. Harold took charge of the book section, singling out William Plomer's *Sado*, a novel with a homosexual theme set in Japan, for an especially sensitive review. But it soon became apparent that Harold's editorial skills were too highbrow for Mosley's more rough-and-tumble conception of a political weekly. As he bluntly put it, 'the new men necessary to our cause' failed to appreciate Harold's 'literary artistry in writing an article entitled: "Lift High the Marigold"'.[12]

But like the New Party, *Action* was doomed, its circulation plummeting from 160,000 to barely 15,000 within ten weeks. Some of Harold's friends were in despair. '*Action* seems to me about the limit,' wrote Mortimer. 'It's not only squalid but ineffective . . . Altogether the New Party has been grotesque . . . It is depressing to see a person one is fond of making an incredible fool of himself.' Harold too was suffering: 'Hell! Heaven! I am going through a bad period. A period of ill success.' Standing at the elections of October 1931 for the Combined English Universities, he warned his potential constituents of the dangers of a 'proletarian revolt', to be averted only by 'the Corporate, the Organic, State'. His warning was ignored. Dreading the result, he lost his deposit, coming fifth out of five candidates and attracting only 461 votes.[13] Harold's constituency was already a relic of a past era: a two-member seat contested on the basis of proportional representation, its constituents, graduates of redbrick universities, being required to vote by post. As for *Action*'s demise, he acknowledged his responsibility, a combination of bad management and his own unsuitability to run a weekly. Harold began to distance himself from Mosley, at least in the privacy of his diary.

It [the New Party] is not a party but rather a sly little movement. I am loyal to Tom since I have an affection for him. But I realise that

his ideas are divergent from my own. He has no political judgment.
He believes in fascism. I don't. I loathe it. And I apprehend that the
conflict between the intellectual and the physical side of the N.P. may
develop into something rather acute . . . I beg Tom not to get muddled
up with the fascist crowd. I say that fascism is not suited to England.
In Italy there was a long tradition of secret societies. In Germany there
was a long tradition of militarism. Neither had a sense of humour. In
England anything on those lines is doomed to failure and ridicule.

The year 1931, Harold reckoned, had been 'the most unfortunate' of his
life. He had incurred enmities: with Beaverbrook, the BBC and the
Athenaeum. His connection with Mosley had caused him untold harm. His
reputation was in tatters. 'I am thought trashy and a little mad . . . reckless
and arrogant.' Yet his *joie de vivre* endured. 'What fun life is!' he concluded.[14]
Disenchanted though he was with the New Party, Harold gave 'Tom' a
last chance, accompanying him to Rome in January 1932 to inspect the face
of Italian Fascism. They passed through Paris, meeting up at the Hôtel
Napoléon, where Harold found Mosley in his 'blue pyjamas' looking washed
out, having been 'doing *jeux de société* till 8 a.m.' Once in Rome Harold
spent his time boning up on *fascisti* pamphlets. 'My Benzie would dislike
being a fascist,' he told Vita, as he saw a 'Jesuit system', all its 'toddlers in
black shirts'. There was no meeting of minds. Mosley spoke of forming
'Young England' clubs, corresponding to the SS of the Nazis: Harold maintained that the movement must be 'constitutional'. Harold held that Fascism
destroys 'individuality' and 'liberty': Mosley could not 'keep his mind off
shock troops and the roll of drums'.[15] From Rome Harold went on to
Munich and Berlin. Rumbold and his ex-colleagues gave him a warm
welcome, so much so that once again he pined for the diplomatic life. The
last round of German elections had left both Rumbold and Harold with the
strong impression that 'Hitler has missed the boat'. 'His patriotic appeals
fall upon ears too tired and hungry for so potent a stimulus.' No longer
representing 'the soul of Germany', Hitlerism was a 'doctrine of despair',
'a catastrophe' for the country. German politics was simply 'fascinating',
Harold thought. German politics was certainly 'fascinating', but Harold's
reading of it was wide of the mark. At the last national elections held in
September 1930, the Nazis had polled 6.5 million votes and their seats in
the Reichstag had leaped from 12 to 107: from ninth the Nazis had become
the second party in the country. Two months after Harold left Germany, in
March 1932, presidential elections were held, Hindenburg securing 18.6
million votes as against 11.3 for Hitler. None of this indicated that 'Hitler
had missed the boat'. The 'soul of Germany' was still up for grabs. Rumbold

felt, and Harold did not disagree, that 'the only certain thing' about them 'is uncertainty'. A year later Hitler came to power.[16]

By the end of January Harold was back at 4, King's Bench Walk, his mind firmly made up. 'The New Party,' he felt, 'is as dead as a doornail . . . it is no longer new and no longer a party.' He had stuck with it so long out of 'personal affection and belief' in Mosley, but also because he was convinced that only a radical solution could salvage something from Britain's current economic and parliamentary malaise. He abhorred the drift towards Hitlerism, and would not follow Mosley into the wasteland of Fascism. Violence had no place in British political culture. By resorting to it, he predicted, Mosley would be 'detested by a few and ridiculed by many'. Harold did not rule out the prospect of a corporate state in the future, but it would not be brought about by 'direct action'. By training and temperament, he wrote to Mosley, the British have become possessed of 'indirect minds'. They parted amicably. 'The ice cracks at no single moment.' The New Party was disbanded in April 1932; in October, Mosley founded the British Union of Fascists, spelling ultimate ruin to his political career.

Had Harold deserted Mosley? Typically, he thought not, though of course he had, and for the noblest of reasons. Equally typically, Mosley's conscience was clear. Harold, a *vox tremula*, was 'quite unsuited for politics', for the 'rough and tumble of a new movement advancing novel ideas *contra mundum*'. Attracted by the thought, Harold was 'repelled by the process; he loved the end, but could not bear the means'. He should have kept to diplomacy and *belles-lettres*.[17] There was some truth in Mosley's observations. Harold was among the last of the intellectuals to abandon Mosley. Did this signify indecision, or exaggerated loyalty to old friends? It was said, all too often, that Harold possessed 'a soft centre'. Leo Kennedy, the *Times* foreign affairs correspondent, told him that to he also lacked 'balance', that his 'great talents were going to waste', that to be successful one must join 'a political machine'. 'I reply that I loathe success.' Look at John Reith and Samuel Hoare (then secretary of state for India), he told Kennedy, those typically successful men; 'how far better to be a noble failure'. Yes, Kennedy replied, failures may be noble but they lack influence. 'Which is true,' Harold conceded. He made much the same point when he went down gallantly at the Combined English Universities: '[I] feel more than ever glad that I should have courted disaster with the New Party than achieved success under this Tory ramp.'[18] These were not the most convincing of credentials for a budding, ambitious politician.

'See you tomorrow,' Harold cried. 'Still excited about Sissinghurst and not as appalled as I thought I should be. Oh my dear dear love – what fun the

Mars have!' While he was settling accounts with Beaverbrook and Mosley, he and Vita had made an audacious decision, one that called for boldness and vision in equal measure: the acquisition of Sissinghurst Castle, their last, and grandest, home. It was a formidable undertaking: not a castle in the traditional sense of the term, but rather a moated Tudor-Elizabethan manor-house. The centuries had taken their toll: the estate – some four hundred acres – which in the past had been used as a camp for French prisoners of war, a parish poorhouse, and a general junk yard – was run-down, the grounds surrounding the house a veritable rubbish tip. When their youngest son first saw it, he exclaimed: 'But we haven't got to live here, have we? There's nowhere to live.' Apart from the detritus that had invaded every corner, there was no electricity, no running water, no drainage except for sump pits, and not a single inhabitable room. But Vita saw it as a 'Sleeping Beauty's Castle', crying out for rescue. She had decided: 'I think we shall be happy here.'[19]

Long Barn no longer suited Vita's purposes. Rumours, unfounded as it turned out, that a local poultry farmer planned to buy up the fields around Long Barn alarmed her, as it did Harold. Unable to buy the plots of land themselves, they looked for alternatives. In any case, both thought that Long Barn and its garden had been improved to their full potential. So what better than to start from scratch in an old, decrepit house that, moreover, had ancient Sackville ties dating back to Elizabethan times. When Harold reviewed the situation, he stressed this point. 'Through its veins pulses the blood of the Sackville dynasty . . . It is, for you, an ancestral mansion.' There can be no doubt that this family connection weighed heavily upon Vita. Knole had been denied her; Sissinghurst, within striking distance of Knole, would be an ideal substitute. There was, however, the problem of raising £12,375 to close out the deal, together with an additional £15,000 to put the estate in working order. Harold was broke: in debt to the tune of £800, and with the income tax authorities claiming another £3,000. 'God did not fashion me in the semblance of an accountant,' he groaned. 'I am depressed by this.' Spending at the rate of £6,000 a year, approximately double the rate of their joint income, and unable or unwilling to economise, they searched desperately for financial salvation. Eventually, it came from moneys underwritten by the Knole estate. The decision to buy Sissinghurst was Vita's: Harold tagged along, a willing and helpful partner. Sissinghurst belonged to her alone, not Harold, not even jointly. The proof of her authority was 'indelibly branded into the woodwork of the farmcarts and garden tools' in the form of her initials, 'V. S-W'.[20]

Restoring this property was a herculean task. The sale was made in May 1930; by mid-October, the Nicolsons were able to spend their first night there, in the top of the tower, on camp beds, reading by candlelight. Harold recalled his first meal at Sissinghurst. 'I am not an exacting man, but there are four things that I hate. One is soup from tablets; another is sardines; a third, tongue; and the fourth is cheese in wedges.' Washing up by candlelight in cold water was also a new, and alien, experience.[21] Harold was not cut out for the pioneering life. Such was the ruinous state of their new acquisition that the Nicolsons continued to exploit the comforts of Long Barn, utilising what spare time they had to repair the eyesore that Sissinghurst had become. It was two years before Sissinghurst was made habitable again, in fact the process never really came to an end. Vita and Harold lived in the South Cottage, where he set up his study: Vita commandeered the first floor of the tower as her den, a sanctum she obsessively guarded against all-comers, including her sons; Nigel and Ben were quartered in the Priest's House, which also contained the dining-room and kitchen. The stables were converted into the Long Library, known to the Nicolsons as the Big Room. Their cook, Mrs Staples, lived with her family in one half of the Main House; Jack Cooper, their chauffeur-handyman, and his family, in the other. No guest rooms were planned for visitors. A lake was put in; and the arduous task of creating a garden from the rubble began. Harold described it as 'a succession of privacies . . . formal in outline, with a controlled abandon in its planting'. He designed it; Vita planted and replanted it, never satisfied, always experimenting, 'a painter in flowers'.[22] It resulted in one of the great show gardens of England.

The Nicolsons lived at Sissinghurst for the rest of their lives. Long Barn too remained in their possession. They used it until Sissinghurst was ready to be lived in, and hung on to it for a few more years, reluctant to sell. The year 1936 brought financial salvation, though in the most tragic circumstances. Lady Sackville died at the age of seventy-four, bringing to a sorrowful end her perverse, wayward relationship with Vita and Harold. 'Vita is much harassed and shattered, but inwardly, I think, relieved.'

Bonne Mama was cremated, her ashes scattered by Harold into the sea. 'B.M.,' Harold eulogised, 'all who love you are happy that you should now be at peace', as 'a handful of dust' slid out of the container on to the waves. Lady Sackville's death gave the Nicolsons a measure of financial security, at least temporarily. Vita came into her inheritance: a gross income amounting to £5,000 a year: Nigel and Ben were award an annuity of £1,000, granting them independence. They were now under no pressure to sell Long Barn. It was first rented to Charles and Anne Lindbergh, and later used as a home for refugee children during the war. In the winter of 1943 Vita decided finally to sell Long Barn, to 'a film magnate', Harold plaintively noted. Its contents, including some 3,000 books, were sold off, raising £1,471. 'My dear home,' Harold reminisced, 'all the happy days of youth passed among those poplars and meadows.'[23]

After having broken with the New Party, Harold felt like 'a little curly straw upon a brown torrent'. He was pretty much at a dead end. He had heard on the grapevine that his old colleague, Sir Robert Vansittart, now Permanent Under-Secretary, wanted him back at the Foreign Office. It was an intriguing offer. But Harold was determined never again to work abroad. 'No Legation for me,' he assured Vita. There were books to write and an American tour in December was scheduled. Still, the idea tempted him. 'If the request were renewed in November 1933, and I would have some sort of assurance that it would not mean being sent abroad, then I might consider it.'[24] Was he thinking yet again of his revered master, Eyre Crowe, who had spent his entire career as a Foreign Office mandarin?

At the beginning of January 1933 Harold and Vita left for a three-month tour of the United States. It was their first time in America: Harold was to return many times, Vita never. Playing the lecture circuit, individually and together, they would cross the North American Continent from coast to coast, from Canada to the deep South. Between them, Harold calculated, they had travelled 33,527 miles, visited 53 cities, and spent 63 nights in sleeping-carriages.[25] They had come to boost their dwindling finances, though they could not have chosen a worse time, with the United States in the throes of an acute and prolonged economic crisis. Although Harold had met and worked effectively with American diplomats and academics, particularly in Paris, and had been suitably impressed with their down-to-earth professionalism, this would be the first time that he would meet typical Americans on their home ground. Like most upper-class Englishmen of his generation, Harold regarded the United States with mixed emotions: on the one hand, a sense of innate superiority towards his less-worldly American cousins; on the other, a feeling of awe at this awkward economic giant that was surely destined to translate its material assets into political, imperial dividends, inevitably at Britain's expense. It would be a bracing experience.

They docked at Brooklyn on 5 January to be greeted by a battery of cameras and enquiring reporters. To their astonishment, it appeared they were better known in America than in Britain. Harold was billed as 'robust, handsome, witty', 'one of the cleverest men in England'; Vita as 'Junoesque', 'Portia-like', and of course as 'Orlando'. Their lecture agency, Coulston Leigh, had left no stone unturned to promote them as the literary couple *par excellence*, ensuring that their books, *The Edwardians*, *All Passion Spent*, *Public Faces* and *Some People* engaged the public's attention. At their hotel, surrounded by publicity agents, 'Press people arrive. Bootleggers ring up.

Social hostesses ring up', to be followed by another procession of 'journalists, flowers, bell-hops, photographers, telephones'. With no time to unpack
or change, they were shunted off to a suite at the Waldorf Astoria where
they dined with Charles and Anne (Morrow) Lindbergh and other New
York luminaries, the party lingering on into the small hours. Finally, at 1
a.m., Harold retired. His American tour had begun. 'Oh brave new world!'
Harold purred, after his first day in New York.[26]

Harold's favourite lecture topics were 'The Future of Diplomacy', 'English
Biography', and 'Europe and the Postwar Generation'; Vita would lecture
on subjects as varied as 'Travels through Persia' and 'D. H. Lawrence and
Virginia Woolf'. Together – and their joint lectures attracted the most attention – they would enlighten audiences, often of 2,000 or more, on 'What
we think about Marriage' or 'How to bring up Children' or 'Changes in
English Social Life'. In Washington Harold was received at the White
House. He met Alice Longworth, the eldest daughter of Theodore Roosevelt,
and was taken by 'her sense of background', something that he felt was
'missing in this country'. Mount Vernon also impressed him by its 'simple
magnificence', its furnishings indicating 'a high level of culture and taste'.
Not so United States senators, who 'all look stout, solid, blear-eyed and
sulky'.[27] He found Charleston utterly charming, but for old-world reasons.
'The old atmosphere is lazy, untidy, dignified, lotus-eating, anti-noise and
rush . . . It is the most unamerican thing I have met . . . It is not [that]
they are pro-English, or like the English; it is that they *are* English of a
peculiar sort – a sort of West Indian plantation flavour has remained undi-
minished.' He chanced upon another piece of England when he crossed into
Canada on the Peace Bridge, overlooking Niagara Falls. 'I get a lump in my
throat. I am no longer on foreign soil.'[28]

Travelling the length and breadth of America was a refreshing journey
of discovery. Los Angeles was 'a ghastly place', but in Hollywood he met
the stars: Gary Cooper, 'a nice shy quiet modest young man, devoid of any
brains'; and later, Leslie Howard, an Englishman who, to Harold's trained
eye, looked 'like an assistant master at some inferior private school. Glasses
and bad teeth', but for all that, 'a nice man'. Just past Palm Springs, he and
Vita stayed at the Smokey Tree Ranch, the guests of hired cowboys, where,
clad in sensible English suits, they patted horses, enjoyed barbecues, and
were treated to camp-fire singsongs. From there they visited the Grand
Canyon, 'twenty Matterhorns blazing with alpine glow and situated many
thousand feet below one'.[29]

These were exhilarating new adventures. But the lecture circuit could
also be soul-destroying. Harold found the experience, particularly 'all this
slushy adulation', socially very trying. 'I thank God daily that I am not an

1. Harold Nicolson and Vita Sackville-West at a flower show in Sevenoaks, 1914.

Harold at the Paris ace Conference, 1919.

3. Vita in 1918,
painting by William Strang.

4. Violet Trefusis in 1919.

5. Vita with Nigel and Ben at Long Barn, 1924.

6. Sissinghurst Castle from the air in 1932.

7. Vita and Harold at Smoke Tree Ranch, California, 1933.

8. Harold as the New Party candidate for the Combined English Universities at the general election of 1931.

9. Harold after his election as MP for West Leicester, November 1935.

10. Harold and Vita at Sissinghurst, 1938.

The MP for West Leicester setting is lathe ready for an evening's helping in the war production.

12. Harold at his typewriter at Sissinghurst.

13. Canvassing in North Croydon, 1948.

.. Bertrand Russell, Harold Nicolson and Lord Samuel at the BBC before the discussion 'Why defend liberty?' on 24 January 1951.

15. Vita and Harold in 1959.   16. (*Inset*) Harold with Nigel and grandson Adam in 1962

American,' he wrote to his mother: 'they have great qualities of frankness and kindness and cheeriness. But oh my God! the cultured American woman is hell!' At a Women's Club luncheon party in Toledo, a lady remarked that when she first saw the Grand Canyon, her initial thought was: 'My, if only Beethoven could have seen this. You see I am very musical.' In the background President Roosevelt's inaugural speech was being broadcast. Harold: ' "Do you realise that you have just heard one of the most startling pronouncements in the whole of American history." Toledo lady: "Well, isn't that too interesting. Not that I reely care for the radio myself".' Nor, to his mind, were there the right intellectual stimuli. 'Dining with the intelligentsia of Springfield, Mass., the conversation languished.' And he noted, 'the oddest thing about Americans is that they never listen': it was all 'chatter,: interrupt'.[30] Regarding American audiences in the mass, his derisiveness too readily spilled over into an exercise of patriotic flag-waving:

> If you cut out the territorial aristocracy and the types which have gathered round them in England, and also cut out our scholars and intellectuals – one would be left with a residue which would be no better than, and possibly worse than, our audiences. What appals me is the sense that the only alternative to these audiences is either the vulgarity of big business or the morons of the farming community. America seems to have so few alternatives: England so many. [31]

But then, there is no such thing as America, Harold proclaimed; it is 'merely a term for a certain surface of the earth. At best, they are a most unfortunate mistake.' Nor was he impressed with the way the American government was coping with its grave economic crisis. Roosevelt, the innovative New Dealer, was damned as little more than an Episcopalian 'theocrat' and 'a fraud' to boot. 'I have the impression that they are really terrified of the social mess they have created. And this makes them pathetic . . . Poor people . . . One feels that they are all surface rotting plants and cannot stand a storm. Whereas we, with all our faults, are homogeneous and deep-rooted.' He would not let up, even though he could not have been unaware that Britain – where unemployment was rampant and hungry people on the march – was coping less well with its economic crisis. After all, he had closed ranks with Mosley for that reason. Yet he chose to put on show his British stiff upper lip in contrast to those whimpering Americans. 'These people are bust. They have all lost money in the depression . . . They are like spoilt children whining over a cake. They lack character. They cannot take the ups with the downs. They are reconciling me to the Public School Spirit. I am becoming more English and patriotic every day. We are the only people on this earth. Jingoism flames to my head.'[32] Was this the aristocrat in him coming to the fore, remote in thought and feeling from the masses? The patrician always living beyond his means, yet always being saved from bankruptcy by the generosity of others. If so, it was a depressing blind spot in an otherwise compassionate person.

In all likelihood there was one specific aspect of Anglo-American relations that accounted for Harold's superior airs. He had long reconciled himself to the fact that the global balance had shifted in America's favour, that the United States had replaced Great Britain as the world's foremost power. But, he assumed, 'US opinion is unenlightened and clumsy', and 'we, therefore, have got to have patience and wisdom enough for two'. Should an international incident occur, it would be intolerable to have 'the Babbits of the Middle West jumping exultantly upon our face'. It was an all too familiar daydream: London would play Athens to Washington's Rome.

On the whole they found their American trip an enriching experience, above all its enhancing of their 'oratorical powers'. Nor should it be forgotten that they had come to America to make money. The tour 'has been a financial success', Harold reported back to Mortimer. 'Not overwhelmingly so since the living expenses are appalling – but we shall bring back a pretty pile.' On 15 April they embarked in the *Bremen* for England. 'Exhausted, bored, exasperated, amused', were Harold's final, partial words on his American adventure.[33] By the end of the month he had returned to his normal routine, commuting between his flat at King's Bench Walk and his castle at Sissinghurst.

The books Harold had spoken about appeared with enviable regularity. *Carnock* (1930), *People and Things* (1931), *Public Faces* (1932), *Peacemaking* (1933) and *Curzon* (1934) – a book a year! All of these works relied heavily upon his own experiences, his personal recollections, his recorded version of the events he described. Certainly this applies to his diplomatic trilogy – the biographies of his father and one-time chief Curzon, together with his memoir and critique of the peace conference. These books were bound by a common theme. *Carnock* was an act of filial commitment, showing how a traditional and high-minded diplomatist, motivated by the time-honoured code of conduct of the Old Diplomacy, was frustrated and defeated by the alien, aggressive, ultra-nationalistic methods of a parvenu power, Germany; *Peacemaking* shows the failure of the New Diplomacy – 'the diary, shaming as it is, does represent exactly what we all felt and thought and did in Paris';[34] while *Curzon* shows the triumph of the Old Diplomacy over the New. Over and again, Harold would emphasise the dangers of imprecision when conducting diplomacy. The historical message is clear. His often shrewd accounts of events that he had witnessed, his perceptive eye, observing, dissecting, noting the minutiae of his subjects' bearing, mannerisms of speech and dress, and how they typically shed light on the character of a person, lends to these books valuable insights and makes them profitable reading today.

Harold's novel, *Public Faces*, also drew from his own career at the Foreign Office. A modern reviewer would rank it as a curiosity, a period piece. Its characterisation is weak – particularly that of its heroine, Jane Campbell, Parliamentary Under-Secretary at the Foreign Office – its dialogue contrived. It is a story not lacking in drama, however. Against the background of a chaste relationship between Jane and John Shorland, assistant private secretary to the Foreign Secretary, Walter Bullinger, it tells in eerily prophetic terms of a Middle East crisis involving Britain, Persia, an Arab country and a disputed mineral concession, of British jet planes and atomic bombs, of horrific scenes of tidal waves and 80,000 dead when a mysterious (British) atomic bomb accidentally explodes off the American coast, of the Washington embassy being looted in revenge, and finally of Britain squaring up to an international coalition, on the brink of a general war. The crisis is defused only when John and Jane go public about the appalling devastation that would result from Britain's new-found power, thereby releasing worldwide 'mass fear' that inhibits the powers from embarking upon a suicidal war. Harold had perfected the 'deterrent theory'.

His other book, *People and Things*, was a collection of the talks he had given for the BBC, a timely riposte to Reith's impudence.

This remarkable output bears ready witness to Harold's phenomenal self-discipline and fluency in style. But there was one major project that he long contemplated but never realised. It took shape at the beginning of 1934. In February Harold visited James Joyce at his 'stuffy and prim' flat in the rue Galilée, Paris. Inevitably, they spoke of *Ulysses*, ' "Oolissays" as he calls it,' and how, hidden in a prayer book, his *magnum opus* – banned in Ireland, Britain and the United States for its so-called obscene content – had been blessed by the Pope. Surrounded by a group of worshippers, Joyce, Harold sensed, 'has little contact with reality': there was something illusory about him. He reminded Harold of 'a very nervous and refined animal – a gazelle in a drawing room . . . brittle and vulnerable'. From Paris Harold moved on to Munich and Vienna, lecturing to well-read audiences who, he was delighted to note, 'had been influenced by his books'.[35] Encouraged by these polite compliments, his 'self-confidence as well as fluidity' grew. He then retired to Somerset Maugham's Villa Mauresque at Cap Ferrat, picked up 'his beloved Proust', and, suitably inspired, the idea took root that he too would write a *magnum opus*, a multi-volume fictional autobiography. He had 'found himself'. All other plans, or daydreams – returning to the Foreign Office as Secretary of State – were to be shelved to make way for 'THE IDEA'. 'Thus I see six volumes ahead of me – *à la recherche du temps perdu*'.[36]

To his publisher, Michael Sadleir, Harold described in great detail how he envisaged bringing his *magnum opus* to fruition. He would repeat the method of *Some People*, 'a technique which I invented'. Each volume would tell of a central character, sometimes a real, sometimes an imaginary, figure. Around these central personages he would develop either his own ideas and experiences, or the general atmosphere of the 'Victorian, Edwardian, pre-war, post-war epochs'. In his first volume he would bring to life his uncle, Lord Dufferin, and his memories of Clandeboye: other volumes might centre on B.M. and 'Sligger'. This vastly ambitious project would run to ten years and eight volumes. Harold asked Sadleir not to proclaim it to the world, 'since it sounds pretentious, and I may well find, when I embark upon it, that it is beyond my powers'.

No sooner had Harold thought of the project than doubts began to creep in. True, as he conceded, he possessed a superb memory and an acutely observant nature. But was he capable of revealing the whole truth about himself and his contemporaries? Civilised behaviour surely required a degree of discretion. He sought absolute sincerity in his writing, but would not this lead to his 'wounding people less pachydermatous' than himself? 'And once I start introducing fictional situations, I may end by just writing a bad novel.' The only defensible standard was to expose himself 'to any amount of shame but to disguise other people so that they will not be involved in my humiliations'. At all costs, he had to resist the temptation to make his narrative half true. Proust, he thought, had not been honest enough. 'If I do not possess his talent, I do possess far more courage.' But there was another, far deeper, pitfall. He had no doubt that he possessed enough energy and talent to carry the undertaking through, 'but am I sufficiently ruthless? That may be the *pierre d'achoppement* [stumbling-block].' He was not a religious man, but he appealed to a higher authority, probably jocularly but perhaps seriously: 'Please God make me able to do my *magnum opus*.'

Two volumes eventually appeared, *Helen's Tower* (1937) and *The Desire to Please* (1943). The general title of these works, 'In Search of the Past', manifestly echoed Proust. As for the contents, Harold had penned lively histories of his uncle, Lord Dufferin, a nineteenth-century Viceroy of India, and his great-great-grandfather, Hamilton Rowan, a celebrated Irish patriot of the late eighteenth century, but little more. Interesting and informative certainly, written with all of Harold's fluency and skill, but hardly Proustian in scope or subtlety or style. His master-work, however, progressed no further. He mulled over a third volume, one that would deal with the Great War. But he quickly scrapped the idea. 'I do not feel in the mood during this war, to continue my "Search of the Past" series.' Instead, he began a study of the Congress of Vienna, in the hope that it would be 'of some slight value' at the forthcoming peace conference.[37]

In this way, his *magnum opus* petered out. Was this due to a lack of sufficient energy, an absence of talent, or was he simply short on ruthlessness? It was a question he constantly agonised about. Energy and talent he possessed in abundance, though clearly his ambition to reinvent Proust outran his literary skills. But he was deficient in ruthlessness, as he candidly admitted. He was still toying with 'the theory' of entering politics, as he revealingly put it. Harold was sensible enough to appreciate that he would never climb to the top of the greasy pole. But even to reach the pinnacle of his ambition, to occupy the Secretary of State's chair at the Foreign Office, would be beyond his reach unless he vigorously applied more than an average degree of bloody-mindedness and self-promotion. He never did. He once noted: 'I never write letters to the press since all forms of self-advertisement are meretricious . . . Once a civil servant always a civil servant.'[38] Perhaps in the long run this is all to his credit. But it would backfire to blight his political career.

In June 1934 Harold was invited by Elisabeth Morrow to write a biography of her late husband, Dwight, an American corporate lawyer, banker and diplomat, who had died suddenly at the height of his career in October 1931. Harold was acquainted with the Morrows. He had met Anne (Morrow) and her husband Charles Lindbergh on his first trip to New York. But perhaps more to the point, Harold had met Dwight Morrow himself, in 1930, at the time of the London naval negotiations. And although he knew little of high finance, and had only a passing command of American diplomacy, Harold had come to admire Morrow and was keen to take up the offer. 'The idea appeals to me,' Harold immediately responded.[39] He was also tempted because, surprisingly, he was at a loose end, the offer having been sprung upon him when he had more free time on his hands than he cared for. He promptly set to work. His methodology is of some interest. He worked from a large loose-leafed notebook into which he inserted, in strict chronological order, the sequence of Morrow's career, relying on printed sources, Morrow's personal papers (there is no evidence that he consulted other collections of private papers), and interviews with his subject's family and friends. At the back of his notebook, he would add character traits such as 'Humour', 'Mannerisms', 'Dress', 'Family Relations', and so on. Harold's aim, as he said, was to retire to a Greek island and write his biography without reference to any other source except his irreplaceable notebook.[40]

Harold arrived in New York on 21 September 1934, two days before Bruno Hauptmann was arrested for the kidnapping and murder of the Lindberghs' son, Charles Jnr. The publicity generated by this sensational case absorbed America. Daily, the Morrows and the Lindberghs were forced to relive their personal tragedy as the press and radio reported it in ever more lurid detail. This dreadful affair overshadowed Harold's stay, though the family's composure was such that they did not allow it to disrupt the smooth running of their household. The Lindberghs were to become close friends of the Nicolsons. Charles, the 'Spirit of St Louis', was an international celebrity, having, at the age of twenty-five, been the first pilot to fly the Atlantic solo direct from New York to Paris.

Harold began his research at the Morrow estate at Englewood, New Jersey. He worked to a rigid timetable. He rose at 7.30, breakfasted at 8.15, and immediately 'plunged into' the thirty filing cabinets of Morrow's papers until lunch was served at 1.30. It was work again until 3.00, when he allowed himself a break to walk 'through fading woods' until 4.30. After 'tea and ginger biscuits', he was hard at it again until 7.30. He then bathed, dined till 9 p.m. and resumed work until it was time to retire at 10.30. This exacting routine was tempered partly by the luxury of his quarters and the wonders of American plumbing. His suite consisted of a large bedroom and sitting-room, sumptuously appointed, 'connected by a super-bathroom'.[41]

Always a gregarious creature, Harold formed an easy relationship with the family, in particular with Anne, the Morrows' Geisha-like second daughter, 'shy, Japanese, clever, gentle . . . an adorable little person', and her husband, Charles Lindbergh. 'Slim' and 'schoolboyish', the world-famous aviator fascinated Harold. 'On the one hand, he is a mechanic and quite uneducated. On the other, he is shrewd and intelligent,' endowed with 'a sense of humour'. 'Eccentrically rude', his legendary reputation for 'sulkiness and bad manners' was due entirely to his 'loathing of society' that impinged remorselessly upon his privacy. Harold thought him 'a very decent man,' though 'of course, in England he would be a bedint'. Not above injecting a measure of Bertie Wooster-like Englishness into the household, Harold befriended the Lindberghs' surviving son, Jon, training him to say politely, 'Hello, old buffer.'[42] As for the object of his visit, he quickly drew some cutting assumptions regarding Dwight Morrow's character. 'Morrow is a Protean figure,' Harold judged. 'There was about him a touch of madness, or epilepsy, or something inhuman and abnormal . . . He had the mind of a super-criminal and the character of a saint.' Brutally frank thoughts passed through his mind when he met a clutch of 'school-marms' in Pittsburgh who showered Morrow with high praise. 'I longed to say, "this is all nonsense and you know it. Dwight Morrow was a shrewd and selfish little *arriviste* who drank himself to death".' But Harold merely sat there, 'silent and glum'. Yet for all Morrow's failings, Harold felt that he 'was a very great man'.[43] It would take all of Harold's tact and skill and integrity to square this particular circle.

There were occasional distractions from work. Although Harold was inclined to agree with Lindbergh that British class distinctions and class privileges were 'ghastly', his barbed comments about American society reveal a true representative of those distinctions and privileges. The Round Table – an informal circle of New York intellectuals that met at the Algonquin Hotel – invited Harold to dine with them. He was not impressed. 'The conversation was like that of the masters' table at a third-rate private school.' Snubbing the literati, ex-ambassadors and academics present, he went on: 'It is strange that the Americans, who have such a passion for talking, should have no idea of conversation.' He would speak of the 'smarminess of Americans', of their 'eternal superficiality'. 'They know,' he wrote to Vita, 'we possess some quality which they can never attain to and which they admire and resent.' If Harold harboured grave doubts about the intellectual and social graces of Americans, as well as lamenting their shortcomings in the arts of diplomacy, he was forcibly smitten by the vitality of American architecture. 'The new Rockefeller Centre is more lovely than any human contrivance I have ever seen. Immeasurable fountains spurt below: immeasurable perspectives soar, flood-lit, above.' But he could not resist adding to Raymond Mortimer that 'these gigantic phallic symbols would be disturbing – had I not found consolations. Three or four. That is very odd. I think it is my LITERARY REPUTATION.'[44]

After a two-month sojourn in England, Harold returned to America in February 1935. He completed a draft of the book, 110,000 words, at the Casa Mañana, the Morrows' estate at Cuernavaca, Mexico. Reading it afresh left him despondent. 'Heavy as lead . . . it just crawls along in prose.' It was partially Morrow's fault, for although his character was interesting, the things he did were 'very dull'. How was it possible to make 'dealing with New York Underground Railways' exciting? More complications arose. Commissioned biographies hold a built-in problem. Elisabeth Morrow, Dwight's widow, 'a little, neat woman . . . worships her husband's memory'. Would she attempt to control what Harold wrote? Harold thought not, believing that she was 'intelligent enough' not to intervene in such matters. And so it proved. Elisabeth Morrow showed herself to be most accommodating; but there were other interested parties who would not be so unassuming. The House of Morgan and the State Department both intervened:

the former, indignant at Harold's lack of understanding of the workings of Wall Street; the latter, incensed at his shallow handling of the intricacies of American–Mexican relations. This was a formidable combination. Intimidated, Harold lay awake 'in torments of rage'. There was no meeting of minds, principally with 'old J. P. Morgan'. 'You see, I regard bankers and banking as rather low-class fellows.' But the outcome was never in doubt. Harold surrendered. 'I daresay I shall manage to tone it down a trifle', mainly, he rationalised, for the sake of Mrs Morrow. But even after amending it, his finished work seemed to him 'soft and flabby', 'very sugary sort of stuff'.[45]

Morrow came out to guarded reviews. 'A remarkable study,' said one, only to emphasise that 'the financier never comes to life'. It throws 'casual light' on Morrow's financial career, said another, making the valid point that Harold, unfamiliar with American life, looked upon it 'as a modified form of English life'.[46] It was the least successful of Harold's books. And Harold knew it. Unfamiliar with the basic themes of Morrow's life, particularly the dog-eat-dog world of American *haute banque*, but no less with the psyche of contemporary American society, he had strayed too far for comfort from his home ground: the familiar settings of the Foreign Office, upper-class English mores, European history and literature. But above all, he had compromised one of the golden rules that he applied to all biographers and historians. Harold laid down three principles of biography: 'It must be history; it must be true . . . about an individual; and it must be well-written.' Paraphrasing a well-known quip, he noted, 'It is not geography which deals with maps. Biography deals with chaps.' Yielding to the House of Morgan illustrated yet again that lack of ruthlessness that had stymied his plans for a Proustian-like epic; and that would also reflect adversely on other aspects of Harold's career.

By the time the Morrow biography was published, Harold was one year off fifty, 'fifty, filthy fifty,' he blurted out. Now well into middle age, his youthful days were receding ever more into distant memory. He had still not found himself. Would he return to diplomacy or journalism? Would he take his place in the vanguard of English men of letters – with the Proust project still hanging fire? Would he eventually find a rewarding career in politics? Consumed by the notion that he had spread himself too thin, that he had not made a compelling mark in any of his chosen fields, Harold presumed that he was squandering his undeniable talents. 'I am still very promising and shall continue to be so until the day of my death,' Harold groaned, on reaching fifty.[47] These open questions remained – until his final days.

Harold's inner doubts were in no measure reflected in his outward appearance. Although not conventionally handsome, he was an attractive man. He sported a short, neatly trimmed, triangular brown moustache, and was blessed with long eyelashes – 'those absurd eyelashes of yours,' Vita would gushingly say – and twinkling, alert eyes. From afar, the impression might be that he was something of a dandy, an appraisal that would prove illusory upon close inspection. One friend noted his 'Anthony Eden-style black hat, splendid frogged top-coat with Persian lamb collar, well tailored, double-breasted blue serge suit and blue shirt', an entrancing vision spoiled only by his 'fly buttons being wide open, displaying two prominent shirt-tails'.[48] Invariably, however, he remembered to decorate his buttonhole with a carnation, and to be seen smoking his pipe. Cherubic in appearance, perky, debonair and urbane in manner, he affected an agreeable puckish air.

Harold generally enjoyed robust health until late in life. There were a few scares. As a young man, the venereal diseases he had contracted caused him some alarm. He was prone to colds and attacks of giddiness. On one occasion, in Persia, he had suddenly fainted; but on examination his blood pressure was found to be normal and his heart in sound order. With middle age came the certainty of growing old. Mockingly, he compared himself to a dead mouse floating in the lily-pool, 'static, obese and decaying'. A visit to Clandeboye, however, brought back golden memories of his carefree youth, now long gone.[49] In March 1934 he became seriously ill. While holidaying in Fez, he complained of an ear infection. Treated by a local doctor, who prescribed 'a black unguent (perfumed oil)', he returned to England and spent the next fortnight in a nursing home, having succumbed to a bout of 'staphylococcus poisoning'. 'Spend the interval writing my Will . . . These may be the last words I ever write on my beloved Tikki.'* He recovered swiftly enough, but not before an attack of gastric influenza left him bedridden for another week. 'My God,' he confided to Raymond Mortimer, 'how I do hate being ill. I feel I could face sudden death with an ingratiating smile. But I am a coward in face of the jerks and nightmares of serious illness.'[50] There were also some commonplace ailments of middle age. A weak bladder was one. On returning with friends from a weekend at the Astors' estate at Cliveden, he panicked and jumped off the train when he saw that there was no lavatory carriage. 'I fear they must have seen me advancing with speed towards the GENTLEMEN. What a bore that sort of thing is.' And Harold also had a weight problem. As a young man he had weighed in at 10½ stone

---

* 'Tikki being the name of one of his typewriters: the others were titled 'Rikki' and 'Tavi'. One must assume that Harold took these nicknames from Rudyard Kipling's lively, energetic, cobra-devouring mongoose, Rikki-Tikki-Tavi. Perhaps also the clatter of Harold's swift typing technique resembled the sound of 'Rikki-Tikki-Tavi', a self-indulgent exercise in onomatopoeia.

(66 kilograms). Now, averaging between 12 and 13 stone (75–82 kilograms), he was put on a 'severe diet' – though it was not one a modern dietician would recognize. For breakfast: a choice of ham, corned beef, grilled kidneys, fish and tomatoes; for lunch he promised 'to manage himself'; for dinner, 'I fear we must have clear soup every day.' Then lobster, crab or prawns 'for a treat', followed by 'a joint, vegetables in water, and stewed fruit without sugar'. And at all meals 'water cress or salad' must be served. 'I shall have no toast and no bread', but rather 'gluten biscuits and Cambrunnen'.[51] Harold never succeeded entirely in ridding himself of his more portly shape.

Harold's domestic life had settled down to a civilised routine. Remodelling Sissinghurst absorbed much of his time; as did the London social, political and literary circuit, with its offshoot, the country house weekend. Vita retreated more and more into her Elizabethan Tower, concentrating on her literary work, perfecting her reputation as an enterprising, talented gardener. Their sexual proclivities were, as ever, indulged, but on parallel courses. A natural subject of mutual concern was their sons' future. Ben and Nigel, passing through Eton and on to Balliol, were now growing into manhood. Harold, outgoing and companionable by inclination, related more easily to the boys, whether reading aloud to them, amusing them with his deft caricatures, or drawing them out in worldly-minded conversation. Vita was more remote, more private. Nigel confessed that he 'never knew her well', and had only dared to intrude into her sitting-room in the tower half a dozen times in thirty years. Ben despised her snobbishness and aristocratic background. Slovenly and unkempt in dress, lackadaisical in manner, at mealtimes he would remain deliberately silent, reprimanding his mother in his own way. In later life, after Vita's death, Ben would refer to her as 'a remarkable writer *manquée*', saying that before her 'true quality' could be revealed it was necessary to peel away the layers of 'snobbery, the assumptions of superiority'.[52]

Of the two boys, Ben caused the most anxiety. Harold worried about him becoming a 'grim prig'. At Eton, his schoolwork was below average, while Nigel did 'brilliantly'. At home for the holidays, Ben would sprawl idly on the sofa roasting chestnuts in the fire. Harold suggested that he should read a book, for self-improvement. 'Oh yes, I must,' Ben responded, but remained where he was. 'Would you like to go up?' Charles Lindbergh asked Ben, who had accompanied Harold to America. After his maiden flight, Ben returned to earth 'safe and aloof and lethargic and drawly and incompetent', in exactly the same state of mind as when he had taken off. 'He is very charming however,' Harold briefed Vita, 'and very affectionate – and I expect his mind will take shape some day, as you say.' Progress came too slowly for Harold's – and Vita's – taste. But Ben had a mind of his own, even if it went undetected by his parents. Although he had no formal training in the subject, he was set on becoming an art historian. Harold consulted one of his friends, Kenneth Clark, then Director of the National Gallery. First, Ben should travel, 'master the galleries of Europe'; later, perhaps, a job of sorts might be found for him. Ben heeded the advice. He explored the galleries and private collections of Europe and North America. He spent several months at I Tatti, Florence, as a pupil of Bernard Berenson, the most coveted of references. Back in London, Clark found him an unpaid job at the National Gallery, and later appointed him Deputy Surveyor of the King's Pictures. Ben's career as one of the foremost art historians of his generation had begun.[53]

ELEVEN

The Member for West Leicester

Always fully occupied, never lacking in projects, Harold still hankered after a public career. In February 1935 he asked Henry 'Chips' Channon – the socialite and recently elected Conservative member for Southend-on-Sea – to find him a seat in Parliament. There was no response. Four months later, he allowed his name to be put forward as the Conservative candidate for an impending by-election at Sevenoaks. 'If it fails,' he promised himself, 'I think I shall abandon the idea of going into politics.' Instead, he would focus upon his *magnum opus*. The Sevenoaks Conservative Association turned him down. Was Harold fitted temperamentally for a political career? Christopher Hobhouse, a young friend from Harold's New Party days, thought not. You have 'not got a political mind', he told Harold, being far 'too fastidious and too critical to have the essential faculty of belief in democracy'. Harold had no convincing answer to these charges, except to say that 'He is right.' To himself, Harold conceded that his desire to enter public life was not motivated by feelings of 'real political ambition or aptitude', but stemmed 'partly from a sense of curiosity, partly from a feeling of duty, and partly because I have not got sufficient confidence in my own literary gifts'. Despite everything, he still aspired to become 'the Proust of England'. Yet he hesitated. Was he sufficiently gifted to claim such dignity? Fearful of literary failure, unsuited for politics, he vacillated. Michael Sadleir came to his rescue, assuring Harold that in time he would unquestionably acquire 'a permanent literary reputation'. Appropriately flattered, Harold resolved to devote such years as remained to him to his *magnum opus*.[1]

If Harold was excited at the prospect of becoming an MP, Vita pointedly paraded her indifference. Harold was at a loss to understand her aloofness. Could she not grasp 'that this may mean a final decision regarding politics versus literature'? 'Strange, very strange,' he mused.[2] But it was not all that strange. And Harold's painful experience of Vita's hostility to his diplomatic career should have told him so. Clearly, he wished to cut a public figure of sorts. There was, apparently, something of a 'doer' in Harold: simply talking or thinking would not suffice. Two months after being snubbed by the Sevenoaks Conservatives, he dreamed that Sir Robert Vansittart had asked him to rejoin the Foreign Office. The dream prompted a spell of acute nostalgia. Perhaps he could 'creep back somehow into the Service'. He approached Lancelot Oliphant, but the discouraging reply he received led him to understand that his ill-starred flirtations with Beaverbrook and Mosley 'have rendered me damaged goods'.[3]

If not the Foreign Office, then back again to Westminster. At the beginning of October 1935, 'Buck' De La Warr, a National Labour peer, and a cousin by marriage, offered Harold a 'safe' seat in the National Labour interest at West Leicester. Harold jumped at the offer. But what attracted him to National Labour? He was certainly not a socialist, at least not in any meaningful definition of that term. 'Yes,' he would own up, 'I fear my socialism is purely cerebral; I do not like the masses in the flesh.' So of course, Real Labour was out of the question. As were the Tories, whom he claimed to despise, denouncing them as reactionary and uncaring (even though he had recently proposed himself as a Conservative candidate). He had also dallied with the National-Liberals, but again to no consequence.[4] It later emerged that Harold saw himself as an Asquithian Liberal, rating Asquith as 'by far the greatest man I have known', if, he hastened to add, greatness 'is a matter of mind and behaviour, and not of producing effects'. He admired Asquith for his 'integrity, probity, courage, and tolerance', above all for his 'intellectual distinction'. But he also revered Asquith for other qualities, for Asquith 'hated war', as did 'all good Liberals'. 'Good Liberals aren't fighters,' Harold continued, commending Asquith for his lack of 'aggression . . . he simply couldn't trample on people'.[5] Harold might have been writing a pen-portrait of himself. But as Asquithian Liberals were no longer a living organism, certainly not as defined by Harold, this counted for nothing in contemporary politics. Harold would wander aimlessly along the political spectrum, from the New Party to National Labour, stopping off to check out the Conservatives or the Liberals on the way, without ever ideologically coming to rest at any one particular point.

Did Harold have a political credo? He made one attempt to commit himself in public. It took the form of an imaginary conversation between himself and a fellow passenger on a train journey between London and Leicester: published as *Politics in the Train*, it served as the main policy statement of National Labour.[6] He told his sceptical companion how much he disliked sectional parties and bureaucrats, those that 'place their own interests or theories above the interests of the country as a whole'. He was a proud imperialist: only by accepting imperial responsibility can the 'British race best express its genius'. Although he favoured the organic state, he did not believe in 'rendering Britain a totalitarian State'; in fact, he abhorred all forms of 'isms' and 'dictatorships'. National Labour, he proclaimed, represented 'the future point of view': it would base its policy on 'Internal Reorganisation' and 'External Peace'. Badgered by his anonymous travelling companion as to why he believes in National Labour, Harold answers: 'National, because I believe in reality. Labour, because I believe in idealism.' Turning to social matters, Harold made clear that, although not a member of the working class, he sympathised deeply with the plight of the poor: he belonged, as he fetchingly put it, to a 'progressive left wing'. Although he considered Eton 'the most perfect educational system in all the world', he deplored the class system of education: he hated the cleavage between public and council schools. Favouring equal education for all, he wanted people of any class to enjoy the privileges of the capitalist class. He aimed at bringing Eton to the masses. So, Harold's incredulous companion queried, 'Your aim is to create a million of half-baked high-brows?' 'Yes,' Harold optimistically replied.

None of this convinced Harold's prospective voter, who clearly treated his long discourse (28 pages) as yet another party political manifesto. By the end of the journey, a frustrated Harold came to see the gentleman seated opposite him 'as The Enemy', as a person of 'inelastic mind'. As the train drew up at Leicester station, Harold said politely, 'So long.' But his fellow traveller persisted: 'why on earth do you belong to . . . ?' Harold 'slammed the door' shut.

Unable to convince Everyman, the same question remains. Did Harold actually have a political credo? Off the record, he was more forthcoming. As a compassionate man, he favoured improving the lot of the masses. 'I have always been on the side of the under-dog,' he proclaimed, adding significantly, in a neat balancing act, 'but I have also believed in the principle of aristocracy.' Here was the rub. Once he sensed that his class values were under threat, he revealed his true colours.

I have hated the rich but I have loved learning, scholarship, intelligence and the humanities. Suddenly I am faced with the fact that all these lovely things are supposed to be 'class privileges'. The snobbishness of the British people (that factor upon which the aristocratic principle relied and often exploited) has suddenly turned to venom. When I feel that my whole class is being assailed, I feel part of them, a feeling I have never had before . . . We imagine that we are fighting [in the Second World War] for liberty and our standards of civilization. But is it perfectly certain that by these phrases we do not mean the cultured life which we lead? I know that such a life, as lived by

Vita and myself, is 'good' in the philosophical sense. We are humane, charitable, just and not vulgar. By God, we are not vulgar! Yet is it any more than an elegant arabesque upon the corridors of history?[7]

This was not so much a political credo as a cry of desperation. Harold could only stand by helplessly as his 'class privileges' were swamped by a rising tide of 'venom'. It mattered little that he was 'on the side of the underdog'. Like an old-style Whig, he would patronise the lower orders, content to ameliorate their plight as long as they knew their allotted place in a society anchored by his 'principle of aristocracy'.

Although Harold was determined to embark on a political career, he was singularly ill suited to do so. He knew little of domestic politics, of the minutiae of economic or financial or social affairs, while his constituents evinced only a passing interest in foreign affairs – his pet subject. Having nothing in common with the middle- or lower-class voters he sought to win over, he flinched from the hustle and bustle, the cut and thrust of electioneering. The hustings held no appeal for him, particularly when facing 'working men and women lowing in disgust and hatred'. 'I loathe and hate every moment of this Election,' he noted after a campaign meeting in West Leicester. 'The evening meetings are such absolute HELL that they hang on one's soul all day like a lump of lead.'[8] An unforeseen hitch arose. At the last moment the Liberals decided to put forward a candidate, Mr H. E. Crawfurd. Had he known, Harold declared that he would not have stood because he objected 'to turning down Liberals'; but also because he knew '[Crawfurd] would do me down'. In any case, it would be a close-run race. Harold put his chances at '48 per cent'. He was not helped by Vita, who refused to appear at West Leicester. 'She says this is a matter of principle. I find it difficult to discover what the principle is.' But an old friend, Alfred Duff Cooper, financial secretary to the Treasury, made 'an amazing speech' on his behalf. 'I learnt a lot from Duff's technique, which I shall imitate.'[9] Voting took place on 14 November. The contest could not have been more tightly fought. After a recount, Harold squeezed in with a majority of only eighty-seven. Wild yells were heard from the hall. The victor made a short speech. He was seized by his supporters, some kissing him, others shedding tears of joy. Outside the Constitutional Club a crowd waited for him in the rain. 'Here he is,' they shouted, and dragged him out of the car. 'Pandemonium let loose.' It was only after the ritual champagne toasts that Harold was allowed to retire to bed in the early hours.[10]

'I put all my philosophy of life into that Election,' he told Vita.[11] But how can a comprehensive 'philosophy of life' be expressed by an Asquithian Liberal, disguised as a National Labourite, propping up a National

Government controlled by the detested Conservative Party? By 1935 there was no question that it was the Conservatives, under the stolid-looking but astute Stanley Baldwin, who ruled, and National Labour, led by the perceptibly failing Ramsay MacDonald, who trailed far behind, a pitiful rump, its eight members swallowed up in the Conservative-dominated National Government. One has to conclude that Harold was jobbed into Parliament by an aristocratic relative in the time-honoured fashion. And he knew it. He knew that 'Buck' De La Warr had manoeuvred him into a party that barely existed. Only three months after his election, he referred to it as 'a poor little thing, it is quite dead'.[12] Was it by chance that Harold had tied his political fortunes to National Labour, a party on paper only, with no political future, again misreading the political map as he had with the New Party? At heart, Harold wished to be a Member of Parliament for its own sake, to make his mark in public life beyond the privacy of his study or the hectic merry-go-round of London high society where he excelled as a brilliant raconteur and a charming, sophisticated dinner companion. All these pursuits were hugely enjoyable and would not be neglected, for they slotted in well with his overall philosophy of life: to preserve – as he repeatedly said – his class privileges, but also to serve his country as befitted a minor aristocrat, while lending a helping hand whenever appropriate to the lower orders.

Harold's first day in Parliament began, symbolically, at lunch with Sibyl Colefax and Victor Cazalet and his sister, Thelma, two Conservative MPs. Together they drove to the House of Commons where he was allocated his peg in the cloakroom. Fussed over by Lady Astor, he took his seat in the Chamber, was shown the House of Lords, and witnessed the re-election of the Speaker, Captain Edward Algernon Fitzroy. 'Then suddenly it was over, and I realized that I had actually sat on the green benches and that I was now one of the fish in the most famous of all aquariums and would henceforth revolve round and round like the other fish in that subaqueous light.'[13] He resolved to lie low, say nothing: he would study procedure and atmosphere for the coming four months. 'After that I shall begin to push and probe and pull. That suits me lovely.'[14] He looked forward to a government reshuffle in February, and a government job. Then he met Churchill in the smoking-room. 'Harold,' Winston yelled, waving his arms. 'Welcome! Welcome! When I saw your result on the tape, I said to myself, "That means he goes straight into the Cabinet", and then I remembered that all of your Party were already in the Cabinet and that they must have at least one follower on the back benches.' Standing there feeling sheepish, all Harold could do was graciously acknowledge the smiles and laughter from the crowd that invariably gathered around Churchill on these gay occasions. Baldwin gave more room for hope. Are you going to devote the rest of your life to politics? he asked Harold. 'I say that I am. He says, "That's right – I am on the lookout for my successors".'[15] Harold never rose to the bait, probably aware that he was being shamelessly flattered – or tactfully ignored!

Harold was offered one job, as Ramsay MacDonald's Parliamentary Private Secretary. He refused outright. Harold excused himself to Vita: 'I dread an orgy of vain outpourings . . . I fear that Ramsay is a vain and slightly vindictive old man,' mocking the old man's ambition 'to make the Party "a living forrrce".' Earlier, MacDonald had addressed the eight members of his faction on the future of National Labour, 'somewhat like King Charles I addressing the Cavaliers from the Whitehall scaffold'. MacDonald championed the idea of 'Tory Socialism', a notion that momentarily intrigued Harold. 'You eight people,' he harangued them, 'are the seed-bed of seminal ideas. The young Tories are on your side. Work hard: think hard: and you will create a classless England.'[16] 'A classless England?' Harold must have asked himself, only to immediately reject the notion as absurd. He would never disown his 'principle of aristocracy'.

In a sense it was fortunate for Harold that foreign affairs came to dominate Parliament, and increasingly the public agenda, until the outbreak of war in September 1939. On these matters he was able to speak with authority and from experience not given to many MPs. His first opportunity to do so came sooner than planned. On 19 December 1935 Harold rose from his 'beloved green bench' to deliver his maiden speech. It was a dramatic moment. The Foreign Secretary, Sir Samuel Hoare, had just resigned in the most startling circumstances over his role in the so-called 'Hoare–Laval affair'. The result of prolonged Anglo-French negotiations, the Hoare–Laval proposals were designed to bring to an end the Italo-Ethiopian war that had been raging since October 1935. By them Ethiopia would be allotted an outlet to the sea, either Zeila or Assab; Italy would be rewarded with territorial gains – and a large zone in the south and south-west in which, acting under the auspices of the League, she would have economic primacy. According to this deal, roughly two-thirds of Ethiopia would be subject to Italian control. Great issues were at stake: revitalising the Anglo-French alliance; restoring the authority of the League; saving Italy from the clutches of Germany; and confronting Germany with a united Europe. The Cabinet approved this plan on 2 December.[17]

Hoare stopped over in Paris to clinch the trade-off with his French counterpart, Pierre Laval. No sooner had agreement been reached than the plan was leaked. It was castigated by the press in Paris and London, and angrily denounced in Parliament. The government, alarmed by the outcry, backtracked. Baldwin, making 'one of his take-you-into-my-confidence' speeches to Parliament, officially buried the scheme. Hoare's personal story was one of high tragedy coupled with high farce. Immediately after the talks he left Paris for Zuoz in Switzerland. Hoare, a skater of international quality, had a blackout on his first day on the ice. He fell and broke his nose. While his colleagues were deciding his future, he remained bedridden. They paid their respects but made clear where his duty lay. On 19 December Hoare delivered his farewell speech as Foreign Minister to a packed House of Commons.

Harold thought it 'excellent. His voice just breaks at the end.' Nervous, afraid that his 'knees will knock together', Harold was called soon after Hoare had crept out of the Chamber.[18] He spoke for sixteen minutes. Typically, he lambasted Italian diplomatic standards, their 'level of integrity' being 'far removed' from that of the British, a complaint that he had been airing since 1919. But he was not concerned with preserving the territorial independence of Ethiopia, 'a bad client' and not 'worth such an effort'. Nor did he see anything 'criminal or Imperialistic' in affording Italy 'preferential rights' in Ethiopia, comparing it without prejudice with French preponderance in Morocco. All in all, he thought the plan 'a very brilliant essay in vivisection'. But if Harold voiced no complaint against the substance of the plan, he did take extreme issue with how it was concocted. It was the 'procedure' that greatly troubled him, not the entirely reasonable terms of the pact. By negotiating it in 'the foetid saloons of the Quai d'Orsay', Britain had reneged on its commitment to the League of Nations; it had resurrected the 'Old Adam' of pre-war diplomacy. Parading his background in diplomatic technique, Harold ruled that it was 'a terrible mistake' for foreign ministers to conduct negotiations. In fact, refining his argument to a debatable extreme, he insisted that the Foreign Secretary should not be allowed to leave the country without a vote of both Houses of Parliament. 'Diplomacy is not the art of conversation,' he ruled. 'It is the art of the exchange of documents in a carefully considered and precise form and in such a way that they cannot be repudiated later . . . Diplomacy by conference is a mistake.' Of course, Harold made clear that Britain should strive for a peaceful solution to the dispute, but only, he cautioned, 'under the aegis of the League'.[19]

Harold took the Foreign Office – and cabinet – view of the crisis. To put it bluntly, he was by no means shocked at the idea of rewarding Italian aggression by carving up Ethiopia to Italy's benefit. His main grievance was that the professional diplomats had been shunted aside to make way for self-seeking politicians, rank laymen in the art of bringing a negotiation to a successful conclusion. His homilies that 'Diplomacy is not the art of conversation . . .', or that 'Diplomacy by conference is a mistake', would be repeated in all his writings on diplomatic practice. A child of the Paris peace conference, he accepted the notion of Summit Diplomacy, but only when the details of an agreement had been painstakingly hammered out by those competent to do so. Only then should the politicians be wheeled in to affix their signatures to a document: only then would the 'Old Adam' of darker days be laid finally to rest. Out to preserve the perceived prerogatives of his chosen profession, Harold's standpoint smacked of exclusivity. It was also progressively out of touch with changing values in the conduct of international affairs; and would become increasingly so.

Still, it was a laudable speech, delivered in a breezy manner. Mr Thurtle – Old Labour – led the conventional round of congratulations, warming to Harold's 'able and attractive speech', to his 'extremely interesting style'. But he was less happy with Harold's 'rather . . . spurious brand' of politics, and advised him to be 'far-seeing enough to change his party' so that he may 'long remain in this House both to instruct and to delight us'. Others followed suit: Eustace Percy – 'the best maiden speech he has ever heard'; 'Jimmy' Thomas – 'You did fine, Harold, you did fine!' Duff Cooper was 'particularly polite', and Austen Chamberlain 'congratulates me', while Stanley Baldwin and Ramsay MacDonald sent him complimentary messages. Even 'Chips' Channon noted his approval. 'What a day!' Harold sighed, when at last he was allowed to retire.[20]

In the 1930s Italy was perceived as a serious threat to Britain's position in the Mediterranean, menacing the routes to India and the Far East. Yet many British politicians and diplomats regarded her with conspicuous disdain, seeing her as an upstart state determined to outdo its betters by any means, however unscrupulous, set on pushing its way into the front rank of the Great Powers, a distinction for which it was patently unsuited. Harold was no exception. But he harboured no such mixed feelings about Nazi Germany. Germany was a Great Power and could neither be ignored nor treated with contempt. In February 1934 Harold had visited Munich and visited the local Nazi headquarters, the 'Brown House', 'which is yellow'. He saw 'many ugly uniforms', adding that 'the passion for uniforms is greater even than in 1912'. The country had been swept up in a mood of military madness. 'Here is no pretense whatsoever of observing the Treaty of Versailles and Germany might just as well be allowed to rearm . . . Germany is again the Germany of before the war but with a new fanatical look in its eye.'[21] Just over a year later Germany renounced unilaterally the disarmament clauses of the Versailles treaty. The Western powers failed to respond effectively to Hitler's provocative *démarche*; nor was there any comment from Harold who, at the time, was in America tidying up the Morrow biography.

By the spring of 1936 the future of the demilitarised Rhineland was under discussion in the Foreign Office, the prospect of it being used as a bargaining chip in a broad-ranging appeasement of Europe gaining much support. Of course, Harold was not privy to the details of this discussion, but he must have been aware of it. On 27 February 1936 he addressed the Foreign Affairs Committee of the House on Anglo-German relations. His message was unambiguous. Germany was an 'aggressive power and wants war'. He predicted that 'trouble would come' by 1939 or 1940. To deter her, it would first be necessary to rearm, 'so as to speak with authority'. Then, Germany would be confronted with two stark alternatives: either 'encirclement' or adherence to the League's Covenant. 'Chips' Channon, who was present, was moved by Harold's 'brilliant address. It was shrewd, but alarming and we almost heard the tramp-tramp of the troops.'²² Harold's reasoning, although enticingly impressive, was seriously flawed. Rearmament, clearly, was a long-drawn-out process. Britain, having only recently taken the first tentative steps along that road, was plainly ill equipped to challenge Germany 'with authority'. But more to the point, what if Hitler, in his current buoyant mood, should take what he gathered was about to be offered and what he believed was rightfully his?

These game plans were frustrated by Hitler's sudden, though by no means unexpected, move into the Rhineland on 7 March, violating the Versailles and Locarno treaties and marking a new and dangerous phase in European diplomacy. Two days later Harold recorded the general mood in the House as 'one of fear. Anything to keep out of war . . . On all sides one hears sympathy for Germany. It is all very tragic and sad.' 'What a mess we are in,' Harold complained to his mother, explaining that Britain's international obligations to France were now little more than casualties of the counterfeit peace that was being forced upon Britain. 'We are afraid of Germany . . . Therefore we must break our word and bow to force.' To Vita, he forecast 'Only humiliation and rancour.'²³ Several days later Harold appeared before a select audience at Chatham House. In some ways, he made an astonishing contribution to the symposium, 'Germany and the Rhineland'. As if to brush aside the rising tide of pro-German sympathy, he made clear that Germany had become 'a mental case', that 'in the German temperament of to-day there is a strong strain of insanity'. As for the Nazi system, it was 'a blot and a scourge to humanity'. But the strongest words were reserved for Hitler, 'a factor of appalling instability and of the very greatest danger'. Hearing 'voices' from on high, guided by some destiny, 'be it God or Wotan', Hitler believes 'mystically, blindly, that he is guided by this deity, this destiny which dictates for him the actions which he should take'. Leading his people along the path of destiny with 'the certainty of a somnambulist', he calls upon his people 'to advance into orgies of self-sacrifice . . .

to fling themselves in droves from the precipice of suicide'. Unlike many, Harold was not taken in by the fiction that Hitler was a puppet manipulated by extremists. He recognised the *Führerprinzip* for what it was: 'Germany *is* Hitler at this moment, and Hitler *is* Germany.'

Nonetheless, Harold was at a loss to furnish an effective outcome to the crisis. When challenged by Lord Arnold that Germany had only asserted 'German sovereignty on German territory', Harold replied yes, 'Germany was right in principle, wrong in practice.' Still, all his sympathies were with the French, as he argued that the Locarno arrangements should be revamped into an Anglo-French-Belgian alliance. But this was intended to deter future German aggression, not to defuse the current crisis. And under no circumstances was it designed to guarantee the so-called French eastern system, a series of contractual obligations that France had concluded with Poland and the Little Entente countries (Czechoslavakia, Romania and Yugoslavia), and more recently the Soviet Union. Harold recognised the logic of the German drive towards the east, that it would lead to 'a hegemony in Europe, and that this will be a world danger'. But though it was 'a terrible danger', Harold admitted that British public opinion would not countenance being 'drawn into a conflict over Poland or Czechoslovakia, or the Eastern States'. All that Harold could suggest as immediate practical measures were to force Germany, '*at any cost*, to apologise for her action'; to augment the German reoccupation with 'an international force'; to withdraw the British ambassador from Berlin – or indeed, all League ambassadors; and finally, to boycott the Olympic Games (due to be held in Berlin in August). But as Harold well knew, these were merely 'gestures', and would in no way influence a megalomaniac Hitler who personified the collective paranoia that had engulfed Germany.

When the House debated the crisis, Harold restated the main themes of his Chatham House speech, though his language was far more parliamentary. Do not be seduced by the current spectacle of German power, he pleaded, there is no need 'to fall upon our knees', or 'bow our foreheads in the dust', or 'say "Heil Hitler"'. France 'will never become our enemy', will never wage 'an aggressive war'. 'Do we know the same about Germany?' he asked. Reverting to the July crisis of 1914, he warned against repeating Grey's (alleged) mistake of not making Britain's position crystal clear at the time.

We must act in such a way that the countries of Europe – Germany above all – must say, 'This time they really mean it.' We must say, if the frontiers of Holland, Belgium or France are crossed by any country, especially by Germany, we will within such and such a time bring so many forces, ships and aeroplanes in their defence. We must also say to France, 'This is an absolute assurance backed by the whole public opinion of this country'.

There was one rider. As Chatham House was told, so was the House of Commons: under no circumstances should Britain commit itself in eastern Europe.[24]

The Rhineland crisis blew over in a flurry of barren diplomatic exchanges, culminating in a series of questions for Hitler. Asked pointedly whether Germany 'recognises and intends in future to respect the existing territorial and political status of Europe, except in so far as this might be subsequently modified by free negotiation and agreement',[25] Hitler skilfully evaded replying to the British questionnaire. By the end of May these initiatives had run their full, and fruitless, course. Throughout the crisis, Harold, in public, had faithfully conformed to the traditional line in British policy, following Eyre Crowe's guiding principles: defence of the Lowlands; preserving, even strengthening, the Anglo-French entente; abandoning eastern Europe to its own devices. Yet to his diaries – and to a closed session of the Foreign Affairs Committee of the House – he had ventured upon another alternative: 'encirclement', a concept that should have been anathema to Harold, who railed against the pre-1914 style of diplomacy at every opportunity. 'Encirclement', if it meant anything at all in its current European context, meant involvement in eastern Europe. In day-to-day, practical terms, it implied shielding France's eastern system. Moreover, Harold was in no doubt that France was fully justified in erecting its system of alliances in eastern Europe. So what exactly was Harold's policy? Like most anti-appeasers at the time, he thought it more prudent to follow public opinion than to lead it. 'We are determined never again to promise something that our public will not allow us to execute.'[26] For this reason, he refused to publicly advocate an alliance system. There was another, perhaps more pertinent, point that all anti-appeasers had to confront. Harold abhorred Germany's internal regime, its brutality, its vulgarity, its lack of democracy, its institutionalised anti-Semitism, its potential for violence. But it was not within the province of the British government to impose upon Nazi Germany a system of government more compatible with liberal standards in western Europe. Nor could Germany be ignored. It would remain the most powerful continental power, restless, energetic, seeking to overthrow the status quo. Better to draw the sting from German demands through negotiation than fatalistically slip down the path of confrontation and war, a war that Britain was ill prepared for. Diplomacy, it was persuasively argued, could not be conducted by saying 'No!' to everything.[27]

The essential problem facing Harold was how to deal with Germany within the context of contemporary international relations. How do you restrain a Great Power? Harold was at a loss to give a cogent answer. He was not alone. If he had any misgivings about the general line of British policy, they remained well disguised. He had nothing but high praise for Eden, who had not 'made a single mistake' over the Rhineland affair. Although he toyed with joining various 'ginger groups', one with 'Winston as leader, together with "Buck" and Kenneth Lindsay', and another with Duncan Sandys (Churchill's son-in-law), his loyalty to the government was never in question. Neville Chamberlain was applauded for 'one of his superb speeches', while there was no hint of criticism of Baldwin, who was discreetly handling the impending constitutional crisis over Edward VIII in a businesslike fashion. In May there were rumours in the press that he was to be given a ministerial post in a government reshuffle. Harold's first inclination was to refuse it, if offered, on the extraordinary grounds that it would be unfair for a raw National Labour member to leapfrog over the backs of the more deserving Conservative faithful. Ambition soon surfaced, however. 'I may find that if the proposal is put to me it will be almost impossible to refuse it.' As no proposal was ever put, Harold was delivered from his moral dilemma.[28]

Harold rarely intervened in matters unrelated to foreign affairs. On the few occasions when he dared, he seemed to be struggling. Discussing the record of the Ministry of Health, he embarked upon a discourse about nutrition, or malnutrition, paupers and pauperisation. It would have been difficult for members to grasp the exact meaning of his preference for 'wide-spread pauperization' to the subsistence of '4,500,000 paupers'. Although he argued for free milk for all schoolchildren and expectant mothers, a humane plea, his speech, rambling in content, lacked conviction.[29]

Harold also tried his hand at educational matters, though not in England. He was asked to serve on a government commission to report on African education, particularly on the affairs of Makerere College, Uganda. It was headed by 'Buck' De La Warr, then parliamentary Under-Secretary of State for the Colonies, and included Rob Bernays, his closest friend at Westminster, and five educational experts. It was the kind of exciting new adventure – mysterious countries, spectacular scenery and convivial company – that Harold most enjoyed. Flying everywhere, Harold apologised to Vita for having to renege on his promise never to endanger his life in such a risky, gravity-defying pursuit. The trip, inevitably, also turned into a sightseeing tour. At Ujiji, Tanganyika, he arrived at the spot where Stanley rediscovered Livingstone. Natives, 'almost completely naked', leaning on their spears, would stare at the Commission 'in respectful amazement'. He saw Kampala, and flew over the Flamingo Lake, 'probably the loveliest thing I have seen'; but was no less impressed by the magnificence of Lake Victoria. At Khartoum, Harold was shown the steps where General Charles George Gordon was cut down by the Mahdi's forces in January 1885.

If Harold was in awe of Africa's natural beauty, his daily contacts with its natives, indigenous and otherwise, and its climate, proved far less enchanting. He had provided himself with a tropical kit, particularly some 'nice blue underwear which I so much admire'. But he felt 'hot all the same'; and, characteristically, he distrusted 'all these niggers'. At one school, he saw raised 'a forest of horrid pink hands'. These derogatory comments were repeated – one might say *ad nauseam* – in his correspondence with Vita. Typically, Harold reacted with aristocratic disdain to the British expatriates he encountered. After dining with one of the heads of Makerere College, their host, 'the perfect type of a second-rate school and the second-rate Oxford college', played the gramophone, inflicting on his guests comic dialogues that poked fun at 'Poonah and pukkha punkhas', interspersed with absurd jokes about 'the 'varsity and Oxford accent'. 'We find this profoundly depressing and sit there with our faces buried in our hands.' Apart from these diversions, there was much uphill investigative work, with Harold reputedly acting as the intellectual driving force behind the Commission's final report. It did not change fundamentally the British outlook or practice on native education, except in some secondary details: its most important recommendation led to Makerere College being transformed into the inter-racial University of East Africa.[30] Harold returned to Sissinghurst exhausted and with a sense of relief. His sojourn in the wilds of East Africa had only confirmed his enduring belief that true civilisation began and ended in a few select capital cities of Europe.

'"'E was like that, you know, 'arold," ' Jimmy Thomas, the down-to-earth Colonial Secretary, told Harold, ' "not afraid of people, if you know what I mean. And now 'ere we 'ave this little obstinate man, with his bloody Mrs Simpson. Hit won't do 'arold, I tell you that straight. I know the people of this country. I *know* them. They 'ate 'aving no family life at Court." ' It was in this manner that Harold learned what the man in the street would have thought – if only he had known – of Edward VIII's affair with Mrs Wallis Simpson, an American lady from Baltimore. She had been introduced to the Prince by Lady (Thelma) Furness, one of the Prince's mistresses and a fellow American. Before long, Mrs Simpson had become the supreme passion of his life. But not only was Mrs Simpson an American and the mistress of the King, she was also a divorcee, and, to cap it all, she was all set to divorce her second husband. This was the most combustible of combinations, threatening to provoke a grave constitutional crisis.

Harold had first met the future King in August 1921 at a luncheon party at Lady Cunard's, noting appreciatively the Prince's 'sandy eyelashes', but was put off by his 'furtive giggling' with another royal guest, his cousin, Prince Louis Mountbatten: it was 'David' this and 'Dickie' that. Harold's feelings towards the Prince of Wales vacillated sharply. At one dinner party, at Lady Colefax's, he was suitably impressed: 'he talks a great deal about America and diplomacy . . . [and] knows an astonishing amount about it all . . . One finds him modest and a good mixer.' At another, this time at the Savoy Grill, it was quite a different story. As usual, the Prince was extremely talkative and charming. 'I like the little man with his white eyelashes and his little red hands,' Harold commented, 'but he is not my sort of pal and I do not like being advertised in his company.' Harold, realising that the Prince was 'in a mess', and rattled by his 'really very right-wing' views, preferred, if possible, to avoid all 'social intimacy' with him, an option often impossible to achieve.[31]

On 20 January 1936, exactly a week after the supper party at the Savoy Grill, George V died and the Prince of Wales succeeded to the throne as Edward VIII. It was an open secret in upper-crust circles that the new King held the strongest of hopes that he would be able to marry Wallis Simpson and make her his Queen. Her estranged husband, Ernest Simpson, no longer in control of his own fate, had filed for divorce, the decree nisi proceedings to be heard in Ipswich in October. A constitutional time bomb was set to explode in late autumn. Harold was not an intimate of either the King or Mrs Simpson, but his standing in London society, his welcome presence at most fashionable dinner tables and social gatherings, enabled him to observe the unfolding drama from close at hand. That spring he was invited to Mrs Simpson's apartment at Bryanston Court to meet the King. Over port, he succumbed yet again to Edward's boyish charm. 'I must say, he is very alert and delightful.' On reflection, however, Harold was saddened by the occasion. 'Mrs Simpson is a perfectly harmless type of American, but the whole setting is slightly second-rate.' Somewhat later, Ramsay MacDonald, another man of the people, but one who enjoyed the attention of high society hostesses, reminded Harold of the moral dimension of the King's infatuation. 'The people do not mind fornication, but they loathe adultery,' he was told. By now, Harold was thoroughly exasperated by the irresponsible conduct of the King, though some of his frustration rubbed off on Mrs Simpson: 'It irritates me that this silly little man *en somme* should destroy a great monarchy by giggling into a flirtation with a third-rate American.'[32]

It was said of Edward VIII that he was 'incapable of deep reflection and prone to erratic judgement', a 'thinking man' whose 'thoughts did not always run deep'. Old-time courtiers, Sir Alan 'Tommy' Lascelles for one, were in despair at the King's offhand behaviour, his neglect of his official duties, his casual attitude to state papers. Traditionalists like Harold viewed such conduct as scandalous.[33] Nor would Edward's intellectual shallowness have appealed to him. Rather than listen to an encore of a Chopin piece played by Artur Rubinstein, he preferred to hear Noël Coward sing 'Mad Dogs and Englishmen': although relaxing to the company present, it left some with the impression that Lady Colefax's salon was frequented by 'a race of barbarians'. Wallis Simpson – 'bejewelled, eyebrow-plucked, virtuous and wise' – emerges (temporarily) in a more positive light from Harold's jottings. She was 'really miserable', Sibyl Colefax told Harold on 18 November, having just returned from Fort Belvedere – the King's retreat near Sunningdale, on the edge of Windsor Great Park – where she had had a frank tête-a-tête with Mrs Simpson. When asked why she wouldn't fulfil her duty and leave the country, Wallis replied: 'If I did so the King would come after me regardless of anything.' Nor had the King 'ever suggested marriage', she said. At the time, Harold believed her, and thought Mrs Simpson 'perfectly straightforward and well-intentioned', an impression confirmed when he received 'a sensible letter' from her.[34]

But Mrs Simpson's frank tête-à-tête with Lady Colefax was at best disingenuous, at worst duplicitous. On the evening of 27 October, the same day that her decree nisi had been granted, the King had presented Mrs Simpson with a magnificent engagement ring from Cartier, a Mogul emerald set in platinum, engraved on the back, 'WE [Wallis joined to Edward] are ours now'. Could there be any clearer declaration of intent? As everyone who was anyone knew of Edward's firm intention to marry Mrs Simpson it would be stretching naïvety to breaking point to assume that he had not told Mrs Simpson of his purpose. Years later she confessed that she had been willing to do anything 'to prevent his going. I lied to our friends, I lied to the King.' One of Harold's 'only three sins' was 'untruthfulness'. Secrets were hard to keep in the highly charged atmosphere of late 1936. It soon became apparent to him that Mrs Simpson had deceived Lady Colefax. Harold's judgement was swift: 'I am distressed since I felt sorry for Wallis Simpson and hoped that she was a decent person. But after having lied like that to Sibyl . . . I cannot feel that she be anything better than a fool or a minx.'[35]

The British public at large had been shielded from the mounting scandal by a carefully orchestrated media blackout. But with the Privy Council threatening to resign, Harold judged that public opinion would turn against the King. 'The upper classes mind her being an American more than they mind her being divorced. The lower classes do not mind her being an American

but loathe the idea that she has had two husbands already.' These speculations were soon put to the test. On 1 December the crisis broke. The Bishop
of Bradford, aptly named the Reverend A. W. Blunt, spoke out at his annual
diocesan conference, reminding the King that he needed 'God's grace if he
is to fulfil his duty faithfully . . . We hope that he is aware of this need . . .
[and] that he will give more positive signs of his awareness.' His sermon
(which was also aimed at the King's neglect of his church-going duties) was
published in the provincial press. 'Poor England,' Harold grieved. Scanning
the papers in the Reading Room of the House, he noted that the offending
article had been cut out of the *Yorkshire Post*. 'But we cannot be ostriches
any longer,' he informed Vita.[36] Two days after Blunt's lesson, the national
press circulated the story. For months the American public had enjoyed
newspaper headlines referring to Mrs Simpson as the 'King's Moll'. Now
it was the turn of the British public to relish such sensationalism, though
the headlines it read were more tastefully phrased.

That same day Baldwin, looking 'ill and profoundly sad', told the House
that no constitutional crisis 'has yet arisen'. Immediately after hearing
Baldwin's statement, Harold dashed off to Islington where he gave a public
lecture on biography. It was an opportunity to sound out public opinion.
Out of an audience of four hundred only ten joined in the singing of 'God
Save the King'. 'I do not find the people angry with Mrs Simpson. But I
do find a deep and enraged fury against the King himself. In eight months
he has destroyed the great structure of popularity which he has raised.'
Meanwhile, Wallis Simpson had fled the country for the relative safety of
Cannes, from where she issued a statement that she would be willing, 'if
such action would solve the problem, to withdraw forthwith from a situation that has been rendered unhappy and untenable'. Was this generous offer
to retire from the affair made tongue-in-cheek? Wallis Simpson knew that
Edward would never give her up, was adamant in his intention to marry
her. While in Cannes she spoke to him several hours a day on the telephone.[37] What else did they speak about?

Baldwin met the King on eight occasions in attempts to resolve the crisis.
At first, Baldwin tried to persuade Edward to halt the divorce proceedings.
Edward refused. He would never abandon Mrs Simpson, he told Baldwin,
and would make her his wife once her divorce became final. 'I am going to
marry Mrs Simpson, and I am prepared to go.' Edward floated the idea of
a morganatic marriage, first put to him by Wallis. Baldwin, backed fully by
the Cabinet and the Dominions, would not hear of it. He told Edward there
remained only two options: abdication or marriage to Wallis. 'So, Mr Baldwin,
you leave me no choice.' Churchill saw another. 'No pistol' should be held
at the King's head, he pleaded. But the House shouted him down to cries

of 'Twister' and 'Drop it'. In any case, it was far too late for compromises. Edward had already decided to abdicate. Baldwin, raising his whisky-and-soda, said: 'Well, Sir, whatever happens my Mrs and I wish you happiness from the depths of our souls', at which the King burst into tears, and Baldwin followed suit. 'What a strange conversation piece,' Harold observed, 'those two blubbering together on a sofa!'[39]

By 10 December the royal drama had run its full course. The Speaker of the House read out the Act of Abdication in 'a quavering voice', followed by the Baldwin, who was greeted by cheers, and who told 'the whole story'. 'It was Sophoclean,' Harold recorded, 'and almost unbearable. There was no question of applause. It was the silence of Gettysburg.' He met Baldwin in the corridor of the House immediately afterwards. 'You see,' Baldwin said, gripping Harold by the arm, 'the man is mad. MAD. He could see nothing but that woman . . . He lacks religion . . . I told his mother so . . . I love that man. But he must go.' The Abdication Bill was rushed through Parliament in one morning's work. 'King's Abdication Bill,' announced one clerk, echoed by another: '*Le Roi le Veult* [the King wishes it]'. 'Thus ends the reign of King Edward VIII,' Harold recorded, promptly reverting to business as usual: 'Back to my steak-and-kidney pie. Down to Sissinghurst.' It was the beginning of the reign of 'Albert the Good' (Edward's brother, as George VI), earnest, dignified, embodying sound family values.[39]

Harold was encouraged at the outcome. 'What a *solid* people we are under all our sentimentality!' He had long ago come to the conclusion that the Windsors – as they had now become – had ruled themselves out of court, so to speak. The Duke was little more than an obstinate, self-centred, 'silly little man' who had neglected his official duties and who had almost destroyed the institution of monarchy for the sake of a manipulative, self-serving, lying American. Vita was more outspoken, particularly towards Mrs Simpson. 'Darling, I now *hate* Mrs. S. That all this should have happened for such a 2½ d. piece of trash! Of course she should never have allowed it, and any decent woman would have prevented it.' To Harold's distress, and her own, she also reported on the 'foolish and irresponsible' generational gap that had opened up in their family: Ben thought the whole affair 'great fun'; while Nigel's attitude can best be summed up as, 'what does it matter if they do [divorce], what does it matter if we lose the Dominions and if the Monarchy loses the respect of the people.' To relieve the general gloom, Vita passed on the latest 'silly joke' circulating about Mrs Simpson: '[she] is writing a book called "The Unimportance of Being Ernest"'.[40]

Harold's contacts with the Duke and Duchess of Windsor over the coming years were sporadic. He did perform one last service for Wallis Simpson. On her hurried flight to Cannes, she had inadvertently left some notes –

that reflected 'greatly to her credit' – at a hotel in Evreux. Upon hearing this story, Harold offered to retrieve them; and did so, giving thanks at the Cathedral after having successfully completed his high-minded mission.* As for the Duke of Windsor, Tommy Lascelles had predicted that he would fritter away his time. 'He will probably be quite happy in Austria. He will get a small *schloss*; play golf in the park; go to night clubs in Vienna; and in the summer bathe in the Adriatic. There is no need to be sorry for him.' Harold concurred.[41] But when Harold saw 'the late King of England and the merry wife of Windsor' at Somerset Maugham's Villa Mauresque in August 1938, he was struck by Windsor's 'glamour and his charm and his sadness . . . They have a villa here and a yacht and go round and round.' In his faintly cockney accent, the Duke excused their late arrival: 'Oim sorry we were a little loite.' Harold thought the Duchess looked 'very well for her age', but that the Duke's 'eyes looked less like fried eggs than formerly'. Harold was careful to address him as 'Your Royal Highness' and her as 'Duchess, sharp-like', as protocol strictly demanded. Later, he visited the Duke at his villa: 'He is full of chat. It is rather pathetic.' Harold noticed his Prince of Wales banner hanging in the hall. What was it doing there? 'When I became King,' the Duke explained,'they had to toik it down as there was no Prince of Woiles; so I did not see whoy oi shouldn't have it here.' Harold didn't bother to explain. Many years later, nothing seemed to have changed. They met in London. Harold saw 'an arrested adolescent' chattering away aimlessly. 'He pretends to be very busy and happy, but I feel this is false and that he is unoccupied and miserable . . . In fact he does nothing: scarcely ever reads and doesn't play cards . . . I see his charm but it is now so faded and I hope I never set eyes on him again.'[42]

But the Windsors' ill-advised visit to Germany in October 1937, where they were received by Hitler and other Nazi leaders, could by no means be depicted as frittering away their time. Its political connotations were clear, even if discounted by the Duke. It must have left Harold considerably on edge. He himself refused to travel through Germany 'because of Nazi rule', telling 'Chips' Channon that 'We stand for tolerance, truth, liberty and good humour. They stand for violence, oppression, untruthfulness and bitterness', distinguishing traits that obviously had eluded the notice of the Windsors. It must have confirmed for Harold what many suspected: that the Windsors had fallen heavily for the 'champagne-like influence of

*Many years later, it was made known to Harold that the notes he had so painstakingly retrieved had been carelessly lost by the Windsors. For Harold's account of his journey to Evreux; and for notes lost, see *ND*, i, 10 July 1937, 304–7, and *ND*, iii, 9 Nov. 1955, 290.

Ribbentrop'.* Rumour had it that Ribbentrop – otherwise known as 'Ambassador Brickendrop' – 'had *used* Mrs Simpson'. Even Channon admitted that the King 'is going the dictator way, and is pro-German, against Russia and against too much slip-shod democracy'. It has been persuasively suggested that Edward differed in many aspects from the government's foreign policy, and foolishly allowed his tongue to wag in an 'unconstitutional' fashion. In Germany, these indiscretions created an impression of warm sympathy and an exaggerated idea of his power and influence. But there is no evidence to indicate that the former King's views, however 'pro-German', influenced government policy. After due consideration, Harold concluded that Edward believed more than he should have in German integrity and in his ability to influence the course of events.[43]

'So ends a full and historic year,' Harold observed. Vita's literary career was well on course – having completed *Saint Joan of Arc* she had started *Pepita*; the boys were progressing famously; their financial troubles were apparently over; Sissinghurst was 'developing splendidly'. Harold was still beset by self-doubt, having dispersed his energies and having no sense of reaching a secure harbour. 'I am still very promising and shall continue to be so until the day of my death.' Would he have changed anything? 'NO,' he insisted. His life was 'as gay as an Alpine meadow patinated with the stars of varied flowers'. So it had been 'a happy year, a useful year'. There was one snag: it was 'clouded by menace on the Continent.'[44]

* Ribbentrop's 'champagne-like influence' on the Windsors appeared to come to the fore again when France collapsed in May–June 1940. On active service with the British army, though demoted from Field Marshal to Major-General, Edward fled to the south of France after the débâcle, and from there to Spain and then on to Lisbon. The Duke's views were well known. Like some in Whitehall, he too favoured a negotiated peace with Nazi Germany. Were the Germans aware of this? Almost certainly. At any rate, they plotted – with Ribbentrop at the Foreign Ministry at the centre of things – to keep him in Europe. Victim to their own fantasies, they most likely hoped to reinstate him as King once they had conquered Britain. However far-fetched a prospect this was, Churchill refused to allow the Duke back into England. Instead, he dispatched him to the Bahamas as Governor, where he remained, out of harm's way, until 1945.

TWELVE

'The Foreign Office Mind'

Harold's parliamentary reputation grew, mainly because he spoke authoritatively on foreign affairs, a topic about which he could reasonably claim some expertise. There was one minor blip. In November 1936 he was called upon to second the Address to the Throne. He was not happy at the honour inflicted upon him. 'Hell! Hell!' he groaned. Clad in his diplomatic uniform, which made him look 'ridiculous', he rose and immediately 'lost and annoyed the House'. He had been asked to follow precedent and mention previous holders of his constituency who had won distinction. As Ramsay MacDonald had represented Leicester (from 1906 to 1918), Harold began with a fulsome tribute to his leader, a panegyric that was greeted with hoots and yells and cries of 'Order! Order!' 'At one moment,' 'Chips' Channon recalled, 'I feared that he was breaking down . . . He sat down, at long last, in complete silence.' Harold acknowledged his gaffe; as did the press reports. Knowing that he had been 'silly and tactless', he felt utterly 'depressed' about the whole affair.[1]

Little attention was paid to the gist of Harold's speech, a 'well-phrased' review of Britain's foreign relations. Despite recent events in Ethiopia and Spain – where a civil war had broken out in July – and the consequent erosion of the League's prestige, his survey was moderately upbeat. Naming Russia, Germany, France and, more grudgingly, Italy, Harold considered that Britain's relations with the powers of Europe 'have considerably improved'. Looking ahead, he predicted that Britain's 'security and independence', its 'authority and influence', maintained by an effective defence posture, 'will be directed to the appeasement, political and economic, of the world'. It was a policy that would lead to general disarmament, 'whatever Signor Mussolini might say', he added mischievously. Rejecting 'entangling alliances' – a dig at the French – Harold opted for 'regional agreements' freely negotiated on the Locarno model. And, as a cry of faith, he visualised 'a League of Nations so fortified, so reconstituted and so reformed' as to unite the British people behind it.

Hardly any of this was borne out in the coming years. Relations with Germany and Italy rapidly deteriorated; Russia's world outlook was marked by acute paranoia; even France proved to be an awkward partner. The powers continued to rearm, including Britain, whose programme was gradually picking up speed, if at a slower pace than most. The only 'regional agreement' reached, the Munich settlement of September 1938, turned out to be an unmitigated disaster, while in the last days of peace Britain opted for an 'entangling alliance' with Poland. Nor would there be a refortified, reformed League; instead, it would fade away into obscurity. Perhaps in seconding the Address, Harold thought it prudent to inject a degree of optimism. Probably a wise decision for a working politician yet to consolidate his reputation, even if it bore no relation to international reality.

From its outset, the Spanish civil war absorbed the attention of the international community. It served as a kind of litmus test for whether democracy would survive or Fascism triumph. The war had begun on 18 July 1936 when military commanders in Spanish Morocco, prompted by extreme resentment at the growing socialist and anti-clerical policies of the recently elected Popular Front government in Madrid, took up arms against it. The fighting spread rapidly to the mainland, and it did not come to an end until March 1939. The official line of the powers, sanctioned by the League, was one of non-intervention, a policy wilfully ignored by Italy, Germany, and the Soviet Union. The extreme polarisation of political forces inside Spain, together with the active intervention of Italy and Germany on behalf of the insurgents and the Soviet Union supposedly championing the cause of the Left, turned the Spanish civil war into the ideological *cause célèbre* of the late 1930s.

'The Spanish situation is hell,' Harold noted. He distrusted both warring factions. The Madrid government he classified as 'Kerensky-like' at the mercy of 'an armed proletariat'; but 'Franco and his Moors' were 'no better'. Conscious that the conflict accentuated the division of Europe into Left and Right, he asked, 'Which way do we go?' He could offer no immediate clear-cut answer. In private, his views inclined towards a more robust anti-Franco line, the belief that the government had been 'weak and confused over the Spanish question'. At a dinner party at Philip Sassoon's he murmured to Eden that he wanted 'the Reds to win'. The destruction of Guernica, the ancient Basque capital, on 26 April 1937 by bombers of the German Kondor Legion reinforced his feelings. 'Only that ass Teenie [Victor Cazalet] goes on sticking up for Franco,' he wrote to Vita. 'I could have boxed his silly ears . . . I do so loathe this war. I really feel that barbarism is creeping over the earth again and that mankind is going backward.' In public, however, he firmly supported the government's policy of non-intervention, praising Eden, its glamorous advocate on the world stage. Britain, Harold instructed the House, can no longer indulge in its 'missionary foreign policy' of the nineteenth century 'to impose our views, our judgments, our standard of life and conduct upon other countries'. Without a trace of irony, he fell back on commonplaces, advising the House that the best way forward was to maintain traditional British interests, the 'preservation of peace' and 'the arrangement of the balance of power', although he failed to spell out how this was to be accomplished in the current climate of European affairs.[2]

When the Foreign Affairs Committee met in July to discuss the Spanish situation, Harold, now its vice-chairman, was agitated to find an 'enormous majority' passionately 'anti-Government and pro-Franco', a setting that allowed 'a lot of the younger Tories to blow off steam'. Harold told Eden that he opposed granting 'belligerency rights' to either side, as this would only serve Franco's cause. Eden agreed. He in turn admitted that non-intervention had 'largely failed'.[3] This could not have surprised Harold: with the Italians, Germans and Russians roaming the Spanish battlefields, no amount of subtle hair-splitting could disguise this fact. But was there any alternative, short of allowing the Spanish war to spread to an all-out European conflagration? It was a Micawber-like policy, regretfully followed in the hope that something better would turn up. One point weighed heavily upon Harold's mind. He confessed to Churchill that he felt 'terribly hampered' in deciding 'about foreign policies' because he had 'no conception whatsoever as to our real defensive capabilities'. Churchill fed him an (inflated) assessment of Germany's air strength, which, if augmented by the Italian air force, 'a very excellent striking machine', led Harold to the inescapable conclusion that 'we are indeed not in a position to go to war without very active Russian assistance'. Nor did Harold's opinion materially change over the coming months. Malcolm MacDonald, Secretary of State for dominions (and later for colonies), whose judgement he valued, reiterated that Britain was too weak to gamble on war. 'It would mean the massacre of women and children in the streets of London. No Government could possibly risk a war when our anti-aircraft defences are in so farcical a condition.'[4]

During the winter of 1937–38 Harold was invited to participate in a kind of 'brains trust' on foreign affairs at All Souls College, Oxford. Its purpose: to set out guidelines that would neutralise the menace of the totalitarian states. Organised by Sir Arthur Salter, the Gladstone Professor of Political Theory and Institutions at Oxford, it was dubbed 'Salter's Soviet' by Lionel Curtis, one of its more energetic members. It was a mixed bunch. A. L. Rowse, a fierce critic of the government's policy, rubbed shoulders with its most loyal defenders, Lord Allen of Hurtwood and Arnold Toynbee. Figures such as Harold Macmillan, Basil Liddell Hart,

H. A. L. Fisher, Norman Angell, Gilbert Murray, E. L. Woodward and Geoffrey Hudson were included; while others, Geoffrey Dawson, Robert Brand, Lord Lothian and Leopold Amery, remained on its fringes, consulted from time to time. Between December 1937 and May 1938 it convened nine times, usually at weekends at All Souls, occasionally at Harold's flat at King's Bench Walk or Norman Angell's chambers, housed in the same block.

There could be no meeting of minds between the young firebrands, Rowse and Hudson, and the pacifist Lord Allen, or the rest of the company, far more conservative in approach. For all that, a programme of sorts was floated, sponsored mainly by Curtis who argued that 'twenty years of peace were worth any price'. It would be a package deal.

We offer Germany: i) *Anschluss* [the Union of Austria with Germany, forbidden under the treaty of Versailles]; ii) arrangements granting cantonal status to Sudetenland by Czech government; iii) recognition of Germany's colonial rights; iv) admit Germany's prior economic interests in eastern Europe.

We demand from Germany: i) assurance that extension of German interests in eastern Europe would not entail any attack upon the autonomy of other countries; ii) that Germany agree to limitation of arms under which she would be the strongest power in central Europe but unable to dominate the collective force of other powers, i.e. preponderance but not supremacy; iii) and that Germany not support Italian aims in Mediterranean and Africa.

This was too much for Harold, who shocked Curtis by his 'anti-German stance'. Harold put on record his belief in Germany's 'aggressive ambitions', underscoring the 'heroic motive' that inspired German youth and that conditioned them to sacrifice themselves in the pursuit of power. Nor would he hear of granting Germany economic privileges in eastern Europe. To do so 'would so strengthen Germany that she would first dominate Europe and then us and the world'. In a cutting aside, Harold calculated that the 'Soviet' polarised into 'the traditionalists of our policy (namely to oppose the strong and to protect the weak) and an experiment in a new policy of trying to conciliate the strong'. 'We are somewhat inconclusive,' Harold owned up. After several months the 'Soviet' dispersed, agreeing to maintain a resolute policy in the Far East and the Mediterranean, to hasten rearmament, to push for more efficient air defences, and to avoid isolating the Soviet Union. They were skirting the main issue, however. Would firmness, taking a stand against the dictators – with Hitler particularly in mind – deter them or provoke them into embarking upon more reckless adventures? No consensus was possible on this crucial point, the primary purpose of convening the 'Soviet' in the first place. The split between the 'realists and the moralists', as Harold put it, was complete.[5]

After only a year as a Member of Parliament Harold sensed that his parliamentary reputation was in decline. 'I am not at my ease in the Chamber,' he acknowledged. Lacking in 'combative instincts', he felt that he was 'not sufficiently virile' to impose his authority upon the House. He had started well enough, but his seconding of the Address had been a fiasco. He gave himself another year to make good: '1938 will decide. At present I am still, for the majority of the House, an open question. This time next year that question will have been answered one way or the other.' His unease persisted well into the New Year: 'For the moment I am still rather frightened of the House.'[6] But as the tempo of international affairs quickened, crisis following crisis, his opportunity came sooner than expected.

On 15 February 1938 news reached London that at Berchtesgaden, the Austrian Chancellor, Kurt von Schuschnigg, browbeaten by Hitler, had effectively handed over the direction of Austrian affairs to Germany. At about the same time, in Berlin, Hitler took the nazification of the German army and Foreign Office a step further.* 'Adventurism is now in the ascendant in Germany,' Harold declared to the Foreign Affairs Committee, advising his audience not to panic but '[to] keep a stiff upper lip, not throw sops or slops about, wait, and, above all, rearm'. At dinner, two days later, a downcast Vansittart – recently sidelined to the hollow post of chief diplomatic adviser to the government – did not improve Harold's temper. No war 'yet', Harold noted. If, somehow, we can play for time and 'gain two years of peace, then we are almost home'. It was an overly optimistic assessment, neutralised by his final thought: 'There is no doubt that Germany is out for *Weltmacht*, and

---

*Those days also saw fundamental changes in the command structure of the German army. Its two foremost generals, General Werner von Blomberg, the Minister of War and Commander-in-Chief of the Armed Forces, and General Freiherr Werner von Fritsch, Commander-in-Chief of the army, had been forced to resign, the former owing to an ill-considered marriage to a lady with a police record for soliciting, the latter resulting from a trumped up homosexual charge. Hitler, constantly at odds with the old-style conservative generals, seized his chance. He assumed von Blomberg's position as Commander-in-Chief of the Armed Forces and abolished the post of War Minister. Instead, he set up a separate High Command of the Armed Forces, the Oberkommando der Wehrmacht (OKW), commanded by the subservient General Wilhelm Keitel. In effect, it acted as Hitler's personal staff.

Making a clean sweep of it, Hitler sacked Constantin von Neurath, the more traditionally minded Foreign Minister, and replaced him with the sycophantic, vain and arrogant Joachim von Ribbentrop, who had already failed miserably as the German ambassador in London.

will carry that through with grim determination.' Just three days after his cheerless dinner, Anthony Eden resigned as Foreign Secretary, ostensibly over Chamberlain's precipitate and inept handling of Anglo–Italian relations.[7]

There was nothing Harold could do about the doleful events in Germany – except enliven the pages of his diary. But Eden's resignation affected him deeply. He had loyally upheld Eden's handling of British foreign policy. 'Don't be worried, my darling,' he assured Vita, 'I am not going to become one of the Winston brigade. My leaders are Anthony [Eden] and Malcolm [MacDonald].' But however much he admired MacDonald, as he had come to the unavoidable conclusion that National Labour had 'ceased to exist as a separate entity', Eden emerged as his front runner.[8] Harold was determined to defend the position of Eden, whose resignation speech, muddled and indecisive, had not gone down well. Harold would enlighten the House instead: the Foreign Secretary, he revealed to the restless members, had resigned not over 'a little point of procedure', but on 'a great question of principle'. This was not the opinion of almost all other observers, including cabinet ministers. Bruised pride, vanity and pique played as large a part in Eden's decision to resign as did 'a great question of principle'.[9] Harold himself, in time, would become aware of the flaws in Eden's character.

But for the moment, Harold was Eden's man. He lashed into Italy, 'a country which has continuously, consistently, deliberately and without apology, violated every engagement into which she has ever entered'; it had perfected 'the corkscrew' method of negotiation. Above all, he deeply regretted that 'our great principles of policy', our regard for 'the rule of law and order, the theory of the League of Nations, the belief in the sanctity of treaties' should be 'butchered to make a Roman holiday'. His speech was warmly received by other critics of the government. Lloyd George called it 'a fine Parliamentary performance'; Churchill congratulated him: 'That was a magnificent speech. I envy you your gift.' Naturally, for adherents of the government it was deemed 'violent' and 'foolish', damaging to 'the cause of peace'.[10] But Harold had no doubt that Chamberlain was blindly leading the country into a political and diplomatic minefield:

> The Government may say what they like, but their policy is nothing less than the scrapping of the ideas which have been built up since the war and the reversion to the old pre-war policy of power politics and bargaining. This means: (1) that we shall have to buy the friendship of Italy and Germany by making sacrifices. (2) That this friendship will not be worth 2d once it is bought. And (3) that in doing so we shall sacrifice the confidence of France, Russia, the United States and all the smaller countries. I mind it dreadfully.

There were other aspects of the affair that he frowned upon. 'Tricky' Chamberlain no longer inspired trust. Nor, unfortunately, did his own party, that had behaved 'like worms and kissed the Chamberlain boot with a resounding smack'. As for all the Tories and die-hards, they were hugging themselves, jubilant at having flushed out 'all the nonsensical notions of the past and having got back the good old Tory doctrines'.[11]

Harold's pessimism intensified when, on 12 March, German forces crossed over into Austria and Hitler, addressing a rapturous crowd from the balcony of Linz Town Hall, proclaimed the *Anschluss*. 'No question of an *Anschluss*, just complete absorption,' commented Harold. Depressed by the Cabinet's spineless response, he agonised: 'How can I continue to support a Government like this?' Although he still sat on the government benches – praiseworthy loyalty to a party that existed in name only – he emerged as a leading critic of the government's foreign policy and its leader. Why do 'we just run about and squeal?' he asked Vita. 'I do not really trust Chamberlain's intelligence. He is no more than an iron-monger [his family fortune derived from screw-manufacturing]. We are going to let Germany become so powerful that she will begin to dictate to us. Then the row will come. But I cannot possibly support the Chamberlain point of view.'[12] The *Anschluss* passed off to whispers of protest. But Spain was still a burning issue. Four days after Hitler's coup, with Franco's troops on the offensive, it afforded Harold an opportunity to speak out forcefully.

He began by expressing his 'deepest sympathy' with the Spanish govern-ment and his 'deepest hatred' for Franco. A Franco victory, he pointed out, would gravely menace Britain's interests and security. A free Spain, he stressed, had traditionally been of immense strategic advantage to Britain. Sounding a note of alarm, he asked the House to imagine the danger of Gibraltar and the Straits 'slipping into Mussolini's hands'. He wanted no more paper resolutions. 'It is essential that this country . . . should display to the world an affirmation of strength.' But what kind of 'affirmation'? Harold sat down without committing himself. A message was passed along to him from the Prime Minister: 'What do you want us to do?' Harold passed back his reply: 'Occupy Minorca.' Chamberlain flung back his head 'with a gesture of angered despair'.[13] Listed among a group of 'insurgents' who, allegedly, were aiming for a government reshuffle, to bring in Churchill at the Admiralty and reinstate Eden at the Foreign Office, Harold's loyalty to Chamberlain had sunk to its nadir. A move was set in motion to remove him as vice-chairman of the Foreign Affairs Committee. At first, the vote went unanimously in his favour, except for 'one little vicious hand' raised against, that of Nancy Astor. But as the pressure mounted – are you 'pro-Chamberlain or pro-Eden?' – he was left with no option but to resign.[14]

In October 1936, Vansittart, then in a position of influence, wanted to send Harold off to the Balkans 'on a sort of unofficial mission'. Its purpose: to impress upon those countries that Britain will stand firmly against a German *Mitteleuropa*. In the second half of April 1938 Harold fulfilled his commission, but on behalf of the British Council. He was to enlighten the Balkan peoples on subjects as diverse as 'Are the British Hypocrites?' and 'The Foundations of British Foreign Policy', two topics, Harold may well have reasoned, that went hand in hand given the current state of British policy. There was also much socialising. He lectured to eager audiences, ate well, and on one occasion embarrassed himself when, lunching with King Carol of Romania, a bottle of sal volatile spilt in his pocket and left a deep wet stain on the plush seat of his chair. 'What will the butler think?' he wondered. There was also an unspoken political motive to his visit. The Foreign Office had indicated that he should also exploit his time to bolster morale in the region, now dangerously exposed to German penetration after the *Anschluss*, the German *Mitteleuropa* of which Vansittart had warned. Harold found something 'pathetic' in 'how these people long for British friendship', and even more in 'how they exaggerate my importance and the meaning of my visit'.[15] For Harold reckoned, with sound reason, that should Germany strike again into central or south-east Europe, Britain would again stand by helplessly. The one country on Germany's immediate timetable, Czechoslavakia, was not favoured by Harold's goodwill tour.

The Czech crisis did not spring upon Western statesmen. In some ways, it had been on the European agenda since the Paris peace conference. It now simmered menacingly for the coming months. However tackled, it presented a problem of considerable complexity, one not given to foolproof solutions. A democratic, multinational state, its problems were formidable. Involved in border disputes with all its neighbours, it was rent internally by national and religious discord. Bound by treaties to France and the Soviet Union, it was a vital link in the so-called encirclement of Germany. Eduard Beneš, its President, an adept politician and diplomat, was burdened by a high-handed, overbearing reputation; in some circles he was judged to be a tool of French policy. Many, probably a majority of Englishmen conversant with European affairs, were troubled at the Czech government's treatment of its ethnic minorities. In particular, the long-standing grievances of the Sudeten Germans received much sympathetic coverage.

The Sudetenland, an area of some 11,000 square miles in northern Bohemia, lies to the east of the mountain range that forms a strategic barrier between

Germany and Czechoslovakia. Populated by almost three million ethnic Germans, and formerly part of the German Confederation, it had been incorporated into the newly created state of Czechoslovakia in 1919. From the outset, the Sudeten Germans complained, often not without justification, that the Prague government discriminated against them on national, economic, social and religious grounds, a condition that considerably worsened with the onset of the economic depression in the early 1930s. Harold, for one, believed that these wrongs needed to be addressed. He understood perfectly well that the independence of Czechoslovakia was a British interest, just as he knew that Britain was 'not strong enough to defend it'. What remained? To persuade Chamberlain to adopt a 'Salter's Soviet' formula: 'namely pressure on the Czechs, to give greater assurances to the Sudeten Germans, coupled with some assurances that if they do that we will protect their future'.[16]

One reason for the acceptance of Sudeten German claims was the personality of Konrad Henlein, at one time a gymnastics instructor, now leader of the Sudetendeutsche Partei (SDP). A smooth customer, personable in manner, he presented himself as a moderate hemmed in by extremists. Primed by his masters in Berlin, Hitler had told him shortly after the *Anschluss* to raise his demands to a degree unacceptable to the Czech government, which he dutifully did at Karlsbad on 24 April 1938, demanding full equality of status between Germans and Czechs; delimitation of the German areas; full autonomy; removal of all injustices and reparations for damage suffered by the Germans since 1918; the right of Germans to proclaim their 'Germanism' and their adherence to the ideology of Germany; and the complete revision of Czech foreign policy. To the outside world, he claimed to want only justice for his people, greater autonomy in running their own affairs. He visited London on three occasions to meet leading figures in British public life. Even such distinguished 'anti-appeasers' as Churchill and Vansittart were taken in, and came away favourably impressed with his performance.

On 13 May 1938 Harold threw a tea party at 4, King's Bench Walk. On the table were temptingly displayed 'five heaped up plates of sandwiches, four pyramids of scones, and a Dundee cake'. The guest of honour was Konrad Henlein. This was a duty of labour, urged upon Harold by Vansittart. Other MPs were present: Duncan Sandys, Sir Edward Spears, Godfrey Nicholson and Captain J. R. Macnamara, all Conservatives. As it was a humid afternoon, the windows were left open. Down below, journalists gathered, straining to overhear snatches of the conversation in both German and English (Henlein spoke no English). Henlein said that, despite his militant Karlsbad speech, he sought no more, but no less, than cantonal autonomy for the Sudetenland, leaving finance, foreign affairs and defence in the hands of the Prague government. Should Beneš prove obdurate, he saw no alternative but German occupation which he knew would lead 'to a general war'. In accordance with Vansittart's wishes, Harold made clear that 'we earnestly hoped that Herr Henlein would not return to Czechoslovakia with the impression that not a single British soldier would fight for the Czechs . . . and that on his shoulders rested the grave responsibility for avoiding a second European war'. In this statement, Vansittart, and his mouthpiece, Harold, were overstepping the guidelines of current British policy. Not that this made much difference in the long run. Henlein was playing a double game. Only a day before his tea party with Harold, on 12 May, Henlein had been in Berlin receiving further instructions on how best to dupe the British.

But the essential point is not what Henlein said, but how his hosts deciphered his soft words. For Harold, at least, this suggested that perhaps the 'Salter's Soviet' recipe offered the most equitable way of resolving the Czech question. The Foreign Office too believed that Henlein's conversations may have done some good. When Harold learned that Lord Runciman, a distinguished, elderly Liberal peer, was being sent to Prague to mediate between the parties in dispute, Harold took heart: 'They are sending Runciman on a mission to Prague to induce the Czech government to make further concessions to the Sudetens. I am delighted by this.'[17] But Harold was in no doubt where to draw the line: carefully monitored concessions were one thing; the dismemberment of Czechoslovakia, its absorption into a Greater Germany, was quite another. His starting point was down-to-earth *realpolitik*: Britain would fight for Czechoslovakia 'to prevent Germany dominating Europe'. But he soon moved on to take the high moral ground, with Czechoslovakia raised to the status of 'a test case in the spiritual conflict between Liberty and the Nazi theory'.[18]

At the height of the crisis, on 23 September, when Britain was on a virtual war footing, Harold completed his monograph, *Diplomacy*. It defines diplomacy as 'the management of the relations between independent states by the process of negotiation', as 'common sense and charity applied to international relations', as 'akin to sound banking' that 'depends on credit'. It sets out the virtues of a proficient diplomat: 'truthfulness, precision, calm, good temper, patience, modesty, and loyalty'. It speaks of the British 'mercantile-style' of diplomacy, so distinct from the German 'warrior-style', which fed off its political philosophy of 'mystic union', its tenet that '*raison d'état*' takes precedence over everything, its belief 'in force, or the threat of force' as the main instrument of negotiation. It accepts that the framing of policy is the prerogative of the elected government, but stresses that its implementation should be left in the competent hands of professional diplomats. And finally, and logically, it deprecates summit diplomacy.[19] These thoughts ran through Harold's mind as he traced the unfolding of the Czech crisis to its lamentable outcome.

As September 1938 passed, Harold's alarm grew. The milestones are all too familiar: Hitler's hysterical Nuremberg speech; Neville Chamberlain's flights to Germany; the Western powers' manipulation of the Czechs; and the last crisis-laden days, leading to the well-timed appeal by Mussolini (and Roosevelt) for a conference at Munich where the concluding humiliating scene was enacted, Sudeten German regions being surrendered to Germany. Harold followed this drama with mounting concern, but also, occasionally, with sighs of relief.

By Harold's yardstick, Neville Chamberlain, who had 'no conception really of world politics', was quite unsuited to conclude a successful negotiation. Yet such was the general fear of war that when Chamberlain set out on 15 September for Berchtesgaden to confront Hitler, the first of his three flights to Germany, he felt 'enormous relief', tinged by a shade of 'disquiet'. 'I shall be one of his most fervent admirers if he brings back something which does not constitute a Hitler triumph,' Harold wrote. His sense of relief was short-lived. It soon became apparent that Chamberlain, who 'didn't care two hoots whether the Sudetens were in the Reich or out of it', had brought back an agreement that, in principle, ceded to Germany the Sudeten German areas, provided the cession be achieved peacefully. Anglo-French pressure mounted on the Czechs to accept this arrangement. At one stage, 'Baffy' Dugdale, a National Labourite and a member of the Executive of the League of Nations Union, rang up Harold to tell him that she had been 'sick twice in the night over England's shame', and had thrown up again after having read in *The Times* that 'the terms submitted to the Czechoslovak Government could not, in the nature of things, be expected to make a strong *prima facie* appeal to them'. Thereupon, she had resigned from the Party. Harold's conscience was pricked, not to the point of resignation, but to the point of a note of protest to 'Buck' De La Warr about National Labour's pusillanimity in remaining silent: Harold would consider his position.[20]

In a roundabout way it improved when Chamberlain returned empty-handed from the second round of talks held at Godesberg on 22–23 September. Angered by Hitler's tactics of hiking up his demands, Chamberlain had broken off the negotiations and returned to London. Attempts were made to whip up support among opposition MPs to stiffen Chamberlain's resolve, but to little effect. Divided and ineffectual, they were incapable even of issuing a joint declaration, Eden shying off at the last moment. On the other hand, Chamberlain enjoyed virtual *carte blanche* from his Party for his peace efforts and, as it turned out, from public opinion. It was an uphill struggle for those hard-liners who met at Churchill's apartment at Morpeth Mansions. 'This is hell,' Harold said to Churchill as they faced each other in the lift. 'It is the end of the British Empire.' They discussed tactics should Chamberlain decide to 'rat again'. 'We do not think he will rat, and therefore we shall then "rally behind him" (poor man). We shall press for a Coalition Government and the immediate application of war measures.' War seemed imminent. Outside, trenches were being dug in Green Park; from the Admiralty, an order was issued to put the Fleet on alert. At Sissinghurst, a room was converted to serve as a gas-proof air-raid shelter; in the calf-orchard, a trench was dug. Harold gamely feigned indifference. 'I know one of the party who will not be there. He will be in his bed minus gas-mask and with all the windows open.'[21]

On the evening of 28 September Harold broadcast on the Empire Service of the BBC an account of that day's events in the House of Commons. It had convened to hear Chamberlain clarify the chain of events that had led up to the crisis. As the Prime Minister entered the Chamber he was greeted with shouts of applause from his supporters, many of whom rose in their seats and waved their order papers. The opposition remained seated and silent. And so did Harold, ostensibly a government supporter. Chamberlain told of the tangled negotiations with the French, the Czechs and the Germans. He turned to his last conversation with Hitler. The Führer had convinced him that he was prepared 'to risk a world war' on behalf of the Sudeten Germans. 'As he said these words a shudder of horror passed through the House of Commons.' All through the briefing, messages were being passed back and forth among the members. At 4.12 p.m. a note on Foreign Office paper reached Sir John Simon, who tugged at Chamberlain's coat, interrupting his discourse. There was a momentary hush. Chamberlain's 'whole face, his whole body, seemed to change . . . he appeared ten years younger and triumphant'. 'Herr Hitler,' he announced to a keyed-up House, 'has just agreed to postpone his mobilisation for twenty-four hours and to meet me in conference with Signor Mussolini and Signor Daladier at Munich.' The House erupted in a great roar of cheers and rose to pay tribute to the man who had saved the peace. Harold felt ashamed. The entire performance reminded him of 'a Welsh Revivalist meeting'. He again remained seated, but heard clearly a Conservative member behind him who hissed, 'Stand up, you brute!' Harold returned home that night with 'an immense sense of *physical* relief', though his 'moral anxieties' were in no way diminished. No doubt he would have appreciated a ditty circulating in the Foreign Office mocking the Prime Minister's 'senile visit' to Canossa, his futile shuttle diplomacy: 'If at first you can't concede/Fly, fly, fly again.'[22]

As news of the Munich pact trickled through, Harold met Vansittart at the St James's Club. Its terms, laid down by the four powers, Britain, France, Germany and Italy, on 29 September – without the encumbrance of Czechoslovakia or the Soviet Union – were most severe. It called for the secession of the Sudetenland to Germany to be carried out between 1 and 10 October, plebiscites to be held in some areas, and the transference of these territories to be supervised by an international commission: it also stipulated that no military installations were to be destroyed. (In its annexe, the agreement called for a settlement of Polish and Hungarian claims and a guarantee – never ratified – of Czechoslovakia's new frontiers. On 2 October Poland duly occupied Teschen, a rich industrial region; later, Hungary annexed a broad strip of southern Slovakia and Ruthenia.)

Vansittart advised Harold to forget the past. Recriminations will only 'create splits', he argued, 'What we have got to do is to come together for the next danger.' Should Chamberlain form a 'Government of Reconstruction', it would be Harold's duty to serve under him. Harold balked at such an outrageous suggestion. 'Now that is very noble of Van . . . I really do admire him. But I shall have [a] hit at the old boy tomorrow, nonetheless.' The occasion was a speaking engagement at a luncheon sponsored by the National Labour group in Manchester. The press reported Harold as saying that the 'Government had been guided by the advice of Sir Horace Wilson, which was never inconvenient, rather than that of Sir Robert Vansittart, which was always right but which the Government found inconvenient.' In fact, Harold had said nothing of the kind. Re-reading his speech, he had toned down its temper, cutting out all personal attacks. But, as required, he had sent a copy of his original draft to the National Labour office, which had promptly released it to the press. His actual speech went down well, but Harold realised instantly that the fallout from this incident would rally the Chamberlainite loyalists against him. Matters worsened when Harold voted against a resolution of the National Labour Executive pledging support to the Prime Minister. Unfriendly letters began to appear in the Leicester newspapers attacking him for his dishonourable behaviour.[23]

Probably the high point of Harold's parliamentary career was his attack on the government's foreign policy after the Munich agreement. His stand was uncompromising. It brought him much credit from the oppositionists, but little joy from his constituents at West Leicester. He spoke with great authority, for in 1919 he had served on the committee at the Paris conference that had laid down the Sudetenland frontier. Hitler, he stated, had three aims: to swallow the Sudeten Germans; to destroy Czechoslovakia; and to dominate Europe.

'We have given him all those three things.' Harold would, possibly, have met the first of Hitler's demands, though with 'unutterable sadness', for the Sudetenland 'was not worth a war'. But by Chamberlain's capitulation on the first point a deadly chain reaction had been set off that led, inexorably, to total surrender. 'The essential thing, the thing which we ought to have resisted, the thing which we still ought to resist; the thing which I am afraid it is now too late to resist is the domination of Europe by Germany.' He referred to 'this humiliating defeat, this terrible Munich retreat' as 'one of the most disastrous episodes that has ever occurred in our history'. It is the '*Führerhaus* in Munich', not Great Britain, that controls Europe's destiny today. 'The tiger is showing his teeth; the cage door is open; the keeper is gone; and they [the countries of Europe] must make their terms . . . we have given away the whole key to Europe.' In a few months, Harold forecast, 'Germany will have the whole trade of Europe in a stranglehold.' He belittled Chamberlain's specious 'bit of paper', that had supposedly brought 'peace with honour', as 'a little after dinner extravaganza'. Was this 'Peace with honour?' he might have asked, as he vilified the Poles, 'those ghouls of the Middle Ages who used to strip the wounded on the battlefield'. As for the guarantee, he castigated it as 'the most farcical diplomatic hypocrisy that was ever perpetrated'. He then called the attention of the House to Sir Eyre Crowe and the Foreign Office mind:

This is the first time in the history of the British people for 250 years in which openly, avowedly and dramatically they have made friends with the strong against the weak. For 250 years at least the great foundation of our foreign policy, what Sir Eyre Crowe called 'a law of nature,' has been to prevent by any means in our power the domination of Europe by any single Power or group of Powers. That principle has necessarily had the corollary that we should always support the small Powers against the strong. By that paper signed lightly, happily perhaps, tragically for certain, in the late hours of the morning, the Prime Minister of Great Britain put his signature to a statement that that policy after 250 years had been abandoned.

I know that those of us who try to be consistent are accused of having 'one-track' minds, I know that in these days of realism principles are considered as rather eccentric and ideals are identified with hysteria. I know that those of us who believe in the traditions of our policy, who believe in the precepts which we have inherited from our ancestors, who believe that one great function of this country is to maintain moral standards in Europe, to maintain a settled pattern of international relations, not to make friends with people whose conduct is demonstrably evil, not to go out of our way to make friends with them but to set up some sort of standard by which the smaller Powers can test what is good in international conduct and what is not – I know that those who hold such beliefs are accused of possessing the Foreign Office mind. I thank God that I possess the Foreign Office mind.[24]

There were other powerful anti-government speeches, by Churchill and Duff Cooper (the only cabinet minister to resign), but they hardly dented the government's huge majority: by 366 to 144, the House declared its confidence in the government's policy. Thirty Conservative MPs abstained; thirteen remained in their seats, Harold, a National Labour rebel, among them. So their 'St. Vitus antics' – as the fawning Chamberlainite, 'Chips' Channon, put it – had little effect. Nor was their case strengthened by the fact that their counter-proposals – increased rearmament, grand coalitions, a revivified League, or claiming the high moral ground – were barren of new ideas. For those preoccupied with the making of British foreign policy, tormented by the memories and horrors of the Great War, inclined – also on moral grounds – to satisfy Germany's 'legitimate grievances', above all conscious of Britain's defence weaknesses and of French lack of will, this was insufficient. The terms of the settlement stuck in the throat of many ministers. These men were not cowards, neither were they indifferent to the German menace. One of them, Walter Elliot, who agonised over the Munich agreement, but who didn't resign, wrote: 'That fearful timetable is a great crime and scandal, for which those of us who accepted it will be justly condemned, and I believe some day punished . . . That does not get me away from my desperate question – if I could rub out that agreement . . . would I do it? In the present state of our forces – French and British – I cannot say that I would. Therefore I accept the Munich terms . . .' It is also worth noting that on 23 September, as the Godesberg talks were breaking down, the Chiefs of Staff presented the Cabinet with a paper that stated: 'To attempt to take offensive action against Germany until we have had time to bring our naval, military and air forces, and also our passive defence services, on to a war footing would be to place ourselves in the position of a man who attacks a tiger before he has loaded his gun.'[25]

Given the basic facts as known to ministers there was a tragic inevitability to the Munich settlement, however disgraceful the betrayal of Czechoslovakia.

By 13 October Harold's local storm had exhausted itself. At West Leicester he survived a vote of no confidence, without having 'to pledge eternal fidelity to Chamberlain', but that left the Conservative ladies of the branch 'really enraged'. He loathed attending his constituency surgery. 'It is really rather hell here . . . Tiresome people come and interrupt me all morning and in the afternoons I have to address women's meetings. They sit there all solid and sullen and do not understand a word.' Harold would be the first to admit that he lacked the common touch: unfortunately, 'tiresome people' were lurking everywhere, in every constituency, and it was they who ultimately decided the fate of politicians, however aristocratically inclined. But his position was anomalous for another reason. Elected to support the government, he had become one of its most vociferous critics. His adversarial qualities found modest expression in a ginger group – 'All good Tories and sensible men' – headed by the ineffectual Eden, rather than in the one led by the more pugnacious Churchill who, Harold thought, was 'more bitter than determined, and more out for a fight than for reform'. Harold's coterie would merely meet from time to time, exchange views, and organise itself 'for a revolt if needed'. This was stretching reality, as Harold well knew. 'I was not made to be a rebel,' he eventually conceded. In any case, the ever-bashful Eden, their nominal leader, declined 'to come out against the Government', missing 'every boat with exquisite elegance'.[26]

In the anxious minds of most European statesmen, 'Waiting for Hitler' characterised the months that followed Munich. But unlike Vladimir and Estragon, Harold did not kill time, clinging to the hope that relief might be just around the corner. Convinced that Germany aimed 'first to conquer eastern Europe and then turn westwards', he busied himself in activities best suited to his talents: lecturing, broadcasting and writing, as well as his required parliamentary duties. In April 1937 he delivered the Rede lectures at Cambridge: his subject, 'The Meaning of Prestige'. Unusually for Harold, he read these lectures from a manuscript, not, as he usually did, speaking from detailed notes, or simply extemporising; fortunately, his transgression 'went undetected'. Later in the year he addressed the Jewish Literary Society in Leicester on 'Biography'. 'It goes very well. Afterwards some of the Jews put their hats on or cover their heads with napkins. I am alarmed at this, scenting some Hebrew ceremony, but they merely have coffee.'[27] Writing was Harold's natural medium. He wrote for scholarly journals, *Foreign Affairs* or *The Nineteenth Century and After*; and also, if the price was right, for more fashionable, self-proclaimed highbrow weeklies. On leaving the Foreign Office he had turned down an offer from the *Spectator* on the grounds that he loathed churning out articles, even though he had already committed himself to such an onerous task for the American magazine, *Vanity Fair*, for the agreeable sum of £1,200. At the end of 1938 he was again approached by the *Spectator*. On this occasion he agreed to contribute a weekly piece, calling it 'Marginal Comment'. By the time he wrote his last article in 1952, his column had become something of a national institution, at least for the readers of that reputable journal. Remaining faithful to his comment to Michael Sadleir – 'I hate anthologies unless they are written by myself' – 'Marginal Comment' spawned three anthologies of his essays in book form, a rich harvest from such modest beginnings.[28]

Harold was already a seasoned broadcaster, having begun his career at the BBC in 1929. His talks, particularly his celebrated broadcast with Vita on 'Marriage', as well as his commentaries on the Munich crisis, had brought him national prominence. From 1938 to 1939 he took upon himself a regular Monday evening slot from 9.45 to 10 p.m., stimulating his listeners with an eclectic miscellany of topics that included 'Good Manners', 'English Public Schools', 'Covent Garden Gala', 'Mass Observation', 'Ma Visite en France' and 'When I Was Young', among others. He also tried his hand at television, still in its experimental stage. He was paired with James Francis ('Frank') Horrabin, the well-known cartoonist for the *News Chronicle* and left-wing socialist, to introduce a series on 'This Rough Island Story'. 'A very difficult technique,' he said after his first appearance before the cameras, 'but I enjoy it'; his second, however, went 'very badly'. Another 'difficult technique' he failed to master was the latest fad in literary style. On meeting James Joyce in Paris, he had observed that the renowned author was divorced from reality. Trying to read and understand *Finnegans Wake* only confirmed his earlier judgement. 'I really cannot make head or tails of it. It's worse than a letter from Sibyl Colefax – One cannot read it; one has just got to prop it up on the mantelpiece and take it in.' On the other hand, the older he got, the closer he felt to his perennial hero, Lord Byron. 'I am like him,' he boasted, adding thoughtfully, but 'without his cruelty or genius'.[29]

It was while Harold worked for the BBC that he formed a friendship with Guy Burgess, although they had met previously at social get-togethers. By then, Burgess, a graduate of Trinity College, Cambridge, and a member of the exclusive intellectual secret society, the Apostles, had been recruited as a Soviet mole. Addicted to drink and casual homosexual dalliances, dishevelled in dress, careless in his personal hygiene, Burgess hardly fitted the perceived image of a pillar of the BBC Yet he functioned as a producer in its Talks Department, a position that brought him into close contact with Harold during the late 1930s. He flaunted anti-Nazi sentiments, a point of view that greatly appealed to Harold (as it did to Churchill). After one of Harold's talks at the height of the Munich crisis, they repaired to the Café Royal, where they met James Pope-Hennessy, and together shared their grief 'over England's shame'. On another occasion, outraged at Downing Street's veto of a talk on Mediterranean naval strategy to be given by Admiral Sir Herbert Richmond – a distinguished naval historian and outspoken critic of the Admiralty – Burgess threatened to resign: Harold urged him not to do so.[30] There is no hard evidence that Harold had an affair with Burgess – although the suspicion did arise after Burgess (and fellow Apostle Donald Maclean) defected to Moscow in May 1951. Given Burgess's notorious reputation, his aggressive homosexual behaviour – he was once arrested for soliciting in a public lavatory – Harold, far more discreet, would have recognised Burgess as an unpredictable, potentially ruinous partner.

In Harold's social circle, homosexuality remained a topic for weighty discourse. Lunching at the Travellers' Club with Alan Pryce-Jones, Tissilot Furstenberg, Malcolm Bullock and Desmond Shawe-Taylor, the company discussed, 'somewhat to Jones's horror, homosexual practices at public schools. We discover the whole system was quite different at Eton, Wellington and Sherborne.' Harold did not elaborate. But he did not confine himself to insightful chats on the subject, as a letter from one Friedel (?) bears ready witness: 'Stupid-stupid-stupid. Yes I am. And I am lonely as I had never been before. All I wish now and have so often wished all through the year is to spend a few more hours with you . . . Your presence makes me feel being a baby, because you are so crashingly masculine. To cover up my timidity and embarrassment I behaved towards you as I did. Time marches on. Is it too late?'[31]

Self-indulgence was a feature of Harold's lifestyle. He made at least one attempt to curb his taste for high living by travelling third class instead of first. It was a modest exercise in self-discipline, but it failed in its aim; and probably had the reverse effect. Indulgence of oneself in pleasurable pursuits might well explain Harold's desire to join the exclusive Other Club. Founded in 1911 by Churchill and F. E. Smith (Lord Birkenhead), and co-sponsored by Lloyd George, its membership consisted of MPs and peers, press lords, authors, top military brass, even actors; its purpose was 'to dine' on alternate Thursdays when Parliament was in session. The dinners were generally held in the Pinafore Room at the Savoy. Churchill invariably 'presided', taking his seat in the middle of the table with his back to the window overlooking the Thames. In time, Churchill became its *genius loci*. Not only Churchill's toadies were included, but if he wanted you in, you became a member. On the surface, the Other Club would appear to be an ideal spot for Harold to shine. He possessed all the necessary qualities to be a popular member: he was well-connected, an amusing dinner companion, a witty raconteur, characteristics tailor-made for the purpose of the Club. Above all, he hero-worshipped Churchill. On familiar terms with Churchill for many years, Harold had also, on occasion, performed useful services for the great man. Checking Churchill's pen-portrait of Curzon in his *Great Contemporaries*, and choosing language that was bound to please, he was unable to find 'a single word which goes beyond reasonable criticism', relishing particularly the phrase about Curzon as being 'able to domineer but not to dominate', complimenting Churchill for his 'brilliant summary of that metallic but brittle temperament'. Yet Churchill refused him entry to his select fraternity. 'Winston carefully considered the possible admission of Harold Nicolson and felt that nothing should be done at present'.[32] Nor was anything done in the future. This was odd. Could it have been because of Harold's homosexuality? A possible, but highly improbable, explanation. These matters barely interested Churchill. In any case, sexual peccadilloes were not an obstacle to membership, as many of the Club's stalwarts would no doubt have admitted, if forced to. Harold Macmillan offered a more persuasive answer, one that spoke much to Harold's character:

Winston relished argument and passionate disagreement, if need be. The inner group would say, 'Winston, you are talking balls. The way you must act is like this.' Winston would listen, complain that they were all against him, even cry, and then do what he thought best as a result of the discussion. Now, Harold was not on these terms. He would look at Winston with adoring eyes like a faithful spaniel. This was not what Winston liked or admired. He did not care for deference . . .[33]

Being shunned by Churchill did not dampen Harold's appetite for self-indulgence. In October 1938 he acquired a small yacht of nine-foot draught, manned by a crew of two. Named the *Mar*, it cost £2,000, money which the cash-strapped Harold had borrowed from Vita. It lay at Southampton all that winter. Harold was overjoyed 'with his silly little boat (oh my dear – how I love the sound of foam against a boat!)'. Having made 'his squalid little tub . . . quite habitable', he embarked from Plymouth on 4 August, accompanied by John Sparrow, a fellow of All Souls, and joined later by Nigel, intending to sail round Land's End to the west coast of Scotland. Off Penzance, bad weather drove them back into the English Channel where they put in at Falmouth, St Michael's Mount and Weymouth, crossed over to Cherbourg, anchored at St Peter Port, Guernsey, and returned to Plymouth Sound on 22 August. That evening Harold heard the news that Germany and the Soviet Union proposed to sign a non-aggression pact. War was imminent. Harold never sailed in the *Mar* again. Hit by a bomb, it became a casualty of war.[34]

By the outbreak of war in 1939, Sissinghurst Castle had been restored for modern living. The bare essentials, mains for water and electricity, had been installed; the living quarters, the Main House and the Long Library, the Priest's House and the South Cottage – Harold's den – and the Elizabethan Tower – Vita's sanctuary – were in day-to-day use, ample enough both for owners and servants, though weekend visitors were at a disadvantage as no private guest rooms had been arranged. There were some mishaps. 'I do wish Sissinghurst were not quite so inflammable,' complained Vita. 'It's as bad as Dottie [Wellesley].' Her beloved tower had caught fire. Helped by a downpour, it was quickly extinguished; but the 'awful mess' had left her 'poor room' quite 'uninhabitable'. Would the insurance company pay for the damage, or will they begin 'to think we do it on purpose?' In the summer of 1938, lightning struck the tower. Vita, perversely, 'blamed' poor Harold. All Harold had done was to insist on putting in a conductor, a reasonable and conventional safety precaution. According to Vita's logic, however, it endangered her tower by attracting the lightning. Harold put it another way: 'A more generous attitude would be to say that unless the conductor had been put in the Tower would now be a heap of bricks.'[35]

The garden too – all six acres of it – was in essence finished, and, as has been observed, 'merely required time for it to achieve its present maturity'. The family and selected guests could explore the Rose Garden, or the Nuttery, or the Herb Garden; or they could stroll down the various walks, named Lime, Yew and Moat; or they could inspect a statue of Dionysus, a Greek altar, a medieval wall, and a dovecote, scattered around the grounds. To the northern and eastern sides a moat lent the whole a reminder of bygone days. The walks were laid out by Harold with meticulous precision, using stakes and strings to attain the symmetry he so desired. Vita was not always pleased with the result. 'What do think?' Harold asked her, pointing out the central path of the Lime Walk. 'It's just like platform 5 at Charing Cross,' she tartly replied. Vita was more taken with the life-cycle of a garden, allowing wild flowers to invade it, contending with seasonal change, watching plants die and be replenished, regarding a garden as 'eternally moribund, eternally renascent'.[36] There was one striking innovation. In the spring of 1939 the 'shillings' began to arrive. On 7 May Harold noted that in two days eight hundred visitors had paid their twelve pence to enjoy the garden at Sissinghurst: a breakthrough that realised £53, and that would continue in the future. Neither Harold nor Vita begrudged this new practice. Apart from its material benefits, Vita viewed it as a 'pleasure, even a form of flattery'.[37]

Following in Harold's footsteps, Nigel, also at Balliol, only obtained a third (but in Modern History) at Oxford. 'Stunned' by the news, Harold, as any caring parent would, took it personally, 'like a blow in the face'. Some months earlier his spirits had lifted at the news that Nigel insisted on buying the Shiant Islands. Advertised as, 'Uninhabited islands for sale. Outer Hebrides. 600 acres. 500ft basaltic cliffs. Puffins and seals. Cabin', they appealed to Nigel's 'romanticism and melancholy', but also to his sense of pride in family history as the Nicolsons 'were originally robber-barons in the Minch', the sea channel dividing the Inner and Outer Hebrides. Harold took Ben with him on a visit in August 1938. He was 'entranced' at what he saw, and profoundly moved by what he felt. 'It is strange how excited I am by my first view of Skye . . . and think that perhaps my ill-adjustment to English life has been due to this Celtic strain . . . nothing is so ridiculous as the Sassenach who pretends to be a Highlander. Yet deep inside me is a dislike of the English . . . and my joy at knowing that by origin I belong to these solemn proud hills is certainly not anything but deeply sincere.'[38] From all the available evidence, Nigel, now working in Newcastle with Tyneside Council Social Services, was the favoured son. Ben, the elder, posed certain problems. As Assistant Surveyor of the King's Pictures, he was making his mark in his chosen calling. No doubt, his achievement and growing expertise as an art historian was a source of parental pride. What most disturbed Harold about Ben was his son's taciturn, laconic character, his overly 'anti' attitude, together with his barely disguised hostility towards Vita, characteristics that were the antithesis of Harold's outlook on life in almost every respect: it could not but sour their relationship.

Erskine (Eric) Arthur Nicolson, the middle brother, was enmeshed in a domestic upheaval of his own, much to Harold's chagrin. He had lived contentedly on a farm at Burrator, on the edge of Dartmoor, until his wife, Katherine, insisted that he abandon farming and run a laundry instead. Eric said: 'Either I have to take on a job which I shall loathe; or else I have to refuse K. a change of life which she longs for. If I refuse, our life at Burrator will become hell. If I accept, my own life will be ruined.' As Katherine held the purse-strings, and was of a nervous disposition, Eric capitulated. Harold exploded. 'How I hate and detest women . . . they let us down all the time. They are beasts. I loathe them.' Despite the surface parallels with his own situation, Vita, naturally, was excluded from this blanket generalisation. But it was the case of his elder brother Freddy, the 2nd Lord Carnock (another favoured son), that gave Harold cause for the gravest concern. Holder of the Legion of Honour, a major in the 15th Hussars, wounded and mentioned in dispatches, Freddy had served with distinction in France. A barrister by profession – whose rooms at the Inner Temple Harold was still using – Freddy was slowly sinking into a state of drunken stupor. 'We discuss Freddy's drinking,' Harold sadly commented, 'we dread a scandal.' The scandal would soon come.[39]

Vita was still writing prolifically – though it has been noted that 'her [literary] ambitions outran her talents'. Secure in her tower retreat, her works appeared steadily: *Sissinghurst* (1931), a lyric poem, dedicated to Virginia Woolf; *All Passion Spent* (1932), a novel – based loosely on Lady Carnock – that tells of an old lady who acted as a consort to her husband, a diplomat, but who, upon his death, lived out her remaining years according to her own beliefs; *Family History* (also 1932), a not very distinguished novel that turns on the destructiveness of possessive love and justifies the separate development of marriage – as practised by Vita and Harold; *St Joan of*

Arc (1936), a biography that Virginia Woolf called a 'good hack work'; and *Pepita* (1937), her extremely well received biography of her Spanish grandmother: 10,000 copies were sold in two months.[40] Harold's list for the 1930s was no less impressive, and more enduring. It ranged from his diplomatic trilogy, *Carnock*, *Peacemaking* and *Curzon*, to his first Proustian venture, *Helen's Tower*, and included a novel, *Public Faces*, his journey to America with *Dwight Morrow*, a monograph on *Diplomacy*, and a commentary on *Why Britain is at War*.

Wrapped up in their literature and gardening, realising their ideal of 'the separate development of marriage', the Harold–Vita partnership grew stronger than ever. In an intriguing aside – that resonated with echoes of the Trefusis affair – Harold pointed to a certain asymmetry in their relationship. 'I know it bores you to realise that we are married,' he told Vita, 'you believe so much in passion that sometimes you underestimate love.' Not so Harold: 'I know that the central thing in myself (the actual mainspring which makes all the little cogs go round and round so busily) is my love for you. It is the rock on which my life is founded.' The billets-doux they assiduously exchanged are always revealing, often charming, sometimes cloying in tone. A cynic might conclude that they had formed a mutual admiration society of two. 'You know, darling,' Vita wrote knowingly, 'one ought to be very grateful for being a highbrow.' Each one was willing to sacrifice something precious for the sake of the other, Harold proclaimed, without a hint of tongue-in-cheek: 'It is really true that I would rather you finished a long poem than I became Secretary of State. And I know (with absolute conviction) that you would be more pleased if I were appointed to the Cabinet than if you finished a long poem. Yet each of us would hide their pleasure at the other's success.'[41]

Harold's remarks about 'passion' and 'love' and Vita's boredom with their marriage reveal his unease that Vita might again cause 'the actual mainspring' of his life to break down. Violet Trefusis remained *the* potential threat. 'I do so dread that woman,' Harold cried, fearing 'her capacity for causing distraction and wretchedness'; she was, he knew, 'absolutely unscrupulous and waiting to pounce'. However many times Vita assured Harold that it would never happen again, she too recognised the danger. 'Lushka, what a dangerous person you are,' she wrote in August 1940, 'I think we had better not see too much of each other . . . we must not play with fire again.'[42] Others took Vita's fancy, Mary Campbell or Hilda Matheson, and most dramatically of all, Virginia Woolf; but none would threaten Harold in the same way that Violet had. Vita would not allow it. Perfectly content with her increasingly reclusive life at Sissinghurst, she and Harold enriched their relationship – punctuated by an occasional 'muddle' on both sides – by respecting faithfully the idiosyncratic rules they themselves had devised.

The general euphoria that had swept Parliament and the country after Munich soon faded. Contrary to the high expectation of 'peace with honour', Anglo-German relations worsened. Hitler, frustrated at being denied a war at Munich, his self-confidence dangerously inflated, was less inclined to talk his way out of a crisis. In November, the Germans perpetrated their organised pogrom against the Jews, *Kristallnacht*. Another indication of the barbaric nature of Nazidom, it was harshly criticised by enlightened British public opinion, a reaction beyond the comprehension of Hitler and his acolytes. That winter, there were rumours of an imminent German strike into the Low Countries. Harold, fearful at what the New Year held, labelled it 'This Year of Destiny'. His faith in Chamberlain's judgement, never high, plummeted to a new low. 'What would you have done if you had been in Chamberlain's place at Munich?' he was asked. 'I should never have allowed myself to be manoeuvred into so impossible a position,' Harold retorted.

I should not have acclaimed myself as having brought peace with honour. I should have got out of that aeroplane, slowly and sadly, and I should have said, 'We have avoided war, but at the price of honour. There is no cause for rejoicing'.

Later, he compared Chamberlain to 'a sort of fetish', who had rendered 'cowardice dignified'. In January, Chamberlain and Halifax visited Rome, but came away empty-handed, after being contemptuously dismissed by Mussolini as 'the tired sons of a long line of rich men'. Apparently unaware of Mussolini's true feelings, Chamberlain returned to London buoyant at Mussolini's 'friendliness': Harold heard him say how much 'he loathed Hitler but rather liked Mussolini'. Even after an 'astonishing' statement by Chamberlain in the House, which Harold interpreted as 'a complete negation of his "appeasement" policy', grave reservations remained: 'I still have the awful doubt that he (being so abysmally ignorant of foreign policy) may not have understood what was meant by his statement.'[43]

On 15 March 1939, German armed forces occupied Bohemia and Moravia, tearing up the Munich agreement, destroying what remained of Czechoslovakia, despite the assurance of a British guarantee of its frontiers. Shortly afterwards, Memel was annexed to the Third Reich. A month later Mussolini, who was also crying for the return of Nice and Corsica, occupied Albania. Harold's reaction was sharp. All of Chamberlain's theories had 'collapsed', he ruled. 'What remains of his prestige?' he questioned. 'We do not know where they will strike next.' Hitler, already master of central Europe, and with overt designs on eastern Europe and the Balkans, 'will reduce us to the status of dependent parasites'. In despair, he castigated the propertied classes 'who will swallow any humiliation to retain their present comforts': it was either 'war or surrender'. He pooh-poohed as 'amateurish' the 'guarantee system' that Chamberlain had set up, referring to the pacts of mutual assistance to Poland, Greece and Romania, later extended to Turkey: at the same time, the first tentative moves were taken to conclude an agreement with the Soviet Union. 'We are increasing our liabilities by leaps and bounds without taking similar action to increase our assets. I am becoming convinced that he [Chamberlain] is a very stupid man.' By 'similar action', he meant, as he suggested to Eden, the formation of 'a Black Sea or Dardanelles Pact with Turkey or Russia alone which would be integrated into other pacts by Turkey's membership of the Balkan entente'. This struck Eden as 'a good idea'. Russia was the key. For some time now Harold had been advocating an 'encirclement' policy, an Anglo-French-Soviet front to rein in Germany, another name for the 'Grand Alliance' strategy advocated by Churchill. Was Chamberlain capable of carrying it out? Harold doubted it. He relied too readily on a 'kitchen cabinet' – Simon, Hoare and Halifax, reinforced by the omnipresent Sir Horace Wilson – that inspired little faith. His 'secretiveness is really appalling', Harold noted; 'he only works with his well-disciplined group of yes-men'. But the gravity of the situation appeared to reinvigorate Harold. 'I feel twenty years younger,' he remarked, echoing Churchill's famous *mot*.[44]

After his parliamentary success at the Munich debate, Harold's interventions in the House sparked off less interest. His language was as fluent as ever, but his message was off-key, and he failed to command the attention indispensable for an effective parliamentarian. Subsequent to the destruction of Czechoslovakia, he lauded Chamberlain's image in Germany as a peacemaker, 'one of our greatest assets'. He assumed, on the basis of a conversation with one German, that a majority of the German people rejected the Nazis' anti-Semitism and were shocked by Hitler's rape of Prague. Would they resist Nazi rule? Apparently blind to his verbal acrobatics, Harold gave an emphatic No! 'Eighty-five percent of the German people are absolutely and entirely behind the Nazi Government.' As a sweetener, he called once again for an 'encirclement' policy. A month later, he was canvassed by 'Baffy' Dugdale to speak out over the May White Paper affair. This government declaration of policy limited Jewish immigration into Palestine to a maximum of 75,000 over the coming five years, and then was to be subject to Arab consent – or veto, as the Zionists put it. Jewish land purchases were also to be severely restricted, excluding the Jewish

Agency from 94 per cent of mandatory Palestine. The Zionists and their supporters naturally considered this document as flatly contradicting the Balfour Declaration and the terms of the mandate, effectively nullifying the promise to establish a Jewish National Home in Palestine.[45]

Harold felt strongly about this. Apart from his great admiration of Chaim Weizmann, the Zionist leader, he considered the Chamberlain government's reneging on its contractual obligations as part and parcel of its shameful appeasement policy: having sacrificed the Czechs, it was now going to sacrifice the Jews to the Arabs. On the eve of the debate he, together with Leo Amery, had dined with Weizmann, who was looking 'more like Lenin than ever'. 'Calm, dignified, and wretched', Weizmann, a master lobbyist, put his case with his customary persuasive skill. It was sufficient for Harold, 'feeling so helpless and ashamed', to condemn the Palestine settlement as 'a terrible act of treachery . . . We are just handing the Jews over to the Arabs and giving up our mandate.' Harold did not speak in the two-day May White Paper debate.[46]

Harold was quite aware that his parliamentary appearances lacked sparkle. He was depressed. Why have I 'no power and so little influence?' he asked. Bob Boothby's answer was brutally frank. At first, he told Harold, your speeches were 'passionate and convincing', listened to 'in pin-drop silence': even when 'you lectured' to the House, it remained 'impressed'. Now 'you appear not to bother any more. You seldom speak at all. You write gay little articles about the House of Commons being like a public school. The assumption is that you have been nobbled by the Powers that be; or that you no longer care.' Harold would not deny the essential truth of Boothby's criticism:

I have slipped out of gear in the House of Commons. I could give all sorts of explanations of that, but they are not real excuses. The real fact is that old things like myself [he was fifty-three] are capable of bursts of hysterical heroism but are not good at the constant fight. I lack (as do so many of my kind – those possessed of what we may call the literary temperament) a lust for battle. We have no combative qualities.

I am not ambitious. That would be all very well were it not for another thing. I really do not believe (one never knows oneself) that I have any ardent appetite for success. But I do know that failure makes me miserable. I love the House since I am a sociable person and much enjoy observing the oddities of my fellow beings. I find the House rather like one of those marine diving-bells in which one can sit and watch the vagaries of the deep-sea fish. Yet I am also conscious that I ought to devote more time and will-power to my Parliamentary career. [47]

This was an astonishing confession for a working politician to make. Lacking ambition and drive, viewing Parliament as a superior social club where he could indulge in abstruse intellectual exercises, such as observing 'the vagaries of the deep-sea fish' – a revealing depiction of his more ambitious contemporaries – was a point of view more in keeping with the gentlemanly, relaxed approach to politics of a bygone age, where you came or went, or spoke or remained silent, as it suited your mood. It was quite out of keeping with the cut-throat politics of the twentieth century; and it ensured that Harold's political career would ultimately end in failure.

Whatever his failings as a politician, his feelings of fair play had not deserted him, although this too at times would work to his disadvantage. At a luncheon party at the Sinclairs', Chamberlain was subjected to violent criticism. Harold, bravely, sprang to the defence of the man he himself had so often fiercely criticised. Archie Sinclair, the Liberal leader, joshed him: 'Harold, no more of your lost causes.' 'How I like these people,' a delighted Harold responded. It was typical of Harold to play at seeing both sides of a question, an academic's prerogative, but not necessarily a politician's.

There were other lost causes that he sustained. The Executive of the League of Nations Union was one. 'Practically dead', and guided by 'old ladies' – Gilbert Murray and Lord Lytton were two that he mentioned – '[they] have ceased merely to have bees in their bonnets and have actually become huge bumble-bees themselves'.[48] National Labour, his own party, was in no better shape. Other causes, however, were well worth championing. Arthur Koestler's wife, Dorothy Asher, 'with tears pouring down her cheeks', pleaded with Harold to help rescue her husband from Franco's prisons. Koestler, while reporting on the Spanish civil war for the *News Chronicle*, had been arrested by the nationalist forces and incarcerated at Seville, and was daily awaiting execution. Harold intervened with the Foreign Office. Two months later, in June 1937, Koestler was released. Later, he was interned as a political suspect in a French concentration camp. Again, Harold interceded. 'It was impulsive and unfair of the *Sûreté* to clap Koestler into a camp. He is as anti-Nazi as can be and his one desire is to help the allied cause in any way he can.' Set free in 1940, Koestler eventually made his way to England where he joined the British army. Harold's interest in the welfare of refugees and deprived children extended to co-operation with Eleanor Rathbone, the mainstay of such work in Britain. Active on committees that she had set up, the Children's Minimum Campaign Committee (serving for a time as its vice-president) and the National Committee for Rescue from Nazi Terror, his efforts, although not always officially rewarded, were highly commendable and worthy of note.[49]

* * *

All that summer, the German pressure on Poland that had begun the previous autumn mounted steadily, terminating in the war crisis of August 1939. Eden's group thought of initiating a press campaign to prevent another Munich over Danzig and the Polish Corridor, the focal points of German designs. The idea was to conscript John Walter Astor IV, owner of *The Times*, to stymie the government's machinations. This was ironic, as it was *The Times*, under the editorship of Geoffrey Dawson – an arch-appeaser and crony of Chamberlain – that had printed a highly contentious leader differentiating between the 'independence' and 'integrity' of Poland, implying that 'an unconditional guarantee of all existing Polish frontiers' should not be an aim of British policy. It led to a tremendous brouhaha in the Commons, forcing Chamberlain to distance himself from Dawson's verbal fidgetiness.[50] Not that it mattered much, as, like most Eden initiatives, this too was shot down before it left the ground.

'Is War Inevitable?' Harold asked in June 1939. 'The only hope for peace,' he wrote, 'is to convince the Axis Powers by a tremendous military and diplomatic effort (I should almost call it an offensive) that we are determined on resistance; and at the same time to issue a manifesto of peace terms comparable to the Fourteen Points of President Wilson as will indicate to the world that we are definitely prepared to meet all reasonable aspirations.' Would such a formula work? As it ultimately depended upon Hitler, a 'fanatic' and a 'mystic', a revivalist leader unable to escape 'his own legend', whose 'capacity for hatred is superhuman' and 'ambition is without bounds', Harold knew it would not. Yet he hesitated. 'War is almost inevitable,' he told his readers, leaving them (and perhaps himself) a tiny window of hope.[51]

Even this morsel of comfort was dashed by news of the Ribbentrop–Molotov pact. On learning of it, Harold, at ease on the *Mar* at Plymouth Sound, rushed back to London to hear a statement by Chamberlain. 'Like a coroner summing up a murder case,' Harold thought. 'I cheered [him] as much as I could, having a weak spot for lost causes.' But after seeing Churchill and Lloyd George, they all agreed that Chamberlain was 'a hopeless old crow . . . personally to blame for this disaster'.[52] It came at daybreak on 1 September as German armies crossed into Poland. Later the same day, Churchill was asked to join 'a small War Cabinet', a sign interpreted by all that Chamberlain meant business. When the House convened that evening, Chamberlain, visibly under tremendous emotional stress, read out 'very slowly' the allied dispatch delivered to Berlin. It was in the nature of a warning: unless Germany gave a firm pledge to suspend all military activities and withdraw its troops from Poland, Britain would instantly honour its obligations. But why was no time limit set? wondered Harold, as did many others.[53]

The same question was repeatedly asked throughout the following day.

One problem was how to work out a co-ordinated response with the French. They procrastinated all day. In touch with the Italians, Bonnet, the French Foreign Minister, slippery, evasive, not above lying when it suited him, was desperately searching for another conference formula, looking for a twenty-four, perhaps forty-eight, hour time limit to the proposed allied ultimatum. By now the temper of the Cabinet and the House was far beyond such diplomatic shenanigans. When the House met again that evening, Chamberlain's statement was loosely phrased. Was there to be another Munich? Arthur Greenwood, the Labour spokesman, rose to answer him. From the Tory benches, Leo Amery shouted, 'Speak for England'.* Chamberlain turned round, 'as if stung'. To a scene that could hardly have been improved upon by any dramatist, the House adjourned in 'indescribable confusion'. The Cabinet reconvened. Churchill reported to his more intimate associates that it had been 'a very stormy Cabinet'. The metaphor was well chosen. Outside, a fierce storm darkened London, torrential rain flooding its streets. Inside 10, Downing Street, the Cabinet had decided to present the ultimatum at nine o'clock the following morning, to expire two hours later. 'Right gentlemen,' said Chamberlain quietly, 'this means war.' No sooner had he spoken than a deafening thunderclap silenced the proceedings, accompanied by a blinding flash of lightning that lit up the cabinet room.

No German answer to the allied ultimatum was forthcoming. On the morning of 3 September Harold made his way to Ronnie Tree's house at Queen Anne's Gate, where the Eden group – 'enlivened' by the company of Bob Boothby, Duncan Sandys and Leo Amery – had gathered. At 11.15 a.m they heard Chamberlain's announcement to the nation that Britain was at war. On their way back to the Commons, the air-raid sirens sounded– a false alarm, it later transpired. Edward Spears drove up. They all clambered in. Anyone looking inside would have seen an unusual sight: 'I sit on Amery's knee and Anthony sits on mine'. In the Chamber an ill-looking Chamberlain made a 'restrained speech', the all-clear siren interrupting the ensuing debate. Immediately after the session, Harold motored back to Sissinghurst with Victor Cazalet. A convoy of evacuees overtook them. From one of the trucks, an elderly lady accompanying the children leaned out, shook her fist, and shouted: 'it is all the fault of the rich'. 'The Labour Party will be hard put

---

*There is some confusion as to who made this famous outburst, one that has gone into all the history books. Harold recorded that it was Bob Boothby, who cried out: 'You speak for Britain.' Not surprisingly, Boothby confirmed this to Nigel Nicolson (see *ND*, i, 419, n. 1). Other available evidence points to Leo Amery. See Barnes and Nicholson, eds., *Amery Diaries*, ii, 570: entry for 2 Sept. 1939; and Rose, '*Baffy*',150: entry for 2 Sept. 1939. Surprisingly, 'Chips' Channon (James, ed., '*Chips*', 260–65) remained silent. I have chosen to adopt the majority opinion.

to it to prevent this war degenerating into class warfare,' Harold recorded presciently.[54] When he finally arrived home, he found Ben and Nigel waiting for him. Ben, aged twenty-five, thought the news 'a tragedy', an unwelcome interruption to his studies; Nigel, three years younger, who had just come down from Oxford, 'was immensely exhilarated'.[55] Both were of an age to serve in the army; and both did, until final victory in the spring of 1945. In a symbolic act, given what lay ahead, the flag flying above the Elizabethan Tower was lowered.

THIRTEEN

The War Years

No sooner had the war started than Harold was asked by Allen Lane, head of Penguin Books, to explain to the nation *Why Britain is at War*. He wrote the 50,000–word Penguin Special in three weeks. Michael Sadleir, Harold's regular publisher, called it 'a masterpiece'. An instant success, it soon sold over 100,000 copies to satisfy a curious public. It began with an intriguing comparison, matching Hitler's methods with those of George Joseph Smith, the notorious 'Brides in the Bath' murderer of 1915, as they progressed from choice of prey, to assurances of good intention, to seizure and murder of the victim, to preparations for the next exercise in butchery. Harold denied that the iniquities of the Versailles treaty had propelled Hitler to power, as so often presumed, claiming that by 1922 a majority of the German people had reconciled themselves to the treaty. The passions of war were subsiding, but had been rejuvenated by the vindictive, hard-line French ex-President, Raymond Poincaré. By recklessly occupying the Ruhr in 1923, against British advice, Poincaré's adventurism had galvanised German nationalist fervour, destroyed the German middle class, and paved the way for the rise of Hitler. These were dubious assumptions, but characteristic ones for a Foreign Office veteran who, like his one-time chief Curzon, viewed Poincaré as a most baneful force in European politics: they took little account of the first German economic miracle of the mid- to 1920s; or of the devastating effects of the world economic crisis of 1929. Nor was it exactly prudent to reproach past leaders of Britain's only ally in its war of survival against Nazi Germany, even if partially blameworthy.

Harold was on firmer ground when he moved away from contemporary Germany history to justifying Britain's motives for going to war. In phrases that evoked the celebrated state paper of his guiding light, Eyre Crowe, he spoke of a small island empire dependent for its survival not only on protecting the sea lanes to its overseas possessions, but also on preserving the balance of power on the European mainland. Germany, then and now, threatened to violate these immutable principles. Britain's reaction by going to war was prompted by 'a sound biological instinct . . . the instinct of self-preservation'. By vividly contrasting the savage nature of the Nazi dictatorship, its 'ruthless nihilism', with the English conception of 'decency and fairness', of 'the Anglo-Saxon Ideal', Harold introduced a moral dimension to the conflict. 'We entered this war to defend ourselves. We shall continue to, to its most bitter end, in order to save humanity.' Once they had emerged victorious from the war, Harold warned, they must not repeat the mistakes made at Versailles (perhaps overlooking his previous remark that the German people had largely accepted the treaty by 1922). 'Only by imposing a just peace, one that does not outrage their pride or drive them to desperation can we guarantee thirty years to establish a new world order so powerful that even Germany will not dare to defy it.' But what kind of 'new world order'? It turned on rectifying the defects of the League of Nations, of organising its own armed force and the need for its members to sacrifice a degree of national sovereignty. Harold optimistically looked forward to a 'United States of Europe'; but whether Britain would play an active part in it remained a moot point. On one point, however, Harold was crystal clear: a social revolution was pending. Whatever the outcome of the war, 'we can be certain that the rich will lose . . . Their privileges and fortunes will go.'[1] His premonition that the war would generate 'class warfare', that the prerogatives of his class would be severely eroded, if not entirely swept away, haunted him throughout the war.

Apart from being a wartime best-seller, praise for Harold's Penguin Special came from an unforeseen authority. RAB (Richard Austen) Butler, Under-Secretary of State at the Foreign Office, hailed his book 'as a work of art and perfectly correct'. Coming from Butler, this was a glowing commendation. Butler was on the wrong side of the divide in the appeasement debate. As his chief, Halifax, sat in the Lords, he became the government spokesman on foreign affairs in the Commons, valiantly defending its policy. An enthusiastic Chamberlainite, he regarded Munich not as a means of buying time but as a way of settling differences with Hitler. An unrepentant appeaser down to the outbreak of war, Butler opposed the Polish alliance signed on 25 August 1939, claiming it would have 'a bad psychological effect on Hitler'. Now he was claiming that Harold's critique of Chamberlain's diplomacy, and in particular the ruinous influence of Sir Horace Wilson – widely seen as Chamberlain's *éminence grise* – was wholly valid. Butler's candour was refreshing. Had he been a secret opponent of appeasement all along, as Harold now suspected? Or was he carefully selecting his words to suit his audience, as a less forgiving man than Harold might readily have assumed? In fact, Butler remained Chamberlain's man. After Chamberlain's downfall, he drank to 'the King over the water' and described Churchill as 'the greatest political adventurer of modern political history'.[2] If nothing else, Butler was a survivor; at least, he survived the discredited Chamberlain's fall from grace. No doubt, Harold was flattered to hear his soft words. But he would gain a more lasting satisfaction from knowing that his record of Britain's misguided diplomacy had struck a sympathetic chord in hundreds of thousands of readers.

Harold was usually to be found at King's Bench Walk, attending to his parliamentary duties, writing his articles, watching the progress of the war, or lack of it, with mounting concern. At weekends, he would relax at Sissinghurst. Travelling between his two homes could be tiresome. Harold recorded one maddening experience. As early morning trains to Paddington lacked dining-cars, he was compelled to eat 'a sausage-roll', an ordeal which made him 'absolutely despair about the prospects of the present war'.[3] Could this be a sample of the class warfare he so feared? When in London, he sat on two committees, one headed by Duff Cooper that dealt with the fate of German refugees, the other a parliamentary Air-Raid Precautions Committee, of which he was chairman. Never having served in the armed forces, fire-watching was the closest Harold came to seeing active service. It could be exciting; it could also be dull, particularly if there was no alert and he had slept all night on an iron bed. Awakening early, he would creep out of his bunker, aching in every limb, knowing this was going to be a 'bad day', a feeling confirmed when he discovered that he had lost one of his 'jade links'. Back at King's Bench Walk, after a bath and a brief nap, he was accosted by a policeman who summoned him for having left a light on the night before. 'It will not be at all agreeable if the papers run a headline, "Member of the Government arrested for contravening Blackout". And I, who all my life, have been obedient to rules.'* Other members of the family had also volunteered for war duties: Vita – despite having told Harold that she did not 'care about this war' – serving on the Kent Committee of the Women's Land Army; Ben as a private at an anti-aircraft battery outside Rochester; and Nigel as an officer-cadet at Sandhurst.[4]

Harold wanted to find a wartime job commensurate with his talents. The Foreign Office, impressed with the success of *Why Britain is at War*, was keen that he should strengthen its Political Intelligence Department, a post tailor-made for Harold's skills. Halifax was enthusiastic for the appointment, but it was stymied by Horace Wilson – one of the sinners in Harold's work – who 'stamped upon' the idea. Nor did Harold make a significant impact

---

* At the time of the fire-watching incident Harold was a junior minister at the Ministry of Information: see **ND**, 11 July 1941.

in Parliament. Apart from the odd question here and there, enquiring about the activities of German propagandists in Britain, he remained silent. The Eden group, made up of Conservative dissidents, but with Harold in constant attendance, still functioned, usually over dinner at the Carlton. The general feeling of the company was that Chamberlain had to be removed and that Churchill should replace him. Ineffectual, except in empty table-talk, it would act only when exceptional circumstances left it no option. Like many of his associates, Harold was in despair at Chamberlain's lucklustre leadership. When urged to attack 'these people at the helm', he wavered, unwilling to disrupt national unity: 'I do not want to do so as yet.'[5]

Even so, no one could deny that the war was going badly. Poland had fallen in less than a month, partitioned along the old Curzon line (with minor variations) between Germany and the Soviet Union. In the west, the Allies were reluctant to take offensive action. Would Britain emerge victorious from the conflict? An air of gloom pervaded Harold's thoughts, relieved briefly by a visit to France in October as a member of the Anglo–French Parliamentary Committee. Commissioned to gauge French political will and military capacity to withstand an expected German onslaught, Harold was agreeably surprised at the upbeat mood of Britain's allies, and first line of defence. Although French soldiers manning the Maginot Line looked like 'troglodytes', the Commission was impressed by their morale and the Line's technical efficiency. 'We've got them already, and they know it!' Paul Reynaud exclaimed. Enormously encouraged by what he had seen and heard, further exchanges with Édouard Daladier and Leon Blum only confirmed Harold in his optimistic reading of French preparedness. 'All of these conversations convince me that we are much too defeatist in London and that these people are absolutely certain of victory . . . They are convinced that if we can stick it for six months the whole German edifice will collapse.' Back in England, Harold soon reverted to his former gloomy self. From his study in the South Cottage at Sissinghurst, he contemplated the war. That the Germans had not devastated London from the air, or launched an offensive through Holland, brought him a sense of relief. Yet the depressing fact remained that 'this war is costing us six million pounds a day and that I am not really certain that we shall win it, fills me with acute sadness at times. We all keep up a brave face and refuse to admit that defeat is possible. But my heart aches with apprehension.'[6]

French confidence was misplaced: it was not the German, but the allied edifice that collapsed in just over six months. Initially, Harold was encouraged by immediate British successes at sea. 'We have won the war at sea,' he rashly predicted. One major success, however, brought mixed feelings. It was wholly typical of Harold to express sympathy for the doomed officers and crew of the German 'pocket' battleship, the *Graf Spee*, trapped by a British task force at Montevideo harbour: there being no escape, its commander, Captain Langsdorff, scuttled his vessel four miles off the River Plate, to Harold's obvious distress: 'There will be no sense of triumph or defeat whatever happens to the *Spee*.' (The *Spee*, it should be remembered, had inflicted heavy damage on British merchant shipping in the South Atlantic.) Four months after this incident, Harold, at the Ministry of Information's request, toured Grenoble, Lyons, Besançon, and Paris. Extemporising in French, he spoke in generalities on 'War Aims', praising the virtues of democracy, damning the iniquities of totalitarianism. His talks were enthusiastically received: at Grenoble, the audience gave him a standing ovation. While in Paris, Harold learned that the 'Winter War' had been brought to an end, Finland finally surrendering to Soviet demands. The notion of opening a second front against the Soviet Union, however faint, is so surrealistic that it defies rational analysis. But influential opinion in Britain, Churchill included, was not averse to coming to the aid of the helpless Finns. British intervention, fired up by anti-Soviet sentiments, would have realised concrete benefits: control of the Norwegian coastline; depriving Germany of Swedish iron ore; and so striking a decisive blow 'at Germany's war-making capacity equal to a first-class victory in the field or from the air', to quote Churchill. Now there was no question of saving Finland, but these ideas resurfaced over dinner at Maxim's towards the end of Harold's French tour. 'Unless we seize Narvik and Baku we shall not win the war,' said Bob Boothby to Harold, who listened attentively.[7]

On 5 April 1940, a British naval force sailed towards Norwegian waters, ground troops being held in reserve should the Germans respond. Four days later the Germans did respond: ruthlessly and with frightening efficiency. By the end of the day, despite a strong British naval presence, they had occupied Denmark and were in control of all major Norwegian ports, from Oslo to Narvik. Having lost the initiative, the British never regained it. Reeling from the relentless pressure of German land and air strikes, they could only evacuate one bridgehead after another. The Norwegian campaign, which dragged on for almost two months, was a disaster. By the beginning of May it was apparent that a great political crisis was in the making. There was much talk of a genuine National Government, but not with Chamberlain at its head. If not Chamberlain, who else? Lloyd George's name was freely bandied about. Harold's favourite, Churchill, was low in credit. Holding him responsible for the Norwegian débâcle, 'another forlorn failure', 'The Tadpoles and the Tapers' were asserting that it 'was all the fault of that wicked Winston!!!' 'That is hell,' Harold recorded, though he seemed to have conceded Churchill's fall from grace as inevitable. After speaking to some Labour members, he agreed 'that we should only win the war under a Labour Government'.[8]

On 7 May the House convened to debate the government's handling of the Norwegian campaign. It did so acutely conscious that the Norwegian fiasco was symptomatic of an impotent government, unable to cope with wartime 'supply and labour conditions', incapable of furnishing inspiring leadership at a time of crisis. When Chamberlain entered the Chamber he was greeted with derisive cries of 'Missed the bus' (commenting on Hitler's apparent reluctance to go on the offensive, Chamberlain had remarked only days earlier: 'One thing is certain: he has missed the bus.') Chamberlain was subjected to crushing indictments of his premiership. Sir Roger Keyes, splendid in his full admiral's uniform, chastised the government in an emotional tirade, his tongue-lashing earning him 'thunderous applause'. Amery, looking at Chamberlain, quoted Cromwell's merciless words to the Long Parliament: 'Depart I say, and let us have done with you. In the name of God, go!' Set the country an example, pleaded Lloyd George, and sacrifice 'the seals of office'. Harold noted an atmosphere of 'resolute fear' in the House, 'not hysteria or cowardice'. He took heart from 'the spirit of the House', certain that the government was 'very rocky and anything might happen'. In response to this across-the-board offensive, Chamberlain fought back by appealing to his followers. '"I have friends in this House",' he blustered, Harold noting the 'leer on his face'. Churchill did much better, defending the government's (and his) policy, while distancing himself from his cabinet colleagues, 'this confused and timid gang', in Harold's words.

Harold now attended the so-called Watching Committee, a group of peers and MPs, including a majority of the Eden group, that met under the chairmanship of Lord Salisbury. They determined to oppose the government. So did Labour, who forced a division on a three-line whip. As the MPs entered the lobbies the Tory faithfuls howled 'Quislings' and 'Rats': 'Yesmen,' shouted back the dissidents. The government scraped home by eighty-one 'Ayes'. It was a Pyrrhic victory and widely construed as a vote of no confidence. Josh Wedgwood, the veteran nonconformist socialist, was observed waving his hands and singing 'Rule Britannia', his victory chant being taken up by others. 'Go, go, go!' cried elated members. Chamberlain rose and walked out of the Chamber, 'pale and angry'.[9]

The situation was confused. Would Chamberlain resign, or not? On the following day, 9 May, Harold's Watching Committee considered its options. It agreed: '1. That a Coalition Government is essential; 2. That Labour will not enter such a Coalition if Chamberlain, Hoare and Simon remain; and that therefore; 3. They must go.' The rebels would support 'any Prime Minister who enjoys the confidence of the country and is able to form an all-Party Government'. On the same day the National Labour caucus met, but typically failed to pass a resolution. The next day, as news trickled through of German armies driving into Luxembourg and the Low Countries, Harold drifted restlessly from one meeting to another, walking the streets between the Travellers' Club and King's Bench Walk, eyeing newspaper posters declaring, 'Brussels bombed, Paris bombed, Lyons bombed, Swiss railways bombed.' Late that afternoon, he returned to Sissinghurst. He was met by Vita and his sister, Gwen. 'It is all looking too beautiful to be believed, but a sort of film has obtruded itself between my appreciation of nature and my terror of real life. It is like a tooth-ache. We dine alone together chatting about indifferent things.' At nine o'clock they heard Chamberlain's statement announcing his resignation, his comments concluding with a 'fierce denunciation of the Germans'. Compassionate to the last, Harold thought the statement 'magnificent', all his pent-up 'hatred' for Chamberlain subsiding. That evening, Churchill kissed hands to become Prime Minister, after Halifax had ruled himself out. Churchill's elevation to the premiership was very much Harold's preferred choice, as he had long seen that controversial, erratic, but highly gifted and pugnacious politician as Britain's wartime leader. 'This is the final fight,' Harold remarked. 'I go to bed and shall, I hope, sleep.'[10]

A week later, on 17 May, while working at Sissinghurst, Harold received a phone call from the Prime Minister's Office. Churchill came on the line. 'Harold, I think it would be very nice if you joined the Government and helped Duff [Cooper] at the Ministry of Information.' 'There is nothing I should like better,' Harold replied. 'Well, fall in tomorrow,' Churchill commanded. Harold's official title was Parliamentary Secretary to the Ministry of Information: headed by Duff Cooper, its offices were located at Senate House, the University of London's administrative centre at Malet Street. Duff Cooper, a friend of his, welcomed him warmly, 'and I mean more than politely pleased', he clarified to Vita. Vita 'liked' Duff, 'but as you know he's a little white mouse compared with you', she shot back.[11]

Harold's first days in office were overshadowed by the German armies' lightning breakthrough to the Channel ports, hemming in the British Expeditionary Force at Dunkirk and leading to the fall of France in June. There was talk of a German invasion and the possibility of evacuating Kent, which would take the brunt of a German assault. Harold, fearing the Germans 'may bring off a smash and grab at several points' by landing at Hastings and Faversham, wrote to Vita: 'You will be in danger. You are a brave person and have a sense of responsibility. It would not be you to run away and leave your people behind . . . you must stick it out if you are allowed to.' As the extent of the disaster in France became known, his mood switched to one almost of apathy. 'I am quite lucidly aware that in three weeks from now Sissinghurst may be a waste and Vita and I both dead. Yet these probabilities do not fill me with despair. I seem to be impervious to both pleasure and pain. For the moment we are all anaesthetised.'

Within days his mood switched again:

> I don't think that even if the Germans occupied Sissinghurst they would harm you, in spite of the horrified dislike which they feel for me. But to be quite sure that you are not put to any humiliation, I think you really ought to have 'a bare bodkin' [a lethal tablet] handy so that you can take your quietus when necessary. I shall have one also. I am not in the least afraid of such sudden and honourable death. What I dread is being tortured and humiliated.

Whether Harold knew it or not, his name had been included in the 'Special Search List' (better known as the 'Black Book'), a list of prominent Britons who were to be arrested (and worse) in the event of a successful German invasion.[12]

In Duff Cooper's absence, Harold, would, as he put it, 'creep into the House' and take his 'seat on the Front Bench'.[13] No sooner had he sat down than he learned from Walter Elliot, 'a good friend', that Lord Davidson 'is seeking to destroy my position'. Apart from Davidson's alleged machinations, Harold was depressed by the serial attacks of the press upon the Ministry. 'What worries me is that the whole press, plus certain pro–Munich Conservatives, have planned and banded together to pull Duff Cooper down.' Despite these intrigues, Harold pressed on. Mainly concerned with morale-boosting subjects, he would respond to questions on propaganda – at home and abroad, the performance of the BBC, problems of censorship, the contents of films, war aims and post-war plans. Often, he would be cross-examined on less profound topics: the purpose of Noël Coward's trip to the United States, or the kind of music to be aired for factory workers.[14]

This continuous sniping at the Ministry of Information did not raise Harold's spirits. He also disappointed himself, as he was quite aware that his offhand manner, the 'abundant and slightly flippant dilettantism' that he so often displayed, impaired his parliamentary reputation and accounted for his 'comparative failure in life'. He admitted that the Ministry was 'ill-organised' and that 'mistakes' had been made. There would be no easy remedy, however.

> If our propaganda is to be as effective as that of the enemy, we must have at the top people who will not only command the assent of the

Press, but who will be caddish and ignorant enough to tell dynamic lies. At present the Ministry is too decent, educated and intellectual to imitate Goebbels. It cannot live by intelligence alone. We need crooks . . . I am prepared to see the old world of privilege disappear. But as it goes, it will carry with it the old standards of honour. [15]

Was Harold effectively talking himself out of a job? He must have known that a Ministry of Information was something of an anachronism in British politics. It came and went with the Second World War. Its Minister, Duff Cooper, believed there was no room for such a creature in the 'British scheme of government'. It was staffed by a band of 'brilliant amateurs' conscripted for wartime duty, whose frustration bubbled over every time their clever schemes were shelved by their superiors, stodgy civil servants. The Ministry attracted widespread criticism. 'Cooper's Snoopers', as his officials were unkindly dubbed, were thought by the press to be omnipresent: it smacked of 'Big Brother'. Nor was Churchill, who fancied himself a propagandist of no mean ability, much help. Both Duff Cooper and Harold complained that the Prime Minister rarely gave his support in their interminable squabbles with the Foreign Office and the three service departments. Nor was Duff Cooper the ideal person to head the Ministry: his reputation as a womaniser given to drink and gambling went before him, rendering him liable to gossipy criticism: would he ever distinguish between business and pleasure? To cap it all, he was not in the best of health. May 1941, a critical month, found him at his home in Bognor, recuperating from an illness. Harold often filled in for him on the front bench. He was only too pleased to do so, but overall it did not add to the lustre of the Ministry.[16]

But what precisely was the purpose of the Ministry of Information, a question constantly, and hostilely, raised by the Beaverbrook press? Was it an organ for 'compulsory censorship', as suggested in a Commons debate, brainwashing the public with carefully monitored information, concealing from it unpleasant facts? Not so, replied Harold. 'Our policy is perfectly consistent, both in aim and in method.' It was, he assured the House, a policy diametrically opposed to that of Dr Goebbels. Harold's Ministry aimed to win the confidence and the trust, not only of the British people, but of the whole world. Raising Britain's credit, nurturing its unblemished reputation 'will not only be of great value to us in time of war but will give us the moral authority when peace comes to play our part, which will be a grave and responsible part, in the reconstruction of the world'.[17]

The subject of war aims was raised repeatedly, but was always fobbed off with the same answer: 'No statement yet possible, but matter under consideration.' To Lord Robert Cecil Harold spoke in vague generalities: 'restoration of occupied territories and some form of collectivisation'. There was a general reluctance to enter into a public discussion on war aims. Churchill gave the lead: to disclose 'precise aims' would be compromising, whereas proclaiming vague principles 'would disappoint'. Nor had the Ministry of Information anything to offer a jittery public. As Harold observed: 'I think we have managed to avoid losing this war. But when I think how on earth we are going to win it, my imagination quails . . . If only we could show people some glimmer of light at the end of the tunnel, we could count upon their enduring any ordeal. But the danger is that there is no light beyond the light of faith.'[18]

All the same, Harold was invited to draft a paper on war aims for internal, off-the-record study. 'People will ask, what are we fighting for?' Harold began. And offered them, 'Free Trade and pooled resources' to lessen international tension, and 'socialism' and 'reconstruction' at home to provide 'equality of opportunity'. Duff Cooper, his chief, agreed with the main thrust of his arguments, but both were aware that it would be well nigh impossible for a Coalition Cabinet to swallow 'this apple of discord' unless served up as tastefully as possible. All of which brought Harold back to his first, instinctive reaction. Switching metaphors, he thought: 'better leave this sleeping tiger to sleep in its own way.' Some months later, his paper was still on hold. He told Halifax that it must emphasise 'home reconstruction' and 'say that we accept Socialism'. Halifax's response was entirely predictable; and it depressed Harold. 'He does not seem to think that the thing in the last resort will ever see light.'[19] One factor remained constant in Harold's thoughts, high on his wartime agenda: 'Home reconstruction' and 'socialism'. It would reappear later, in a different form, in his support for the path-breaking Beveridge Report.

In his frequent broadcasts, Harold presented Britain's war aims to a far wider audience. Playing on the 'moral authority when peace comes' theme, Harold, speaking to French audiences, told his listeners that Britain was fighting to defend

the rights of man – the right of man to seek happiness in his own way . . . to express his thoughts freely and to have access to the thoughts of others, the right of man to be protected by law against the State . . . to worship as he desires . . . to enjoy a private family life. And I mean also the right of nations, however small, to preserve its own independence and its own neutrality . . . to direct its own political, social and economic life according to its own traditions, temperament and interests . . . to preserve its own individual character. [20]

'I am speaking to you in the French language and as one who has loved France all his life and will love her till he dies,' he added. 'Have courage,' he implored, 'since France is eternal.' The shameful capitulation of France, its moral authority betrayed by its upper classes, had deeply affected Harold, a lifelong Francophile. 'What a collapse for a great nation!' he recorded, sick at heart: would it mean 'the end of France?' Reluctantly, he approved of the British destruction of French naval forces anchored off Oran and Mers-el-Kabir on 3–4 July 1940, conscious that it would boost Britain's political credit in the free world. 'Our action against the French Fleet has made a tremendous effect throughout the world. I am as stiff as can be.'[21]

Harold eventually met the 'eternal' France he so passionately believed in over lunch at the Savoy Hotel. His first impression of General Charles de Gaulle did not augur well. The General accused his Ministry of 'being Pétainiste'. '*Mais non*,' Harold protested, as calmly as possible, '*nous travaillons pour la France entière*.' '*La France entière*,' snapped de Gaulle, making 'a great Boulangiste gesture', '*c'est la France Libre. C'est moi!*' 'I am not encouraged,' Harold sadly recorded. Proud, aloof, endowed with a sense of mission and reverence for the grandeur of France, de Gaulle was the most refractory of allies for Churchill (and even more so for Roosevelt). In contrast, Harold quickly, and ardently, embraced de Gaulle's 'Free French' movement, so much so that on one occasion he kept well 'out of earshot' of Churchill in the smoking-room of the House, bitter at Churchill's shabby treatment of the General.[22]

The Battle of Britain was fought largely in the skies over Sissinghurst. Harold would watch the German planes 'coming in wave after wave', buzzing and zooming, engaged in 'terrific dog-fights', flashing like 'silver gnats above us in the air'. Enemy aircraft crashed nearby. Vita saw one 'catch fire and fall': 'That's one less to go after Hadji,' she thought triumphantly. During the Blitz, Harold often slept in his office at Senate House. 'I sleep perfectly once I am there,' he assured Vita, until one night he awoke to the sounds of 'Splaaassh! Craash! Tinkle! Tinkle!', no longer in bed, but stretched out on the floor. 'We had really been struck on the boko [nose],' Harold reflected. Bombs also fell on the Inner Temple, blowing out the windows of his flat at King's Bench Walk, destroying some of its panelling. Earlier, Ben's flat had suffered a similar fate. These near misses, and the momentous air battles above, stirred Harold's innate patriotism. Self-confident, he ruled, 'WE SHALL WIN THIS WAR.'[23]

The blackout and Blitz affected Harold's social life. 'The suspension of social life renders me as isolated as in Persia,' he grumbled. 'I must struggle to get away from this vegetable existence.' This was not entirely accurate. Harold would lunch or dine regularly at Lady Colefax's table; and things picked up considerably when she introduced her so-called 'ordinaries' –

weekly dinner parties at the Dorchester for about thirty guests, who would then be discreetly billed for their repast. Meanwhile, as a distraction, he would 'slack generally' at long weekends and read detective novels. Old friends disappeared: Oswald and Diana Mosley behind bars, imprisoned under the wartime 18B Regulations. Others sought refuge abroad, causing Harold much anguish. Although he refused to attack them in public, he felt deeply 'ashamed' at Christopher Isherwood and W. H. Auden, 'two people whom I admire so much', running off to the United States and remaining 'when we are in such dire distress'.[24]*

Most tragic of all was Virginia Woolf's suicide. As yet unaware of the tragedy, Harold, concerned at Vita's 'muzzy moods' – a tactful reference to her 'melancholia' and excessive drinking – was cautiously questioning aspects of their relationship. He felt 'such a failure', unable to help her when she was 'in trouble', incapable of dealing with her 'eccentricities', at a loss to cope with the 'rather cruel and extravagant' side of her personality. Perhaps, he asked her, 'you would have been happier married to a more determined and less sensitive man'. These gloomy thoughts were cast aside – though not forgotten – when Vita's letter (crossing his) arrived, telling him that Virginia had drowned herself. 'I simply can't take it in – that lovely mind, that lovely spirit.' Harold hurried down to Sissinghurst. They spoke (prob-ably about their relationship), comforted each other, but never mentioned Virginia's death – the reason for Harold's last-minute visit. 'We are funny people, though, you and I,' Vita acknowledged. Knowing that 'Virginia meant something to you which nobody else can ever mean', Harold urged Vita 'to dismiss the physical aspect' from her mind, 'concentrate only upon the great joy that friendship has been to you'. Both mourned for Virginia; but no less they commiserated with Leonard. 'My heart absolutely aches with sympathy for Leonard,' grieved Harold. Years later Vita would write of Virginia Woolf as one of the two people she missed most (the other being Geoffrey Scott). 'Oh God, how I wish I could get Virginia back!' Could she have saved her? Vita thought so. 'I still think I might have saved her if only I had been there and had known the state of mind she was getting into. I think she would have told me, as she did tell me on previous occasions.'[25]

During the spring of 1941 British policy suffered one disastrous setback after another. In March, the long-anticipated pro-allied Balkan front crum-bled when Bulgaria, Hungary and Romania joined the Axis powers; Turkey,

*Harold would not have been pleased with Auden's poem, 'September 1, 1939', widely interpreted as a brazen apologia for the Third Reich, which he saw, crudely, as a product of the Versailles treaty. Its lines on Germany read: 'Those to whom evil is done/ Do evil in return.'

withstanding all pressure, remained neutral. On 6 April, German troops poured into Yugoslavia and Greece, sweeping up the allied armies as they advanced and trapping 10,000 British troops. Three weeks later, the swastika flew over the Acropolis. By the end of May, German paratroops had overrun Crete. This was not the repetition of 'the Norwegian fiasco' that Churchill feared; it was a disaster of even greater magnitude. And it was compounded by failure to exploit British military successes in North Africa, for on 3 April Rommel began to drive the British army out of Libya. Churchill's responsibility for the débâcle was considerable. Later that year, he admitted that Greece had been an 'error of judgment'. The humiliation of the rout cut deep. At home, criticism was harsh. Churchill's parliamentary skills carried him through, even securing a vote of confidence in the House by an overwhelming majority of 447 to 3. But if Churchill survived, Harold did not. In the wake of an unavoidable government reshuffle, Churchill asked Harold to place his office as 'Parliamentary Secretary at my disposal', offering him, as a sop, a governorship of the BBC.[26]

Harold was already in a grim mood, for other reasons. 'No sign of anything but *murs calcinés* and twisted girders,' he glumly noted, after surveying the ruins of the House of Commons, its Chamber completely gutted in a raid on 10 May. Politically at a low ebb, he was 'slightly' shell-shocked to find himself virtually bankrupt. On learning that he paid £1,100 in taxes, he grumbled: 'I cannot possibly live on £400 a year', a princely sum for the working classes, but 'to me it appears an utter impossibility'. To tide things over he asked Ben for a loan of £500. Ruminating on his reduced situation led him into deep waters.

> It meant nothing to me that Derby House and Stafford House and Chatsworth should become shabby and then dead. I achieved a different and no less self-indulgent form of elegance which seemed to me likely to survive my own lifetime. It consisted of comparatively modest establishments in the country and in London, and a gay combination of the Café Royal, Bloomsbury, rooms in the Temple, the Travellers' Club, the garden at Sissinghurst, foreign travel, the purchase of books and pictures and the unthinking enjoyment of books and wine . . . And now this tide of self-sacrifice is lapping at our feet. We shall have to walk and live a Woolworth life hereafter. I feel so poor. I hate the destruction of elegance. The drabness of Berlin or Moscow will creep into my lovely London streets.

There is no trace of irony here. Powerless, except to utter a heartfelt cry at the cultural and social desert that beckoned, Harold feared the worst.[27]

These depressing thoughts were brought to a head by Churchill's letter. 'Bewildered and shaken', Harold was inconsolable. Expressions of sympathy poured in, from Duff Cooper, Leo Amery, Philip Noel-Baker, Gladwyn Jebb, Malcolm MacDonald, and others. Harold was grateful for this widespread support, but he was supremely conscious that Churchill had out-manoeuvred him. Having meekly accepted a new job as a governor of the BBC 'robs me of all claim to have been ill-treated': he hated the idea of being 'bought off with favours'. More to the point, Harold was aware that his political ambitions had suffered an irreversible setback, the consequence of a fatal combination of personality traits and political expediency. 'My political career is at an end,' he concluded. 'The reason is not due to any error of energy, intelligence, or morals on my part, but partly due to the fact that I am alone without a party, and partly to my eternal lack of self-assertiveness which is what leads head waiters and customs officials to pass me by with an indifferent glance.' For some years he had been viewed as a 'might-be', now he would always be looked upon as 'a might-have-been'. Harold considered his future: 'I now know that I shall never write a book better than I have written already, and that my political career is at an end.'[28]

Harold's pessimism, in part, was entirely understandable. His literary output never diminished, at times to his satisfaction, at times less so. But politically he no longer counted, if he ever had. He read a 'rude article' about himself in *Truth* saying that he had 'the mincing manner of a French *salon*' and that he should retire from public life and bury himself in books. 'All rather true,' he owned up. 'But I happen to enjoy public life. I could never be merely an observer.' In fact, that was how it turned out. Regrettably, he spent the remainder of his time at Westminster as an observer from the back benches. For this, he could blame no one but himself. Wholly expendable, lacking a firm and vibrant political base, he invited his own political suicide the moment he hitched his fortunes to National Labour, a terminally ill organism. He had committed the same folly with Mosley's New Party. Too soft-centred to walk out on old friends, he stuck with National Labour knowing that it had no future. When asked to become its leader, he refused. 'How silly and out of proportion it all is!' he remarked. He saw what had happened to those who had claimed to lead the rump faction: 'Buck' De La Warr as an official at the Ministry of Supply, supervising home flax production; Malcolm MacDonald in exile in Canada, as Britain's High Commissioner. In private, Harold wished that 'we should die decently and quietly', and set the burial date for 1 January 1942. By then, the National Labour Executive had exhausted even Harold's infinite patience. It launched into an all-out attack on Churchill, who, according to its luminaries, 'will never win the war'. Harold listened to this diatribe in absolute disgust.

'Winston is the embodiment of the nation's will,' he told his diary. Were there other alternatives to National Labour? He toyed with the idea of a peerage. After all, as his friend Rob Bernays reminded him, 'you never realise that you are a national figure', and pausing for effect, added, 'of the s-s-s-s-second d-d-d-d-d-degree'. He was urged to join the Conservatives, but refused. The Liberal Party 'is my spiritual home', he proclaimed, though he could hardly have been unaware that it too was a spent force in British politics. Eventually, he opted to run as an Independent, a choice that also offered faint chance of success. 'In fact,' he confessed, 'I have ruined my political career by not knowing enough about politics at the start.'[29] For the remainder of the war Harold wandered the corridors of Westminster, easily identifiable, not least by himself, as a political orphan.

Harold's new job as a governor of the BBC was less demanding, but also less rewarding, than his previous one as a junior minister. He soon formed an alliance on the Board with Lady Violet Bonham Carter (Asquith's only daughter) as they vowed not to be treated as mere figureheads. This did not amount to much. There was a minor contretemps over the appointment of William Haley as the BBC's editor-in-chief. Harold and Lady Violet took umbrage on the grounds that they had not been consulted, and threatened resignation. The affair petered out harmlessly enough. Not only were there no resignations, but Haley went on to become Director-General of the BBC. 'Rather shattered' at the outcome, Harold held his colleagues to severe account. Although they breathed the same air, they inhabited different worlds. His world was moved by virtues such as 'truth, beauty, tolerance, fairness, generosity, courage, faithfulness, and taste', all desirable qualities that possessed, for him, 'a certain absolute validity'; it was augmented by other intellectual values, 'intelligence, wit, humour, knowledge'. Reliving the Haley incident, Harold felt 'in dealing with these men the same gap in commu-nication as I do when I hear people talking about batting averages or foot-ball pools or racing form. I believe that they are quite unaware of the standards which to us seem the axioms of life.'[30] He was, unfortunately, also referring to the very people the BBC aspired to serve. Throughout his life, Harold failed to bridge his 'gap in communication', fully content with preserving his 'axioms of life'.

Free of ministerial duties, Harold found his timetable no less crowded, though less stressful. His new schedule allowed him to spend more time at Sissinghurst, a gratifying bonus. He resumed his weekly stint as a fire-watcher at Westminster. Some of his valuable leisure hours were spent working at a light-engineering factory in London, not, however, with conspic-uous success: 'I am worse than ever. I file a thing too short and another too long . . . I go away at 9 covered in oil and frustration.' Instinctively, Harold was drawn back to writing. As a governor of the BBC he was not allowed to broadcast, a drawback partially compensated by the renewal of his weekly column, 'Marginal Comments', for the *Spectator*. But he planned more formidable tasks. Immediately on leaving office he began editing his 1939 diary for publication. Unsure whether or not it would be of any use as 'most of the juicy bits' would have to be cut out, he was warned off by 'Bobbitty' Cranborne (later fifth Marquess of Salisbury): 'It would cause a great deal of political embarrassment to Anthony [Eden],' a concerned Cranborne – who had served as Eden's Under-Secretary at the Foreign Office – pointed out, adding, 'Appeasement is, I hope, dead, but the appeasers are not.' It was never published. Shortly afterwards he began work on another chapter of his Proustian venture, *The Desire to Please*, the story of his Irish ancestor, Hamilton Rowan. Unhappy at its progress – it 'is simply not interesting enough' – Harold eventually released it in 1943.[31]

At the same time Harold began work on a new edition of *Peacemaking*, its more up-to-date 'Introduction' looking forward to another round of peacemaking. This theme was expanded in his researches for a new project, *The Congress of Vienna*. Here again, its contemporary relevance drew Harold forward. At Vienna in 1815 the victorious powers had fashioned a peace settlement that had lasted for almost a century before a Great Power conflagration had again engulfed all Europe. What lessons, if any, could be inferred from their success – and, no less apposite, from the failure of the powers at Versailles? Some problems appeared to be intractable. Harold stumbled into the quagmire of Poland. At a loss to explain how it had brought the disputants to the verge of war in 1815, he was equally conscious that it threatened to do so again in the present conflict. Despite the intricacies of the Polish question, Harold found the book 'immense fun to do', fully aware that the subject of peacemaking after a great war 'should be of interest and usefulness'.[32] *The Congress of Vienna* is one of Harold's more serious works: attractive in style, it can be read for profit today.

While engaged on this work, Harold was shown Edmund Wilson's telling review of his literary *oeuvre*. Harold could expect little mercy from Wilson, a renowned American writer and critic. An authority on Proust, Yeats and Stein, he was also a persuasive advocate of 'socially responsible' fiction, influencing the works of radical authors such as Upton Sinclair, John Dos Passos and Theodore Dreiser. His book on revolutionary writing, *To The Finland Station*, was widely considered a classic of its kind. A one-time assistant editor of the *New Republic*, he now contributed regularly to the *New Yorker*. Wilson never questioned Harold's genuine literary gifts, as he produced 'vivid and readable', 'neat and bright' books that were 'often engaging' and 'sometimes brilliant'. He thought *Some People* equal to the works of Evelyn Waugh or Max Beerbohm, but added cuttingly, it was 'the one very good book' that Harold had written. The sting, elegantly implanted, came in his last sentence: 'I have been opening every new book of Nicolson's with an eagerness which, though gradually diminished, is still always stirred by the hope of finding something else as good.' For Wilson, Harold's talents were fundamentally flawed. Trapped by his aristocratic antecedents, inhibited by his puritan upbringing, incarcerated for most of his life in the Foreign Office, socialising only with people of his own class, Harold had no conception 'of any other kind of life': the real world moved on, but not for Harold. Frozen in time, he stood, 'well-brushed and well-bred', staring out of an embassy window with his devoted governess at his side. Thus his diplomatic books 'tell in general a schoolboy story in which England is always St George', while when writing his biographies of the poets 'he is forced by a reflex action to detach himself socially from their company by a quiet but well-placed accent of amusement, disapproval, disdain'.

There is a touch of exaggeration in Wilson's remarks, but there is also, as Harold disarmingly admitted, much truth. Buckling before this assault, he acknowledged his faults in a candid *mea culpa*:

It seems absurd to me that any man of Wilson's great intelligence should regard me as 'well-brushed and well-bred' or suspect that I could ever be shocked by the depravity of men of genius. I believe he has got the *symptoms* wrong, but I have a nasty feeling that he has got the *illness* right. There is something (is it a hatred of emotion, or merely a lack of muscles in the mind?) which renders most of my writing superficial. I am sorry about this since I must have written ten million words in my day and it is sad that they should be so valueless. But when I read the article a third time, my irritation disappeared. I felt glad that Wilson should have devoted an article to books which he had clearly read carefully, and his nice remarks about *Some People* made up for classing of the rest as 'unsatisfactory'. But if in truth I have gone through life regarded by the respectable as a Bohemian and by the Bohemians as conventional, there must be something very very wrong.

Vita was not so understanding. How can you deny the circumstances of your birth, education, experience and consequent outlook? she asked. Wilson should have stated this as 'a fact', not as 'an adverse criticism'. Critics, she went on, repeatedly make a common error, 'which is to demand that a writer shall be something he is not. It is no good expecting a gentle person of sensibility and culture to care for the rough-and-tumble.' But like Wilson, she saw Harold's 'merits' and his 'shortcomings' as a writer as proceeding from his character. 'I think, for instance, that your almost morbid dislike of emotion is at the root of much of what E. Wilson is trying to say; only he has not got the clue to the puzzle.' Vita had given the game away. She had also pointed a finger at Harold's failure to sustain a successful political career. Perhaps he would have been better off staring out of an embassy window.[33]

In his diary Harold entitled 1942 'A Year, I hope, of Recovery'. After the ignominious reverses of 1941, he was clearly buoyed up by Soviet successes in repelling the German advance before Moscow – though his first thought had been that the Soviets would be 'bowled over by a touch' – and by the entry of the United States into the war: Americans, he maintained, 'will not rest until they have avenged it [Pearl Harbor]'.[32] His initial optimism soon faded. Further humiliations and disasters followed in quick order. There was an ominous sign in December 1941 when the capital ships, *Repulse* and *Prince of Wales*, were sunk by Japanese aircraft off the Malayan coast. Some weeks later the German battleships, *Scharnhorst* and *Gneisenau*, triumphantly ran the British gauntlet, 'sailing past our front door' through the English Channel. By March 1942 the British Empire in the Far East had collapsed: Singapore had surrendered, its garrison yielding to a force less than half its number; Hong Kong had fallen; Japanese armies, having occupied Malaya and Burma, had advanced to threaten India. In North Africa, Rommel, his army reinforced, struck eastwards, driving British forces out of Cyrenaica. That June, Tobruk capitulated, 33,000 troops again surrendering to a numerically inferior enemy force. Axis armies, now deployed on the borders of Egypt, menaced the Suez Canal and British possessions in the Middle East. These were military disasters of the first magnitude. A mortified Churchill recalled: 'Defeat is one thing; disgrace is another.' Harold wondered why 'our troops had not fought well in Malaya . . . the blackest mark in the whole history of the British army'. 'Why? Why?' he cried.[35]

By the end of the year Harold's mood had improved. Invited to Downing Street for lunch, he was greeted by a radiant Churchill, clad in a romper suit of air force blue, who waved before the company a letter from the King saying how much he and the Queen were thinking of 'Winston these glorious days'. And 'every word in his own hand', Churchill muttered. It celebrated the victory at El Alamein, a name Churchill refused to acknowledge. 'It must be called the Battle of Egypt,' he growled, ordering Harold, who he assumed wielded much influence at the BBC, to 'see to that at once'. As the guests were about to scatter, Churchill promised them 'more jam to come. Much more jam. And in places where some of you least expect.' Three days later, on 9 November, Harold heard of the Anglo–American invasion of French (Vichy-controlled) North-West Africa. His first thoughts were of de Gaulle, who had not been informed of the landings, and whose immediate reaction was '*profondément mortifié*', but who was mollified by Churchill and emerged from their meeting 'wreathed in smiles'. Harold's admiration of Churchill knew no bounds. 'What a brilliant piece of timing and strategy it all is! How 'I envy Winston at the Guildhall . . . in the House . . . [he] holds the House in the hollow of his hands . . . But how he has deserved it all!' Writing to Vita, Harold bestowed on Churchill the ultimate accolade: 'I do not think that, except for Winston, I *admire* anyone as much as I admire you.'[36]

While the Allies were making gains in North Africa, Harold was involved in a traffic accident outside St James's Palace that almost proved fatal. He was on his way from the Travellers' Club to meet Sir Arthur Penn, the Queen's private secretary, at Buckingham Palace. Penn, also Regimental Adjutant of the Grenadier Guards, was custodian of its official diary, drawn up by Nigel, who was now a serving officer in its 3rd Battalion. Harold, a diarist himself, was naturally keen to judge his son's skills. Hurrying along in the blackout, he stepped off the kerb and was knocked down by a taxi. The cab-driver, believing the injuries were mortal, wished to take Harold to hospital. Harold refused: take me to Buckingham Palace instead, he told the astonished cabby. In a state of shock, he arrived at Penn's quarters, bedraggled, bleeding, with a cracked rib, and without his spectacles. He was given a stiff whisky and soda. After resting, and declining an invitation from the Queen to stay overnight, he returned, 'feeling rotten', to King's Bench Walk. For weeks afterwards Harold was bandaged up, 'like Amenhotep the Second'. One after-effect that Harold did complain about was an increase in his deafness, a disability that worsened over time.[37]

For a man in his mid-fifties, Harold was in reasonably good health. He was concerned at the first signs of a prostate condition and, always inclined to portliness, was continually watching his weight. He had one scare. At the end of 1943, he dined with Guy Burgess at the Reform Club before boarding the night train for Cornwall. In the lavatory he fainted. On gaining consciousness, he murmured: 'I did not expect to die in the place where I first met Robbie Ross.' He refused to cancel his journey. Escorted by Burgess, he made his way to Paddington station. Safely tucked up in his sleeper, he took an aspirin and slept through the night until he reached his destination. (The cause of his collapse went unrecorded. It was probably a combination of low blood pressure and a taxing work schedule.)[38]

But Harold coped well with arduous wartime journeys abroad. Sponsored by government offices, he was sent to Ireland (March 1942), Sweden (October 1943), and North Africa (April-May 1944) on speaking tours, lectures, receptions, luncheons, and banquets following each other with tedious regularity. In Sweden, his hosts attached far more importance to him than he claimed for himself; in North Africa, Harold pitched into his ritual act of appeasing de Gaulle, who greeted him 'with what for him is almost warmth', but who was, as usual, trapped in a familiar '*profondément mortifié*'state.

These trips passed off without noticeable incident. Not so his visit to Dublin, where he appeared in a debate before students of University College. Harold thought he had made a good speech. Provoked by an intemperate attack by one of the panel on old-style British imperialism, he had put aside his notes and spoke extempore. 'Imperialism is dead,' he said, 'and I devoutly hope buried . . . it would be much wiser to think of the British lion as an elderly, replete, self-satisfied, moth-eaten animal, whose tail in the last twenty years has been so frequently twisted that few hairs remain, but an animal which at this moment is alert and angry.' Garbled reports appeared in the Irish press. Headlines described Britain as 'a moth-eaten lion', neglecting to highlight the patriotic excerpts of Harold's talk. A motion was put down in the Commons calling for Harold's dismissal from the BBC for spreading 'defeatism'. In a 'short, personal statement', he defended himself before the House. Describing his Dublin speech 'as the best speech I have ever made', and emphasising that it had been greeted by the audience with 'cheers', he went on to elucidate its main themes: that the war was being fought to defend principles 'shared by every Christian country'; and that whatever happened, 'we should not rest until victory was ours'. At one point he lost the House, as hecklers cried out, 'Don't overdo it.' But if not the most convincing of his parliamentary performances, it was persuasive enough to have the motion withdrawn. Harold emerged with his reputation firmly intact. And indeed, the charge of lack of patriotism levelled against him was patently absurd. His faith in Britain was unshakeable, in some ways touching in its naïvety.

I have much pride in my own people and much faith in the future. I really do believe that we in England have set an example to the world. I think that we may solve the social and economic problems of the twentieth century with as much wisdom and tolerance as when we solved the political problems of the nineteenth. Surely this is worthwhile? [39]

As 1943 progressed, an air of guarded optimism infiltrated Harold's thoughts. There was good reason for his subtle change in spirit. After the decisive battle at Stalingrad, the Red Army took the offensive, steadily pushing the German invaders back towards Poland and Germany; that July, Mussolini was ousted from office, and soon after Anglo-American forces invaded Sicily and the Italian mainland; in May, forty-one U-boats were sunk in the Atlantic, a turning-point in the pivotal sea war; while the Americans, after the battle of Midway in June, began methodically to exert a stranglehold on the Pacific war. Victory seemed only a matter of time.

Harold was concerned with more routine matters. He intervened forcefully in a debate on Foreign Office reform, a subject close to his heart, having long been in favour of fusing the Diplomatic with the Consular and Commercial Services. But Nancy Astor disturbed his train of thought. Her mind, as Harold pointed out, 'works from association to association, and therefore spreads sideways with extreme rapidity', so that arguing with her was like 'playing squash with a dish of scrambled eggs'. Undeterred, Lady Astor babbled on about the underprivileged, women whose rights were being trampled upon and who were being excluded from the service. Harold took an opposite view, and argued, not very convincingly, against women being granted equal status with men, though he was prepared to concede that women should be eligible for 'selective posts'. In general, he supported the proposed reforms. He recognised that merging the services would provoke a degree of discontent. To resolve these difficulties he proposed a kind of 'staff college', as 'a filter' to smooth over any disquiet felt by aggrieved officials. There were other aspects of the proposed reforms about which he held strong opinions. Having seen too many 'incompetents' being sent 'to agreeable places of exile', he spoke out effectively against this self-defeating practice. He also disapproved of compulsory retirement at the age of sixty: 'Diplomats, like wine,' he assured the House, 'improve with age.' And finally, recalling his own strapped financial past (and present), he approved wholeheartedly of 'the superannuation rule', praising it as 'the fairest' of all the rules of the new reforms, and the one that 'will produce the most beneficial results'.[40]

War aims cropped up again. When Harold heard of the Atlantic Charter, an eight-point declaration of Anglo-American war aims,* he was not impressed. 'Not as good as Wilson's 14 points,' he noted, 'but better than

---

* From 9 to 12 August, Roosevelt met Churchill in Placentia Bay, off Newfoundland. An eye-catching public display of Anglo-American solidarity, its Charter, couched in generalities, spoke of 'a peace which will afford to all nations the means of dwelling in safety within their own boundaries, and that will afford assurance that all the men in all lands may live out their lives in freedom from fear and want'. Most divisive of all was article 3, respecting the rights of 'all peoples to choose the form of government under which they will live'. Churchill subsequently contended that it applied only to the enslaved countries of Europe, and not to the peoples of the British Empire. Roosevelt thought otherwise.

nothing.' Some time later he was asked by the Army Bureau of Current Affairs to write a pamphlet, *The Last Peace and the Next*, which reflects Harold's general ideas on the post-war world.[41] In Parliament, he was far more specific. Anglo-French relations in particular concerned him. Harold emerged as a trenchant critic of the government's policy towards France. He accused it of reneging on its commitments. It had repeatedly maintained that France 'should be fully restored to her position of independence and greatness', yet all its actions 'run counter' to these aims. He readily admitted to the 'misunderstandings, outrages and affronts' that had marred Anglo-French relations since the beginning of the war. Although aware of de Gaulle's wayward behaviour, he took particular exception to General Jan Smuts's 'cruel and ungenerous' remarks about France. Smuts, a man whom Harold greatly admired, had questioned in public whether France would ever recover her position as a Great Power. Smuts was adamant: 'in Europe, we are left with Great Britain and Russia'. This was not Harold's view. He pleaded with the House not to discount the cardinal lesson taught by Eyre Crowe that Britain must oppose any country that seeks by power to dominate western Europe. Before very long, Churchill would ask, 'What will lie between the white snows of Russia and the white cliffs of Dover?' Harold spoke of Britain being hemmed in by 'a young Eagle apt to indulge in flights of fancy', and 'an enormous Bear', menacingly 'reticent' in its attitude towards its neighbours. But there were already clear signs of Russia's intentions, known to the Foreign Office, that, if fulfilled, would have confirmed its role as the paramount power in central and eastern Europe. As American commitment to a post-war Europe was still uncertain (and was to remain so), that left only France as a viable partner, as 'an equal, an Ally and a friend', in Harold's turn of phrase. In August 1944 he was at Sissinghurst when he heard the news that 'Paris is free', and freed, 'at least in appearance', by the Parisians themselves. Together with Vita and their cook, Mrs Staples, they toasted 'the future of France' with a glass of gin. More than anything, Harold wished to see '*Une France pure et dure*'.[42]

As the war drew to its close, Harold , like most observers, watched nervously as Soviet armies advanced relentlessly westwards into Poland and southeast Europe. How best to measure up to the Soviet threat was the question uppermost in their minds. Resolving the German question was the most immediate problem. Harold deplored the use of the term 'unconditional surrender', which had 'some strange historical connotation' in America,*

---

*The term is attributed to General Ulysses S. Grant, who earned the nickname 'Unconditional Surrender Grant' at Fort Donelson in February 1862 during the American Civil War. He told the defeated troops: 'No terms except unconditional and immediate surrender can be accepted.'

but was misunderstood in Germany. He much preferred the expression, *la victoire intégrale*, and was pleased to note that Churchill too, despite his lapse at Casablanca, when he had supported Roosevelt's formula of unconditional surrender, was fond of the phrase 'total victory'. Ferreting out the nuances of meaning between 'total victory' and 'unconditional surrender' would be a matter of semantic debate, far removed from events on the ground. By September 1944 the German question had in effect been resolved, and largely in the Soviets' favour. That month Britain, the United States and the Soviet Union signed a protocol that divided Germany into zones of occupation. Whatever happened, a Soviet military presence in Germany was assured, at some points little more than 120 miles from the Rhine. Whispers of this arrangement had already reached Harold's ears. He was reconciled to the partition of Germany – for that was what it amounted to – even though, as Gladwyn Jebb told him, the Foreign Office frowned upon such an arrangement. '[It] is bound to come owing to the zones of occupation and relief,' Harold noted.[43]

But it was the Polish problem that attracted most attention. By this time there were two Polish governments: a Provisional Government-in-Exile, based in London from June 1940, in defence of which Britain had gone to war; while in Lublin, the Soviets, as the Red Army crossed the Curzon Line, had set up a creature of their own, the Polish Committee of National Liberation. The fate of the Polish Underground Army, anti-Soviet in allegiance, which in August 1944 rose up against their Nazi occupiers to liberate Warsaw, was a frightening indication of Soviet intentions. As German forces moved in to destroy the uprising, Stalin waited, though his armies were within easy striking distance of the beleaguered city. Despite desperate appeals from the British, Stalin refused to rescue what he termed 'power-seeking criminals'. What a tragedy, Harold wrote, 'that such immense power should be in the hands of people so ruthless and unreliable'. By now it was common knowledge that Soviet ambitions included control over the Baltic States; establishing itself in the Balkans; resurrecting the Curzon Line as the Soviet–Polish frontier; and pushing Poland westwards, to the Oder, at Germany's expense.[44]

Poland was the immediate issue when Churchill met Stalin in Moscow in October 1944, at the so-called 'Tolstoy' conference. Harold was all too familiar with the ramifications of the Polish question. In his book, *The Congress of Vienna*, written as the two leaders were conferring in the Kremlin, he warned of 'the danger of substituting French [read German] domination for the domination of Russia', and of 'the menace of Russian expansion towards the west'. The Polish question had split the Allies at the Congress of Vienna: it had done so again in the aftermath of the Paris peace conference.

Would it once again threaten allied unity? 'They have NOT settled the Polish question – merely adjourned it,' Harold protested to his diary, only days after the conclusion of the Moscow talks. Was he referring to the statesmen at 'Tolstoy' or at Vienna? It is not clear. What is clear, however, is that Harold had already come to the conclusion that the London Poles were 'insane'. In the House of Commons he pleaded with them: 'You cannot possibly entertain the insane folly of believing that you can ever exist except with friendly relations with Russia. Why be provocative? Why worry about frontiers which you know are quite untenable unless Russia is prepared to uphold them?' And he went on: behave sensibly, realistically, place yourselves 'in a relation of dignity and virtue' towards your more 'powerful neighbour'. In Moscow, Churchill made much the same point, if in more picturesque terms, to Stanislaw Mikolajczyk, Prime Minister of the Poles-in-Exile. Mikolajczyk had been dragged to Moscow to be browbeaten into accepting the Curzon Line. 'Should I sign a death warrant against myself?' he asked. 'You ought to be put in a lunatic asylum!' Churchill snapped back. 'You hate the Russians. I know you hate them.'[45]

At the Yalta conference (4–11 February 1945), the last and most notorious of the wartime summits, the German question was tidied up: military plans were co-ordinated for the final onslaught on Nazi Germany; German industry was to be shorn of its military potential; a reparations committee was set up; major war criminals were to be tried. Lastly, the zoning of Germany was confirmed. Over Poland, Stalin refused to budge, except to scatter paper promises. Having settled on the Curzon Line to his satisfaction, he did not disguise his intention to extend Poland's frontier with Germany up to the Oder–Neisse line. It was the same story in the Balkans, where, even as the parleying at Yalta continued, the Soviets were tightening their grip. Turning to the Far East, Stalin promised to intervene in the war two to three months after Germany's surrender, receiving in return territories it had lost during its war with Japan in 1904–5. Other matters were dealt with: voting procedures for the Security Council and the United Nations. And finally, a much-publicised 'Declaration on Liberated Europe' was signed, affirming 'the right of all peoples to choose the form of government under which they will live'.

Immediately after the conference twenty-two Conservative MPs put down an amendment remembering that Britain had taken up arms in defence of Poland and regretting the transfer of the territory of an ally – Poland – to another power – the Soviet Union – noting also the failure to ensure that those countries liberated by the Soviet Union from German oppression would have the full right to choose their own form of government free from pressure by another power, namely the Soviet Union. Harold voted against it! 'I who had felt that Poland was a lost cause, feel gratified that we had at least saved something.' Praising the settlement as 'the most important political agreement that we have gained in this war', he considered the alternatives. To stand aside, to disapprove but do nothing, would be 'unworthy of a great country'. Recalling Castlereagh's and Talleyrand's machinations at Vienna, he knew that to oppose the Russians by force would be insane. The only viable alternative was 'to save something by negotiation'. The Curzon Line, delineated after 'a solid, scientific examination of the question' at the Paris peace conference, was 'entirely in favour of the Poles'. Should Poland advance beyond that line, 'she would be doing something very foolish indeed'. Churchill and Eden came in for the highest praise. 'When I read the Yalta communiqué, I thought, "How could they have brought that off? This is really splendid!"' Turning the Conservative dissidents' amendment on its head, Harold revealed Yalta's most lasting achievement. Russia, dazzled by its military successes, revengeful and rapacious, might well have aimed to restore its 'old Tsarist frontiers'. It had not done so. 'They have agreed in a very important way to modify the Tsarist frontiers. They have agreed at Yalta to make a concession to Poland.' Harold spoke with conviction. But to salute Stalin's perceived altruism in this matter rendered his reasoning contrived and decidedly off-key. The truth was more prosaic. Stalin had dealt himself an unbeatable hand. As two exiled Soviet historians laconically put it: 'The presence of 6.5 million Soviet soldiers buttressed Soviet claims.'

Harold's warm support of the Yalta agreement rested on the Crimean Declaration that promised 'the right of all peoples to choose the form of government under which they will live'. 'No written words could better express the obligation to see that the independence, freedom and integrity of Poland of the future are preserved,' Harold said. But could Stalin be trusted to carry out his obligations? Harold thought so. 'Marshal Stalin has made many promises . . . to his Allies: and as far as my knowledge goes every one of those has been kept.' Ever since the war, Harold assured the House, Stalin had demonstrated 'that he is about the most reliable man in Europe'. These sentiments, to a later generation alarming in their naïvety, were soon to change as the harsher realities of the Cold War set in. But for the time being Harold was in good company. On returning from Yalta, Churchill reported to his Cabinet. He felt convinced that Stalin 'meant well to the world and to Poland', and he 'had confidence' in him: Stalin 'had kept his word with the utmost loyalty'. (Hugh Dalton, who was present at the cabinet meeting, put it more dramatically. He reported Churchill as saying, 'Poor Neville Chamberlain believed he could trust Hitler. He was wrong. But I don't think I'm wrong about Stalin.') Opposition to the Yalta agreement was muted, confined mainly to discredited 'Munichites' who now sprang to the defence of Poland. When the Commons voted 396 to 25 in favour of his policy, Churchill was 'overjoyed'. After the debate he approached Harold in the smoking-room: "'Harold, you made a powerful speech. A most powerful speech. You swung votes. I thank you. I congratulate you. I give you" – and here he made a sort of offering gesture – "my congratulations.'"[46]

Harold's faith in Stalin's word proved true in one important respect. At the 'Tolstoy' conference the fundamental issue had not been the Polish question – for all its high drama – but the Balkans. At one of its sessions, the two leaders had put their signatures to the so-called 'Percentages Agreement', Churchill's 'naughty document' that cut up the Balkan countries into spheres of influence, apportioning Britain – in accord with the United States – primacy in Greece, the Soviet Union in Romania and Bulgaria, and earmarking equality of status in Yugoslavia and Hungary. Events in Greece came to a head in December 1944 when British troops entered Athens to separate warring monarchist and communist factions. Treat it as a conquered city where a rebellion has broken out, Churchill instructed the local British commander, General Robert Scobie. Britain would 'hold and dominate' Athens, establishing its position in the eastern Mediterranean, a vital strategic-imperial area. Stalin adhered 'strictly and faithfully' to the Percentages Agreement, Churchill hearing more protests from the State Department than from the Kremlin.

Harold, a committed Hellenophile – 'they are perhaps the most charming race in the world' – supported Churchill's interventionist policy. 'Not that we intervened forcibly too soon, but a day too late.' He derided the idea of a devious British conspiracy, 'an evil act of policy devised by the reactionaries on the Front Bench'. 'Knock all their heads together,' he advised the government, 'and say, "Shut up, stop fighting".' The Greeks would understand: 'They are used to English people coming in. They expect it. Our intervention is part of their history.' Would anything ever shatter the Greeks' 'inherited attitude of liking towards the British people'? Harold thought not. Here was a voice from the Old Foreign Office, a far cry from the new world order in the making, which, ostensibly, he welcomed. If it was not quite the gunboat diplomacy of far-off days, it was a close approximation to it.[47]

On matters of diplomatic procedure Harold spoke with considerable authority. Years in the Foreign Office, participation in the Paris peace conference, and later as a servant of the League of Nations, lent weight to his views on these questions. Harold judged the Dumbarton Oaks plan of August–October 1944, which led to the foundation of the United Nations, according to three essential tests: 'First, has it got the power? Second, is it well designed?' About these points, Harold had no doubt: the draft proposals were 'unsurpassed in skill, in ingenuity': it was 'about as perfect a machine as could be devised', 'a masterpiece'. As for the third, 'is it going to be used in the right way?' he queried. He harboured serious reservations. It was 'the more questionable Clause', the right given to the five permanent members of the Security Council (the United States, the Soviet Union, Britain, France and China) to veto proposals for action, that troubled him most. It was a fatal flaw: it would paralyse the capacity of the United Nations to maintain international peace and security. 'Every big Power will have its satellite, and every satellite will have its big Power.' But despite Harold's caveat, how else could the Great Powers have safeguarded their national interests? He offered no alternative. Perhaps this particular circle was impossible to square. He feared that 'these organisations can cope with small opposition, they become hesitant when the opposition is serious'. Still, to a certain degree the exigencies of the Cold War vindicated Harold. The crucial decision to intervene in the Korean war was made possible only because of a temporary boycott of the Security Council by the Soviet Union. It was a decision of which Harold thoroughly approved.[48] His anti-veto discourse was to be his last major speech in Parliament.

As early as December 1940 Harold had argued that Britain's war aims should place greater emphasis on 'home reconstruction', even telling a startled Halifax that 'we accept Socialism'. The first significant indication of 'home reconstruction' was provided by Sir William Beveridge's report, a plan for universal social security covering unemployment benefits and family allowances. By creating a financial safety net from abject poverty, it was seen as a blueprint for a new welfare state. Harold was committed to its essentials, 'a popular issue', he thought. In August 1942 he met Beveridge and put to him the idea of a national health service. And although Beveridge dodged the subject, and despite some differences of approach, Harold was heartened by what he had learned: 'I come away more cheerful and encouraged than I have been for weeks.' The Beveridge Report was published in December 1942 and debated in the House the following February. The government gave it lukewarm backing, electing to delay its implementation until after the war. This was a serious mistake; and in a roundabout way it determined Harold's future. The report proved to be extremely popular, particularly with the armed forces: it sold over half a million copies. When the House considered its recommendations, the Labour backbenchers put down an amendment urging a more positive stand by the government. Although the amendment was defeated by 338 votes to 121, all Labour

members not in office, with two exceptions, voted for it. Harold felt that
the government's evasiveness 'merely creates suspicion' as to its ultimate
intentions. Fearing for Churchill's position, he hoped the die-hards would
not 'drag out Winston tomorrow to crack the whip of National Unity . . .
If only he had refused to head the Conservative Party.'[49] Harold's suspicions
were well grounded. The vote was important in persuading the electorate
that Labour was best suited to create a just society after the war. In this
manner, it prepared the ground for Churchill's shock defeat at the polls in
July 1945.

At Sissinghurst, Vita, in a 'pre-1792' mood, was anything but heartened
at Beveridge's message. She thought it 'dreadful', allowing the proletariat
'to breed like rabbits because each new rabbit means 8/- a week – as though
there weren't too many of them already'. By giving everybody 'everything
for nothing', it completely discouraged 'thrift or effort'. Let's hope it 'gets
whittled away like an artichoke'. Was she prepared to tolerate old age
pensions? Yes, but only grudgingly: 'I suppose so, in default of euthanasia
which I should prefer, as also for mental deficients.' Despite her immod-
erate language, there is no evidence that Vita was bluffing. Judging from
these remarks, she can only be classified as a dyed-in-the-wool reactionary.
She made her position abundantly clear in her so-called '*Manifesto*'. 'I hate
democracy. I hate la populace. I wish education had never been introduced.
I don't like tyranny, but I like an intelligent oligarchy. I wish la populace
had never been encouraged to emerge from its rightful place. I should like
to see them as well fed and well housed as T. T. [dairy] cows – but no more
thinking than that.' This was far removed from Harold's standards and
values. Yet their relationship effortlessly overcame this clash of outlooks. 'It
is,' as Vita elegantly put it, 'like a deep, deep lake which can never dry up
. . . I don't honestly think that as much can said for most marriages, do
you? Of course I suppose it could be said of the bourgeois bedint marriage
founded on habit; but not for a difficult unorthodox marriage like ours, with
rather subtle and difficult people involved.'[50] However else one decodes this
stylish formula, it undoubtedly worked for them.

Harold and Vita, 'subtle and difficult', continued to nurse their 'difficult
unorthodox marriage', Harold working mainly in London, Vita guarding
her privacy at Sissinghurst. The two boys were away at war: Nigel, an officer
in the Grenadier Guards, saw service in North Africa and Italy; Ben, after
serving in an anti-aircraft battery at Chatham, obtained a commission in the
Intelligence Corps, served in the Middle East, and was invalided home from
Italy in 1945 after a road accident which broke two bones in his spine.
Harold, more accessible, more empathetic than Vita, dined with them at a
Greek restaurant prior to their embarkation overseas. For the next two and

a half years he kept up a correspondence with them. Every Sunday he wrote them a joint letter from Sissinghurst, some 3,000 words long. Perhaps as an intellectual exercise, Harold stirred up a somewhat pointless controversy involving Nigel. He argued, contentiously, that 'works-of-art are irreplaceable, whereas no lives are irreplaceable', refining his point in a 'Marginal Comment' by stating that 'he would rather his son was killed at Cassino than that the Monastery should be destroyed'. Unknown to him at the time, Nigel was taking part in the battle for Monte Cassino. In the event, the Benedictine Monastery was destroyed and Nigel survived. Harold's muddled order of priorities irritated his constituents, an unforeseen fallout that undermined his position at Leicester.[51]

'Darling,' Vita wrote, 'Knole has been bombed.'

I mind frightfully, frightfully, frightfully. I always persuade myself that I have finally torn Knole out of my heart, and then the moment anything touches it, every nerve is alive again. I cannot bear to think of Knole wounded, and I not there to look after it and be wounded with it. Those filthy Germans! Let us level every town in Germany to the ground! I shan't care. Oh, Hadji, I wish you were here. I feel hurt and heartsick.

The same day that Vita wrote these words, Hadji dined with Lord Rothermere and elaborated upon the 'works-of-art for lives' trade-off.

Harold attended assiduously to his parliamentary duties but, as he noted wryly, it is 'Impossible to speak in the House of Commons except on technical matters. My only technical speciality is in Foreign Affairs and that is the one subject it is impossible to mention in public.' Feeling 'lost in isolation', he rode the social merry-go-round. It gave him much pleasure and enjoyment: it also generated a disagreeable feeling that he was frittering his life away at a time of national crisis. 'I often wonder whether my grandson, reading this diary after many years, will not be irritated by my constant record "lunch here, dined there".' Out of office, he patrolled the fringes of power, moving from salon to salon, from the Travellers' to the Reform, from the Ritz to the Savoy. The usual names appeared, Lady Colefax leading the pack. A cluster of notables followed: the Devonshires, the Camroses, the Rothermeres, Lady Cunard, Lady Furness (the Duke of Windsor's ex-lover), Mrs George Keppel (Edward VII's mistress), Sir Edward Marsh, Sir James Rothschild, Sir Roderick Jones (chairman and managing director of Reuters), Kingsley Martin, and others. Guy Burgess showed up, 'like Ovid among the Goths'. He lunched with Violet Trefusis, past intimacies not forgotten but put aside: 'I suppose she is amusing, but her stories are ruined by the fact that they are not true.'[52]

Towards the end of 1943 Harold began to fear that he would lose his seat at the forthcoming elections, scheduled to take place at the end of the war. It was 'the Mosley business' that first alerted him. It was only natural that he should feel sympathy for Mosley, a long-standing friend and one-time colleague, who had been incarcerated since May 1940 under Regulation 18B, first at Brixton, later at Holloway. 'In a courageous act of friendship', Harold attempted to visit him, but Mosley turned him away, annoyed at the tenor of Harold's overseas broadcasts. (Harold was not as forgiving regarding other sympathisers or collaborators of the Nazi regime: he believed that John Amery 'ought to be hanged', that P.G. Wodehouse should be prosecuted, and that William Joyce, 'Lord Haw Haw', should be tried, though not in an English court.) In November 1943 the Mosleys were released from prison on humanitarian grounds, Mosley's physical condition having seriously deteriorated. Sixty-two MPs voted against the release, fifty-five from the Labour benches. It confirmed for Harold 'the prejudice and passion of the proletariat'. If nothing else, the debate, vindictive in tone, had 'destroyed all confidence in the governing class . . . It has widened the class breach. I see quite clearly now that I shall not stand a dog's chance in keeping my seat in West Leicester. The whole working class will vote solid against me.'[53] There were other, no less ominous, signs that the working class would no longer tolerate a Conservative-led government. For one thing, the newly formed Common Wealth Party, pledged to run against all 'reactionary candidates', had won two recent by-elections. And at Blackheath, Harold found, scrawled on the wall of the station lavatory, the graffito, 'Winston Churchill is a bastard'. 'Yes,' he was told, 'the tide has turned.' 'But how foul,' Harold responded. 'How bloody foul!' He could only conclude that 'Winston has become an electoral liability'.[54]

The war in Europe came to an end on 8 May 1945. At Sissinghurst, Vita, Harold and Ben climbed the turret stairs and hoisted the flag to its rightful place above the tower. 'It looks very proud and gay after five years of confinement.' Back in London, Harold found Trafalgar Square packed with cheering crowds. Along Whitehall, loudspeakers had been affixed to all government buildings. Harold was escorted into Palace Yard where, as Big Ben struck three, 'an extraordinary hush' came over the assembled multitude, waiting to hear Churchill's victory speech. '"The evil-doers," the Prime Minister intoned, "now lie prostrate before us." The crowd gasped at this phrase.' 'He was very good,' thought 'Baffy' Dugdale, 'I don't think anyone but him could have got away with "Advance Britannia!" But he did, at the end there was a mighty roar.' After listening to 'The Last Post' and singing, in a very loud voice, 'God Save the King', Harold made his way to the Chamber to await Churchill. Churchill came in, 'looking coy and cheerful', responding to the cheers, 'not with a bow exactly, but with an odd jerk of the head and with a wide grin'. The House then retired to St Margaret's Church 'to give humble and reverend thanks to Almighty God for our deliverance from German domination'. The Speaker read out the names of Members who had laid down their lives, among them Robert Bernays, Harold's most intimate parliamentary colleague. 'I was moved. Tears came into my eyes. Furtively I wiped them away. "Men are so emotional", sniffed Nancy Astor, who was sitting next to me. Damn her.' That evening he went to a party at 'Chips' Channon's. He loathed it, feeling isolated among 'the Nurembergers and the Munichois celebrating *our* victory over *their* friend, Herr Ribbentrop'. He left hurriedly. Making his way back to the Inner Temple along Fleet Street he saw 'the best sight of all – the dome of St Paul's rather dim-lit, and then above it a concentration of searchlights upon the huge golden cross. So I went to bed. That was my victory day.'[55]

Only days later Labour decided against renewing the Coalition. On 23 May Churchill reluctantly tendered his resignation to the King, reconciling himself to the prospect of a general election. Polling day was set for 5 July.

As a working MP Harold's predicament was self-evident: he was functioning in a political vacuum. National Labour existed in name only. Harold had wanted to bury it some time ago; but it staggered on, punch-drunk, waiting for the final knock-out blow. Five weeks before the general election it dissolved itself, assuming the name 'National Campaign Committee', a gesture without much meaning.[56] At a loss for an eye-catching slogan, Harold finally petitioned the voters of West Leicester to 'Support Churchill and vote for Harold Nicolson, the National Candidate', a loosely worded appeal that confused rather than clarified Harold's position. It would have little impact. Harold's political identity crisis was not the only reason that he approached the challenge of re-election in a mood of deep pessimism:

I am frankly dreading the General Election. I dislike the falsity, the noise, the misrepresentation, the exhaustion and the strain of the whole thing. I am bad at posing as a demagogue. I dislike being abused and heckled. I have not the combative instincts which lead some people to enjoy the conflict. And above all, I have no prospect of success . . . Times are not normal. People feel, in a vague and muddled way, that all the sacrifices to which they have been exposed . . . are all the fault of 'them' – namely the authority or the Government. By a totally illogical process of reasoning, they believe that 'they' mean the upper classes, or the Conservatives, and that in some manner all that went well during these years was due to Bevin and Morrison, and all that went ill was

due to Churchill. Class feeling and class resentment are very strong.
I should be surprised, therefore, if there were not a marked swing
to the left. I am not sure that I think this would be a bad thing . . .
In any case, even a slight swing to the left will sweep away my 87
majority. [57]

His analysis was valid, as far as it went. But Harold would have done
well to recall that 'class resentment' looked back to the inter-war period of
high unemployment, hunger marches and poverty stricken areas, all under
Conservative-dominated administrations, topics that were largely ignored in
his diaries and letters.

Harold's campaign opened on 18 June. It went as badly as he expected.
Vita turned up at Leicester, setting a precedent. A morale-booster for
Harold, she spoke at a women's meeting and sat on the platform beside
Harold at two of his evening rallies. But in the long run, her intervention
had little effect: Vita hated grassroots politics even more than Harold. As
the electioneering got under way, his campaign making little impact, Harold
revealed the darker side of his character. He wrote to Vita : 'I am sure my
canvassers say, "What, vote for a Jew like Janner. What are you thinking
of?"'[58]* Convinced – mistakenly, of course – that the Board of the staunchly
Labour *Daily Mirror* was dominated by Jews and hence was subverting the
armed forces into 'a general distrust of authority', he noted that 'The Jewish
capacity for self-destruction is really illimitable.' Given that the basic facts
about the Holocaust were already well known, this reads as a most outrageous comment. His campaign continued downhill, 'One bad meeting'
followed by one that 'was not so bad'. 'Anyway,' he consoled himself, 'it will
not be a dishonourable defeat.' He was already looking around for another
job, perhaps as chairman of the British Council, even better as a member
of the House of Lords: 'I should like that,' he affirmed.[59]

On 26 July Harold learned that he had lost his seat by 7,215 votes. That
night, before retiring, he took two aspirins: 'I feel as if I had been run over
by a tram, but mainly owing to the physical exhaustion and nervous strain.'[60]
Intellectually, at least, Harold had prepared himself for the day of judgment:

I shall earn all your [Nigel's] sympathy when the day comes that I cease
to be a Member of Parliament. I have loved my ten years at Westminster,
and have found there a combination of genial surroundings with useful

---

*Barnett Janner (1892–1982): Born in Lithuania, brought up in Glamorgan, Wales:
prominent parliamentarian, solicitor and Jewish communal leader. Knighted in 1961;
Life Peer, 1970.

activity which is the basis of all human happiness. If I learn that my political career is over (perhaps for ever), I shall accept it with philosophic resignation and devote such years as may remain to me to serious literary work. I have a domestic retreat of the utmost felicity and a second string to my bow. My God! what right have I of all men to complain? [61]

After his defeat, Harold received many letters of condolence. Past and present diplomats wrote in, as did friends from the political-literary-social world he graced. A constituent, Mrs Dell, sorry 'to lose such a real friend', expressed the feelings of many voters at West Leicester: 'We, as small shopkeepers, will miss your kindness and help shown to us in the most difficult times we have passed through. It has been a real shock to the older people.' Nothing, however, gave him greater pleasure than Churchill's generous tribute to his contribution to Parliament. 'The House,' Churchill was reported as saying, 'will be a sadder place without him – and smaller.' So closed, as Harold put it, 'a very happy chapter' in his life. [62] It was the end of his political career, but not of his political ambitions.

FOURTEEN

The Edwardian

'I avert my eyes,' said Harold, as he watched the newly elected MPs filing into the House of Commons. 'I do NOT like having ceased to be a Member . . . it rather bites to feel that at 11.0 this morning the new House will assemble and I will not be there.' This was not the only affront Harold suffered. He had also been banished from his comfortable lodging at King's Bench Walk, his chambers being required for practising barristers. Ben found alternative accommodation for Harold at 10, Neville Terrace, South Kensington. The sight unnerved Harold: 'I saw in front of me what is in fact the ugliest house I have ever seen – being a miniature replica of the Charing Cross Hotel.' Ben and Nigel moved in, temporarily relieving the gloom. Residing at 'Devil Terrace' or 'this bloody tenement', as Harold called it, brought him little pleasure, a marked contrast to the delights he had enjoyed at the Inner Temple. (Later, his brother Freddy, a chronic alcoholic, joined him, presenting him with an additional, intensely private, source of anguish.) To make matters worse, he had recently endured considerable physical discomfort. Regressing to his nursery-style parlance he told how he had 'broke a toof and was stung in the eye by a waps'. Harold was fifty-eight years old. He had lost his precious seat in the Commons, his desirable flat at K.B.W., and had suffered facial 'disfigurement'.[1] It was not the most auspicious of beginnings to a new era.

Harold viewed the advent of a Labour government, 'an amazing statement of public opinion', with a sense of bewilderment. What does it really mean? he asked. It was not the dread of social revolution, something he had anticipated for some time and claimed not to fear. 'It may be the conflict within me between the patrician and the humanitarian. I hate uneducated people having power; but I like to think that the poor will be rendered happy. This is a familiar conflict.' He was delighted at Bevin's appointment as Foreign Secretary. 'I hate the thought of our appearing small in the councils of Europe.' Bevin, he learned from a top official at the Office, 'reads with amazing rapidity, remembers what he reads, cross-examines the experts, and having once mastered his brief, acts with vigour.' When Bevin arrived for the Potsdam conference, he said: 'I'm not going to have Britain barged about.' A bold statement, but the British, like the Americans, had few trump cards to play. When Harold heard of the territorial clauses of the conference he thought them 'terrific', but only in the sense that 'If any country other than Russia had acquired such tremendous annexations there would be an outcry. Even as it is, people will be considerably shocked.' At the Potsdam conference (17 July–2 August), appropriately code-named 'Terminal', the Western Allies implicitly acknowledged Soviet primacy in eastern Europe by, *inter alia*, accepting Polish and Soviet administration of certain German territories (Poland had been moved westwards up to the Oder–Neisse line), and agreeing to the transfer of the German population of these territories, and other parts of eastern and central Europe (over 10 million people), to Germany. Still, faithful to his high-minded, traditional diplomatic code of conduct, Harold argued that agreements, however dishonourable, once signed, should be honoured: 'our attempts to wriggle out of it [later, at the Paris conference of August 1946] suggest weakness and deprive us of that moral authority which we might possess and ought to possess.'[2]

While at Potsdam, the Allies gave Japan a stark choice: unconditional surrender or total destruction. On 6 August an atom bomb, nicknamed 'Little Boy', was dropped on Hiroshima with obliterating effect, destroying houses and buildings within a 1.5 mile radius, and causing 80,000 immediate deaths (another 60,000 would die within a year). Three days later a second bomb, 'Fat Man', was dropped on Nagasaki. Japan sued for peace. By 14 August, it had capitulated to the allied terms of surrender. The war in the Far East had come to an end. 'A happy, happy day,' Harold noted (obviously unaware of the horrific effects of weapons of mass destruction). But Harold was 'amused' in a different sense. Reporters contacted him wishing to know whether he had been blessed with prophetic vision. In his *roman-à-clef*, *Public Faces* (1932), he had told of jet planes and a mysterious (British) atomic bomb that had accidentally exploded off the eastern seaboard of America, causing untold destruction and resulting in 80,000 deaths. Temporarily diverted by these enquiries, Harold returned to his work in progress to complete the first draft of *The Congress of Vienna*.[3]

Out of office and Parliament, Harold was obliged to return to journalism, broadcasting and literature to earn his living. How would he allocate his time? 'Now that I have dropped out of public life, I do nothing of any real importance. I do my "Marginal Comments" once a week; my *Daily Telegraph* reviews once a week; my *Figaro* once every other week; and my many broadcasts. I also, when in London, have a succession of Boards and Committees [including the National Trust, the National Portrait Gallery, the London Library, the Classical Association, War Memorials, and the Royal Literary Fund].' He soon quarrelled with the *Daily Telegraph*, the literary editor refusing to publish a commissioned review of a book on European federal union, a concept Harold favoured. 'I cannot allow them to treat me with such lack of seriousness.' But he hung on for another few months, and then switched to the *Observer*: 'It is quite evident that the *Daily Telegraph* public is not worth writing literary articles for.' He was required to write one review a week, alternating with George Orwell. In the early 1950s he was joined by A. J. P. Taylor. Both were reviewers of the highest quality, though Taylor was more inclined than Harold to shock his readers. The *Observer*'s literary pages became a focus, a weekly must, for what today would be termed the 'left-leaning, chattering classes'. Harold and Vita were now working for the same concern, for Vita had first reviewed for the *Observer* in 1935. In 1946, she began her weekly column, 'In Your Garden'. This feature brought her popular fame; it was more widely read than anything else she wrote.[4]

The element of self-doubt was embedded in Harold's character, first as a political animal, now as a literary figure. 'It is sad that at my age one is bored by the way one writes and yet too old to write differently or better. I well know that I cannot hope to rise above my own level. All that I can strive to do is not sink below it.' Yet the diaries, letters and articles multiplied. He might 'struggle', as he did with a piece on Churchill for *Time* magazine, but other essays flowed more easily: 'Men and Circumstances', an exercise weighing up the pros and cons of the 'great men' versus 'accident' theories of history; or, 'Peacemaking at Paris, Failure or Farce', an analysis of the 1946 conference.[5] There were also books: *The Congress of Vienna* (1946) and *The English Sense of Humour* (1947). *The English Sense of Humour* was really an extended, and not very funny, essay of seventy pages, depicting humour as a form of self-protection. Testing the wit of the magazine, *Punch*, it claimed that the proletariat (and Gladstone) lacked the kind of humour of its masthead symbol, the anarchic glove puppet Mr Punch, while those of other classes evidently savoured it. Ben thought its 'exterior superior to the interior': Raymond Mortimer also chimed in, believing it 'very bad and sham philosophy'.[6]

At the end of April 1946 Harold flew to Nuremberg. The purpose of his trip, arranged by the Foreign Office, was to cover the show trials of Nazi war criminals before the International Military Tribunal (IMT). It was felt that Harold was most suited to write about them for British and French journals. He dreaded the prospect. The thought of seeing men, however odious, humiliated, 'caught like rats in a trap', depressed him. In the dock, these one-time masters of Europe constituted a pathetic sight: Hess, lifeless, 'not attending'; Ribbentrop, 'utterly broken'; Rosenberg, 'a dim and middle-aged creature with hanging head'; Jodl, resembling 'a reliable coachman of Victorian days'; von Papen, 'haggard and untidy'; von Neurath, 'shrunk and aged'. Only Goering, striking the 'attitude of Rodin's *Penseur*', radiated a semblance of the authority that had once made him the second man in Germany. Harold inspected their living quarters. 'Ah yes,' the Commandant told him, 'no mother has ever cherished her children as I cherish these men. I must keep them fresh for the last day.' Harold was then taken to a storeroom that exhibited specimens of Nazi atrocities, a lampshade made of human skin, a human head reduced to the size of an orange. But most horrifying of all was a series of photographs depicting Jewish women, 'stark naked', lined up 'at the edge of a trench, the corpses of their predecessors filling the upper half of the trench like sprats spilled from a fishing smack', and then summarily mown down by their guards, their bodies flopping helplessly in the trench until they lay still. After such obscene images, the ruins of Nuremberg took on a wholly different significance. Harold, however, was nothing if not compassionate. On hearing the verdicts of the IMT, he was sufficiently moved to say, 'I cannot bear it . . . to hear those men being bumped off one by one.'[7]

Harold heard the sentencing while in Paris. He had been sent there by the BBC to report on an international conference of twenty-one powers convened to draft texts of peace treaties with Italy, Romania, Bulgaria, Hungary and Finland.[8] Two weekly broadcasts were planned, each of fifteen minutes, the first to be heard on the Home Service and simultaneously relayed to the Commonwealth, the second in French on the Overseas Service. Harold reckoned he would be speaking to about 20 million people. At what level should he pitch his talks to appeal to such a vast, disparate audience? After careful deliberation, he finally decided: 'I shall invent a woman.' The talks were immensely successful, and earned him high praise from many quarters: 'They have been outstanding,' reported the *Irish Times*; RAB Butler thought his talks had 'an immense effect'; another fan pointed out that 'the British public only interpret the Conference through my talks'.[9]

Harold's broadcasts were aired as the Cold War was warming up. The Russians came in for strong criticism. At the recently held Council of Ministers meeting in Paris, Bevin, incensed at Molotov's asinine obstructionism, rose to his feet, his hands knotted into fists, and started towards Molotov, saying, 'I've 'ad enough of this, I 'ave.' But Harold did not think them 'wholly in the wrong'. They were 'not yet the enemy, and it is our job to be patient and wise and sensible', he counselled. The problem, as Harold saw it, was that Soviet officials, unversed in 'the courtesies of international intercourse', lacked the social graces of Western diplomats. 'We take as deliberate insults remarks which are merely stock-in-trade remarks and part of the current terms of Russian propaganda.' As if to prove his point, Molotov made a really 'dreadful speech . . . Not a single argument of any sense at all; just the old utterly meaningless slogans trotted out.' Despite protests from his Foreign Office friends, including Gladwyn Jebb, irritated by his overly charitable attitude, Harold was unrepentant: 'There is much to be said for the Russian point of view.' Attlee arrived for the opening ceremony, but made a lamentable entry: 'so small, so *chétif* [puny or pitiful, or both] . . . How different from Lloyd George.' Harold, a veteran of the 1919 conference, and, apparently, the only man in Paris who remembered those days, assumed the character of a 'Rip van Winkle', conjuring up rose-tinted impressions of a conference that he himself had never ceased to criticise. The late appearance of Bevin – who had collapsed with a heart attack and was incapacitated for a few days – revived his spirits.

Now look 'ere, 'arold, when I took this job on I knew it wouldn't be a daisy. In fact, no Foreign Secretary has had to keep so many plates in the air at the same time. But what I said to my colleagues at the time was this: 'I'll take on the job. But don't expect results before three years.' Now it's patience you want in this sort of thing. I am not going to throw my weight about 'ere in Paris. I am just going to sit sturdy 'ere and 'elp.

After listening to this unaffected declaration of intent, a delighted Harold (or 'arold) could only comment: 'My God! How I like that man!'[10]

The future status of Trieste, navigation rights on the Danube, and the question of Italian reparations, were among the controversial topics discussed at the conference. And although at Paris the Soviet Union was usually outvoted, in the long run, as eastern Europe and the Balkans fell into the Soviet orbit, the Russians realised their aims. Harold had never been an advocate of 'Open Diplomacy'. At Paris, he had witnessed 'a public performance, not a serious discussion', Molotov's mischief-making only adding to the carnival-like atmosphere. In a memorable turn of phrase, he defined the new diplomacy: 'Instead of Open Covenants openly arrived at, we have open insults openly hurled.' Harold left Paris in a pessimistic frame of mind. 'How sad it is that I shall see a third world war in my lifetime.'[11]

Kenneth Lindsay was the only survivor of the seven National Labourites to sit in the 1945 Parliament: representing the Combined English Universities, he ran as an Independent candidate. Of his former colleagues, three had retired from politics; the others, including Harold, had failed at the polls. Despite this setback, Harold still harboured political ambitions. He first looked to the Conservatives, but judged that Churchill would neither offer him 'a safer seat' nor put him 'in the Lords'. Next, it was Labour's turn. Ivor Thomas – soon to be a junior Labour minister – suggested that he might go to the Lords if he took the Labour whip. Harold seriously considered Thomas's proposition, but rejected it. 'To join the Labour Party for the sake of a peerage would not be understood, nor should I feel quite happy myself inside. But it does mean a sacrifice to refuse as I hate not being in Parliament.' Early in the New Year a Combined English Universities seat became vacant on the death of Eleanor Rathbone, the same seat that Harold had fought and lost in 1931. Unable to drum up sufficient backing for his Independent candidature, he was persuaded to back down. Such was his desperation that he recanted and told the Lord Chancellor, William Jowitt, that he would be willing to take the Labour whip if he were offered a peerage. But this tactic too ran into the ground. He saw no immediate prospect of advancement. 'What a jam your poor old tumbledown is in,' Harold confessed to Vita. 'The Cranfield gets further and further away.'* 'I had looked upon Cranfield at first as a *pis aller*, as a retirement, as a consolation prize. And now that it is being taken away from me, I realise that I had come to love the consolation prize even more than I desired the prize itself.'[12]

But the 'consolation prize' proved too tempting. In February 1947 he joined the Labour Party, though not without serious misgivings. 'My ships are now burnt. What a row there will be.' He assured his friends and himself that his move was 'in no way impulsive' and that he had been considering it for 'about two years' (although there is no evidence for this). To Violet Bonham Carter he insisted that he entertained no thought of 'self-advancement', but 'I do hate being out of public life and not being able to do anything in Parliament.' To that extent, at least, 'my motives were selfish, and as such I suppose to be deplored'. 'You will remain a captive Wooden Horse,' Lady Violet replied, unimpressed. Richard Crossman, a prominent member of Labour's 'Keep Left' faction, said to him, 'I hear you have joined the Labour Party', adding teasingly, 'which part of it have you joined?' Harold admitted to the essential truth of Crossman's aside: 'If I find the Party too rigid and the atmosphere too uncongenial . . . I shall just lie and retire quietly into my library and garden.'[13]

Harold knew that his decision would leave him open 'to much obloquy,

---

*After considering several fanciful titles, Lord Sissinghurst or Lord Benenden, Harold had decided that *if* he were offered a peerage, he would dub himself Lord Cranfield, a defunct Sackville title.

misinterpretation, ridicule and attribution of false motive': bereft of conviction or principle, his critics would say, he was moved purely by the prospect of a peerage. 'If I scrape my conscience,' Harold conceded, 'I must admit that there is some truth in that accusation. I hate being out of Parliament. I do not want to fight an election. I should be at ease in the Upper House and able to do some good. If there were no prospect of my getting a peerage within a reasonable time, would I fight an election as a Socialist? I might.' At any rate, he 'could never have become a Tory', and 'it would be madness to join to become a Liberal'. So, the only alternative was Labour: 'the only angle to fight communism', he convinced himself, 'is the Labour angle'. More than anything, he feared that his friends would doubt his integrity. But then, 'God' would grant him absolution, because He 'knows that my integrity is a solid thing within me'. (An odd remark, for Harold was not religious in any traditional sense of that term, having once informed Vita that 'I believe in evolution as a religion. It is my only religion.') What would his friends think? What would his family think? The press, thankfully, took 'his betrayal of the nation quite calmly'. But an unnamed Tory did little to soothe his conscience, pointing out that his friends on that side of the House would continue to regard him with 'affection', but would no longer trust his judgement. However, the unknown Tory went on, should Harold be rewarded with a peerage, he would stand guilty of 'moral turpitude'. 'So that if I get a peerage, it will be said that I joined the Labour Party to become Lord Bowlingreen . . . So that if I get it, instead of being an honour and the crown of my career, it will be a crown of thorns and a badge of shame.'

Harold's family reacted much as he anticipated. Nigel was 'struck dumb', though full of admiration for 'his resilience'; his mother experienced 'a cruel blow': 'I never thought that I should see the day when one of my own sons betrayed his country'; and as for brother Freddy, he assumed that Harold would 'now resign from all [his] clubs'. Vita, in her own inimitable way, was not wholly hostile, 'especially if it leads to Lord Cranfield'. 'Of course, I don't really like you being associated with those people. I like Ernest Bevin and Philip Noel-Baker. I have a contemptuous tolerance of Attlee, but I loathe Aneurin Bevan, and Shinwell is just a public menace. I do not like people who cannot speak the King's English.'[14]

Ten months later, on 17 December 1947, he appeared before the selection committee of the Labour Party at North Croydon, a by-election pending. Ten people turned up to listen to him. Disarmingly, Harold listed all his disadvantages, from Tom Mosley to his lack of combativeness to his being a paid-up member of the upper class. It scarcely mattered. Harold was the only candidate. Nominated by eight votes to two, he prepared for his campaign, scheduled to open on 23 February. Boarded out at a local hotel, sitting in an icy bedroom, hungry, in front of a spluttering gas fire, Harold found its material comforts sadly wanting. He found a 'tiny bedint restaurant' where he assuaged his appetite with a dish of fish and chips and a cup of coffee. 'But somehow that is not a diet to which I am accustomed.' Dispirited, 'cold and lonely' (Vita was away in North Africa, lecturing for the British Council), he would occasionally escape from the drabness of North Croydon to the elegance of the Travellers', where he would meet up with more congenial companions and unavoidably partake of a 'very gay' dinner party.[15]

As the campaign progressed his spirits rose and fell. 'I actually enjoy canvassing,' he surprisingly conceded at one point. He warmed to Ella Boln, a Labour Party activist, a 'dear old fuz buz', who had smacked his hand hard with a ruler as punishment for having forgotten to display his red rosette in his lapel. But before long, Harold's relish for the hustings vanished. He could hardly be accused of striking up a rapport with his constituents. 'I do not like the masses in the flesh,' Harold remarked, damning them as 'congenitally ignorant'. 'My God! It is dispiriting canvassing these dumb idiots. They have no knowledge and interests at all. They are just sheep.' He toured the streets of Croydon in a car with loudspeaker, booming out 'I am Harold Nicolson', only to notice that 'Not a soul even paused in their shopping or looked aside.' He hated every moment of the campaign, crying out against the innate 'falsity' of the elections, the necessity of simulating 'friendship and matiness with people whom one does not wish ever to see again. My hands are still aching (and have to be washed) after shaking hands with a hundred enthusiastic workers.' Harold knew his chances of winning were slender to an extreme, as did the Deputy Prime Minister and Leader of the House, Herbert Morrison. 'Ultimately,' he consoled himself, 'I do not think I should enjoy the present House of Commons anything as much as I enjoyed the last one. I should be kept too busy to do my books. I should cease to have any private life at all. And in the end I should be happier to get my peerage and have the ideal mixture between public and private life.' In short, he wished to lose honourably and gain his Cranfield.[16]

Polling took place on 12 March. Harold received 24,500 votes, increasing the Labour vote by 2,000, but running second to the Conservative candidate by 12,000 votes. The same day he wrote to Vita: 'I did well on the whole . . . And I should not like to represent Croydon, which is a bloody place. Nor should I like to be in the present House. All has turned out for the best, and what is more, it is OVER, and without disgrace.' This was an immediate, knee-jerk reaction, reflecting his joy at being rid of 'bloody Croydon' once and for all. But nothing could disguise the fact that he had come unstuck, and in full view of the public (the by-election had commanded wide national interest). 'Since Croydon,' he told his diary, only a month after his defeat, 'I have been haunted by a sense of failure, inadequacy, super-ficiality, and of old age.' He would refer to his North Croydon 'crucifixion'. And after reading the latest Labour Party manifesto, he saw the truth: 'How I wish I had not been such an impulsive fool as to join the Labour Party. It was certainly the cardinal error of my life. But I cannot redeem it now.'[17]

Three weeks after his undoing at North Croydon, Harold, in a revealing passage, railed against the whole 'ungainly', 'loathsome' procedure he had just endured. Praising the 'comforts of obscurity', and rejecting 'the aura of falsity' of his role as 'one of the central figures in a harlequinade', he thought 'any election odious to a person of sensibility'. He was, he confessed, 'temperamentally unable to give even a faint breath of fanaticism to my conviction'. 'Accustomed to self-analysis and self-criticism', he had sold himself 'cheap', flinging 'friendliness like confetti in the air', making public display of something 'so intimate and cherished'. Of North Croydon, he said, 'It possesses for the stranger no identity, no personality, no pulse even, of its own . . . there is but little local patriotism or character.' Nor were his staff anything more than 'ardent technicians'. Comparing himself to a thor-oughbred on its way to Epsom, his main regret was having been 'a disap-pointment to my trainer and stable-hands'.[18] This piece, published as a 'Marginal Comment', nettled his supporters, those who had given their all to get him elected, Ella Boln, for instance. No doubt his crushing sense of frustration was more than he could bear, and prompted his splenetic tirade. But these telling comments divulge much about Harold. After all, he had only participated, by choice, in a routine, standard democratic process. Harold's intemperate outburst cost him any chance of gaining a peerage under a Labour (or, as it turned out, Conservative) administration.

As time passed, and his name failed to decorate the Honours List, Harold, loathing the commonplace name of 'Nicolson' as lacking in social distinction, was intrigued to discover in himself 'a fat grub of snobbishness'. He went on:

I don't mind it for myself . . . But I hate it for Viti. Thus if I were made a real peer, I could change it to 'Cranfield'. But if a life peer, I could not change my name, and 'Lord Nicolson', and even more so, 'Lady Nicolson', would sound absurd. Now, really at my age I ought not to mind such things. And yet I am conscious of that little grub or slug inside me. How little one knows oneself, even when one probes and pokes and is amused. [19]

Harold would be denied both a 'real' and a 'life' peerage. The 'fat grub of snobbishness' would continue to gnaw at his *amour propre*.

* * *

At about this time Harold described himself in the *Picture Post* as a 'diplomat; writer; rentier; pacifist; typical early Georgian; sentimental; emotional; optimistic; indulgent; superficial; feebly hedonistic; hemmed in by religion, class, good-taste, public school, Oxford; patriotic; nationalist; bad pituitary, worse adrenals: no sense of synthesis; no community-feel; plump, romantic, rosy, deaf, curly, very foolish.' He forgot to add, 'shy'. 'Shyness,' he had ruled, thinking of himself, 'is the protective fluid within which our personalities are able to develop into natural shapes'; anyone 'who is not shy at twenty-two will at forty-two become a bore'. Harold was no longer forty-two. By now in his early sixties, he ruminated upon the twists and turns of his life. Conscious that his physical powers were on the wane, he felt no decline in his intellectual faculties. 'I do not notice that my curiosity, my interests or my powers of enjoyment and amusement have declined at all.' But in passing sixty, he had, unfortunately, lost all sense of adventure. 'It is unlikely now that the impossible will happen.' It pained him that he had not achieved either in the literary or the political world that status which his talents and hard work seemed to justify.

He would not indulge in self-deception:

> In literature, the explanation is simple: although hard-working, I am not intelligent enough to write better than I do. In politics, it has been due partly to lack of push and even of courage, and partly to a combination of unfortunate events (Mosley, National Labour . . .) Now how much do I mind all this? I have no desire for office or power in any sense . . . I have no wish to be prominent or grand. But of course I am disappointed by my literary ill-success. Nor do I quite relish the idea that my reputation rests not so much on my political or literary work, as upon my journalistic and broadcasting work.

On the other hand, he could look back on a long life 'dashed with sunshine and gay with every colour. And to have three people in my life such as Viti and Ben and Nigel is something greater than all material success. For if happiness is the aim of life, then assuredly I have had forty years of happiness . . . For which I thank my destiny.' [20]

'It is the greatest of human tragedies,' Harold thought, when considering the drawbacks of growing older. He had put on weight and developed a paunch. 'I notice that it affects the way I walk. I move more slowly, and with a swinging movement like an elephant. It is dreadful when one notices the movements and gait of an old man.' He had also lost much hair and was troubled constantly by dental problems. 'My tooth rotten and I arrange to have it out . . . There is no pain and two broken fangs are cut out.' A week later, he was still 'eating slops'. He became increasingly conscious of the trials of ageing. 'Easily tired, no sex passions, get breathless when I run upstairs, deafness increasing.' For all that, he reasoned that 'I am good for a long time yet.'[21]

But there were other reasons for concern. Reviewing books – to the uninitiated an innocuous pastime – could result in unforeseen repercussions. To his astonishment, Harold was challenged to a duel by Adrian Conan Doyle. Apparently, or so the young Conan Doyle alleged, Harold had insulted his distinguished father in one of his reviews. 'I think it is I who have the choice of weapons,' Harold quipped. Do take it seriously, Harold was advised, and write the aggrieved son a 'soothing letter'. Harold compromised. A letter was duly sent, bringing this bizarre affair to an amicable end. Far more lethal were Harold's perennial financial problems. He wavered between Mr Micawber's classic extremes of 'happiness' or 'misery'. Annual income, for 1949–50, £4,352 17 0: annual expenditure, £3,011 1 9, including £1,439 11 2 in tax and surtax, but excluding (undetermined) costs for medicine, clothes, presents, subscriptions and coal. Harold's main income derived from his books, his royalties for the said year amounting to £1,471 17 0.[22]

On 3 June 1948 he was given an opportunity to generate a more substantial income when he was invited to write the official biography of George V. Harold consulted Vita. Would you be granted 'a free hand'? she asked. Harold, in doubt, held back for a few days. Sir Alan 'Tommy' Lascelles, George VI's private secretary and a close friend, humoured him: 'I should not be expected to write one word that was not true. I should not be expected to praise or exaggerate. But I must omit things and incidents which were discreditable. I could say this in the Preface if it would ease my mind.' There were other considerations. A 'Life and Times' of George V would engage his energies for the coming three to four years. It would mean, in effect, abandoning all hope of a political comeback, a considerable sacrifice given Harold's constant hankering for a role in Westminster. There was also the question of his current project, a biography of Benjamin Constant, the Franco-Swiss novelist and political writer; and a prior commitment to lecture to British troops confined in Berlin during its blockade by the Russians. Typically, he found time to honour both obligations, polishing off Constant in two months *and* flying to Berlin to cheer up the troops. After a few days of indecision, he wrote to Tommy Lascelles accepting the assignment. Elvira Niggeman, his secretary, approved. She put it neatly into perspective: it would not only serve as 'the anchor' of his middle age, it would also prevent him doing 'silly things like Croydon'.[23]

George V occupied Harold for the next three years. So engrossed was he in the book that he made only fleeting references to foreign affairs in general, including the Korean war, the pivotal international event of the early 1950s. Harold, granted full access to the King's papers, was shown over the Royal Archives at Windsor Castle by Sir Owen Morshead, its Librarian. Usually accompanied by Elvira Niggeman, he worked there from April 1949 until August 1951. The (relatively) contemporary nature of the book impelled him to adjust his methodology. As a rule he would prepare all his notes in chronological order, and, once satisfied, would begin writing. Now, anxious to interview witnesses still alive – including Queen Mary – he began virtually at the end of the King's reign, with the 1931 crisis that led to the formation of the National Government. On re-reading what he had written, he resolved 'to slide from my early chirrupy overture into a wider and more solemn note'. 'My gift,' he thought, 'is to explain things at length and convey atmosphere.' Vita was less certain. She found the book 'interesting', his exposition 'lucid', but she pounced with particular delight on 'the 'Hadji-bits', not those passages that were swallowed up by his 'police-court manner'. 'I think the austerity which you have imposed upon yourself is slightly over-done.' Stitch in 'a few bright flowers here and there', she advised.[24]

The final draft of *George V* was finished on 19 September 1951. George VI approved. As did Queen Mary: 'They have done it beautifully, so digni-fied' (though it's not clear whether she was referring to its production or to its contents). And so did Harold: 'I have enjoyed it immensely. It has been a most congenial task': he compared himself '(modestly) with Gibbon'. For Eddy Sackville-West's benefit, he drew a pen-portrait of George V in sharper colours: 'Of course, he was a Philistine in many ways, and in many ways a rather harsh Naval Officer.' Harold did not find George V intellec-tually stimulating: the late King, he remarked, wrote no better than 'a railway porter', while his diaries, a major source for Harold, were 'pure pastiche'. Addicted to shooting and philately, as Duke of York 'he did nothing at all but kill animals and stick in stamps'. Other aspects of George's lifestyle were far removed from Harold's. York Cottage on the Sandringham estate was George's preferred residence. But Harold saw it as 'a glum little villa', its appearence and appointments 'indistinguishable from those of any Surbiton or Upper Norwood home'.[25] In other words, to relapse into Nicolsonion jargon, here was a 'bedint' King living in a 'bedint' cottage pursuing 'bedint' hobbies.

Did Harold harbour any 'mystic feeling about the Monarchy'. No! he answered unreservedly, 'I regard it merely as a useful institution.' But this was only partly true. Hugh Trevor-Roper, Regius Professor of History at Oxford University and no favourite of Harold's, who hadn't read the book, but perhaps sensed its tone, told Nigel that 'I do not waste my time reading Royal hagiography.' At the time, Nigel thought that 'pretty bad'. But in a later correspondence with 'Tommy' Lascelles, Nigel, who had just completed editing three volumes of Harold's diaries, wrote: 'People reading his diaries will be astonished to find that the hagiography, which is an accepted part of royal biography, should have mesmerized his mind.' A discerning reader of Harold's diaries, published and unpublished, will unavoidably reach the same conclusion. Clearly, Harold identified with the institution of monarchy, taking it for granted as God-given, pre-ordained.[26]

Harold had set out to resolve two questions: 'How does a Monarchy function in a modern State?'; and 'To what extent were the powers and influence of the Monarchy diminished or increased during the twenty-five years of King George's reign?'[27] The first question, with the reader drawn forward by Harold's powerful narrative style, he answered satisfactorily; regarding the second, the reader is generally left to draw his own conclusions, though the King is usually given the benefit of the doubt that he did not breach constitutional precedents when dealing with the three great political crises of his reign: the parliamentary battles of 1910–11; forsaking Curzon for Baldwin to replace Bonar Law as Conservative Prime Minister in 1923; and in dealing with the events that led to the formation of the National Government in 1931.

George V was published on 14 August 1952 to huge acclaim. Widely praised for its scholarship and style, it sold 10,000 copies within a fortnight and earned Harold £4,000 (by June 1953, it had reached 24,632 copies). 'My life's work is finished,' he asserted. 'Never have I witnessed such a chorus of praise,' he crowed, though he expected 'the counter attack to begin shortly'. It never came. Nancy Mitford, the novelist, called it 'the very best biography of any English King'; James Pope-Hennessy, the writer and a close friend, considered it 'a serious historical work and a major biographical success'; G. M. Trevelyan, the historian, thought it Harold's 'best book – and to me his most interesting'. (Harold thought differently, placing *Carnock* first, *Some People* second, and *George V* a good third.) *George V* brought him fame and literary distinction – and its success compensated, in a muted form, for his failure at North Croydon. It also, paradoxically, brought him yet again to the brink of bankruptcy: the tax authorities, requiring an extra £1,800, were eating into his income. His accountant, Michael Venning, suggested that he turn himself into 'Harold Nicolson Publications', a commonplace device that would allow him to claim more expenses. Harold refused: in a noble, but self-defeating, gesture, he declined 'to adopt this farcical disguise in order to cheat Inland Revenue'. Instead, he turned to Vita for a loan, offering to pay it off at 4 per cent interest.[28] There is no mention of Vita acknowledging his request – but one must assume that she responded favourably as Harold did not raise the subject again.

There was another side-effect. As a reward for *George V*'s success Harold was dubbed a Knight Commander of the Royal Victorian Order, 'that beastly K. C. V. O.' as he called it. 'How much more I would have liked a Regency Clock,' he told Vita, who found the title 'absurd'. 'Had I remained in the diplomatic service I would have received it as a matter of course twenty years ago.' But he could find no rational grounds to refuse it. To have done so would appear 'churlish, snobbish and conceited'; so he accepted, 'in bitterness'. But he instructed his publishers *not* to introduce him as 'Sir' to his readers. It became known as his 'bedint title'. He claimed to loathe it: 'A knighthood is a pitiful business, putting me in the third eleven . . . I feel as if I had got a fourth prize in scripture when I should have liked the Newcastle [a prestigious classics scholarship at Eton]. So one is really much more snobbish and vain than one imagines.'[29] This brought to a full circle a most humiliating episode in Harold's story, from lobbying for an august peerage to being fobbed off with a 'bedint' knighthood. But it was one brought on solely by Harold's vanity, by the false image he had created of himself. No Lord by the name of Cranfield ever entered the House of Lords.

Harold always took pride in his family. 'United and loving', it would serve him as an emotional anchor in times of personal crisis. 'It is perhaps the best thing that life can give.' There were occasional lapses that spoiled this idyllic outlook. By the beginning of 1951 Harold's mother, Lady Carnock, in her late nineties, a diabetic, 'resigned but blind', her memory failing, was sinking fast. Murmuring, 'My darling, darling Harold', she died on 23 March. 'I dislike having ceased to be anybody's son,' Harold observed, now definitely classing himself among 'the older generation'. On the same day that Lady Carnock died, Harold's brother Freddy (the second Lord Carnock) was taken off to a nursing home, a confirmed alcoholic. For the past few months he had been living with Harold at Neville Terrace, having taken over Ben's rooms. Daily he would retire to the local pub, the Anglesea Arms. Night after night Freddy would be carried home in a state of drunken stupor, and Harold's servant, Stanley Parrot, would put him to bed, often having to call a doctor to sedate the elderly and enormously corpulent peer. There were unsightly scenes. Freddy, incontinent, 'makes water all over the floor and on my trousers'. The strain on Harold during these months must have been intolerable. 'I am nearly ill with the ugliness of it all,' he cried in desperation. Freddy hung on for another few months, deteriorating rapidly, 'a tragic spectacle'. He died at the end of May at the age of sixty-nine. 'Poor old Freddy, condemned to a life so ineffective and miserable,' Harold recorded. 'Such a wasted, lonely end . . . I feel aching pity for him.'[30]

Just when he needed them most, his immediate family kept their distance, partly at Harold's choosing. 'I want to hide my shame,' he confessed. In any case, Ben and Nigel were busy furthering their own careers; and although Ben 'has always been beastly about my mother', Harold was, by now, reconciled to his eldest son's awkward personality. It was Vita's pointed indifference that caused Harold most pain. She had always affected a remoteness, even contempt, towards Lady Carnock; while she had never concealed her opinion that Harold had made a terrible mistake by taking Freddy in. Fuming at her insensitivity, Harold told her that conventional family ties must be 'a bedint thing rather than an aristocratic feeling. You toffs think so much about Norman blood that you forget about the wretched Freddies . . . Why are you such an angel to the Trouts [a nickname for some highborn friends] when you have no feeling at all about Aunt Cecilie [Vita's aunt] and never thought for one moment of sending flowers to my Mum?' 'You have no sense of family obligation,' he told Vita, and in fact 'you dislike it'.[31] It was a gap in their relationship they would never fully bridge.

The year 1951 put Harold under pressure of a different kind. The headlines for June of that year were monopolised by the sensational news that Guy Francis de Moncy Burgess and Donald Maclean, now revealed as Soviet spies – they had been recruited while students at Trinity College, Cambridge – had broken cover and fled the country for Russia. Burgess, notorious for his homosexual promiscuity, excessive drinking habits and boorish behaviour, was a long-standing friend of Harold's from the 1930s. Towards the end of the war he had proposed that he move into Harold's flat at King's Bench Walk, a plan Harold thought too risky to countenance. But their friendship survived: it was even bandied about that Burgess procured 'friends' for Harold. At North Croydon he had suddenly showed up to lend support, a touching gesture that 'amused' Harold. Their last recorded meeting was in January 1950. 'Drunk as usual,' Harold noted wearily, 'what a sad, sad thing this constant drinking is. Guy used to have one of the most rapid and acute minds I knew. Now he is just an imitation (and a pretty bad one) of what he once was.' Talk was rife of a third man, an accomplice of Burgess and Maclean who had warned them of imminent arrest. Make it 'Six', Harold guessed, 'because it might involve Philip Toynbee, Anthony Blunt, and perhaps even my poor silly Ben'. Harold clearly harboured suspicions about Blunt, but did he *know* that Blunt was a traitor? In a roundabout way, Blunt later confessed to Harold that he was one of the 'Six'. Blunt, who had retained his connection with MI5, told him that if Burgess returned home to see his mother he would be arrested: there would be a state trial, and his friends (including Harold) would be called as witnesses. As a result he, Blunt, would undoubtedly lose his job as Surveyor of the Queen's Pictures and as head of the Courtauld Institute.[32]

The Burgess affair threw Harold into a 'real depression'. It also roused Vita's suspicions: 'I shouldn't like to think it was anything that you were keeping from me.' Harold put her mind at rest: 'No my darling, I am not hiding anything from you. I have not become involved in a spy ring nor have I become connected in any way with Guy's disreputable habits.' Harold simply shrank from seeing 'his old profession being made a fool of and degraded': moreover, he hated to think that Philip Toynbee had 'the same sinister effect on Donald Maclean (politically and morally) as he might have had on Benzie'. (Toynbee, Ben's 'Mephisto', was an eternally damned figure in Harold's eyes.) What would be the effect on the lower classes, Harold wondered, if people such as they, well-educated, well-informed, of a privileged background, could 'throw over everything in their hysterical love for holy Russia'? Harold maintained contact with Burgess even after his defection, the only one of the spy's former friends who chose to keep in touch. He did so because he 'felt sorry' for Guy, who 'had acted on impulse'. 'My principle was not to desert friends in distress,' he explained – a noble tenet, even if in this instance it lacked judgement. Towards the end of his life Burgess wrote to Harold disclaiming as 'nonsense' the rumours circulating that he intended to return to England. Stimulated by the 'enormous respect given here for things of the mind', Burgess was content to stay where he was. For all that, he craved to see London once more, to be kept up to date with the latest 'news and gossip'. Burgess remained in Moscow until his death in 1963, pining for his old haunts, poring over out-of-date cricket scores, ordering his suits from Savile Row, a sad, pathetic and dissolute figure.[33]

Reflecting on 1953, Harold decided that it 'had been a good year'. Vita's health had improved (she suffered from arthritis in her back and hand, and had also damaged a bone at the base of her spine, complaints that limited her movement): *George V* continued to sell: peace seemed less precarious (on 27 July 1953 a final armistice had been signed, bringing to an end the Korean war): and the economic situation had improved, as Britain moved out of the post-1945 austerity years. Nor did Harold have to return every evening to his 'bloody tenement' at Neville Terrace. He now resided at flat C.1 Albany, by the Royal Academy, Piccadilly, one of the most prestigious addresses in London, where he remained until 1965. At first, Nigel and John Sparrow took rooms with him at C.1, and when Nigel moved out, Colin Fenton, of the 'falcon eyes and exquisite manners', an undergraduate whom Harold had met at All Souls, moved in. In December 1952, Harold wrote his last 'Marginal Comment' for the *Spectator* feeling that he had exhausted his skills as a weekly columnist: 'People should refrain from dancing once the joints begin to creak.' But his workload was as heavy as ever, reviewing, writing, lecturing, broadcasting – often as one of the high-brow panel of the 'Brains Trust' – attending committees. His sons' careers were prospering, grounds for particular pleasure. Ben edited the *Burlington Magazine* with conspicuous distinction; under his direction, it soon became the most respected scholarly journal of the history of the fine arts in the English language. 'Ben doing well,' Harold acknowledged, 'and is as happy as his nature will allow.' Meanwhile, Nigel had joined forces with George Weidenfeld to form the publishing firm, Weidenfeld and Nicolson. He was also set on following Harold into Parliament. After two failures, at Leicester and Falmouth, he finally entered the House as Conservative MP for Bournemouth East in February 1952. His sons' financial situation had also materially improved. By a settlement with the Sackville estate each one received 'about £15,000' (and Vita £30,000). 'Oh, I am so happy,' Harold rejoiced, 'everything seems sunlit.' But 'above all', Harold was delighted by Nigel's 'excellent marriage'.[34]

Nigel first introduced Miss Philippa Tennyson-d'Eyncourt, aged twenty-four, to Harold not as 'an intellectual' but as 'a real bunny'. Harold responded: 'That is exactly what will suit him', remembering her as 'exceedingly pretty'. 'You will find us shy, eccentric, untidy, but most benevolent,' Harold reassured Philippa, as an introduction to her first visit to Sissinghurst. When Sir Gervais and Pamela Tennyson d'Eyncourt (christened the 'Tenniscourts' by the Nicolsons) came down, Harold took Sir Gervais for a walk in the gardens. He questioned Sir Gervais about 'a dowry'. 'My dear Harold,' Sir Gervais replied, 'dowries went out with the First World War.' A deflated Harold now thought of him as 'a typical City gent plus White's plus Pratt's. Not my sort at all. He feels me as unpleasant as I feel him.' Nigel and Philippa were married in July 1953 at St Margaret's, Westminster. 'Red-letter day or black-letter day?' Harold asked himself. Clearly a 'Red-letter day', as he came to love Philippa 'as a daughter'. The union brought Harold and Vita three grandchildren, Juliet (b. 1954), Adam (b. 1957), and Rebecca (b. 1963). Harold was overwhelmed: 'I feel all different being a grandfather, and thirty years younger . . . I am so happy that I find myself singing.' Nigel and Philippa's marriage, however, survived only until 1970. Nigel blamed mainly himself. Apart from 'the house, the children and the dogs', he found that they shared few common interests; moreover, Philippa became progressively bored with his constituency duties, while Nigel, over time, found 'the wear and tear of proximity' exhausting: he required his own 'space', and 'it was with increasing relief that I sought the privacy of my own bedroom'. 'I was unsympathetic,' he admitted frankly, 'I turned away from her.'[35]

'Well, I'm blowed,' said Harold, when he learned of Ben's engagement to Luisa Vertova, an art historian, who had worked for Bernard Berenson as his assistant librarian – by chance, Harold and Vita had met her as early as 1950 on one of their visits to I Tatti. They were married in Florence in August 1955. Vita thought she was 'perfectly suited' to Ben, and particularly liked her for being 'a Florentine'. Harold was impressed with her lively character. 'Will her intelligence and good nature triumph over Ben's absent mindedness and inattention? I think all will be very well if they have a child.' Their daughter, Venessa, was born in 1956. Harold welcomed her as 'Venessa Pepita [Vita's Spanish-born grandmother], a citizen of the world'. A minor contretemps preceded the birth. Ben wanted his baby born in a public ward: he thought it wrong for the rich to demand special treatment. As always, Harold saw in Ben's presumed waywardness 'the satanic shadow of Philip Toynbee'. Ben's marriage slowly crumbled. Luisa's 'bourgeois' ways were crushing him: she fussed too much. They were also sexually incompatible, Ben claiming that 'sex has died in him'. Luisa 'wants sexual relations and Ben doesn't', Harold noted. 'No nerves can stand the gap between demand and supply. I do see Ben's point of view, but it is not one that makes a good case for the ordinary public.' It was Ben's 'guttersnipe friends' who were to blame for the crisis, Harold judged, adding, 'I never knew a man with such destructive capacity as Philip.' Vita, finally realising how unsuitable Ben was for marriage, told Luisa, 'You must divorce Ben'. Luisa said 'ingratitude' was Ben's worst failing: he took everything for granted; never uttered a word of appreciation or thanks.[36] Ben and Luisa divorced in 1962. Unkempt and shabby in appearance, Ben continued to flourish professionally as editor of the *Burlington*, still favouring his 'guttersnipe friends', Toynbee in particular, much to Harold's distress. His relations with Vita never improved, often snubbing her in company. On 22 May 1978, after dining at his club, the Beefsteak, he made his way to the booking-hall of Leicester Square underground station where he collapsed and died instantly of a massive stroke. He was only sixty-three. Five hundred people attended his memorial service at St James's, Piccadilly.[37]

'As a family,' Nigel noted much later, 'our marital record is dismal.'[38] He might well have excluded Harold and Vita's marriage from that cheerless verdict, for despite its odd, and for many, puzzling nature, it survived for forty-nine years, until Vita's death.

After the war had ended, and once free of *George V*, Harold found more time for travel, both for business and pleasure. Invited by the British Council to lecture on 'Constitutional Monarchy', one of the themes of *George V*, he visited Copenhagen, Rome, Athens, Düsseldorf and Frankfurt am Main. In Paris, at the Sorbonne, he was surprised to see Violet Trefusis, 'looking seventeen', among the packed audience.[39] There were also home-based trips. In his capacity as vice-chairman of the National Trust's Executive Committee, he and Vita, escorted by James Lees-Milne, the historian of architecture and adviser to the National Trust on historical buildings, toured National Trust properties in the West Country. They inspected some forty properties. Lees-Milne noted: the Nicolsons 'do not care for classical buildings, only liking the Gothic or Elizabethan'. Shortly afterwards Harold and Vita toured the West Country again, stopping over at Long Crichel House, Dorset, where Eddy Sackville-West, Raymond Mortimer, Eardley Knollys and Desmond Shawe-Taylor shared quarters. In August 1952 they went off on a garden tour of Wales and Ireland; Vita was welcomed everywhere, now famous for her weekly gardening column in the *Observer*. They broke their journey at Clandeboye, County Down, cherished by Harold since his boyhood, but for Vita 'an ugly' pile.[40] If these excursions could be classified as 'business trips', there were also 'lovely holidays' in France, touring the Dordogne, or visiting Carcassonne and Perpignan. At the end of a trip to Provence, fully exploring for the first time its 'wonderful landscapes' and 'interesting buildings', Harold wrote to Vita: 'Always we shall look back with joy and gratitude to these eighteen days of happiness together'; and to Philippa, who had accompanied them: 'what a joy for Vita and me to have someone so gay and lovely with us'.[41]

In the spring of 1953, Elvira Niggeman, Harold's secretary, greeted him with the splendid news that 'Honours are being showered upon you.' She was referring specifically to his honorary fellowship at Balliol, a distinction he treasured above all others. But other honours were piling up. There were honorary doctorates at the Universities of Newcastle, Glasgow and Trinity College, Dublin (to add to those he had acquired from Athens and Grenoble).[42] In April 1953 he was elected as one of the keynote speakers at the Royal Academy Banquet. Nervous, he neither ate nor drank before he rose to address the distinguished audience. His speech did not go down well; it gave the impression of 'nervous pomposity'. No one, not even old friends, congratulated him afterwards. 'I return miserable and humiliated to Albany.' Some months later, asked to deliver the prestigious Chichele lectures at All Souls, Harold scored a minor triumph. An august occasion, it was also his birthday, 21 November: 'I am 66 today, no HELL I am 67.' Despite his increasing deafness, his lectures were delivered with conspicuous success, and were later published as *The Evolution of Diplomatic Method*.[43] Already nominated as chairman of the London Library, he also assumed the presidency of the Classical Association, a clutch of eminent dons and academicians, for 1951–52. A few years later, in October 1958, he was made an Associate of the New York Academy of Literature.[44]

Harold was also favoured by foreign countries, particularly France. Just after the war he had been invested with the Legion of Honour at the French embassy. René Massigli, the French ambassador, introduced Harold as: '*Ecrivain, diplomate et homme politique de renommé mondiale, qui n'a pas cessé un instant de croire en la France et en sa destinée. La France possède en lui un magnifique champion de sa cause.*' ('Writer, diplomat and politician of international renown, who never ceased for a moment to believe in France and its destiny. In him, France has a magnificent champion of its cause.') In 1960 he was promoted as 'Commander de la Légion d'honneur', and came away from the ceremony 'pleased with extra piece of ribbon. I really did think I was indifferent to such tinsel.' But the German government, at Konrad Adenauer's instigation, also rewarded Harold, according him Das Grosse Verdienstkreuz mit Stern, a prize for enlightening the British public that 'good Germans' really do exist.[45]

There was one distinction that he hesitated about accepting. At the beginning of 1956 his name was put forward as a candidate for Professor of Poetry at Oxford. In theory, anyone could stand, but since the election of Cecil Day-Lewis in 1951, it had become the custom to appoint a poet. Standing against him were W. H. Auden and Professor Wilson Knight, a Shakespearean scholar. His first instinct was to say 'No'. Although Harold held Auden in contempt for 'having bolted to America during the war', he admired him as 'an honourable poet'; and, as he frankly put it to Vita, 'I am not a poet' myself. But carried away by the name of Oxford, even on 'a pot of marmalade', he was bewitched by the Oxford ethos: 'Oh dear, I should like to be Professor of Poetry at Oxford! . . . it would be a great and glamorous honour.' So he agreed to let his name go forward, even though, perversely, he refused to let his supporters canvass on his behalf. 'I expect they will choose Auden in the end and I rather hope they do.' And they did, by 216 votes to 192. 'I am delighted by this result,' Harold told his diary, 'my vote is most honourable and there is no humiliating defeat'.[46]

On 25 July 1956 Harold was a guest at a party given by Bob Boothby. Political gossip dominated the conversation, particularly about Eden, who had succeeded Churchill as Prime Minister in April 1955. Eden, the gossipers decided, was a dud, with no leadership qualities. Aneurin Bevan, a Labour frontbencher present, said that 'the decay of the present government is due entirely to Eden who is incompetent and tricky'; Boothby, a leading Conservative backbencher, joined in: 'Eden is loathed by his colleagues and bullies them.' A day later, Egypt's President, Gamal Abdel Nasser, nationalised the Suez Canal. Eden's handling of the ensuing crisis, highlighted by his incompetence and trickery, would lead eventually to his downfall. At first, opinion was unanimous in condemning Nasser's move. Harold's first reaction – 'That is a pretty resounding slap in our face' – was entirely predictable, and wholly representative of public opinion. Kept fully conversant with events in Parliament and government through Nigel, now MP for Bournemouth East, and Hugh Thomas, a young Foreign Office official – later, Lord Thomas, a distinguished historian, who would write a dispassionate and judicious history of *The Suez Affair* – Harold feared 'a fearful loss of prestige' for Britain and 'increased tension' in Anglo-American relations. Apart from Eden's bumbling, his Foreign Secretary, Selwyn Lloyd, inspired little confidence; his pretentious sabre-rattling at the Foreign Affairs Committee was anathema to Harold's diplomatic style. Should Britain use force or even threaten it? Harold was not 'absolutely sure'. One thing was self-evident: 'The Government have shown their accustomed irresolution and confusion of purpose.'[47]

As the crisis moved through its well-documented stages – from the London Conference of the eighteen 'most-interested nations' to the Suez Canal Users Association – 'provocative and likely to lead to war', said Hugh Thomas – to the final Anglo-French-Israeli attack on Egypt – Harold's position hardened against government policy, and in particular against its head, the conniving Eden. All efforts to achieve a negotiated settlement petered out in deadlock. Harold knew why: France 'clearly wants a showdown with Nasser because of Algeria', and was dragging Britain along. On 29 October Israel, in a three-pronged strike, swept into the Gaza Strip and Sinai, driving swiftly towards the Canal and Sharm el-Sheikh. Harold's first, instinctive reaction was to see this as 'a preventive war', to protect Israel from Fadayun attacks on its territory. Matters changed dramatically the following day when Harold heard of the Anglo-French ultimatum to Cairo and Jerusalem to end the fighting, withdraw their troops behind a ten-mile strip along the Canal, and allow allied forces to occupy key points along the disputed waterway. 'Eden is mad! Eden is mad!' inveighed Hugh Thomas, reflecting informed opinion in the Foreign Office. Harold, on hearing the news of this transparent ploy, wrote: 'we have sacrificed our principles and practically destroyed UNO and the Charter': it was 'an act of insane recklessness'. The destruction of the Egyptian air force left him suitably unimpressed: 'Success does not render a dirty trick any less dirty.' Harold now suspected 'a conspiracy . . . a very nasty plot', with the French masterminding it. 'It is truly one of the most disgraceful transactions in the whole of our history': a 'dishonest' Eden had put Britain 'in breach' of international law. On 5–6 November, Anglo-French forces landed at Port Said and Port Faud. A day later the operation was halted and a cease-fire declared. 'It is about the worst fiasco in history,' Harold recorded. 'Nasser regarded as a hero and a martyr . . .

our reputation is tarnished . . . at the first serious threat from Bulganin, we have had to climb down.'[48]

Nikolai Bulganin, the Soviet Prime Minister, had certainly taken a hard line. Notes of the most menacing nature had been issued to the aggressor nations – Britain, France and Israel – threatening the use of 'every kind of destructive weapon' unless they withdrew. Was this a cover-up for the Russian invasion of Hungary to crush a people's rebellion? Harold thought so. No less pertinent, allied action in Egypt deprived the government of any moral right to indict the Soviet Union. 'The Russians have sent seven divisions into Hungary and are closing in on Budapest. But we have no right to speak a word of criticism.' In the House, Eden and Selwyn Lloyd made 'revoltingly unctuous statements' about Hungary. For Harold, this was rank hypocrisy. He indulged in a telling comparison. In Hungary, 'when people rise against foreign oppression, they are hailed as patriots and heroes', but in Cyprus, 'the Greeks whom we are shooting and hanging are dismissed as terrorists. What cant!' (As was to be expected, Harold adopted an increasingly pro-Hellenistic line in the Greek-Cypriots' struggle for enosis, the union with Greece.)[49]

Whether the Russians were bluffing or not, more cogent considerations persuaded the government to back down. Suez was the most divisive issue in British politics since Munich. With Hugh Gaitskell appealing to the Tory dissidents (including Nigel) to vote against the government, and mass demonstrations in Trafalgar Square calling for its resignation, Eden's administration was seemingly teetering on a political precipice. Isolated in the international arena, Eden, misinterpreting the signals emanating from Washington, had virtually destroyed Anglo–American relations. Eisenhower, up for re-election as President on 6 November, would not countenance lending his support, however guarded, to any foreign adventures. When there occurred a disastrous run on sterling, the Americans refused to lend their support unless Britain withdrew its forces from Egypt. Harold Macmillan, Chancellor of the Exchequer and the strong man in Cabinet, once hot for military action, now blew cold, informing his colleagues that he could no longer 'be responsible for Her Majesty's Exchequer' unless there was a cease-fire. By 22 December the evacuation of Anglo-French forces from Egyptian territory was complete. A discredited Eden, broken in body and mind, had already left London for Jamaica to winter at Goldeneye, the holiday home of Ian Fleming, the creator of James Bond. On 9 January he resigned to be replaced by Macmillan. These were the last acts of what, to put it cruelly, took on all the attributes of a second-rate *opéra bouffe*. How 'tragic to see great imperial countries ending their pretensions in comic style' was one well-phrased verdict.[50]

Harold put it differently: 'Our smash-and-grab raid got stuck at the smash.' He placed the blame for this fiasco squarely on Eden's shoulders.

A stalwart of 'the Eden group' of the late 1930s, Harold had turned full circle, uncovering failings in his one-time chief that many others had long suspected. The 'utterly disgraceful tale' of collusion between France and Israel, to which Britain was a party, flew in the face of everything he held dear. He had long advocated an ethical-style diplomacy, one based on 'moral influence' and founded on 'Truthfulness–Precision–Calm–Good Temper–Patience–Modesty–Loyalty', not backstairs conspiracies that brought his revered Foreign Office into disrepute and shamed his country. He coldly listed Eden's failings: 'breaking election pledges; lying; bringing about international isolation; endangering relations with US; blocking the Canal and disrupting oil supplies; and robbing Israel of fruits of its victory'. Eden, he calculated, had done more 'to dishonour his country than any man since Lord North'.[51]

Nigel's opposition to the Suez adventure – he had abstained on a vote of confidence in the government – put him at odds with the ultra-conservative Conservative Association at Bournemouth East, threatening his parliamentary career. The chairman of the Association, a Major S. Grant, ex-Indian army, took a resolutely hostile line against Nigel. A new candidate, Major James Friend, was chosen to stand at the next election, but was forced to withdraw when it was discovered that he was a paid-up member of the League of Empire Loyalists, a far-right organisation that had publicly insulted Harold Macmillan. Throughout all these manoeuvrings Nigel refused to resign. On 26 February 1959 a new ballot was held to decide whether Nigel should be reselected as Conservative candidate for Bournemouth East: he lost by 91 votes. Just prior to the voting *Punch* published a cartoon by David Langdon showing a mother shouting 'Lolita!' at her coquettish daughter, while a group of Bournemouth residents looked on with extreme disapproval. 'Was Lolita, the *ragazzina pericolosa*, responsible?' wondered Nigel.[52] Harold, profoundly disturbed at the prospect of his son's political fortunes fading away, would have answered unhesitatingly in the affirmative.

Nigel's publishing firm, Weidenfeld and Nicolson, had contracted to publish an English edition of Vladimir Nabokov's controversial novel, *Lolita*, telling the story of a flirtatious twelve-year-old nymphet with whom a middle-aged man, Humbert Humbert, falls in love and whom he eventually seduces. It had already appeared in New York and Paris, but was effectively banned in Britain owing to the so-called deviant nature of its contents: any attempt to publish it would invite legal proceedings. Nigel, when he finally read the book (he had not done so before the contract was signed) was 'shocked' at what it revealed; it seemed to him to be 'saturated in lust'. He thought it would do him infinite harm politically. Bigwigs in the Conservative Party had warned him he would be 'in the dock' if Weidenfeld and Nicolson went ahead and published, while a leading Bournemouth cleric signalled that publication would do him 'irreparable damage'. Nigel, seeking an acceptable compromise, proposed exposing the book in a test case trial of a single copy. Weidenfeld hesitated, but eventually gave way. Ultimately, they were saved from prosecution by a decision of the Director of Public Prosecution not to take legal proceedings. Published in the summer of 1959, *Lolita* was a huge success. Within a month it had sold 100,000 copies. 'It was a triumph for George,' Nigel acknowledged. For him, less so. As his 'two great controversies' had peaked simultaneously, it was assumed that the row over *Lolita* had ruined his chances of success at Bournemouth.[53] This was certainly Harold and Vita's view.

Harold, like Raymond Mortimer, saw in Nabokov's work some literary merit. Though he read it with 'disgust and loathing', hating it, he thought it 'talented and brilliantly written'; Mortimer, more sympathetic, read it as 'a work of literature, a cautionary tale with a moral purpose'. Vita was even more restrained, holding it to be 'funny in parts'. But all were agreed that it would be regarded by the public as 'corrupting and obscene'. Harold wrote to Nigel: 'It has been my custom hitherto to pat little girls on the head . . . Since *Lolita* I avert my gaze, not wishing to be suspected of *libido senilis*. I am sure that the publication of that book will ruin your political prospects.' Together with Vita, he thought 'poor Nigel . . . too innocent and honest for this world'.[54] If Nigel was 'too innocent and honest', Harold blamed George Weidenfeld for brazenly exploiting those worthy qualities, claiming that Weidenfeld was aiming simply at a *succès de scandale* in order to make money. He abused Weidenfeld in the most shameful manner, flinging racist epithets about in reckless abandon – 'that filthy oily Jew', 'that Jewish twerp', 'that slimy Jew' – advising Nigel to break with 'that reptile'. 'Why is it,' he moaned, 'that my two sons make such ghastly friends? Philip Toynbee and Weidenfeld have done them dreadful harm.'[55]

Harold was more concerned at the collapse of Nigel's political career – perhaps hoping that it would blossom as compensation for his having withered – than the fate of Weidenfeld and Nicolson. (In any case, Nigel left the firm in January 1964.) But the root of the matter was that Nigel was no Tory backwoodsman, and it can be safely presumed that his liberal tendencies were never likely to appeal to the loyal Tory faithfuls at Bournemouth, particularly with the likes of Major Grant running the Association. Suez and *Lolita* apart, Nigel supported the anti-hanging lobby and welcomed the path-breaking proposals of the Wolfenden Committee, which recommended that homosexual acts between consenting adults over the age of twenty-one (except in the armed forces) should no longer be a criminal offence. Harold was convinced that Wolfenden 'will seal [Nigel's] fate at Bournemouth'.

What did Harold make of the Wolfenden proposals? He could hardly remain indifferent. After due consideration, he reckoned that the general public was not yet prepared to accept such innovative legislation, 'but they will be so before long and meanwhile the persecution will die out'.[56] In 1967, Leo Abse's Sexual Offences Act was passed, incorporating the main recommendations of Wolfenden. It came just too late to benefit Harold.

On 21 November 1956 Harold celebrated his seventieth birthday. The previous day he had received a letter telling him that 255 of his friends and admirers had clubbed together to present him with a cheque of £1,370 (approximately £21,000 at today's value) as a mark of their esteem: 'we hope that you will not disapprove, and will accept this cheque simply as proof of the affection felt for you by your friends'. Harold reacted with 'stunned amazement'. Going through the list of subscribers, he found, to his intense embarrassment, names that he didn't recognise. In a private room at the Garrick, he was hosted at a celebratory dinner by seven of his most intimate friends – Raymond Mortimer, John Sparrow, Rupert Hart-Davis, James Lees-Milne, Lawrence Jones, Alan Pryce-Jones and Colin Fenton. That night Harold retired 'full of champagne and gratitude'. When the champagne had worn off, he wrote to one of the contributors, Francis King, of how he intended to spend their generous gift: he would buy a 'super television set' and take 'luxury cruises'. However, he saw no compensation in getting old: 'Who wants reverence or all passion spent.'[57]

Financial constraint was certainly a factor inhibiting their taking 'luxury cruises', but their cash flow problems continued, particularly Harold's, despite their friends' handsome largesse. Strapped for ready funds, they sold off some of their silver for £4,000, including a Napoleon travelling set. It was a never-ending saga. In 1960, Harold was faced with a surtax demand of £1,500, a peremptory claim 'which 'knocks me out'; and the following year, with an income tax bill for £1,400.[58] Sustained by Harold's birthday gift, they refused to be daunted by liquidity problems. Their holiday cruises went ahead. Each winter, from January 1957 to January 1962, Harold and Vita indulged themselves. Escaping from the inclement English weather, and thankful for 'such a phenomenon as free time', they embarked on six winter cruises. Their journeys took them to Java, to the Caribbean and the west coast of South America via the Panama Canal, to the Far East and Japan, to Cape Town and South Africa, to Rio de Janeiro, Buenos Aires and Montevideo, and again to the West Indies.[59]

The Nicolsons stopovers at their various ports of call were considerably eased by Harold's diplomatic contacts. Often Rolls-Royces were put at their disposal to carry them to tourist attractions; receptions were held;

introductions to important personages made. Aboard ship, Harold swam practically every day, health and weather permitting; otherwise they rested, or occasionally played Bingo, or watched movies. Mainly they used their ample free time to read and write. Harold described those days as 'a halcyon existence'. It personified the essential nature of their partnership: busy with their own projects, they occupied separate cabins and met for meals and trips ashore. Harold worked on his articles and book reviews, kept a special travel diary (later published as *Journey to Java*), and began work on a new book, *The Age of Reason* (1960), an ambitious, readable, but rather slapdash enquiry into eighteenth-century intellectual life, dealing with political and social trends and figures such as Saint-Simon, Louis XIV and Peter the Great. Harold thought it 'a rotten book . . . it is very dull, and so second-hand that it is second-rate'. It was not well received: even Raymond Mortimer gave it faint praise. In turn, Vita began work on the *Daughter of France* (1959), a biography of *la Grande Mademoiselle*, Anne-Marie Louise d'Orléans, Duchess of Montpensier, an idea she had been toying with for years. Although it sold well, the final result disappointed her: 'my book is so bad. It really is.'[60]

All too often Harold's first-hand contacts with foreigners confirmed his worst prejudices. 'What an ugly and loathsome race!' he said of the Japanese, after visiting Tokyo and Kyoto; and how ill-mannered. In South Africa he was appalled by the Apartheid system, 'the complete police state', ashamed at 'the humiliation and injustice' to which the Black and Coloured populations were exposed 'by those bloody Boers. It makes my blood boil.' Weighing up an intolerable situation, he wrote to Nigel and Philippa: 'You know how I hate Negroes . . . But I do hate injustice more . . . God bless our little island! God bless her as a jewel of justice!'[61] Safely on board ship, the Nicolsons kept pretty much to themselves, observing rather than mixing. They took 'a fierce dislike' to a young Argentinian girl, aged about twelve, whose ostentatious posturing they watched 'with horror', revolted by her offensive 'self-consciousness'. On one home-bound journey they were joined by Evelyn Waugh and his daughter, 'a charming girl'. True to form, Waugh flaunted his notorious rudeness of manner. An American admirer approached him, wishing to shake his hand. Waugh flinched: 'I'm afraid not. I hate physical contacts with social adventurers and vulgarians.'[62]

Harold too was not above snubbing passengers when he sensed they were intruding upon his privacy. But with some he struck up an easy, tension-free dialogue. On the trip to Rio there were Sir Philip Magnus-Allcroft, 'a clever Oxonian and an excellent writer' (among his books, biographies of Kitchener, Gladstone, and King Edward VII), and his wife, Jewell, 'a real person, obstinate and kind'. This agreeable relationship was eroded, in private, by Harold's bigotry. 'Philip walks into the dining room with only bum-bags on [Bermuda Shorts?]. I am disgusted and tell him to dress. It is the insensitiveness of the Jews that I find one of their many abominable traits. It is nonsense to say one cannot generalize. About the Chosen Race one can.' Back in London, Harold attended a dinner at Fishmongers' Hall, its principal guest, the Lord Mayor of London, Sir Bernard (Nathaniel) Waley-Cohen. Something in Waley-Cohen's appearance or behaviour inflamed Harold. He exploded: 'Such a Jew you never saw; he arouses my sympathy for Eichmann.'* These shameless outbursts represent the murkiest side of Harold's character, for which no excuses can or should be made. They became more common with advancing years. Not only against Jews. Nigel tells the following story.

> I was lunching with him in the Travellers Club which had just engaged its first black man as a waiter. He was an usually handsome youth, dignified not only by his looks but by his manner, yet my father ostentatiously took out a silk handkerchief to wipe the spot on his plate where the man's thumb had momentarily rested. I protested strongly. 'Yes, I know,' he replied, 'but I cannot tolerate the dark races.'

And if one adds to the list, Coloureds, Japanese, Turks, Persians, Arabs, Slavs, Catholics, and the vast army of hostile 'bedints' lying in wait, it amounts to a resounding indictment of Harold's racist-social prejudices.[63]

1955 was a disagreeable year for Harold. Accompanied by Colin Fenton, he travelled to Lisbon at the end of February to lecture at the British Institute. At a reception he developed a nose-bleed. A doctor recommended an injection, so 'a dear old lady arrived and shoved some sort of stuff into my bottom'. Before long, the 'dear old lady' had metamorphosed into 'an old hag' who had clumsily inserted the needle too close to the sciatic nerve, causing him dreadful pain. A few days later, on 10 March, he suffered a minor stroke, to be followed by another two months later. 'He had lost all power in his left hand . . . his poor mouth was all twisted, also his speech was so thick that I [Vita] could only just understand what he said'. Harold consulted Dr Hunt of Harley Street and found his heartbeat was 'irregular', his 'arteries not those of a young man'. The doctor advised Harold to 'Avoid hot baths, heavy meals, stooping or lifting weights.' 'Otherwise,' he added helpfully, 'lead an ordinary life.' After the immediate effects of the strokes

---

*Adolph Eichmann was the principal military logistical officer who planned and carried out the extermination of European Jewry. Captured in Argentina by Israeli agents in 1960, he was put on public trial in Jerusalem for war crimes. For many, it was their first exposure to the horrifying details of the Holocaust. Found guilty, Eichmann was hanged, his body cremated, and his ashes scattered in the Mediterranean.

had worn off Harold noticed that his 'mental and physical powers' were in no way impaired. But the fact remained: 'at any moment I may pass out and become paralytic'. Ongoing troubles worsened. He decided not to confide in Vita that his prostate condition had deteriorated. But he could not hide his progressive deafness. This was particularly frustrating, for when attending committees and banquets he found that he was unable to follow the proceedings or catch after-dinner speeches. All in all, Harold became acutely conscious that old age was creeping up on him, 'slouch, slough, slop' it came, remorselessly, without pity. 'I am curiously unfrightened by death,' wrote Harold at the end of 1955. 'I dread pain and squalor but not just a plain stroke. But God knows how much I love life and how much I hate the idea of parting from my darling.' He began the New Year with the inscription, 'Probably the year of my death. 1886–1956, R.I.P.' He survived, to welcome 1958 on a more hopeful note: 'May Well Be My Last Year of Active Life.'[64]

Harold, naturally, was concerned at the state of his own health; but he was equally, if not more, concerned at Vita's, 'which is always unpredictable'. For years she had suffered from arthritis of the spine, a debilitating condition: 'You see I used to be so strong, but now I dare not make a rash movement and am also frightened of falling down.' Prone to fevers, she was confined to her cabin for three weeks with high temperatures on their second winter cruise. The following year she fell ill again, with viral pneumonia: 'I do feel very ill,' she complained. Bedridden for eight weeks, it was the first sign of a cancerous growth, that went undetected at the time. Later, she developed a heart condition; and in December 1960 she was admitted to a nursing home, where she was subjected to penicillin injections.[65] The state of her health was now a subject of grave concern. The Nicolsons took their last cruise to the West Indies in January 1962. On the train journey from London to Southampton, Vita sustained a severe haemorrhage, concealing the fact from Harold for a month, but confiding in her friend, Edith Lamont, who luckily accompanied them. Diagnosed with malignant abdominal cancer on her return to England, she was operated upon, appeared to be making a recovery, but suffered a relapse and died at Sissinghurst on 2 June 1962. Her body was cremated, the ashes laid to rest in the Sackville crypt at Withyham. 'She dies without fear or self-reproach,' Harold recorded.[66]*

It might be said that after Vita's death, Harold was living on borrowed time. His published diaries cease at this point. 'My brain is a mush of sorrow

*Vita bequeathed Sissinghurst and its gardens to Nigel; the South Cottage to Harold for his lifetime. Faced with heavy death duties, Nigel decided to offer the property to the Treasury in part-payment of the duties, on the understanding that they would transfer it to the National Trust. For years Vita had opposed such a possibility: 'So long as I live, no National Trust or any other foreign body shall have my darling. No, no.

and fear,' he wept, a day after Vita's funeral. Wandering through the gardens at Sissinghurst, he picked flowers 'in a mist of tears'. 'I really must pull myself together,' he told himself. But he was unable to do so. Utterly miserable, he would 'blub when alone', 'sob bitterly' when he woke up, his brain 'a puddle of tears'. 'Let it die,' he said of 1962. 'This beastly year is ending and I cry bitterly when I think of my darling. I am glad that nobody sees me crying since I am not manly about it . . . Oh my darling I finish this *année funeste* in tears for you. I have wept buckets for you.'[67]

Yet on another level, he seemed to function normally – at least for a short while. He continued reviewing, meeting people, attending luncheons and dinners. In August, accompanied by John Sparrow and James Pope-Hennessy, he set off on a month's trip to Bergamo, by Lake Como. Joined by Nigel, he watched his last book, *Monarchy*, being printed and bound at a printing works in Bergamo. A convoluted attempt to explain the theory of monarchy, it was the least successful of his books. He would report on his experiences to Philippa, who, in the role of a surrogate Vita, tended diligently and lovingly to his cares, signing off one letter as 'Your devoted old blubberbox'. In the New Year, without a travelling companion, Harold crossed the Atlantic in the *Queen Mary*. On arrival, he complained about the state of his health: 'my legs are groggy and my sorrow unceasing. I wish I hadn't come.' But he persevered. In New York he stayed at the Knickerbocker Club, saw old friends, W. H. Auden and Anne Lindbergh, and met many prominent Americans, Adlai Stevenson, Alan Dulles and Walter Lippmann among them. He visited Washington, appeared at a number of well-attended receptions arranged by his old friend, Minna Curtiss, putting an unnecessary strain upon him, or so Nigel thought. On the train to Boston a nosy clergyman asked him if he believed in God. 'No!' responded a tetchy Harold, incensed at God intruding upon his privacy.[68]

By February he was back at the Albany. On 21 May he complained of loss of memory: 'I cannot recall the names of my closest friends.' Four days later he suffered his third stroke. 'I am very ill and wretched.' He was drifting in and out of *compos mentis*. Male nurses were hired to care for his daily needs, his favourite being Tony King, for whom he formed an emotional attachment. Normally exacting in his dress and personal habits, he began to neglect his appearance: his behaviour, usually impeccable, was now unpredictable, visitors all too often leaving his side shaken by his rudeness. With his decline,

---

Over my corpse or my ashes, not otherwise.' But, she added, 'Nigel can do what he likes when I am dead.' (See *ND*, iii, Vita's diary, 29 Nov. 1954, 268.) Which is what he did. It was not until April 1967 that the final details were ironed out and Sissinghurst became National Trust property, with Nigel as its 'resident donor'.

came a falling off in his table manners, once so exemplary. He would demand a second helping before others had finished their first, choking on his food, mumbling embarrassing groans and grunts while wiping his plate clean. No longer able to cope with journalism, he abandoned plans for another book, *The Age of Romance*. His diary, once crammed full of fascinating insider information, of engaging social, literary and political gossip, became little more than an engagement book. Its last entry is dated 4 October 1964.[69]

In the spring of 1964 Harold, attended to by Tony King, took his last cruise, appropriately enough through the Mediterranean to Greece, Rhodes – where he refused to go ashore 'as it has painful memories' – and Sicily. He chose – by chance, or as a gesture of Zionist solidarity? – an Israeli ship, the MS *Moledet* ('Homeland'): 'Servants speak Jewish [i.e. Hebrew] but very attentive.' There was one last excursion abroad. In June he spent some days in Paris, with Tony King, who had never been there before. Staying at the elegant Hôtel Crillon, overlooking the Place de la Concorde, they visited the obvious tourist sites: the Eiffel Tower, Napoleon's Tomb at the Invalides, and of course Versailles, reviving old memories. Not only was Harold's condition declining, but financial constraints made it impossible to maintain him any longer at the Albany. Nigel negotiated the serialisation and book rights of Harold's diaries to the *Observer* and Collins, a deal that brought in £9,000 and granted the family more leeway in treating Harold's growing infirmity. John Sparrow and Nigel conspired to persuade Harold to leave his apartment at the Albany and retire to Sissinghurst, where he could be under constant supervision, and which would cut costs in providing for him. He finally succumbed in May 1965 and took up quarters in the South Cottage: he would never leave Sissinghurst again.[70]

Nigel lived through Harold's last years. He recalled:

It pained me to watch his gradual decline . . . He stopped writing, then reading, then talking. He would hide behind a newspaper when friends like Gerry Wellington, Robin Maugham, Gladwyn Jebb, or Richard Church came to visit him, and he would watch television all afternoon and evening, whatever the programme, moved to tears by any emotional scene, even when a goal was scored by Wolverhampton Wanderers, of whom he had never previously heard. Once he asked me, 'What's all this business in Vietnam?' when the war had been reported on television for years.

When Nigel, who edited the three volumes of his diaries, showed him the typescript of the first, Harold was incapable of remembering names, dates or events; he read the second volume, and then forgot that he had.

The diaries were a great publishing and commercial success. Harold was pleased, making the pertinent remark, 'It's rather sad to think that of all my forty books [in fact, thirty-three, including the three anthologies of 'Marginal Comments'], the only ones that will be remembered are the three I didn't realise I'd written.'[71]

For his eightieth birthday, a number of close friends gathered at Sissinghurst to celebrate the occasion. Harold appeared, 'looking very smart in a blue suit'. They dined off pheasant and drank champagne. Nigel asked whether he had any regrets in his life. Yes, 'that Vita is dead'; and about joining Mosley, 'but I suppose it was a useful experience'. 'What about leaving the Diplomatic Service?' 'No!' he replied emphatically. Harold retired early, at ten o'clock. Before they went their different ways, his guests agreed to meet again to commemorate his ninetieth birthday.[72] Eighteen months later, on 1 May 1968, as he was undressing for bed, Harold collapsed and died of a fatal heart attack, aged eighty-one.

In accordance with his revised instructions, his ashes were laid, not by Vita's in the Sackville vault at Withyham, but in Sissinghurst's churchyard, a posthumous, perhaps teasing, reminder of the class gulf that separated their families and that had always intimidated him. Later in the month, a memorial service was held for both Vita and Harold in St James's Church, Piccadilly. John Sparrow delivered the eulogy; the Poet Laureate, Cecil Day-Lewis, read from the poem that Vita had written for Harold in the Second World War, looking back on their lives:

I loved you then, when love was Spring, and May . . .
But now when autumn yellows all the leaves,
And twenty seasons mellow our long love,
How rooted, how secure, how strong, how rich,
How full the barn that holds our garnered sheaves!

Harold too had attempted a retrospective of their lives, written also during the war. Less romantic, it was no less to the point. 'But we agree that we have had the best of both the plutocratic and the Bohemian worlds, and that we have had a lovely life,' apart from the fact, he pointed out, 'that we remained Edwardian for too long'.[73]

FIFTEEN

A Retrospective View

Harold George Nicolson was a man of rare talents. As a diplomat a glittering career beckoned – an embassy certainly, perhaps even the top job in the service, that of Permanent Under-Secretary at the Foreign Office. But his talents extended well beyond the conference chamber, for he was a renowned politician, journalist, broadcaster, historian, biographer, diarist, novelist, lecturer, literary critic, essayist and gardener. Few men could boast such gifts. Yet he ended his life plagued by self-doubt, fearful of being counted as second-rate, despondent at not having realised his full potential. 'I am attempting nothing; therefore I cannot fail,' he once acknowledged.[1] What went wrong? It was a question that haunted Harold throughout his adult life.

Born in the late Victorian age, when Britain was at the pinnacle of her imperial power and economic strength, the scion of an obscure aristocratic family of Scottish origins (though with grander connections), Harold benefited from all the advantages the circumstances of his birth could offer. It was almost predestined that he would enter the Foreign Office, which he did, and he pursued, on the whole, a diplomatic career with considerable success. Persuaded – some would say, blackmailed – to leave a profession for which he was eminently suited, he entered another, politics, for which he was patently ill-suited. Deep down he knew it. It was not that he lacked ambition. Harold desperately wanted to move from the shadowy margins of public life to its brightly lit centre. But he had no appetite for grassroots politics: he lacked the burning passion, the combative instinct, the common touch that would bring his ambition to fruition. He also lacked judgement. His political adventures, first Mosley, then National Labour – two counterfeit parties – and finally Real Labour, as a springboard to that bastion of aristocratic privilege, the House of Lords, all dented his credibility as a politician with a future. Was he actually a democrat in the contemporary sense of that term? After his North Croydon 'crucifixion' he castigated in public the democratic process: 'any election', he claimed, is 'odious to a person of sensibility' – such as himself, he might well have added. Of course, Harold was a compassionate man, for 'the underdog', delighted when Labour took power in 1945, though his enthusiasm quickly soured. But equally he championed 'the principle of aristocracy'. 'I do not like the Labour Party,' he eventually announced, 'I am a mixture of an aristocrat and a Bohemian. The bedintness of the Labour people is as repugnant to me as is their gentility. I feel ill at ease, self-conscious, insincere, unauthentic, in their presence . . . I am glad therefore to have an excellent excuse to withdraw into my Round Tower.' Which is precisely what he did. Like a Whig grandee of old, Harold favoured government *for* the people but not necessarily *by* the people.[2]

Having resigned under pressure from the Foreign Office, and having been crucified at North Croydon as a working politician, Harold could always fall back on literature. For a while, he frittered away his time as a gossip columnist. He loathed it, dismissing it as a bedint occupation catering for bedints. He moved into quality journalism, exploiting his gift for most forms of literary prose, and for fourteen years wrote elegant and fastidious 'Marginal Comments' for the *Spectator*, mainly on the political, social and literary establishment within which he moved. At times, he was not above putting forward preposterous ideas, as when he argued that the novel had become *passé*, an empty theory easily shot down by Philip Toynbee, his *bête noire*.[3]

As a reviewer (for *Books This Week, Daily Express, Action, Daily Telegraph* and *Observer*) he was generally fair-minded and charitable, sticking to his brief, reluctant to impose his own views and prejudices upon the reader. He could be cruel. He panned Hugh Trevor-Roper's book, *Essays on History*: 'I am not very kind to him since I dislike his bad manners and harshness.' (Trevor-Roper replied in full, with a devastating critique of the third volume of Harold's diaries.)[4] He was a prolific and felicitous writer. He wrote many readable and some delightful books. John Betjeman once called him 'the greatest living master of English prose' – a rash judgement with Evelyn Waugh and Anthony Powell still around – while Somerset Maugham thought he could describe a person's exterior better than any novelist alive. Others were less flattering. 'The enemies of scholarship are tact and urbanity,' wrote Ben, perhaps casting a gentle dig at his father? And Peter Quennell said that Harold sacrificed 'seriousness for flippancy', unable to resist introducing a funny anecdote regardless of whether it was apropos: this made scholars not take his work seriously.[5] There is a touch of exaggeration here. As a writer, Harold was deft rather than subtle. He was scrupulous in his scholarship. Unlike Lytton Strachey, he never manipulated facts, of events or character, to sacrifice them on the altar of cynical, if shrewd, epigrams. His diplomatic trilogy, two innovative biographies, *Carnock* and *Curzon*, which fused his personal recollections with historical narrative, and *Peacemaking*, together with *George V* – a superior 'Life and Times' – and *The Congress of Vienna*, remain among the most readable and informative of his books, profitable also to the contemporary reader.

Having spent twenty-odd years in the Foreign Service, and possessing the eye of a keen observer, Harold felt eminently qualified to write and speak extensively on diplomatic method and practice, most notably in *Diplomacy* and the somewhat repetitive *The Evolution of Diplomatic Method*. Generously admitting his debt to Sir Ernest Satow's *Guide to Diplomatic Practice*, and keeping dutifully to the guidelines his late master, Sir Eyre Crowe, set out, Harold provides a clear, concise account of the development of diplomatic technique while offering some illuminating insights into the diverse diplomatic styles of the powers. But in all, it became evident that Harold much preferred the Old to the New Diplomacy. Lamenting the disastrous turn diplomatic technique had taken, he favoured the cosy, leisurely style of the Congress of Vienna of 1814–15 to the hustle and bustle of the Paris peace conference of 1919, to say nothing of the media-obssessed summit diplomacy of the post-1945 era.

Although Harold wrote many more books, some are little more than period pieces, others of interest only to the learned specialist. His two novels, *Sweet Waters* and *Public Faces*, scarcely bear out Betjeman's rush to judgement. Not so *Some People*, his original stab at autobiography, generally recognised, and rightly so, as his most charming and lasting book. Harold rated *Carnock*, *Some People* and *George V* as his best books, in that order. When Igor Stravinsky told him that 'your best book is that of your father', he 'swelled with pride'.[6] What emerges with startling clarity from this story is his extraordinary self-discipline, industry, powers of concentration, fluency of style. Having begun one book, *Curzon*, in May 1933, he handed in the completed manuscript the following January. His total output was prodigious: thirty-three books (even though some were little more than extended essays), tens of thousands of letters, articles, speeches and lectures. And then there were his diaries, written almost on a daily basis from 1910 to 1964. One project, long contemplated but never completed, was his Proustian epic, an over-ambitious enterprise on too grand a scale for Harold's talents.

Harold had once remarked, ironically, that he would be best remembered for his diaries, the three books he hadn't intended to write – as it turned out a self-fulfilling prophecy. But of course he had intended to write them, for he did not believe in a 'purely "private" diary', it being 'too self-centred and morbid'. His ideal audience would be his 'great-grandchildren at the age of twenty-five . . . One should have a remote, but not too remote, audience.' Thinking of Pepys – whom Harold passed off as 'a mean little man. Salacious in a grubby way' – he reflected that to be a great diarist 'one must have a little snouty sneaky mind'. If so, Harold also 'sneaked' around a great deal. His diaries contain the usual ingredients that connoisseurs of this genre hunger for: country house weekends, high-society luncheon and dinner parties, get-togethers in London's clubland, post-prandial *bons mots*, political gossip and literary chit-chat. Given his background and interests, they could be nothing less than a lively record of the Great and the Good – and sometimes the Ugly. Harold took pride in his discreetness: 'I do not think it right to record day by day all the turpitude or sexual aberrations of my friends [or his own]. I love them too dearly for that.' There were other aspects of life that went unrecorded. Of the profound social and economic changes that were sweeping Britain at the time, there is little of merit – except in a negative sense. By choice and inclination, Harold shied away from the world 'of democratic fish and chips'. [7]

There was criticism. 'What a pitiable little engagement book it is!' complained Harold, modestly. James Pope-Hennessy thought it 'too boring for words' and advised not 'going on with it'. Trevor-Roper, in his usual lordly way, found in it 'Not a single heretical thought, not a single arresting phrase, not a single profound judgment.'[8] But a more rigorous examination of the diaries reveals Harold as a perceptive, often witty, observer of the social mores of the world that he knew, honoured, and revered. Relentlessly he pursued, and brought to life, not only the social butterflies, but also the political and literary mandarins of the so-called Establishment, that charmed and closed circle that claimed to rule in the name of Britain. Here was his most lasting contribution to our understanding of those times.

If Harold was constantly plagued by self-doubt, Vita sustained him. Indeed, it might be said that they sustained each other. They massaged each other's egos, formed a kind of two-person mutual admiration society. It was 'Us and Them' – apart from the gilded few – whether vulgar American millionaires or Persian 'savages' or the bedints of Leicester or North Croydon. Their correspondence, his diaries, are replete with songs of praise about their work and manner of life, about how wonderful and talented they were, and how perfect their relationship. They often detected in each other's writings compelling aspects that went unnoticed by others. As befitted 'subtle and difficult people', 'gifted and charming', and of course 'very, very, intelligent', theirs, they comforted themselves, was 'no bourgeois bedint marriage'. Whatever else it was, Vita dominated. Of nobler birth, holding the purse-strings, owner of Sissinghurst, more volatile in character, she was at times given to violent outbursts. Harold would complain of the 'crushed life' he led, wondering whether Vita would have been happier had she married 'a more determined and less sensitive man'. It was Harold Macmillan who noted that 'Harold enjoyed being a martyr, was slightly masochistic'.[9]

'How queer,' Vita once pointed out. 'I suppose Hadji and I have been about as unfaithful to one another as one could well be from the conventional point of view, even worse than unfaithful if you add in homosexuality, and yet I swear no two people could love one another more than we do after all these years.'[10] Harold put it somewhat differently, claiming that Vita and his homosexuality were the two most important things in his life. Bound together by other interests – a common social outlook, their aristocratic parochialism, mutual respect and deep pleasure in each other's company, literature, the rebuilding of Long Barn and Sissinghurst, gardening, and their immediate family, Ben and Nigel – they pursued their lovemaking by remote control, by prolonged absences and open-minded letters. Their serial infidelities, sufficient to destroy conventional marriages, presented no threat to their relationship – at least, once the Trefusis affair had died down – and became a topic for either good-natured bantering or open encouragement. The Harold–Vita partnership prospered, drawing strength and stability from its unconventional nature.

Harold was a compassionate man, certainly in no way malicious. An amusing, at times scintillating, conversationalist, he had a gift for friendship, though his intimates were limited to his own narrow social circle. A sceptic by nature, he was not religious in any meaningful way. The English hymnal, he believed, contained much 'twaddle', and both he and Vita described themselves as 'good pagans'.[11] Harold would have shrunk with horror had anyone accused him of being a vulgarian: just the thought would have been anathema to him. Yet he was capable of making the most vulgar and odious of remarks about those excluded from, and who would never enter, his own charmed circle, whether Jews or Blacks or 'bedints'. A more than willing captive to the hidebound prejudices of his class and social background, Harold saw 'bedints' lurking everywhere: bankers were 'rather low-class fellows; 'Ascot or City' people were regarded with disdain; trade unionists were simply 'ghastly'; the middle and working classes were pigeon-holed as 'dumb idiots', or 'sheep', or 'congenitally indolent'. Naturally, all this was in distinct contrast to himself and Vita, 'as we prefer the upper-class to the middle-class even as we prefer distinction to vulgarity'.[12] Unfortunately for him, the 'bedints' were on the move. Fearful that the rising tide of vulgarity would eventually engulf him, he remained forever on the watch. But Harold cast this particular net much wider than local 'bedints'. And it would bring him little credit. He saw nothing but 'servile and inglorious decay' in Turkey; he 'hated' the Arabs; and thought the Japanese 'an ugly and loathsome race!' More at ease in Europe than in

America, he claimed that the United States had 'the hands of a giant with the limbs of an undergraduate, the emotions of a spinster and the brains of a peahen'. He frowned upon 'candlesticks' (Roman Catholics), referring disparagingly to John Kennedy's election as President.[13]

It has been suggested that Harold 'tempered his [anti-Semitic] prejudice with a sense of guilt'. Perhaps. But there was no such dubious suggestion regarding Blacks. He detested the coloured races, regarding them as simply 'inferior . . . a challenge to white hegemony. They had produced no art . . . almost no history. They were born to occupy an inferior station in life. They were dirty. There were far too many of them.' While lunching with Nigel at the Travellers' Club he confessed, eyeing with suspicion a black waiter, 'I cannot tolerate the dark races.'[14] Imbued with the genteel anti-Semitism and racial bigotry of his class, he would confide to his diary, even after the Holocaust: 'The Jewish capacity for destruction is really illimitable. I loathe anti-semitism, but I do dislike Jews.' Or, while on a visit to South Africa: 'You know how I hate niggers . . . But I do hate injustice more than I hate niggers'.[15] Yet, almost in the abstract, his bigotry was tempered by a strain of compassion. He genuinely 'loathed' institutionalised anti-Semitism and 'hated' the terrible injustices inflicted upon Blacks by the Apartheid system. But as though struck down by a mental block, he was unable to grasp that his own prejudices could so easily be the prelude to the very things he claimed he most detested. No matter from which direction one approaches Harold, one recoils with disgust at his racist outbursts, too routine to be passed off as a transient phenomenon.

Harold achieved much; but he aimed for much more. He had spread himself too thinly. Suffering 'from the sad defects of every epicurean', he sombrely recognised his failings – if such they were. When told that he lacked 'the competitive spirit, that he never 'threw the whole of [himself]' into what he believed, he agreed that this was so. 'It is, I suppose, a profound disbelief in myself coupled with a rather self-indulgent and frivolous preference for remaining an observer.' 'What is ironical,' Ben remarked, 'is that neither of them will live in history, except as creators of Sissinghurst and for the Diaries.'[16]

But there was a more fundamental cause than frivolity or self-indulgence of Harold's perceived failure to realise his full potential. 'Vain and proud I am,' he once proclaimed, 'but I am not conceited.'[17] Harold's conceit, however, was of a special kind: it fed off the 'grub of snobbishness' that he felt gnawing away inside him. Harold, the quintessential (minor) aristocrat, had slipped his 'anchors in a drifting life'. A child of his times, who was fed with 'silver spoons' from birth, Harold was in many ways an emblematic figure of his class and age: he would not have wanted it any other way.

Yet here he was, bedded out for ever in 'alien soil', unable or unwilling to cope with a changing society that he scorned and in many ways rejected. The Second World War, like the First, hastened the collapse of the traditional social order that he held sacred. The drab age of meritocracy was eating away at his glittering 'principle of aristocracy'. How symbolic that Sissinghurst Castle, once the exclusive preserve of the Nicolsons, should have fallen to the 'bedints' of the National Trust. But not only Sissinghurst. In Ireland, the great family patrimonies of his childhood fared no better. Close by Clandeboye estate lies the Clandeboye Lodge, 'a quality three-star hotel', within easy distance of Blackwood Golf Course; Killyleagh Castle now offers its visitors 'self-catering apartments . . . a unique holiday experience'; while Shanganagh Castle was recently closed down by the Irish Prison Service as 'a place of detention'.

A close friend of Harold's, Rob Bernays, once told him that he never realised that he was 'a national figure, [but] of the second degree'. But let John Sparrow, who knew him well, have the last word. His eulogy at St James's Church was wiser and more charitable, and far more apt. After touching upon the rich variety of his interests and his contributions to public life, Sparrow saw Harold as 'a nineteenth-century Whig leading an eighteenth-century existence in the twentieth century'.[18]

ABBREVIATIONS

BC   Berg Collection, New York Public Library
BL   British Library
CHAR Churchill Papers, Archives Centre, Churchill College, Cambridge
CP   Constable Papers, Special Collections Department, Temple University Library, Philadelphia
CRP Curzon Papers, British Library, London
DBFP Documents on British Foreign Policy (HMSO)
DNB *Dictionary of National Biography* (OUP, CD-ROM, 1995)
HRC Nicolson Papers, the Harry Ransom Research Center, University of Texas at Austin
KC   Misc. Correspondence, King's College, Cambridge
LL   Harold and Vita Correspondence, Lilly Library, University of Indiana, Bloomington
LLGP Lloyd George Papers, House of Lords Record Office
LP   Loraine Papers, Balliol College, Oxford
NA   National Archives, Kew, London, for all FO, CAB, CSC and INF references
ND   *Harold Nicolson. Diaries and Letters* (Atheneum, New York, 1966; 1967; 1968) three volumes, ed., Nigel Nicolson
ND   Unpublished Harold Nicolson Diaries, Balliol College, Oxford
PD   *Parliamentary Debates* (Hansard), Commons, 5th Series
PoM Nigel Nicolson, *Portrait of a Marriage* (Atheneum, New York, 1973)
RMP Raymond Mortimer Papers, Special Reading Room, Firestone Library, Princeton University
SP   Sissinghurst Papers, Sissinghurst Castle, in the keeping of the late Nigel Nicolson
V–H *The Letters of Vita Sackville-West and Harold Nicolson*, ed. Nigel Nicolson (G. P. Putnam's Sons, New York, 1992)

NOTES

1. 'Silver Spoons'

1. Leonard Woolf to Malcolm Muggeridge, 14 Oct. 1966, commenting on publication of the first volume of the Nicolson Diaries. In Frederic Spotts, ed., *Letters of Leonard Woolf* (Weidenfeld and Nicolson, 1989), 546.
2. Harold Nicolson, *Helen's Tower* (New York, 1937), 1.
3. See Janet Wallach, *Desert Queen. The Extraordinary Life of Gertrude Bell: Adventurer, Adviser to Kings, Ally of Lawrence of Arabia* (Phoenix, 1997), 32–33; and Hughe Knatchbull-Hugesson, *Diplomat in Peace and War* (London, 1949), 75.
4. See Kenneth Younger, ed., *The Diaries of Sir Robert Bruce Lockhart, 1915–1938* (1973), 9.
5. Details of his family background from Harold Nicolson, *Helen's Tower*, and *The Desire to Please. A Story of Hamilton Rowan and the United Irishmen* (New York, 1943).
6. See *ND*, i, 30 Mar. 1932, 113.
7. Details in Harold Nicolson, *Sir Arthur Nicolson, Bart. First Lord Carnock. A Study in the Old Diplomacy* (Constable, London, 1930), 7–9.
8. *Carnock*, x.
9. *Some People* (1927; OUP paperback edn 1983), 2.
10. See *Helen's Tower*, 106, 177; *Some People*, 9, 10; and *Small Talk* (Constable, 1937), 46.
11. *Helen's Tower*, 9–10, 29, 160–63; and 'When I was Young', *The Listener*, 2 Feb. 1939.
12. See *Carnock*, 70; Byron Farwell, *Burton. A Biography of Sir Richard Francis Burton* (Penguin Books, 1990), 356–57; and *Marginal Comments, 1941–44*, 'King Boris' (Constable, 1944), 188.
13. See *Helen's Tower*, 31–32, and *Carnock*, 153.
14. For details of Harold's Paris visit, see *Helen's Tower*, 7–9, 14, 15–16, 19–20, 23–26.

15. See ibid., 79, 117–18; and *The Desire to Please*, 1.
16. See James Lees-Milne, *Through Wood and Dale. Diaries 1975–78* (John Murray, 1998), 258.
17. See letters to Vita, 7 Aug. 1936 and 16 Mar. 1942, LL; and Lees-Milne, *Harold Nicolson*, i, 8–9.
18. See Nicolson's biography of Hamilton Rowan, *The Desire to Please*. For quotations, ibid., 14, 87, and *Helen's Tower*, 82–83.
19. Nicolson, *The Desire to Please*, 5.
20. See *Helen's Tower*, 81–82; and *The Desire to Please*, 11.
21. See *The Desire to Please*, 1, 5, 6, and *Helen's Tower*, 80; for 'candlesticks', *ND*, iii, 9 Nov. 1960, 387.
22. *The Desire to Please*, 62, and *Helen's Tower*, 82.
23. For the passage on the Grange, see *Helen's Tower*, 261, 262; *Some People*, 4, 22; *ND*, i, 152–53; his article, 'Thucydides', 5 Mar. 1948, in *Comments, 1944–1948* (Constable, 1948); letters to his mother (no exact dates, but 1896 and 5 Feb. ?), SP; and Nicolson to Jocelyn Brooke, 17 Oct. 1950, HRC.
24. See the entry on Benson, *DNB*; and Jonathan Gathorne-Hardy, *The Public School Phenomenon* (Penguin Books, 1979), 101, 264.
25. *Helen's Tower*, 263–64.
26. See *Some People*, 22–23, 25–26; Gathorne-Hardy, *Public School*, 118, 251; and David Newsome, *A History of Wellington College, 1859–1959* (John Murray, 1959), 264, n. 26.
27. For Persius quotation, see Nicolson's 'Introduction' to Bertram Pollock, *A Twentieth Century Bishop. Recollections and Reflections* (1944); for further impressions of Pollock, *Some People*, 31–33.
28. For 'exact of hellenists', *Some People*, 32; and Harold's letter home, 13 Dec. 1903, SP.
29. See letters home, Sep.–Dec. 1903, SP; and Lees-Milne, *Harold Nicolson*, i, 12–13.
30. See his broadcast of 10 Jan. 1939, 'When I Was Young', *The Listener*, 2 Feb. 1939.
31. For 'linseed oil', *Some People, 22;* also Nicolson's article, 'Corporal Punishment', 2 May 1947, *Comments, 1944–1948*.
32. Quotations in *Some People*, 32; *The Desire to Please*, 12; *Small Talk*, 160; also Lees-Milne, *Harold Nicolson*, i, 7.
33. See *ND*, i, 113; Newsome, *History*, 264 n.26; *Some People*, 23.
34. Quoted in Gathorne-Hardy, *Public School*, 245.
35. Said to James Lees-Milne, in *Ancestral Voices* (1975), 187.
36. Gathorne-Hardy, *Public School*, 240–41.

37. See *Some People*, 22–23, and Harold Nicolson's 'Introduction' to Pollock, *Twentieth Century Bishop*.
38. Letter from Harold to his mother, 19 Mar. 1901, SP; and *ND*, ii, 55.
39. See *Some People*, 21–22, and Lees-Milne, *Harold Nicolson*, i, 5.
40. Harold to 'My Dear Family', 24 Feb. 1910, SP.
41. Letters to his family, Feb.–Aug. 1904, SP.

2. 'Effortless Superiority'

1. Quotations in Stephen Koss, *Asquith* (Hamish Hamilton, 1985), 8; and Noel Annan, *The Dons. Mentors, Eccentrics and Geniuses* (HarperCollins, 2000), 61.
2. As 'immutable', Koss, *Asquith*, 8 ; for 'brain-power', Jan Morris, *Oxford* (Oxford, 1979), 65; Asquith's 'perspective' in Roy Jenkins, *Asquith* (Fontana Books, 1967), 20 ; ditty on Jowett attributed to Tennyson: Libretto from *The Masque of Balliol*, quoted in John James, *Balliol College. A History* (Oxford 2nd edn, 1997), 222; and A. G. Gardiner, *Prophets, Priests & Kings* (1927), 57.
3. 'Deadlocked', in Annan, *The Dons*, 73; 'inoculate', Morris, *Oxford*, 47.
4. Letters to his family Oct.–Nov. 1904, SP.
5. See Harold Nicolson, 'A Portrait of Winston Churchill', *Life*, 16 April 1948: copy in CHUR 4/15B, CHAR.
6. Lees-Milne, *Harold Nicolson*, i, 24.
7. See Nicolson's essay, 'The Boat Race', in *Comments, 1944–1948*.
8. Quoted in Lees-Milne, *Harold Nicolson*, i, 22.
9. As the 'hub', Annan, *The Dons*, 78; and 'presumed homosexuality', James, *Balliol*, 233–35, 259–61.
10. Quoted in Lees-Milne, *Harold Nicolson*, i, 22.
11. See *Some People*, 46.
12. For 'fastidious', see Nicolson, 'Alan Leeper', *The Nineteenth Century* (Oct. 1935); 'one honour', *ND*, iii, 241, and 'pot of marmalade', *ND*, iii, 296; 'Balliol made me . . .', from *Verses* (1910), 'To the Balliol Men Still in Africa'.
13. Nigel Nicolson, *Long Life* (Phoenix Books, 1997), 63.
14. For the above passage on Russia, see Nicolson, *Carnock* (1930; 4th edn, 1937) , 204–5, 226–28; his essay, 'Tzarist Russia', in *Friday Mornings, 1941–1944*; Sir Nevile Henderson, *Water under the Bridges* (Hodder and Stoughton, 1945), 31–33; Kenneth Harris interview with Nicolson, *Observer*, 12 Nov. 1961; for his Tory candidature, *ND*, i, 207, 25 June 1935; see also Harold Nicolson, 'National Character and National Policy', Montague Burton International Relations Lecture, University College, Nottingham, 1938, and 'The Values of Europe', *The Listener*, 2 Jan. 1958.

15. Quoted in Lees-Milne, *Harold Nicolson*, i, 34. Maximilian Harden (b. Witkowski): founder and editor of *Die Zukunft*, a sensational political weekly of considerable influence. A vigorous supporter of Bismarck, he savaged mercilessly Wilhelm II and the mores of his social circle.

16. *ND*, i, 104.

17. See Nicolson's sparkling essay, 'Jeanne de Hénault' in *Some People*. Also Duff Cooper, *Old Men Forget* (1953), 40–41; Norman Rose, *Vansittart. Study of a Diplomat* (1978), 9; and *ND*, i, 104.

18. See Nicolson's essay, 'On Learning Foreign Languages', in *Small Talk*.

19. For details of Harold's grades, see CSC (Civil Service Commission)/10/3084, NA. Eustace Percy scored a total of 2,643 marks, Harold 2,486. Harold's grades for individual subjects were: 325 for English composition; for English, 396; for Italian (translation, composition and oral), 235; for French (translation, composition and oral), 315; French, 'critical questions', 115; German (translation, composition and oral), 309; Roman history, 219; modern German history, 263; political science, 309. For Harold's acceptence into the Civil Service, see CSC/11/203, NA.

20. David Kelly, *The Ruling Few* (London, 1952), 77.

21. See Zara Steiner, *The Foreign Office and Foreign Policy, 1898–1914* (Cambridge University Press, 1969), 174–75.

22. Nicolson, *Peacemaking* (University Paperback, 1964), 230.

23. Letter to his family, 19 Oct. 1909, SP.

24. Steiner, *Foreign Office*, 16.

25. Lord Vansittart, *The Mist Procession* (Hutchinson, 1958), 43.

26. These developments may be followed in Steiner, *Foreign Office, passim*.

27. Letter to his family, 19 Oct. 1909, SP.

28. Quoted in Kenneth Bourne, *Palmerston: The Early Years, 1784–1841* (Allen Lane, 1982), 418.

29. Letters to his family, 5 and 19 Jan. 1910, SP; and *Carnock*, 326.

30. See Harold Nicolson, 'The Origins and Development of the Anglo-French Entente', *International Affairs* (July 1954); and *Carnock*, 308.

31. Castlereagh's 'State Paper of 5 May 1820', printed in H. Temperley and L. A. Penson, *Foundations of British Policy* (London, 1938), 49–63; Crowe's 'Memorandum on the Present State of British Relations with France and Germany', in G. P. Gooch and H. Temperley, eds, *British Documents on the Origins of the War, 1898–1914* (London, 1926–38), iii, Appendix A.

32. See *Carnock*, 327–28; and Sibyl Crowe and Edward Corp, *Our Ablest Public Servant. Sir Eyre Crowe, 1864–1925* (Merlin Books, Braunton, Devon, 1993), xxiii, 491.

33. Quotations in Steiner, *Foreign Office*, 108, 118 n.2, 123; see also entry for Tyrrell in *DNB*.

34. *Carnock*, 335.

35. Letter to his family, 13 Dec. 1909, SP.

36. *Carnock*, 328.

37. ND, 18–19 May 1910.

38. See his essay, 'The Edwardian Week-End' in *Small Talk*; according to the *OED*, 'jade' also refers to 'an inferior or worn-out horse', or 'a disreputable woman'.

39. Letter to his family, 19 Feb. 1909, SP.

40. Lord Gerald Wellesley, later seventh Duke of Wellington (1885–1972): entered Diplomatic Service, 1908; served at St Petersburg, Constantinople, Rome; retired from service, 1919; Surveyor of King's Works of Art, 1936—.
Arthur Michael Cosmo Bertie, second son of seventh Earl of Abingdon (1886–?): honorary attaché at British embassy, St Petersburg, 1906–7; promoted to Major in First World War, DSO, MC; various diplomatic appointments, 1918–25; emigrated to Northeren Transvaal, 1925.
Gerald Hyde Villiers (1882—): joined Foreign Office, 1903; head of Western Department, 1921; resigned, 1929.
Gerald Hugh Tyrwhitt-Wilson, fourteenth Baron Berners (1883–1950): honorary attaché Diplomatic Service, 1909–20; noted muscian, artist, author.
Alan Frederick Lascelles (1887–1981): sat twice, in vain, for Foreign Office; royal courtier; assistant private secretary to George V, Edward VIII, George VI; private secretary to George VI and Elizabeth II.
Archibald John Clark Kerr, first Baron Inverchapel (1882–1951): diplomat; ambassador to Stockholm, 1935; to Baghdad, 1935–38; to China, 1938–42; to Moscow, 1942–46; to Washington, 1946–48.

41. ND, 18 Aug. 1910, and Lees-Milne, *Harold Nicolson*, i, 47.

42. For these matters see John Grigg, *Lloyd George: The People's Champion, 1902–1911* (University of California Press, Berkeley, 1978), 190–288 *passim*; and Kenneth Morgan, *Lloyd George* (1974), 65–71.

43. Letter to his family, 19 Jan. 1910, SP.

44. Letters to family, 19 Nov. 1909, and 30 Mar. 1910, SP.

45. Quoted in Lees-Milne, *Harold Nicolson*, i, 45.

46. Letter to his family, 13 May 1910, SP.

47. ND, 29 June 1910, and 1 Oct. 1913.

3. Vita

1. This passage, unless stated otherwise, follows *PoM*, Part 1, 49, 55–58, 61–64, 65–73; Victoria Glendinning, *Vita. The Life of Vita Sackville-West* (1983; Penguin edn, 1984), 3–35, *passim*; Vita Sackville-West, *Knole and the Sackvilles* (1922), 4; David Cannadine, 'Portrait of More than a Marriage', in *Aspects of Aristocracy* (Yale University Press, 1994), 211–17. Also *Knole* (National Trust, 1986).
2. For this affair, see T. C. Hinckley, 'George Osgoodby and the Murchison Letter', *Pacific Historical Review* (1958), 27, and C. S. Campbell, 'The Dismissal of Lord Sackville', *Mississippi Valley Historical Review* (1958), 44.
3. See *ND*, iii, Vita to Harold, 7 Dec. 1950, 196.
4. Quotations in *V–H*, 24; and James Lees-Milne, 'Vita Sackville-West', in *Fourteen Friends* (John Murray, London, 1996), 47.
5. See Vita Sackville-West, *The Edwardians* (Hogarth Press, 1930), 12–15, quoted in Michael Stevens, *V. Sackville-West. A Critical Biography* (Michael Joseph, 1973), 24.
6. Vita Sackville-West, *Knole and the Sackvilles*, 18–19, 28–33.
7. Vita to Lydia Lopokova (Mrs John Maynard Keynes), 6 Mar.?, KC.
8. Quoted in Glendinning, *Vita*, 33.
9. Quotations in *V–H*, 8–9, 336, 350.
10. *PoM*, 27, and **ND**, 29 June and 2 July 1910, and 1910 *passim*.
11. Quoted in Glendinning, *Vita*, 22, 28.
12. *PoM*, 29, 75; and Diana Souhami, *Mrs Keppel and her Daughter* (Flamingo Press, 1977), 97.
13. *PoM*, 77–78, and *V–H*, 21.
14. See *PoM*, 32, 82, 84–86; and Harold to his Dear Family, 10 Dec. 1912, SP.
15. See *PoM*, 33, 64; and Glendinning, *Vita*, 37.
16. *V–H*, 6, 7, 26, 30.
17. Quotations in **ND** for Aug. and Sept. 1912; *PoM*, 33, 75–76, 88, 90; *V–H*, 22; and Vita to Harold, 6 June 1913, LL, quoted in Souhami, *Mrs Keppel*, 109.
18. Quotations in *PoM*, 92, and *V–H*, 42–45.
19. *PoM*, 93.
20. *PoM*, 88, and *V–H*, 19 n.1.
21. *V–H*, 23.
22. **ND**, Sept.–Dec. 1912–Jan. 1913.
23. For the background to these events, see Joseph Heller, *British Policy towards the Ottoman Empire, 1908–1914* (Frank Cass, London, 1983); for

Grey's quote, Viscount Grey, *Twenty-Five Years* (Hodder and Stoughton, London, 1925), i, 174.

24. **ND**, 18 Oct. and 14 Dec. 1912; and *V–H*, 38–39.

25. Quotations in *V–H*, 21, 33–34, 39, 41.

26. See **ND**, 1912–13, in particular entries for 14 and 18 March, 7 May, 21 Dec. 1912, and 26 April 1913 ; also *Some People*, 49–50, where Firbank appears as Lambert Orme.

27. **ND**, 9, 15, and 20–29 Oct. 1913; also *PoM*, 38, 97.

28. See Glendinning, *Vita*, 69, and *PoM*, 97.

29. **ND**, 16 Nov. 1913; and Glendinning, *Vita*, 73.

30. Harold to his Dear Family, 10 Dec. 1913, SP; and Nicolson, *Peacemaking, 1919* (University Paperback, 1964), 35.

31. See Crowe and Corp, *Our Ablest Public Servant*, 129.

32. See *Peacemaking* (dedicated to Crowe's memory), 211.

33. For Tyrrell's distrust of Nicolson, see Steiner, *Foreign Office*, 139 and n.7; Nicolson to Cambon quoted in A. J. P. Taylor, *The Struggle for Mastery in Europe, 1848–1918* (Oxford, 1954; 1960), 479; and Lichnowsky on Office rivalries, *Carnock*, 394.
In some circles, Tyrrell had also gained a reputation as an intriguer. Richard von Kühlmann, a German diplomat stationed in London, told Harold that in 1912 he had 'worked hand-in-glove with Tyrrell – and behind the back of my father and even Grey'. In **ND**, 5 Dec. 1929.

34. Grey, *Twenty-Five Years*, i, 310.

35. Minute by Eyre Crowe, 25 July 1914, in *British Documents on the Origins of the War* (1926), xi, no. 101, p. 82, ed. G. P. Gooch and Harold Temperley.

36. Following *Carnock*, 425–26.

37. See ibid., xv–xvi, 258–59; Hobbes, *Leviathan*, Part 1, ch. 4.

38. See Steiner, *Foreign Office*, 149 n.1, and Lewis Namier, *Vanished Supremacies* (Peregrine Books, 1962), 120; also Harold's review of Kühlmann's memoirs, *Spectator*, 24 June 1949, quoted in Namier, 121, n.1.

39. Kühlmann's recollections in *ND*, 31 March 1928, and 5 Dec. 1929; von Bülow quoted in Taylor, *The Struggle*, 453.

4. War Games

1. *V–H*, 22 Aug. 1917, 58.

2. See Harold Nicolson, *Diplomacy* (1939; Oxford Paperbacks, 1969), 3.

3. Nicolson, *Peacemaking, 1919*, 159–60.

4. See NA, FO.371/3148, no.117931, Nicolson's minute of 5 July 1918;

and for his 'lamenting', FO.371/3448, no.179302, minutes of 25 Oct. 1918.

5. See NA, FO.371/3448, no.164553, Nicolson's memorandum on 'Bulgaria, the Balkans, and Turkey', 28 Sept. 1918.

6. See NA, FO.371/3136, nos 177085, 177223: memorandum by Leo Amery, 20 Oct. 1918, and minutes by Namier and Nicolson, 7 Nov. 1918, and Hardinge and Cecil (n.d.); also V. H. Rothwell, *British War Aims and Peace Diplomacy, 1914–1918* (Clarendon Press, Oxford, 1971), 248–49.

7. See NA, FO.371/3258, a note by Nicolson for 'Persia Committee, 14 Feb. 1918, FO.371/3260, no.103815; a memorandum by Nicolson on 'HMG's policy in Persia', 8 June 1918; FO.371/3261, no.133775, memorandum by Nicolson 'Summarizing the Persian situation from March 1917–July 1918', 16 July 1918; and FO.371/3274, no.138234. Also a memorandum by Nicolson, 11 Aug. 1918, in the Cecil Papers at the British Library, quoted in Rothwell, *British War Aims*, 197, 213.

8. See Nicolson's memorandum of 28 Sept. 1918, NA, FO.371/3448, no.164553. In the event, both agreements were revised, though perhaps not in the manner that Harold envisaged. For other papers Harold submitted on the same topics, see FO.371/3094/ 3099/ 3101/ 3106.

9. See *V–H*, Harold to Vita, 22 Aug. 1917, 58. And a memorandum by Balfour, 20 Sept. 1917, NA, CAB/1,P–22; FO.371/3086, no.230895 and FO.371/3440, no.40497, memoranda by Nicolson, 8 Dec. 1917 and 10 Mar. 1918.

10. See NA, FO.371/2806, no.263816, Nicolson's minute of 29 Dec. 1916; also David Lloyd George, *War Memoirs* (London, 1938), v.1, 509–13, 653, 659–60, and Rothwell, *British War Aims*, 64.

11. See NA, FO.371/1917, nos 164776, 165197, 170014, Nicolson's 'useful summary', 23 Aug. 1917.

12. See L. S. Amery, *My Political Life* (Hutchinson, London, 1953–55), ii, 92; Roger Adelson, *Mark Sykes: Portrait of an Amateur* (1975); Nicolson, *Curzon. The Last Phase, 1919–1925 A Study in Post-War Diplomacy* (1934), 86 n.1; and Nicolson, *Comments, 1944–1948*, 'The Balfour Declaration', 221–25.

13. For disliking Jews, *ND*, ii, 13 June 1945, 469; and for Butlin's, Nigel to Raymond Mortimer, 30 April 1969, RMP.

14. For the complexities of Gentile Zionism, see Balfour's speech to the House of Lords, 21 June 1922, PD, 5th series, v. 50, cols. 1009–19; Mayir Vereté, 'The Idea of the Restoration of the Jews in English Protestant Thought', *Middle Eastern Studies* (Jan. 1972); and Norman Rose, *The Gentile Zionists* (Frank Cass, 1973).

15. See *ND*, ii, 149; also Stanley Olson, ed., *Harold Nicolson. Diaries and Letters, 1930–1964* (New York, 1986), 150.
16. Quoted in Lees-Milne, *Harold Nicolson*, i, 94–96. No reference, or date, is given for this quotation. I was unable to trace it in the Lilly Library; perhaps it was mislaid, or perhaps I overlooked it. Judging from its context it was written in the late spring of 1918, just as the Vita–Trefusis affair was coming to the boil (see below), which may explain the sense of pathos that exudes from this letter.
17. Quotations in Harold to Vita, 18 Oct. 1918, LL; **ND**, 13 March 1918; also Lees-Milne, *Harold Nicolson*, i, 87, 91.
18. *V–H*, 4 Sept. 1918, 69–70. The report is contained in Harold's letter.
19. For his memorandum on Holland, *V–H*, 61–62; for Belgian claims, see NA, FO.371/4357, a memorandum by James Headlam-Morley, and minutes, 3 Nov. 1918, also CAB.29/1, P–32, a memorandum by Curzon, and minutes, 19 Nov. 1918.
20. In these connections see NA, FO.371/3448, no.164553, a memorandum by Nicolson on 'Bulgaria, the Balkans, and Turkey', 28 Sept. 1918; FO.371/3160, no.198694, a memorandum by Nicolson on 'Britain, Roumania, Italy, and Bulgaria', autumn 1918; FO.371/4353, memorandum on 'South East Europe and the Balkans, 20 Nov. 1918', by Nicolson, Allen Leeper and Namier, and helped by Professor Robert Seton-Watson ; FO.371/3106, a memorandum by Nicolson to Supreme War Council on 'Present situation in Greece, Italy, Austria, Switzerland, and Roumania', 2 Dec. 1917; CAB.29/1, 1919, a memorandum by Curzon, with minutes by Nicolson and Toynbee, 2 Jan. 1919.
21. Nicolson's appreciation of Allen Leeper in *The Nineteenth Century* (October 1955); and FO.371/4353 for memorandum of 20 Nov. 1918; also Crowe and Corp, *Ablest Public Servant*, 316.
22. See NA, FO.372/1487/T14067, and 14067/319D; also FO.372/1569/T30392D.
23. The memorandum, 10 March 1918, and minutes in NA, FO.371/3440, no.40497.
24. See *Peacemaking, 1919*, 8–9; and ND, for Oct.–Nov. 1918, and *V–H*, Harold to Vita, 11 Nov. 1918, 73.
    Such was Harold's enthusiasm for Venizelos, that he dedicated his biography of *Byron* (1924) to the wily Greek politician.
25. **ND**, 8 Nov. 1918.

5. Personal Distractions

1. *V–H*, Harold to Vita, 11 Sept. 1914, 54–55; and Lees-Milne, *Harold Nicolson*, i, 77.
2. Nigel was born on 19 January 1917 at their home at Ebury Street, London. A year and half earlier, in November 1915,Vita had given birth to a stillborn son.
3. *V–H*, 57, and *PoM*, 193–94.
4. Anne Scott-James, *Sissinghurst. The Making of a Garden* (Michael Joseph, 1975: 6th edn 1983), 21.
5. For Lady Sackville's largesse, and the gardener, see ibid., 23; and Glendinning, *Vita*, 77, 79, 81, for the Rolls-Royce, Ebury Street and Brook Farm.
6. See BL Manuscripts Room, Add.68905, ff.5, Harold to Eddy Sackville-West, 29 Oct. 1928.
7. Quoted in Lees-Milne, *Harold Nicolson*, i, 92.
8. *V–H*, 60.
9. *V–H*, Harold to Vita, 25 Oct. 1919, 99.
10. For 'turning point', Glendinning, *Vita*, 88; and lack of sexual 'finesse', *PoM*, 136, Souhami, *Mrs Keppel*, 141, and Glendinning, *Vita*, 87. For 'diseased husband' and 'frightfully opty', Harold to Vita, 15 Mar. 1918, LL, parts of which have been quoted in Souhami, *Mrs Keppel*, 126, and Glendinning, *Vita*, 90; and for Violet as godmother, *PoM*, 39. For Violet seeing into Vita's 'soul', ch.3, p. 13.
11. Violet and Vita at Long Barn, *PoM*, 103–5; and Harold to Walpole, 25 Apr. 1918, HRC.
12. Souhami, *Mrs Keppel*, 173–74.
13. For sending funds, *PoM*, 153–54; '*not* your fault', *V–H*, Harold to Vita, 18 Mar. 1919, 78; and 'a little cottage', *V–H*, Harold to Vita, 2 Sept. 1918, 69.
14. For 'Wanderlust', *V–H*, Vita to Harold, 11 May 1918 and 5 Dec. 1919, 66–67, 103; for fighting for Vita, *V–H*, Vita to Harold, 1 Feb. 1920 and 17 Aug. 1926, 104–5, 158–59; and for Harold as a 'martyr', see Lees-Milne, *Through Wood and Dale*, 236.
15. For blaming Violet, *V–H*, Harold to Vita, 9 Sept. and 5 Dec. 1918, and 22 May 1919, 71, 73–74, 85–87.
16. '*Je t'aime*', Souhami, *Mrs Keppel*, 143; as 'good friends', *PoM*, 123, *V–H*, Vita to Harold, 9 Feb. 1920, 109; Vita and Violet's impending marriage, *V–H*,Vita to Harold, 1 June and 5 Dec. 1919, 88, 102; discarding Victorian values, *V–H*, 88–89; as a 'madwoman', *PoM*, 114, and Glendinning, *Vita*, 105.

17. For 'cross-dressing', *PoM*, 103, 110–11, 116.
18. Harold 'appalled' but forgiving, Harold to Vita, 21 Feb. 1919, LL, and Glendinning, *Vita*, 107; and for Lady Sackville, *PoM*, 157, and Souhami, *Mrs Keppel*, 200.
19. Quotations in *PoM*, 148–51, and *V–H*, Harold to Vita, 25 Oct. 1919, 99–100.
20. See *PoM*, 117–19; Souhami, *Mrs Keppel*, 171; and **ND**, 28 Feb. 1921.
21. See *PoM*, 119–24, and Souhami, *Mrs Keppel*, 176.
22. *PoM*, 119–29, and Glendinning, *Vita*, 108.
23. *PoM*, 130–31.
24. **ND**, 1 and 15 Feb. 1921.
25. *V–H*, Harold to Vita, 3 Dec. 1919, 101, and Vita to Harold, 5 Dec. 1919, 102–3.
26. Souhami, *Mrs Keppel*, 147; *V–H*, 15 Sept. 1919, 98; and Harold to Vita, 17 Jan. 1919 and 19 July 1920, LL, parts of which quoted in Souhami, 192.
27. Quoted in Glendinning, *Vita*, 106.
28. Quotations ibid., 96, and *PoM*, 103–4.
29. See *V–H*, 8, 9, and Souhami, *Mrs Keppel*, 218.
30. See *PoM*, 137, 145, 162, 187–88.
31. As published in the *Listener* (26 June 1929).
32. For 'crushed life, *ND*, iii, 8 Oct. 1958, 352; 'dual personality', *ND*, ii, 31 Mar. 1941, 156. For these matters, see also *PoM*, 140, 180, 191, 230.
33. Railing at the 'Sackville toffs', Harold to Vita, 17 April 1951, LL; for his 'hating' his name and his 'fat grub', *ND*, iii, 141; and on 'Harold's parents', Glendinning, *Vita*, 45.
34. See Lees-Milne, *Harold Ncolson*, i, 261, and Glendinning, *Vita*, 329, 368–69, 374.
35. 'Hateful muddle', Harold to Vita, 14 Feb. 1919, LL; 'unreal and inanimate', *V–H*, 2 Feb. 1919, 77; and '*Viti, Viti*', **ND**, 21 Feb. 1921.
36. Harold to Alvide Lees-Milne, 16 June 1959, BC.

6. Back to Diplomacy

1. *Peacemaking*, 44, and Crowe to Ronald Graham, 18 July 1918, NA, FO.371/3747.
2. See J. L. Salcedo-Bastardo, *Hope of the Universe* (UNESCO, 1983), 44.
3. See *Peacemaking*, 230, 269, 271, 274, 279; and Nicolson, 'The Foreign Service', *Political Quarterly* (April 1936).
4. *Peacemaking*, 122–23, 257.
5. From Nicolson, 'Cure for Overwork', in *Small Talk*.

6. See Nicolson, 'Allen Leeper', *Nineteenth Century and After* (Oct. 1935), and *Peacemaking*, 105, 230.

7. For Crowe, see Crowe to Clema (his wife), (undated, but shortly after Vita returned from the south of France), Eyre Crowe Papers, MS Eng. c.f.3023, ff.104v, 105, Bodleian Library, and *Peacemaking*, 230. For Vansittart, Forbes-Adam and Hardinge, see Harold to Vita, 11 Jan. and 16 Feb. 1919, LL; and *V–H*, Harold to Vita, 4 July 1919, 94–95.

8. See 'The Political Reconstruction of the Balkans and Turkey in Europe. Record of a conversation with members of United States Delegation regarding Bulgaria, Macedonia, Greeko-Bulgarian Frontier, Thrace, Dobrudja, Albania, Italian Treaty, Greece, Serbia, Constantinople and Asiatic Turkey ', a summary by Nicolson, 9 Jan. 1919, in NA, FO.608/30. Also *Peacemaking*, 106–7, 226, 228–29, 231, 242, 259–60, 266, 274.

9. *Peacemaking*, 312.

10. For these matters, see Harold to Vita, 24 Jan. 1919, LL; Harold to Vita, 4 May 1919, *V–H*, 83; and *Peacemaking*, 238–39, 268, 327, 335.

11. In *Peacemaking*, 65, 133–37, 248, 270–71, 315.

12. For Harold and Wilson, see ibid., 52–53, 164, 199, 249, 270.

13. See Harold to Vita, 21 Mar., 13 and 16 May 1919, LL; and for praising Lloyd George, *Peacemaking*, 333, 340, 358, and Harold to Sir Arthur Nicolson, 8 June 1919, *Peacemaking*, 359.
Lloyd George's most notable attempt to soften the German treaty is contained in the so-called Fontainebleau memorandum of 25 March 1919. Text in David Lloyd George, *The Truth about the Peace Treaties* (London, 1938), i, 404–16.

14. Quotations in *V–H*, Harold to Vita, 4 May 1919, 83, and *Peacemaking*, 335.

15. *Peacemaking*, 263.

16. Harold to Sir Arthur Nicolson, 9 and 23 Mar. 1919; also, in same sense, letters to Vita, 22 and 24 Mar. 1919, printed in *Peacemaking*, 281, 287–89.

17. For Molyneux, *V–H*, Harold to Vita, 15 Sept. 1919, 98; de Gaigneron, Lees-Milne, *Harold Nicolson*, i, 123; and Proust, *Peacemaking*, 275–76, 318–19.

18. For Proust, see Lees-Milne, *Prophesying Peace* (London, 1977), 30, and *Peacemaking*, 352–53, 361; and for Chatham House, Norman Rose, *The Cliveden Set* (Jonathan Cape, 2000), 104–5.

19. *Peacemaking*, 289.

20. For the Bela Kun interlude, see Harold to Vita, 9 April 1919, LL, and *Peacemaking*, 292–308; also *Some People*, 2.

21. *Peacemaking*, 311, 317, 364.

22. Ibid., 108, 350 (a letter to Vita, 28 May 1919).

23. See Margaret MacMillan, *Peacemakers. The Paris Conference of 1919 and its Attempt to End War* (John Murray, 2002), 197–98; and *Peacemaking*, 358.

24. *Peacemaking*, 358, 359 (letter to his father, 8 June 1919).

25. See ibid., 365–71, and Harold to Vita, 28 June 1919, *V–H*, 91–94.

26. See *Peacemaking* (revised edition, 1943) , 'Introduction' and 'As It Seems Today'; Nicolson, 'Modern Diplomacy and British Public Opinion', *International Affairs* (Sept.–Oct. 1935); Nicolson, 'Causes and Purposes', *The Nineteenth Century and After* (Oct. 1939), 391–92; Nicolson, *Why Britain is at War* (Penguin Special, 1939), 144–49; Nicolson, 'Peacemaking', Fourth Montagu Burton Lecture (University of Leeds, 19 Mar. 1946).

27. Quotations in *Why Britain is at War*, 21, 147.

28. Ibid., 147.

29. For Bulgarians, Romanians, Turks, French and Germans, *Peacemaking*, 1964 edition, 33, 34, 136, 266, 326 ; for Wilson, ibid., 52, 164–71, 195–96, 198.

30. Ibid., 187.

31. See *V–H*, Harold to Vita, 14 July 1919, 95–96, and '*Fête de la Victoire*', in *Small Talk*.

32. Quotations in *Peacemaking*, 1964 edition, 328, 363, and *V–H*, 84–85 (a bowdlerised version of this letter appears in *Peacemaking*, 344). For Vita's ignorance about the League, *PoM*, 140.

33. For Teschen, see *DBFP, 1919–1939*, Series 1, v.VI, no.83; and Harold to Vita, 19 July 1919, LL, also quoted in Lees-Milne, *Harold Nicolson*, i, 136.

34. See *DBFP*, Series 1, v.IV, no.18, pp. 43–46, 'Note by Mr. Nicolson of an Allied Meeting in Paris', 6 Aug. 1919; and James Joll, *Europe since 1870. An International History* (Weidenfeld and Nicolson, 1973), 265; also Lees-Milne, *Harold Nicolson*, i, 138.

35. For Venizelos, see Richard Clogg, *A Concise History of Greece* (Cambridge, 1993), 93–94; and Harold to Vita, 8 Aug. 1919, *V–H*, 97–98.

36. For Italy and Lloyd George, **ND**, 22 June 1922; and for Greece, Clogg, *Concise History of Greece*, 95.

37. Harold to Vita, 19 Nov. 1920, LL (parts of which quoted in Lees-Milne, *Harold Nicolson*, i, 155).

38. For this passage, see Harold's papers, *DBFP*, Series 1, v.XII, nos 439 (20 Nov. 1920), 488 (20 Dec. 1920); and *DBFP*, Series 1, v.XVII, nos 7 (8 Jan. 1921), 12 (18 Jan. 1921). Also, Report of Allied Conference held at 10, Downing Street, 2 Dec. 1920, *DBFP*, Series 1, v.VIII, no.97, 827–40. And **ND** for Jan.–Feb. 1921.

39. Quotations from *DBFP*, Series 1, v.XII, no.488, and v.XVII, nos.12, 24; also **ND**, 18 and 27 Jan. 1921.

40. See **ND**, 22 Feb. 1921, and *DBFP*, Series 1, v.XVII, no.41.
41. See **ND**, 1 and 16 Feb. 1922. A more anodyne version of this incident appears in *Curzon*, 180–81.
42. See **ND**, 2 March and 24 June 1922.
43. **ND**, 5 Sept. 1922; and Clogg, *Concise History of Greece*, 97.
44. **ND**, 18 Sept. 1922.
45. **ND**, 21 Sept. 1922; and *Curzon*, 273–74.
46. **ND**, 28 Sept. 1922: the original memorandum has not been traced in the PRO. Also 'The Attitude of the Balkan States towards the Problem of Constantinople and the Straights', 14 Sept. 1922, LLGP, Box 78, folder 2, no.2.
47. See the Anglo-French-Italian Conference held at Downing Street, 2 Dec. 1920, *DBFP*, Series 1, v.VIII, no.97, p. 933.
48. For above passage, see **ND** for 1921–22, in particular entries for 28 Feb., 4 July and 1–14 Oct. 1921; also Lees-Milne, *Harold Nicolson*, i, 166.
49. Harold to Michael Sadleir, 17 Jan. 1938, CP; and Vita to Harold, ? Jan. 1920, LL.
50. Harold to Michael Sadleir, 12 and 29 Apr. 1921, CP; and **ND**, 11, 18, and 31 Mar., and 21 Apr. 1921.
51. For Harold's opinion of Strachey's *Landmarks . . .* , Michael Holroyd, *Lytton Strachey. A Biography* (Penguin edn, 1980), 475; for Strachey's reaction to *Verlaine*, see Lees-Milne, *Harold Nicolson*, i, 164, relying on a recollection of Raymond Mortimer. Also Edmund Wilson, 'Through the Embassy Window', *New Yorker*, 1 Jan. 1944); and Harold Nicolson, *The Development of English Biography* (Hogarth Press, London, 1927), 11.
52. Harold to Michael Sadleir, 6 Aug. 1921, CP.
53. Harold to Michael Sadleir, 26 Oct. 1920, and **ND**, 20 June 1921.
54. As frankly described by Harold to Michael Sadleir, 6 Aug. 1921, CP.
55. *Sweet Waters*, 260–61, 277.
56. **ND**, 16 Jan. and 16 Mar. 1922, and Michael Sadleir to Harold Nicolson, 22 Feb. 1922, CP.
57. Harold to Michael Sadleir, 8 Aug. 1922, and Michael Sadleir to Harold, 6 Sept. 1922, CP.
58. For this passage, see **ND** for March 1923; Anne Oliver Bell (assisted by Andrew McNeille), *The Diary of Virginia Woolf, 1920–1924* (1978), ii, 239; Virginia Woolf to Joan Pernel Strachey (Lytton's elder sister, Principal of Newnham College, Cambridge), 3 Aug. 1923, in Nigel Nicolson and Joanne Trautmann, eds, *The Letters of Virginia Woolf, 1923–28* (London, 1976), iii, 62; and Lytton Strachey to John Maynard Keynes, 16 Apr. 1923, quoted in Holroyd, *Lytton Strachey*, 855; and Lees-Milne, *Harold Nicolson*, i, 203.

59. For 'meanest intelligence', Harold to Raymond Mortimer, 8 Sept. 1925, RMP, Box 3, folder 1; 'flabby old sod', Harold to Vita, 31 Dec. 1926, LL; 'bitchy old woman', Holyrod, *Lytton Strachey*, 19; 'drooping Lytton', *V–H*, Vita to Harold, 3 Aug. 1938, 304; 'aping him', Harold to Raymond Mortimer, 14 July 1927, RMP, Box 3, folder 2.

60. For 'sly minds', Harold to Raymond Mortimer, 22 July 1925; 'gift from heaven', Harold to Raymond Mortimer, 27 Aug. 1925; 'flabby vulgarity', Harold to Raymond Mortimer, 19 Aug. 1925, all in RMP, Box 3, folder 1. For 'tawdry', Virginia Woolf to Lytton Strachey, 21 Mar. 1924, Nicolson and Trautmann, *Letters of Virginia Woolf*, iii, 95; and 'against shams', Harold to Raymond Mortimer, 24 Aug. 1925, RMP, Box 3, folder 1.

61. ND, 4 July 1923.

62. For Marsh's role, see Harold to Michael Sadleir, 16 Dec. 1922; Harold to Edward Marsh, 29 Dec. 1922, HRC; and ND, 30 Dec. 1922.

63. Wilson, 'Through the Embassy Window'.

64. See ND, 28 Dec. 1923, and 31 Dec. 1925; also Harold to Raymond Mortimer, 3 Sept. 1925, RMP, Box 3, folder 1.

65. ND, 12 Mar. 1924.

7. 'But you see Britannia *has* ruled here'

1. See Harold to Vita, 18 Nov. 1922, LL; and *Some People*, 141, for a more picturesque version.

2. For Harold's crowded daily timetable, Harold to Vita, 23 Nov. 1922, LL; his clash with Curzon, ND, 2 Jan. 1923, and Lees-Milne, *Harold Nicolson*, i, 190. And in general, for Harold's participation at Lausanne, see also the Curzon Papers, FE 112/298, at the British Library.

3. See ND, 22 Nov., 4 and 8 Dec. 1922; and Nicolson, *Curzon*, 40–48, 302–3, 304.

4. For Harold's 'patience' and Athens atrocities, see ND, 22 Nov. 1922 and Clogg, *Concise History of Greece*, 100; also 'managing the Cretan', *Curzon*, 345.

5. See *DBFP*, Series 1, v.XVIII, nos 287, 307, 329; ND, 22 Dec. 1922; and *Curzon*, 345.

6. Quoted in *Curzon*, 299, n.1.

7. Harold's memorandum printed in *DBFP*, Series 1, v.XVIII, Appendix 1; for Curzon's reaction, ND, 13 Oct. 1922; for Curzon's proposals, *Curzon*, 312, n.1: they also included demilitarisation zones on both shores of the Straits and an international commission to supervise navigation rights.

8. *Curzon*, 324–25.

9. *V–H*, 117–18, Harold to Vita, 2 Jan. 1923.
10. Quotations in **ND**, 7 Jan. 1923; *V–H*, Harold to Vita, 24 Jan. 1923, 119; and *Curzon*, 348.
11. *DNB*.
12. Quotations for Harold, Tyrrell and Curzon in **ND**, 26 Feb. 1934 and 15 Mar. 1947; Young, *Diaries of . . . Lockhart*, ii, 698–99. Harold was gracious enough to add in these diary jottings that Tyrrell had 'suffered greatly in his domestic life and I bear him no ill will'. And for Curzon on Tyrrell, see Curzon to Grace Curzon, 22 Dec. 1922, quoted in Steiner, *Foreign Office*, 118, n.3.
    The above story of Tyrrell being sent home in disgrace has been denied by another of Curzon's aides, Lord William Cavendish-Bentinck, who claimed that Tyrrell was sent home as a result of a nervous breakdown. See Lees-Milne, *Through Wood and Dale*, 271.
13. See *V–H*, 115, Harold to Vita, 25 Nov. 1922. Harold later admitted to having 'dolled up' this story in one or two details, though not in its essence. See Nigel Nicolson's 'Introduction' to *Some People* (Oxford, paperback edn, 1983), xi.
14. See **ND**, 1 Feb. 1922; Young, *Diaries of . . . Lockhart*, ii, 575; Nicolson, 'Allen Leeper' and *Curzon*, 195.
15. See Lord D'Abernon, *An Ambassador for Peace* (Hodder and Stoughton, 1929), ii, 147, 165–66; *Curzon*, 344, 349; and *V–H*, Harold to Vita, 1 Feb. 1923, 120.
16. See *V–H*, Harold to Vita, 1 Feb. 1923, 120.
17. **ND**, 21 Jan. 1923.
18. Quotations in Harold to Vita, 18 Dec. 1922, and Vita to Harold, 19 Dec. 1922, LL, also quoted in *PoM*, 201; and Bell, assisted by Andrew McNeille, eds, *Diary of Virginia Woolf*, ii, 187, 216–17, and Nicolson and Trautman, eds, *Letters of Virginia Woolf*, iii, 150. Also Leonard Woolf, *An Autobiography, 1911–1969* (Oxford, 1980), ii, 303.
19. Quotations in Glendinning, *Vita*, 139–42, 232.
20. See *ND*, i, 24 Oct. 1934, 185–87; and iii, 2 Oct. 1957, 339.
21. Quotations in Vita to Harold, 12 Jan. 1923, LL, also quoted in Lees-Milne, *Harold Nicolson*, i, 196; also Bell, *Diary of Virginia Woolf*, ii, 19 Feb. 1923, 235.
22. Correspondence: Vita to Harold, 19 Dec. 1925, and Harold to Vita, 2 Sept. 1926 in *PoM*, 205, 206; *V–H*, Vita to Harold, 28 June 1926, 150 and 17 Aug. 1926, 158–59; *V–H*, Harold to Vita, 7 July 1926, 150, n.7.
23. By Nigel Nicolson, *PoM*, 207.
24. For details and summing up of Vita's affair with Virginia, *PoM*, 39, 207. Other quotations in Nicolson and Trautmann, eds, *Letters of Virginia*

Woolf, iii, 484–85, and Bell, *Diary of Virginia Woolf,* iii, 239. For other signs, see Nicolson and Trautmann, 9, 36, 242, and iv, 36.

25. Harold to Lady Sackville, 2 May 1931, LL.
26. ND, 31 Dec. 1923.
27. See ND, Sept.–Oct. 1923.
28. ND, 12, 15 and 29 Jan. 1924.
29. See ND, 23 and 31 Mar. 1924.
30. *DNB.*
31. Minutes in NA, FO.371/9183, C.2028/1346/18, including a memorandum by J. C. Sterndale Bennett on 'British Policy in the Rhineland', that set out how Poincaré had succeeded in his so-called devious tactics. Also, MacDonald's letter and Poincaré's reply, *The Times,* 3 Mar. 1924.
32. General Staff memorandum on 'The Future of the Rhineland', NA, FO.371/9813, C.5185/1346/1; Foreign Office reaction: minutes of Lampson, Sterndale Bennett and Crowe, April 1924, in NA, FO.371/9813, C.5185/1346/18; and Harold's minutes of 27 Aug. and 15 Oct. 1924, in NA, FO.371/9819, C.13663/2048/18, and FO.371/9819, C.15288/2048/18.
33. For Jubaland, see ND, 7 and 31 Mar. 1924; for Italy, Greece and Albania, see *DBFP,* Series 1, v.XXVII, nos 15 and 51, pp. 28–31, 85–87.
34. For degree, ND, 5 May 1924.
35. See ND, 16 Aug. 1924; and David Marquand, *Ramsay MacDonald* (Jonathan Cape, 1977), 342–51.
36. For quotations see ND: Mosley, 10 and 31 Mar. 1924; Curzon, 18 Mar. and 28 Sept. 1924; Asquith, 11 Oct. 1924, and 6 Jan. 1925; Churchill, 7 June 1925; Shaw and Belloc, 12 Mar. and 22 Sept. 1924; and Elgin Marbles, 4 Apr. 1924.
37. See Lees-Milne, *Through Wood and Dale,* 159.
38. For quotations see ND, 4 Feb., 25 June, 2, 14 and 21 July 1925; and *Some People,* 55–56, for entering 'the Areopagus'.
39. For Lord Carnock's heart attack, ND, early Mar. 1924; for the 'row' and 'bless them', ND, 4 Apr. 1924, and Glendinning, *Vita,* 138; and for Harold on Geoffrey Scott, Lees-Milne, *Harold Nicolson,* i, 238.
40. For Ben, ND, 12 Oct. 1924; for holidays, ND, 25–27 Mar. and 11–31 July 1924, and ND, 3–20 Apr. 1925.
41. See ND, 1 July 1925; and Harold to Liddell Hart, 11 Feb. 1955, HRC.
42. For Beerbohm and Rothenstein, ND, 28 Mar. 1925, and Lees-Milne, *Harold Nicolson,* i, 224.

8. 'Not really interested in foreign politics'

1. References in **ND**: in a 'rut', 31 Dec. 1924; Hardinge and Tyrrell, 18 Mar., 24 Apr., 12 Sept. 1924 ; adoring Crowe, 25 Sept. 1924; MacDonald turns on Foreign Office, 18 Oct. 1924; and Zinoviev affair, 24–25 Oct. 1924.
2. **ND**, 31 Oct. 1924.
3. For avoiding Curzon, **ND**, 31 Oct. 1924, and for policy discussion, 22 Jan. 1925. Harold's paper, 'British Policy considered in relation to the European Situation', in *DBFP*, Series 1, v.XXVII, no.205, pp. 311–18. The paper was registered as C.2201/459/18, but was not preserved in its relevant file, NA, FO.371/10753. A severely abridged version appeared in *The Times*, 2 Mar. 1925.
4. For Harold on Chamberlain, **ND**, 20 Feb. 1924 and 4 Aug. 1925.
5. For Curzon, **ND**, 20, 25 Mar. and 9 June 1925.
6. For references, see **ND**: 'Tyrrell reigns', 21 May 1925; 'feeling bored', 24 May 1925; 'ignored', 4 Aug. 1925; offered Tehran, agonises and accepts, 23 and 24 Sept. 1925; and 'not servile,' 17 Oct. 1925.
7. Harold to Francis Henry King, 28 Apr. 1952, HRC.
8. For St Tropez, see **ND**, 14 Aug. 1925, and Harold to Mortimer, 24 Aug. 1925, RMP, Box 3, folder 1. For unbearable parting, letters to Mortimer of 16, 17, 24 (two), 27 and 29 Aug. 1925, RMP, Box 3, folder 1.
9. For 'restless', Harold to Mortimer, 14 Aug. 1926; 'starved', Harold to Mortimer, 1 Jan. 1926; 'guardsman', Harold to Mortimer, 5 Nov. 1926; of 'supreme importance', Harold to Mortimer, 3 Nov. 1926; 'middle-aged', Harold to Mortimer, 29 Dec. 1926, letters in RMP. Also **ND**, 31 Mar. and 4 July, 1926, for 'silent and wretched'.
10. Harold to Vita, 20 Dec. 1926, RMP.
11. See Lees-Milne, *Ancestral Voices*, 222, 276.
12. Quotations in *PoM*, 182–85; and Lees-Milne, 'Vita Sackville-West', in *Fourteen Friends* (John Murray, 1996), 55.
13. For 'prig', see Harold to Mortimer, 29 Jan. 1927, RMP; and for Ben and Vita, interview with Nigel Nicolson, 1 July 2002.
14. Quotations in *V–H*, Harold to Vita, 17 Sept. 1928, 202–3; and Harold to Ben, 6 Mar. 1933, and Harold to Vita, 8 Nov. 1933, LL.
15. For George V, see David Cannadine, *In Churchill's Shadow* (Allen Lane, Penguin, 2002), 247; for Oscar Wilde, Max Egremont, 'Siegfried Sassoon's War', in Wm. Roger Louis, ed., *Still More Adventures with Britannia. Personalities, Politics and Culture in Britain* (I.B. Taurus, 2003), 90: and for Beauchamp, *DNB*; *V–H*, Vita to Harold, 26 Feb. 1927, 292; Cannadine, *The Decline and Fall of the British Aristocracy* (Yale University Press, 1990), 381, and *In Churchill's Shadow*, 247; and *V–H*, 292.

16. The 'love poems' included some sonnets dedicated to Mary Campbell, Vita's lover. Virginia Woolf was enraged at Harold's interference. 'Damn Harold. And why should you attach any importance to the criticism of a diplomat.' The collection was eventually published as *King's Daughter* (1929) by the Hogarth Press. See *V–H*, Vita to Harold, 11 Aug. 1929, 221–22; Virginia to Vita, 1 Sept. 1929, in Nicolson and Trautmann, eds, *Letters of Virginia Woolf*, iv, 85; Bell, *Diary of Virginia Woolf*, entry for 4 Sept. 1929, iii, 252–53; and Glendinning, *Vita*, 219.

17. See **ND**, 11 Dec. 1923; and Michael De-la-Noy, *Eddy. The Life of Edward Sackville-West* (1999), 112.

18. See *Orlando*, 162 *passim*, and Harold to Vita, 13 Oct. 1928, LL.

19. See Lord Berners, *Far From the Madding War* (Constable, 1941), 160–62; Mark Amory, *Lord Berners* (Chatto and Windus, 1998), 193; and Richard Rumbold, *Little Victims* (1933), 184–87, 189–93, 206; 'fling it away', **ND**, 2 Mar. 1933; 'quite frankly', Harold to Mortimer, 15 Mar. 1934, RMP; and for Waugh, *TLS*, 24 Oct. 2004.
Rumbold wrote in his diary in June 1933, as *Little Victims* was being published: 'Harold understands me better than anybody else, understands the good in my nature [of] which other people are only dimly conscious.' See William Plomer, ed., *A Message in Code. The Diary of Richard Rumbold, 1932–1960* (1964), 34.

20. See Roy Campbell, *Collected Poems* (London, 1955), i, 196.

21. See Chapter 1, pp. 2–3.

22. Harold to Sir Percy Loraine, 31 July, 14 and 16 Aug. 1926, LP.

23. See **ND**, 1 Feb. 1926; for Russian activities, Nicolson to Austen Chamberlain, 10 Sept. and 29 Oct. 1926, NA, FO.371/11504, E.5537/5537/34, E.6458/6458/34.

24. Quotations in Harold to Loraine, 3 July, 28 Aug. and 4 Dec. 1926, LP. Harold had used remarkably similar language when describing the Turks.

25. *V–H*, Harold to Vita, 26 June 1926, 147.

26. For Buchan-Hepburn, Harold to Mortimer, 22 Aug. 1926, RMP, and *V–H*, Harold to Vita, 7 Sept. 1926, 160–61; for Ashton, Harold to Mortimer, 12 and 26 Feb. 1927, RMP.

27. Harold to Mortimer, 3 Dec. 1925, and 1 Jan. 1926, RMP.

28. For ample leisure time, **ND**, 1926–27; for Vita's arrival, **ND**, 1 Mar. 1926; on Tehran, Vita Sackville-West, *Passenger to Teheran* (1926; Penguin edn, 1943), 63 ; for Shah's birthday: Vita to Virginia Woolf, 15 Mar. 1926, in Louise de Salvo and Mitchell A. Leaska, eds, *The Letters of Vita Sackville-West to Virginia Woolf* (Macmillan Papermac, 1985), 126; journey to Isfahan and coronation, *Passenger* . . . , 91–92, 107–8 .

29. See *PoM*, 209–11.
30. Vita to Mortimer, 10 Feb. 1927, RMP.
31. *V–H*, Harold to Vita, 1 July 1926, 150.
32. See Nicolson to Sir Austen Chamberlain, 30 Sept. 1926, in *DBFP*, Series 1a, v.II, no.447, pp. 812–20.
33. See *DBFP*, Series 1a, v.II, no.447 n.9, and Sir Austen to Mr Clive, 29 Nov. 1926, no.458, pp.837–41; also Gordon Waterfield, *Professional Diplomat* (John Murray, 1973), 136.
34. *ND*, 3 Nov. 1925.
35. Quoted in Waterfield, *Diplomat*, 136.
36. Harold to Mortimer, 29 Dec. 1926, RMP.
37. Quotation in *Curzon*, 404. Also *Diplomacy*, 24, 116.
38. See Vita's account of their journey in *Twelve Days. An Account of a Journey across the Bakhtiari Mountains in Southwestern Persia* (Hogarth Press, 1928).
39. 'Babbling idiocy', **ND**, 2 April 1927; other quotations in Harold to Mortimer, 29 Dec. 1926, and 18 Nov. 1929, RMP, and *V–H*, Harold to Vita, 28 June 1926, 30. Also Nigel Nicolson to Mortimer on *Some People* (undated, but 1969), and 25 May 1969, RMP.
40. See **ND**, 15 July 1927: Tyrrell made this aside to Harold at one of Sibyl Colefax's luncheon parties.
41. Quotations in Waterfield, *Diplomat*, 119, 136, 138.
42. For George V, see Nigel Nicolson's 'Introduction' to *Some People* (Oxford, paperback edn, 1983), ix, and for Connolly, *V–H*, Harold to Vita, 16 May 1928, 195, and Jeremy Lewis, *Cyril Connolly. A Life* (Jonathan Cape, 1997), 196.
43. See Nicolson and Trautmann, eds, *Letters of Virginia Woolf*, iii, 392; and Virginia Woolf's largely favourable review in *New York Herald Tribune*, 30 Oct. 1927.
44. Edmund Wilson in the *New Yorker*, 1 Jan. 1944; John Raymond in *New Statesman and Nation*, 10 May 1968.
45. Nigel Nicolson to Mortimer, 1969, RMP; and Constable's account for 1–31 July 1927, amounting to £278 12 2.
46. Nigel Nicolson to Mortimer, RMP, and Nigel Nicolson's 'Introduction'.

9. From Diplomacy to Grub Street

1. For the eclipse see Bell, *Diary of Virginia Woolf*, iii, 142–44; for imperialism, Paris and de Murville, **ND**, 16 and 21 July 1927.
2. **ND**, 25 Oct. 1927.
3. Above based on **ND**, 20, 21, 23 and 24 Aug. 1927; 26 and 30 Sept. 1927;

and 14, 18 and 25 Oct. 1927; and for 'Little one', Harold to Vita, 24 Oct. 1927, LL.

4. **ND**, 31 Dec. 1927.

5. *V–H*, Harold to Vita, 3 Nov. 1927, 185, and Vita to Harold, 4 Nov. 1927, 186.

6. For Vita's pressure, *V–H*, Vita to Harold, 12 July 1928 and 25 June 1929, 198, 215–16; for Virginia Woolf's advice, Virginia to Vita, 18 Feb. 1927 and 23 Feb. 1929, in Nicolson and Trautmann, *Letters of Virginia Woolf*, iii, 332, and iv, 29 ; and 'successful diplomatist', Harold to Virginia Woolf, 7 Mar. 1928, BC.

7. Harold to his parents, 7 July 1928, SP.

8. Quotations in *DBFP*, Series 1a, v.V, Nicolson to Sir Austen Chamberlain, 20 July 1928, no. 99; for variations on the same themes, ibid., 79, 80, 91, 92, 115, 116, 119, 134.

9. Quotations in Nicolson, 'Diplomacy Then and Now', *Foreign Affairs* (October 1961), 44; and *DBFP*, Series 1a, v.VII, Harold to Arthur Henderson, 20 Nov. 1929, no.87, pp.168–69. Lindsay minuted this dispatch, 'Lunatic', though it is not entirely clear to what passage he was referring.

10. 'Bumble bee' in *V–H*, Harold to Vita, 3 Aug. 1928, 199–200. For Rumbold, see Martin Gilbert, *Sir Horace Rumbold. Portrait of a Diplomat* (Heinemann, 1973), 377–79; and Rose, *The Cliveden Set*, 138.

11. *V–H*, Harold to Vita, 15 Mar. 1929, 211.

12. For Hindenburg, *V–H*, Harold to Vita, 28 June 1928, 196–97, and Harold to his family, 7 July 1928, SP; for the Yorks, *V–H*, Harold to Vita, 25 May 1929, 214–15; and for Keynes, **ND**, 3 Apr. 1928.

13. See **ND** for 4–10 Nov. 1927, and 1928–29. Also *V–H*, Harold to Vita, 7 Nov. 1927, 186, and 14 Apr. 1928, 192–93; and Harold to Vita, 16 Apr. 1928, LL.

14. *V–H*, Harold to Vita, 8 Dec. 1928, 207–8.

15. **ND**, 2 July 1929 for '*Juli 1914*'; and for 'oily', see, for example, **ND**, 4 Dec. 1958.

16. See Harold to Vita, 13 Oct. 1928, LL; and Glendinning, *Vita*, 189–90.

17. **ND**, 1 Nov. 1928.

18. 'Best book', *V–H*, 11; for Harold's first impressions, see Harold to Vita, 26 Nov. 1929, LL, and Harold to Mortimer, 18 Nov. 1929, RMP.

19. For Sandy Baird, De-la-Noy, *Eddy*, 128; for Bobby, **ND**, 10 and 15 Jan. 1928.

20. For Cyril and Tray, *V–H*, Harold to Vita, 16 and 18 May 1928, 195, 214; and Lewis, *Connolly*, 201. For Vita: Vita to Harold, 8 July 1928, LL; *V–H*, 12 July 1928, 198; and Glendinning, *Vita*, 190.

21. See Spotts, ed., *Letters of Leonard Woolf,* 233 n. 2.
22. Vanessa's observations in Quentin Bell, *Virginia Woolf* (1972), ii, 141–43.
23. See Oswald Mosley, *My Life* (Nelson, 1968), 243; and Robert Skidelsky, *Oswald Mosley* (Nelson, 1975), 166.
24. See Vita to Virginia, 12 Jan. 1929, in De Salvo and Leaska, *Letters of Vita Sackville-West to Virginia Woolf,* 324; for Eddy, De-la-Noy, *Eddy,* 117; and Christopher Isherwood, *Christopher and his Kind* (Eyre Methuen, 1977), 10, 29, 32.
25. **ND,** 30 Jan. 1929.
26. See **ND,** 9 Jan. and 6 Aug. 1929; and *V–H,* Harold to Vita, 11 Aug. 1929, 220–21.
27. For politics and Mosley, *V–H,* Harold to Vita, 8 Aug. 1928, 201; **ND,** 30. June 1929 ; Harold to 'Mummy', 2 June 1929, SP.
28. Harold to 'Darling Mummy', 6 Jan. 1929, SP.
29. See, for example, **ND,** 15 Dec., 1928; *V–H,* Harold to Vita, 8 and 26 Aug. 1929, 220–21, 222–23 and 14 Nov. 1929, 223–24; Harold to 'Mummy', 24 Aug. 1929, SP.
30. See *V–H,* Harold to Vita, 22 July 1929, 218–19, and Young, ed. *Diaries of . . . Lockhart,* i, 99–100; and for 'purse-strings', Harold to 'Mummy', 4 Aug. 1929, SP.
31. **ND,** 11 Sept., 1929.
32. See *V–H,* Vita to Harold, 11 Aug. 1929, 221–22, and Vita to Harold, 24 July 1929, LL; brushing off bloom of diplomacy, Virginia Woolf to Vita, 17 Sept. 1929, in Nicolson and Trautmann, eds, *Letters of Virginia Woolf,* iv, 88; and 'almost ashamed', quoted in Glendinning, *Vita,* 190.
33. See **ND,** 7 Sept. 1929, and Lindsay to Harold, 14 Dec. 1929, SP; Rumbold to Harold, 16 Sept. 1929, SP.
34. Quotations in *V–H,* 8 and 26 Aug., 1929, 220–23; Harold to Mortimer, 18 Nov. 1929, RMP; and *ND,* i, 1 Jan. 1931, 104. Once, he came away depressed after visiting the Foreign Office 'where my young feet used to prance so hopefully' (**ND,** 7 Mar. 1932).
For further random examples of his yearning after the diplomatic life, see *ND,* i, 79, 104, 169; Olson, *Harold Nicolson,* 37; and Nigel Nicolson, *Long Life,* 1.
35. Harold's vow in *V–H,* Harold to Vita, 14 Nov. 1929, 223–24; for his projected income and financial difficulties in 1930, Harold to Vita, 5 Dec. 1929, and 30 July 1930, LL; 'untold sums', **ND,** 15 Dec. 1928; the BBC, Harold, a note of 18 Dec. 1929, SP: the contract was signed by Hilda Matheson, Director of Talks at the BBC, and one of Vita's lovers;

and Harold to Evelyn Wrench, Dec. 1928, BL, Add. 59543, f. 112. For B.M.'s largesse, see Glendinning *Vita*, 224, 234–35, 247.

36. See Nigel Nicolson, *Long Life*, 210–11; Derek Hudson, 'Harold Nicolson', *Quarterly Review* (2 April 1967); and Cannadine, 'Portrait of More than a Marriage . . .', in *Aspects of Aristocracy*, 231.

37. *V–H*, Harold to Vita, 16 Dec. 1929, 225, and **ND**, 19 Dec. 1929.

38. 'Modern pictures' *V–H*, Harold to Vita, 16 Dec. 1929, 225; 'bedint' and 'privileges', Harold to Vita, 5 Nov. and 10 Dec. 1929, LL.

39. For 'bedints', Harold to Vita, 24 Aug. 1930, LL; and **ND**, 31 Dec. 1929.

10. Interregnum

1. Wasted assets, in **ND**, 7 Feb. 1930; loathes journalism, **ND**, 11 Oct. 1930, and *ND*, i, 57, 18 Oct. 1930: also, *ND*, i, 31 Dec. 1930, 62 ; Gilliat in **ND**, 22 Aug. 1930; and 'urinal', **ND**, 17 Aug. 1931.

2. A selection of these articles appeared in *Marginal Comment, January–August 1939* (Constable, 1939); *Friday Mornings, 1941–1944*; and *Comments, 1944–48*.

3. For book-reviewing, **ND**, 11 May 1933, *ND*, i, 147, and Harold to John Lehmann, 21 Feb. 1949, HRC; 'Marginal Comment', *ND*, i, 22 Dec. 1938, 383; Reith and BBC, *DNB*, and **ND**, 29 June 1931; and 'reputation', *ND*, i, 31 Dec. 1930, 62.

4. See **ND**, 2 March 1931; *ND*, i, Harold to Mosley, 4 Mar. 1931, 69, and 18 June 1931, 78–79. Harold spurned Beaverbrook's offer to become editor of the *Evening Standard* mainly because of an unexpected upturn in the Nicolsons' finances: Vita's French royalties had suddenly brought in £2,600. It turned out to be a temporary relief, however. See *ND*, i, 14 Sept. and 27 Oct. 1933, 154, 156.

5. For approaches by parties, see letters from Sir John [?], 1 Dec. 1930, Thomas Tweed, 30 Dec. 1930, and E. T. Wise, 5 Mar. 1931, all in LL; his BBC talk in Skidelsky, *Mosley*, 240; for Vita's 'creeps' and Harold's 'conviction', **ND**, 23 Feb., 1932, and Vita to Mortimer, 5 Jan. 1931, RMP; and for 'famous names', Norman Rose, *Churchill: An Unruly Life* (1994), 81.

6. See Skidelsky, *Mosley*, 249–50: the 'observer' was Hugh Dalton.

7. Democracy 'is dead', in **ND**, 26 Jan. 1931; leading lights, **ND**, 15 Feb. 1930 ; and fantasy scenario, **ND**, 6 Jan. 1932.

8. **ND**, 12 Sept. 1931, and *ND*, i, 27 Apr. 1931, 71.

9. For new strategy and 'philosopher-kings', *ND*, i, 5 May 1931, 73, and **ND**, 12 Sept. 1931.

10. For two stools, **ND**, 25 Sept. 1931, also Skidelsky, *Mosley*, 266–67; advises caution, *ND*, i, 28 May 1931, 75, and **ND**, 28 Apr. and 12 Aug.

1931; for Prince of Wales, **ND**, 20 July 1931 and 23 Feb. 1932; 'Hitlerism', *ND*, i, 10 June 1931, 77; 'uniforms', *ND*, i, 21 Sept. 1931, 91; 'Biff Boys' in Richard Griffith, *Fellow Travellers of the Right* (Oxford, 1983), 33; and 'better class', **ND**, 22 July 1931; also Skidelsky, *Mosley*, 263.

11. See **ND**, 5 May and 31 Aug. 1931; also Skidelsky, *Mosley*, 264–65.

12. **ND**, Aug.–Dec. 1931; and Skidelsky, *Mosley*, 264–65, 278.

13. For circulation, *ND*, i, 86; Mortimer to Eddy Sackville-West, quoted in Lees-Milne, *Harold Nicolson*, ii, 24; Harold suffering, *ND*, i, 2 Nov. 1931, 96 ; Harold's election statement in LL; dreading the result, Harold to Hugh Walpole, 31 Oct. 1931, HRC.

14. *Action*'s demise, and distancing himself, *ND*, i, 97, entries for 2 and 24 Nov. 1931; 'thought trashy' and 'What fun', *ND*, i, 31 Dec. 1931, 99–100.

15. For Rome visit, *ND*, i, 1–7 Jan. 1932; 104, 105, 106, also Harold to Vita, 7 Jan. 1932, LL.

16. For Berlin trip, **ND**, 24 Jan. and 6 Feb. 1932; *V–H*, Harold to Vita, 25 Jan. 1932, 232–34; and *ND*, i, 22 and 24 Jan. 1932, 108.

17. Quotations for leaving New Party in **ND**, Note to Mosley, 20 May 1932; *ND*, i, 30 Jan. 1932, 108; and *ND*, i, Harold to Dr Robert Forgan (a New Party recruit from the Parliamentary Labour Party), 15 Apr. 1932, and entry for 19 Apr. 1932, 114–15. Mosley's reaction in *My Life*, 80.

18. **ND**, 18 Dec. 1931, and *ND*, i, 28 Oct. 1931, 96.

19. Quotations in *ND*, I, Harold to Vita, 7 May 1930, 48; Nigel Nicolson, *Sissinghurst Castle. An Illustrated History* (National Trust, 1964), 45; and Nigel Nicolson, *Long Life*, 209.

20. 'Ancestral mansion' in *ND*, i Harold to Vita, 24 Apr. 1930, 47–48; broke, **ND**, 11 Feb. and 10 June 1931; spending, *ND*, i, 147; initials, in Nigel Nicolson, *Long Life*, 209.

21. See *ND*, i, 48, and *Long Life*, 210.

22. See Nigel Nicolson, *Long Life*, 210–11, and Nigel Nicolson, *Sissinghurst Castle Garden* (National Trust, 1994).

23. B.M.'s death, *ND*, i, 30 Jan. and 8 Feb. 1936, 241, 243; selling Long Barn, *ND*, ii, 26 Dec. 1943, 335, and Glendinning, *Vita*, 330.

24. Harold to Vita, 27 Sept. 1932, LL.

25. See *ND*, i, 129.

26. See *ND*, i, 129, and 5 Jan. 1933, 131–32.

27. For Washington, see *V–H*, Harold to Vita, 16 Feb. 1933, 239, also *ND*, i, 16 Feb. 1933, 137; for Mount Vernon, *ND*, i, 27 Jan. 1933, 134; and senators, *ND*, i, 27 Jan. 1933, 135.

28. For Charleston, *V–H*, Harold to Vita, 18 Feb. 1933, 239–41, also *ND*, i, 17 Feb. 1933, 138–39; and 'foreign soil', *ND*, i, 3 Mar. 1933, 140–41.

29. Hollywood, in Harold to his 'Darling Mummy', 27 Mar. 1933, SP, also

ND i, 25 and 26 Mar. 1933, 143–44; 'Smokey Tree Ranch and Grand Canyon, *ND*, i, 28 and 29 Mar., and 1 Apr. 1933, 144–46.

See also Harold's 'What Struck Me Most in America', in *Small Talk*, where he devotes much of his essay to his stay at the Smokey Tree Ranch, commenting on the American 'instinct for equality' and 'simplicity' and comparing them favourably with 'the snobbishness of Europe . . . an arid and inhuman thing'. Admirable as these comments are, it remains highly doubtful whether he would exchange one for the other.

30. Soul-destroying, in Harold to 'Darling Mummy', 5 Mar. 1933, SP ; 'slushy adulation', Harold to Vita, 23 Feb. 1933, LL; 'Springfield, Mass.,' in *ND*, i, 24 Jan. 1933, 133; in Toledo, Harold to Mortimer, 5 Mar. 1933, RMP, also *ND*, i, 4 Mar. 1933, 141–42; and 'chatter', *V–H*, Harold to Vita, 1 Oct. 1934, 261.

31. Harold to Vita, 23 Feb. 1933, LL.

32. 'Unfortunate mistake', in Harold to Mortimer, 15 Mar. 1933, RMP; for Roosevelt, Harold to Mortimer, 15 Mar. 1933, RMP; 'rotting plants' in Harold to Mortimer, Mar. (undated) 1933, RMP; and 'spoilt children', Harold to Ben, 23 Feb. 1933, LL.

33. 'Pretty pile', in Harold to Mortimer, 6 Apr. 1933, RMP; 'oratorical powers', *V–H*, Harold to Vita, 23 Feb. 1933, 242–43 ; and 'exhausted', Harold to Mortimer, Mar. (undated) 1933, RMP.

34. Harold to Michael Sadleir, 11 Oct. 1932, CP.

35. For Joyce, *ND*, i, 4 Feb. 1934, 164–65; and visits to Munich and Vienna, *ND*, i, 5 Feb. 1934, 165–66, 168.

36. For the passage on Proust, see Harold to Michael Sadleir, 22 June 1935, CP; **ND**, 10 Feb. 1934; and *ND*, i, 11, 18 and 19 Feb. 1934, 168–170.

37. See Harold to Michael Sadleir, 6 Oct. 1943, and 23 Aug. 1944, CP.

38. For abandoning Proust, see *ND*, i, 11 Feb. 1934, 168; and 'self-advertisement', **ND**, 21 Aug. 1935.

39. See **ND**, 26 June 1934, and *ND*, i, 26 June 1934, 176.

40. In *ND*, i, 195.

41. See Harold to Mortimer, 16 Oct. 1934, RMP, and Harold to 'Darling Mummy', 30 Sept. 1934, SP.

42. For Anne and Charles Lindbergh, *ND*, i, 30 Sept. 1934, 180; Harold to Vita, 13 and 15 Oct. 1934, LL; and Harold to 'Darling Mummy', 7 Oct. 1934, SP. For Jon, Harold to 'Darling Mummy', 30 Sept. 1934, SP.

43. For Morrow, see *ND*, i, Harold to Vita, 26 Oct. and 17 Nov. 1934, 186, 189–90.

44. For 'ghastly', see Harold to Vita, 13 Oct. 1934, LL; Round Table, Harold to 'Darling Mummy', 4 Nov. 1934, SP ; 'smarminess', in *ND*, i, Harold to Vita, 17 Nov. 1934, 189–90 ; 'quality', Harold to Vita, 13 Oct. 1934,

LL; and 'Rockefeller Centre', Harold to Mortimer, 16 Oct. 1934, RMP.

45. For 'crawls along', *ND*, i, Harold to Vita, 16 Feb. 1935, 197–98; on Elisabeth Morrow, *ND*, i, 23 Sept. 1934, 179; formidable combination, *ND*, i, 1, 2, 4, 5 and 7 June 1935, 203–5; 'torments', *ND*, i, 4 June 1935, 205 ; 'low-class fellows', *ND*, i, Harold to Vita, 1 June 1935, 203 ; 'tone it down', *ND*, i, Harold to Vita, 2 June 1935, 204; and 'very sugary', *ND*, i, 7 June 1935, 205.

46. For reviews, see, R. L. Duffus, *New York Times Book Review* (6 Oct. 1935), and Ian F. D. Morrow, *International Affairs* (Nov. 1936).
   In an academic study of Harold's diplomatic works, the author sees *Morrow* as a link between the 'Old' classical diplomacy and the 'New' diplomacy, fashioned also by legal and financial know-how. An accurate assessment in itself; but does it go far enough in evaluating the Morrow biography? See Derek Drinkwater, 'Professional Amateur: Sir Harold Nicolson's Writings on Diplomacy' (thesis, University of Queensland, 1977), 43–44.

47. Quotations in Lees-Milne, *Harold Nicolson*, ii, 87, and *DNB*.

48. Physical details in CSC (Civil Service Commission)/11/203, NA; quotation in Lees-Milne, ii, 203.

49. For giddiness and fainting, *ND*, i, 17 Apr. 1938, 335, and Lees-Milne, i, 300; 'obese' in, *ND*, i, 31 Jan. 1932, 109; and Clandeboye *ND*, i, 1 Sept. 1936 , 271.

50. See Harold to Mortimer, 25 Apr. 1934, RMP, and *ND*, i, 25 Mar. 1934, 171–72.

51. For weak bladder, Harold to Vita, 2 Mar. 1936, LL; and dieting, Harold to Vita, 5 June 1931, LL.

52. See Nigel Nicolson, *Long Life*, 1–2, 9; *PoM*, vii; interview with Nigel Nicolson, 1 July 2002; Ben Nicolson to Philip Toynbee, 18 Sept. 1968. These remarks were made in response to a critical review by Toynbee of the third volume of Harold's published diaries. I am grateful to Ms Janice Rossen of Austin, Texas, for bringing this letter to my attention.

53. 'Prig' in Harold to Mortimer, 29 Jan. 1927, RMP; roasting chestnuts, Harold to Vita, 11 Nov. 1929, LL ; maiden flight, *ND*, i, 12 July 1935, 208–9; and for Clark, Harold to Vita, 31 Mar. 1936, LL, and *ND*, i, Harold to Vita, 11 June 1936, 264.

11. The Member for West Leicester

1. For this episode, see Robert Rhodes James, ed., *'Chips', The Diaries of Sir Henry Channon* (1967; Penguin edn, 1970), 35; **ND**, 10 June 1935; *ND*, i, 19 June, 205–6; and Harold to Michael Sadleir, 22 June 1935, CP.

2. *ND*, i, 25 June 1935, 207.

3. See **ND**, 16 and 23 Aug. 1935; and *ND*, i, 16 Aug. 1935, 210, and Harold to Oliphant, 24 Aug. 1935, 212.

4. Offered West Leicester in **ND**, 3 Oct. 1935, and *ND*, i, 3 Oct. 1935, 214; for his 'cerebral socialism', *ND*, iii, 7 May 1948, 139; and for contacts with National Liberals, see correspondence between Harold and Lord Hutchinson, 8 Aug. 1934, and 10 and 27 May 1935, LL.

5. From 'Sir Harold Nicolson Talks to Kenneth Harris', *Observer*, 12 Nov. 1961.

6. See *Politics in the Train* (Constable, 1936): sold as a sixpenny pamphlet.

7. *ND*, ii, 13 Jan. 1940, 57.

8. Quotations in **ND**, 30 Oct. and 9 Nov. 1935; and *ND*, i, 1 and 7 Nov. 1935, 221, 223.

9. Liberal intervention, Harold to Raymond Mortimer, 1 Nov. 1935, RMP, and *ND*, i, 13 Nov. 1935, 223; '48 per cent' in *ND*, i, Harold to Vita, 7 Nov. 1935, 222; on Vita, **ND**, 27 Oct. 1935; and Duff Cooper, *ND*, i, 2 Nov. 1935, 222.

10. See *ND*, i, 14 Nov. 1935, 224–5.

11. *ND*, i, 15 Nov. 1935, 226.

12. Harold to Vita, 18 Feb. 1936, LL; also in *ND*, i, 18 Feb. 1936, 243–44.

13. See Harold to Vita, 27 Nov. 1935, LL.

14. Harold to Vita, 20 Nov. 1935, LL.

15. For Churchill, *ND*, i, Harold to Vita, 4 Dec. 1935, 228–29; for Baldwin, **ND**, 4 Feb. 1936.

16. As Ramsay's *PPS*, ND, i, Harold to Vita, 18 Feb. 1936, 234–44; mocking the idea, Harold to Vita, 18 Feb. 1936, LL; and no future for National Labour, *ND*, i, 28 and 30 Jan. 1936, 241, 242. For Tory Socialism, *V–H*, Harold to Vita, 20 Nov. 1935, 279–80.

17. Details of Hoare–Laval plan in NA, CAB.23/82, C.P.235; and for the Cabinet approving it, see cabinet conclusions for 2 Dec. 1935, CAB.23/82.

18. For Baldwin's 'confidence' speech; Harold's reaction to Hoare's speech; and Harold's 'knees', see *ND*, i, 19 Dec. 1935, 232–33.

19. See *PD*, Commons, v. 307, cols 2076–81, 19 Dec. 1935; **ND**, 16 Dec. 1935; *ND*, i, 19 Dec. 1935, 232–33; and Harold to Vita, 10 Dec. 1935, LL. Also Harold's article, 'A Case of Conscience', *The News-Letter* (Dec. 1935), LL.

20. *ND*, i, 19 Dec. 1935, 232–33; and James, *'Chips'*, 64.

21. **ND**, 4 Feb. 1934.

22. For the Rhineland discussions, see Rose, *Vansittart*, 189–92: in particular, NA, FO.371/18851, C.7533/55/18 (a memorandum of 21 Nov. 1935 by Orme Sargent and Ralph Wigram), and CAB.24/260, CP.42,

43(36). And for Harold to Foreign Affairs Committee, **ND**, 27 Feb. 1936, and James, *'Chips'*, 77.

23. Mood in House, *ND*, i, 9 and 10 Mar. 1936, 248–49; to mother and Vita, Harold to 'Darling Mummy', 12 Mar. 1936, SP, and Harold to Vita, *ND*, i, 10 Mar. 1936, 249.

24. See Harold Nicolson, 'Germany and the Rhineland' (Royal Institute for International Affairs, March–April 1936): Harold's address was given on 18 March; also *PD*, Commons, v.310, cols 1468–72, 26 Mar. 1936; and Nicolson, 'Has Britain a Policy?', *Foreign Affairs* (July 1936).

25. See 'Questions to be Addressed to the German Government', NA, CAB.24/262, C.P.127 (36).

26. See his Chatham House address, also for his justification of French policy; for 'encirclement', see *ND*, i, 27 Feb. 1936, and James, ed., *'Chips'*, 77.

27. These sentiments, typical of the anti-appeasement camp as a whole, were made by Sir Robert Vansittart. See his minutes of 1 Dec. 1935, NA, FO.371/18852, C.8852/55/14.

28. For Eden see Harold's Chatham House address, and Harold to Vita, 22 Mar. 1936, LL, where he speaks of Eden's 'tremendous triumph' in the House; for 'ginger groups', **ND**, 25 June and 13 Sept. 1936; and moral dilemma, **ND**, 21 May 1936, also Olson, *Harold Nicolson*, 21 May 1936, 97–98.

29. See *PD*, v.325, cols 775–79, 18 June 1937.

30. For his East Africa trip see Harold to Vita, 13 Jan. 1937, LL; and letters to Vita, Jan.–Feb. 1937, LL; also *V–H*, Harold to Vita, 27 Feb. 1937, 293–94; and *ND*, i, 23 Jan. to 22 Feb. 1937, 291–95. Also *Higher Education in East Africa. Report on the Commission appointed by the Secretary of State for Colonies* (HMSO, Sept. 1937).

31. Quotations in **ND**, 22 Aug. 1921, and 13 Jan. 1936; also *ND*, i, 13 Dec. 1935, 232.

32. For 'second-rate', *ND*, i, 2 April 1936, 255; Ramsay MacDonald, **ND**, 23 July 1936; and 'silly little man', Harold to Vita, 6 Oct. 1936, LL; also Olsen, *Harold Nicolson*, 104.

33. See Michael Bloch, *The Reign and Abdication of Edward VIII* (Bantam Press, 1990), 29, also *DNB*. And *V–H*, Harold to Vita, 15 Dec. 1936, 289–90.
   Sir Alan Lascelles had acted as private secretary to the Prince of Wales, 1920–29; and would serve King George VI in the same capacity, 1936–43.

34. For 'a race of barbarians', *ND*, i, 11 June 1936, 263–66; for 'bejewelled', *ND*, i, 13 Jan. 1936, 238; and for 'well-intentioned' and 'sensible', *ND*, i, 18 and 26 Nov. 1936, 279–80.

35. For Mrs Simpson's engagement ring and her lies, see Greg King, *The*

Duchess of Windsor. The Uncommon Life of Wallis Simpson (New York, 1999), 184, 192; 'three sins' in Nigel Nicolson, *Long Life*, 3; and 'fool or minx', see **ND**, 30 Nov. 1936, and Olson, *Harold Nicolson*, 106.

36. For public opinion, *ND*, i, 30 Nov. 1936, 280; and 'ostriches', Harold to Vita, 2 Dec. 1936, LL.

37. No constitutional crisis, in *ND*, i, 3 Dec. 1936, 281–82; also **ND**, 4 Dec. 1936. Mrs Simpson's statement printed in James, ed., *'Chips'*, 121, foot of 39; and speaking on telephone, *'Chips'*, 118–19.

38. Morganatic marriage, King, *Duchess of Windsor*, 201; for Baldwin–Edward meetings, Bloch, *Reign*, 70–74, 102–6, 167–69, 192–94, 208. For 'blubbering together', *ND*, i, 7 Dec. 1936, 282–83; also James, ed., *'Chips'*, 117. This story was told to Harold by Oliver Baldwin, the Prime Minister's son.

39. 'Sophoclean' in *ND*, i, 10 Dec. 1936, 284–86, and Olson, *Harold Nicolson*, 108, and cheers, James, ed., *'Chips'*, 125; *'Le Roi le Veult'*, *ND*, i, 11 Dec. 1936, 287; for 'Albert the Good', *V–H*, Harold to Vita, 10 Dec. 1936, 289.

40. *'Solid'* in *ND*, i, Harold to Vita, 9 Dec. 1936, 284, and *V–H*, Harold to Vita, 10 Dec. 1936, 289; for Vita's opinion, Vita to Harold, 10 Dec. 1936, LL.

41. For Lascelles, see *V–H*, Harold to Vita, 15 Dec. 1936, 290. True to Lascelles's intuition, after the abdication the Windsors first stayed at the Schloss Enzesveld, the home of Baron Eugene de Rothschild near Vienna: they then moved on to the Schloss Wasserleonburg, near the Wörther See, for the summer of 1937.

42. See Harold to Vita, 5 Aug. 1938, LL; **ND**, 9 Aug. 1938; and *ND*, i, 5 Aug. 1938, 352. And for final assessment, **ND**, 3 March 1953, and *ND*, iii, 9 Nov. 1955, 290. (I have merged these two entries.)

43. For refusing to travel in Germany, and 'champagne-like influence', see James, ed., *'Chips'*, 143, and *ND*, i, 20 Sept. 1936, 272–73; using Mrs Simpson in Norman Rose, ed., *'Baffy', The Diaries of Blanche Dugdale, 1936–1947* (Valentine Mitchell, 1973), 10 Dec. 1936, 34; the King as 'pro-German' in *'Chips'*, 107; 'Ambassador Brickendrop', Ian Kershaw, *Hitler, 1936–1945. Nemesis* (Penguin, 2000), 23; for the King and foreign policy, see Frances Donaldson, *Edward VIII* (Weidenfeld and Nicolson, 1974; Omega edn, 1978), 193, 205 ; and for Harold's conclusions, *Daily Express*, 30 Oct. 1962.

44. See *ND*, i, 31 Dec. 1936, 288. Harold had been overly enthusiastic about the literary quality of Vita's work. It was not well received. Virginia Woolf, whose opinion Vita valued above all others, thought *Saint Joan of Arc* 'massive and wholesome', 'a good hack work' (Glendinning, *Vita*, 284].

12. 'The Foreign Office Mind'

1. See *PD*, Commons, v.317, cols 17–21, 3 Nov. 1936; *ND*, i, 4 and 7 Nov. 1936, 277–78; and James, ed., *'Chips'*, 97.
2. For 'Kerensky', *ND*, i, 8 Aug. 1936, 270; as anti-Franco, **ND**, 12 Apr. 1937; to Eden, Harold to Vita, 24 Nov. 1936, LL; on Guernica, *V–H*, Harold to Vita, 29 Apr. 1937, 294–95; and his comments to the House, *PD*, v.322, cols 1091–95, 14 Apr. 1937, and v.326, cols 1889–94, 19 July 1937.
3. See *ND*, i, 15 and 27 July 1937, 307–310: in the narrative I have telescoped these two meetings together.
4. See **ND**, 15 Nov. 1937; also *ND*, i, 15 Nov. 1937, 312, and 29 Mar. 1938, 332.
5. For 'Salter's Soviet', see, **ND**, 18 and 19 Dec. 1937, and 15–16 Jan., 6 Feb., 8 Mar. and 15 May 1938; Sidney Astor, ' "Salter's Soviet": Another View of All Souls and Appeasement', in *Power, Personalities and Policies: Essays in Honour of Donald Cameron Watt*, ed. Michael Fry (Frank Cass, 1992), and Rose, *The Cliveden Set*, 185–86.
6. See *ND*, i, 31 Dec. 1937, 315–16, and 17 Feb. 1938, 322.
7. See *ND*, i, 15, 17 and 20 Feb. 1938, 322–23.
8. For his 'leaders', *ND*, i, Harold to Vita, 25 Feb. 1938, 325–26: ; and 'separate entity', **ND**, 20 July 1938.
9. See Norman Rose, 'The Resignation of Anthony Eden', *Historical Journal*, 25, 4 (1982); *ND*, i, Harold to Vita, 22 Feb. 1938, 323–34; and David Carleton, *Anthony Eden* (Unwin Paperback, 1986), 119–31.
10. For Harold's speech, see *PD*, Commons, v.332, cols 99–104, 21 Feb. 1938; *ND*, i, 22 Feb. 1938, 323–25; and James, ed., *'Chips'*, 182.
11. *ND*, i, Harold to Vita, 25 Feb. 1938, 325–26.
12. For supporting the government, *ND*, i, 15 Mar. 1938, 331; and Harold to Vita, 10 and 14 Mar. 1938, LL.
13. See *PD*, Commons, v.333, cols 521–525, 16 Mar. 1938; *ND*, i, 16 Mar. 1938, 331–32. Harold made the same point to Sir Alexander Cadogan, Permanent Under-Secretary at the Foreign Office, adding to the taking of Minorca the taking of Ceuta, a city in Spanish Morocco. (Quoted in Astor, '"Salter's Soviet."', 159.)
    Minorca, the second largest of the Balearic islands, had been a focus of attention for British strategists since the War of the Spanish Succession (1702–13); and Britain had indeed occupied it for prolonged periods since the early eighteenth century.
14. For 'insurgents', James, ed., *'Chips'*, 190–91; and Foreign Affairs Committee, *ND*, i, Harold to Vita, 25 Feb. 1938, 326–27 and 7 Apr. 1938, 333.

15. For Vansittart's 'mission', **ND**, 8 Oct. 1936; and for Balkan tour, *ND*, i, 16–26 Apr. 1938, 334–38.

16. See **ND**, 22 Mar. 1938.

17. For Henlein, see a letter from Harold in *The Times*, 5 June 1953, categorically refuting specious claims made by Sir Walford Selby in his memoirs, *Diplomatic Twilight* (1953), 73, about Henlein's visit and Vansittart's role in this affair. (For Selby's largely inaccurate memoirs and animosity towards Vansittart, see Rose, *Vansittart*, 267–68.) Also for the Henlein visit, see Harold to Vita, 14 May 1938, LL; *ND*, i, 13 May 1938, 340–41; and Nicolson, *Why Britain is at War*, 78–79. For Foreign Office attitude, see David Dilks, ed., *The Diaries of Sir Alexander Cadogan, 1938–45* (Cassell, London, 1971), 77. For Runciman, ND, 24 July 1938.

18. **ND**, 4 Sept. 1938; also Olson, *Harold Nicolson*, 131.

19. See *Diplomacy* (Oxford, 1939, 3rd edn, 1969), 3, 20, 25–27, 41, 52, 55, 78–79, 143.

20. For 'no conception', *ND*, i, 26 Aug. 1938, 358; fervent admirer, **ND**, 15 Sept. 1938 and *ND*, i, 14 Sept. 1938; for 'two hoots', Keith Feiling (quoting from Chamberlain's diary), *The Life of Neville Chamberlain* (Macmillan, 1947, 367), and for conscience pricked and 'Baffy', Harold to Vita, 19 Sept. 1938, LL, *ND*, i, 20 Sept. 1938, 362, and Rose, *'Baffy'*, 100.

21. Eden 'shying off' in *ND*, i, 19 and 29 Sept. 1938, 361, 371–72; at Morpeth Mansions, *ND*, i, 22 and 26 Sept. 1938, 363–65, 366–68; and at Sissinghurst, Vita to Harold, 20 Sept. 1938, LL, *ND*, i, 26 Sept. 1938, 366, and Vita to Harold, *ND*, i, 27 Sept. 1938, 368.

22. For the Commons session, see *ND*, i, 28 and 29 Sept. 1938, 369–72, and James, ed., *'Chips'*, 211–14; 'fly again' quoted in Bruce Lockhart, *Comes the Reckoning* (London, 1947), 9.

23. For Vansittart's advice, *ND*, i, 30 Sept. 1938, 373; for Harold's Manchester speech and misquote, see *The Times*, 2 Oct. 1938, and *ND*, i, 1–4 Oct. 1938, 373–75.

24. For the Munich debate see *PD*, Commons, v.339, cols 30–162, 169–308, 337–454, 3–5 Oct. 1938. Harold spoke on 5 Oct., *PD*, Commons, v.339, cols 426–434.

25. For Elliot, quoted in Rose, *'Baffy'*, 112; and for Chiefs of Staff, NA, CAB.53/41. CoS Paper, 770.

26. At West Leicester, Harold to Vita, 19 Oct. 1938, LL, *ND*, i, 13 Oct. 1938, 376, *V–H*, Harold to Vita, 10 Oct. 1938, 307–8, and *The Times*, 10 Oct. 1938; for ginger group, **ND**, 8 Nov. 1938, also *ND*, i, Harold to Vita, 9 Nov. 1938, 377–78; not a 'rebel', **ND**, 30 Apr. 1962; and for Eden, *ND*, i, 24 Nov. 1938 and 18 July 1939, 380–81, 406.

27. See **ND**, 23 April 10 Oct. 1937.
28. See Harold to Evelyn Wrench, ? Dec. 1928, BL, Add. 59543, f. 112; for three anthologies, p. 329, n2; and Harold to Michael Sadleir, 22 Nov. 1945, CP.
29. Lists of radio talks for 1938–39 among the Sissinghurst Papers; for television, **ND**, 11 and 15 May 1939; for James Joyce, **ND**, 28 Apr. 1939, and Chapter 8, p. 21; and Byron, **ND**, 28 Dec. 1938.
30. For meeting Burgess, Harold to Vita, 16 June 1938, LL, and *ND*, i, 17 Mar. 1936, 252; for 'England's shame', *ND*, i, 19 Sept. 1938, 361; and for Richmond, *ND*, i, 23 Nov. 1938, 380.
31. At the Travellers' Club, **ND**, 22 Nov. 1937. Also Friedel to 'Dear Mr Harold Nicolson', 21 Sept. 1939, LL. The syntax and contents of the letter, together with the name, 'Friedel' (barely decipherable), indicates that the writer was young and not an English-speaker.
32. Travelling 'third class' in **ND**, 7 Feb. 1938; for *Great Contemporaries*, Harold to 'Dear Winston Churchill', 21 July 1937, CHAR 8/548. For Other Club, see Rose, *Churchill*, 196 and p. 376, n14; and for being refused admission to the Other Club, letters of 24 Mar. and 4 July 1936, CHAR 2/252/63, and CHAR 2/256/20.
33. Quoted in Lees-Milne, *Through Wood and Dale*, 235.
34. For the *Mar*, Harold to Vita, ? Oct. 1938, LL; *V–H*, Harold to Vita, 8 May 1939, 311; and *ND*, i, 4–22 Aug. 1939, 408–11.
35. For fire, *V–H*, Vita to Harold, 18 Jan. 1937, 291; and lightning, Harold to Vita, 7 July 1938, LL.
36. Much has been written about the garden at Sissinghurst, see in particular, Scott-James, *Sissinghurst: The Making of a Garden*; Jane Brown, *Vita's Other World* (1985) and *Sissinghurst. Portrait of a Garden* (1990); and Tony Lord, *Gardening at Sissinghurst* (1995). Also *Sissinghurst Castle Garden* (National Trust, 1994), and Nigel Nicolson, *Sissinghurst Castle*, 46 and *Long Life*, 211–13.
37. **ND**, 7 May 1939, and Glendinning, *Vita*, 301.
38. For 'stunned', **ND**, 29 July 1938; for Shiant, **ND**, 18 Mar. 1937, *ND*, i, 31 Dec. 1936, 287–88, and 9 and 10 Aug. 1938, 352–53; and Nigel Nicolson, *Long Life*, 235–37. The three islands cost £1,400, moneys that Nigel raised from his inheritance of £11,000, courtesy of Lady Sackville: the islands remain in the family to this day.
39. For Eric, Harold to Vita, 2 Dec. 1936, LL; and for Freddy, **ND**, 24 May 1938.
40. For literary 'ambitions', Michael Holroyd, *Works on Paper* (Abacus, 2003), 86. Also Glendinning, *Vita*, 251–52, 284, 289.
41. For 'highbrow', Vita to Harold, 24 Aug. 1939, LL: an extract from this

letter has been published in *ND*, i, 413; and for asymmetry and sacrifice, Harold to Vita, 11 July 1938, LL, and *ND*, i, 348–49.
Vita did finish another epic poem, *The Garden* (1942–46). Although written in the manner of *The Land*, it was not as successful.

42. Quotations in *V–H*, 4 Dec. 1924, 125–26; Souhami, *Mrs Keppel*, 221; *PoM*, 181. Also see Glendinning, *Vita*, 164, 306–7.

43. Losing faith in Chamberlain: Harold to Vita, 24 Oct. 1938 LL; *ND*, i, 30 Nov. 1938, 381–82; **ND**, 7 Mar. 1939. Also *ND*, i, 20 Jan. 1939, and Harold to Vita, 7 Feb. 1939, 389–90, 390–91.

44. For 'war or surrender', **ND**, 8 Apr. 1939; as 'stupid man', **ND**, 13 Apr. 1939; for 'similar action', **ND**, 13 Apr. 1939; and 'yes-men', **ND**, 18 and 21 Apr. 1939; and as 'younger', **ND**, 14 Apr. 1939.

45. For details, see Cmd. 6109: *Palestine: A Statement of Policy* (HMSO, May 1939).

46. For verbal acrobatics, *PD*, Commons, v.345, cols 2524–27, 3 Apr. 1939; and May White Paper, **ND**, 18 May 1939, and Olson, *Harold Nicolson*, 17 May 1939, 150.
For May White Paper parliamentary debate, *PD*, Commons, v. 347, cols 1937–2056, 2129–2190, 22 and 23 May 1939. In the Commons debate the government suffered, in effect, a vote of no confidence, its massive majority cut to 89. It is worth noting that a year later, in the vote over the abortive Norwegian campaign, the government scraped through with a majority of only 81, a vote that led to the collapse of Chamberlain's government.

47. 'No power', in *ND*, i, 29 Dec. 1938, 383; for Boothby's criticism, **ND**, 6 June 1939; and for Harold's *mea culpa*, *ND*, i, Harold to Boothby, 7 June 1939, 402–3.

48. Defending Chamberlain, **ND**, 25 March 1939; League of Nations Union, *ND*, i, 10 Nov. 1938, 378.

49. For Koestler, see *ND*, i, 21 April 1937, 298, and *The Times*, 2 June 2003. His experiences in Spanish and French prisons provided the material for two of his books, *Spanish Testament* (1937), and *Scum of the Earth* (1941).
I am grateful to Professor Susan Pedersen of Harvard University for bringing the Rathbone connection to my attention. The Children's Minimum Campaign Committee sought to obtain free or subsidised milk and meals for deprived children. Harold was a firm advocate of these benefits. See his attempt to persuade the House in *PD*, Commons, v.325, cols. 775–80, 18 June 1937.

50. Eden's press campaign, **ND**, 29 June 1939; brouhaha in Commons, **ND**, 3 Apr. 1939.

51. See Harold's article, 'Is War Inevitable?', *The Nineteenth Century and After* (July 1939).
52. *V–H*, Harold to Vita, 25 Aug. 1939, 314–15.
53. The following passage is drawn from **ND**, 25 Aug.–3 Sept. 1939; *ND*, i, 22–23 Aug. and 1–3 Sept. 1939, 411–12, 416–22; John Barnes and David Nicolson, eds, *The Leo Amery Diaries* (1980; 1988), ii, 570–71; Rose, *'Baffy'*, 150–51; James, ed., *'Chips'*, 260–65. There is a detailed account of these events in D. C. Watt, *How War Came: The Immediate Origins of the Second World War* (1989), ch. 30.
54. For these incidents, see *ND*, i, 3 Sept. 1939, 420–22.
55. See Nigel Nicolson, *Long Life*, 81.

13. The War Years

1. See Michael Sadleir to Harold, 18 Nov. 1939, CP; Nicolson, *Why Britain is at War*, in particular 21, 132, 133, 135–41, 145–49, 155, 156–57, 159. Also *ND*, ii, 25 Sept. 1939, 21, 37.
   Crowe's paper, 'Memorandum on the Present State of British Relations with France and Germany' (January, 1907), appears in G. P. Gooch and H. Temperley, *British Documents on the Origins of the First World War* (1929–38), iv, Appendix A.
2. James, ed., *'Chips'*, 306–7, and Rose, *Churchill*, 261.
3. See **ND**, 30 June 1940.
4. For Vita, Ben and Nigel, Vita to Harold, 18 Oct. 1939, LL, and *ND*, ii, 29.
5. For Political Intelligence Department, Harold to Vita, 12 Oct. 1939, LL; the odd question, *PD*, Commons, v.352, col.1044, 19 Oct. 1939; and wavering, Harold to Vita, 24 Oct. 1939, LL.
   For the Eden group, *ND*, ii, 3 Oct. 1939, 38, and 17 Jan. and 17 Apr. 1940, 58, 72. The group usually met without Eden, who was now a member of the government as Secretary of State for Dominions, though without a seat in Cabinet.
6. For visit to France, see *ND*, ii, 29–31 Oct. 1939, 40–45; and for depressing fact, *ND*, ii, 25 Nov., 46.
7. 'Won the war at sea', *ND*, ii, 27 Mar. 1940, 64; on the *Graf Spee*, *ND*, ii, 14 Dec. 1939, 50–51; for Harold's French tour, *ND*, ii, 8–16 Mar. 1940, 60–63; and at Maxim's, *ND*, ii, 14 Mar. 1940, 61–62.
   Narvik, a coastal town in northern Norway, was considered to be a key factor in disrupting Swedish iron-ore supplies to Germany; seizing Baku, on the Caspian, would deny Germany and Russia its rich oil reserves.

8. For Lloyd George, *ND*, ii, 30 Apr., 3 and 4 May 1940, 74–74; for Churchill, Harold to Vita, 1 May 1940, LL, and *ND*, ii, 30 Apr. 1940, 74; and for Labour, *ND*, ii, 30 Apr. 1940, 74.

9. The above account is based on *ND*, ii, 7–8 May 1940, 76–80; James, ed., '*Chips*', 299–300; Rose, '*Baffy*', 168–69. See also Rose, *Churchill*, 260–61. The House divided technically on a motion of adjournment, which in fact was a vote of censure on the government's conduct of the war. The actual figures for the division were 281 for the government, 200 against. Amongst those who voted against were 33 Conservatives and 8 other supporters, while another 60 Conservatives abstained.

10. See *ND*, ii, 9–10 May 1940, 80–84.

11. Joins government, *ND*, ii, 17 May 1940, 86, and as 'white mouse', Harold to Vita, 18 May and Vita to Harold 19 May 1940, LL.

12. 'In danger', Harold to Vita, 4 June 1940, LL (other extracts of this letter are in *ND*, ii, 92–93); 'anaesthetised', *ND*, ii, 15 June 1940, 95–96. 'The bare bodkin' in *ND*, ii, 26 May 1940, 89–90: 'the bare bodkin' was eventually supplied by a Swiss doctor, Pierre Lansel, an acquaintance of Raymond Mortimer.

For the 'Special Search List', see *Invasion 1940. The Nazi Invasion Plan for Britain by SS General Walter Schellenberg* (St Ermin's Press, 2000), Introduction by John Erickson. Schellenberg, Chief of Bureau IVE of the RSHA (Reichssicherheitshauptamt), the department responsible for counter-espionage, 'hurriedly and carelessly' compiled the 'Black Book' in May 1940. Drawn up in no particular order of priorities, it contains many anomalies: for example, Lytton Strachey, and the spy, Sidney Reilly, both long dead, make an unexpected appearance.

13. **ND**, 21 May 1940.

14. For Davidson, see **ND**, 28 May 1941; and for 'questions', *PD*, Commons, v.366, p. 459; also v.375, pp. 349–50.

John Colin Campbell (first Viscount) Davidson was a Tory stalwart, the intimate of Bonar Law and Baldwin. A former chairman of the Conservative Party, he had acquired a reputation as something of a wheeler-dealer, a behind-the-scenes manipulator. Although he officially retired in 1937, he was employed at the Ministry of Information at the same time as Harold.

15. 'Failure in life', ND, 24 Aug. 1940; and effective propaganda, *ND*, ii, 3 Aug. 1940, 104–5.

16. See Cooper, *Old Men Forget*, 285–88, and John Charmley, *Duff Cooper* (Macmillan PaperMac edn, 1987), 29, 92–94, 141–53.

17. Beaverbrook intrigues, **ND**, 5 Aug. 1940; and Commons speeches, *PD*, Commons, v.371, col.1826, 27 May 1941; also v. 367, cols 1315–18, 18 Dec. 1940.

18. For fobbed off, *PD*, Commons, v.365, col.480, 10 Oct. 1940; also v.369, col. 1144, 11 Mar. 1941, and v.371, col. 22, 22 April 1941; vague generalities, Harold to Lord Cecil, 21 Sept. 1940, BL, Add. 51186, f. 83; Churchill, in Rose, *Churchill*, 303, and *ND*, ii, 22 Jan. 1941, 139; for 'imagination quails', *ND*, ii, 8 Nov. 1940, 126; and 'light of faith', *ND*, ii, 2 Mar. 1941, 149.

19. I was unable to trace his paper in the files of of the MoI, but its general contents, and its fate, can be seen in *ND*, ii, 12, 16 July and 3 Dec. 1940, 101, 102–3, 130.

20. Quotation from broadcast on 24 Apr. 1941 (in French): other talks on ? Mar. (in English), 28 Apr. (in German), and 1 July 1941(in English). Transcripts in NA, INF 1/175.

21. 'End of France', *V–H*, Harold to Vita, 26 June 1940, 325; and British attack, *ND*, ii, Harold to Vita, 10 July 1940, 100.

22. On meeting 'eternal' France, *ND*, ii, 20 Jan. 1941, 138, and *V–H*, Harold to Vita, 21 Jan. 1941, 333–34; 'out of earshot', **ND**, 1 July 1942.

23. For sleeping perfectly, Harold to Vita, 17 Sept. 1940, LL; Senate House 'Splaaassh', *ND*, ii, 8 Nov. 1940, 126; King's Bench Walk, *V–H*, Harold to Vita, 16 Oct. 1940, 331–32, and *ND*, ii, 2 Jan. 1941, 136; Ben in Harold to Vita, 18 Sept., LL; and 'WIN THIS WAR', Harold to Vita, 24 Sept. 1940, LL.

24. 'Vegetable existence' in *ND*, ii, 31 Jan. 1941; for slacking, **ND**, 23 Aug. 1940; and for deeply 'ashamed', Harold to Vita, 9 Apr. 1940, LL, and Harold to John Lehmann, 4 June 1943, HRC; also *ND*, ii, 2 Apr. 1940, 65.

25. For Virginia Woolf: **ND**, 31 Mar. 1941; *V–H*, Vita to Harold, 31 March 1941, and Harold to Vita, 2 Apr. 1941, 335–37; *ND*, ii, Vita to Harold, 2 Apr. 1941 (in reply to Harold's 'more determined' letter), Harold to Vita, 3 Apr. 1941, and Vita to Harold, 8 Apr. 1941, 158–59. For afterthoughts on Virginia: *V–H*, Vita to Harold, 8 Nov. 1949, 391–92, and *ND*, iii, 14 Oct. 1953, 247.

26. See Churchill to Harold, 18 July 1941, CHAR 20/22A; 'error of judgment', Rose, *Churchill*, 278–80.

27. 'Twisted girders', *ND*, ii, 16 May 1941, 166; virtually bankrupt, **ND**, 31 May 1941; and 'a Woolworth life', *ND*, ii, 4 June 1941, 170.

28. See **ND**, 21 July and 25 Aug. 1941; *V–H*, Harold to Vita, 22 July 1941, 340–41; and *ND*, ii, 19 July 1941, 179–80.

29. For *Truth*, *ND*, ii, 28 July 1941, 183; as leader, *ND*, ii, 18 Feb. 1941, 146 ; for burial date, **ND**, 15 Aug. 1941; Churchill attacked, *ND*, ii, 14 Jan. 1942, 205; for peerage and 'national figure', *ND*, ii, 30 Mar. 1943, 286–87, and 27 Sept. 1944, 401–2 ; and 'spiritual home', *ND*, ii, 1 Nov.

1942, 256; as an Independent, *ND*, ii, 19 Mar. 1944, 356; and for 'ruined' career, *ND*, ii, 1 Nov. 1942, 256.

30. See *ND*, ii, Harold to Lady Violet Bonham Carter, 28 Aug. 1943, 313–14.

31. As factory-worker, *ND*, ii, 8 July 1942, 234; publishing 1939 diary, **ND**, 2 and 16 Aug. 1941, and Harold to Paul Emrys-Jones, 8 Aug. 1941, BL, Add. 58247, f. 1; and for Proustian venture, *ND*, ii, 22 June 1942, 229.

32. Peacemaking, in **ND**, 14 June 1942; and *Congress of Vienna*, **ND**, 6 and 21 Sept. 1944, and *ND*, ii, 6 Jan. 1945, 429.

33. See Wilson, 'Through the Embassy Window'; and *ND*, ii, Harold to Nigel and Ben, and Vita to Harold, 21 and 23 Feb. 1944, 350–52.

34. 'Bowled over', *ND*, ii, 22 June 1941, 174; and Pearl Harbor, *V–H*, Harold to Vita, 10 Dec. 1941, 343.

35. For 'front door', *ND*, ii, 16 Feb. 1942, 211; for 'disgrace', Rose, *Churchill*, 286; and 'Why? Why? in *V–H*, Harold to Vita, 24 Feb. 1942, 344.

36. Churchill's lunch and de Gaulle, *ND*, ii, 6 and 9 Nov. 1942, 257–61; 'holds the House', Harold to Vita, 8 Oct. 1940, LL; 'ultimate accolade', *V–H*, Harold to Vita, 24 Sept. 1942, 346–47.

37. See **ND**, 24 and 26 Nov. 1942; also Lees-Milne, *Harold Nicolson*, ii, 156–57.

38. See Lees-Milne, ii, 166, who recounts this story.

39. For Ireland, see *PD*, Commons, v.378, cols 2167–69, and *ND*, ii, 16–18 Mar. 1942, 216–20; for Sweden: *V–H*, Harold to Vita, 27 Oct. 1943, 355, *ND*, ii, Harold to Nigel and Ben, 7 Nov. 1943, 325–28, and *PD*, Commons, v.393, cols 1232–37, 10 Nov. 1943; and for North Africa, *ND*, ii, 21 Apr.–11 May 1944, 361–70. His patriotism not in doubt, see *V–H*, Harold to Vita, 9 Dec. 1942, 349–50.

40. For Foreign Office reform, *PD*, Commons, v.387, cols 1388–95, and v.390, cols 1073–74, 18 Mar. and 22 June 1943; and *ND*, ii, Harold to Nigel and Ben, 18 Mar. 1943, 285. And for wider implications of the Foreign Service Act of 1943, see D. C. Watt, *Personalities and Policies. Studies in the Formulation of British Foreign Policy in the Twentieth Century* (Greenwood Press, Westport, Conn.), 188–89.

41. Atlantic Charter, **ND**, 14 Aug. 1941; ABCA pamphlet, *ND*, ii, 7 Jan. 1944, 343.

42. For France, the Soviet Union and the United States, see *PD*, Commons, v.395, cols 1599–1604, 15 Dec. 1943, v.400, cols 786–91, 24 May 1944, and v.403, cols 678–85, 29 Sept. 1944, also *ND*, ii, Harold to Nigel and Ben, 11 Jan. 1944, 344, and 23 and 25 Aug. 1944, 394–95; for Churchill, Rose, *Churchill*, 315.

43. For Harold's (and Churchill's) attitude to 'unconditional surrender', see *PD*, Commons, v.403, col. 684, 29 Sept. 1944, and *ND*, ii, Harold to

Nigel and Ben, 18 Jan. 1945, 429; and Harold reconciled to zones, *ND*, ii, 19 Apr. 1944, 359–60.

44. 'Ruthless', *ND*, ii, 30 Aug. 1944, 397.

45. For Russian expansion, see *The Congress of Vienna* (Readers Union, Constable, 1948), 26–27; debating the 'Polish question', **ND**, 21 Oct. 1944; the London Poles as 'insane', *PD*, Commons, v.403, cols 678–85, 29 Sept. 1944; and for Churchill–Mikolajczyk exchange, Rose, *Churchill*, 311.

46. Harold's Yalta speech in *PD*, Commons, v.408, cols 1477–83, 28 Feb. 1945; also **ND**, 13 Feb. 1944. Some of Harold's more telling points were prompted directly by a friendly chat he (and Buck De La Warr) had had with Churchill on 27 February. Churchill consumed 'a large brandy' and began talking. See *ND*, ii, 27 and 28 Feb. 1945, 436–38. For Soviet historians, see Timothy Garton Ash, 'From World War to Cold War', *New York Review of Books* (11 June 1987). And for Churchill's faith in Stalin, see his report to the Cabinet, 19 Feb. 1945, NA, CAB.65/51; John Colville (Churchill's private secretary), *The Fringes of Power. Downing Street Diaries, 1939–55* (1985), 562, who recorded his master as saying: 'Chamberlain had trusted Hitler as he was now trusting Stalin (though in different circumstances)'; and for Dalton, see Dalton Diaries (deposited at the London School of Economics), 23 Feb. 1945.

47. See *PD*, Commons, v.406, cols 984–88, 8 Dec. 1944; and Rose, *Churchill*, 312.

48. See *PD*, Commons, v.410, cols 115–120, 17 Apr. 1945, and *ND*, ii, Harold to Nigel and Ben, 17 Apr. 1945, 449. For Korea, *ND*, iii, 28 Nov. and 31 Dec. 1950, 195, 197.

49. 'Popular issue' and meets Beveridge, *ND*, ii, 29 July and 28 Aug. 1942, 237, 239; army identifies with report, *ND*, ii, 31 Jan. 1944, 346; debate in House, *ND*, ii, 16–18 Feb. 1943, 281–82.

50. Reaction to Beveridge, *V–H*, Vita to Harold, 2 Dec. 1942, 349, and *ND*, ii, Vita to Harold, 3 Dec. 1942, 264–65; '*Manifesto*', *V–H*, Vita to Harold, 7 Feb. 1945, 361; 'bedint marriage', *V–H*, Vita to Harold, 18 Jan. 1944, 356–57.

51. For Nigel and Ben, *V–H*, Harold to Vita, 24 Sept. and 2 Oct. 1942, and *ND*, ii, 254; for Monte Cassino, *ND*, ii, 16 Feb. and 19 Mar. 1944, 349, 356, and Nigel Nicolson, *Long Life*, 102.

52. Knole bombed, *V–H*, Vita to Harold, 16 Feb. 1944, 357, and *ND*, ii, 16 Feb. 1944, 349; 'technical speciality', **ND**, 23 July 1943; Harold's 'grandson', *ND*, ii, 21 June 1942, 228–29; and Burgess and Trefusis, Harold to John Lehmann, 4 June 1940, HRC, and **ND**, 4 Oct. 1944.

53. 'Act of friendship', Mosley, *My Life*, 410; working class prejudice, **ND**,

1 and 3 Dec. 1943; Amery and Joyce, **ND**, 7 Dec. 1945; and Wodehouse, *PD*, Commons, v.406, cols 1582–84, 15 Dec. 1944.

54. *ND*, ii, 7 Feb. 1944, 347.

55. *ND*, ii, 7 and 8 May 1945, 456–59. The other spectator was Blanche Dugdale, see Rose, *'Baffy'*, 221.

Bernays, a member of a parliamentary delegation visiting troops in Italy in January 1944, was reported missing in a flight from Rome to Athens via Brindisi. It is presumed that his light plane crashed over the Adriatic.

56. See **ND**, 15 Aug. 1941, 15, 19, 23 July 1943, and 9 Jan. 1945; also *ND*, ii, 31 May 1945, 466.

57. *ND*, ii, 27 May 1945, 465.

58. See Harold to Vita, 3 July 1945, LL. These thoughts were not included in the published letter, see *ND*, ii, Harold to Vita, 3 July 1945, 474.

59. For 'disliking Jews', *ND*, ii, 13 June 1945, 469: these were not off-the-cuff remarks; see also **ND**, 19 Mar. 1932, 'What I hate about Jews is their love of destruction.' For election campaign, *V–H*, Harold to Vita, 21 June 1945, 362–63, and *ND*, ii, Harold to Vita, 3 July 1945, 474; for British Council, *ND*, ii, 5 June 1945, 468, and Lords, **ND**, 13 Mar. 1945.

60. For 'two aspirins', *ND*, ii, 26 July 1945, 478–79.

61. 'Day of judgment', *ND*, ii, Harold to Nigel, 27 May 1945, 464–66.

62. For condolences and Mrs Dell, Harold to Vita, 1 Aug. 1945, LL, and **ND**, 29 July 1945; Churchill, *ND*, ii, 1 Aug. 1945, 479; 'happy chapter', *ND*, ii, 26 July 1945, 479.

14. The Edwardian

1. See **ND**, 1 and 15 Aug. 1945; Harold to Vita, 1 Aug. 1945, LL; and *ND*, iii, 49 and 21 Nov. 1946, 80.

2. Advent of Labour, *ND*, iii, 27 July 1945, 30; for Bevin, **ND**, 28 July 1945, and *ND*, iii, 8 Aug. 1945: 'barged about', quoted in Alan Bullock, *Ernest Bevin. Foreign Secretary 1945–1951* (Heinemann, 1983), 25; Potsdam as 'terrific', **ND**, 3 Aug. 1945; and honouring agreements, *ND*, iii, 18 Aug. 1946, 74.

3. 'Happy day', **ND**, 15 Aug. 1945 ; Harold 'amused', *ND*, iii, 7 Aug. 1945, 31.

4. Allocating time, *ND*, iii, 10 Nov. 1947, 113; *Daily Telegraph* and *Observer*, **ND**, 5 Apr. 1948, and *ND*, iii, 26 Jan. 1949, 163; and for Vita, Glendinning, *Vita*, 346–47.

5. Self-doubt, **ND**, 23 Nov. 1947; articles in *Foreign Affairs* (Apr. 1945; Jan. 1947).

6. Ben, *ND*, iii, 6 Dec. 1946, 81, and Raymond Mortimer, Lees-Milne, *Harold Nicolson*, ii, 203.

7. For Nuremberg, see *ND*, iii, 25 Apr.–3 May 1946, 57–63, 78, and **ND**, 1 May 1946.

8. The proceedings of the conference may be followed in Bullock, *Bevin*, 259, 282, 287, 300, 312, 318–19; and *ND*, iii, 26 July–16 Oct. 1946, 65–79.

9. 'Invent a woman', *ND*, iii, 27 July 1946, 68; high praise, **ND**, 23 Aug. 1946, and *ND*, iii, 2 and 22 Oct. 1946, 78, 79.

10. For Russia not 'wholly in the wrong', *ND*, iii, 9 and 18 Aug. 1946, 71, 74; 'dreadful speech', *ND*, iii, 11 Oct. 1946, 79; Bevin 'incensed', Bullock, *Bevin*, 282; Harold unrepentant, *ND*, iii, 9 Aug. 1946, 72; Attlee, *ND*, iii, 29 July 1946, 69; and liking Bevin, *ND*, iii, 6 Sept. 1946, 75–76.

11. For 'Public performance', *ND*, iii, 5 Aug. 1946, 71; defines New Diplomacy, *ND*, iii, 67; and 'third world war', *ND*, iii, 22 Aug. 1946, 75.

12. 'Safer seat', **ND**, 30 July 1945; Labour whip, **ND**, 22 Aug. 1945; Combined English Universities and Jowitt, *ND*, iii, Harold to Vita, 8 Jan. 1946, 49–51.

13. See **ND**, 3, 5, and 13 Mar. 1947: the latter entry includes correspondence between Harold and Violet Bonham Carter, 12–13 Mar.

14. For scraping his conscience, *ND*, iii, 28 Feb. 1947, 90–91; 'evolution', Harold to Vita, 20 Nov. 1929, LL; the press, *ND*, iii, 12 Mar. 1947, 94; unnamed Tory and 'crown of thorns', *ND*, iii, Harold to Vita, 26 Mar. 1947, 94; 'struck dumb', *ND*, iii, Nigel's Diary, 5 Mar. 1947, 92; mother and Freddy, *ND*, iii, 13 Mar. 1947, 94; and Vita , *ND*, iii, Vita to Harold, 7 Mar. 1947, 93.

15. Nominated, *ND*, iii, 17 Dec. 1947, 119–20; material comforts and 'bedint restaurant', *V–H*, Harold to Vita , 24 Feb. 1948, 379–80, and *ND*, iii, 25 Feb. 1948; and the Travellers', *ND*, iii, Harold to Vita, 28 Feb. 1948, 128.

16. Enjoys canvassing, *ND*, iii, 29 Feb. 1948, 128; Ella Boln, **ND**, 4 Mar. 1948; not liking 'the masses', quotations in *ND*, iii, 55, 139, and Harold to Vita, 4 Mar. 1948, LL (quoted in Olson, *Harold Nicolson*, 331); 'Not a soul', **ND**, 4 Mar. 1948; 'friendship and matiness', *V–H*, Harold to Vita, 10 Mar. 1948, 381; Herbert Morrison, *ND*, iii, 4 Mar. 1948, 130; and consoling himself, *ND*, iii, Harold to Vita, 5 Mar. 1948, 131.

17. For 'a bloody place', see *ND*, iii, Harold to Vita, 12 Mar. 1948, 132–33; 'sense of failure', **ND**, 18 Apr. 1948; and 'cardinal error', *ND*, iii, 15 June 1950, 190–91.

18. See 'Losing a By-Election', in *Comments, 1944–48*, 301–5; also printed in *ND*, iii, 19 Mar. 1948, 133–37.

19. See *ND*, iii, 28 May 1948, 140–41.

20. Character traits in **ND**, 25 Aug. 1945: this confession first appeared in

an appendix to his novel, *Public Faces*, though here, for effect, he used an archaic form of spelling; for 'A Defence of Shyness', see Nicolson, *Small Talk*; and for contemplating life at sixty, *ND*, iii, 21 Nov. 1946, 80–81.

21. For 'human tragedies', *ND*, iii, 28 Apr. 1952, 224; 'gait of an old man', *ND*, iii, 28 May 1950, 190; also *ND*, iii, 29 Dec. 1949, 178–79; dental problems, **ND**, 17, 18, 26 July 1951; and 'no sex passions', **ND**, 21 Nov. 1951.

22. Details in **ND**, Dec. 1950: he earned £1,022 from the BBC; his royalties came to £1,471 17; and he received from the *Spectator* £819, and the *Observer*, £1,040.

23. See *ND*, iii, 141–42, and 3 June 1948, also Harold to Vita, Vita to Harold, 8 and 9 June 1948, 142–45; for doing 'silly things', *ND*, iii, Harold to Vita, 8 June 1948, 143. (In *George V* Harold did not include a Preface, but in his 'Author's Note' he wisely makes no mention of Lascelles's precautionary caveat.)

24. Korean war, *ND*, iii, 183; Royal Archives, *ND*, iii, 17 Apr. 1949, 168, and 8 Aug. 1951, 208; methodology, *ND*, iii, 9 Dec. 1948, 156, and 21 Mar. and 17 Apr. 1949, 166–68; 'chirrupy overture' and 'gift', *ND*, iii, 8 Aug. 1949, 174, and 7 Nov. 1948, 155; and Vita, *ND*, iii, 24 July 1950, 191 and n. 3.

25. For George VI's and Queen Mary's approval, *ND*, iii, 201, and Harold to Michael Sadleir, 29 July 1952, CP; for 'Gibbon', 5 Apr. 1952, **ND**, also *ND*, iii, 19 Sept. 1951, 209; 'pastiche', **ND**, 16 Apr. 1951; on George V, his diaries and the monarchy, Harold to Eddy Sackville-West, 15 Oct. 1952, BC, and *ND*, iii, 17 Jan. 1950, 184; for killing 'animals', *ND*, iii, Harold to Vita, 17 Aug. 1949, 174; on York Cottage, Harold Nicolson, *King George V: His Life and Reign* (1952) (Pan Books, 1967), 86–88. See also David Cannadine, 'From Reverence to Rigour', *TLS*, 23 Jan. 2004.

26. For Trevor-Roper, see Nigel to Raymond Mortimer, 13 Nov. 1968, RMP; for Nigel's final verdict, see Nigel to Lascelles, 11 Feb. 1967, placed in **ND**; and Harold to Eddy Sackville-West, 15 Oct. 1952, BC. See also Nicolson's, *Monarchy* (1962).

27. Author's Note to *George V*, p. 5.

28. For copies sold, *ND*, iii, 217, and **ND**, 9 Oct. 1954; 'life's work', **ND**, 18 May 1952; 'chorus of praise', *ND*, iii, 14 and 17 Aug. 1952, 226–27, and Harold to Compton Mackenzie, 1 Aug. 1952, HRC; Harold's 'best book', *ND*, iii, 3 Sept. 1955, 287; bankruptcy, *ND*, iii, 2 Jan. 1952, 218; 'Harold Nicolson Publications', **ND**, 6 Jan. 1953; and Vita's loan, *ND*, iii, 16 June 1955, 284.

29. For 'beastly', *ND*, iii, Harold to Vita, 16 June 1955, 284; accepts knighthood, **ND**, 31 Aug. 1952, and *ND*, iii, Harold to Sir Alan Lascelles, 31

Aug. 1952, 229; 'Regency Clock' and 'churlish', *V–H*, Harold to Vita, 4 Sept. 1952, 406–7; 'absurd' and 'twenty years ago', **ND**, 7 Jan. 1953; instructing publishers, Harold to Constable, 21 Dec. 1952, CP; 'bedint title', **ND**, 7 Jan. 1953; and 'a pitiful business', *ND*, iii, 7 Jan. 1953, 235–36.

30. Loving family, see, for example, *ND*, iii, 31 Dec. 1945, 29 Dec. 1946, and 31 Dec. 1955, 46, 82, 292; for Lady Carnock, Harold to Vita, 16 Mar. 1951, LL, **ND**, 9 Jan. 1951, and *ND*, iii, 12, 23 and 28 Mar. 1951, 204; and Freddy, **ND**, 19 and 23 Mar. and 28 Sept. 1951, and 16 and 31 May 1952, and Nigel Nicolson, *Long Life*, 183; also *ND*, iii, 31 May 1952, 225. Harold's second brother, Erskine (Eric) Arthur Nicolson, succeeded Freddy as third Lord Carnock.

31. See Harold to Vita, 16 Mar. and 7 Apr. 1951, LL.

32. For Croydon, *ND*, iii, Harold to Vita, 5 Mar. 1948, 131; 'Drunk as usual', **ND**, 12 Jan. 1950, and *ND*, iii, 25 Jan. 1950, 184; 'Make it "Six"' and 'depression', **ND**, 8 and 11 June 1951; Blunt's 'confession', **ND**, 13 July 1960. For moving into King's Bench Walk and procuring, private information.

33. For Vita's suspicions, Vita to Harold, Harold to Vita, 11 and 12 June 1951, LL, also *V–H*, Harold to Vita, 12 June 1951, 399–400; for 'Mephisto', Harold to Raymond Mortimer, 12 Sept. 1951, RMP; 'sorry' for Guy, *ND*, iii, 25 Feb. 1959, 365; disclaiming as 'nonsense', Burgess to Harold, 23 May ? (the year is not marked on the letter, but from its contents it is clear that it was written after 1961, Harold's seventy-fifth birthday. I am grateful to Andrew Lownie for bringing this letter to my attention).

34. For a 'good year', **ND**, 31 Dec. 1953; Vita's complaints, *V–H*, Vita to Harold, 19 Dec. 1944, 359, *ND*, iii, 273 and 17 Apr. 1955, 281; the Albany, *ND*, iii, 17 July 1952, 226–27, and 255; 'Marginal Comment', *ND*, iii, 217; Ben 'as happy', **ND**, 31 Dec. 1953; Nigel as MP, *ND*, iii, 6 and 7 Feb. 1952, 219–20; the Sackville estate, **ND**, 19 Feb. 1952; and 'excellent marriage', **ND**, 31 Dec. 1953.

35. For 'real bunny', *ND*, iii, 30 Mar. 1953, 238; 'find us shy', *ND*, iii, 1 Apr. 1953, 239; 'Tenniscourts' in De-la-Noy, *Eddy*, 251. For 'dowry', Nigel Nicolson, *Long Life*, 282; 'City gent', **ND**, 14 Apr. 1953; 'Red-letter day', *ND*, iii, 30 July 1953, 244; Philippa 'as a daughter', **ND**, 19 Oct. 1954; as grandfather, *ND*, iii, 9 June 1954 and 12 Sept. 1957, 259, 338; and Nigel blames himself, *Long Life*, 283–84.

36. 'Well, I'm blowed,' *ND*, iii, 13 Apr. 1955, 281; Ben marries, *ND*, iii, 8 Aug. 1955, 285; Luisa as 'a Florentine', *ND*, iii, 8 Aug. 1955, 286; Harold impressed, **ND**, 25 Sept. 1955; 'Pepita', *ND*, iii, 9 Aug. 1956, 307–8;

'satanic shadow', **ND**, 2 Feb. 1956; Ben's marriage crumbles and 'gutter-snipe friends', **ND**, 4, 14, 26 Aug. 1958; Vita's advice and Ben's 'ingratitude', Lees-Milne, *Through Wood and Dale*, 170.

37. For Ben's unkempt appearance and relations with Vita, Interview with Nigel Nicolson, 1 July 2002; also *DNB* and *Long Life*, 281.

38. See Nigel Nicolson, *Long Life*, 285, also 278–84 for an overall view of Ben's and Nigel's marriages.

39. For Copenhagen, Rome and Athens, see **ND**, 20 Feb.–19 Mar. 1952, and *ND*, iii, 21–22 Jan., 22–23 Feb. and 28 Feb.–12 Mar. 1952, 218, 220–21, 221–23, also *V–H*, 401–5, and Lees-Milne, *Harold Nicolson*, ii, 256–59, 263; for Paris, **ND**, 19 May 1952; and for Düsseldorf, **ND**, 3–19 Sept. 1952.

40. To the West Country, **ND**, 4–15 Aug. 1947, and *ND*, iii, 5–14 Aug. 1947, 103–6, and Lees-Milne, *Caves of Ice* (1983), 192–201; Long Crichel House, **ND**, 20–23 Aug. 1951; and garden tour, **ND**, 16–22 Aug. 1952, and *ND*, iii, 17–18 Aug. 1952, 227.

41. For the Dordogne, **ND**, 13–29 Aug. 1954 and 31 Dec. 1954, also *ND*, iii, 17–25 Aug. 1954, 261–64; for Carcassonne and Perpignan, **ND**, 30 Sept.–19 Oct. 1956, and *ND*, iii, 22 Oct. 1956; in Provence, Harold to Richard Church, 26 Oct. 1955, HRC, **ND**, 7–23 Oct. 1955, and *ND*, iii, 10–18 Oct. 1955, 288–89.

42. 'Showered upon you', *V–H*, Harold to Vita, 7 May 1953, 410–11; Balliol, **ND**, 5 May 1953; for Newcastle, *ND*, iii, 4 July 1953, 242–43; Trinity, **ND**, 2 July 1953; and Lees-Milne, *Harold Nicolson*, ii, 270.

43. For Royal Academy, *ND*, iii, 30 Apr. 1953, 239–40; and Chichele lectures, **ND**, 21 Nov. 1953.

44. London Library, *ND*, iii, 25 Oct. 1951, 211; and Classical Association, New York Academy, Lees-Milne, *Harold Nicolson*, ii, 249, 313.

45. Legion of Honour, *ND*, iii, *H–V*, 8 July 1947, 101, and 'such tinsel', **ND**, 28 May and 2 June 1960 ; 'good Germans', **ND**, 15 Oct. 1958, Harold to Vita, 23 Oct. 1958, LL, and *ND*, iii, Harold to Vita, 16 Oct. 1958, 352.

46. See **ND**, 24 and 26 Jan. 1956; Harold to Vita, 1 Jan. 1956, LL; and *ND*, iii, Harold to Vita, 25 Jan. and 7 Feb. 1956, and 29 Jan. and 9 Feb. 1956, 296–97, 298.

47. For Bevan and Boothby, **ND**, 25 July 1956; 'resounding slap', *ND*, iii, 27 July 1956, 306; Harold feared, *ND*, iii, 31 July 1956, 306; Selwyn Lloyd, use force, and government 'irresolution', *ND*, iii, 31 July and 2 Aug. 956, 306–7.

48. For 'lead to war', **ND**, 12 Sept. 1956; France 'wants a showdown', **ND**, 11 Sept. 1956; 'preventive war', *ND*, iii, 29 Oct. 1956, 311; 'Eden is

mad!', **ND**, 30 Oct., 1956; 'sacrificed our principles', *ND*, iii, 31 Oct. 1956, 312; 'a conspiracy' and 'dishonest' Eden, *ND*, iii, 2, 3 and 4 Nov. 1956, 313–15; 'worst fiasco' and Bulganin, *ND*, iii, Harold to Vita, 7 Nov., 1956, 317–18.

49. For no moral right, *ND*, iii, 4 Nov. 1956, 315; and 'What cant!', *ND*, iii, 29 Oct. 1956, 311.

50. In 'comic style', Thomas, *The Suez Affair* (1967; revised edn, Pelican Books, 1970), 183.

51. 'Smash-and-grab', in *ND*, iii, Harold to Vita, 8 Nov. 1956, 318; for collusion, **ND**, 14 Nov. 1956, and *ND*, iii, Harold to Vita, 15 Nov. 1956, 319; for ethical-style diplomacy, see his *Diplomacy* (Oxford, 1939; 3rd edn 1969), ch. 5, 'The Ideal Diplomatist'; and for Eden's failings, **ND**, 9 Nov. 1956, and Lees-Milne, *Harold Nicolson*, ii, 341.

52. These events can be followed in *Nigel Nicolson, Long Life*, 168–76.

53. Nigel recounts these events ibid., 195–202.

54. For Harold, Mortimer and Vita on *Lolita*, *ND*, iii, 4 Dec. 1958, 356, and Vita to Aileen Pippett, 12 July 1959, BC; '*libido senilis*', in *ND*, iii, Harold to Nigel, 17 Jan. 1959, 363; 'disgust and loathing', **ND**, 12 July 1959; and 'poor Nigel', Vita to Aileen Pippett, 12 July 1959, BC.

55. Blaming Weidenfeld and 'ghastly friends', **ND**, 4, 18, 20 and 27 Dec. 1958, and 26 June 1959.

56. 'Seal [Nigel's] fate', *ND*, iii, 11 Nov. 1958, 355; on Wolfenden, **ND**, 21 Nov. 1958.

57. See **ND**, 21 and 14 Nov. 1956, *ND*, iii, 20 and 24 Nov. 1956; Elvira Niggeman to Vita, 21 Nov. 1956, 319–21; and Lees-Milne, *Harold Nicolson*, ii, 297–98; winter cruises, Harold to Francis King, 24 Nov. 1956, and to Compton Mackenzie, 26 Nov. 1956, HRC (two of the contributors), and 'no compensation', Harold to Francis King, 24 Nov. 1956, HRC.

58. See **ND**, 25 Apr. 1958, 24 Feb. 1960 and 17–18 July 1961; also Vita to Harold, 18 July 1961, LL.

59. These journeys, in the above order, may be followed in detail in **ND**, Jan.–Mar. 1957; Dec. 1957– Feb. 1958; Jan.–Mar. 1959; Dec. 1959–Feb. 1960; Jan.–Feb. 1961; and Jan.–Feb. 1962. Also *ND*, iii, 26 Jan.–17 Mar. 1957, 330–32; 6 Dec. 1957–24 Jan. 1958, 340–46; 5 Jan.–9 Mar. 1959, 361–67; 3 Jan.–4 Feb. 1960, 377–80; 20 Jan.–4 Feb. 1961, 391–93; 19 Jan.–8 Feb. 1962, 405–7.

60. 'Rotten book', *ND*, iii, 13 Mar. 1960, and Harold to Vita, 10 May 1960, 383; for *Daughter of France, ND*, iii Vita to Harold, 26 Feb. 1958, 346–47.

61. For Japan, *ND*, iii, 12 Jan. 1960, 378, and Harold to Francis King, 10 Dec. 1962, HRC; South Africa, *ND*, iii, Harold to Nigel and Philippa, 24 Jan. 1960, 378–79, and Harold to Francis King, 2 Feb. 1960, HRC.

62. For Waugh and snubbing passengers, see Lees-Milne, *Harold Nicolson*, ii, 341.

63. For Magnus-Allcroft, *ND*, iii, Harold to Philippa, 24 Dec. 1957, 341–42, and **ND**, 2 Feb., 1961; Waley-Cohen, **ND**, 19 Apr. 1961; hates Arabs, **ND**, 14 Jan. 1963; anti-Catholic, *ND*, iii, 4 Nov. 1958, 355; and black waiter, Nigel Nicolson, *Long Life*, 4.

64. Sciatica and first strokes, **ND**, 1, 6, 7 April, 15 and 29 May and 5 July 1955; *ND*, iii, Harold to Vita, 28 Feb. and 3 Mar., 1955, 278, and Vita's diary, 11 Mar. 1955, 279; doctor's advice, **ND**, 6 Apr. 1955; physical and mental powers, *ND*, iii, 19 June 1955, 284; prostate, **ND**, 30 Jan. 1954; 'slouch, slough, slop', *ND*, iii, Harold to Vita, 12 Jan. 1955, 274; see also *ND*, iii, 22 Sept. 1961, 400; 'unfrightened by death', **ND**, 31 Dec. 1955, 1 Jan. 1956 and 1 Jan. 1958.

65. For 'unpredictable', **ND**, 9 Nov. 1958; arthritis, *V–H*, Vita to Harold, 19 Dec. 1944, 359; second cruise, *ND*, iii, 6 Dec. 1957–21 Jan. 1958, 340–46; bedridden, *ND*, iii, 13 Apr.–24 June 1959, 367–69; heart and nursing home, **ND**, 8 Aug. and 2 Dec. 1960.

66. See **ND**, 19 Jan.–2 June 1962, and *ND*, iii, 19 Jan.–2 June 1962, 405–15.

67. See **ND**, 6, 25, 28, 30 June, 11 and 27 July, 1 and 31 Dec. 1962.

68. Trip to Bergamo, **ND**, 23 Aug.–24 Sept., 192; 'blubberbox', Lees-Milne, *Harold Nicolson*, ii, 348; in America, **ND**, 12 Jan.–12 Feb. 1963.

69. Loss of memory and stroke, **ND**, 21–25 May 1963; Tony King and dress and personal habits, Lees-Milne, *Harold Nicolson*, ii, 350–52.

70. Mediterranean cruise, **ND**, 31 Mar.–16 Apr. 1964; and Paris, **ND**, 12–16 June 1964; financial constraints and book rights, Nigel Nicolson, *Long Life*, 15; leaves Albany, *ND*, iii, 24, and Lees-Milne, *Harold Nicolson*, ii, 351.

71. Last years and pertinent remark, *Long Life*, 15–16.

72. From a note by Kenneth Rose (one of the guests), 21 Nov. 1966, quoted in Lees-Milne, *Harold Nicolson*, ii, 353–54.

73. For Vita's poem, see Nigel Nicolson, *Long Life*, 17, and Harold's retrospective, *ND*, ii, 2 Sept. 1940, 110.

15. A Retrospective View

1. Nigel Nicolson, *Long Life*, 290.
   I have only referenced those quotations that have not appeared previously in the narrative.

2. See *ND*, iii, 31 Dec. 1949, 178; and for grandee, see David Southgate, *The Passing of the Whigs, 1832–1866* (1962), 322–23, quoted in A. N. Wilson, *The Victorians* (2002), 584.

3. See Philip Toynbee, 'Is the Novel Dead? The Defence Brief', *Observer*, 5 Sept. 1954.

4. See **ND**, 13 Oct. 1957, and Hugh Trevor-Roper, 'Lord Cranfield as He wasn't'.

5. Betjeman in Lees-Milne, *Harold Nicolson*, ii, 295, Somerset Maugham, *Diaries*, i, 13 Dec., 1934; Ben, *DNB*; and Peter Quennell, in Lees-Milne, *Through Wood and Dale*, 209.

6. See *ND*, iii, 3 Sept. 1955, 287, and 4 Dec. 1958, 355–56.

7. One evening, Harold explained to Vita, Nigel and Ben that his diary was 'a mere record of activity put down' for his 'own reference only' (*ND*, i, 23 Aug. 1938, 357). But the evidence speaks against him. See his 'Marginal Comment' on keeping a diary, *Spectator*, 2 Jan. 1942; *ND*, ii, 28 Dec. 1941, 198–99; *ND*, iii, 9 Nov. 1947, 113, and 3 Jan. 1953, 236; also Trevor-Roper, 'Lord Cranfield . . .'

8. As 'pitiable', *ND*, iii, 27 Nov. 1956, 321; 'boring', *ND*, iii, 3 Jan. 1953, 235–36; and 'Not a single', Trevor-Roper, 'Lord Cranfield . . .'

9. See *ND*, ii, Harold to Vita, 31 Mar. 1941, 156, and iii, Harold to Vita, 16 Oct. 1958, 352; and for Macmillan, Lees-Milne, *Through Wood and Dale*, 236.

10. See *V–H*, Vita to Harold, 4 June 1941 and 18 Jan. 1944, 339, 356–57; and Valentine Cunningham, 'A Prideful Pair of the Terribly Self-Possessed', *Observer*, 2 Aug. 1992.

11. See *V–H*, 13.

12. Quotations in *ND*, i, 203, and iii, 386, 387; Nigel Nicolson, *Long Life*, 4; Olson, ed., *Harold Nicolson*, 118, 331: this abridged volume contains previously unpublished extracts from Nicolson's diaries.

13. For the Turks, see Harold to Family, 10 Dec. 1913, SP; for the Arabs, ND, 14 Jan. 1963; for the Japanese, *ND*, iii, 364; for 'candlesticks', *ND*, iii, Harold to Vita, 9 Nov. 1960, 387; and for the United States and Americans, *ND*, i, 133, and iii, 243.

14. See Nigel Nicolson to Raymond Mortimer, 30 Apr. 1969, RMP, and Nigel Nicolson, *Long Life*, 4.

15. For disliking Jews, *ND*, ii, 469; and hating niggers, *ND*, iii, 379. See also Cannadine, 'Portrait of More than a Marriage', 219–20.

16. For 'epicurean', *ND*, iii, 31 Dec. 1949, 179; lacking 'competitive spirit', *ND*, ii, 1 Jan. 1940 and 8 May 1943, 55, 293–94; and for 'ironical', Ben to Philip Toynbee, 18 Sept. 1968. (I am most grateful to Janice Rosen for making this letter available to me.)

17. See *ND*, i, 19 June 1935, 209.

18. Sparrow's eulogy is summarised in Lees-Milne, *Harold Nicolson*, ii, 354–55.

BIBLIOGRAPHY

Harold Nicolson: Major Works

Paul Verlaine (1921)
Sweet Waters (1921)
Tennyson (1923)
Byron: The Last Journey (1924)
Swinburne (1926)
Some People (1927; 1944; 1959; OUP paperback edn, 1983)
The Development of English Biography (Hogarth Lectures on English
    Literature: 1927)
Sir Arthur Nicolson, Bart. Lord Carnock. A Study in the Old Diplomacy (1930)
People and Things (1931)
Public Faces (1932)
Peacemaking, 1919 (1933; revised edn, 1943; 1964)
Curzon. The Last Phase, 1919–1925. A Study in Post-War Diplomacy (1934)
Dwight Morrow (1935)
Politics in the Train (1936)
Small Talk (1937)
Helen's Tower (1937)
Diplomacy (1939; OUP paperback edn, 1969)
Why Britain is at War (Penguin Special, 1939)
The Desire to Please. A Story of Hamilton Rowan and the United Irishmen (1943)
The Congress of Vienna (1946; 1948)
The English Sense of Humour (1947)
Benjamin Constant (1949)
King George V: His Life and Reign (1952 Pan edn, 1967)
Good Behaviour (1955)
Sainte-Beuve (1957)
Journey to Java (1957)

The Age of Reason (1960)
Monarchy (1962)
Diaries and Letters (3 vols, 1966–68)

Harold Nicolson: Articles

(I have listed only those articles used in preparing this book)

'Modern Diplomacy and British Public Opinion', *International Affairs* (September–October 1935)
'Allen Leeper', *Nineteenth Century and After* (October 1935)
'Germany and the Rhineland', *Royal Institute for International Affairs* (March–April 1936)
'The Foreign Service', *The Political Quarterly* (April 1936)
'Has Britain a Policy?', *Foreign Affairs* (July 1936)
'British Public Opinion and Foreign Policy', *The Public Opinion Quarterly* (January 1937)
'National Character and National Policy', Montague Burton International Relations Lecture (University College, Nottingham, 1938)
'After Munich', *Nineteenth Century and After* (November 1938)
'Marginal Comments', *Spectator* (1939–52)*
'Is War Inevitable?', *Nineteenth Century and After* (July 1939)
'Causes and Purposes', *Nineteenth Century and After* (October 1939)
'The Diplomatic Background', in *The Background and Issues of the War* (Oxford, 1940), ed., H. A. L. Fisher
'Men and Circumstance', *Foreign Affairs* (April 1945)
'Treaty Making, 1946', *Current Affairs* (4 May 1946)
'Peacemaking', Fourth Montague Burton Lecture (University of Leeds, 19 March 1946)
'Peacemaking at Paris: Success, Failure or Farce?', *Foreign Affairs* (January 1947)
'The Origins and Development of the Anglo-French Entente', *International Affairs* (July 1954)
'The Values of Europe', *The Listener* (2 January 1958)
'Perspectives on Peace: A Discourse' (Carnegie Endowment for International Peace, 1960)

*Three anthologies of 'Marginal Comment' were published: *Marginal Comment, January–August, 1939* (1939); *Friday Mornings, 1941–1944* (1944); and *Comments, 1944–48* (1948).

'The Old and the New Diplomacy', Annual David Davies Memorial Lecture (March 1961)
'Diplomacy Then and Now', *Foreign Affairs* (October 1961)

Books and Articles

(I have included only those works that I found particularly useful in preparing this book. Unless stated otherwise, the place of publication is London.)

Addison, Paul, *The Road to 1945. British Politics and the Second World War* (1975)
Amery, L. S., *My Political Life* (1953–55), 3 vols
Amory, Mark, *Lord Berners* (1998)
Amory, Mark, ed., *The Letters of Ann Fleming* (1985)
Anon 'Socialite – Blunt' *The Times* (28 November 2002)
Astor, Sidney, '"Salter's Soviet": Another View of All Souls and Appeasement', in *Power, Personalities and Policies: Essays in Honour of Donald Cameron Watt* (1992), ed., Michael Fry
Barnes, John, and Nicholson, David, eds, *The Leo Amery Diaries* (1980; 1988), 2 vols
Bell, Anne Oliver, *The Diary of Virginia Woolf, 1915–19; 1920–24; 1925–30; 1931–35; 1936–41* (New York, 1978), vols ii, iii, v
Bell, Quentin, *Virginia Woolf* (1972), 2 vols
Berners (Lord), Gerald Hugh Tyrwhitt-Wilson, *Far From the Madding War* (1941)
Bloch, Michael, ed, *Deep Romantic Chasm. Lees-Milne Diaries, 1979–1981* (2000)
Boothby, Robert, *I Fight to Live* (1947)
—— *Recollections of a Rebel* (1978)
Branson, Noreen, and Heinemann, Margot, *Britain in the Nineteen Thirties* (1970)
Briggs, Asa, *The History of Broadcasting in the UK: The Golden Age of Wireless* (1965)
Brogan, Sir Denis, 'The Sage of Sissinghurst', *Spectator* (17 May 1968)
Brown, Jane, *Vita's Other World. A Gardening Biography of Vita Sackville-West* (Penguin, 1986)
Bullock, Alan, *Ernest Bevin. Foreign Secretary, 1945–1951* (1983)
Bury, John, 'The Ben Nicolson and Philip Toynbee Lunch Club' (talk given on the occasion of the 40th anniversary of the Club, 1 July 1992)
Busk, Sir Douglas, *The Craft of Diplomacy* (1967)
Butler (Lord, 'RAB'), *The Art of the Possible* (1971)

—— 'Problems of Diplomacy, Past and Present' (Arthur F. Yencken Lectures: Australian National University, March 1971)

Calder, Angus *The People's War* (1969)

Campbell, Roy, *Collected Poems* (1955), vol. 1

Cannadine, David, *The Decline and Fall of the British Aristocracy* (1990; Picador edn, 1992)

—— 'Lord Curzon as Ceremonial Impressario', in *Aspects of Aristocracy* (New Haven: Yale University Press, 1994)

—— 'Portrait of More than a Marriage', in *Aspects of Aristocracy*

Carey J. 'Darling We're Wonderful', *Sunday Times* (14 June 1992)

Carlton, David, *Anthony Eden* (1981; paperback edn, 1986)

Cesarani, David, *Arthur Koestler* (1999)

Charmley, John, *Duff Cooper. The Authorized Biography* (Papermac edn, 1987)

Church, Richard, 'V. Sackville-West: A Poet In A Tradition', in *Eight for Immortality* (1941)

Clogg, Richard, *Arnold Toynbee and the Koraes Chair. Politics and the Academy* (1986)

—— *A Concise History of Greece* (Cambridge, 1993)

Cockett, Richard, *Twilight of Truth: Chamberlain, Appeasement and the Manipulation of the Press* (1989)

Cooper, Alfred Duff, *Old Men Forget* (1953)

Craig, Gordon A. and Gilbert, Felix, *The Diplomats, 1919–1939* (New York, 1965), 2 vols

Crowe, Sibyl and Corp, Edward, *Our Ablest Public Servant. Sir Eyre Crowe, 1864–1925* (Braunton, Devon: Merlin Books, 1993)

Cunningham, Valentine, *British Writers of the Thirties* (Oxford, 1989)

—— 'A Prideful Pair of the Terribly Self-Possessed' (*Observer*, 2 August 1992)

De Courcy, Anne, *The Viceroy's Daughters. The Lives of the Curzon Sisters* (2000)

De-la-Noy, Michael, *Eddy. The Life of Edward Sackville-West* (1999)

De Salvo, Louise and Leaska, Mitchell A., *The Letters of Vita Sackville-West to Virginia Woolf* (Macmillan Papermac, 1985)

Dilks, David, ed., *The Diaries of Sir Alexander Cadogan, 1938–1945* (1971)

——, ed., *Studies in Britain's Foreign Policy in the Twentieth Century* (1981). 2 vols

Donaldson, Frances, *Edward VIII* (1974)

Driberg, Tom, *Guy Burgess. A Portrait with Background* (1956)

Drinkwater, Derek, 'Professional Amateur. Sir Harold Nicolson's Writings on Diplomacy' (University of Queensland, Unpublished Thesis, 1977)

Edel, Leon, *Bloomsbury: A House of Lions* (Penguin edn, 1981)

Eden, Anthony (Earl of Avon), *Full Circle: Facing the Dictators: The Reckoning* (1960–65), 3 vols

France, Peter and St Clair, William, *Mapping Lives. The Uses of Biography* (Oxford, 2002)

Gasalee, Stephen, *The Language of Diplomacy* (Cambridge, 1939)

Gathorne-Hardy, Jonathan, *The Public School Phenomenon* (Penguin edn, 1979)

Gaze, John, *Figures in a Landscape. A History of the National Trust* (1988)

Gilbert, Martin, *Sir Horace Rumbold: Portrait of a Diplomat* (1973)

Gilmour, David, *Curzon* (1994)

Gladwyn, Lord, *Memoirs* (1972)

Glendinning, Victoria, *Vita. The Life of Vita Sackville-West* (1983; Penguin edn, 1984)

Gooch, G. P., and Temperley, Harold, eds, *British Documents on the Origins of the War* (1926–38), 11 vols

Granzow, Brigitte, *A Mirror of Nazism: British Opinion and the Emergence of Hitler, 1929–1933* (1964)

Gregory, J. D., *On the Edge of Diplomacy* (1928)

Griffith, Richard, *Fellow Travellers of the Right* (Oxford, 1983)

Hankey, Lord, *The Supreme Control: At the Paris Peace Conference, 1919* (1963)

Harding, Lord *Old Diplomacy* (1947)

Harris, Kenneth, 'Prime Ministers at Close Range – Interview with Harold Nicolson' (*Observer*, 12 November 1961)

Harvey, John, *The Diplomatic Diaries of Oliver Harvey* (1970–78), 2 vols

Haskell, Francis, 'Benedict Nicolson (1914–1978)', *Burlington Magazine* (July 1978)

Headlam-Morley, Agnes, Bryant, Russell and Ciencials, Anna, eds, *A Memoir of the Paris Peace Conference, 1919* (1972)

HMSO, *Documents on British Foreign Policy, Series 1, 1a*

Holroyd, Michael, *Lytton Strachey: A Biography* (Penguin edn, 1980)

Hudson, Derek, 'Harold Nicolson', *Quarterly Review* (2 April 1967)

James, John, *Balliol College. A History* (Oxford, 1988; 2nd edn 1997)

James, Robert Rhodes, ed., *'Chips'. The Diaries of Sir Henry Channon* (1967; Penguin edn, 1970)

—— *Memoirs of a Conservative: J. C. Davidson's Memoirs and Papers, 1910–1937* (1969)

—— *Victor Cazalet. A Portrait* (1976)

—— *Anthony Eden* (1986)

Jebb (Lord), Gladwyn, *Memoirs* (1972)

Kennedy, Paul, *The Realities behind Diplomacy* (1981)

Koss, Stephen, *The Rise and Fall of the Political Press in Britain* (1984), vol. 2

—— *Asquith* (1985)

Kronenberger, Louis, 'Diary of a U Man', *Atlantic Monthly* (5 November 1966)

Lee, Hermione, *Virginia Woolf* (Vintage Books, 1997)

—— 'The Muse and the Widger', *Guardian* (22 June 2002)

Lees-Milne, James, *Another Self* (1970)

—— *Ancestral Voices* (1975)

—— *Prophesying Peace* (1977)

—— *Harold Nicolson. A Biography* (1980–81), 2 vols

—— *Caves of Ice* (1983)

—— *A Mingled Measure. Diaries, 1953–1972* (1994)

—— 'Vita Sackville-West', in *Fourteen Friends* (1996)

—— *Through Wood and Dale. Diaries, 1975–78* (1998)

Lentin, Antony, *Lloyd George and the Lost Peace: From Versailles to Hitler, 1919–1940* (2001)

Lewis, Jeremy, *Cyril Connolly. A Life* (1997)

Lindbergh, Anne Morrow, *The Tower and the Nettle. Diaries and Letters, 1936–39* (New York, 1976)

Lloyd George, David, *The Truth about the Peace Treaties* (1938), 2 vols

—— *War Memoirs* (1938), 2 vols

Louis, William Roger, *In the Name of God, Go!* (New York, 1992)

Lyall, Sir Alfred, *The Life of the Marquess of Dufferin and Ava* (1905), 2 vols

MacKnight, Nancy, ed., *Dearest Andrew: Letters from V. Sackville-West to Andrew Reiber, 1951–62* (1980)

MacMillan, Margaret, *Peacemakers: The Paris Peace Conference of 1919 and its Attempt to End War* (2001)

Maisel, Ephraim, *The Foreign Office and Foreign Policy, 1919–1926* (Sussex Academic Press, 1994)

Marquand, David, *Ramsay MacDonald* (1977)

Maurois, André, *Aspects of Biography* (New York, 1929)

Miller, J. D. B., 'The Shape of Diplomacy' (Inaugural Lecture as Professor of International Relations, Australian National University, Canberra: 17 September 1963)

Mosley, Nicholas, *Rules of the Game. Beyond the Pale: Memoirs of Sir Oswald Mosley and Family* (Dalkey Archive Press, Illinois, 1991)

Mosley, Sir Oswald, *My Life* (1968)

Muggeridge, Malcolm, *The Thirties* (1940)

Neilson, Keith, ' "My Beloved Russians": Sir Arthur Nicolson and Russia, 1906–1916', *International History Review* (1987), IX

Newsome, David, *A History of Wellington College, 1859–1959* (1959)

Nicolson, Nigel, ed., *Harold Nicolson. Diaries and Letters, 1930–1939; 1939–1945; 1945–1962* (Atheneum Press, New York, 1966–1968), 3 vols

—— *Portrait of a Marriage* (New York, 1973)

—— 'Portrait of a Love Betrayed?', *The Times* (22 September 1990)

——, ed., *Vita and Harold. The Letters of Vita Sackville-West and Harold Nicolson* (G. P. Putnam's Sons, New York, 1992)

—— *Long Life: Memoirs* (1997)

—— 'Virginia Woolf, My Mother's Lover', *Sunday Telegraph* (20 August 2000)

Nicolson, Nigel and Trautmann, Joanne, eds, *The Letters of Virginia Woolf* (1976–80), vols 2–6

Olson, Stanley, ed., *Harold Nicolson. Diaries and Letters, 1930–1964* (New York, 1980)

Otte, T. G., *Harold Nicolson and Diplomatic Theory* (1998)

—— 'Nicolson', in *Diplomatic Theory from Machiavelli to Kissinger* (2001), eds, G. R. Berridge, M. Keens-Soper and T. G. Otte

Parker, Peter, *Ackerley. A Life of J. R. Ackerley* (1989)

Pearce, Joseph, *The Friends and Enemies of Roy Campbell* (2001)

Phillips, John and Jullian, Philippe, *Violet Trefusis. Life and Letters* (1976)

Pimlott, Ben, ed., *The Second World War Diary of Hugh Dalton* (1986)

Plomer, William, ed., *A Message in Code. The Diary of Richard Rumbold, 1932–1960* (1964)

Pollock, Bertram, *A Twentieth Century Bishop: Recollections and Reflections* (1944): Foreward by Harold Nicolson

Pryce-Jones, Alan, *The Bones of Laughter* (1987)

Quennell, Peter, ed., *A Self-Portrait of James Pope-Hennessy* (1981)

Raitt, Suzanne, *Vita and Virginia. The Work and Friendship of Vita Sackville-West and Virginia Woolf* (Oxford, 1993)

Raymond, John, 'Not So Urbane', *New Statesman and Nation* (10 May 1968)

Riddell, Lord, *Intimate Diary of the Peace Conference and After* (1933)

Robbins, Keith, 'Konrad Henlein and the Sudeten Question and British Foreign Policy', *The Historical Journal*, 12, 4 (1969)

Rose, Norman, ed., *'Baffy'. The Diaries of Blanche Dugdale, 1936–1947* (1973)

—— *Vansittart: Study of a Diplomat* (1978)

—— 'The Resignation of Anthony Eden', *Historical Journal*, vol. 25, no. 2 (1982)

—— *Churchill: An Unruly Life* (1994)

—— 'Harold Nicolson: A Curious and Colourful Life', in *Still More Adventures with Britannia* (2003), ed., William Roger Louis

Roskill, Stephen, *Hankey, Man of Secrets* (1970–74), 3 vols

Rothwell, V. H., *British War Aims and Peace Diplomacy, 1914–1918* (Oxford, 1971)

Rumbold, Richard, *Little Victims* (1933)

Sackville-West, Lionel, *My Mission to the United States* (1895)

Sackville-West, Vita, *Knole and the Sackvilles* (1922)

—— *Passenger to Teheran* (1926; Penguin edn, 1943)

—— *Knole and the Sackvilles* (1949)

—— *Knole* (National Trust, 1948)

Salter, Sir Arthur, *Memoirs of a Public Servant* (1961)

Scott-James, Ann, *Sissinghurst. The Making of a Garden* (1975; 6th edn, 1983)

Shurrock, John B., *Harold Nicolson and Alfred Duff Cooper: The Historian as Politician in the Age of Appeasement* (Graduate Thesis, West Virginia University, 1975)

Skidelsky, Robert, *Oswald Mosley* (1975)

Souhami, Diana, *Mrs Keppel and Her Daughter* (1977)

Spotts, Frederic, ed., *The Letters of Leonard Woolf* (1989)

Steiner, Zara, *The Foreign Office and Foreign Policy. 1898–1914* (Cambridge, 1969)

Stevens, Michael, *V. Sackville-West. A Critical Biography* (1973)

Stuart, Charles, ed., *The Reith Diaries* (1975)

Taylor, A. J. P., *Beaverbrook* (1972)

Thomas, Hugh, *The Suez Affair* (1967; revised edn, Pelican Books, 1970)

Toynbee, Philip, 'Is the Novel Dead? The Defence Brief', *Observer*, (5 September 1954)

—— 'By God, We Are Not Vulgar', *Observer* (25 August 1968)

Trevor-Roper, Hugh, 'Lord Cranfield as He Wasn't', *Spectator* (6 September 1968)

Vansittart, Lord, *The Mist Procession* (1958)

Waterfield, Gordon, *Professional Diplomat* (1973)

Watt, Donald Cameron, *Personalities and Policies: Studies in the Formulation of British Foreign Policy in the Twentieth Century* (Greenwood Press, Connecticut, 1975)

—— *How War Came: The Immediate Origins of the Second World War* (1989)

Wilson, Edmund, 'Through the Embassy Window', *New Yorker* (1 January 1944)

Windsor, Duke of, *A King's Story* (1951)

Woolf, Leonard, *An Autobiography, 1911–1969* (Oxford, 1980), 2 vols

—— 'The Public Faces of Harold Nicolson', *Biography*, 5 (1982), 240–52

Woolf, Virginia, *Orlando* (1928)

—— 'The New Biography', in *The Essays of Virginia Woolf, 1925–1928* (1994), v.iv. ed., Andrew McNeille

Young, Kenneth, ed., *The Diaries of Sir Robert Bruce Lockhart, 1915–1938; 1939–1965* (1973; 1980), 2 vols

Foreign Office dinner party 127;
invites HN to Hackwood 130;
forsaken by George V 281; passed
over by Baldwin 134; death and
funeral 136; *see also* Nicolson, Harold:
Curzon. The Last Phase...
Curzon Line 258, 259, 260
Cyprus 92, 120*n*, 290
Czechoslovakia/Czechs: World War I
and after 61–3, 70, 89, 92, 94; and
Teschen 103–4; and France 197; and
Sudeten Germans 63, 210, 214–16,
217, 218, 219; German invasion 229,
230

D'Abernon, Edgar Vincent, Lord 122
Daily Express 122, 163, 301
Daily Mail 122, 134
Daily Mirror 267
Daily Telegraph 166, 270, 271, 301
Daladier, Édouard 218, 239
Dalton, Hugh 260
D'Annunzio, Gabriele 105
Dansey, Pat 83
Dardanelles, the 49, 109
Davidson, John Colin Campbell, 1st
Viscount 243, 342*n*14
Dawes, Charles G.: Plan 129, 155
Dawson, Geoffrey 210, 233
Day, Professor Clive 91
Day-Lewis, Cecil 288, 299
de la Oliva, Josefa ('Pepita') (*née* Durán)
39
De La Warr, Herbrand ('Buck')
Sackville, 9th Earl 189, 192, 199, 217,
249, 344*n*46
De La Warr, John West, 5th Earl 38
Dell, Mrs (HN's constituent) 268
Denman, Lord: Committee 69
Dickinson, Oswald ('Ozzie') 74, 76, 82
Dillon, D. J. 149
Diplomatic Service 28–9, 30, 31
Dos Passos, John 251
Dost Mohammed 143
Douglas, Lord Alfred 111
Douglas, Norman: *South Wind* 150
Dreiser, Theodore 251
Drinkwater, John 110

Drummond, Sir Eric 102
Duff Cooper, Alfred *see* Cooper, Alfred
Duff
Dufferin and Ava, Frederick Temple-
Hamilton Blackwood, 1st Marquess
of 1, 3, 6, 7–8, 180
Dufferin and Ava, Lady Hariot ('Lal')
(*née* Rowan Hamilton) 3, 5, 7, 8
Dufferin and Ava, Terence Temple, 2nd
Marquess of (*formerly* Lord Terance) 7
Dugdale, Blanche ('Baffy') 217, 230, 265
Dulles, Alan 297
Duncan, Harold Handaside 28, 149
Durán, Pedro 39

Eden, Anthony: praised by HN 199,
208–9; and non-intervention in
Spanish Civil War 209; resigns as
foreign secretary 212; ineffectual
opposition to Chamberlain 217, *see
also* 'Eden group'; agrees with HN on
Russia 230; and publication of HN's
diaries 251; at Yalta 260; becomes
prime minister 288; and Suez Crisis
288, 289, 290–1
'Eden group' 213, 214, 222, 233, 234,
239, 341*n*5
Edward VII 78, 294; death and funeral
35, 44
Edward VIII (*later* Duke of Windsor)
169, 264; Abdication Crisis 199,
200–4; visits Germany 205–6; visited
by HN 204, 205; exiled by Churchill
206*n*
Egypt 52, 108, 253; and Suez Crisis
289–90
Eichmann, Adolf 295 *and n*
Eisenhower, Dwight D., US President
290
Elizabeth I 38, 85
Elizabeth, the Queen Mother 157
Elliot, Walter 168, 221, 243
Emily (Vita's maid) 52
Enver Bey 50
Ethiopia 193, 194, 207
Evening Standard 161, 162, 163, 165,
170; 'London Diary' 161, 166, 168
Feisal, Sherif 131